Twentieth-Century America

The Intellectual and Cultural Context

Longman Literature in English Series

General Editors: David Carroll and Michael Wheeler
Lancaster University

For a complete list of titles see pages xii–xiii

Twentieth-Century America

THE INTELLECTUAL AND CULTURAL CONTEXT

Douglas Tallack

Longman

London and New York

Longman Group UK Limited,
Longman House, Burnt Mill, Harlow,
Essex CM20 2JE, England
and Associated Companies throughout the world.

*Published in the United States of America
by Longman Inc., New York*

First published 1991

BRITISH LIBRARY CATALOGUING IN PUBLICATION DATA
Tallack, Douglas
  Twentieth-century America : the intellectual and cultural
  context. – (Longman literature in English series).
  1. United States. Cultural processes
  I. Title
  306.0973

  ISBN 0–582–49454–0
     0–582–49455–9

LIBRARY OF CONGRESS CATALOGING IN PUBLICATION DATA
Tallack, Douglas.
    Twentieth-century America : the intellectual and cultural context
  / Douglas Tallack.
      p. cm. — (Longman literature in English series)
    Includes bibliographical references and index.
    ISBN 0–582–49454–0. — ISBN 0–582–49455–9 (pbk.)
      1. United States—Intellectual life—20th century. 2. Arts,
  American. 3. Arts, Modern—20th century—United States.
  4. Politics and culture—United States—History—20th century.
  I. Title. II. Series.
  E169.1.T254 1991
  973.9—dc20
                                                            90–41577
                                                                 CIP

Disc conversion in 9½/11 pt Bembo
Produced by Longman Singapore Publishers (Pte) Ltd.
Printed in Singapore

Contents

List of Plates

Acknowledgements

We are grateful to the following for permission to reproduce illustrations: The Cleveland Museum of Art, Hinman B. Hurlbut Collection, 1133 22 (Plate 1); Collection of Whitney Museum of American Art (Plate 2, purchase with funds from Gertrude Vanderbilt Whitney, 31.95); Visual Arts Library — Phillips Collection (Plate 3); Metropolitan Museum of Art, Alfred Steiglitz Collection (Plate 4); The Museum of Modern Art, New York (Plate 5, acquired through the Lillie P. Bliss Bequest; Plate 9, purchase); Yale University Art Gallery (Plate 6, a gift of Collection Société Anonyme); Visual Arts, Joslyn Art Museum (Plate 7); Friends of American Art Collection, The Art Institute of Chicago (Plate 8); The University of Iowa Museum of Art (Plate 10, gift of Peggy Guggenheim, 1959.6); Tate Gallery (Plates 11 and 12); The Estate and Foundation of Andy Warhol (Plate 12); Simon/Neuman Gallery, New York (Plate 11); Vijak Mahdovi and Bernard Nadel-Ginard Collection, Boston, Massachusetts, Mary Boone Gallery, New York (Plate 13); Architectural Association Slide Library (Plate 14, photographer V. Bennett; Plate 15, photographer H. T. Cadbury-Brown; Plate 16, photographer R. McCabe; Plate 18, photographer A. Higgott; Plate 20, photographer A. Minchim; Plate 21, photographer Tom Clark); British Architectural Library (Plate 17); Buffalo and Erie County Historical Society (Plate 19); Susan Griggs Agency (Plate 22); SITE Projects, Inc. (Plate 23).

We are grateful to the following for permission to reproduce copyright textual material: Henry Holt and Company, Inc. for an extract from p. 60 of *The Letters of Robert Frost to Louis Untermeyer* Copyright © 1963 by Louis Untermeyer and Holt, Rinehart and Winston, Inc; the author's agent on behalf of the Estate of John Dos Passos for an extract from the poem 'Nineteen Nineteen' in *USA* (Penguin 1966); Warner Chappell Music Limited/Fred Ahlert Music Corporation for an extract from the song 'Rosie the Riveter' (Redd Evans/John J. Loeb), © Paramount Music Corp. Lyrics reproduced by permission of Famous Chappell Ltd/Ahlert — Copyright © 1942. Copyright Renewed 1969. John J. Loeb Company All Rights Reserved.

Editor's Preface

The multi-volume Longman Literature in English Series provides students of literature with a critical introduction to the major genres in their historical and cultural context. Each volume gives a coherent account of a clearly defined area, and the series, when complete, will offer a practical and comprehensive guide to literature written in English from Anglo-Saxon times to the present. The aim of the series as a whole is to show that the most valuable and stimulating approach to literature is that based upon an awareness of the relations between literary forms and their historical context. Thus the areas covered by most of the separate volumes are defined by period and genre. Each volume offers new informed ways of reading literary works, and provides guidance to further reading in an extensive reference section.

As well as studies on all periods of English and American literature, the series includes books on criticism and literary theory, and on the intellectual and cultural context. A comprehensive series of this kind must of course include other literature written in English, and therefore a group of volumes deals with Irish and Scottish literature, and the literatures of India, Africa, the Caribbean, Australia, and Canada. The forty-seven volumes of the series cover the following areas: pre-Renaissance English Literature, English Poetry, English Drama, English Fiction, English Prose, Criticism and Literary Theory, Intellectual and Cultural Context, American Literature, Other Literatures in English.

David Carroll
Michael Wheeler

Longman Literature in English Series

General Editors: David Carroll and Michael Wheeler
Lancaster University

Pre-Renaissance English Literature

★ English Literature before Chaucer *Michael Swanton*
English Literature in the Age of Chaucer
★ English Medieval Romance *W. R. J. Barron*

English Poetry

★ English Poetry of the Sixteenth Century *Gary Waller*
★ English Poetry of the Seventeenth Century *George Parfit*
English Poetry of the Eighteenth Century 1700–1789
★ English Poetry of the Romantic Period 1789–1830 *J. R. Watson*
★ English Poetry of the Victorian Period 1830–1890 *Bernard Richards*
English Poetry of the Early Modern Period 1890–1940
English Poetry since 1940

English Drama

English Drama before Shakespeare
★ English Drama: Shakespeare to the Restoration, 1590–1660
Alexander Leggatt
★ English Drama: Restoration and Eighteenth Century, 1660–1789
Richard W. Bevis
English Drama: Romantic and Victorian, 1789–1890
English Drama of the Early Modern Period, 1890–1940
English Drama since 1940

English Fiction

★ English Fiction of the Eighteenth Century 1700–1789
Clive T. Probyn
★ English Fiction of the Romantic Period 1789–1830 *Gary Kelly*
★ English Fiction of the Victorian Period 1830–1890 *Michael Wheeler*
★ English Fiction of the Early Modern Period 1890–1940
Douglas Hewitt
English Fiction since 1940

English Prose

English Prose of the Renaissance 1550–1700
English Prose of the Eighteenth Century
English Prose of the Nineteenth Century

Criticism and Literary Theory

Criticism and Literary Theory from Sidney to Johnson
Criticism and Literary Theory from Wordsworth to Arnold
Criticism and Literary Theory from 1890 to the Present

The Intellectual and Cultural Context

The Sixteenth Century
★ The Seventeenth Century, 1603–1700 *Graham Parry*
★ The Eighteenth Century, 1700–1789 *James Sambrook*
The Romantic Period, 1789–1830
The Victorian Period, 1830–1890
The Twentieth Century: 1890 to the Present

American Literature

American Literature before 1880
★ American Poetry of the Twentieth Century *Richard Gray*
American Drama of the Twentieth Century
★ American Fiction 1865–1940 *Brian Lee*
American Fiction since 1940
★ Twentieth-Century America *Douglas Tallack*

Other Literatures

Irish Literature since 1800
Scottish Literature since 1700

Australian Literature
★ Indian Literature in English *William Walsh*
African Literature in English: East and West
Southern African Literature in English
Caribbean Literature in English
★ Canadian Literature in English *W. J. Keith*

★ *Already published*

Author's Preface

The main challenge in writing a book entitled *Twentieth-Century America* is apparent in a single bewildering entry in the Chronology. In 1933 Nathaniel West's *Miss Lonelyhearts*, Gertrude Stein's *Autobiography of Alice B. Toklas*, and Sidney Hook's *Towards an Understanding of Karl Marx* were published, and the Marx Brothers' *Duck Soup* and Cooper and Schoedsack's *King Kong* were released by Hollywood. Unemployment was at thirteen million, a celebratory World's Fair was held in Chicago, Prohibition was repealed, and Roosevelt's first New Deal got underway. The avant-garde Black Mountain College was opened, but 1933 was also the year when social realism was revived through the Federal Arts Projects. Since events in Europe cannot be ignored, we must add that Hitler became Chancellor of Germany and the Bauhaus was closed.

Twentieth-century America is a heterotopia, writ large and, stereotypically, in neon as well. In *The Order of Things* (1966), one of the inaugural texts of our time, the French theorist, Michel Foucault, defines a heterotopia as a 'place' in which classifications are perfectly comprehensible in their own terms but combine to produce a taxonomy which is startling because, as he puts it, 'the common ground on which such meetings are possible has itself been destroyed.' The loss of common ground is one legacy of the modernist revolution, and a representative post-modernist like Foucault has hardly helped to repair the loss. And yet the multi-facetted concepts of modernity and post-modernity, along with the contentious relationship between them, do offer the best way of responding analytically to the discontinuities which, at a micro- and macro-level, seem to have characterized the years since the 1880s. The aim should not be to smooth out the kind of discontinuities evident in the entry for 1933, but to examine them and also to confront certain problems thrown up by a book on twentieth-century America.

To take one problem. In coming right up to the 1980s, I want at least to broach some of the issues provoked by writing a survey, not simply of a period which is literally getting longer, but from the point of view of a post-modern era in which European thinkers like Foucault and Jean-François Lyotard, and Americans like Richard Rorty and Charles Jencks, have seriously questioned grand narratives of social and artistic progress (or regress). Notwithstanding post-modern scepticism, patterns have emerged for me, and with them commitments and changes of mind. I am, for example, much more sympathetic to the New York Intellectuals than I was before writing this book. Historically, I now see the vital periods as the late nineteenth century, when the shift from production to consumption took place; the formative 1910s, rather than the more glamorous 1920s; the 1930s, when the crisis of both capitalism and socialism and the advent of totalitarianism set the intellectual agenda for post-war America; and the often denigrated 1950s, when the experiences of the 1930s were reflected upon with impressive intellectual results. The last of these preferences accounts for the long centrepiece on such thinkers as Hannah Arendt, David Riesman, Reinhold Niebuhr, C. Wright Mills, and Herbert Marcuse. I happen, also, to think highly of some of the academic post-structuralism of the 1980s, not least because it may yet rescue the 1960s from the intellectual and cultural blight of an Anglo-American New Right – one of the more unfortunate results of the special relationship.

Organizing this book around the key debate between modernity and post-modernity has pedagogical as well as analytical value. I hope that my approach will provide readers, who might otherwise be over-whelmed by the diversity and sheer quantity of material that could potentially be surveyed, with a number of important arguments. These can be tested against the many works that are regrettably omitted, either for lack of space or, in the notable instance of works of twentieth-century music, because arguing a case with any honesty requires a certain level of familiarity with the formal demands of a mode of expression. Foregrounding the concepts of modernity and post-modernity also enables links to be made between developments in many spheres, thereby providing a context for the imaginative literature which for many readers has been their entrée to twentieth-century America. In other words, when space necessitated selectivity, I have gone for arguments in preference to coverage and information. By way of compensation, though, I have made full use of the generous appendices which are so valuable a feature of the Longman Literature in English series. In particular, I have written the Notes on individual figures to complement, rather than repeat, my text, and have at least included a section on twentieth-century American music in the General Bibliographies.

Arguments only make sense when they are argued out, and so I have often halted the onward push of a survey to stay with a work long enough to explain why it matters. It would be insulting to present a text like Arendt's *The Origins of Totalitarianism* (1951) or a film like John Ford's *Stagecoach* (1939) as merely symptomatic of a broader intellectual and cultural history. For the same reason, I have insisted on attending closely to the crucial debate over political pluralism in mid-century America, despite the undoubted rival attractions of the Beats and Counter-Culture radicals, both of whom would push the narrative of the century onwards towards utopian conclusions. As the intellectual historian, Morton White, remarks in *Social Thought in America*, 'a work in which an effort is made to place ideas in a historical and social context *must*, to some degree, offer a logical analysis of those ideas, whether they are philosophical or not.' Close analysis is indispensable, and is not at all at odds with the politics of culture/culture of politics angle which I have adopted as a structural principle for the book.

An argument about modernity and post-modernity, then, is traced in chapter after chapter, often coming up to the 1980s, at which point readers can compare cinematic and architectural post-modernism, or evaluate the turn towards a post-structuralist concern with difference, marginality and textuality on the part of, for example, white and black feminist theorists and artists. Describing how different figures engaged with the issues of modernity and post-modernity is a way of showing that these are not merely categories over which critics haggle for definitive possession. My particular interest in Part One is in the complex and politically ambiguous struggle within selected art forms between the claim, central to modernism, that each discipline should purify itself, and the counter-pressure towards increased inter-disciplinarity exerted through the continuing communications revolution and the blurring of art forms in 'happenings', mixed media works and so forth. In the Introduction, Conclusion and throughout Part Two, I have drawn attention to a related question, the usage of 'modernism' and 'post-modernism' in social and political theory as well as aesthetics.

Part One of this book is devoted to the three art forms I have been most excited by and (equally important) know most about: cinema, where the influence of technology can be introduced; painting, where some of the most purist arguments about representation (literally) surface; and architecture, the most material of the arts. The longer Part Two turns to intellectual history and the history of intellectuals and, perhaps, needs some further comment. Chapter 4 charts the attempts by intellectuals as varied as William James, Randolph Bourne and the Southern Agrarians to understand the relationship between the country's culture and politics in the transitional period between Victorianism and Modernism. Chapter 5, which runs from the 1930s to the present, concentrates upon debates over culture and politics between American liberalism and the Left. Chapter 6, as already acknowledged, is an intellectual centrepiece insofar as it explores the theme of totalitarianism and reinterprets the 1930s for the post-war world. The imbalance between Parts One and Two is partially accounted for by my decision to write separate chapters on blacks and women and to integrate aesthetic concerns more directly with political issues. I have defended this inconsistency in the appropriate chapters (7 and 8).

In the Introduction I have tried to give a broader sense of twentieth-century American culture and have certainly wanted to stress the motor force of capitalism. In the rest of the book, however, I have had to slight social history and, instead, come at the United States through the preoccupations of artists and intellectuals: for example, the 'kaffee klatches', TV and radio world of the 1940s and '50s in Betty Friedan's *The Feminine Mystique* and David Riesman's *The Lonely Crowd*; the freeways, the 'strip' and the shopping mall in the work of Robert Venturi and John Portman; and religion in William James, Reinhold Niebuhr and Martin Luther King. At least, though, the gap between intellectuals and artists and American life has been less noticeable than in Europe. American intellectuals (including Americanized European intellectuals like Arendt and Marcuse), have been constantly exercised by mainstream developments in American life, so much so that a good deal of American thought might best be described as 'criticism', in the broadest sense. In this connection, I take the slightly anomalous status of critics like Bourne or Lionel Trilling to be a strength rather than a weakness of American intellectual history.

In selecting figures who bear closely upon mainstream American developments (whether these occurred in Washington DC or Hollywood), I have, however, become aware of a serious deficiency, not simply in American intellectual history but in myself. Quite probably most readers of this book also share my disturbing ignorance of the specialized knowledge which has accumulated within mostly scientific professions this century, and especially since 1945. As my Conclusion suggests, this is not a healthy state of affairs, though it is one that the best contemporary intellectuals are beginning to address, in the United States as in Europe. If this book were to have a sequel, it would have to examine developments in the biological sciences, law, linguistics, information technology and cybernetics, and so on – but without abandoning the critical edge of cultural politics which the professions cannot, or will not, provide but which the humanities can and should provide.

The following people were good enough to comment on parts or all of the book that I *have* written: Nicholas Alfrey, Peter Boyle, Donald Fixico, Phillip Hammond, Liam Kennedy, Brian Lee, Peter Messent, Elaine Millard, Eric Mottram, David Murray, Frank Piekarczyk, Robert Reinders, Jill Tallack, Imelda Whelehan, Michael Wheeler (my very supportive academic editor), David Wragg, Sue Wragg, and, especially, Richard King.

In references throughout the book the place of publication is London unless otherwise stated.

Douglas Tallack
University of Nottingham

Introduction: Modernity

The American century

If we take Gertrude Stein's point, that the United States is the oldest country in the world because it has been in the twentieth century the longest, then the locus of the debate over the meaning and direction of modernity should come as no surprise. America is still both the object of analysis and prophecy and the place where many of the arguments circulate.

During the revived debate over modernity during the 1980s, no one has been more impassioned in identifying what is at stake, or more provoking in selecting texts and artefacts for discussion, than the American political and cultural commentator, Marshall Berman. In *All That Is Solid Melts Into Air* (1982), he provides this recognizable and compelling definition of modernity:

> There is a mode of vital experience – experience of space and time, of the self and others, of life's possibilities and perils – that is shared by men and women all over the world today. I will call this body of experience 'modernity'. To be modern is to find ourselves in an environment that promises us adventure, power, joy, growth, and transformation of ourselves and the world – and, at the same time, that threatens to destroy everything we have, everything we know, everything we are. Modern environments and experiences cut across all boundaries of geography and ethnicity, of class and nationality, of religion and ideology: in this sense, modernity can be said to unite all mankind. But it is a paradoxical unity, a unity of disunity: it pours us all into a maelstrom of perpetual disintegration and renewal, of struggle and contradiction, of ambiguity and anguish. To be modern is to be part of a universe in which, as Marx said, 'all that is solid melts into air'.[1]

By the intriguing but rather vague term, 'modernity', Berman means a relationship between 'modernism' and 'modernization'; between, on the one hand, 'visions and ideas . . . that aim to make men and women the subjects as well as the objects' of history and, on the other hand, socio-economic processes: demographic movements (for example, immigration and migration), industrialization, growth of cities, technological advances, and, above all, the extraordinary expansion of the capitalist market. The mid-term, modernity, is, in Berman's words but with another nod towards Marx, 'the dialectics of modernization and modernism': it is *historical experience*, a meld of objective forces and subjective responses (p. 15). The word dialectic also suggests a direction, a way out of the contradictions of capitalism. Yet Berman seems to write against this story with an end. His argument, that modernism must (in order to be modernism) remain in a tense, often ironic, relationship with socio-economic modernization, is strung out along an open-ended narrative, which eschews utopian, but also dystopian, conclusions.

In contrast to commentators from across the American political spectrum who advocate pre-modern communal values as an antidote to modern times, Berman insists that whatever the perils, there is no going back, even if we wanted to. The pre-modern world is gone forever and with it an unambiguous loyalty to family, community, region, and religion. Modernity has been our inescapable condition since the industrial revolution and it is a condition that will go on. Going-on is the important thing for Berman, and it is this quality which makes his a very American book, even though only the final section is devoted to explicitly American themes and locations.

If we are provoked – into agreement or disagreement – by Berman's account of what it means to be modern and tempted to insert our own examples of its 'possibilities and perils' then, at the start of a book on 'the American Century', it may be helpful to rehearse some responses: a 'way out' of modernity, or a 'way in', or a way of refusing these alternatives. Following Berman's advice, do we maintain a grip on modernity (make it *our* modernity) by returning to earlier modernists? Among others, Berman cites Baudelaire, Marx, Nietzsche, and Dostoyevsky, but Walt Whitman, William James, William Carlos Williams, Louis Sullivan, Charles Ives, Charlie Chaplin, and Joseph Stella make a more varied American pantheon. Berman recommends applying their lessons to what he elsewhere calls the contemporary 'signs in the streets'. Or do we take a more positive attitude towards high and late modernism, those twentieth-century developments that Berman feels have failed us because of their cultivation of formal autonomy? If so, we shall need to argue that the relationship between, say, Abstract Expressionism or the International Style and socio-economic conditions is more dialectical than Berman thinks, less of a retreat in the face of the market; in which case Jackson Pollock and Mies van der Rohe emerge as modernists capable of rivalling the earlier and, in Berman's view, genuine modernists.

To take another tack, do we refuse Berman's qualified optimism about 'development' (the ambiguous motor for change in his spirited account) and reject the freedoms of the modern world as so many illusions, desires which have been manufactured for our consumption by 'the culture industry'? A materialist and probably Marxist theory of culture would then be an option, but one which may have difficulties getting back to base. Alternatively, we may look to community, tradition and, eventually, to religion as the only reliable guides in an increasingly secular world – though still with the nagging doubt that these, too, are hardly immune from modernization. The 'personal' letters distributed through the computerized mailing lists of televangelists like Jerry Falwell, Oral Roberts and Pat Robertson trade on, and make a mockery of, the need for stable beliefs and community felt by ordinary Americans. If we follow Berman and eschew nostalgia, this does not, of course, mean that we have to accept his assertion that modernity cuts uniformly across geography, religion, race, ethnicity, and gender. In particular, it will be worth asking whether twentieth-century feminism and black political culture tell a different story, one in which social change and protest have created different communities and allegiances to replace those traditional, pre-modern ones which so often oppressed rather than protected people. Or, finally, do we see a viable response in a break with the modernist tradition which Berman endorses, a break which announces the new aesthetic and new politics of post-modernism, with its very different relationship with post-industrial society. This would mean questioning or deconstructing the apparently straightforward oppositions which Berman employs: self/society, culture/economics, subjective/objective, even modernism/modernization.

This is not an exhaustive list of the options pursued by the figures surveyed in this book: architects, film-makers, painters, philosophers, theologians, critics and theorists, some openly engaged with the dilemmas of modernity and post-modernity, others reflecting upon them indirectly through their own disciplines and art forms. Nevertheless, the questions Marshall Berman poses, and the concepts he foregrounds, can serve as a point of reference and, perhaps more importantly, as a reminder of what is at stake when we reflect upon modernity and post-modernity in their American context.

For the remainder of this Introduction, I want to do two things. First, through some excursions into social, economic and technological history, convey something of the contradictory mixture of cultural richness and poverty which has characterized the United States since its full-scale entry into modernity in the late nineteenth century. And, second, identify some of the issues precipitated by the socio-economic and technological developments of this period, because I go along with Berman's observation that 'it is modern capitalism, not modern art and culture, that has set and kept the pot boiling' (p. 123). Indeed, so rapid was the modernizing of America, that even in the era of high aesthetic modernism (roughly 1890 to 1930) capitalism and its technology were creating the depthlessness and relational quality which have since been identified as defining characteristics of the post-modern. In this respect, quite possibly the key factor is highlighted not by the well-worn synonym for modernity – Henry Luce's phrase, 'the American Century' – but by Luce's occupation. He made his millions out of mass circulation magazines, and was among the first of the media tycoons. As such he was a product of the communications revolution that entered a new phase in these early years of the modern age, and had a decisive effect on the formation of twentieth-century American culture.

Culture and communications in Middletown

In his novel, *Sister Carrie* (1900), Theodore Dreiser starts the twentieth century with a train journey from a small town to a city:

> They were nearing Chicago. Signs were everywhere numerous. Trains flashed by them. Across wide stretches of flat open prairie they could see lines of telegraph poles stalking across the fields toward the great city.[2]

Railroad tracks, telegraph lines, an expanded postal service, roads carrying more and more automobiles in the early decades of the new century, and, most importantly, ubiquitous signs – all of these in-betweens or, more technically, mediations, connected cities with each other and with other small towns besides Carrie Meeber's hometown. Among them was Muncie, Indiana, the site of Robert and Helen Lynd's renowned sociological case study, *Middletown: A Study in Contemporary American Culture* (1929). As the Lynds report, by the mid-1920s, 'the rise of large-scale advertising, popular magazines, movies, radio, and other channels of increased cultural diffusion from without are rapidly changing habits of thought.'[3]

Most of this book will be devoted to the kind of place Carrie was travelling to, but, first, something of the kind of place she was leaving and the broadly religious world-view it represented for the seven out of ten Americans who still lived in small towns or on farms in the 1890s. Talking to inhabitants who remembered nineteenth-century Middletown, the Lynds reconstruct a typical pre-industrial community:

> Standard time was unknown; few owned watches, and sun time was good enough during the day, while early and late candle lighting served to distinguish the periods at night . . . Social calls were unknown, but all-day visits were the rule, a family going to visit either by horseback, the children seated behind the grown-ups, or in chairs set in the springless farm wagon. Social intercourse performed a highly important service; there were no daily papers in the region, and much news traveled by word of mouth. (pp. 11–12)

People also got news when they went to church, both from each other and, more formally, from the minister's sermon. Religious observance was strict in nineteenth-century Middletown.

'And then in the fall of '86 came gas', the Lynds announce, their perhaps inadvertent pun inaugurating a theme generalized by later social historians and cultural commentators. This is historian, Robert Wiebe, in *The Search for Order*, writing about the Lynds' nineteenth-century base-line:

> The great casualty of America's turmoil late in the century was the island community. Although a majority of Americans would still reside in relatively small, personal centers for several decades more, the society that had been premised upon the community's effective sovereignty, upon its capacity to manage affairs within its boundaries, no longer functioned.[4]

At our end of this story of lost communities, we find novelist and essayist, Joan Didion, only mostly joking in *The White Album* (1979) when she connects community and communications and speculates that the only surviving community in Los Angeles is on the freeway at rush-hour.

The Lynds' punning reference to the 'fall' has a particular significance in *Middletown*. Funded by the Institute of Social and Religious Research, the Lynds ended up describing the decline of religion in the 1920s, even in 'middle America':

> As changes proceed at accelerating speed in other sections of the city's life, the lack of dominance of religious beliefs becomes

more apparent. The whole tide of this industrial culture would seem to be set more strongly than in the leisurely village of thirty-five years ago in the direction of the 'go-getter' rather than in that of 'Blessed are the meek' of the church; by their religious teachers Middletown people are told that they are sinners in need of salvation, by speakers at men's and women's clubs they are assured that their city, their state, and their country are, if not perfect, at least the best in the world, that it is they who make them so, and that if they but continue in their present vigorous course, progress is assured . . . In theory, religious beliefs dominate all other activities in Middletown; actually, large regions of Middletown's life appear uncontrolled by them. (p. 406)

It should be admitted here – and it requires a substantial digression to do so – that the Lynds misread the signs of religion's demise. They are perceptive on the 'fall' into the secularized 1920s and on the American ideology which effortlessly joined religion and business. Moreover, in their identification of 'channels of increased cultural diffusion from without' the Lynds have, arguably, understood the forces of social change as well as any other twentieth-century American commentators. Yet their analysis has been confounded by the undoubted persistence of religion in some regions (notably the South) and among some groups (notably blacks), but mostly by the revival of religion after the Second World War and especially since the 1960s. A necessarily schematic outline of religion in modern America will allow us to run important lines forward into later chapters.

The combination of evolutionary thought and the modernization which we shall shortly describe recommended a liberalization of religion as the best answer to secularization. The alternative was the débâcle of fundamentalist outrage in Dayton, Tennessee, in 1925 when John Scopes was tried for teaching evolution in a school. Defending lawyer, Clarence Darrow, lost the case, won the appeal, and left fundamentalism and its champion, former Populist presidential candidate William Jennings Bryan, humiliated. The more sensible route for religion was the Social Gospel movement of city clergy in the 1870s and 1880s. Washington Gladden's 'applied Christianity' was an alternative to the hypocritical 'gospel of wealth' of Andrew Carnegie. Following Gladden, Walter Rauschenbusch argued in *Christianity and Social Crisis* (1907) for the kingdom of God on earth and, at the very least, for an alliance between reform movements and theology. Christianity would be reasonable and practical, he further maintained in *A Theology for the Social Gospel* (1917). In a related vein, in *Social Idealism and Changing Theology* (1913), Gerald Birney Smith advocated the democratization of religion. Harvey Cox's *The Secular City*, published in 1965, is at some chronological distance from the specific concerns and contexts of Gladden, Rauschenbusch and Smith, but is, none the less in the same broad tradition of thinking. 'The era of the secular city', Cox writes, 'is not one of anticlericalism or feverish antireligious fanaticism . . . The forces of secularization have no serious interest in persecuting religion. Secularization simply by-passes and undercuts religion and goes on to other things. It has relativized religious world-views and thus rendered them innocuous.'[5] Cox set himself the task not of revitalizing religion but of adapting God to the society he saw around him, some thirty years after the Lynds described the forces which produced Cox's secular and urban society.

The Secular City became an embarrassing best-seller since it marked the reversal of the trend which Cox described. He admitted as much in later writings. The subsequent revival of religion which the Lynds and, more culpably, Cox failed to foresee, has been of two broad kinds. The more evident kind has been born-again Christianity, which has been fundamentally anti-modern yet caught up in, as it exploits, the most blatant forms of modernization – for example in what has been called 'the electronic church'. Religious revivalism and the moral majority are certainly important themes for social and political historians. As it is often remarked, in 1980 all three Presidential candidates, Reagan, Carter and Anderson, were born-again Christians. Of greater relevance to the intellectuals and artists covered in this book is the more diffused religion of the post-1945 period which, in sometimes ambiguous ways, accompanied the diffusion of pre-modern culture which the Lynds rightly link with the mass media. In a special issue of *Daedalus* on religion (1982), Martin Marty documents this more decentred revival, and observes that America's official and legal 'secular, nonreligious culture . . . houses an impressive number of religious institutions that attract the loyalties of three out of five citizens, and the weekly participation of two out of five – and are likely to continue to do so indefinitely'.[6] No one denies the weighty contributions of William James, Reinhold Niebuhr and Martin Luther King. However, the 'new religious consciousness' amongst post-1960s intellectuals, which includes a revived Harvey Cox speculating on what a post-modern theology might look like, also deserves discussion.[7]

Back with the Lynds and the early decades of the century, we can see *Middletown* not simply as social history, but as revealing a particular concern for the present book. This is the dilemma of so many twentieth-century American intellectuals, critical (even moralistically so) of capitalism's incursions into community life, yet accepting, in the title of Thomas Wolfe's 1940 novel, that 'you can't go home again'. This tension is also to be found in the best literary engagements with middle America, from Willa Cather, Sherwood Anderson and Sinclair Lewis onwards. It is when Anderson and Lewis lost their critical edge

and came home that their work generated a folksy rhetoric indistin-
guishable from that which Hollywood predictably disseminated at
times of crisis – notably during the Depression of the 1930s. Anderson,
for example, is so far from the tense ambiguities of *Winesburg, Ohio*
(1919), but so close to the 1930s populist cinema of Frank Capra in his
eulogy, 'The American Small Town' (1940):

> Day after day, under all sorts of circumstances, in sickness and
> health, in good fortune and bad, we small-towners are close to
> one another and know each other in ways the city man can never
> experience. A man goes away and comes back. Certain people
> have died. Babies have been born. Children of yesterday have
> suddenly become young men and women. Life has been going
> on. Still nothing has really changed.[8]

In calling Muncie 'Middletown' the Lynds do not simply present it
as in some ways typical of middle America, a characterization that has
persisted in research projects such as their own sequel, *Middletown in
Transition* (1937), and in much twentieth-century American literature;
they also ironically reveal that this representative town was anywhere
but in the middle or centre of things. W.B. Yeats's modernist
pronouncement that 'the centre cannot hold' finds a surprising
endorsement in the dislocation of Middletown amid the babble of radio
signals and the onslaught of advertising slogans. Local newspapers,
once content to report from abroad that 'Pipe ignites clothing – man in
London burns to death', in 1924–5 carried detailed foreign news
reports, though these were systematically supplied by outside agencies
like the Associated Press (p. 473). Two-thirds of the Middletown
morning paper consisted of advertising, much of it promoting the
goods and services of out-of-town companies, while the popularity of
radio, especially in the 1930s, and motion pictures from the 1920s
onwards were conclusive proof of the decline of a culture centred on
the locality:

> Today nine motion picture theaters operate from 1 to 11 p.m.
> seven days a week summer and winter; four of the nine give
> three different programs a week, the other five having two a
> week; thus twenty-two different programs with a total of over
> 300 performances are available to Middletown every week in the
> year. (p. 263)

As the image of small-town America has grown more powerful, its
geography has become more and more dislocated, as Bill Bryson
relates in *The Lost Continent* (1989), an account written for a British
readership of his return to the Midwest of his youth:

Every town, even a quite modest one, has a mile or more of fast food places, motor inns, discount cities, shopping malls – all with thirty-foot-high revolving signs and parking lots the size of Shropshire. Carbondale [Illinois] appeared to have nothing else. I drove in on a road that became a two-mile strip of shopping centres and gas stations, K-Marts, J.C. Penneys, Hardees and MacDonald's. And then, abruptly, I was in the country again. I turned around and drove back through town on a parallel street that offered precisely the same sort of things but in slightly different configurations and then I was in the country again. The town had no centre. It had been eaten by shopping malls.

If driving is disorientating, then taking a walk in a town apparently without sidewalks turns out to be an esoteric pastime, requiring Bryson to negotiate parking lots, garage forecourts and 'little white-painted walls marking the boundaries between, say, Long John Silver's Seafood Shoppe and Kentucky Fried Chicken . . . What you were supposed to do was get in your car, drive twelve feet down the street to another parking lot'.[9]

The Lynds were among the first twentieth-century American intellectuals to doubt that Middletowners could resist the onset of a mass culture which, in the years since they wrote, has continued to expand under economic and technological imperatives. Just as the late nineteenth-century reformer, Henry George, had recognized that progress could bring poverty, and wealth could threaten rather than ensure democracy, so the Lynds delineate the paradox that the concentration and exercise of cultural power (what the Italian Marxist, Antonio Gramsci, called hegemony) was accompanied by undeniable advances in the general standard of living. By 1920 American women could expect, on average, to live 56.5 years, compared with 51 years in 1900; for men, life expectancy rose from 48 to 54 years in the same period. Diphtheria, typhoid and tuberculosis had been combatted by medical advances, though cancer, heart disease and diabetes were killing more people, and the numbers of murders and deaths in car accidents were rising steeply. The availability of consumer goods was the most marked sign of progress, though buying 2 billion cigarettes in 1899 (hardly any were bought twenty years earlier) and 43 billion by 1921, or 151,000 pairs of silk stockings in 1899 and 217 million pairs in 1921, suggests the ambiguities of progress. These figures are given substance by the sheer clutter of Middletown. As a book, *Middletown* is more full of objects than any nineteenth-century English novel, though the principle of built-in obsolescence can be deduced from the many broken consumer goods which litter Middletown houses and yards.

When discussing the advent of modernity, we invariably take the easy option and home in on crisis years: 1910 according to Virginia

Woolf, 1915 for D. H. Lawrence, and 1922 for Willa Cather. In Ernest Hemingway's fiction the break comes with the experience of the First World War. In contrast, the war barely figures in the pages of *Middletown*. Where it does, the inhabitants recall the war as a time of co-operation and community, an anti-modernist interlude amidst the inexorable development of a capitalist culture. The 1920s may have seen American writers and artists establishing outposts in Paris and adding a new dimension to modernism, but the changes affecting Middletown were already clearing away the pre-modern sources of resistance. One consequence of this accelerated chronology of modernization in the United States, is a less oppositional, but sometimes more engaged, relationship between American modernists and material changes than was the case in much European modernism. As we shall see when discussing cinema, painting and architecture, this had its advantages as well as its drawbacks. What is undeniable is that these material changes were no mere backdrop to artistic experimentation. They produced a mass culture based on the market, the phenomenon with which all twentieth-century writers and artists had to contend.

In trying to summarize the reasons why *Middletown* is such an appropriate 'place' to begin a survey of twentieth-century American intellectual and cultural history, four related themes may be identified. First, the threat to Culture (with a capital C) represented by the materialism and insistent 'middleness' of modern America; second, the loss of centrality, and with it identity, within the very communications network which disseminated the safe, conservative, provincial, middling, image of small-town America; third, the spectre of what Max Weber called 'the iron cage' of rationality and Herbert Marcuse termed 'one dimensionality'; and then a fourth theme which counters the overall negative impression which books like *Middletown* convey. Almost in spite of themselves, the Lynds revealed the sheer excitement and range of possibilities of mass communications: the variety which motion pictures, radio, popular magazines, and advertising were bringing to small town life, and, by implication, the innovations which these new cultural forms permitted. It will be the purpose of the chapters in Part One to detail some of these innovations while yet maintaining the critical perspective of Robert and Helen Lynd.

The iron cage of capitalism

We gain a sharper perspective upon twentieth-century American thought and culture by recognizing that the years of modernism were not just the years of the kinetoscope, skyscrapers, factories, trains and the telegraph, but also the period in which most of the concepts and interpretive models through which we understand modernity in general were formulated by European social theorists: by Max Weber, Emile Durkheim, Georg Simmel, Sigmund Freud, and by Marx to the extent that he remained in dialogue with these later figures. Of all of these, Weber, with his image of the iron cage, is the pre-eminent theorist of modernity, and notwithstanding the prominence of Marx and Freud, it is Weber who sets the agenda for intellectual and cultural history in twentieth-century America. For that reason alone he requires early introduction.

According to Weber, 'the reality in which we move' was defined by capitalism, 'the most fateful force in our modern life', and a force nowhere more important than in the United States.[10] It is the concept of rationalization which, Weber argues, gives an unmistakable shading to Western capitalist development. Rationalization therefore provides a handle upon the ambiguous relationship between communications and culture which is at the heart of the Lynds' book and the recognizably modern America they describe. As far back as the late eighteenth century, New England towns, which were in the vanguard of the first stage of industrial capitalism, were experiencing the bleaching out of personal and not explicitly economic associations by the growth of a market which linked one place with another and with the few large centres of trade. The 'purposeful pursuit of profit' (Weber's phrase) under market conditions became *the* orientation of action during the subsequent century, because, as Weber explains, to function, that is to say to be rational in its own terms, capitalism depends upon calculability. Products, services, labour, time, and space – all are given a numerical value through the agency of money so that they can be 'taken into account'. Neither capitalism nor money are themselves sufficient to explain the consolidation of a rationalized culture; rather, they are part of an interlocking and developing *system* (itself a key concept by the early twentieth century). Calculability is not simply a matter of assigning a monetary value; it involves the predictability which comes with control of labour, the factory, the machinery, and the sources of power, and, outside the productive process, of the administrative and distributive structures that surround the expanding market. Within this sphere of calculability, the logic of rationality can still be subdivided. For example, the kind of control exercised within the factory – known in its developed form as 'scientific management' – depends upon the prior control of labour that comes with a free market. Labour must be, in Weber's words, 'formally free', so that control can be exerted economically rather than physically, the latter calling up the inefficient system of slavery. Apart from registering the logic of a process leading, apparently inexorably, to our present, the point to stress is the paradox that the deterministic character of the 'specific and peculiar rationalism' of capitalism was set in motion by free activity, and is maintained by a continuing and quite reasonable belief that as modernization increases control over the environment so it brings greater individual freedom, as well as more wealth and better health.

Frederick Winslow Taylor's time-and-motion studies, which he began in the 1880s and wrote up in *The Principles of Scientific Management* (1911), sought to institute rational control within American factories. Scientific management exemplified the self-conscious belief in the rationality of the system, such that continual recalculation of the constituent elements and attention to their compatibility would improve efficiency. The information derived from Taylor's empirical studies had the effect of translating a substantive productive activity into *knowledge*. Knowledge could then be transferred from factory to office and from there into the bureaucratic network run by the new professionals, who used the new technologies of communications to process increasingly standardized blocks of information. The outcome of modernization was far more dramatic, and of course more ambiguous, than even Mark Twain could envisage in *A Connecticut Yankee in King Arthur's Court* (1889), in which he sends his nineteenth-century inventor back to initiate a sixth-century apocalypse.

In *The Search for Order*, Robert Wiebe reminds us that rationalization in the face of the apparent chaos of urban-industrial America was not a plot hatched by the Carnegies, Rockefellers, Goulds and other monopoly capitalists (the so-called 'Robber Barons'). It was a way of thinking about the world that also attracted Progressive reformers, who were seeking to regulate the economic and social system for liberal purposes. The rationalization of avenues of communication (through such means as settlement houses and newspapers) became, for social worker Jane Addams and urban sociologist Robert Park, the means for translating the small-town togetherness which they had known as children into the 'Great Community' of the city – in their case, Chicago.[11] City planning, social theory, national economic reform, the welfare state, even cultural reform – these were among the activities engaged in by Progressives from the 1890s through to the First World War. The most famous utopian novel in American literature, Edward Bellamy's *Looking Backward* (1888), anticipated the movement for reform not through the rousing rhetoric of revolution but by espousing rationalist principles and proposing a national bureaucracy and a disciplined industrial army as answers to 'the labor problem'. Similarly, Bellamy's descriptions of the new, orderly Boston of the year 2000 was a stimulus to the 'City Beautiful' movement of the early twentieth century. City planning reached a peak in Daniel Burnham and Edward Bennett's *Plan of Chicago* (1909), while the major architectural expression came when the skyscraper and the standard American grid-plan met, initially in the 1880s with Chicago School architects, Louis Sullivan, John Root and Burnham himself, and then from the late 1930s when the European Modern Movement arrived in the persons of Bauhaus architects, Walter Gropius and Mies van der Rohe.

We can examine the relationship between rationalization and architecture in a later chapter. However, rationalized production processes, use of new technology, and new business methods leading to the growth of bureaucratic organizations are better illustrated by the American railroad corporations of the late nineteenth century and the then emerging communications industry. These enterprises contributed physically to the spread of the market and the setting in place of the comprehensive system that Weber describes. By 1880 the United States had the longest railroad network in the world and in the next decade the length of track doubled to 200,000 miles as the links in the system were completed. In the light of Weber's insights into rationality (knowledge, predictability, calculability), these physical links ought to be understood as the basis for a prevailing cast of mind: only if the elements in a system are connected can they be counted (upon) and this, in turn, is the basis for rational behaviour within the system.

As the tracks linked buyers and sellers so they underlined the impersonality of the system, much as the flow-charts of Frederick Taylor constituted individual workers as interchangeable units, lacking in autonomy. John Jay Chapman's frequently quoted remark that the story of the small town after the Civil war was the story of the arrival of the railroad may also be understood as a loss of autonomy. The very existence of a town came to depend upon whether the tracks came or not and the period is littered with the stories of ghost towns. But when the tracks did come the centre of a town's economy (and its culture) shifted somewhere else; dependence, rather than much-hallowed American independence, became the norm. Autonomy has its spatial and temporal co-ordinates and both were 'incorporated' by the extension of a railroad network.

The regulation of time is usually associated with an urban environment but while it is true that city life multiplied interactions and so necessitated the standardization of time (the need to be 'on time'), the impetus came from economic and technological sources. This is where we perceive the significance of the railroad as an industry *and* a form of communication. Slight time differences between towns in the same state or county made little difference. Before the introduction of standard time in 1883, Indiana had 23 time zones, Wisconsin 39. Space dominated time. But when the railroad criss-crossed the continent it revealed the irrationality of time, from a certain modern point of view. Local times were, at first, repeated in the timetables of railroad corporations, alongside railroad time which was itself keyed to cities; those cities varied according to the constituency of the railroad and where its offices were located. This situation could not continue and it was the railroads, acting under economic imperatives, which brought about standard time zones across the USA. Where time was once located physically, it became legitimated according to other criteria as local communities were forced either to adjust to the standard time used on the railroad timetables or to risk being 'out of time'.[12]

On the occasions when Max Weber's own point of view stands clear from his account of capitalist rationality, we are faced with the picture of a gradual 'disenchantment' of the world, bringing a loss of individualism and community, and the dismantling of the mystery of craft-skills. When describing changes in the glass-blowing industry in Middletown during the thirty-five years spanned by their case study, Robert and Helen Lynd refer to 'batteries of tireless iron men doing narrowly specialized things over and over' and to 'the speeding-up process of the iron man' (pp. 39 and 40). They bring to mind the fatalistic image of the iron cage which dominates the closing pages of Weber's *The Protestant Ethic and the Spirit of Capitalism* (1904–5):

> This order is now bound to the technical and economic
> conditions of machine production which to-day determine the
> lives of all the individuals who are born into this mechanism, not
> only those directly concerned with economic acquisition, with
> irresistible force. Perhaps it will so determine them until the last
> ton of fossilized coal is burnt . . . No one knows who will live in
> this cage in the future, or whether at the end of this tremendous
> development entirely new prophets will arise, or there will be a
> great rebirth of old ideas and ideals, or, if neither, mechanized
> petrification, embellished with a sort of convulsive self-
> importance. (pp. 181 and 182)

Variations on the image of the iron cage appear in the work of many twentieth-century thinkers and artists, not least Hannah Arendt, Theodor Adorno, Max Horkheimer, Herbert Marcuse and other European exiles who came to the United States from the 1930s onwards to escape persecution by the Nazis. Indeed, it has been the theme of most leading intellectuals and artists this century that not only people, work, products, places, and time, but also culture itself, has taken on meaning according to the dictates of capitalist rationality.

However, two other points may be taken from Weber's peroration: first, the hope for 'new prophets' or a return to old ideas, alternatives which were mentioned earlier in connection with Marshall Berman's book, and which will be the concern of later chapters; and, second, the implication, in the images of 'fossilized coal' and the iron cage as the sources, respectively, of power and materials, that Weber's pessimism is related to an outmoded technology. As we shall see, the period under discussion witnessed the institution of new technologies, notably in the field of communications. Like the print technology of the fifteenth century, the communications revolution of the nineteenth century and beyond changed habits of thought and ways of seeing the world, and also brought new forms of cultural expression: radio, motion pictures, photography, phonographic records, and so on. Of course, these new forms had (and, with new electronic technologies, still have) the potential to extend cultural control, and to create more novelty, in the sense of the trivial refashioning of standardized options ('novelty goods'). Yet a degree of indeterminacy enters with technological change. Motion pictures and photography, for instance, which simply did not exist prior to the invention of the camera, possess the potential for liberation and novelty, in the literal sense of something unknown. We can gain some understanding of this crucial doubleness, a version of the active/passive paradox outlined by Marshall Berman, by tracing the transition from the rationality of a nineteenth-century production economy to that of a twentieth-century consumer economy. In commenting upon such matters as credit, techniques of marketing and selling, and technologies of communication, we can also glimpse, in the drive towards rationalized practices and formations, the shape of a different, post-modern, society – one that would not be formally identified until the 1960s.

The American economy was, if unstable, extraordinarily productive into and then through the 1920s. Between 1919 and 1929, GNP rose by 40 per cent. By then the United States had been the world's leading industrial power for at least three decades, with an output which exceeded that of Britain, France and Germany together. Because of the excess production from American farms as well as industries, and because of labour unrest at the wage and factory system in the context of post-First World War socialist movements in Europe, an image of a new society was required, a society characterized by abundance and, therefore, by consumption and leisure.

The logic of rationalization, which had already been extended beyond the factory gates to administrative and legal spheres, also encompassed that of consumption. Advertising was the chief means for achieving this end. Expenditure on advertising was around $9.5 million in 1865; in 1900 it was $95 million; in 1919 $500 million; and in 1929 an astounding $1.78 billion. Since the late eighteenth century and Thomas Jefferson, the distant farmer had been the epitome of a producer, but this figure, too, was drawn into the orbit of consumerism as city-based newspapers and magazines achieved mass-circulation status. The mail-order houses of Montgomery Ward and Sears and Roebuck had been utilizing the postal service since the 1870s, but the institution of Rural Free Delivery in 1898 and parcel post in 1913 turned their catalogues into portable department stores. The 500 pages of Ward's 'Great Wish Book' brought a whole new world of city goods, especially fashion, into isolated farmhouses. Mail-order catalogues were used as textbooks in rural schools, and as substitutes for the gossip formerly to be found in the general store, witness this letter addressed to Mr Ward:

> I suppose you wonder why we haven't ordered anything from you since the fall. The cow kicked my arm and broke it and besides my wife was sick, and there was the doctor bill. But now, thank God, that is paid, and we are all well again, and we have a fine new baby, and please send plush bonnet number 29d8077.[13]

Richard Sears converted rural consumers into agents by rewarding them with premiums if they introduced their neighbours to the company. 'Iowaization', as his scheme was called, even converted folkways into rationalized channels of commercial communication, and is one of the clearest illustrations of the decisive influence of capitalist economic relations upon cultural relations.

Distance from the product in quite a different sense could also be resolved by the credit facilities offered by Marshall Field, Macy's, Wanamaker's and the other large department stores which came to prominence in the late nineteenth century. Just as money, as a supposedly neutral means of exchange, allowed work, for example, the routine tasks demanded on a Ford Motor Company production line or in the glass-blowing plant in Middletown, to be converted into the phantasmagoric world of consumer goods, so credit made such compensation almost immediate. Advertising, credit and the mass communications upon which they were based, changed the economic and cultural face of the United States, much as Thorstein Veblen had predicted they would in his discussion of 'conspicuous consumption' in *The Theory of the Leisure Class*, published in 1899. Processed foods carrying brand names and distributed through chain stores across the country; electric refrigerators and washing machines; wristwatches; radios; and thirty million cars: no longer the Model T, first marketed in 1910, but a whole range of models which were changed each year – these were among the products bought by Americans in the 1920s.

Inspire, educate and entertain: the dissemination of mass culture

The Lynds' announcement that Middletown in 1924–5 no longer produced the bulk of what it consumed ranks with those of Woolf, Lawrence, Hemingway, Cather or any other commentator on modernism. The goods in Middletown stores had become commodities. In Marx's classic explanation, a product lost its substance, any uniqueness which it might have possessed in a local, craft economy prior to mass production, by being passed through the market system of exchange. Its value was determined by exchange and not use. Furthermore, with the expansion of credit facilities and advertising, images or even product numbers (as in the letter quoted above) circulated rather than the goods themselves, making it vital for the maintenance of consumer confidence that the product be both described in the abstract and be describable. It should be noted, though, that this degree of control was not dependent upon a more objective, truthful relationship between object and representation, in spite of the claims of journalists, advertising people and some modernist writers, but was legitimated by a logic of rationality which, as we have seen, arose out of industrial, commercial and technological developments dating back to late eighteenth-century America. The identity of a product, perhaps even of a person, lost its presumed essential, self-evident quality, and became relational, dependent upon other elements in the system. This would have far-reaching and unexpected implications.

Standardization also operated when the product itself was a reproducible image and here we have the point of intersection between goods as commodities and cultural products as a new kind of leisure commodity. There was a growing audience for cultural goods, as there was a growing consumer market, and this was particularly so in American cities. Chicago, for instance, had grown from a village of 350 people in 1833 to a city of over two million by 1910. This concentration of people, along with with good urban transportation and expanding literacy, created a market for news and entertainment.

The idea of pre-digested information was institutionalized in DeWitt Wallace's *Reader's Digest*, founded in 1922. Wallace admired and sought to emulate Henry Ford by applying mass production techniques to the world of print. He also pioneered direct and postal selling in the effort to 'inspire, educate and entertain'. (In the post-Second World War era, especially, these laudable aims were thought to be quite compatible with the tough State Department line adopted whenever American foreign policy was big news in the daily papers.) The 'tabloid', which made its first American appearance in 1919 in the form of the *New York Illustrated Daily News* further demonstrates the commodification of news, which could be sent down the telegraph or telephone line, packaged, and distributed by road, rail and, by the late 1920s, by aeroplane. By 1926 the circulation of the *Daily News* had topped the one million mark. Physically manageable in crowded locations and, through its large headlines and 'leads', a short-cut to what was new, the tabloid also sought to be entertaining. The New York *Evening Graphic* announced in 1924 that it would 'dramatize and sensationalize the news and some stories that are not news . . . We want this newspaper to be human, first, last and all the time. We want to throb with those life forces that fill life with joyous delight.'[14] Two points can be made here. First, the way that the ordinary, the human and the real, become a composite quality to be constructed and projected – onto ordinary Americans. And, second, by way of a comparison with the advertising industry, that, curiously, out of standardization could come excess. Indeed, the *look* of the front page became vitally important, adding a new dimension to news.

One magazine, Henry Luce's *Life*, actually had its origins in a technical invention, the camera. Photography would present the world more directly than any words and its influence was in every verb in *Life*'s manifesto: 'To see life; to see the world; to witness great events; to watch the faces of the poor and the gestures of the proud; to see strange things – machines, armies, multitudes, shadows in the jungle and on the moon.'[15] Students of literature might think of Joseph Conrad's stated intention of making the reader 'see', but, far from endorsing this modernist aesthetic of immediacy, *Life*, with its worldwide coverage of people, places and events poses the question of authenticity: Was the reproduction of the Himalayas in *Life*, or the voice on the radio the real thing?

In 1941, just over twenty years after the Westinghouse Company had opened KDKA, the first broadcasting station, there were 955 stations, and two television stations. In 1924 Americans spent $350 million on radios and spare parts. Between 1922 and 1932 the proportion of homes with radios jumped from 0.2 to 55.2 per cent; by 1939 it was up to 88.5 per cent. The speed of communication also increased the rate of consumption and put pressure upon the producers of radio programmes. Inevitably, this led to the recycling of material and variations upon a format. Mass communications had other effects, though. People were put in the same cultural place at the same time: a movie theatre or around the family hearth but tuned in to the radio:

> Often whole families would place the headset into a soup tureen and cluster with their ears close to this primitive loudspeaker. What they heard was 'AWK . . . RAACK . . . hello out there . . . hello ouBriee . . . crackle . . .snap . . . wee . . . this Is . . . ROAR . . . HISS . . . STAtion 8 xkCRASHhiss . . . RoArrr . . . pop.' (quoted in Marquis, *Hopes and Ashes*, p. 16)

Once communications had been improved, radio could give instant access to the same images and messages, as illustrated by the phenomenon of the fad. Throughout the 1920s crossword puzzles, mah-jong, the Charleston, and stunts like goldfish swallowing caught on with amazing rapidity. The special power of radio was exemplified by 'The War of the Worlds', broadcast on Halloween 1938 in which Orson Welles left millions of Americans convinced that Martians had landed in New Jersey. The novelty of radio is hard to recapture, the feeling of being a part of and yet apart from the scenes being broadcast.

In the early days, radio had been thought of rather like a telephone, a situation that called for arbitration. According to Herbert Hoover, who in 1922 was Secretary of State:

> Obviously, if ten million [radio] telephone subscribers are crying through the air for their mates they will never make a junction; the ether will be filled with frantic chaos, with no communication of any kind possible. In other words, the wireless telephone has one definite feature, and that is for the spread of certain predetermined matter of public interest from central stations.'[16]

In the light of disputes about satellite television and deregulation in the 1970s and 1980s, first in the USA and then in Europe, we can appreciate the ambiguous cultural politics which the invention of radio brought about. Should information be controlled or permitted to 'flow' or disseminate? In which direction does freedom of information lie? As the Lynds realized in the 1920s, radio contributed to a general political problem: people knew more but had more difficulty in judging information when they did not know its source and there was so much of it 'in the air' and on the page. The fear that 'alien' (usually communist and Jewish) propaganda would infiltrate American homes over the airwaves was voiced by Henry Ford's *Dearborn Independent*, an ironic response from the man who famously proclaimed that 'society lives by circulation and not by congestion'. In the 1930s the political scene was deeply affected by radio: in Europe where fascist and communist leaders made expert use of the new medium, and in the USA, in a different register, in the fireside chats of Franklin Roosevelt and the radio church of Father Coughlin.

In addition to worrying about the mass media's effects on the political process, American intellectuals, from Randolph Bourne in the 1910s through to Dwight Macdonald from the 1930s onwards, were concerned about the media's influence on the process of cultural Americanization. Between Bourne and Macdonald, a generation of intellectuals voted with their feet. According to Malcolm Cowley, post-war intellectuals like Harold Stearns, Harry Crosby, e.e. cummings, Hemingway, John Dos Passos, and others followed the lead of Henry James, Gertrude Stein, Eliot, and Pound and self-consciously 'performed autopsies . . . wrote obituaries of civilization in the United States [and] . . . shook the standardized dust of the country from their feet. Here, apparently, was a symbolic struggle: on the one side, the great megaphone of middle-class culture [*The Saturday Evening Post*]: on the other, the American disciples of art and artistic living'.[17]

A related, but differently focused, post-mortem on mass society was conducted by leading Southern intellectuals, among them Donald Davidson, John Crowe Ransom, Allen Tate, and Robert Penn Warren. Their critique, which arose out of the impact of modernization upon a society that explicitly characterized itself as traditional, was at its most explicit in the manifesto of the Southern Agrarians: *I'll Take My Stand*, published in 1930. According to the 'Statement of Principles', all the contributors 'tend to support a Southern way of life against what may be called the American or prevailing way; and all as much as agree that the best terms in which to represent the distinction are contained in the phrase, Agrarian *versus* Industrial'.[18] This opposition, like that between the traditional and the modern, turns out, on inspection, to be a good deal more complicated, not least because the Southern Agrarians were modernists of a sort (see pages 174–76), just as Southern industrialists were modernizing, albeit in the context of pre-modern social relations based upon the plantation. Nevertheless, in the criticism of Davidson, Ransom, Tate, Warren, and their colleagues, we undoubtedly have an example of an important group of intellectuals who sought to base their resistance to modernity upon claims made for the past. Richard Godden succinctly translates the North/South economic division into cultural terms, pointing out that 'a culture committed to wage labour and its attendant forms of accumulation generates a commodity aesthetic' whereas 'a culture, or a cultural fragment, which resists wage labour and the consequent spread of the shop window, will generate an aesthetics of anti-development'.[19] Similarly, in their careers as New Critics, Southern Agrarians determinedly opposed any kind of aesthetics which was dependent upon mechanical reproduction; their aesthetics was thus a defence of literature (in particular) against the media of a mass society.

In one of his late papers, 'Science as a Vocation' (1918), Weber pessimistically enters this familiar modernist debate:

> The fate of our times is characterized by rationalization and
> intellectualization and, above all, by the 'disenchantment of the
> world.' Precisely the ultimate and most sublime values have
> retreated from public life either into the transcendental realm of
> mystic life or into the brotherliness of direct and personal human
> relations. It is not accidental that our greatest art is intimate
> rather and not monumental.[20]

Weber's distinction between 'intimate' and 'monumental' points to one strain in modernism as it responded to rationalization and became a private and difficult art. It advanced aesthetic criteria: for example, the hard or the impressionistic image in Pound and Cezanne, respectively; narrative epiphanies in Joyce; cleansing the language of the tribe in Mallarmé and Hemingway. Yet modernism's fiercely individualistic ethic and unerring insights into questions of representation (the necessity of *creating* the immutable or even the real, rather than merely reflecting either), served to undermine any of the universal or eternal claims which art has traditionally made when opposing the flux of change. This does not mean that these relativizing tendencies in modernism and their ambiguous relation to the commercial processes of product differentiation issued directly into post-modern pastiche and play. Even hindsight, and our realization that the struggle for style and uniqueness is a feature of the market as well as the artist's garret, still cannot reduce modernist writers and artists to the status of mere symptoms of post-modernist problematics. Besides, cultural 'institutions', such as expatriation in the 1920s, and larger and more prestigious American galleries and exhibitions from the early 1930s onwards, underpined modernism, marking it off from mass culture in a distinctively modernist way.

A reaction against modernization and mass culture was only one strain in modernism, however. Aside from the European Futurists, with their enthusiastic and shrill embracing of technology, a number of American intellectuals and artists, for instance Randolph Bourne, Lewis Mumford, Joseph Stella, and Frank Lloyd Wright, refused to turn away from modernization. As Americans, they were much closer to its processes than many Europeans. They were conscious of the dangers of the mass media, but did not dismiss the possibility that what they were witnessing was less the closure of a one-dimensional culture than the openness of a democratic culture. The image of the undifferentiated, threatening masses which dominates a European book like Ortega Y Gasset's *The Revolt of the Masses* (1930) jarred with an American faith in 'The Art and Craft of the Machine' (Wright's formulation) and the potential for individual self-improvement within a democratic rather than aristocratic frame of beliefs. Besides, it was (and is) difficult to opt single-mindedly for one of these interpretations rather than the other when faced with the pot pourri of American culture: music of different kinds – classics, jazz, popular tunes; news – of fads and of political developments in Germany, Italy and Spain in the 1930s; comics and soap operas; photographs exhibited not in such and such a gallery but between the covers of *Life*; films – mediocre productions scripted by Scott Fitzgerald and genre-films which have consistently attracted critical attention; operatic performances sponsored by Texaco; and what-you-need-to-know guides to art, history and science. If twentieth-century American culture is a heterotopia (to borrow Foucault's term again), it is a fascinating one. But more than this: the appearance by the 1930s of novel cultural forms demonstrates that the communications revolution had affected the production as well as the distribution and reception of culture. Specifically, things that could not be done before could now be done with the refinement of colour printing and radio transmission. Understood in a less precise way, as the intersecting of different dimensions of life, better communications meant that Midwestern grain elevators could enter the consciousness of Bauhaus architects and American Cubist-Realists. In other words, different strains of modernism became possible, besides the intimate and private one. In all its manifestations, though, modernism had still to grapple with the politics of a culture which had its motor in new material conditions, and which was no longer rooted in pre-modern locations.

Warren Susman has addressed the perennial division between freedom and domination, activity and passivity, and the two meanings of novelty that we have introduced. He has done so in the context of the communications revolution which, for most of this century, has had its forward wave in the United States. Consequently, his conclusion supplies a perspective upon the politics of culture/culture of politics axes that this book will explore:

If the culture of abundance has become manipulative, coercive, vulgar, and intolerable . . . why did this happen? Did it have to follow? Were there alternatives? Only a historical view – a vision of that culture as it developed and changed over time and in interaction with the traditional culture itself – can provide hope of getting at these crucial issues . . .

To see the utopian possibilities in the culture of abundance and to insist on a dialogical or dialectical reading of both its repressive and its liberating possibilities is not to commit oneself to the culture itself, to accept all that it proposes, or even to agree that its end can be achieved only within this particular economic and social structure.[21]

We can reasonably add that demographic changes – an important aspect of modernization in the United States during the years of massive immigration and migration to cities – produced recipients of mass culture but also potential sources of new ideas, new resistances. There were few blacks and recent immigrants in Middletown in the 1920s, but there were a great many in New York and Chicago, and they represented an 'emergent culture' within the 'dominant culture', to make use of Raymond Williams' useful terms.

The society of the spectacle

Arguments about mass culture, modernism, and the politics of both are a staple of the twentieth-century thought and culture which we shall be covering. However, an important aim of this introductory chapter remains that of establishing a dynamic relationship between modernization and articulated ideas and formal works of art which can then be drawn upon in later chapters. Questions of representation and temporality, which are central to the innovations of modernist art, literature and thought, were also precipitated by the process of modernization. When the 'ether' was 'filled with frantic chaos' (Herbert Hoover's words), and cities were filled with signs (Vachel Lindsay's 'hieroglyphic civilization'), discontinuities, decenterings, and novelties were encountered in the communications network itself. As such they are an undeniable part of historical *experience*, though whether we agree with Marshall Berman and describe this experience as modern or have to introduce the term post-modern to describe some aspects of the experience remains to be seen. Here we might note, but postpone comment upon, the interesting career of Yeats's line, 'Things fall apart; the centre cannot hold': it appears as an epigraph in Arthur Schlesinger Jr's end-of-ideology study, *The Vital Center* (1949); in Philip Rieff's end-of-modernism/pre-post-modernism jeremiad, *The Triumph of the Therapeutic* (1966); and then in Joan Didion's post-modernist collection, *Slouching Towards Bethlehem* (1968).

In his anatomy of the consumer culture, *The Theory of the Leisure Class*, Thorstein Veblen comments that people were on the move and that this affected forms of representation:

> In such places as churches, theaters, ballrooms, hotels, parks, shops, and the like [in] order to impress . . . transient observers, and to retain one's self-complacency under their observation, the signature of one's pecuniary strength should be written in characters which he who runs may read.[22]

But signs, too, were 'on the run'; they were, in Theodore Dreiser's words from *Sister Carrie*, 'everywhere numerous' on billboards, in movie theatres, in newspapers and magazines. Cities and towns were full of dealers in signs, and while the dollar sign and what it crudely represents is a central theme of both *The Theory of the Leisure Class* and *Middletown*, it is apparent that Veblen and the Lynds were also interested in the way that money functioned as a sign system, keeping goods and people on the move and constantly changing their appearance. America by the 1920s had become the first example of what Guy Debord calls 'the society of the spectacle'.

One of the most noticeable institutions in this society was the department store. This description of Wanamaker's Chicago store conveys some of the magic and novelty of display, which expanded cultural life even as the profit motive narrowed it:

> 129 counters totalling two-thirds of a mile in length, with fourteen hundred stools in front of them. Lighting was supplied by leaded glass skylights by day, gas chandeliers by night. In 1896, Wanamaker built a nearly life-sized replica of the Rue de la Paix in his store – 'a consolation for Americans who could not go to Paris.' In 1911, Wanamaker opened a new twelve-story structure featuring a Grand Court, and the second largest organ in the world, the latter punctuating the shopping day with sacredness.[23]

Rachel Bowlby writes shrewdly on the department store and her title phrase, 'just looking', makes a connection that we can explore in the next chapter:

The transformation of merchandise into a spectacle in fact suggests an analogy with an industry that developed fifty years after the first department stores: the cinema. In this case, the pleasure of looking, *just* looking, is itself the commodity for which money is paid.[24]

Going back to Thorstein Veblen's statement, the consolidation of railroad and urban transport systems meant that as well as metaphorically climbing the ladder of social mobility, more and more people were literally on the move as well. In consequence, they saw things differently. Now, of course, we take for granted the unexpected sights which occur when a train 'cuts' straight through a landscape rather than respecting its unique features. Yet when separated from the landscape, modes of perception and then of representation alter. The passenger, seemingly passive, just looking, looks out sideways from the compartment but with far from routine results: discrete objects are blurred and streaked; they carry a 'tail', the visual equivalent of the 'elongated' noises of rail travel: whistles, the sound of a train passing in the opposite direction, and so on.

There is an important difference between this modern view of the landscape and the relationship between sight and the landscape in mainstream romanticism. For example, in *Nature* (1836), Emerson claims that raising one's eyes from the foreground to the horizon has the effect of transcending (by blurring) the property divisions, thereby recreating the original landscape. Passengers on a train, however, are themselves on the move, allowing for no fixed or central point of perception and therefore no certain relation. Moreover, where for Emerson, perception was thought to be an unmediated process, best achieved when in isolation, the passenger sees the landscape by means of the train. In *The Railway Journey*, Wolfgang Schivelbusch makes this intriguing observation about mediation and movement:

> The outer world beyond the compartment window is mediated to the traveler by the telegraph poles and wires flashing by – no longer does he see only the landscape through which he is travelling, but also, continuously, these poles and wires that belong to the railroad as intimately as the rails themselves do. The landscape appears *behind* the telegraph poles and wires; it is seen *through* them . . . The hurtling railroad train appears here as the very motion of writing, and the telegraph poles and wires are the calligraphic instruments with which the new perception inscribes the panoramic landscape upon the real one.[25]

The intervention of the train, its rails and the signalling system between the observer and the landscape and, more obviously, between places of departure and destination, remove what were thought to be the normal continuities and produce discontinuities, a montage effect which anticipates developments in aesthetics: the replacement of a mimetic and narrative relationship between a visual or verbal sign and object by the juxtapositions of modernism. It is precisely this disconnectedness which the Marxist critic Georg Lukács criticizes: 'The loss of the narrative interrelationship between objects and their function in concrete human experiences means a loss of artistic significance.' What he has to say also applies to the 'constructedness' of the newspaper and the pot pourri that was radio programming: 'Lifeless, fetishized objects are whisked about in an amorphous atmosphere.'[26]

It is true that the ceaseless round of commodity differentiation in advertising, as well as the speed of travel and pace of metropolitan life can leave people and objects disconnected, and can dull rather than excite the senses. However, Lukács, in common with critics of mass culture from the left and right, takes for granted that there is an underlying narrative which gives meaning to surface objects and events, and that genuine art is in touch with this narrative. Yet this is precisely what is at issue in the communications revolution that only became fully manifest in the 1920s and 1930s. The kinds of developments in consumer capitalism which the Lynds detail in their 'Study of Contemporary American Culture' and which the German critic, Walter Benjamin, theorizes in his essay, 'The Work of Art in the Age of Mechanical Reproduction' (1936), question such oppositions as depth and surface, necessity and randomness, and reality and representation, together with the aesthetics of discrimination that accompanies these oppositions. As Dreiser's *Sister Carrie* demonstrates, and Georg Simmel explains in his essay of 1903, 'The Metropolis and Mental Life', urban life is so crowded with impressions and images that we are kept at the surface of life. Our confidence in a fundamental (deeper) temporal order based upon a fixed point of perception is challenged. Radio had the same effect, Catherine Covert argues: 'The jumble now included bands, orchestras, national rites, and public functions interspersed mindlessly with "explanations" by announcers. Radio broadcasting provided "the biggest crazy-quilt of audition" ever perceived by human ear' (Covert and Stephens (eds), *Mass Media Between the Wars*, p. 208).

In *The Lonely Crowd* (1950), which is the heir to *Middletown* in taking American 'sudsology' and the media society entirely seriously, David Riesman picks up the sense of anxiety as the formerly 'inner-directed', nineteenth-century individual becomes attuned to the 'torrent' of 'words and images'. 'Increasingly', Riesman adds, 'relations with the outer world and with one-self are mediated by the flow of mass communication.' Appropriately, he presents this shift in technological terms. Where the inner-directed character – the hero or perhaps anti-hero of Weber's *Protestant Ethic* – is kept on the right track by his/her 'psychological gyroscope', the 'control equipment' of the other-directed character is 'like a radar'. Identity and location become problematical for the person who is 'at home everywhere and nowhere.'[27]

The examples cited – railway travel, radio, modernist aesthetics, and social theory – may seem to be too specific to warrant larger claims about changing modes of perception and representation. The interconnections between different spheres of activity, which are so characteristic of twentieth-century American culture, suggest otherwise. For example, in the 1920s, 1930s and 1940s, modernist architecture was being seen on screen (and therefore seen everywhere) as Hollywood sets made use of internal and external architectural motifs derived from the work of Le Corbusier, Mies, Gropius, and Wright. The nineteenth-century train traveller experienced a more direct sense of interconnectedness. The spacious city railroad stations were architecturally similar to department stores, and made much use of glass and, later, electric lighting. In anticipation of today's shopping malls, the railway stations were multi-functional, housing restaurants and shops, and providing space for cultural events.

The expansion of the sign system, as one network intersected with another, raises spatial and temporal questions normally discussed in terms of modernist aesthetics; this in spite of a dominant tradition of modernist aesthetics stemming from the philosopher, Henri Bergson, which contrasts subjective perception and mechanistic, rationalized notions of space and time. When the name of a destination city was displayed on a railroad information board, travellers must have wondered where the city limits were drawn. Was a destination city somehow part of the traveller's home or departure city once the distance between them had shrunk with faster travel? Similarly, well before structuralism gave intellectual prominence to Saussure's insight that identity (including an individual's identity) arises differentially rather than referentially, the complexities of communications made any traveller who consulted the map of a subway system (for example in Boston after 1897) a party to the shift in thinking. The pre-history of subway mapping confirms the importance of the move towards abstraction and system in representation. Prototype maps attempted to reflect the surface reality but looked like a picture of multi-coloured spaghetti. Under ground, travellers could not relate and made more sense of a map which systematically distorted above-ground reality. The most successful designs represented stations as widely separated when they were, in actuality, on opposite sides of a street. In the 'code' of the map, the meaning of one entity (a station) depends upon its relation to, or difference from, another entity in the system. Each element in the system, each sign or mark, carries with it the traces of the whole sign system, but the rules that legitimate the system are also part of it. I hasten to add that the indeterminacy of sign-systems is not a paradox to be shunted off for resolution into the domains of faith, the occult or the ineffable. It is the unexpected outcome of the process of rationalization and systematization which was given theoretical prominence by Weber.

Where Weber remained a theorist of modernity, some of the insights more properly associated with post-modern theorists came to Weber's contemporary, Thorstein Veblen, when he chose not to burrow beneath the surfaces of life but to cultivate superficialities. *The Theory of the Leisure Class* describes in hyperbolic detail the replacement of an apparently tangible reality by codes – of behaviour, of dress and, back of it all, of consumption; consumption, that is, under the direction of mass advertising, in which, by definition, only representations of products can appear and circulate free from reference to use-value. Veblen's 'conspicuous consumption', facilitated by money and, even more intangibly, by credit, illustrates the peculiar functioning of 'the medium', understood not as a mere in-between but as a system or code in which signs refer to other signs. At the time when language had become a new kind of social fact, especially in the multi-signposted and billboarded American cities of the early twentieth century, so with Veblen, but more explicitly with Saussure, language also became the theoretical model for explaining proliferating sign-systems.

These speculations recall my initial question about the centrality of Middletown, or indeed, of any centre, including that of the individual self. It is not simply that by the 1920s the small town had lost its pre-eminent position in American culture to the large city; the communications network made it difficult even to locate the new centre of the economy in Chicago, New York or wherever, since cities were also subject to the new time/space continuum and the circulation of commodities. Instead, as we have seen, attention switched to relations between the elements in any system. In *The Education of Henry Adams* (1907), an autobiography written in the third person, Adams remarks on the consequences of communications:

> He and his eighteenth-century, troglodytic Boston were
> suddenly cut apart – separated forever – in act if not in sentiment,
> by the opening of the Boston and Albany Railroad; the
> appearance of the first Cunard steamers in the bay; and the
> telegraphic messages which carried from Baltimore to
> Washington the news that Henry Clay and James K. Polk were
> nominated for the presidency. This was in May, 1844; he was six
> years old; his new world was ready for use, and only fragments
> of the old met his eyes.[28]

Adams linked the railroad, as well as steamships, with the telegraph, and it is true that the telegraph did follow the physical tracks of the railroad. None the less, the transportation revolution should, strictly speaking, be distinguished from the communications revolution, which brought still more alterations to ways of seeing (time). The telegraph, which ushered in this new phase, was invented in 1844 but was not in widespread use until after 1900. In 'Technology and Ideology: The Case of the Telegraph', James Carey expertly draws out the implications of telegraphic communications when describing the moving of markets from space, where local market conditions determined the price of a commodity, into time, where all markets (national and international) determine price because, by means of the telegraph, everyone can be in possession of the required information about supply and demand at the same time. With the refinement of 'futures' trading, which the telegraph permitted, next year's goods, as well as simply the goods in other geographical markets entered the concern of dealers. Carey concludes that 'time as a new region of experience, uncertainty, speculation, and exploration was opened up', but the point worth emphasizing is that this was the outcome not of stream-of-consciousness techniques in the modernist fiction of Joyce, Woolf or Faulkner, or of investigations into the irrational by philosophers and psychologists, but of *a logical extension of rational calculability in the commercial sphere*. This is the same contradictory process we noted earlier when discussing the excess which standardization produced in mass-circulation newspapers, and the curious concept of time which standard time zones enforced.

James Carey points out that the crucial change which the telegraph brought about was that the commodity being bought and sold did not actually have to move at time of purchase and so 'was *sundered from its representations*' (p. 317). The separation of the object from its representation in a telegraphic message or a mail-order catalogue; the separation of the traveller from the 'real' world; the alienation of workers from their work and their territorial communities and relocation in what Daniel Boorstin calls 'consumption communities'; the enclosure of the shopper in a large department store or in a movie theatre: all of these illustrate the creation of systems of meaning which 'incorporated' what were thought to be separate sectors of American society in the years after the Civil War.

Not surprisingly, Marxist theory reorientated itself in the 1920s away from a straightforward economic determinism towards the idea of cultural domination, or, to use the technical term, hegemony. We can return to this critique in later chapters. However, the distinction between controlled and controller which is at the heart of such a critique of mass culture, the idea of some one or some company outside of, say, the fashion industry or even the communications industry, manipulating the whole charade, is rendered problematical by the sheer extent of any one system, let alone the overlapping of different systems. Equally, without clear boundaries it is difficult to identify the artistic or political source of transcendence, the way out of Weber's cage of rationality, or even the point of view from which a way out could be seen. A final example will help to explain how indeterminacy was produced by what were conceived of as determinate systems of thought and operation.

The shift from a production to a consumption economy which we have been describing depended, in large part, upon persuading women to consume. Veblen was among the first to depict women as consumers, most clearly in the chapter on fashion in *The Theory of the Leisure Class*. Women, he maintains, are the chief victims of the cultural domination and economic oppression that is effected by means of fashion: 'The corset is, in economic theory, substantially a mutilation, undergone for the purpose of lowering the subject's vitality and rendering her permanently and obviously unfit for work' (p. 121). On the other hand, fashion illustrates very clearly the arbitrariness which results when signs are separated from objects within a system of signification. An item of clothing in what the Lynds, quoting local terminology, call the 'style show', takes on its meaning not from a relation to that which it represents outside the style show or from some essence residing in it, but from that which it is not, its competitor or a variation within the same catalogue. There is no relation to an older use-value, but there is a relation to the 'old', the 'old' being the superseded image. 'The object of study,' Henry Adams remarks prophetically, 'is the garment, not the figure' (*Education*, p. xvi).

The great uncertainty of fashion arises from this lack of a firm referent, and while Marx's distinction between use-value and exchange-value is one important way of interpreting the constant differentiation of commodity which late capitalism demanded and fashion exemplifies, we should also acknowledge that the very distance from use-value makes space. As Baudelaire recognized, fashion is social and historical through and through: as such it reflects power relations but in the case of women, especially, creates an arena which need not be an extension of the biological. 'Anatomy is destiny', Freud wrote in an unguarded moment; but anatomy is not necessarily the determinant of fashion. Objecting to deterministic theories of fashion (including Veblen's) Elizabeth Wilson writes that 'clothing marks an unclear boundary ambiguously, and unclear boundaries disturb us.'[29] An item of clothing can be *given* meaning and, to this extent, there is the potential for activity, even creativity, within the seemingly closed system of fashion. Women can use fashion as well as be used by it, though the distinction between the two is often difficult to determine: was the clothing worn by the 'flapper' in the 1920s a sign of emancipation from Victorian values or a sign of further exploitation? Or, to put it differently, who derived pleasure from shorter skirts and how do we 'take account' of pleasure? Whether or not this is thought to be a significant example, the underlying issue here, as in all of the examples discussed in this book, is one of power, rather than of truth and falsity. This reorientation is one legacy of the modernist revolution, and is therefore the main reason why this book will pay only passing attention to the pre-modern world and the fundamental truths it is thought to embody.

Going back to Weber, for a moment, we can fully accept the sombre portents of his prophesy – 'mechanized petrification, embellished with a sort of convulsive self-importance' – while taking up the idea that his pessimism was very much tied to a nineteenth-century machine technology and to sources of power ('fossilized coal') that were being superseded even as he wrote. Even the powerful image of all-encompassing rationalization – the iron cage – may be inappropriate given that the bars of the cage have become, in one sense at least, 'wire-less', a point very nicely made by Henry James in 'In the Cage' (1899), his story of a London telegraphist. In his discussion of the telegraph, James Carey identifies this transition to a different way of thinking:

> The telegraph not only allowed messages to be separated from the physical movement of objects; it also allowed communication to control physical processes actively . . . Telegraphic messages could control the physical switching of rolling stock . . . The world of signifiers progressively overwhelms and moves independently of real, material objects. (pp. 305 and 319)

As it happens, the main intellectual source of this key insight in twentieth-century thought was roughly contemporaneous with many of the new technological developments, as well as with a modernism that sought to recreate in art the values that had hitherto given a centre to life. In Saussure's *Course in General Linguistics*, delivered as a lecture series between 1906 and 1911 but influential only with the advent of structuralism in the 1960s, we find this seminal statement:

> In language there are only differences. Even more important: a difference generally implies positive terms between which the difference is set up: but in language there are only differences *without positive terms*.[30]

In some ways, then, the Lynds' America was ahead of the productions of artists and intellectuals, many of whom took on an adversary role *vis-à-vis* their society. They were right to attack the corrosive effects of a mass culture, and, as we shall see in the next chapter on cinema, the opportunities for reconceptualizing time and space were too often seen purely in commercial terms and wasted or turned into opportunities for control. But 'the mechanization of perception', as Wolfgang Schivelbusch has it, and the rationalization of social and economic life described by Max Weber, were also vital and stimulating aspects of the experience of modernity. They produced novelties and contradictions which have given a distinctive quality to modernist thought and culture in America. However, books like *Middletown, The Theory of the Leisure Class* and *The Education of Henry Adams*, reveal modernizing processes as underway so early and so vigorously in the United States that the conditions were already being set for post-modernism to 'dissolve its own boundaries and become coextensive with ordinary commodified life itself, whose ceaseless exchanges and mutations in any case recognize no formal frontiers which are not constantly transgressed'.[31] In the latter part of many of the chapters which follow, we can consider how, 'in our time' (to co-opt Ernest Hemingway's modernist expression), intellectuals and artists have tried to take account not just of the 'possibilities and perils' of modernity, but, additionally, of the 'post-modern condition' in which the very oppositions which structure modernity have been deconstructed.

Notes

1. Marshall Berman, *All That Is Solid Melts Into Air: The Experience of Modernity* (1982), p. 15.

2. Theodore Dreiser, *Sister Carrie* (Columbus, Ohio, 1969), pp. 8–9.

3. Robert S. Lynd and Helen M. Lynd, *Middletown: A Study in Contemporary American Culture* (1929), p. 81.

4. Robert Wiebe, *The Search for Order, 1877–1920* (New York, 1967), p. 44.

5. Harvey Cox, *The Secular City: Secularization and Urbanization in Theological Perspective* (1965), p. 2.

6. Martin E. Marty, 'Religion in America Since Mid-Century', *Daedalus*, 111, (1982), p. 161. See, also, the rest of this special issue of *Daedalus*, and Sydney E. Ahlstrom, *A Religious History of the American People* (New Haven, 1972).

7. See *The New Religious Consciousness*, edited by Charles Y. Glock and Robert N. Bellah (Berkeley, 1976).

8. *The Sherwood Anderson Reader*, edited by Paul Rosenfeld (Boston, 1947), pp. 740–41.

9. Bill Bryson, *The Lost Continent: Travels in Small Town America* (1989), pp. 41 and 42.

10. Max Weber, *The Protestant Ethic and the Spirit of Capitalism*, translated by Talcott Parsons (1985), p. 17.

11. See Jean B. Quandt, *From the Small Town to the Great Community: The Social Thought of Progressive Intellectuals* (New Brunswick, New Jersey, 1970).

12. See Alan Trachtenberg, *The Incorporation of America: Culture and Society in the Gilded Age* (New York, 1982), ch. 4; and James Carey, 'Technology and Ideology: The Case of the Telegraph', *Prospects*, 8 (1983), pp. 303–25.

13. Quoted in Mary Beth Norton, *et al.*, *A People and a Nation: A History of the United States, Volume II: Since 1865* (Boston, 1982), p. 454.

14. Quoted in James E. Murphy, 'Tabloids as Urban Response', in *Mass Media Between the Wars: Perceptions of Cultural Tension, 1918–1941*, edited by Catherine L. Covert and John D. Stephens (Syracuse, 1984), p. 63.

15. Quoted in Alice G. Marquis, *Hopes and Ashes: The Birth of Modern Times, 1929–1939* (New York, 1986), p. 133.

16. Quoted in Richard A. Schwarzlose, 'Technology and the Individual: The Impact of Innovation on Communication', in Covert and Stephens (eds), *Mass Media Between the Wars* (see note 14), p. 100.

17. Malcolm Cowley, *Exile's Return: A Literary Odyssey of the 1920s* (Harmondsworth, 1986), p. 53.

18. Twelve Southerners, *I'll Take My Stand: The South and the Agrarian Tradition* (New York, 1962), p. xix.

19. Richard Godden, *Fictions of Capital: The American Novel from James to Mailer* (Cambridge, 1990), p. 143.

20. *From Max Weber: Essays in Sociology*, translated and edited by H.H. Gerth and C. Wright Mills (1970), p. 155.

21. Warren I. Susman, *Culture as History: The Transformation of American Society in the Twentieth Century* (New York, 1985), pp. xxix–xxx.

22. Thorstein Veblen, *The Theory of the Leisure Class: An Economic Study of Institutions* (1970), p. 72.

23. Stuart and Elizabeth Ewen, *Channels of Desire: Mass Images and the Shaping of American Consciousness* (New York, 1982), p. 69.

24. Rachel Bowlby, *Just Looking: Consumer Culture in Dresier, Gissing and Zola* (1985), p. 6.

25. Wolfgang Schivelbusch, *The Railway Journey: Trains and Travel in the 19th Century*, translated by Anselm Hollo (Oxford, 1980), pp. 38 and 40.

26. Georg Lukács, *Writer and Critic and Other Essays*, translated and edited by Arthur Kahn (1978), pp. 131 and 133.

27. David Riesman, with Nathan Glazer and Reuel Denney, *The Lonely Crowd: A Study of the Changing American Character* (New Haven, 1961), pp. 21 and 25.

28. Henry Adams, *The Education of Henry Adams* (New York, 1931), p. 5.

29. Elizabeth Wilson, *Adorned in Dreams: Fashion and Modernity* (1985), p. 2.

30. Ferdinand de Saussure, *Course in General Linguistics*, translated by Wade Baskin, edited by Charles Bally and Albert Sechehaye, in collaboration with Albert Reidlinger (1960), p. 120.

31. Terry Eagleton, *Aginst the Grain: Essays 1975–1985* (1986), p. 141. These comments and those dotted throughout my Introduction (on decentred structures, loss of confidence in meta-narratives, play, pastiche, and depthlessness) will have to suffice as a working definition of post-modernism. Later chapters will refine the definition as appropriate to the text or art-form under discussion.

Part One
The Politics of Culture

Chapter 1
Cinema

The work of art in the age of mechanical reproduction

In *Modern Times*, a 1936 film dealing with mechanization, Charlie Chaplin belatedly confronted the cinematic machinery of sound and spoke on screen for the first time. Hearing Chaplin's nonsensical mixture of English and Italian we are unsure whether he has triumphed over the latest technology or has been confused by it. 1936 was also the year of Walter Benjamin's 'The Work of Art in the Age of Mechanical Reproduction', a seminal essay in thinking about the cinema. Benjamin, too, identifies the threat of mechanical reproduction to the unique 'aura' of the work of art and goes on to remark on the function of mass communications in the totalitarian regimes of the 1930s, a theme in Chaplin's *The Great Dictator* of 1940. Benjamin nevertheless intimates that mechanical reproduction is a source of both new artistic possibilities and a revolutionary, because popular, political culture.

Cinema is founded in technology and has its beginnings in industrial production and commercial distribution. Far from downgrading cinema, in comparison with literature and painting, this points to the complexity, as well as the novelty, of the cultural form which is so much a part of the mental and material fabric of modern times. When photographs moved, and became 'the movies' instead of the simple magic lantern shows of cinema's pre-history, they had enormous popular appeal. The movies seemed to capture the real thing by mechanical, scientific means free from bias and the limitations of words or painted images. The technology which permitted this dramatic advance in representation, and the commerce which distributed the results took preference over the content and certainly the aesthetics of the very first cinematic 'events': Thomas Edison's Kinetoscope, on display at the Chicago World's Fair of 1893; two years later, Louis and Auguste Lumière's Cinematographe, which had its commercial debut in Paris at the Grand Café, Boulevard des Capucines; and Edison's large-screen exhibition in 1896 at Koster and Bial's Music Hall in New York City. In 1910 there were well over five thousand nickelodeons in the United States, and by the end of the silent era there were 'stars' – Rudolph Valentino, Mary Pickford, Greta Garbo, Douglas Fairbanks, and many others – and 'directors', such as D.W. Griffith, Charlie Chaplin, and Erich von Stroheim. There were also 'studios' – Paramount Pictures and 20th Century-Fox for example – and many critics and historians of American cinema maintain that these are the names that really count.

Technology, politics, aesthetics, and economics. These elements come together in the idea of a *language of cinema*, which we can follow from the silent period through the introduction of sound and the full institution, followed by the supposed break-up, of the studio system. 'Language' refers to how a film signifies through editing and *mise en scène*, by which is meant the direction on set: of actors, sound recordists and camera operators, the last of these dealing with the positioning of cameras, choice of lenses, 'shots' and so on. 'Cinema' refers, in Christian Metz's important definition, 'not just [to] the cinema industry (which works to fill cinemas, not to empty them)', but also to 'the mental machinery – another industry – which spectators "accustomed to the cinema" have internalized historically and which has adapted them to the consumption of film.'[1] By the 1920s, 'cinema', in both of Metz's senses, was fast becoming synonymous with the Los Angeles suburb called Hollywood, later to be called 'the dream factory'.

We didn't know what we were doing: realism and modernism in the silent cinema, 1890s to 1920s

Like the silent films, with their madcap chases, congested spaces, and compressed plots, the silent era was full and busy. Working for American Biograph between 1908 and 1913, D.W. Griffith alone made at least five hundred films: westerns, thrillers, gangster movies, and comedies, as well as adaptations of literary classics. The majority were one-to-three-reelers, lasting approximately ten to thirty minutes, one reason why Griffith's *The Birth of the Nation* was such a milestone in 1915. It was twelve reels, lasted three hours, cost the then enormous sum of $110,000 to produce and, depending upon the method of calculation, has earned between $13 million and $100 million.

In the confused arena of silent cinema, we can discern the two main tendencies in cinematic representation – realism and modernism – which, later, would become polarized into 'Hollywood' and the different strands of 'art cinema'. The ridiculous extremes of an early 'short' such as Edison's *Electrocution of an Elephant*, and Griffith's next big film, *Intolerance* (1916), demonstrate that in the former the medium appears to give way before the object, person or event, and so remains closer to the sheer amazement which greeted cinema, while Griffith's dazzling display of camera work gestures towards cinematic modernism.

Modernism can serve as an all-purpose category for expressionism, avant-garde cinema and the other alternatives to mainstream American cinema. This broadly non-realistic cinema dates from roughly the same period as stream of consciousness, cubism and other developments in literary and painterly modernism, but where Joyce, Picasso and their contemporaries were reacting against forms of realism, cinematic modernism and its rival were not successive phases in the history of film. How could they be at a time when 'we didn't know what we were doing', as Cecil B. DeMille is reported to have said of the early days of the movies.

There were realist and modernist tendencies in representation well before Griffith claimed to have invented such cinematic techniques as the close-up and the cut. Some film historians trace the two traditions back to the Lumière brothers (realism) and to Méliès (modernism). However, specific examples are more helpful. In 1903, near the beginning of his decade of pre-eminence, Edwin S. Porter made *The Great Train Robbery*. Where previous Edison films had mostly been a single action in a fixed frame, Porter's explored the all-important relationship between frames, which we now take for granted, of course. For example, early in the film, there is a hold-up, during which a train passes, glimpsed through the window of the telegraph office. When the robbers reappear in the next scene and scramble on to another train the two distinct scenes are linked by a simple narrative. Narrative continuity is adhered to as a principle throughout most of the ten-minute film, though the technique of parallel cutting alerts us to a different concept of cinematic language. During the robbers' escape, cuts to the telegraph office and to the barn-dance, the latter interrupted by news of the robbery, are not necessarily coterminous or sequential in time. Instead the editing intervenes in realistic presentation in order to comment upon cause and effect and the relationship between everyday, legal activities and the irruption of illegal violence. Cross-cut editing, in contrast, is between events taking place at, presumably, the same time in different places: in a typical 1917 Mack

Sennett comedy entitled *Teddy at the Throttle*, the cuts are between the heroine (Gloria Swanson) chained to a railway line; an oncoming train; a precursor of Lassie; the villain looking on from behind a tree; and the rescuer-hero. Cross-cutting enforces realism, making time and place coincide (fortunately without disaster on this occasion) to the exclusion of interpretive commentary.

Then we have Porter's full-size close-up of the leader of the bandits firing at the audience. Packaged separately, exhibitors could show it at the beginning or end of *The Great Train Robbery*. Since all the outlaws are killed by the posse, the exhibitor's choice made a considerable difference to the meaning of the film. Possibly it was perceived that a close-up in which the audience was 'addressed' by a character could not be smoothly integrated into the realistic narrative sequence of, mostly, long and medium shots. Yet it was promoted in the Edison catalogue under the banner of 'Realism. A life size picture of Barnes, leader of the outlaw band, taking aim and firing point blank at each individual in the audience.'[2] This prophetic tension is between the photographic image drawing attention to the work of narrative in joining one frame to another, while, at the same time, authorizing the realism of the film. It would be the achievement of Hollywood to arrange a marriage between realism and narrative which is still going strong.

Early American cinema was a small, as well as a busy, world and in 1907 D.W. Griffith appeared in Porter's *Rescued from an Eagle's Nest*. Once with Biograph, Griffith made the transition to directing with *The Adventures of Dollie* (1908) and, by the time of *The Birth of a Nation* and *Intolerance*, which were made in Hollywood with Reliance Majestic, he had posed much more explicitly than Porter the key questions of cinematic language. Where the revolution in literary language led to the victory of modernism, in both the novel and poetry, the competing aesthetic, socio-economic, and, of course, technological determinants upon cinema increasingly pressed the claims for film as the reproduction of reality. For all the panoply of cinematic devices in *The Birth of a Nation*, more representative of the film as a whole is Griffith's retention of the same shot for the long scene when confederate soldiers approach us down the main street of Piedmont, and then march away to the left. This is consistent with his use of Matthew Brady's photographs of the Civil War, and his own efforts to authenticate the story and the sets. Another of cinema's specific contributions to realism is apparent in the many family scenes where, within the same shot, characters, particularly lesser ones like the young Cameron daughter, are engaged in peripheral activities which seemingly continue off-screen.

Reviews of *The Birth of a Nation* praised the film's capture of the unfolding panorama of battle, but sometimes protested at the experiments with camera angles, the practice of cutting between shots within a single scene, and fade-in and fade-out 'irises': 'such angles dispelled the carefully built-up realism, because the audience, now participant rather than spectator, was instantly made aware of the presence of the camera'.[3] *Intolerance* better illustrates this very revealing reaction, because identification with characters and a single narrative is impeded by the device of linking stories of intolerance among contemporary reformers, the sixteenth-century Medici, the priests of Babylon, and the Pharisees in Jerusalem. Griffith was after unity, but particularly when, later in the film, the repeated link-scene of the woman rocking a cradle gives way to direct juxtaposition of scenes from the four stories, full rein is given to the possibilities of montage.

Montage means editing; but certain kinds of editing – sometimes referred to as creative, as opposed to continuity, editing – have become virtually synonymous with the modernism of Sergei Eisenstein and Soviet cinema in the 1920s and early 1930s. The political and aesthetic turmoil of the post-revolutionary decade in the USSR was a long way from the developing consumer capitalism of the United States, but the sheer unformed-ness of the two cinemas led to some similarities. Certainly, Eisenstein's work shows the influence of the 'eccentrism' which he and other Soviet modernists perceived in the new urban-industrial world emerging simultaneously in the United States and on American film. For Eisenstein montage derived from 'the assembling of machinery, pipes, machine tools . . . Let *units of impression combined into one whole* be expressed through a dual term, half-industrial and half-music-hall'.[4]

Film stock was scarce and the first students of film, Eisenstein included, experimented by re-editing existing films. In Hollywood, formalism took second place to the hunt for more and more subjects to film. After seeing *Intolerance* in the Soviet Union in 1919, Eisenstein acknowledged Griffith's pioneering work with montage but, in *Strike* (1925), *Battleship Potemkin* (1925) and *October* (1928), he explored the modernist implications in Griffith. Of *October*, he asserts that in juxtaposing political speech-making by Mensheviks at the Second Congress of Soviets and images of harps and balalaikas, parallel montage enters 'a new realm': from the sphere of action into the sphere of significance.' Montage, he stipulates, is not 'a *linkage* of pieces' but 'a *collision*', which gives access to the dialectical pattern of history.[5] Whether or not Eisenstein's juxtaposition, in *Strike*, of shots of a massacre of workers with shots of an abattoir is explicable in strictly dialectical terms, his overall position departs from the realist one in its insistence that montage (but also *mise en scène* in certain hands) estranges the spectator from everyday assumptions (for instance about the straightforwardness of narrative), thereby demonstrating how reality, including psychological reality, is constructed. From 1920s German Expressionism onwards, other European cinemas have also fed into modernism, and by the time of the French New Wave and

Alain Resnais's *Last Year at Marienbad* (1961), nameless characters can be depicted caught up in decentred and enigmatic narratives.

When Eisenstein eventually had the chance to visit Hollywood in 1930, modernist cinema had been largely superseded by narrative cinema. Eisenstein's projects for Paramount, one of them an adaptation of Theodore Dreiser's novel, *An American Tragedy*, never reached the screen. It will help to crystallize what happened to this other cinema in the wake of the success of American narrative cinema, if we make use of the influential writings of André Bazin, a very different film theorist from Eisenstein and one who has paid special attention to Hollywood.

Bazin gave a different answer to his own question 'What is cinema?' Looking back at the silent era in such essays as 'The Evolution of the Language of Cinema' and 'The Virtues and Limitations of Montage' he gives theoretical weight to the argument, which we have been tracing through examples, that the inherent qualities of photography and cinema overrode what he called 'anti-cinematic' modernism. These qualities permitted greater progress than even the nineteenth-century novel had made in the attempt directly to represent reality. This preference informs his promotion of 1920s directors Robert Flaherty, Erich Von Stroheim and F.W. Murnau. In Flaherty's documentary film, *Nanook of the North* (1922), montage reverts to the basic editorial function of removing excessive footage. The scene when Nanook waits for the seal is, for Bazin, a return to the first single-shot films of the late 1890s.

Erich von Stroheim championed the cause of realism against montage, and this in spite of his declared indebtedness to Griffith. Stroheim's first film as director was *Blind Husbands* (1919), with his other important films being *Foolish Wives* in 1922, *Greed* in 1925, and *The Wedding March* in 1928. The abstract title of *Greed* invites a comparison with Griffith's *Intolerance* of the previous decade, but the slow-moving camera movements keep attention upon the story and the actors (rather than on the 'idea'), while short shots record the detail which was so important to the Naturalistic novel upon which the film was based, Frank Norris' *McTeague*. Stroheim favoured location shooting to the extent that he sought out the exact locations which had inspired Norris. His use of deep-focus photography, as an alternative form of realism to continuity editing, keeps background as well as foreground in clear view, so the action can proceed in a unified rather than cut-up space.

The Western benefited from the commitment to realism. The actor, Tom Mix, had popularized the genre by importing stunt routines and rapid cutting from comedy. *The Last Trail* (1927) and Mix's other action and hero-centred westerns pointed in one direction, but another was followed by William S. Hart, as actor and director in such films as

The Return of Draw Egan (1917) and *Tumbleweeds* (1925). The combination of long and medium shots and location shooting in *Tumbleweeds*, especially in the land-rush sequence, produces the documentary quality for which James Cruze's *The Covered Wagon* (1923) and John Ford's *The Iron Horse* (1924) are more famous. Ford, more than any of these directors, favoured unobtrusive camera work and so, for all the lyricism which marks him off from Stroheim and Murnau, he is early associated with the tradition that Bazin outlines. Once Hopalong Cassidy (William Boyd) and the 'singing cowboys' had had their day in the 1930s, the realistic tradition resurfaced in a modified form in Ford's 1939 film, *Stagecoach*.

Realism and modernism are not simply part of a descriptive taxonomy. There is a politics to style and form. *Birth of a Nation* is again a revealing example because it is known for both its experimentalism and a specific content: the racist portrayal of black slaves as happy, respectful and loyal, and of northern free blacks as upstarts, trouble-makers and a danger to the honour of white women. One caption describes the Ku Klux Klan as 'the saviour of white civilization'. Some critics play down or excuse Griffith's racism, but those who acknowledge it tend to separate his modernism and his reactionary views. Analogous debates surround the literary modernists, Wyndham Lewis, Ezra Pound and T.S. Eliot. Yet this response to Griffith mostly misses the point that the construction of the film is intimately related to Griffith's historical vision of 'the birth of a nation'. For example, a specific cinematic technique, the 'dissolve', is used in conjunction with the structural device of the two families, the Camerons and the Stonemans, so that public issues can be represented by means of private family histories. Similarly, scenes involving Austin Stoneman, the northern politician, are constructed through camera shots that link his advocacy of the rights of slaves with his lust for his mulatto maidservant and his own personal vanity. The point – more generally – is not that realism and modernism are necessarily radical or conservative politically; if they were, then Eisenstein and Griffith would make a very odd pair. Rather, it is that Griffith's modernist techniques unsettle the process of audience identification, which he otherwise sought through narrative continuity and a commitment to historical authenticity, and so draw attention to the ideological construction of a cinematic world.

The representational, narrative and sheer spectacular qualities of Griffith's work proved to be a more telling influence upon Hollywood than the incipient modernism, which reached a pitch in the visually and formally disconcerting *Intolerance*. It was an influence that Griffith left behind him, however, when, on the basis of the commercial success of *Broken Blossoms* in 1919 and *Way Down East* the year after, he moved away from Hollywood and set up his own studio in Mamaroneck,

New York. Thereafter, he declined in importance, though continued to make films into the early sound period.

Variety: Hollywood and genre

In the early 1920s Griffith was leaving more than just a Californian suburb. Hollywood was a place where Paramount, Universal and other studios were establishing themselves on an industrial footing barely dreamed of by the owners of Biograph, Essanay, and Kalem. By 1918, 80 per cent of all American films were made in Hollywood. The studio system was fully recognizable by the end of the silent era, even if its full effects were not felt until after the coming of sound. The star system was also in place, and in the 1920s Greta Garbo and Rudolph Valentino joined Douglas Fairbanks, Lillian Gish, Mary Pickford, and Clara Bow in their monopoly of Hollywood publicity. Hollywood's international pre-eminence was also signalled by the power of the studios to attract European directors as well as actors in the 1920s and 1930s. Ernst Lubitsch, F.W. Murnau, Paul Leni, and Fritz Lang came to Hollywood for higher salaries but also to take advantage of the technology and the resident expertise. Besides, World War I had decimated the European film industry so that 95 per cent of all films exhibited outside the United States were American films. When discussing cinema, it would be impossible to overestimate the significance of Hollywood's influence on the style and form of American films.

The infrastructure being built up in Hollywood allowed the industry to respond quickly to demand, however unexpected. During the First World War Hollywood adapted to its role as the source of propaganda, and its star system, led by Chaplin, Fairbanks and Pickford, swung into fund-raising action. After the war, Hollywood cashed in with war movies, and, then, in the mid-1920s when the genre seemed moribund, revived it with anti-war films like King Vidor's *The Big Parade* (1925). Once the genre was back in favour, Hollywood risked including comedy sequences in Raoul Walsh's war film, *What Price Glory?* (1926). The spectacular stunts in William Wellman's *Wings* (1927) differentiated the genre further, while retaining generic consistency. This kind of variety in a single genre and, overall, the riches of American cinema in the 1920s, measured by a head-count of directors, actors, and technical experts, would appear to contradict a now common view of Hollywood as the home of standardized production. And so it does – up to a point, which we can appreciate by pausing to discuss comedy and Charlie Chaplin, respectively, the most successful genre of the silent era and the other great name of the period besides Griffith.

The first serious advocate of screen comedy in America was not Chaplin but Mack Sennett. Between 1908 and 1912 Sennett was at Biograph, and worked for some time as an assistant to Griffith. His editing techniques owe something to Griffith, but he took charge of a genre that Griffith tended to downplay, and while at Biograph directed around one hundred short comedies. In 1912 Sennett went to the recently formed Keystone Company and over the next few years was joined by Roscoe 'Fatty' Arbuckle, Wallace Beery, Gloria Swanson (who resented the slapstick roles she was asked to play), Harry Langdon and, in 1914, Charlie Chaplin. While with Sennett, Chaplin made over thirty comedies, most of which he directed with Sennett as 'central producer', the mode of production which Hollywood favoured until around 1930. In this role, symbolized by the watchtower which he had built in the middle of the lot, Sennett forged the frenetic Keystone style that dominated comedy into the early 1920s. The camerawork is highly mobile, as a consequence of following the fast-moving action, while the rapid cutting style reflects the influence of comic strips, vaudeville and French slapstick comedy. Though the chase is the centrepiece of a Keystone Cops film, it does not uniformly ensure narrative progression, as it was increasingly doing in other Hollywood genres. The assemblage of set-piece gags cuts across the forward movement of the film contributing to what the Soviet film-makers admired as 'eccentrism'. Others have suggested comparisons with Dada, Surrealist and Futurist art.

Working against the heterogeneity and potential disorder of Sennett's comedies are principles of coherence. They are specific to different comedians, for instance the emotional restraint that was common to most of Buster Keaton's films, or the pathos that increasingly unified Chaplin's. The box-office success of *The Kid* (1921), Chaplin's first feature-length film, proved the worth of pathos. In the comedies produced by Hal Roach in the 1920s and 1930s, narrative is more noticeable, especially when it is reinforced by a gentle moral and made the vehicle for the development of character; we think, in 1920s films, of the importance of comic personalities, like Laurel and Hardy, Will Rogers, Harold Lloyd, Keaton, and Chaplin.

These individual principles of coherence are contained within general, that is to say, generic principles. The most comprehensive principle for screen comedy is *repetition*. Repetition is necessary, by definition, in a genre but especially in a new genre, such as screen comedy. When the Keystone Cops set off in pursuit of a criminal it is recognized by the audience that at least one of them will be left behind or will fall off and be forced to run after the car. Within a range of variations the audience knows what to expect. Aside from the relating of one film to another by means of repetition, there are local repetitions, which structure the comic action within individual films. At its most obvious, actions (usually falling down or colliding) are repeated, and often they are preceded by a mime of the action. There are, however, scenes in Keystone Cops films where the sheer duration of the local repetition generates a certain unnerving quality that decomposes, without destroying, the larger pattern of generic repetition. We can make more of this dissident element in the development of comedy when we get to Chaplin's films.

With so much going on in 1920s cinema, there is no clear pattern. What we can see, though, is the highly individual 'look' of two 1927 films made by German directors, Leni's *The Cat and the Canary* and Murnau's *Sunrise*, being taken in the direction of continuity and coherence. As we have noted in war movies and in comedy, Hollywood's mode of production through the studio system was capable of absorbing new elements. These brought 'variety', mass culture's version of difference. Interestingly, Universal Studios was attracted to the German director, E.A. Dupont, on the strength of his 1925 film, *Variety*. That film and Murnau's *The Last Laugh* (1924), according to David Bordwell, 'created a vogue for unusual angles and the so-called "free" camera . . . "Well, that's a great shot; why can't we do that?" '[6] However, Hollywood rarely took on board any hint that odd camera angles were *not* to be explained with reference to character and narrative or, as was the case in Soviet cinema, the idea that the individual perspective could be subsumed under the viewpoint of a class.

Chaplin had an uneven relationship with the studios. In 1919 he formed United Artists with Fairbanks, Griffith and Pickford to gain some independence, while the release of the pacifist film, *Monsieur Verdoux* in 1947 attracted the attention of the House Un-American Activities Committee. Interestingly, though, for much of the silent era the gradual refinement of genre as an economic way to entertain, with 'economic' being understood in a formal as well as a financial sense, produced relative harmony between commercial and aesthetic principles. Genre played an important and subtle role in mediating between standardization and difference, between the compulsion to repeat what has been successful in order to obtain the greatest return on the rising costs of capital investment, while, at the same time, accepting that repetition will kill demand. So while Chaplin undoubtedly stands out, his qualities do not isolate him from the mainstream. Up until he signed for MGM in 1927, Buster Keaton was a more eccentric figure than Chaplin, whose work was described by Jean Renoir as 'classical cinema', in which 'nothing is left to chance' and 'the smallest detail takes its place of importance in the overall psychological scheme of the film' (quoted in Bordwell, et al., Classical Hollywood Cinema, p. 3).

Compared with the largely undifferentiated mass of the Keystone Cops, in Chaplin's films there is a narrowing of focus, which dates from The Tramp (1915), where the title-character occupies the whole of the concluding fade-out. Thereafter, this character appears regularly in features and short films, and becomes instantly recognizable through his moustache, walk, shoes, bowler hat, cutaway coat and walking stick. According to André Bazin these 'constants' derive from the 'person', rather than the 'character.' 'Charlie . . . is always free to appear in another film.' The significance of this repetition of character in Chaplin's films lies in the theory, firmly associated with Bazin, that realism is the essence of the cinema. There is an inseparable link between the photographic image and, in this instance, 'the living Charlie'.[7]

Within, even more importantly than across, films, it is repetition which tells us who characters are in relation to their surroundings. In Pay Day (1922), Charlie triumphs over the routine of work on a building site in a series of gags with a lift. In Modern Times, his relationship to society is defined for us by a succession of vans which draw up and cart him off to prison or an asylum. Yet there is a localized repetition in Chaplin's films which troubles the continuity of any narrative and, by extension, the coherence of characters and genre. Bazin instances Charlie, in Easy Street (1917), dodging back and forth behind a bed even when his adversary stands still, and, in Modern Times, tightening up imaginary bolts when the production line has stopped. He concludes that 'when Charlie is involved with an object for some time he quickly contracts a sort of mechanical cramp, a surface condition in which the original reason for what he is doing is forgotten' (What is Cinema?, p. 150).

As so often, Bazin's perceptive observations suggest reasons for objecting to his theoretical explanation. Charlie's repetitions are quite different from the kind of controlled repetition upon which all narrative genres depend. Far from being reassuring, some of Charlie's repetitions approach the unbearable, and we long for some more definable conflict which would at least hold out the hope of a resolution. 'Repetition is an absence of direction, a failure of coherence', Stephen Heath remarks.[8] Charlie's repetitions call up the very beginnings of cinema, when the gaps between the frames were more apparent. Where cinema, as a 'time machine' invented at about the same time as H.G. Wells's fictional one, creates the illusion of movement and brings with it pleasure, the mechanization that takes command over Charlie (and pervades much early comedy) brings to the surface a fundamental disconnection that is not easily assimilable to a character or narrative. Charlie dodging back and forth or continuing to jerk in tune with the machine while having his lunch, undermines the self and any notion of coherent action stemming from the self. In this case, *repetition produces difference*: a lack of identification between viewer and character on screen.

It is true that Charlie can be incorporated into our world as an eccentric or tragi-comic victim. But Charlie's way of being in the film, the very arbitrariness of his movements, reveals the arbitrariness of our world, its mode of production and, especially, its way of turning discontinuity into the continuity of a narrative. In *Modern Times* repetition structures but also un-structures the narrative, so much so that the repetitive economy of production becomes the subject of the film. At one level this is quite apparent. *Modern Times* is Max Weber's theme of rationalization given an ironic twist, from the epigraph onwards: 'A story of industry, of individual enterprise – humanity crusading in the pursuit of happiness.' The smooth continuity of the production line is quickly disrupted by Charlie, distracted first by an itch and then by a fly. His efforts to extricate himself from the production line into whose giant cogs he is threaded – an extraordinary futurist image – sets in motion an aberrational rhythm which exposes rationalized production as an end in itself, end-less repetition. We never know what the factory is producing other than refinements to the production line. When the Billow's automatic feeding machine is rejected by the company president it is because it is not 'practical'.

Mechanized production is undoubtedly challenged by Charlie, but it is replaced by a different and more subtle form of industrial production, the dream factory of Hollywood which, by 1936, had monopolized the reproduction of images and their sequencing into a narrative. Charlie is literally removed from the factory machinery early on in the film, only to be re-moved by the 'machine ensemble' of the media, to borrow Wolfgang Schivelbusch's expression. It is a prophetic moment in the film when, in the prison governor's office, to drown the embarrassing, and entirely inconsequential, noise of his stomach rumbling, he turns on the radio only to hear an advertisement for a cure for gastritis. Even the cures for modern times are manufactured. When Charlie and the gamin (Paulette Goddard) escape from the police and the city streets they end up in a landscaped suburb. And when, sitting by the road, they imagine themselves in a country cottage, the scene comes straight out of the routines of the domestic comedies which had become a staple of Hollywood in the early sound years. The scene concludes when a cow brings milk directly to the newly-weds' door, but the cow is on a production line. Chaplin further underscores the film's self-consciousness about its own production line in Charlie's luddite assault on the factory (a repetition of his disruptive activities in the 1916 film about film-making, *Behind the Screen*). Charlie's actions are not abrupt but very smooth, being choreographed as a combination of a ballet and a swashbuckling routine. In 1936, the system in which Charlie is enmeshed is Hollywood.

The images of coherence which accompanied the growing importance of narrative continuity in American cinema are there in the Lynds' case study which we drew upon in the Introduction:

> In 1890 Middletown appears to have lived on a series of plateaus as regards standard of living . . . . Today [1924] the edges of the plateaus have been shaved off, and every one lives on a slope from any point of which desirable things belonging to people all the way to the top are in view. (pp. 82–3)

When the Lynds returned to Middletown in the middle of the Depression, they were confirmed in their hypothesis that the movies exerted a regulating and unifying influence upon discontinuous lives through the power of visual images. 'Life in its truth as scene', is Christian Metz's neat formulation.[9] Earlier, during the period of mass immigration, the power of the image was advertised as transcending any verbal language tied to a particular culture. D.W. Griffith announced to his production unit: 'We are playing to the world. We've gone beyond Babel, beyond words. We've found a universal language – a power that can make men brothers and end war forever.'[10] Thinking about these different audiences gives an extra dimension to the issue raised by Stephen Heath when he imagines people sitting facing the image of reality on a screen, rarely, if ever turning round to face its source.

Would that reality hang together, though? This question would not have been posed in terms of ideological influence. Rephrased as an economic question, it was uppermost in the minds of producers, directors, actors and everyone who had a stake in the film. The 'flicker' between frames, reminding us, as in home-movies, of how the reality on screen is constructed, suggests the potential for disorder in cinema. In *Modern Times*, Charlie's direct battles with machines and institutions are, in the end, moved along by the narrative and apparently transcended in the freedom of the closing scene. Yet we also remember a few less obvious but, in view of the developing Hollywood style, more resistant images. Among them are the inconsequential comic repetitions: the minister's wife tripping over Charlie's feet – twice; and the furniture and fittings in the shack repeatedly and randomly attacking Charlie. In spite of the pathos of 'Charlie', from *The Tramp* onwards, the development of this character through narrative is continually being sidetracked in favour of unmotivated attacks on those around him. This is the 'eccentrism' of Sennett's comedy resurfacing.

Then there is the opening juxtaposition of sheep and workers in *Modern Times*. It is crude enough, compared with those in Eisenstein's films, but it is the fact that it is left as a juxtaposition and never referred to again that is important. It is not brought into the reality constructed by the narrative (as the fantasia in the suburban house is) because the gaps between the images of sheep and workers are not filled by narrative or by character. That these gaps are rarely noticed in mainstream cinema is the achievement of a certain mode of production and the filmic style it made possible. Both came to fruition in the studio era which lasted from the 1920s into the early 1960s.

We're nearly in the real world: the coming of sound

When Chaplin first spoke on screen it was ten years after Warner Brothers' *Don Juan* (1926) had had music and sound effects added after filming, using the recently developed sound-on-disc Vitaphone system. *The Jazz Singer* followed in 1927 and by the early 1930s technical and operational problems to do with sound-proofing, microphones, and set construction had been overcome and the 'talkies' or 'talkers' had taken over. None the less, the contortions Hollywood went through with the coming of sound are only slightly exaggerated in *Singin' in the Rain* (1952), in which a silent film, *The Duelling Cavalier*, is remade as a musical with a dubbed voice for Lena Lamont and with interpolated modern sequences to allow for song and dance routines. Studios held back at first because sound technology interrupted the smooth economy of the silent cinema, with its signed-up European stars, many with strong accents, and Hollywood regulars, who had no training in learning and delivering lines. There was also a justifiable fear that overseas income would be drastically cut once language became a barrier, and before dubbing and subtitles ensured Hollywood's continued pre-eminence. In fact, once the box-office income of Warner Brothers' part- and then all-sound pictures had made sound inevitable, the studios' heavy investment had the effect of confirming their monopoly. It also cemented links between the studios, the financial institutions which supplied the capital, and General Electric, Westinghouse and Western Electric which had carried out the research and held the patents.

The eight major studios were Paramount, RKO, 20th Century Fox, Loew's (with its subsidiary, MGM), Warner Brothers, Universal,

Columbia, and United Artists. They made three-quarters of all feature films, and all but the last three handled production, distribution and exhibition, so realizing an ideal of control first hinted at by Thomas Edison's bid in 1909 for monopoly through the Motion Picture Patents Company. The star system, with stars tied to studios through contracts, tightened the studios' control over the industry. Division of labour operated in almost exactly the same way in all the major studios, even as the studios were specializing in certain genres: Warner Brothers, for instance, became famous for gangster and social problem films, like the two directed by Mervyn LeRoy: *Little Caesar* (1931) and *I Am a Fugitive From a Chain Gang* (1932). Within studios there was further division into producers, with their teams of directors and other staff. This 'producer-unit', so-called, replaced the 'central producer', whose overall control of as many as fifty films in a single year was thought to have led to too much standardization. Hollywood's quite astounding success, nationally and internationally, meant that, in Robert Ray's summary:

> Henceforth, different ways of making movies would appear as aberrations from some 'intrinsic essence of cinema' . . . Given the economics of the medium, such a perception had immense consequences: because departures from the American Cinema's dominant paradigms risked not only commercial disaster but critical incomprehension, one form of cinema threatened to drive out all others.[11]

Chaplin's reluctance to make 'talkies' contributed to an unhelpful mythology of the 'fall' into sound in the writings of Dwight Macdonald and other participants in the 1930s and 1940s debate over mass culture, to be discussed in later chapters. The silent cinema embodied Art, whereas Hollywood figured as a totally repressive system single-mindedly constituting its audience in its own image. To question this mythology is not to minimize the power of Joseph M. Schenck, Darryl F. Zanuck, Louis B. Mayer, and Harry Cohn. As a group, the movie moguls survived most of their stars and the Great Crash of 1929, the Depression, the Second World War, anti-trust lawsuits, as well as sound, colour and aesthetic innovations. Naked power was wielded too many times for it all to be just apochryphal. Similarly, there is no doubting the basic truth or the genuine fears about the manipulation of mass media in the 1944 analysis of 'the culture industry' by the exiled Frankfurt School Marxists, Theodor Adorno and Max Horkheimer.[12] But their approach, and Macdonald's straightforward canonization of the silent film, and even modernism, are blunt approaches which tell us little about Hollywood films, and therefore not enough about perturbations within the system (for example, Chaplin's repetitions) or the difficulties in transcending it that produced many of the most interesting American films.

The chief difference between the silent and sound eras was simply that one came before the other and before the studio system was fully in place. Sound was not, and is not, in itself, either a liberating or a repressive technology but its management by Hollywood's mode of production turned it in the direction of a certain kind of 'realism', even, in Bazin's theory, a utopia of representation: 'Every new [technical] development added to the cinema must, paradoxically, take it nearer and nearer to its origins', defined as 'the myth [of] an integral realism, a recreation of the world in its own image' (*What is Cinema?*, p. 21). Or, in the words of the director of a recent 3-D Omnimax film: 'We're nearly in the real world'. However, Chaplin's debut as a 'talker' in *Modern Times* suggests that nothing could be less natural than the spoken voice. His words are first spoken silently, then rehearsed in mime, and then (when he cannot remember his words) written on his cuff. When his cuff flies off in the dance routine, there are further delays. His whole performance is akin to modernist critiques of the authorial 'voice' of the nineteenth-century realist novel, and ask us to treat sound as just another dimension of the signifying process.

The maturity of a style: classical Hollywood cinema, 1930s to 1950s

Without thinking, we might well echo Jean Renoir and describe as 'classic' other Hollywood directors besides Chaplin: Frank Capra, Alfred Hitchcock, Walt Disney, Raoul Walsh, John Huston, Howard Hawks, William Wyler, Cecil B. DeMille, Allan Dwan, and John Ford, are regular candidates. We might apply the adjective to John Wayne, Humphrey Bogart, Barbara Stanwyck, Joan Crawford, Clark Gable, and to the movies themselves: probably, *Gone with the Wind*, *Casablanca*, and maybe *The Wizard of Oz*. However, the term 'classic' or 'classical style' has received quite a lot of critical attention as well as casual use, and, again, André Bazin gets us going.[13]

In citing John Ford's *Stagecoach* (1939) as 'the ideal example of the maturity of a style brought to classic perfection' (*What is Cinema?*, vol. 2, p. 149), Bazin subsumes his understanding of realism into the more comprehensive concept of classical cinema. The central formal components of the classic style are coherence and continuity, though at the start of a film we are usually faced with a threat to these qualities.

In William Wyler's *Mrs Miniver* (1942) the pre-text tells us that English country life is endangered by the coming war: the film is set in 1939. Once picked out from the London crowd, a troubled look comes across Mrs Miniver's face, but it is caused only by her doubts about whether to buy an extravagant hat. However, such minor troubles serve to convey the precious normality of everyday life, against which we pick up intimations of war. In the musical, *Top Hat* (1935), Jerry Travers (Fred Astaire) is a bachelor and an American, and is found behind a newspaper, nervy and at a loose end in a 'stuffy' all-male London club. Dale Tremont (Ginger Rogers) is anticipated as the missing element in his life when he startles the members of the club by a burst of dancing. Late that night this turns out to be his introduction to Dale, the sleeping occupant of the flat below. The openings of other genres are also constructed around a missing element. In the western it is the lack of law and order, and the signs of its absence are, accordingly, more violent. The narrative then seeks to remedy this lack.

In Ford's *Young Mr Lincoln*, released the same year as *Stagecoach*, there is an interesting variation. The film opens with a poem which supposes that Lincoln's dead mother returns and asks such questions as 'What's happened to Abe?' and 'What's he done?' The narrative substitutes for the 'what if?' of the poem by stressing Lincoln's indecision in the scenes with Ann Rutledge by the river and by her graveside, and when he cannot judge the pie contest because the apple and peach pie are equally good. In fact the choice has already been made because, as Lincoln (Henry Fonda) says (in his first words): 'Gentlemen and fellow citizens. I presume you all know who I am. I'm plain Abraham Lincoln.' This is not an exceptional Hollywood opening because Hollywood narrative is about what we already know. That is why we recognize a Hollywood movie almost instantaneously if we happen to catch one on television.

Stagecoach begins with the coach entering the screen from the right. Against a different background it crosses the screen in the same direction but followed (we assume escorted) by a cavalry troop. There is a slight change in music. The next shot is of just the cavalry coming over the brow of a hill towards us, silhouetted against mesas and buttes. Then, against a similar background, a war-party of Indians briefly crosses the screen. Without the signal of the menacing 'Indian music', we could miss them because they are virtually transparent compared with the substantial images of the stagecoach and the cavalry. With the credit sequence complete, there is a shot of two riders galloping towards us across a valley and then into a cavalry camp. Inside, the riders, who turn out to be scouts, are telling of an Apache uprising. The telegraph 'begins to chatter', followed by this interchange between Captain Sickels and the telegraph operator:

'Clear the wires to Lordsburg.'
'That's Lordsburg now, sir. They seem to have something very urgent to tell you, sir.'
'Well? What's wrong?'
'The line went dead, sir.'
'What did you get?'
'Only the first word, sir.'
[Reading] 'Geronimo.'

The lack or breakdown of communication afflicts the main characters too. There is no communication between the two outcasts, Ringo (John Wayne) and Dallas (Claire Trevor), and the respectable members of society who sit at the far end of the table at Dry Fork way-station. The narrative is predicated on lack, and the journey to Lordsburg becomes the means for re-establishing communication and resolving the disequilibrium initiated by the appearance of the cavalry and the Indians during the credits. It becomes a Western pilgrim's progress (to Lord's burg) with way stations and danger (the Indians, and then the Plummers) between the beginning and the end. Through the stagecoach, which replaces the telegraph, the characters reach their 'destinations', and this is true for the minor as well as the principal characters. Doc Boone passes his test in sobering up sufficiently to deliver Lucy Mallory's baby; Mr Peacock comes through, learning courage but also sympathy for Doc; and Gatewood's theft from his own bank is discovered once communications with Tonto are literally repaired.

The classical style also depends on *how* we reach the ending, rather than upon the ending per se. In *Stagecoach* our viewing experience is composed of interior scenes, in the coach and in the way-stations, interspersed with scenes of the stage traversing the valley. The shots which make up these scenes of the occupants squashed together in the coach and then of the buttes and mesas (of Monument Valley), are now so familiar that, in our admiration for a 'classic', we tend to take them for granted. But it is precisely in not doing so that we approach an accurate description of what 'classic' might mean. Robert Ray reminds us not to be 'superior' about Hollywood cinema:

> Each shot results from dozens of choices about such elements as camera placement, lighting, focus, casting, and framing (the components of *mise en scène*); editing adds the further possibilities inherent in every shot-to-shot articulation. Not only do things on the screen appear at the expense of others not shown, the manner in which they appear depends on a selection of one perspective that eliminates (at least temporarily) all others. (*A Certain Tendency of the Hollywood Cinema*, p. 32)

The perspective or, in literary terms, the point of view, is achieved through 'establishment shots' both at the beginning of a film and of individual scenes. Howard Hawks's *Scarface* (1932) opens with a four-minute uninterrupted pan and track shot, which begins with the street light on 22nd street, takes us 'through' the wall of a restaurant, introduces characters, and records a murder and the discovery of the body. Only then is there a dissolve to a newspaper office. This establishing shot 'sets the scene': it tells us right from the beginnning what is to be seen. Its authority is based not on verisimilitude (we know the wall of the restaurant is not a real wall) but on our privileged point of view.

The long establishing shots in *Stagecoach*, of the valley but also of Main Street in Tonto, complete a pattern by taking us from inside the story (inside the coach) back to an overview that the characters cannot have. In one sense, this is wholly unimportant, except when posing the question of the point of view from which this 'world' is being seen. Then the motivation behind the choice of camera position is entirely pertinent. In another example, Billy Wilder's *Double Indemnity* (1944), we are taken back into the recent past through an extended flashback, and see Phyllis Dietrichson (Barbara Stanwyck) coming to open the front door to Walter Neff (Fred MacMurray). These shots are not motivated, or at least not according to the 'realist' claim that this story is authorized as Neff's memory.

For the scenes inside John Ford's stagecoach there is much use of a characteristic feature of the Hollywood style, shot-reverse-shot. In a dialogue scene, for example, the camera shoots first over one character's shoulder and then over the other, so including the audience in the situation. The assumption that one shot completes the previous one has the further effect of locating the audience both inside and outside the scene, with the consequence that the space of the scene comes to seem unified, even as it is formally cut up. This viewing experience corresponds precisely with Bazin's claim on behalf of classical cinema. It is a space which is filmically comprehended and understood by the audience which, according to one manual of film editing, is given an '*ideal* picture of the scene . . . the best possible viewpoint, . . . irrespective of the fact that no single individual could view a scene in this way in real life'.[14]

James Monaco reminds us of how disorientating it is to watch Carl Dreyer's *The Passion of Joan of Arc* (1928), 'a film shot mainly in closeups' where the 'setting' is left out, or Roberto Rossellini's *Viva l'Italia* (1960), where we are kept at a distance from the characters.[15] Both films highlight Hollywood's smooth relating of the part to the whole, so that the audience knows which is the 'telling' detail to focus on in encountering a scene for the first and probably the only time. In this way communication is ensured, and the film can thrive on suspense and uncertainty, as at the end of *Stagecoach*, when we are denied a clear view of the gunfight with the Plummers, though we hear the gunshots. So authoritative has been the *mise en scène* throughout that we, as it were, agree to 'wait here' with Dallas while Ringo shoots it out. All of the other 'lacks' in the opening of the film have been remedied, so the logic of classical narrative dictates that the 'place' where the Dallas–Ringo story will be resolved is where we will end up.

Thinking back to the beginnings of the Western helps us to appreciate that between *The Great Train Robbery* and *Stagecoach*, just as between the beginning of *Stagecoach* and its conclusion, Hollywood narrative is the principle which links one image (a photograph) with another, so that they become 'invisible' frames in a continuous temporal structure: the 'movies'. The individual frame is composed from the point of view of narrative. Or as Raoul Walsh emphatically puts it: 'There is only one way to shoot a scene, and that's the way which shows the audience what's happening next' (quoted in Bordwell *et al.*, *The Classical Hollywood Cinema*, p. 163).

Within the pattern of continuity editing there are lots of variations; otherwise the film would be boring. In *Mr Deeds Goes to Town* (1936), made by Frank Capra, the story appears to be a search for the heir to the fortune of financier, Martin Semple, recently killed in a car accident. The trail takes the New York lawyers to Mandrake Falls and Longfellow Deeds (Gary Cooper), and the camera movements reinforce the search-narrative. However, Longfellow Deeds's preoccupation with seemingly unimportant homely matters tells us that he is the centre of a more important narrative than the search for the heir to $20 million. The formal transition to this other narrative is made via the question of lunch rather than money. It is first broached by Deeds's housekeeper and taken up by Deeds himself. The camera, however, keeps one of the New Yorkers, a Mr Cobb, in view, preparing for his eventual conversion to Deeds's (and Mandrake Falls') way of thinking. The rest of the visitors remain New Yorkers throughout. Aside from some hiccoughs in the story (when Deeds gets drunk), it is the narrative centred on Mandrake Falls' values which determines the construction of the individual frames in the film.

Add the star system to these generic imperatives and the power of narrative is dramatically increased. Who a character is may not be initially clear but the fact that the part is played by Gary Cooper, John Wayne or Henry Fonda means that, in most cases, the character becomes what the star was from the outset: one of the great pleasures of Hollywood cinema, but a curious concept of narrative progression none the less.

Having described beginnings and what comes in-between, we can look now at closure. Gangster films of the 1930s and 1940s illustrate an important technique: the repetition of earlier shots but with the narrative linking them in the spectator's mind. At the end of *Scarface* the screen is filled with the neon sign, 'The World is Yours'. It is a repetition of earlier scenes but it also partially echoes the boast of the gang chief murdered by Tony at the start of the film: 'Big Louie: he sit on top of the world.' Later, in the 1949 *White Heat*, directed by Raoul Walsh, Cody Jarrett (James Cagney) will shout 'Top of the World, Ma' as he is blown up. *Stagecoach* ends when Ringo and Dallas ride away from us across the valley as the two scouts had ridden towards us at the outset bringing news of Geronimo. This is the affirmative answer to the question of whether Ringo can prosecute his own ends (the revenge of his brother's murder) while assisting the community. Ringo has helped the stage get through and has killed the Plummers; having done so, he is about to settle down. But while he will get married, it will be to Dallas, a woman who will not alter his character: he could perform the same role again, should a community have need of him.

Yet the moment of closure is also the moment of openness and uncertainty: the audience is leaving the cinema (having liked the film? likely to return?). Hollywood has sought to contain this uncertainty in various ways, two of which are instantly recognizable, 'classic' even: the embrace of the male and female stars and the disappearing into the sunset of the main character or, occasionally, characters. Despite our superiority in looking back at classical Hollywood films, there are very few loose ends which, if tugged, would unravel the 'rightness' of the ending. The point, though, is that the rightness of the ending is a function of the form and style which has drawn the spectator into the filmic space, populated by recognizable, narrative-orientated, in-dividuals. So much so, that when Hollywood took on difficult subjects, such as soldiers returning from the war (*The Best Years of Our Lives*, 1946) or race (*Guess Who's Coming to Dinner*, 1967), individual dramas and not political issues were to the fore.

The problem with these classic endings is not that we have seen them before (that's the point) but that if the embrace creates unity it does so by excluding the larger context of the action, since the couple fill the screen, while the 'sunset' shot widens the perspective but assumes that we know where the hero (as it usually is) is going. We cannot see the expressions on Ringo and Dallas's faces but have no reason to assume that they are not happy ones. It is where they are going that creates a slight uncertainty at the moment of closure. They are going to Mexico but the status of Mexico in the unified space of the film is at the very least ambiguous. The vaqueros abandon the people in the stagecoach and, presumably, make for the Border. Dallas, too, advises Ringo to 'Make for the Border'. Yet this comes after Ringo's description of his ranch 'across the Border. It's a nice place . . . a real nice place . . . trees . . . grass . . . water . . . a cabin half-built.' These are positive images of unity, of home, but they are never actually images on the screen because the film is set in the United States.

That there is a connection between the enclosure of 'space' by the narrative and ideological closure is apparent if, with the classic style in mind, we reconsider the theme of communication, or the lack of it, in *Stagecoach*. What must strike us is how much all the characters seem to know, in spite of the distances between one place and another and the interruptions resulting from telegraph lines going down, bridges being burnt, and newspaper editors who construct the news before the event. Curly knows Ringo's father; Chris, the Mexican station manager, knows about Luke Plummer's murder of Ringo's brother; and there are many more examples, some suggesting a much wider community of knowledge, as when Lucy Mallory recognizes Hatfield's silver cup: 'Isn't this from Ringfield Manor?' Everyone is interconnected: the 'territory' is a community (a space of reliable communications) that has been temporarily fragmented by the Indians but persists regardless of them. But, in a way, that is the significance of the ghostly image of the Indians in the credit sequence. They are not real, which, in formal terms, means not part of the unified space.

Yet, occasionally, the fact that this geographical and filmic space is based not on inclusiveness but exclusiveness is evident. The audience's loss of knowledge in the shoot-out does not really constitute a breakdown of communication of the cinematic machine. On the other hand, the close-up of Geronimo prior to the attack by the wholly de-personalized Indians is mystifying because unmotivated. Momentarily we do not know what is going on and from the point of view of that close-up the subsequent set piece of the attack on the stage is unhelpful: it leaves the Indians as a complete enigma, though their function in the narrative is quite clear. The lack of attention accorded the Indians is in contrast to the attention given Luke Plummer, who has a place/space in Lordsburg: he has a woman to help him by supplying a shotgun, and he is the beneficiary of information-networks in the town. Geronimo and the smoke signals from the hills outside Apache Wells are outside of our frame of knowledge. Consequently, these communications are not seen as signs of community but as part of the threat to it. However, the vaqueros at the way-station, acting under advice from Yakima, Chris's Apache wife, and then Yakima herself, interpret the signs differently – and leave.

In Ford's other film of 1939, *Young Mr Lincoln*, the relationship between the public and private dimensions is more explicitly treated. Politics is introduced in the very low-key hustings scene that follows the establishing shot of Main Street, New Salem, Illinois, only to be rapidly translated into a personal, moral matter. Lincoln helps a family of farmers by giving them credit at his store, receiving in return a barrel of old books, one of which is Blackstone's *Commentaries*. From politics to the law (Lincoln's later profession) but, thence, to morality through match-editing: Lincoln holds up the book, wonderingly says the words, 'Law', and there is a cut to a scene by a river with Lincoln reading the book. The first word in the new scene is 'Law' and, with surrounding nature to assist him, the route from politics to morality and the drama of the individual character is complete: 'By Jing, that's all there is to it. Right and wrong. Maybe I ought to begin to take this up serious.'

Once the film becomes the story of an individual, the narrative style is in a position to resolve all conflicts dramatically. Institutions are by-passed (there is only one reference to slavery), and power relations are simplified into personal relations, as in the legal scenes. After the trial, with Lincoln firmly associated with 'right', the public, historical narrative of Lincoln is introduced through a carefully constructed shot. Coming out of the courthouse, framed by the door and caught by the sunlight, the low angle of the shot makes him look taller and older. Through a shadow effect he even seems to have a beard. He is now Lincoln the public figure and the stage need no longer be merely Springfield, Illinois. The film has established Lincoln's inviolable private credentials, and, thus armed, he can, in the still powerful conclusion, decide to 'go on apiece . . . maybe to the top of that hill,' where the sudden lightning and rain symbolize his confrontation with the storms of history: the political crises of the 1850s leading to the Civil War. In the same mould, the narrative of *Mr Deeds Goes to Town*, with Longfellow Deeds, as we have seen, firmly at the stylistic centre of it, not only brings a moral standard to 'town' but provides a model for resolving the economic crisis of the Depression: personal charity, as Deeds gives away his fortune. Just as the wider public dimension is kept at bay in *Young Mr Lincoln*, so, in Capra's film, the Depression is not even mentioned until well into the film. With the personal dimension established, the close-up of the embrace between Long-fellow Deeds and 'Babe' Bennett at the end of the film is entirely right because there is no historical and societal context to take into account.

Musical endings are possibly the most closed of all. In *The Wizard of Oz* (1939) Dorothy returns to Kansas; even in a musical she had to do that, but while it is still 'black and white' (Oz is in technicolor) it is transformed from the dreary, unsympathetic and even frightening place it had been before she left. 'There's no place like home' are the closing words of the film. In *Top Hat* there is a romantic conclusion with Jerry and Dale coming together, in spite of her initial reluctance and his stated intention to have 'no strings'. In 'backstage' musicals, beginning with *42nd Street* in 1933, the romantic ending coincides with the finale of the show. For Hollywood to produce a show within a 'show' (the film) is the operation of ideology at its most effective since what could 'mask' the mode of production better than Hollywood 'on the town' or 'singin' in the rain', or telling us that 'there's no business like show business' or, more conclusively (in 1974 and again in 1976), that 'that's entertainment'. 'If we were to think about that', Jane Feuer perceptively remarks, 'if we were to think at all, it wouldn't be entertainment any more.'[16]

While André Bazin's description of the classic style has provoked the above analyses, we have moved beyond his realist aesthetic towards Robert Ray's thesis, that Hollywood persistently attempts to resolve at a stylistic/formal level what are very tangible dilemmas: between individualism and community, capital and labour, men and women, and blacks and whites.

A somewhat rebellious frame of mind: challenges to the classical style, 1940s to 1960s

The Western came of age with *Stagecoach* but, like any product, it had to be differentiated from competitors yet still remain recognizable. Some post-war Westerns from the studio era while, for the most part, repeating the pattern of initial disequilibrium and eventual reconciliation, include elements that work against the narrative and its resolution. John Ford manages to include Indians other than as stereotypes in *Cheyenne Autumn* (1964), but has much more trouble in *The Searchers* (1956) because, in the character of Ethan Edwards (John Wayne), he confronts the appalling loneliness and metaphorical blindness at the heart of the hero-figures which John Wayne had played since *Stagecoach*. In the three remaining sections, which take us through to the 1980s, we can best explore this important relationship between sameness and identity through a series of critiques of individual films within their generic contexts. *3.10 to Yuma* (1957) never reaches the heights (or depths) of *The Searchers*, but in some ways is a more typical post-war film, one of a genre of 'problem' films identified by Robert Ray and other critics. A stagecoach is held up by Ben Wade's gang, and a second story, that of Dan (Van Heflin) and his responsibilities to home and ranch, intersects with it. However, unlike *Stagecoach* and also *High Noon* (1952), which it otherwise strongly resembles with its explicit theme song and the continual clock-watching, the focus on Dan and his dilemma of whether to get involved in the community's dispute with Ben Wade, gets muddied by the interest generated by Wade's character and by an increasingly intense relationship between them. It is only Wade's intervention when he helps Dan to get him onto the train which will take him to gaol, that resolves an impossibly contradictory situation. Safe on the train, Dan sees his wife waving to him from the trackside and patently proud of him. It then rains, reminding us that he had undertaken to escort Wade to Contention City and the train in return for the $200 reward that would buy him water rights. The rain and the appearance of Dan's wife resolve disjunctions that relate to their relationship and his with his two sons, but only partially address the interest generated by Wade's character and the confusion as to how the community figures in the conclusion. The only community of any substance in the film is Wade's gang. There are similar imbalances, but no outright challenge to the genre, in other post-war Westerns, notably, *Red River* (1948), *The Man Who Shot Liberty Valance* (1962) (both starring John Wayne, but set off against a different or younger character, played, respectively by Montgomery Clift and James Stewart), *The Gunfighter* (1950), *The Far Country* (1954), *The Tin Star* (1957), and *One-eyed Jacks* (1961).

The archetypal problem film is *film noir*, even if box-office popularity suggests that Hollywood had the last word. Such films as Hitchcock's *Shadow of a Doubt* (1943), Charles Vidor's *Gilda* (1946), Dmytryk's *Crossfire* (1947), Tourneur's *Out of the Past* (1947), Ray's *They Live by Night* (1949) and Welles' *The Lady from Shanghai* (1948) and *Touch of Evil* (1958), illustrate the confluence of internal and external factors and the strain they put upon the classic style. External factors included the war, and its aftermath with men returning to find women in 'their' jobs and 'their' women with other men; the beginning, in 1947, of the McCarthy witch-hunts when Hollywood's liberals were accused of being communists; and the coming of television. The internal factors had to do with generic transformations and discontinuities, technical and aesthetic innovations, most of which centred on the work of Orson Welles; and European cinema, the influence of which dated back to the 1920s but was augmented in the 1930s and 1940s through expatriate directors like Billy Wilder, Otto Preminger, Robert Siodmak, and Michael Curtiz.

Fritz Lang's *The Woman in the Window* (1944) is of particular relevance because it exemplifies a quite common combination of European avant-garde visuals and a Hollywood narrative. Left to his own devices when his wife and children go on vacation, Richard Wanley (Edward G. Robinson), a professor of psychology, is distracted from his routine, initially by a portrait of a woman in a shop window outside his club, and then when he meets the woman (Joan Bennett) who modelled for the portrait. Though a more worldly figure than Wanley, Walter Neff in Wilder's *Double Indemnity* is also seeking an escape from routine when he joins Phyllis Dietrichson to murder her husband under the double indemnity clause. Wanley is very rapidly embroiled: later the same evening he is attacked by the woman's lover, kills him, and in the early hours dumps the body in an isolated spot. More terrors follow (especially for the respectable, professional, male viewer?), culminating in Wanley's suicide, at which point the narrative has gone so far from its innocuous starting point (Wanley had been in 'a somewhat rebellious frame of mind') that an ending must be manufactured or, more accurately, borrowed from Hollywood's stock of happy endings. It has all been a dream, peopled by those around him in the club. Approached by – we assume – a prostitute outside the same shop window, he flees. The visuals, it would seem, have been safely incorporated into a comic melodrama where the family is once again central. The portrait of the woman in the window is replaced by that of his wife and children so that 'normal' social (and economic) relations can be resumed. And yet the very collapse of the dream narrative (which had culminated in his suicide) has the effect of leaving the *noir* style not entirely assimilated.

French critics coined the expression *film noir* to describe those films of the 1940s which were full of dark interiors, and streets that were usually wet and shining in the partial light of street lamps. Characters in dark rooms were partly in, and partly out, of any source of light – a shaded lamp or street-light. As the title of Nicholas Ray's film has it, the characters 'live by night'. *The Woman in the Window* also has the *noir* characteristic of being full of framed and mirror images, the former being especially evident in the scenes outside the woman's apartment block. And, of course, there are the reflections in the window as Wanley gazes at the portrait of the woman, only to encounter the model who posed for it. Interestingly, there is what might be called a *noir* supplement to one of the trademarks of the classic style, the shot-reverse-shot. Outside the shop the space between Wanley and the woman is occupied by the portrait in the window.

What are we to make of this excess of style to narrative requirements? In the musical there are ways of explaining it and, to the extent that we can attribute images to Wanley's state of mind they can be recuperated. However, the framed and mirror images are less easy to explain subjectively because many do not involve Wanley, but convey the pervasiveness of another way of seeing the world. The images also allow for the very frank expression of female sexuality. While this is enclosed by the reassuring ending of *The Woman in the Window* and the violent deaths of Dietrichson and Neff at the end of *Double Indemnity*, the images of women are not so easily laid to rest whether in 'the cemetery at the end of the line' (*Double Indemnity*), or in the substitution of a prostitute for the more unsettling woman in the window. Though still promoting a stereotype of women as a 'fatal attraction', *film noir* creates some (visual) space for women to act, in contrast to the strictly delineated spaces allowed them in Westerns and

– to make a necessary polemical point – in *Fatal Attraction*, one of the box office successes of the 1980s. Since these *noir* camera angles and frames, together with the chiaroscuro effects, appear in a whole range of films (hence the difficulty in agreeing upon a canon for *film noir*), they function as the 'ghost in the machine', that which has to be excluded or contained by narrative closure in order that the coherence of the classical style and Hollywood's vision of the world be maintained. A particular interpretation of these unsettling *noir* moments is that they mark the crossing of a dominant male discourse (which tantalizes itself before returning women to their place) by a counter-discourse precipitated by the interaction of the Hollywood style with post-war America, an interaction motivated by the marketplace's demand for variety.[17]

The larger question posed by these 1940s and 1950s films – whether they undermine the unity of the classical style and consensus ideology – can be finally put with reference to *Citizen Kane* (1941), the *cause célèbre* of Hollywood. The original title of the film was *American* and it is the irony that surrounds Kane's announcements that he is first and foremost an American which, at a thematic level at least, constitutes a threat to consensus. *Citizen Kane* offers a contorted, even *noir* re-telling of the American Dream of success, appending the moral that money and power does not necessarily bring happiness. This, in itself, would not be a problem for Hollywood since the dream of success in America, from the Puritans onwards, has rarely been wholly materialistic. Consequently, when, amidst the bonfire of Kane's unwanted belongings, the camera picks out his sledge, with the inscription 'Rosebud" on it, the dream is preserved and not sent up in flames. Presumably, with more 'character' on the part of the hero, this ending could have been avoided. The dream (and Hollywood narrative) can be rescued providing there is a coherent, knowable character at its centre whom we can identify with or against. Character flaws do not call coherence into question. But the deep focus photography, tilted camera angles, dissolves, and chiaroscuro effects – however familiar they are now – do undermine the coherence, even the psychological coherence, of Kane. The multiple perspectives (of Kane as husband, businessman, object of a newspaper feature, a newsreel and so on), do not add up to a clear point of view. The 'detached, omniscient' perspective proves to be another layer.

Furthermore, the activities of the camera seem to comment ironically upon the desire to see, to know, that we have discussed with reference to Hollywood, but which is given a twist by the lighting and camerawork in *film noir*. In the opening scene the camera ignores the 'No Trespassing' sign on the wire fence of Kane's mansion, Xanadu, and moves closer to the house by a series of dissolves, which yet keep the lighted window in view. As it centres on the glass ball containing a snow scene, and Kane's lips, and enlists the authority of the Word ('Rosebud'), the suggestion is that the camera is getting to the essence of Kane. But the camera is also the agency for the other representations of Kane, most blatantly, in *News on the March*, itself being viewed in the film by the reporters who will seek to reconstruct Kane's life.

Together, *Citizen Kane*, a number of genre films which did not satisfactorily resolve the tasks they set themslves, and *film noir*, as a transgression of genre itself, questioned the classical style. In so doing they posed an implicit challenge to the ideological positions inscribed in classical Hollywood cinema.

A non-Hollywood Hollywood: 1960s to 1980s

'Movies in the seventies have a different resonance than they had in the mid-1950s or the high 1930s', Axel Madsen announces, while for Diane Jacobs, 'a period of cinematic "rebirth" seems to have been gestating within the frenetic activity of the [1960s]'.[18] Even a selective list of the mainstream films upon which these and other estimates are based will provide a rough chronology and help us to get our bearings in the third broad phase of American cinema: *The Graduate* (1967), *Bonnie and Clyde* (1967), *Medium Cool* (1969), *Easy Rider* (1969), *The Wild Bunch* (1969), *Five Easy Pieces* (1970), *Little Big Man* (1970), *M*A*S*H* (1970), *McCabe and Mrs Miller* (1971) *The Godfather* (1972), *The King of Marvin Gardens* (1972), *The Long Goodbye* (1973), *Mean Streets* (1973), *The Conversation* (1974), *Chinatown* (1974), *The Godfather, Part II* (1974), *Nashville* (1975), *Taxi Driver* (1976), *The Deerhunter* (1978), *Days of Heaven* (1978), *The China Syndrome* (1979), and *Apocalypse Now* (1979). We are closer still to home with recent films like *Platoon* (1987), *Full Metal Jacket* (1987), *The Milagro Beanfield War* (1988), *Mississippi Burning* (1988), and *Rain Man* (1988).

These films have revived the hope, expressed by Walter Benjamin among others, that cinema can be a genuinely *popular art*, that is to say, one which disseminates widely a critical outlook on class, race and gender relations, social fragmentation and the arms race, nuclear power and other perils of modernity. Certainly fewer films have been made since the late 1960s so that there is not the vast undertow of studio films. One reason for fewer pictures, though, was the big budget film, a Hollywood tradition which entered a new phase with spectacular disaster movies like *Airport* (1970) and *The Towering Inferno* (1974); the

Jaws and *Star Wars* series and those constructed around Superman, Indiana Jones, Rambo, Shaft, and Dirty Harry; together with one-off successes like *ET* (1982).

While still exploring the question of sameness and difference, a further question can be posed which brings together the individual critiques which follow: What kind of mode of production lies behind Hollywood's more adventurous output since the late 1960s? The answer lies in the changing fortunes of the studios, beginning with the 1946 court decision against Paramount Pictures which led to the separation of production and distribution from exhibition throughout the industry. Also in the late 1940s, labour disputes, taxes levied by Britain on foreign film earnings, the investigations of the House Committee on Un-American Activities and, especially, the growing popularity of television combined to undermine the studio system in the next two decades. Anxiety set in, reflected in an oscillation between economy drives and plumping for the kind of big-budget production that television could not match. The most significant change was from mass production of films under 'the producer-unit' system to the 'package-unit' system, described in detail by Bordwell, Staiger and Thompson in *The Classical Hollywood Cinema*. Individual producers put together packages from the resources of the whole industry rather than drawing on the studio to which they were contracted. The focus for these more independent productions was the individual project rather than the studio, though in practice a production team often did stay together so that standardization still operated across the various packages. The new independence was also under the financial and distributive umbrella of corporations as the studios diversified into new areas (television, video-games, hotels) or were merged with existing corporations outside of the industry: for example, Paramount with Gulf-Western, Warner Bros with Kinney National Services; and Columbia with Coca-Cola. The industry moved into a new phase in 1989 when the Australian Qintex Group bought MGM/United Artists for $1.45 billion, and then the Japanese corporation, Sony, bought Columbia for $3.4 billion. With Columbia's library of 2700 films at its disposal, Sony can integrate the film industry with its large share of the video industry.

The more distanced (but more comprehensive) form of control currently being exerted in Hollywood, goes some way towards accounting for a different pattern of film production. First, block-busters, which brought income but, because of the expenditure involved, could not be risked on a regular basis, especially after the box-office disaster of *Heaven's Gate* (1980). Second, revisionist genre pictures like *Butch Cassidy and the Sundance Kid* (1969), which undercuts the western through gentle irony, two anachronistic heroes, and a non-diegetic musical interlude (the bicycle sequence); but undercuts it only so far. And, third, new departures, the kind of films which would have been difficult to make in the old Hollywood. The income generated by spectaculars, and the subsequent milking of the formula in sequels, cushioned the experimentation that Hollywood has always had to risk but which became more urgent as the stable audience was commandeered by television and cinema had to compete for those sections of the movie-going population which the social changes of the post-war years were rapidly identifying: youth, blacks, women. Television had not only won the mass audience, it was following classical Hollywood in refining the conventions which held the middle ground. It therefore became economically imperative for the new films to appeal more directly to specified audiences, housed in smaller auditoriums rather than in great movie palaces like Radio City. With more people receiving a college education the 'menu' could also cater for a growing interest in the revived European cinema, which, in any case, was already influencing some of the new directors.

The distanced relationship with finance allowed for new directors to replace the old guard of Ford, Hawks, and Hitchcock. Among the newcomers were Peter Bogdanovich, Francis Coppola, George Lucas, Woody Allen, Roman Polanski, Martin Scorsese, Robert Altman, Steven Spielberg, and Terrence Malick. Others, like John Frankenheimer, Arthur Penn and Sam Peckinpah, came out of the late 1950s and early 1960s to make the seminal films of the new Hollywood. The changed economics also gave directorial and production opportunities to stars who could attract finance: Paul Newman, Burt Reynolds and, especially, Robert Redford with his Sundance Institute in the Rocky Mountains. Founded in 1980, Sundance supports small projects, such as *Desert Bloom* and *Promised Land*, as well as Redford's own films, the latest being *The Milagro Beanfield War* (1988). Redford acknowledges the need to keep open some avenues of communication and finance with Hollywood: 'It is not an anti-Hollywood position I'm after.' With more independence, however, film-makers have experienced more insecurity and so, arguably, the pressure to communicate widely, and therefore retain a modified Hollywood style has remained. A 'non-Hollywood Hollywood' is David Bordwell's alternative to Madsen's 'new Hollywood'.

Having lowered expectations, somewhat, it must still be stated that a number of films have gone beyond the muted subversiveness (often arising out of confusion) of *The Searchers*, John Frankenheimer's *The Manchurian Candidate* (1962) and *film noir*, and have been openly critical of consensus, both socio-economic-political and stylistic. *The Graduate* and *Bonnie and Clyde*, together with *Easy Rider* and *Alice's Restaurant* (1969), represent different aspects of the counter-cultural revolt of the 1960s: middle-class youth against the middle-class affluence and hypocrisy of their parents; the values of the underground transposed into the Depression setting of *Bonnie and Clyde*; and the freewheeling yet precarious, even doomed, life of hippies. With the alienated stance towards society often came a formal reaction against the conventionality of the Hollywood style, usually in the name of the French New Wave directors of the late 1950s and 1960s, Alain Resnais, Jean-Luc Godard, Eric Rohmer, Claude Chabrol, and François Truffaut. We see their influence in the use of slow motion, exaggerated close-ups, and freeze framing.

The cross-fertilization of Hollywood continued into the next decade, with Martin Scorcese's *Mean Streets* displaying a mixture of *cinéma verité72 and New Wave artifice. It begins with a succession of amateur snap-shots, and hand-held movie-cameras are used in the festival scenes. Dialogue is not narrative-directed, but rambles. In contrast, there is much stylized camerawork, for example, the use of slow-motion in some of the bar scenes. By no means all of the slow-motion scenes are motivated by the subjective perception of Charlie (Harvey Keitel). Similarly, while his dance routine in the bar is acted out in diegetic synchrony with the rock music, the pool-room fight lasts only as long as the rock track. New Wave stylization and a faith in the reproductive power of photography suggest the two traditions of cinematic language discussed at the beginning of this chapter. They do not mesh, however, but play off one another. We have met this in the multiple perspectives of Citizen Kane but in Mean Streets the suggestion* is that all of us, and not just the famous, live according to how we represent ourselves and how we are represented – verbally, musically, as well as in photographs, moving or still. Michael's attack on Charlie, Teresa and Johnny at the end of the film, and the resulting car crash, is intercut with shots of the other main characters, one of whom is watching a car crash on television, and as the credits roll the representations continue with an announcement in Italian. Aside from not actually knowing whether any of the three people in the car have been killed, we get no sense that the camera is drawing together the many little narratives that have shown signs of interconnecting. On the other hand, the cuts in the closing minutes deny that this is slice-of-life realism. It seems inappropriate to call *Mean Streets* 'post-modernist'; but if it has none of the playful character of a film like *Blue Velvet* (1986) (see below), it nevertheless shares an indeterminacy of perspective, and uses, even if it does not parade, its knowledge of film history in ways that tend to be associated with the post-modern.

French New Wave films made regular genuflections towards classic Hollywood genre pictures, and when the influence of the New Wave worked back across the Atlantic self-referentiality and the practice of 'quoting' from other films became characteristics of American cinema. Self-consciousness also resulted from the repeated exposure given to classic Hollywood films on television and from the training which

Coppola, Lucas, Scorcese, Polanski, and Bogdanovich, for instance, had received in film schools or as film critics. Aside from full-length parodies, for example of the western in *Cat Ballou* (1965) and *Blazing Saddles* (1974), there has been an oblique, ironical re-working of standard Hollywood genres. Continuity – already breaking down in *film noir* – is subjected in Coppola's gangster film, *The Godfather Part II*, to parallel developments and dependence upon *The Godfather*. Television united the two films in chronological order. In *The Conversation*, released in between the two parts of *The Godfather*, Coppola subjects narrative to the complexities that stem from sound being separated from the visuals. The desire to know is accentuated because Harry is a top surveillance expert. As the camera picks out the young couple in Union Square, we are intent upon hearing, even more than seeing, more. The ambiguous information elicited precipitates a narrative in which Harry attempts to decipher 'the conversation' between the two people under surveillance. The initial uncertainty leaves us unsure of the objectivity of events, as when the toilet overflows with blood. In the end, though, the narrative does come together and centres on character: we know that the young couple committed the murder but, more importantly, we know that the chief source of the ambiguity is Harry's character. Coppola's stated intention to work against the Hollywood system from within it is a subversiveness which, in *The Conversation* leaves him too vulnerable to the power of narrative. And in attempting to resist story, Coppola switches to the other node of the classic style and overloads Harry's character with behavioural 'tics'. Thus, Harry's sharp reaction to any casual blasphemy shows his Catholicism surfacing, and almost immediately afterwards, while at his workbench, he misinterprets the crucial sentence on the tape.

What we have been loosely calling modernist cinema has often taken character in the direction of greater subjectivity and, in common with the modernist novels of Joyce, Woolf and Faulkner, has recreated coherence at a deeper psychological level. This has been truer of strands in German Expressionism (*The Cabinet of Dr Caligari* rather than *Waxworks*) and hardly applies at all to Eisenstein. Similarly, in the New Wave, character is often treated psychologically and narrative is often in evidence. However, Godard's use of jump cuts; deliberate, rather than accidental, transgressing of the 180 degree line; and built-in commentary on his own film-making, all make it difficult for the spectator to go with the flow of the narrative. In these respects Godard's *Breathless* (1960) is 'ahead' of its American remake by Jim McBride. Despite differences, Godard is in the tradition of Eisenstein, a cinema which, as Sylvia Harvey puts it, 'is able to produce knowledge about itself' and which is therefore part of 'the *political* defence of modernist aesthetics' (my emphasis).[19] Or as Stephen Heath argues in *Questions of Cinema*, cinema itself can be 'a fracturing of the vision of representation so as to show, as Brecht puts it, that "in things, people, processes, there is something that makes them what they are and at the same time something that makes them other"' (p. 7).

Because post-1960s American cinema remained committed to narrative and even genre, albeit a reworked genre, the influence of modernist cinema has been selective. Robert Altman's films are a more sustained reworking of standard genres (*McCabe*, *M★A★S★H*, *The Long Goodbye*, *Nashville* and *Thieves Like Us*) and so provide a clear indication of what can and cannot be done within a medium which seeks to remain popular. The clearest example is *The Long Goodbye*, based on Raymond Chandler's 1954 novel and a successor to Howard Hawks's *The Big Sleep* (1946). There is straight parody in the gatekeeper who mimics Hollywood stars, but irony is more radical than parody because the subject can turn out to be the narrative's own point of view. This may be the reason why the narrative has difficulty getting underway, whereas in *The Big Sleep* the delays have more to do with what is not as yet known about the case. Philip Marlowe (Elliott Gould), like McCabe (Warren Beatty), mumbles his way through the film so that the consequential and inconsequential are difficult to distinguish. In classic Hollywood even the inconsequential is related to the narrative through the red herrings that litter detective films. *The Long Goodbye*'s title song augments rather than repairs the lack of communication, being heard in snatches, while the camera seems to drift, catching characters unawares.

Altman's film departs most significantly from Chandler's novel and from *The Big Sleep* (novel and film) in the motivation of the characters, and especially Marlowe. The narrative, though seemingly dispersed into at least three plots, does come together in the conclusion (as in *The Conversation*), when it transpires that Lennox did kill his wife and was in league with Eileen Wade. In a similar situation in *The Maltese Falcon* (1941), based on Dashiell Hammett's novel but starring Humphrey Bogart, Sam Spade turns Brigid O'Shaughnessy over to the police, while in Chandler's novels betrayal of the ideal of friendship is a capital offence. Altman's Marlowe kills Lennox but with the same indifference that he displayed going about his nightly business when the film opened. Consequently, it is difficult to identify with him at this point, where we have much less trouble sticking with the more violent Bonnie Parker and Clyde Barrow. The narrative force of Hollywood cinema is dissipated in *The Long Goodbye*, less into enigma and more into an unsuccessful search for an alternative point of identification that will make the narrative cohere.

Altman's *McCabe and Mrs Miller* is a much more traditional genre film, in which we identify more and more with the main character, and do so precisely because he is an anti-hero. The only serious disruption – serious in that our position as spectators is implicated – is right at the end when the camera leaves McCabe dead in the snow to return to Mrs Miller (Julie Christie) in the opium den. Switching to the women (grieving or left behind) is a well-tried way of registering the final impact of the hero in a Western, but closing in on Mrs Miller's face, then on one eye, and eventually losing focus on the viscous surface of her eyeball is excessive to either the psychological or social meanings of the film. This hyperbole of a close-up blocks a switch of allegiance to Mrs Miller as the 'real' centre of the narrative but also blocks out McCabe.

Chinatown, directed by Roman Polanski, is ostensibly even more in tow to classic Hollywood, or at least its noir dimension, than *The Conversation* or *The Long Goodbye*. Inevitably, for a 1970s detective film, there are multiple plots. The difference comes with the slitting of J.J. Gittes' (Jack Nicholson's) nose. More than a comment on his profession ('nosey guy'), the incident signals a switch in the film's focus. Thereafter, the scale of corruption becomes so great, incorporating the personal dimension (incest and rape) and the public scandal of the selling off of Los Angeles' water rights, that the 'private eye' cannot encompass it. Arthur Penn's *Night Moves* (1975) has a similar narrative structure, and both films shade into a sub-genre of 'paranoia' films which includes *Three Days of the Condor* and *The Parallax View*. In Polanski's film, references to Chinatown become more insistent as Gittes becomes more embroiled. At first the references fill in his own background. Gradually, though, we understand Chinatown to be the place where investigative techniques break down. In the terms we have been using to describe classic Hollywood, Chinatown challenges the truth of the privileged point of view to which the basic detective-story narrative gives us access. 'You can't always tell what's going on there.' At what ought to be the denouement, his associate advises him: 'Forget it Jake. It's Chinatown.' Where the film is drawn back into classic Hollywood is in the implication that Chinatown and Evelyn Mulwray (Faye Dunaway), the woman who dies there, are both inscrutable. Chinatown is not inscrutable, but (in language that is appropriate to both the public and private themes) encountering Chinatown and incest produces 'run off' which transgresses boundaries. Is Catherine Mulwray sister or daughter to Evelyn Mulwray? And since Noah Cross is also involved in the water theme, we sense interconnections between the private and public worlds that go well beyond both the ostensible New Deal/ecological politics of the film and mere mystery.[20]

Epistemological questions can be posed without subverting the detective story structure. The young girl's voice-over in Terrence Malick's *Days of Heaven* alternately accompanies what we see on screen and retrospectively comments on it, so that we are not sure where we are. In some respects this is more disconcerting than the more famous unattributed voice-over in Alain Resnais's *The War is Over* (1966). Moreover, the girl's narration survives the three main characters with whom we variously identify (two are killed and she just gets on a train and leaves), but the film never becomes her story and its generic inconsistency is not resolved: social problem film, family melodrama or western?

More variety: Vietnam and beyond

The question of genre has been dramatically foregrounded in the many films about the Vietnam War, principally because 'Vietnam' has proved to be a highly charged and complicated subject for a film to be 'about'. For example, a number of films co-opt other genres as a way of dealing with the fact of defeat and the revelations about massacres, use of chemical weaponry, and loss of leadership and of moral right. *Soldier Blue* and *Little Big Man* (both 1970) and *Missouri Breaks* (1976) show how the Western informs, but can barely survive, Vietnam and the damage it did to the national/Western mission. The science fiction film also intersects with Vietnam. *Dark Star* (1978) tells of the technological destruction wrought by another American 'errand into the wilderness' – of space – and also of the psychological effects upon the space ship's crew, cut loose as they are from their normal co-ordinates. In *American Graffiti* (1973), a small-town movie, Vietnam is only mentioned in the textual coda. Yet the innocence of the small town life of the adolescent characters seems predicated upon the war which ended it.

The *Green Berets* (1968) was the first important film about the Vietnam War. It came out in 1968, during the war, and comes closest to the traditional Hollywood war movie. However, it employs strategies which seek to manage the military and political difficulties that had become apparent by the time the film was made. Blame is shifted onto bureacracy and, more specifically, onto technology as the strategy chosen by Lyndon B. Johnson in 1963 to win the war. The soldiers, and the John Wayne character in particular, stand for on-the-ground tactics; these even permit sympathy for the colonized, and a familiar combination of individualism and the closely knit group – familiar because it is transposed from earlier war movies (*The Sands of Iwo Jima*, 1949, *The Battle of the Bulge*, 1965, and *Anzio*, 1968), and, of course, from the Western. The 'buddy' aspect of *The Green Berets* survives the anti-war turn in later Vietnam films, such as *Go Tell the*

Spartans (1978), *Hamburger Hill* (1987) and *Platoon* (1987), to soften the political critique of American involvement in Vietnam.

The *Rambo* series of the 1980s is a later phase of Hollywood's response to Vietnam, and to defeat. Rambo (Sylvester Stallone) is the reincarnated nineteenth-century individualistic frontiersman, who fights back against the military-industrial complex and the Soviet influence in Vietnam. In *Rambo: First Blood, Part II* (1985), Stallone's character returns to Vietnam and is obliged to rely on himself rather than the paraphernalia of technology with which the military equip him. John Carlos Rowe explains the complexity of ideological layering in the series:

> *Rambo* marshalls countercultural arguments against high-technology America to claim that the war in Vietnam would have been better conducted by freedom fighters like Rambo and Co [a Vietnamese woman], both of whom represent the best virtues of their respective cultures . . . By claiming that our failure in Vietnam was caused by leaders far from the scenes of battle who relied blindly on technological representations of the war, *Rambo* diverts our attention from such obvious political issues as America's anti-communism in the post-World War II period and our commitment to outdated 'balance-of-power' foreign policies.[21]

While we should distinguish the *Rambo* films and *The Green Berets* from an anti-war film such as Michael Cimino's *The Deerhunter* (1978), they share certain preoccupations as well as an ability to transpose the Vietnam War into 'Vietnam' or 'Nam', and thence into a reflection upon 'America'. In *The Deerhunter* the mythology of the frontiersman does not fit the way the war was fought. Michael (Robert DeNiro), as the deerhunter, finds his code of one good shot (echoes of James Fenimore Cooper's Natty Bumppo) distorted into the crazy logic of Russian roulette. To this extent, *The Deerhunter* cannot be mistaken for a Second World War movie; the war is simply so off-centre, at least according to available models of war. As in other Vietnam films, the war is replaced by fascination for an alien reality and its sheer difference from the blue-collar community of Clairton, Pennsylvania. The cinematic realism which we have seen to be the forte of Hollywood action films had to be modified. Structurally, the Vietnam and American parts of the film are not smoothly integrated. The two cultures are represented differently, too. We notice the difference in the sharp cutting sequences and odd angles in the Saigon scenes, compared with the long (and uncritical) shots of the steeltown and the surrounding mountains. But this conceptualizing of Vietnam as not-America, a drug-inspired version of the mysterious Orient, allows a war, in which the United States was the aggressor and the perpetrator of now-proven horrors, to be managed generically. *The Deerhunter* eventually finds its narrative in Michael, who plays professional Russian roulette but only to try and get Nicky back. Nicky cannot come home alive because he has been lured into the other world and that world is portrayed as madness. However, Michael brings Nicky's body back; nothing like Rupert Brooke's image of a 'corner of a foreign field/That is forever England' took hold of the American imagination in the Vietnam era. In bringing Nicky home, Michael, the outsider, reunites the community. The patriotism of the concluding scene, when the survivors are at Nicky's funeral and sing 'God Bless America' is not really a surprise, though it has upset some critics. It is realism and genre regained, though films like *Taxi Driver* (1976) and *Cutter's Way* (1981) disturb the equilibrium with their portrait of Vietnam vets back home.

Francis Ford Coppola's *Apocalypse Now* (1979) is perhaps the most extreme example of what happens to the war movie 'about' Vietnam. Briefly, it is overlaid upon a story of colonialism (Mistah Kurtz from Conrad's *Heart of Darkness* becomes Green Beret Colonel Kurtz) but is given a post-modern detachment, not just in the epic scenes of orchestrated technological warfare 'conducted' by Colonel Kilgore but in the use of traditional Hollywood techniques, like the Chandleresque voice-over and frequent reminders of the Western genre. The superimposition of images early in the film is only an advance warning for the disorientating effects to follow, but the result is, yet again, that Vietnam and its placing in a history of Far-Eastern colonialism begun by the French recede even more from the film's centre than in *The Deerhunter*: 'In this war things get confused out there.' What is left is a melange of genres, yoked together into a universal myth.

Important generic questions have not been entirely monopolized by Vietnam films, of course. Equally interesting, because it recalls questions raised both by the early cinema and by *film noir*'s treatment of women, is a low budget, 1983 film called *Variety*. It was directed by Bette Gordon, with Kathy Acker involved on the script, and suggests that the line between the strict avant-garde American film (which I have had to neglect) and the mainstream need not be so absolute; Jon Jost's gumshoe movie *Angel Heart* (1977) is another example that comes to mind, as is David Lynch's '1950s' film, *Blue Velvet*, and David Byrne's musical, *True Stories* (both 1986). In all of these films, the cross-over point between modernism and mass culture is through genre, since they work through and off recognizable forms. In Gordon's film, the generic continuities are primarily with *film noir*, though the main character is a woman who, in the final scene, is revealed as a *film noir* heroine, but one who takes over the narrative and becomes the pursuer and detective. The other generic cross-over is through the pornographic film. The 'Variety' of the title is the name of a cinema showing pornographic films and the heroine first gets a job in the box-office and then seems to be on the point of acting in one of the films, though this is more the way she is filmed than in actuality; that is, we, as viewers, are positioned as people watching a pornographic film rather than watching others watching such a film. We are involved – in different ways, presumably – with the idea of what (more) can be seen, and so confront very directly the abstractions discussed in this chapter, namely, the relationship between standardization and variety and between realism and modernism. The succession of different screens which the main character is seen on, and through, from the box-office window to the movie camera lens, make us acutely aware of how strange it is to 'go to the pictures'.

Much the same can be said of *Blue Velvet* (*the* post-modern film according to many critics) insofar as we feel that we have seen most of the film before, but in many different films. In just the opening minutes, and in quick succession, we are confronted with a number of utterly *déjà vu* images, among them, a white picket fence; a contemporary suburban street with a post-war fire engine passing down it; a woman watching television, on which there is a close-up of a gun being held; 1950s billboard posters; and a screen-size close up of grass, full of ants (horror movie or natural history documentary?). None of these images engender narratives which are conclusively resolved, not least because 1980s images (today's cars on downtown streets, the hero's gold earring and so on) complicate the idea that this film does begin (historically or metaphorically) in post-war America. We are complicit in the 'knowingness' about narrative in the film. Consequently, instead of story, we are drawn to discrete scenes with no narrative priority attached to any. There is nowhere to put the startlingly discontinuous, but 'known' images. The town in the film is called Lumberton, but even the idea of a lumber room of images can barely accommodate the opening sequence of *Blue Velvet*.

In spite of the variety of contemporary cinema, I am still persuaded by David Bordwell's insistence that while recent American films have made exciting use of New Wave and other European stylistic devices, the determining factor has been the system into which they are integrated. The New Wave techniques are striking in *Bonnie and Clyde* but over the whole film they are mobilized in a very coherent, indeed uniform, way. This is not to say that its violence is not shocking, but it does not radically disturb patterns of viewing a film. The narrative is formally, if violently closed, but, more significantly, the balletic slow-motion massacre and the images of innocence work towards identification on grounds that can be shared by different ideological factions. Although the car-driving, quirky gunfighter in Don Siegel's *The Shootist* (1976) is a candidate for 1970s' anti-heroism, this is never considered because the John Wayne character monopolizes the role of the anachronistic (and innocent) hero. Faced with corporations, cars, paved roads and other signs of progress, films to the left and right of the Hollywood political spectrum can line up together on the side of individualism and innocence. Classic Hollywood found ways of resolving the contradictions in that pairing; so too has Hollywood after the studio days. The power of sentimentality in permitting us to have our progress and regret it is still strong in a film like *Kramer vs Kramer* (1979).

Barry Levinson's *Rain Man* (1989), starring Dustin Hoffman as the autistic savant, Raymond Babbitt, makes for a more interesting final example. Aside from taking on the subject of mental illness, this is latter-day Hollywood faced with making a narrative film around a character who will be 'just the same' at the end. Apart from two jokes – one by Raymond and the other by his brother, Charlie (Tom Cruise), which Raymond recognizes, the film resists finding a cinematic cure. Moreover, while Raymond's mannerisms come very close to turning him into a 'character' (Hoffman is a wonderful character actor), there are scenes which take Raymond's repetitive behaviour beyond being any kind of humour. In all kinds of ways, then, *Rain Man* is a brave film. It is, finally, soft-centred though. The star system survives even the scenes in the mental hospital, where Raymond stands out from the other patients. And the narrative survives, of course, in Charlie Babbitt, who learns from Raymond to make the connections that are mostly beyond his brother. This is less disappointing, however, than is the evasion of the theme of mental illness and the question of whether it should be treated in an institution or in the community. Because of, rather than in spite of, its genre (a 'popular' film), *Rain Man* could have dealt with this theme in a significant way.

One intriguing footnote or perhaps credits note is that as the final credits are screened, so, too, are the random snap-shots that Raymond took on the journey across America with his brother. They are a reminder of the discontinuous frames that so clearly made up the first films. Shown at the end, when we have been 'moved' by the characters, we are encouraged to re-view the film and make the connections, make a narrative.

Hollywood narratives and characters make for a compelling way of seeing the world. My own favourites from 'classic' Hollywood would be the endings of *Young Mr. Lincoln* (1939), *Casablanca* (1943), and *Ride the High Country* (1962). When we criticize such films, we are criticizing ourselves and what we regard as the freedom that comes with, and is signified by, entertainment. To quote Jane Feuer again: 'If we were to think about that, if we were to think at all, it wouldn't be entertainment any more.' While subsequent Hollywood films have dealt more openly with issues like feminism and, especially, female sexuality (*Klute*), institutional corruption (*All the President's Men*), and class (*Five Easy Pieces*), these issues can be partially evaded because, in the end, we are persuaded to see ourselves completed by, and not estranged from, the images of ourselves on the screen.

Notes

1. Christian Metz, 'The Imaginary Signifier', *Screen*, 16 (1975), p. 18.

2. Quoted in Anthony Slide (with the assistance of Paul O'Dell), *Early American Cinema* (New York, 1970), p. 14.

3. Reviews paraphrased by William K. Everson, *American Silent Film* (New York, 1978), p. 9.

4. Quoted in Peter Wollen, *Signs and Meanings in the Cinema* (1970), p. 32.

5. Sergei Eisenstein, *Film Form: Essays in Film Theory*, translated and edited by Jan Leyda (1963), p. 245.

6. David Bordwell, Janet Staiger and Kristen Thompson, *The Classical Hollywood Cinema: Film Style and Mode of Production to 1960* (1988), p. 73.

7. André Bazin, *What Is Cinema?*, translated and edited by Hugh Gray Berkeley, 1967), Vol. 1, pp. 144–45 and 150.

8. Stephen Heath, *Questions of Cinema* (Bloomington, Indiana, 1981), p. 124.

9. Christian Metz, 'History/Discourse', *Edinburgh '76 Magazine* (1976).

10. Quoted from *Hollywood*, written, directed and produced by Kevin Brownlow and David Gill, 1979.

11. Robert B. Ray, *A Certain Tendency of the Hollywood Cinema, 1930–1980* (Princeton, NJ, 1985), p. 26.

12. See Theodor Adorno and Max Horkheimer, 'The Culture Industry: Enlightenment as Mass Deception', in their *Dialectic of Enlightenment* translated by John Cumming (1979), pp. 120–67.

13. Along with Bazin's work (see note 7), this section draws upon Bordwell *et al.* (note 6); Ray (note 11); Steve Neale, *Genre* (1988); and Editors, *Cahiers du cinéma*, 'John Ford's "Young Mr Lincoln"', *Screen*, 13 (1972), pp. 5–43.

14. Karel Reisz and Gavin Millar, *The Technique of Film Editing* (New York, 1968), p. 215.

15. James Monaco, *How to Read a Film: The Art, Technology, Language, History, and Theory of Film and Media* (New York, 1981), p. 162.

16. Jane Feuer, *The Hollywood Musical* (1982), p. 13.

17. See the essays in *Women in Film Noir*, edited by E. Ann Kaplan (1980).

18. Alex Madsen, *The New Hollywood: American Movies in the '70s* (New York, 1975), p. 1; Diane Jacobs, *Hollywood Renaissance* (New York, 1977), p. 11.

19. Sylvia Harvey, *May '68 and Film Culture* (1978), p. 38.

20. See Deborah Linderman, 'Oedipus in Chinatown', *Enclitic* (1982), p. 198.

21. John Carlos Rowe, ' "Bringing It All Back Home": American Recyclings of the Vietnam War', *Working Papers*, No. 3, Center for Twentieth-Century Studies, The University of Wisconsin-Milwaukee, p. 11.

Chapter 2
Painting

Port of New York: realism and modernism in American painting, c. 1900 to 1929

The most straightforward way to survey twentieth-century American painting is to follow mainstream art history (and the terminology of the previous chapter) and talk of a struggle between realism or representationalism and modernism. After aesthetic skirmishes in New York City in the teens between The Eight (or Ash Can School realists) and the early modernists associated with Alfred Stieglitz's 291 gallery, modernism registered some successes, particularly after the Armory Show of 1913. These were short-lived and American modernism came up against the revival of realism in the Depression of the 1930s, but then reemerged in the 1940s with the triumph of Abstract Expressionism. Post-modernism, in such forms as Pop Art and Conceptual Art, reacted against this dominant strain of American modernism, though its excesses are currently reactivating a call for realism and tradition.

It is important to hang on to this story because it illuminates individual works and reveals artistic influences; besides, at present, it is the only convenient way to map the complicated American art scene. At the same time, we can at least entertain the possibility of telling the story differently. Aside from recent developments in art theory, our own experience in front of paintings tells us that realism and modernism must always have invisible scare-quotes around them, to remind us that these modes of representation are historical categories: they developed and gained acceptance at certain periods and not at others.[1] In this connection, the chronology of American art history warrants special comment: its story is more than a simple matter of a cultural time lag. When the critic, Paul Rosenfeld, entitled his groundbreaking celebration of 'fourteen American moderns' *Port of*

New York (1924), he was certainly drawing attention to the port of entry for European modernism; equally, though, he was identifying the encounter with America. The influence of high European modernism of the 1880–1930 period is undeniable, and yet it does not quite fit with what was going on in early American modernism, mostly in New York City through to the end of the 1920s. In contrast, with the re-emergence of modernism in American art after the Second World War, the closeness of the fit between the anxious and intense stance of high European modernism and a new, yet late, generation of American moderns (mostly the Abstract Expressionists) must make us wonder what else is going on, aside from the normal pattern of development and influence within art history. Though it is unwelcome in some critical circles, one hypothesis is that the particular form which 'the tradition of the new' took, and its unexpected acceptance as part of the official culture of post-1945 America, had a good deal to do with the momentous political upheavals of the 1930s and 1940s. What has happened to modernist painting in America might, then, be seen as a mirror image of what happened to realism in Hollywood: it triumphed but did so for more than aesthetic reasons. To explore this hypothesis, we must drop back to the early twentieth century.

'The Great Event in the history of American art' is Harold Rosenberg's verdict on the Armory Show of 1913, at which 1300 works, roughly a third by Europeans and nearly all post-1860, were exhibited at the Sixty-ninth Regiment Armory in New York City.[2] The organizers, the Association of American Painters and Sculptors (AAPS), missed out Arthur Dove, Charles Demuth and Max Weber (no relation), but otherwise exhibited the best new American artists: Alfred H. Maurer, Marsden Hartley, John Marin, Charles Sheeler, Joseph Stella, Stanton Macdonald-Wright, and Abraham Walkowitz. The AAPS achieved less by way of personal encouragement of American modernist painters than did Alfred Stieglitz, who, between 1910 and 1917 at 291, and then at other galleries, gave exhibition space to all of the promising American moderns who were around at the time of the Armory Show, plus Georgia O'Keeffe, who came to New York in 1916. The Armory Show did, none the less, lay an artistic foundation by bringing European modernist paintings to the United States in much larger numbers than Stieglitz or individual dealers could afford. Impressionism, which was already fairly well known, was represented by Manet, Monet and Renoir; Post-Impressionism by Van Gogh, Cezanne, and Gauguin; Neo-Impressionism by Seurat and Signac; Fauvism by Dufy, Matisse and Vlaminck; and Cubism by Picabia, Picasso, Braque, Gleizes, Leger, and Duchamp. The Italian Futurists refused to participate when they were not accorded the same distinction as, for example, Gauguin, Cezanne and Van Gogh, and allocated a separate booth.

The most important formal consequence of so much concentrated exposure to European modernism was a challenge to realism or representational painting, which Peter Wollen quite rightly defines in historical as well as in formal terms:

> The history of art since the Renaissance until the modern period, had been one of homogenisation: the exclusion of words from the picture-space, the restriction of point of view spatially and temporally (homogeneous space and single moment in time), the banishing of discontinuity.[3]

Visitors to the Armory Show encountered the angular shapes of Cubism, which had its collective birth virtually on the eve of the Show, together with a loss of depth, as the brushwork or the arbitrary mis-matching of colours in the many Fauve paintings waylaid efforts to look through the surface to what the painting represented, or what the title said it was representing. Even the popular jokes tell us something about what had been happening to representation in European art, though they inevitably overstate the degree of abstraction and ignore Picasso and Braque's dialogues with more representational styles. Most lay and critical attention at the Armory Show fastened upon Marcel Duchamp's *Nude Descending a Staircase, No. 2* (1912), a blatantly constructed painting in which the figure is virtually lost or reduced to a series of lines. One sort of reaction was summed up by the *American Art News*'s competition to find the nude. Another was symbolized by the visit to the Show of the New York Vice-Commission, which did not win the competition and generally had little to report. One newspaper did re-title Duchamp's painting *Rude Descending a Staircase*.

The coming of the modern in American art is a local as well as a trans-Atlantic matter, which could be one reason for the relative lack of controversy and drama. Very local, since the right to be called 'modern' was being contested in the years up to and beyond the Armory Show on the doorstep of Stieglitz's 291. Robert Henri, the leader of The Eight, had been involved in the early planning of the Armory Show. The other members, besides Henri, were Arthur Davies, John Sloan, George Luks, Everett Shinn, William Glackens, Ernest Lawson, and Maurice Prendergast. The last two and Davies were known more for landscapes than New York scenes, and for their interest in European Impressionism, so, again there was no firm division between realists and modernists. Later, this close inter-relationship allowed artists like Edward Hopper and Stuart Davis, who were students at the time of The Eight's and Stieglitz's gatherings, to avoid the hardening extremes of realism and modernism. In terms of exhibitions, though, there was competition between realism and modernism, dating from 1908 when The Eight and Stieglitz's group held pioneer exhibitions. Both groups were, however, in reaction against the National Academy of Design, with its preference for nineteenth-century portraiture and landscape painting, genteel realism and American Impressionism. For this reason both groups were sometimes called 'modern'. They were equally committed to the development of American art, though Stieglitz's proselytizing on this theme also emphasized the need for contact with European modernism.

The European modernism at the Armory Show and 291 highlighted, by contrast, The Eight's theory of art as reflection, or, better, as a window onto the world, a new urban world. Many of the artists were newspaper reporters and illustrators, who would sketch on the spot and then, in their studios, complete the record of typical urban scenes: a rush-hour crowd and a passing train on the elevated railroad in John Sloan's *Six O'Clock Winter* (1912); and people milling around outside a New York tenement house in *Cliff Dwellers* (1912) by another realist, George Wesley Bellows. We look on at the products of reportage, part of the crowd in George Luks' *The Wrestlers* (1905), and, in Everett Shinn's *Sixth Avenue Elevated After Midnight* (1899), at one end of the railway car, from where we observe a recognizable urban interior. There is a clear sense of depth as the carriage recedes into the 'background' of the painting.

According to art historian, Barbara Rose, after the Armory Show the 'essentially conservative' attitude to form of the realists underwent some modifications, and in the right direction she implies. Expanding upon her instance of Bellows' *Stag at Sharkey's* (1907) and *Dempsey and Firpo* (1924), two similar boxing scenes, we can appreciate the 'new self-consciousness with regard to formal values' (Plates 1 and 2).[4] There is a sharper stylization in *Dempsey and Firpo*. Figures are precise, where the attempt to capture movement in *Stag at Sharkey's* blurs lines. The ropes of the boxing ring are a more obvious sign of a changed style. In the earlier painting, they are not at all obtrusive and contribute to the depth of the painting. In *Dempsey and Firpo*, the ropes become lines, which criss-cross the space, dissecting the action, flattening it into a pattern which brings parts of the background into the foreground.

Later, when we look at urban paintings by Marin, Weber, Stella and other early modernists, we can further distinguish the two modes of representation. This is an appropriate moment, however, to depart temporarily from a descriptive account of realism and to question its claims to reflect the world. As we saw when discussing cinema, modes of representation are not 'essentially' anything (conservative, radical, true or false), but they are historical, and they do have ideological inflections. This is made very apparent in recent feminist art theory which successfully re-casts standard oppositions, not least that between representational and non-representational art.

In *Sixth Avenue Elevated After Midnight* and the two boxing paintings by Bellows, the absence of women at those times and in those places in a modern city at once endorses the paintings as neutral and accurate representations and draws attention to the invisible point of view at work, in the double sense of the point of view of the painter and the spectator. For these are also places of *representation* and *observation* where women are not. A lot is going on in these low-key paintings, not least the positioning of us as very particular, rather than neutral, onlookers. Griselda Pollock's comment, on a different set of paintings of modern life, is apposite:

> To recognize the gender specific conditions of these paintings'
> existence one need only imagine a female spectator and a female
> producer of the works. How can a woman relate to the viewing
> positions . . .? Could [a female artist] have gone to such a
> location to canvass the subject? Would it enter her head as a site
> of modernity as she experienced it?[5]

Switching to the positive rather than critical function of feminist art criticism (what is called gynocritics in literary studies), we can understand the importance of Georgia O'Keeffe in the formative period of twentieth-century American painting. 'With woman suffrage and all', Abraham Walkowitz thought it 'a good idea to have a woman on the walls' of 291.[6] O'Keeffe replied in the best possible way. Her giant, bright flowers look back at the viewer in ways that were striking for a period when women artists and their work were still being compared with flowers, but small delicate ones (Plate 4). Although she often painted from objects (shells and pine-cones as well as flowers), the sheer size of the details in *Red Poppy* and *Black Iris* (both 1926), and *Black Hollyhock, Blue Larkspur* (1930), together with the careful pictorial construction, combine to produce an effect similar to that in the movie close-up. Space and perspective are redefined and force an abstract appreciation from the viewer, even though, in one sense, it is clear what is being represented. In *The Shelton with Sunspots* (1926) and *Radiator Building – Night, New York* (1927), she does something similar, in that objects (skyscrapers) are treated in the stylized realism of what was coming to be called Precisionism. Thinking back to the other Max Weber's distinction between 'intimate' and 'monumental' art, it would seem that O'Keeffe refuses the personal or public options that are often associated with modernist and realist art, respectively. The eroticism of her flowers and the private places amid the canyons in *From the White Place* (1940) have a monumental, epic and impersonal feel to them.

We are getting ahead of the art history. Griselda Pollock's comments on realism are part of the broader claim by Meyer Schapiro that 'all renderings of objects, no matter how exact they seem, even photographs, proceed from values, methods and viewpoints which somehow shape the image and often determine its contents.'[7] Bellows' second boxing painting, *Dempsey and Firpo*, does demonstrate a new-found awareness of form, but more significant is the idea that its authority as a representation derives from previous representations rather than from reference: from relations within a painting and across other paintings, in this example Bellows' own *Stag at Sharkey's* and other paintings of urban sports, realist or proto-modernist, in which, it should be noted, a gender-specific representation persists with striking uniformity. The ambiguous status of representation which was highlighted by modernism, rather than any essential difference between realism and modernism, makes it difficult for us to affirm the claims of Robert Henri's group to be, in Baudelaire's famous phrase, 'painter[s] of modern life'. Far from resolving questions of representation and ideology, however, the gradual ascendancy of modernism sharpened them.

Some downtown stuff: modernism and the city, 1910 to 1930

Besides the idea of a port of entry for European art, Paul Rosenfeld suggests another meaning for 'Port of New York'. In the Epilogue to his book, he admits that 'one could not break with New York', and then goes on to describe the city in painterly terms: 'the very jostling, abstracted streets of the city'; 'the form is still very vague'; and, 'the port of New York lies on a single plane with all the world to-day'.[8] Somewhat obliquely, then, Rosenfeld was one of the first to comment on the encounter between American modernism, experimenting with abstract, conceptual representation, and the coming site of modernity: New York City, a Cubist city according to Francis Picabia, who arrived from Europe a month before the Armory Show.

Among John Marin's fourteen paintings at the Armory Show were four of the Woolworth Building, part of the body of work that followed his decision in 1911 to paint 'some downtown stuff, and to pile these great houses one upon another with paint as they do pile themselves up here.'[9] Similar decisions appear to have been made by Joseph Stella, resulting in his individual Coney Island and Brooklyn Bridge paintings, as well as in the five panels of *New York Interpreted* (1920–22); and by Max Weber who 'converted' to the city around 1914. Of *New York at Night* (1915), Weber remarks that it was 'a web of colored geometric shapes, characteristic only of the Grand Canyons of New York at night'.[10] In this painting and, more so, in *Rush Hour, New York* (1915), Weber combines a Cubist reduction to squares, rectangles, triangles, and other abstractions of three-dimensional space, with colour divisionism, Futurist lines, and the imagery of wheels, in order to convey energy and process. 'Everything moves, everything runs, everything turns rapidly', to quote from Boccioni's *Technical Manifesto of Futurist Painting* (1910).[11] The coincidence of New York and a Cubist-Futurist amalgam excited, in Marin's formulation, an orientation towards the 'great forces at work; great movements', so that his *Brooklyn Bridge* (1910) is not simply piled up but tilts to the left, even as it pulls to the right. Similarly, skyscrapers, identified by Henry James during his visit in 1904 as the prime symbol of New York, were seen by Marin less as 'precise structural units', to be analysed in the manner of Cubist studio or at least interior studies, and more as 'dynamic forces'.[12] 'Dynamism' and 'Electricity' had been considered by Marinetti as possible names before 'Futurism' was chosen. This engagement with the material culture and 'forces' of New York City follows the example of Walt Whitman's poetry, and, in turn influenced Hart Crane's 1930 epic poem, *The Bridge*.

Where Marin's *Brooklyn Bridge* has a more solid attachment to the stonework as well as to the steel strands, the more Futurist-inspired Stella, beginning in 1917 with the first of his studies of the bridge, concentrates on 'the vibrating coils, cutting and dividing into innumerable musical spaces the nude immensity of the sky'.[13] The steel strands of Stella's bridges shine and convey electricity, and the power is in the vertical and diagonal lines rather than in the blocks. Moreover, the blocks in Stella's 1917–18 painting, and in *The Skyscraper* (1920–22), are themselves angled by diagonal converging lines, so that there is 'movement' within them as well as across them. As with Marin and Weber, however, Stella set the tone of early American modernism by taking from Futurism its excitement and celebration of technology, but declining its apocalyptic and proto-fascist politics. In Stella, the politics are mute: 'Steel and electricity had created a new world . . . The steel had leaped to hyperbolic altitudes and expanded to vast latitudes with the skyscrapers and with the bridges made for the conjunction of worlds.'[14]

Beginning in 1917, with Charles Demuth's *Trees and Barns, Bermuda*, and continuing, the same year, with Charles Sheeler's barns series, George Ault's *The Mill Room* (1923) and *Sullivan Street Abstraction* (1928), Louis Lozowick's *Cities* series, and Elsie Driggs' *Pittsburgh* (1927), a group known as the Precisionists sought a different kind of representation of modern American life from Marin and Weber. The Precisionists, are sometimes known as Cubist-Realists because they evinced a Cubist interest in shapes, including the shapes of machinery – *Machinery* is the title of a 1920 painting by Demuth – and buildings, as in Sheeler's *Offices* of 1922 (Plate 3). Similarly, when Sheeler brings the American landscape into art in *Classic Landscape* (1931), he stylizes it. Railroad tracks, chimneys and industrial plant are not fragmented; nor do they 'clash', as in Marin, Weber and Stella; instead, they are chosen for their geometry. The straight lines of the tracks and buildings are accentuated in order to formalize the representation. Even the shadows are hard-edged, and the background is as precisely delineated as the foreground.

A reasonable summary of American art from 1900 to the Depression would be that The Eight and associated realists, who were themselves often journalists, followed the example of that profession and also learned from reformist photographers and sociologists of the city. They worked close to identifiable and self-contained scenes, for example city streets, as in William Glackens, *Shoppers* (1908). They had difficulties, however, with the *processes* of modern urban life, both its increasing rationalization and the more dynamic, even chaotic side that, paradoxically, arose from rationalization and technological innovation. The development of communication systems, as we saw in the Introduction, created its own internal dynamic as more people interacted more frequently. Precisionists, like Demuth and Sheeler, responded to the rationalizing processes per se, falling in with them to such an extent that their formalism merges with a design-aesthetic that was apparently impervious to the economic discontinuities of the Depression. *Classic Landscape* is dated 1931. Marin, Stella and Weber introduce more of a critical edge, mixing Cubist influences with Futurist ones in an attempt to convey the doubleness at work in the larger forces moulding an urban-technological society. One measure of their success is that it is Marin and Stella, along with Stuart Davis and Edward Hopper, and not the more famous Abstract Expressionists, who come in for exemplary praise in Marshall Berman's study of the 'dialectical interplay between unfolding modernization of the environment – particularly the urban environment – and the development of modernist art and thought' (*All That Is Solid Melts Into Air*, p. 309). At the very least, early American modernism comes as a relief from the inward turn of high modernism, presented as a forced retreat in the social theory of Max Weber, but, positively by James Joyce, as the 'luminous silent stasis of aesthetic pleasure'.

Besides a distinction between the representation of process and the representation of scenes, there is a further difference (of degree) between realism and modernism in the early period. Where realism is about recognition and frequently opposes and seeks to reform society on that very basis, 'the shock of recognition' in modernism, which is how Edmund Wilson describes its oppositional stance, is actually more indirect. It is a consequence of *not* taking reality on its own terms. Typically, we are puzzled and can be affronted by an abstract painting when we fail to recognize what it is about. But on what, or whose, terms do we respond to the painting? It is tempting to ignore this question, and to follow the orthodox art history of a halting, but none the less clear, progression beyond realism to modernism. But, sooner or later, we have to say something about our experiences when faced by examples of this art of the empirically unobservable. In the absence of some thing, person, event, or tradition, to which the representation on the canvas can be unambiguously referred, how *do* we respond? From the late 1930s onwards, and particularly in the criticism of Clement Greenberg as he championed the Abstract Expressionists, one very influential answer was that we respond by talking about the formal qualities of the work of art. Conflicting interpretations of what the painting is about become tensions contained in the space of the autonomous work. Students of literature might recognize a parallel in Anglo-American New Criticism.

In relation to a painting by Willem de Kooning, Jackson Pollock, or Barnett Newman (Plates 9, 10 and 11), Greenberg's art theory is much richer than I have suggested, as we shall see later in this chapter. However, it has its problems, not least an a-historical quality. By looking closely at some early American modernist paintings, we have the opportunity to discuss conflicting interpretations of a painting, and of modernism, historically and in terms of ideology. It will be worth keeping in mind two statements. The first is Raymond Williams on modernism as a historical phenomenon:

> The positive consequence of the idea of art as a superior reality was that it offered an immediate basis for an important criticism of industrialism. The negative consequence was that it tended, as both the situation and the opposition hardened, to isolate art, to specialize the imaginative faculty to this one kind of activity, and thus to weaken [its] dynamic function.

And the second is a definition of ideology by T.J. Clark:

The existence in society of distinct and singular bodies of knowledge: *orders* of knowing, most often imposed on quite disparate bits and pieces of representation . . . a set of permitted modes of seeing and saying; each with its own structure of closure and disclosure, its own horizons, its way of providing certain perceptions and rendering others unthinkable, aberrant or extreme. [15]

In our first example, John Marin's *Lower Manhattan (Composing Derived from Top of Woolworth Building)* (1922), we are immediately confronted with modernist 'spaces' that are unobservable in a photograph (Plate 5). Height is flattened, and the buildings 'rebound' off each other, competing for space in a force-field. What is the authority for these spaces that will permit us to interpret them? Standard critical explanations are to hand, the most persuasive off-loading the problem onto the work of the philosopher, Henri Bergson. In these explanations, Bergson's 'Life Force' is what the painting is 'about'.

For a low-altitude explanation, which gets closer to the question of what was, and was not, oppositional about modernism, we can look to the ideologies which informed the spaces which artists probably looked at most days: these being the spaces in the modern society around them and the spaces on their canvasses. There was, for instance, a confidence in progress which was much more apparent in the United States than in Europe in the post-war years. New York, after all, was being built and redeveloped almost as the early modernists painted and drew it. Marin, especially, interprets the city as a dynamic force in its own right, separate from, rather than caught up with, the activities of the philistine business class, which was alternately hostile towards, and mystified by, events like the Armory Show. Incidentally, in Max Weber's city paintings the instability of the juxtaposed buildings comes close to overwhelming this sense of confidence. Quite possibly, the unnerving feeling of constructing art over a void, or on a building site, was a contributory factor in Weber's recourse, in later paintings such as *Adoration of the Moon* (1944), to his own Jewish past in search of a firmer foundation.

This difference between Weber and Marin is not sharp, but it is there and would seem to revolve around the two ideas of *energy* and *power*, which are invariably encompassed in the word 'forces'. Marin insists upon the word 'forces', and it was also part of the cultural talk of the time. As *energy*, forces are self-generated and carry a positive charge in Marin's paintings and in his anthropocentric estimations of New York as a modern city. 'If these buildings move me,' Marin asserts, 'they too must have life' (quoted in P. Conrad, *The Art of the City*, p. 128). As *power*, however, the forces raise the kind of doubts which 'move' Henry Adams, a jaundiced visitor to New York in 1904:

> The outline of the city became frantic in its effort to explain something that defied meaning. Power seemed to have outgrown its servitude and to have asserted its freedom. The cylinder had exploded, and thrown great masses of stone and steam against the sky. The city had the air and movement of hysteria, and the citizens were crying, in every accent of anger and alarm, that the new forces must at any cost be brought under control. Prosperity never before imagined, power never yet wielded by man, speed never reached by anything but a meteor, had made the world irritable, nervous, querulous, unreasonable and afraid.[16]

Power, when it is analysed, and not submerged in concepts such as 'progress', 'development' and 'modernization', is exerted by, and on, someone or some group. It is related to knowledge, and so to ideology in T.J. Clark's definition quoted above, and thence to representation. Forces, understood in terms of power, are in conflict and cannot, other than in the different kind of 'space' created by ideology, be lumped together as progress or regress. When Marin was painting his cityscapes, there were still fears about the accumulation of economic power in monopolies, in spite of the efforts of trust-busting Progressive politicians. Yet Marin is content to leave the city alone and not impose a viewpoint in the manner of perspective, realist art. He seems to have confidence in a free market equilibrium of 'great masses pulling smaller masses, each subject in some degree to the other's power'.[17] Thus, in *Lower Manhattan*, the pasted-on cut-out star with the radiating black lines suggests a centripetal/centrifugal principle amidst the frenetic activity, perhaps even an affinity between modernist 'seeing' and the energy of laissez-faire capitalism. On the other hand, though, there is a point of view on the financial district: 'Composing Derived from Top of Woolworth'. And there is a frame, reinforced, as in many of Marin's paintings by the blank spaces around the edge of the canvas. The point of view and the frames *contain* the field of contending forces, exert power from without. The pasted on star is an image of the motif on the Old World Building beneath the Woolworth, and this suggests, in partial contradiction to the unifying interpretation, an explosion, the flattening of a rival financial power, with the wider ramifications of power at large hinted at by Henry Adams.

Joseph Stella's *Battle of Lights, Coney Island* (1913) is, like Marin's work, undeniably modern in its subject matter, a slap in the face for a genteel tradition horrified by the idea of painting such vulgar abandon (Plate 6). It is also a painting about 'forces', and so differs from the visual record left by photographers and realists like Sloan and, later, Reginald Marsh. Symbolized by Luna Park's electric tower in the centre-top of the painting, electricity is an exciting force, stimulating new concepts of time and space in this place of leisure. Elsewhere in his New York paintings, however, electricity is a force tied to the world of work, a connection that is not made by Marin within his understanding of forces as neutral energy. John Kasson makes the point in his social history of Coney Island, by juxtaposing a photograph of workers on a mine railway 'descending for work', and a cartoon showing one of the rides at Coney Island, captioned 'Thrill seekers descending for pleasure'.[18]

As in Marin, we also have two readings of an urban space. Stella's choice of a carnival day – Mardi Gras – points to collective pleasure as a critique of work and the hierarchies of the surrounding society. 'Carnival', as the concept has come down to us from the writings of Mikhail Bakhtin, overturns hierarchies and transgresses boundaries in pre-industrial societies. In Stella's *Battle of Lights*, the greens and reds of the arabesque designs similarly overspill boundaries, in particular the straight lines of the funfair machinery, and dislocate the protocols of orderly representation. Kasson argues that the switchback rides functioned as a social leveller, a kind of mechanical melting pot in which different ethnic groups, men and women, and at least the working and middle classes were upended and flung together on 'The Mountain Torrent' or in 'The Barrel of Love'.

The problem is that whereas carnival could interrupt the calendar of work in the place of work in a pre-industrial economy, with full industrialization, Coney Island increasingly became a specialized leisure activity, to be indulged in at weekends or on scheduled holidays and located outside the city on Long Island, but linked by a suburban railroad. In Stella's painting, we are unsure whether the depiction of pleasure, at the expense of the direct social/moral commentary of John Sloan and others, breaks or completes the cycle of consumption and production. Does an arabesque, like Wyndham Lewis's modernist vortex, create a new kind of temporality that undermines cause and effect – where does a line begin and end? Or does it reconstitute a spatial pattern susceptible to control and containment, albeit in a much more complex form than in realism? Readers familiar with modernist debates over stream of consciousness in the novel or the epiphany in the short story will probably recognize the argument, and the difficulty of resolving it at a purely formal level. Possibly, though, it is a historical question before it is a formal one, this being Raymond Williams' position on modernism, though one that the high modernist theory of Clement Greenberg rejects. Kasson argues that during a turn-of-the-century interlude between the end of Victorian culture, based on production and the onset of a mass culture of consumption, Coney

Island, as the first of the great amusement parks, did indeed represent a radical challenge to the economic and cultural establishment. Elements of folk culture – notably carnival and festival – came into the wider arena of popular culture. But this challenge was, by the 1920s, incorporated into mass culture, and eventually into the controlled environment of Disneyland and its progeny. Also in that interlude, Stella's Coney Island painting was one of many that broke down the distinction between high and popular art, fulfilling the aspiration of Walt Whitman that America should forge a truly democratic culture. Its nemesis in Coney Island art was Reginald Marsh's figurative, rather than abstract, *George C. Tilyou's Steeplechase Park* (1936) which, though far from sanitized, reinstated pleasure as a spectacle at which we passively look. It would seem that an *oppositional* modernism exists between two kinds of looking or, if we're doing art history, some-*when* between realism and high modernism.

Duchamp's 'Fountain': New York Dada, 1917 to 1930

Between the egalitarian Romanticism of Whitman's *Leaves of Grass* (1855) and Marsh's *Steeplechase Park*, the United States became a mass society, and this enormous fact makes representation a political issue. Dada was sited on the increasingly indistinct borderline between art and mass production, and it is this, rather than its rejection of the idea of art as either a craft or an expression of inner, psychological states, that accounts for its importance.

Nude Descending a Staircase, No. 2 (1912) may have perplexed critics and lay visitors to the Armory Show, but in 1917 Marcel Duchamp posed the question, What is art?, more dramatically still. In the country which was revolutionizing mass production, under the name of R. Mutt, which he borrowed from a New York plumbing company, and under the title, *Fountain*, Duchamp submitted a mass-produced urinal to the Independents Exhibition. The urinal became a work of art, in Duchamp's view, because someone construed it as such and gave it a title at a certain time and in a certain place. 'The choice of these ready-mades was never dictated by an aesthetic delectation', Duchamp later explained. 'The choice was based on a reaction of visual *indifference*, with at the same time a total absence of good or bad taste, in fact a complete anaesthesia' (quoted in Stangos (ed.) *Concepts of Modern Art*, p. 119).

The changeable, rather than eternal quality of art, was explicitly introduced in Duchamp's *The Large Glass, The Bride Stripped Bare by Her Bachelors, Even*. As a glass construction, whatever can be seen through it becomes part of its (temporary) significance. In 1923, after working on *The Large Glass* for eight years, Duchamp put it aside, and it took on a new title: *Delay in Glass*. When it broke in 1927, Duchamp repaired it but the cracks remained part of the 'new' work. After such a 'career', it is difficult to hold onto the idea of the completed work of art, irrespective of whether completeness is legitimized according to referential or autonomous criteria.

The organizers of the Independents Exhibition hid the urinal behind a screen until Walter Arensberg bought it, whereupon it became a centrepiece of the group which met at his salon at 33 West 67th Street. The Arensberg Circle also advertised its Dada credentials through Baroness Elsa von Freytag Loringhoven, who wore sardine cans on her shaved head, which she painted purple. Man Ray, Morton Schamberg and John Covert were the artists most directly involved with New York Dada. In addition, Stuart Davis, Arthur Dove, Marsden Hartley, and the Precisionists, Sheeler and Demuth, found that Dada-ist experimentation with assemblage, kinetic and ready-made art, and its anti-art philosophy, enlivened their own education in modernism. All were experimenting in the materials rather than the subject matter of art. In his 'aerographs', Man Ray explored the link with the commercial world by using an airbrush, which, apart from the particular effects, kept him at a distance from the canvas and focused attention upon the concept of the work of art rather than its realization through a continuous mind-arm-wrist-hand-brush-canvas sequence.

Although Arthur Dove and Marsden Hartley from Stieglitz's group were also part of Arensberg's Dada-ist inspired circle, his was a more diverse and experimental section of the early avant-garde, which was working against the refinement of the medium and the inward turn of high modernism.

Much more derivative than it seems at first glance: Social Realism and American Scene painting in the Depression

The Depression of the 1930s is commonly regarded as encouraging a revival of realism in painting. There was already enough fragmentation about in a massive economic crisis, without the experimentalism of modernism, as modernist painters themselves testified when applying for places on the New Deal Works Progress Administration (WPA) art projects. Beginning in 1933 and, with changes of title and administration, continuing until 1943, these projects employed over three-and-a-half thousand artists, including early modernists like Marsden Hartley and Stuart Davis, as well as Jackson Pollock, Willem de Kooning, Arshile Gorky, and Mark Rothko, who would dominate American modernism after the Second World War. Aesthetic differences between modernists and the still strong realist tradition in American art were officially played down as the WPA projects sought to utilize art to remedy the divisions and uncertainty within society. To this end, art had to come out of the art school, gallery, or avant-garde salon, and into the workplace, the union office, and distant communities, through mural as well as easel painting, and through the teaching of evening classes. Art also had to be understandable to ordinary people and this meant it had to represent people, places and things, preferably American. This determined effort to forge a middle-ground for American art drew in artists from the two main groupings of the 1930, the Social Realists and American Scene painters.

Large sections of the Left, through the John Reed Clubs, the American Artists Congress, and *The New Masses*, linked modernism with decadence and bourgeois individualism. These groups and institutions advocated a proletarian art, generically known as Social Realism, and exemplified by the work of William Gropper, Philip Evergood, Ben Shahn, and Jack Levine. Yet when we compare these painters both with each other and with the Eight, the oddity is that they should have been called realists, so clearly articulated is the point of view from which the representation derives. Reviewing a Ben Shahn exhibition in 1947, Clement Greenberg, who, by then, had little sympathy for Social Realism, puts the matter differently, remarking that it is 'much more derivative than it seems at first glance'.[19] William Gropper's, *Youngtown Strike* (1937) and *Capitalist Cartoon Number 1* (1933) make use of, respectively, the revolutionary art of Daumier and Goya, and magazine illustration in the style of the *New Masses*. Philip Evergood's *American Tragedy* (1937) and *Through the Mill* (1940) are both influenced by magazine art, but do not rely on caricature to the extent that Jack Levine does in *The Feast of Pure Reason* (1937), which depicts a capitalist, a gambler or gangster, and a policeman in conference. What is interesting is that the sources are often the same as those for American Scene painters, most of whom did not share the politics of the Social Realists.

American Scene painters were, however, just as hostile as the Social Realists to modernism. The regionalist, Thomas Hart Benton and his advocate, the critic Thomas Craven, verged on citing modernism as a minor cause of the economic crisis. Benton sought a combination of explicitly American themes and an objectivity conceived in direct opposition to his dalliance with Cubism during his days in New York, when he often visited Stiegitz's 291. Realism would help to provide the substance and integrity which was lacking in an America suffering the upheavals of the Depression and unhealthily centred upon large cities. In Benton's *Political Business and Intellectual Ballyhoo*, the city is where an avant-garde practises its alien politics and art, while *City Scenes* elaborates upon his populist vision of urban depravity and waste. In the latter picture, at least, we can see the overlap between the politically conservative Benton and the social realism of the Left.

Besides Thomas Hart Benton, the most important painters on the regionalist wing of the American Scene were Grant Wood and John Steuart Curry. Grant Wood – known, of course, for *American Gothic* (1930) – presents in *Stone City, Iowa* (1930), *Fall Plowing* (1931), and *Arbor Day* (1932), an ordered, even modelled, world of neat houses and vaguely maternal fields (Plate 7). It is a unified world. The bridge in *Stone City* connects town and countryside; for American Scene painters, no such connection would be possible between a large city and the countryside. *Arbor Day* is also full of connections, in this case stories: the people are all doing something or going somewhere, not in the impersonal manner of the inhabitants of a city, but as part of the routine of a culture. We know from the chiselled ruts in the road that the horse and cart outside the house will presently go down that road and away to the distant horizon. People and landscape share the overall sense of purposeful behaviour. *In the Spring* (1939) reveals a clear admiration for the farmer who is responsible for the ordered landscape behind him. When we get close to Wood's human figures – notably in *American Gothic* – we cannot miss their resolve.

In *American Gothic*, there is also, however, something manic about the farmer's stare and we are left wondering what his sister is looking at – neither us nor her brother nor his slightly sinister pitchfork, but something off to her left, or perhaps not visible at all but inside her head. Those who, in the 1930s and 1940s, interpreted *American Gothic* as an image of mid-American resolution, seem not to have commented upon the macabre title. A similar mixture of respect for traditional values and intimations of psychological disorder, explicable in the modernist vocabulary of Freud, is to be found in Sherwood Anderson and other novelists of the 1920s and 1930s who wrote about small town communities.

Benedict Anderson argues that 'communities are to be distinguished, not by their falsity/genuineness, but by the style in which they are imagined'.[20] American Scene painting aspires to be a community based upon the representational image. Under the pressure of the economic crisis of the 1930s there was a search for the real, for what everyone could agree on, and in representational terms, could recognize, 'free from isms and fads and so-called modern influences', in the words of Works Project administrator, Edward Bruce.[21] The WPA advice that artists should paint only what they knew about and could see (advice that begs exactly the questions that modernism grapples with), and in so doing preserve American culture, had two consequences. It revealed the odd mixture that is *American Gothic*, or even that is Grant Wood's work as a whole, in which there is depth (the roads and fields stretch away to the horizon) and yet the trees, houses and people have a flat, cardboard quality, marked by the sharp shadows they cast. The other consequence, apparent in Reginald Marsh's *Twenty-Cent Movie* and Benton's *Engineer's Dream* (1931) and *Boom Town* (1928), is the contradiction of a supposed folk art mediated by the only plausible common denominator in an industrial society: the media. Stuart Davis called Benton's art 'dime novel American history', though the reliance on comic-strip techniques is a more significant influence.[22]

The intention to paint in the 'round', to borrow E.M. Forster's synonym for realism, is in tension with the claims for representativeness, even universalism. The shafts of light through dark clouds jar with the documentary quality of the open-air baptism scene in John Steuart Curry's *Baptism in Kansas* (1928). Or, to put this another way, there is a tension between regionalism and claims for a national art and culture. In the course of his discussion of the new nationalism of the 1930s, Warren Susman notes that 'it was during this period that we find, for the first time, frequent reference to "an American Way of Life." The phrase "The American Dream" came into common use; it meant something shared collectively by all Americans' at a 'grass roots' level.[23] The most effective rejoinder to the contradictions between this ideal of unity and a complex society in conflict, whether the ideal was expressed officially or through the various realisms of the 1930s, is the work of Edward Hopper. His importance goes beyond his renowned depiction of the other side of the American Dream, the alienation and simple loneliness and dreariness of American life.

American painting: Edward Hopper and Stuart Davis

Hopper objected that American Scene painting was caricature and Social Realism was propaganda. In relation to his own painting, this is a highly illuminating criticism, because caricature and propaganda assume that we agree upon what reality is, and is not. Hopper is undoubtedly committed to representational art, yet there is something visually very disconcerting about all his paintings: urban ones like *Chop Suey* (1929) and *Approaching a City* (1946) or the very famous *Early Sunday Morning* (1930) and *Nighthawks* (1942); but, equally, suburban and coastal ones, from *Sun on Prospect Street* (1934) to *Second-Story Sunlight* (1960). Patently, our uncertainty about reality does not result from being directed away from the people, buildings or objects towards formal relationships, or at least not nearly to the extent that we are in abstract art. Moreover, there are clear points of focus in the barber's pole in *Early Sunday Morning*, the woman in the cafe in *Chop Suey* and the man and woman facing us over the bar in *Nighthawks* (Plate 8). Yet knowledge, the knowability of reality, does not seem to follow from its representation. In *Nighthawks* the downcast eyes of the couple facing us repel our gaze, and we are drawn away, via the man with his back to us who is in fact centrally placed, to the expanse of street and blank windows which make up at least half of the painting. As for *Early Sunday Morning*, it is a relief to have the title to explain the blankness of the storefronts and first floor windows. Someone else must have felt the same. 'It wasn't necessarily Sunday', Hopper recalled. 'That word was tacked on later by someone else.' In fact the whole title was 'tacked on' since Hopper had first called it *Seventh Avenue Shops*.[24] We are not, to turn around an earlier remark, a community united or reunited by recognition of an image, whether it be of Curry's homely Kansas scene in *Father and Mother* (1929), or Joseph Hirsch's *Hero* (1939–40), in which we know, at one level at least, that peddling on the city streets is what happens to discarded soldiers. Of course, the nostalgia now evoked by Hopper's landscapes and city scenes has brought a common recgnition, but nostalgia is a highly suspect kind of knowledge – it is never what it used to be.

Before rejoining the story that will take us out of the 1930s, we need to pause to consider another artist who, like Hopper, is not easy to place. Many of the criticisms which Hopper – apparently a very American artist – levelled at American Scene painting were applied, quite justifiably, to the Social Realists by Stuart Davis. Like Hopper, Davis' career began in the days of The Eight. While still working in that group's style and sharing its radical politics, he exhibited at the Armory Show, again like Hopper, but counted it the seminal event of his career. From 1913 onwards, he, more than any other American artist, explored the relationship between a Cubism- and Dada-inspired modernism and radical politics, an American-European connection which he celebrated in a number of Paris–New York paintings, which combine abstraction and the icons of mass culture. In 1916 he resigned from the *Masses*, along with John Sloan, because the editorial policy of

Max Eastman and Floyd Dell was one-dimensional in its interpretation of what socialist art should be. Ten years later, when the *New Masses* was founded, Davis was on the editorial board, and for most of the Depression he edited the Artists' Congress magazine, *Art Front*. While working on WPA projects between 1933 and 1939, he was instrumental in unionizing artists and was national secretary of the Artists Congress.

Davis, like Berthold Brecht in European modernism, is a test-case of sorts for a radical art that was also experimental. Indeed, his theoretical position on aesthetics and politics is very close to that of Brecht. Having acknowledged the need for literature that is 'absolutely comprehensible and profitable to [the broad working masses]', Brecht warns that: '*popular art*' and '*realism*' are not 'completely transparent, without history, uncompromised or unequivocal'. Realism 'bears the stamp of the way it was employed, when and by which class, down to its smallest details. With the people struggling and changing reality before our eyes, we must not cling to "tried" rules of narrative, venerable literary models, eternal aesthetic laws.'[25]

Davis' 1930s work, particularly a mural like *Men Without Women* (1932), confirms his general support for art that was in the public eye. *American Painting*, begun in 1932 and not finished until 1951, is a more interesting example of what he was after (see cover). The title appears to be ironic in the light of Davis' opinion of American Scene painting, yet the two lines from a contemporary song – 'It dont mean a thing if it aint got a swing' – down the left-hand border, endorse Brecht on the political necessity for popular art. Estranged from their context, though, these words take on a specific charge when linked, but also formally contrasted, with a powerful, but dogmatic, political statement: the large word 'No' overlaid upon an image of seduction and consumption. Davis exemplifies the claim, made by Thomas Crow, that 'from its beginnings, the artistic avant-garde has discovered, renewed or re-invented itself by identifying with . . . the social practices of mass diversion – whether uncritically reproduced, caricatured, or transformed.'[26] We think of Davis' use, in *Garage Lights* (1931) and *Swing Landscape* (1938), and in earlier works like *Lucky Strike* (1921), of advertising and media material, and the objects of daily urban life: Lucky Strike wrappers, billboards, street signs, store fronts, coffee percolators. The blank entrance to the tunnel in Hopper's *Approaching a City* leaves us doubtful whether the city and its inhabitants can be collectively known; the contemporary images in Davis's work are the signs of how the city is known, and this is equally problematical. In his cigarette paintings, for instance, we are distanced from the naturalness and straightforwardness of signs when he chooses not to use the Lucky Strike or Caporals packets as in a collage but, instead, to paint an enlarged packet.

Davis is often treated as the bridge between pre- and post-1930s American modernism. It would be more accurate to say that he is important as much for the version of political modernism that he maintained, as for the fact that he did not renege on modernism. He is the first American painter to sustain an engagement with the politics of representation, and to do so during a decade when the representation of politics was high on the cultural agenda.

The tradition of the new: Abstract Expressionism, 1940s to 1960s

The issues which Davis and also less politically committed early modernists were confronting were shifted on to a different plane by the emergence of the Popular Front in the mid-1930s. The Popular Front will be discussed in detail in Chapter 5 but, briefly, in the context of the rise of fascism, the Popular Front was an attempt by the Soviet Communist Party and its American offshoot to find political ground not just with other Left positions, but also with centrist and liberal ones. The formation of the Front had two effects upon art. First, it diluted intense ideological dispute about the role of art into the stodgy compromises of middle-ground art. And, second, it left radical artists and intellectuals stranded when the truths of Stalinism and the Moscow trials filtered through after 1936, and the Nazi-Soviet Pact was signed in 1939. The first reaction, on the part of these politically marooned artists and intellectuals, was in the form of an essay rather than a painting, but an extraordinarily influential essay.

Clement Greenberg's 'Avant-Garde and Kitsch' was published in *Partisan Review* in 1939, by which time that journal had broken with Stalinism but was still on the left and supporting Trotsky. In advance of Abstract Expressionism, and following on from Alfred H. Barr Jr's two exhibitions at MOMA in 1936, 'Cubism and Abstract Art' and 'Fantastic Art, Dada and Surrealism', Greenberg's essay articulates the first stirrings of 'late' modernism, as it should be called in an international context, but 'high' American modernism. He defends abstract art against representational art and what it leads to: '*Kitsch*: popular, commercial art and literature with their chromeotypes, magazine covers, illustrations, ads, slick and pulp fiction, comics, Tin Pan Alley music, tap dancing, Hollywood movies, etc., etc.' In his barely veiled attack on the Popular Front and all it heralded in the USA and the USSR, Greenberg quotes Dwight Macdonald, another contributor to *Partisan Review* who became important in the post-war debate over mass culture: 'if the masses crowd into the Tretyakov (Moscow's museum of contemporary Russian art: kitsch), it is largely because 'they have been conditioned to shun "formalism" and to admire "socialist realism" '. Greenberg adds, tellingly, that 'It is lucky, however, for Repin [a Russian realist], that the peasant is protected from the products of American capitalism, for he would not stand a chance next to a *Saturday Evening Post* cover by Norman Rockwell.'

Since the Popular Front had revealed how easy it was to co-opt accessible, that is, representational painting, and had itself then been discredited by its association with Stalinism, Greenberg argues that the key to the art-work's resistance to kitsch, whether the capitalist or communist variety, is abstraction. In non-representational art, 'content is to be dissolved so completely into form that the work of art or literature cannot be reduced in whole or in part to anything not itself'.[27]

To those who became part of Abstract Expressionism – Pollock, de Kooning, Gorky, Reinhardt, Rothko, Motherwell, Gottlieb, Newman, Still, and Kline – American society on a war-footing resembled the cultural totalitarianism of the WPA projects and the Popular Front. Adopting an alienated but committed stance, which is wholly contradictory outside of the historical context, these New York artists countered the Popular Front mentality of the 1942 Artists for Victory Exhibition at the Metropolitan Museum, with their own American Modern Artists Show of 1943:

> We artists . . . conscious of the dangers that beset our country
> and our art can no longer remain silent. For the crisis that is here
> hangs on our very walls. We who dedicated our lives to art – to
> modern art – to modern art in America, at a time when men
> found easy success crying 'to hell with art, let's have pictures of
> the old oaken bucket' – we mean to make manifest by our work,
> in our studios and in our galleries the requirement for a culture in
> a new America.[28]

Statements such as this, by Barnett Newman in the catalogue to the American Modern Artists Show, signalled both the re-birth of the avant-garde in America and its adversarial roots in the political dilemmas of the late 1930s. It was part of a subtle cultural shift in which, under the unassailable name of 'quality', art moved away from politics. In *The Vital Center* (1949), probably the most revealing text of the immediate post-war period, Arthur Schlesinger Jr catches the mood of the anti-Stalinist left whose cultural wing had coalesced around *Partisan Review*:

> Anxiety is the official emotion of our time . . . By making choices, man makes himself: creates or destroys his own moral personality. This is a brave and bleak expression of our dilemma. But such a philosophy imposes an unendurable burden on most men. The eternal awareness of choice can drive the weak to the point where the simplest decision becomes a nightmare. Most men prefer to flee choice, to flee anxiety, to flee freedom.[29]

The vital centre of what turned out to be a reborn liberalism would be less anxious, and it now seems that Schlesinger was intent upon giving the new responsibility of the 'end of ideology' generation a more dramatic and dynamic image (see Chapters 5 and 6). The idea of confronting anxiety on a 'tightrope' (another of Schlesinger's metaphors) also fitted the Abstract Expressionists' view of painting as Existential risk-taking, but did so much more closely and honestly. Willem de Kooning's *Woman* series is a good example of what Harold Rosenberg calls 'anxious objects'; even the surface focus of Cubism is hacked about. Moreover, his *Woman I* was painted and repainted between 1950 and 1952 not, so de Kooning insisted, somehow to get it right, but to continue working, making choices and experiencing anxiety as well as creating it in the spectator (Plate 9). Put Greenberg's emphasis upon 'quality' alongside these feelings of anxiety, alienation and embattlement and we come close to understanding Abstract Expressionism, and even why, by the 1960s, it had become central to the official rather oppositional culture in the United States.

Following the lead of Picasso's synthetic Cubism and the geometric abstraction of the New York-based Piet Mondrian, the early Abstract Expressionists investigated form, line and colour, but also texture. Pollock used oil and sand as well as different kinds of paint. The muralist art of the 1930s directly influenced their interest in size as another formal property. However, *Mural* (1943), which took up twenty feet of Peggy Guggenheim's apartment, eschewed the blatant representationalism of nearly all 1930s' murals, and, instead, challenged reference and interpretation in a novel way: it cannot easily be seen all at once; nor can it be divided up, into a narrative, as was the American mural series begun by Thomas Hart Benton in the late 1920s (Plate 10). In Pollock's murals there is no obvious starting or concluding point. Instead, the curved, upright lines which provide the most obvious pattern in *Mural* or the layers of paint in *Mural on Indian Red Ground*

(1950) make us think of the act of painting. In *Eyes in the Heat* (1946), even before his famous 'drip' method was fully in operation, the spectator is drawn into the swirling pattern of colours.

The other dimension of Abstract Expressionism, the expressionist elements in the work of Pollock and his contemporaries, have a source in Surrealism, which underwent a revival from 1939 when Matta, and then Max Ernst, Salvador Dali, André Masson, and the poet André Breton began arriving in New York, part of the intellectual exodus from Europe to the United States which so influenced post-1930s intellectual and cultural history. Ernst was married to Peggy Guggenheim so there was a personal connection with the new American avant-garde through her Art of This Century gallery, which opened in 1942 and exhibited the two traditions of abstract and surrealist art that fed into Abstract Expressionism. Arshile Gorky was the other personal connection, since he had already been part of the Surrealist movement in Europe. He was attracted to the Matta and Miro form of Surrealism in *Garden in Sochi* (1941) and *Waterfall* (1943).

Pollock found other ways for the formal elements to 'run', within a philosophy of 'action' painting. Harold Rosenberg, the other main critic of Abstract Expressionism besides Greenberg, explains this philosophy of composition in *The Tradition of the New*:

> At a certain moment the canvas began to appear to one American painter after another as an arena in which to act – rather than as a space in which to reproduce, re-design, analyze or 'express' an object, actual or imagined. What was to go on the canvas was not a picture but an event.[30]

With a very large sheet of glass laid out on the ground Pollock was filmed in action, painting *Number 29*. Arm movements, dripping or even flinging paint onto a surface already partially covered with sand and pieces of string, replace the movements of the wrist normally associated with painting. The relationship of the painter to the canvas is changed since Pollock paints from all angles, producing a diffused focus and uneven perspective.

Barnett Newman was part of this new avant-garde from the start. Yet, in company with Still, Rothko, Reinhardt, and Gottlieb, his colour-fields are a different kind of Abstract Expressionism from the 'gestural' or 'action' painters, de Kooning, Pollock and Kline. Newman's paintings are as immediately recognizable as Pollock's: large canvasses, like Pollock's, but with clearly defined colour areas, and, often, 'zips', as Newman called them, or sometimes thicker bands, usually in the vertical plane. *Cathedra* (1951), *Adam* (1951–52) and

Who's Afraid of Red, Yellow and Blue II fifteen years later, exemplify Newman's interest in the canvas as a determining factor, with the edges of the canvas being picked up in the parallel zips or bands (Plate 11). Where Pollock would 'frame' his painting late on, Newman accepts the space from the outset. This kind of explanation has the bonus of helping us to 'place' other Abstract Expressionists, for instance Robert Motherwell, somewhere along the spectrum between action and chromatic abstraction.

The increased emphasis on abstraction in the early 1950s paintings of Ad Reinhardt, such as the variations on rectangles and colour in *Brick Painting* (1951–52), appeared, at first, to be a threat to the special tension of Abstract Expressionism. Greenberg's role proved decisive and at a retrospective exhibition at French and Company in 1959, he stressed the importance of the Barnett Newman side of Abstract Expressionism, rather than Pollock's. Heroism is still a mark of quality, but where the heroism of Pollock is tantamount to a physical struggle, with Newman and then Reinhardt's near-black series exhibited in 1959 at Betty Parsons Gallery, and Ellsworth Kelly's *Broadway* of 1958 and *White-Dark Blue* of 1962, it is the risk of how far the artist can go with vast colour fields, a minimal pattern and any signs of the painter. While Newman's zips are not always hard-edged, there are few signs of brushwork.

When Greenberg introduced, in print and through exhibitions, what he called 'post-painterly abstraction', he included Newman and Gottlieb to indicate where the continuity could be found with Ellsworth Kelly, Al Held, Jules Olitski, Kenneth Noland, and Frank Stella. Newman's treatment of the space of the canvas helps us to grasp the significance of, for example, Noland's *Shift* and *Shade* of 1966, which are diamond-shaped paintings, rather than a diamond-shape image on a rectangle or square canvas. Like Stella's aluminium paintings of 1960, Noland's seeks to be its own shape. The irregular shape of *Six Mile Bottom* (1960), with its oblong in the centre, is even repeated in parallel lines across the whole surface. If this is a confrontation with the horizontal and vertical limits of painting, then the methods of staining employed by Noland, following the example of Helen Frankenthaler and Morris Louis, confront the surface. By reaching into the fabric of the canvas, staining seeks to remove even the minimal distinction between the canvas and the paint, let alone the common sense distinction between the representation (in paint) and its object. The most immediate source is Pollock's experiments with different kinds of paint, though when he used enamel paint in the early 1950, light was sent back off the surface, rather than being soaked into the pigment.

The dual concentration on dimensions and surface in post-painterly abstraction is an attempt, deriving from Pollock but going beyond him, to make painting autonomous, as Michael Fried announces in *Three American Painters* (1950), a book on Noland, Olitsky and Stella:

> In a painting such as [Pollock's] *Number One* there is only a pictorial field so homogeneous, overall and devoid both of recognizable objects and of abstract shapes that I want to call it *optical* to distinguish it from the structured, essentially tactile pictorial field of previous modernist painting from Cubism to de Kooning and even Hans Hofmann. Pollock's field is optical because it addresses itself to eyesight alone.[31]

The explanation of the pre-eminence of Abstract Expressionism, which we find in Greenberg, Fried and in the most authoritative art histories, such as Barbara Rose's *American Art Since 1900* and Irving Sandler's *Abstract Expressionism: The Triumph of American Painting*, is indispensable and highly informative – up to a point. That point is reached when the history of modernism is expressed as the ultimate formal quality of *opticality*. Fried's defence of opticality meets the lay response – typically, that a child could have painted a 'Barnett Newman' or that Pollock's compositions make good wallpaper. And yet, curiously, Fried's claims on behalf of Abstract Expressionism and its refinement in post-painterly abstraction, confirm the lay opinion that this is meaningless art. Gottlieb and Rothko made their position clear, stating, as early as 1943, that 'there is no such thing as a good painting about nothing . . . The subject is crucial and only that subject-matter is valid which is tragic and timeless' (quoted in Rose, *American Art Since 1900*, p. 197). They anticipate Rothko's late 1940s and early 1950s paintings; in particular, *Number 22* (1949) is patently an abstract work but one which invokes a mythic significance through the light which edges out, literally, and is just visible on either side of the principal horizontal band. Myth was especially important to Rothko and Gottlieb and, formally, it ties in with their interest in surrealism and 'the fables of savages and the strange beliefs that were so vividly articulated by primitive man'.[32] The subject is mythic, then, and myth, however much it seeks to universalize connections, does not deny signification, whereas 'opticality' is predicated on the refusal of connections in the joint names of autonomy and quality.

Faced with this inconsistency, we can reasonably look for historical connections, rather than just those internal to both the work of art and its art history, in order to interpret the mythic aspirations that find expression in the swirls, lines and drips of Pollock, or the colour-fields of Newman, or the back-lit rectangles of Rothko. As Roland Barthes remarks in *Mythologies*, 'myth is a type of speech chosen by history: it cannot possibly evolve from the "nature" of things'.[33] Oddly, it is Greenberg who gives us a clue to the historical connections when, looking back on the 1930s, he makes the link between form and myth:

> Abstract art was the main issue among the painters I knew in the late 1930s. Radical politics was on many people's minds, but for these particular artists Social Realism was as dead as the American Scene. (Though that is not all, by far, that there was to politics in art in those years; some day it will have to be told how 'anti-Stalinism,' which started out more or less as 'Trotskyism,' turned into art for art's sake, and thereby cleared the way, heroically, for what was to come.) (*Art and Culture*, p. 230)

Through myth, and the philosophy of Existentialism, whose key texts were then being translated, the heroism of alienation and anxiety came to mean authentic individualism, that is to say, freedom. Unlike in classic nineteenth-century bourgeois culture, in which, Marx argues, alienation is mistaken for individualism, this new American culture would be characterized by a self-conscious alienation, free from ideology. In effect, the painters sought a resolution in the 'field' or 'space' of non-objective art of the very tangible issues of the 1930s aesthetics and politics debate. In *How New York Stole the Idea of Modern Art*, Serge Guilbaut argues that the 1930s had taught these artists that 'it had become impossible to represent the diffuse anxiety and fear that defined modernity without falling into the grotesque or the facile, without, in a word, making kitsch' (pp. 196–7).

Guilbaut does not deliver much in the way of analysis of paintings but marshals the contextual evidence expertly to answer the question ruled out of order by formalist criticism: Around twenty years after the Modern Show, why did Barnett Newman's claim that this bewildering avant-garde art should be part of 'a culture in a new America' gain acceptance? It did not look American and Jackson Pollock poured as much scorn on the idea of an American art as on an American mathematics. Moreover, the phenomenal success of the Abstract Expressionists, capped by their promotion in prestigious European exhibitions, came only a few years after their protest against the lack of support to American artists offered by the Metropolitan Museum. Guilbaut's answer is that the Cold War mentality, on top of the 1930s' experience, led the mass media to defend 'without knowing it . . . the concept of modernism with all its attendant ambiguities and contradictions. Though modernism had previously not caught on in the United States, now it slipped in through the back door, as it were, and established itself in the national consciousness' (p. 55).

The undergrowth evidence behind this startling claim is in the work of the Federation of American Painters and Sculptors, and the importance it attached to an international culture; in the growing official sense of responsibility for an art that the Third Reich and Stalinism had tried to destroy; in the leaders and letters pages, as well as the art sections, of influential newspapers; in the role of institutions, not least MOMA; and in the contribution of Clement Greenberg and other prominent experts, in authorizing the modernist pedigree of Abstract Expressionism. Greenberg's 'The Decline of Cubism' (1948) paved the way for American painters to assume the mantle of modernism, but, in the same year, his scholarly argument was put into a different context when René d'Harnoncourt, who became the director of MOMA in 1949, gave an address to the American Federation of Arts in which the 'foremost symbol' for American democracy became 'modern art in its infinite variety and ceaseless exploration' (quoted in Guilbaut, p. 189). From this interpretive angle, the Armory Show of 1913, which introduced European modernism into America, was less a 'Great Event' and more a time capsule whose contents were activated in an unexpected way.

Earlier we noted a similarity between the modernist outlook of Abstract Expressionists and that described by Arthur Schlesinger Jr in *The Vital Center*, which largely summed up attitudes shared by other anti-Stalinist liberals working in the fields of criticism, and social and political thought. In a study of one of those intellectuals, the sociologist, Daniel Bell, Howard Brick makes an important connection with the argument being developed here, when he claims that 'the modernist sense of disabling antinomies . . . provided the intellectual medium for the accommodation he reached with American society'.[34] This will need to be argued out in a later chapter, but, judging from the casualty list of early and accidental deaths (Kline, Newman, Pollock, Reinhardt) and suicides (Gorky and Rothko), the 'antinomies' could not be endured so easily by the artists, as by the theorists of modernism, Greenberg in particular. For the Abstract Expressionists, coming out of the 1930s' disillusion with socialism, there appeared to be no alternative space in which to remain radical other than the canvas or the materials of art. Talking about the sculptor David Smith, Robert Motherwell referred to 'the black abyss in each of us . . . a certain kind, I suppose, of puritanical bravado, of holding off the demons of guilt and depression that largely destroyed in one way or another the abstract expressionist generation'.[35] 'Pollock', John Ashbury observed, 'was gambling everything on the fact that he *was* the greatest painter in America, for if he wasn't, he was nothing'.[36] As far as the individual artists are concerned, perhaps what we are dealing with is the relationship between intents and effects.

Has modernism failed?: 1950s to 1980s

For a 1987 programme, *The State of the Art*, Channel 4's cameras filmed a script conference for the soap opera *Dynasty II: The Colbys of California*. It was chaired by Hollywood producer, Douglas S. Cramer, also known as an art collector, subject of paintings by Andy Warhol, and trustee of the Museum of Contemporary Art in Los Angeles – MOMA's West Coast rival and an institution heavily supported by corporate finance. In a boardroom adorned with modern art, the *Dynasty* team was discussing the authenticity of an art auction scene in the next episode, for which Cramer had sought the advice of David Nash of Sothebys. Cramer stressed that the Rothko impressions commissioned for the series should not damage 'the integrity of the artist'.[37]

All of this seems to confirm the account which Suzi Gablik gives in *Has Modernism Failed?* (1984) of a booming but bureaucratized and compromised art world. The bizarre situation caught by the television cameras provokes two further thoughts: admiration for the severe virtues of the late modernism of Rothko, Pollock and then the post-painterly abstractionists, and, it must be added, for the modernist theory of Greenberg, Rosenberg and Fried; but, equally, a realization that the power of the marketplace over art was actually consolidated when modernist art undermined reference and abandoned even the pretence of use-value. The way was then open for post-modernism to cultivate commerce and thereby erase the link between the work of art and the commodity. Under the broad banner of post-modernism, however, a bewildering plurality of different art forms has sought to avoid the high modernism of Greenberg and the (reluctant) anti-modernism of Gablik, while, at the same time facing up to the accelerating rationalization of capitalism, with its art market sideline. Though it is impossible to survey the whole range of American art after Abstract Expressionism, we can, at least, consider the significance of this rampant pluralism with reference to selected examples.

In Emil de Antonio's 1972 film, *Painters Painting*, Robert Rauschenberg perches on the top of a ladder in his studio and tells how, in 1953, he persuaded Willem de Kooning to let him erase one of his drawings. The result, which took him four weeks to achieve, was then exhibited as *Erased De Kooning Drawing* by Robert Rauschenberg. The break was not acrimonious. The Abstract Expressionists were too serious, too existential, too wracked by doubt, and just too heroic for Rauschenberg, Jasper Johns, the Pop Artists, and those associated with performance and conceptual art. Susan Sontag's reaction against seriousness in her essays, 'Against Interpretation', 'Notes on "Camp"' and 'One Culture and the New Sensibility', written in the first half of the 1960s, was also part of the reaction against modernism. Though she does not use the word 'post-modernism', her attack on the seriousness of high culture and her interest in indeterminate cultural forms and practices (categorized as 'camp') suggest that she was one of the first to realize that something had happened culturally.

When Jasper Johns met Marcel Duchamp in 1960, he had already been working in a neo-Dada manner for a number of years, and was fascinated by the relationship between art objects and real objects. The edge of his mid-1950s paintings of the American flag is the edge of the flag, so, in a sense they are not paintings *of* a flag, yet also not flags as such because of the encaustic surface. Johns followed his flags in 1960 with *Two Painted Bronze Beer Cans* (1960), two real beer cans cast in bronze and painted. The 'field' of 'opticality', so central to modernist claims for the space of art, is questioned because we are not sure what we are seeing.

The quality of opticality is challenged in a different way in the assemblages, for which Rauschenberg is better known than Johns. Painting, assemblage and readymades come together in *Bed* (1955), which is just that, or rather not just a bed but one that has had paint dashed onto the pillow and quilt – Pollock-style. The paint has then dripped, as we would expect because the bed (and *Bed*) is on the wall. The bed, chairs, stuffed animals and birds, which stick out from Rauschenberg's paintings into the space of the spectator, also raise the very interesting question of what, precisely, is the space of the painting. One tendency of modernist painting had been progressively to remove the illusion of depth. At the other end of the modernist movement, Rauschenberg rediscovered Duchamp's ur-modernism and literally expanded the painting's space in the opposite direction.

In other hands, the combination of materials was extended into the pot pourri of performance art upon which the composer John Cage had a decisive impact. In the company of dancer, Merce Cunningham, and poet, Charles Olsen, Rauschenberg was part of Cage's 'happening' in the summer of 1952 at Black Mountain College in North Carolina, in which dance, painting, music, text, and manual and technological events were combined. When Cage remarked that the event 'was purposeless in that we didn't know what was going to happen', he anticipated the anti-narrative happenings of the 1960s and 1970s.[38] Susan Sontag dates them from Allan Kaprow's *Eighteen Happenings in Six Parts* of 1959, which was followed by a number of legendary performances: Jim Dine's *Car Crash* (1960), Robert Whitman's *The American Moon* (1960), Red Grooms's *The Burning Building* (1962), Claes Oldenburg's *Store Days* (1965), and Kaprow's *Spring Happening* (1961), for which a report (by Sontag) has to suffice:

The spectators were confined inside a long box-like structure resembling a cattle car; peep holes had been bored in the wooden walls of this enclosure through which the spectators could strain to see the events taking place outside; when the Happening was over, the walls collapsed, and the spectators were driven out by someone operating a power lawnmower.[39]

Suzi Gablik reserves much of her attack on late- or post-modernism for such examples of performance art as Robert Barry's *Telepathic Piece* (1969), in which he announced that 'during the exhibition I will try to communicate telepathically a work of art, the nature of which is a series of thoughts that are not applicable to language or image'.[40] Against Gablik's protest that Barry plays into the hands of the market, and ends up with a publicity stunt, is the claim that because this kind of conceptual art is a sheer act of mind, it outstrips the more limited because more cautious commercial decisions to market this or that new idea. In the happenings, various forms of material theatricality resist incorporation by the market by refusing the object-status of modernist art. Happenings cannot be housed in museums, and if some can be moved to different venues, they do not remain the same. While it is difficult not to sympathize with Gablik's frustration, we should also note that this variety of post-modernism shares the important preoccupation with boundaries that we find in the Duchamp–Dada practice *within* modernism. By crossing discipline boundaries as well as spatial and temporal boundaries, as in the work of Laurie Anderson, notably her eight-hour *United States* of 1982, post-modernism disrupts the consistency of the medium, and has the opportunity, as Rosalind Krauss puts it, 'to think the expanded field' of society. This expanded field most definitely includes the media; arguably, it is the media.[41]

Rauschenberg and Johns also anticipate the more definable movement of Pop Art which burst into the art world and the wider culture of the early 1960s in the persons of Andy Warhol, Roy Lichtenstein, Claes Oldenburg, George Segal, Jim Dine, Tom Wesselmann, James Rosenquist, and Robert Indiana. Pop Art is a kind of up-to-date 'American Scene' painting; even realism again, at least as Lichtenstein defines realism:

> Art since Cezanne . . . has had less and less to do with the world; it looks inward . . . Outside is the world. Pop Art looks out into the world; it appears to accept its environment, which is not good or bad, but different, another state of mind.[42]

Claes Oldenburg is more positive about the banalities of mass culture and we catch echoes of Walt Whitman's openness and eclecticism:

> I am for the art of red and white gasoline pumps and blinking
> biscuit signs . . . I am for Kool-Art, 7-Up Art, Pepsi Art,
> Sunkist Art, Dro-Bomb Art, Pamryl Art, San-O-Med Art, 39
> cents Art and 9.99 Art. (quoted in Lippard, *Pop Art*, pp. 106–7)

Oldenburg's view was endorsed, and seemingly in the direction of a
critique of consumer capitalism, when Pop Art became popular among
the young. It became part of the general feeling of 1960s liberation
from high culture and political authority. Lichtenstein took art at its
most mechanical and formularized, the comic strip, and created giant
'blown-up', vividly coloured fantasies like *Whaam!* (1963) and *As I
Opened Fire . . .* (1964). Warhol focused on consumables of a different
kind: Brillo boxes, Coca-Cola bottles, Campbell Soup Cans, which
appeared in their normal colours and also in 'fauve' colouring and, of
course, images of Marilyn Monroe (Plate 12). Oldenburg made giant
soft hamburgers and sandwiches, and floppy fans, typewriters, and
other household goods. Pop Art's radical pedigree was enhanced when
the modernist establishment put it down as the incursion of
supermarket values, and commercial techniques of illustration into art.
A less oppositional interpretation of Pop Art follows, however,
when we compare it with the incorporation of mass cultural artefacts
and images in the work of Duchamp and those he influenced. In *Thirty
are Better than One* (1963), Warhol directly recalls Duchamp's
L.H.O.O.Q. (1919), in which the Mona Lisa has a moustache and
goatee beard and is the subject of a rude joke in French. Warhol's is a
serial portrait of a photograph of the *Mona Lisa*, which simply accepts
the image and then reproduces it. Warhol does not want to shock,
which might account for Duchamp's otherwise surprising rejection of
Pop. Even the electric chair, and car and train wrecks of Warhol's
Death and Disaster series are distant images, despite their often close
relationship to the events of the 1960s. Though figurative and topical,
Pop Art ends up being curiously impersonal, too close to the
representation of the mass-produced commodity in advertising.
Warhol's Marilyn Monroe series is, in each case, a repeated silk-
screened image of the image of Marilyn Monroe, a formalism of the
image to go with his formalism of the object in the Campbell Soup
Can series. In the 1920s, the era of America's first consumer boom,
Charles Sheeler's Precisionist attempt 'to divorce the object from the
dictionary and disintegrate its identity' came close to overlapping in an
uncritical way with the design aesthetic of 'department store modernism' (quoted in A. Davidson, *Early American Painting*, p. 187). Warhol
went out of his way to demonstrate that this was not a problem which
bothered him.
Like Pop Art's apparent rejection of Art with a capital letter, the
roll-call of styles and movements which it ushered in can be

interpreted as a rejection of authority and modernist purity in the name of individual freedom. But just as modernism is related, against its proponents' intentions, to specialization, division of labour, and separation of spheres, so varieties of post-modernism are often difficult to distinguish from the heterogeneity of consumer society. A too-intimate relationship with consumer culture cannot generate a critique. The objects which re-appear in art in a significant way for the first time since the decline of realism are self-consciously consumables and so there is no way to differentiate between them; they are all aesthetically equivalent. Any thing will do because 'there is nothing behind it' (Warhol) upon which to base judgement or interpretation.

One response to this problem has been to re-think the concept of the frame or the boundary, as it has come to be called in post-modernist theory. The spare modernist art of Frank Stella and Kenneth Noland evinces an interest in frames, but its refinement of what lies inside discipline boundaries literally hardens the lines. There is seemingly no interest in the transgressions which Duchamp inaugurated with his *Fountain*, and which makers of collages and assemblages from Joseph Stella and Stuart Davis through and beyond Rauschenberg have continued. To stray over the boundary into other representations, including photographic, sculptural, aural, and theatrical ones, is to inhabit modernism but to quite different ends from those that Greenberg envisaged when he defined modernism as 'the use of the characteristic methods of a discipline to criticize the discipline itself – not in order to subvert it, but to entrench it more firmly in its area of competence.'[43]

When modernism seemed on the point of refining itself out of existence – it was at John Cage's 1952 happening that Rauschenberg's white paintings commented on this possibility – the alternative, as Rauschenberg himself demonstrated, did not have to be realism or the return to tradition that Gablik advocates, but could be an art which built into its very area of operation the cultural power of other representations and other media. In opting for a neo-Dada assemblage technique in the 1950s, Rauschenberg, renewed modernism's interest in the politics of representation. In *Break-Through* and *Crocus* he transforms the tabula rasa of art – the canvas – into a palimpsest consisting of the bits and bobs of a consumer society, and is especially taken with the idea of constructing the surface out of printed matter. Newspapers are part of the waste or excess of a culture – every day they are preserved they become more useless. And yet, as the left-over signs after the supposedly neutral language of reportage has performed its task, they are sources of history, or rather sources of how history has been represented, how subjects have been positioned. Ever since Joseph Stella used soiled wrappers, with the logos visible, in his collage series of the 1920s, a strand of American modernism has been commenting on the relationship between art and mass production, often taking considerable pleasure in the juxtapositions of textures, shapes and colours. More persistently than Stella, though, Rauschenberg plays on the idea of the surface as the always already painted/photographed/written and, in general, represented. Earlier we discussed Andy Warhol's *Mona Lisa*. Rauschenberg's *Persimmon* (1964) is superficially similar in that it is a silkscreen of a photographic reproduction of Ruben's *Venus at Her Toilet*. This image, which once we would have considered complete in its own space, is then laid onto other images, for instance of a Coca Cola sign.

In the twenty years since Rauschenberg's most productive period, we have become more accustomed to 'play' in art. A post-modern break-out from the autonomous work has, according to some critics, only reinstated the 'aesthetic' on a grander scale – the idea of the 'text' as a world and not a work, to borrow Roland Barthes's terminology. In literary criticism, so the parallel argument goes, the rejection of Anglo-American New Criticism has only led to a new New Criticism, which genuflects to the deconstructive criticism of Jacques Derrida rather than to the organicism of T.E. Hulme or W.K. Wimsatt. We can take up the broader dimensions of this debate in the Conclusion to this book. It would seem, though, that much depends upon where the intersection between artist and text/world occurs and who the artist is.

As a final example of an artist who functions as a bricoleur, an odd-job woman, situated where different media and therefore different audiences intersect, we can look at the work of Barbara Kruger, one of a group of artists concerned with representations of sexual identity, the others being Dara Birnbaum, Louise Lawler, Sherrie Levine, Jenny Holzer, Cindy Sherman, and Martha Rosler. At its most active the post-modernist art of Barbara Kruger does not repeat the logic of consumer capitalism but deconstructs its representations so as to reinscribe them. 'I am concerned with who speaks and who is silent,' she stated on Channel 4's *State of the Art*. 'I want to be on the side of surprise and against the certainty of pictures and property.' It is at the point of reinscription, where photographs and pasted-on graphics from advertisements are juxtaposed, that critical interventions can be made in the phantasmagoria of images that is both post-modernist art and contemporary life. Within this image-rich environment Kruger's untitled works of the 1980s identify masculine 'ways of seeing'. When discussing the realism of The Eight, it was noticeable how absent women were from many places in large modern cities. In our contemporary cities, women are everywhere, but primarily as representations on billboards, in magazines, and on screen, those 'signs in the streets' that Marshall Berman is inclined to interpret positively but which position women as the subject of (good) 'looks'.[44] In Kruger's poster panels women were at first represented as (to quote her captions) 'deluded' and 'perfect'. She moved towards more critical appropriations. Outsized captions talk back against the authority of the fetishized images: 'You destroy what you think is difference'; 'We are your circumstantial evidence'; 'Your gaze hits the side of my face' (Plate 13). But the 'we' talks back against the 'you' from within the system of representations to show that these are constructed identities, which take on meanings according to contexts, locations and readers.

In its initial questioning of representation, modernism taught that lesson. So, while Suzi Gablik answers the question, Has modernism failed? in the affirmative, the response that this survey recommends is not to answer in the negative, but to take modernism's lessons on representation more seriously still.

Notes

1. For examples of new developments, see Roland Barthes, *Image-Music-Text*, translated by Stephen Heath (1977); Norman Bryson, *Vision and Painting: The Logic of the Gaze* (1983); Benjamin Buchloh, *et al.*, (eds), *Modernism and Modernity: The Vancouver Conference Papers* (Halifax, Nova Scotia, 1983); Victor Burgin, *The End of Art Theory: Criticism and Postmodernity* (1986); T.J. Clark, *The Painting of Modern Life: Paris in the Art of Manet and his Followers* (1984); Francis Frascina (ed.), *Pollock and After: The Critical Debate* (1985); Rosalind E. Krauss, *The Originality of the Avant-Garde and Other Modernist Myths* (Cambridge, Mass., 1985); Griselda Pollock, *Vision and Difference: Femininity, Feminism and Histories of Art* (1988); and Brian Wallis (ed.), *Art After Modernism: Rethinking Representation* (Boston, 1984).

2. Harold Rosenberg, *The Anxious Object* (Chicago, 1966), p. 187.

3. Peter Wollen, 'Manet, Modernism and Avant-Garde', *Screen*, 21, (Summer 1980), p. 24.

4. Barbara Rose, *American Art Since 1900: A Critical History* (1967), pp. 16 and 80.

5. Griselda Pollock (see note 1), pp. 53-4. See, also, Janet Wolff, 'The Invisible *Flâneuse*: Women and the Literature of Modernity', *Theory, Culture and Society*, 2 (1985), pp. 37-46.

6. Quoted in Abraham Davidson, *Early American Modernist Painting, 1910–1935* (New York, 1981), p. 36.

7. Meyer Schapiro, *Modern Art: 19th & 20th Centuries: Selected Papers* (New York, 1978), p. 196.

8. Paul Rosenfeld, *Port of New York* (Urbana, 1966), pp. 287, 292 and 293.

9. Quoted in Peter Conrad, *The Art of the City: Views and Versions of New York* (New York, 1984), p. 128.

10. Alfred Werner, *Max Weber* (New York, 1974), p. 50.

11. Quoted in Norbert Lynton, 'Futurism', in *Concepts of Modern Art*, edited by Nicos Stangos (1981), p. 99.

12. Quoted in Milton W. Brown, *American Painting from the Armory Show to the Depression* (Princeton, NJ, 1955), p. 134.

13. Joseph Stella, 'The Brooklyn Bridge (A Page of My Life)', *Transition*, 16–17 (June 1929), p. 87.

14. Quoted in Alan Trachtenberg, *Brooklyn Bridge: Fact and Symbol* (New York, 1965), p. 133.

15. Raymond Williams, *Culture and Society, 1780–1950* (Harmondsworth, 1963), p. 60; T.J. Clark (see note 1), p. 8.

16. Henry Adams, *The Education of Henry Adams* (New York, 1931), p. 499.

17. John Marin, 'Notes on 291', *Camera Work*, 42 (April–July, 1913), p. 18.

18. John F. Kasson, *Amusing the Million: Coney Island at the Turn of the Century* (New York, 1978), p. 73.

19. Clement Greenberg, 'Review of a Ben Shahn Exhibition', in *Social Realism: Art as a Weapon*, edited by David Shapiro (New York, 1973), p. 297.

20. Benedict Anderson, *Imagined Communities: Reflections on the Origin and Spread of Nationalism* (1983), p. 15.

21. Quoted in George H. Roeder, Jr, *Forum of Uncertainty: Confrontations with Modern Painting in Twentieth-Century American Thought* (Ann Arbor, Michigan, 1980), p. 147.

22. See Karal Ann Marling, 'Thomas Hart Benton's *Boomtown*: Regionalism Redefined', *Prospects*, 6 (1981), pp. 73–137.

23. Warren I. Susman, *Culture as History: The Transformation of American Society in the Twentieth Century* (New York, 1984), p. 154.

24. Quoted in Gail Levin, *Edward Hopper: The Art and the Artist*, exhibition catalogue, (New York, n.d.), p. 6.

25. Berthold Brecht, 'Against Georg Lukács', in Ernst Bloch, *et al.*, *Aesthetics and Politics* (1977), pp. 80 and 81.

26. Thomas Crowe, 'Modernism and Mass Culture in the Visual Arts', in Francis Frascina (see note 1), p. 233. For an analysis of Davis and other 1930s artists, see Heinz Ickstadt, 'The Writing on the Wall: American Painting and the Federal Arts Project', in *The Thirties: Politics and Culture in a Time of Broken Dreams*, edited by Heinz Ickstadt *et al.* (Amsterdam, 1987), pp. 221–45.

27. Clement Greenberg, *Art and Culture: Critical Essays* (Boston, 1961), pp. 9, 13, 14, and 6.

28. Quoted in Serge Guilbaut, *How New York Stole the Idea of Modern Art: Abstract Expressionism, Freedom, and the Cold War*, translated by Arthur Goldhammer (Chicago, 1983), p. 69.

29. Arthur Schlesinger Jr., *The Vital Center: The Politics of Freedom* (Boston, 1962), p. 52.

30. Harold Rosenberg, *The Tradition of the New* (Chicago, 1960), p. 25.

31. Michael Fried, *Three American Painters: Kenneth Noland, Jules Olitski, and Frank Stella* (Cambridge, Mass., 1965), p. 14.

32. Quoted in Irving Sandler, *Abstract Expressionism: The Triumph of American Painting* (New York, 1970), p. 64.

33. Roland Barthes, *Mythologies*, translated by Annett Lavers (Frogmore, St Albans, 1973), p. 110.

34. Howard Brick, *Daniel Bell and the Decline of Intellectual Radicalism: Social Theory and Political Reconciliation in the 1940s* (Madison, 1986), p. 54.

35. Quoted in John Gruen, *The Party's Over Now: Reminiscences of the Fifties: New York's Artists, Writers, Musicians, and Their Friends* (New York, 1967), p. 194.

36. Quoted in Dore Ashton, *American Art Since 1945* (1982), p. 81.

37. See also, Sandy Nairne, in collaboration with Geoff Dunlop and John Wyver *State of the Art: Ideas and Images in the 1980s* (1987), Chapter 2.

38. Quoted in RoseLee Goldberg, *Performance Art: From Futurism to the Present* (1988), p. 127.

39. Susan Sontag, *Against Interpretation and Other Essays* (New York, 1969), p. 267.

40. Suzi Gablik, *Has Modernism Failed?* (1984), p. 41.

41. Rosalind E. Krauss (see note 1). p. 287.

42. Quoted in Lucy R. Lippard, *Pop Art* (1985), pp. 85–6.

43. Clement Greenberg, 'Modernist Painting', in *Modern Art and Modernism A Critical Anthology*, edited by Francis Frascina and Charles Harrison (1982), p. 5.

44. See Marshall Berman, *All That Is Solid Melts Into Air: The Experience of Modernity* (1982), passim; Griselda Pollock (see Note 1); and Janet Wolff (see Note 5). On Barbara Kruger and other contemporary American women artists, see Hal Foster, *Recodings: Art, Spectacle, Cultural Politics* (Port Townsend, Washington, 1985), pp. 99–118.

Chapter 3
Architecture

Architecture at the crossroads

In 1939 modernist art and the modern movement in architecture met formally on American soil in the new building for the Museum of Modern Art (MOMA). The straight lines and unadorned surface of Edward Durrell Stone's building derive primarily from two European sources: Le Corbusier, working mostly in France from the 1910s; and the German school of modern design, the Bauhaus, founded in 1919 in Weimar, decamped to Dessau in 1925, and eventually disbanded by the Nazis in 1933.

Tom Wolfe comments on the coincidence of MOMA's building and contents in *From Bauhaus to Our House* (1981). Having attacked the modern art criticism of Clement Greenberg and others in *The Painted Word* (1975), Wolfe reached a wider audience still with his indictment of modernist architecture as a powerful, elitist, European-inspired, movement. In Britain, the scene of so much that is brutal and incomprehensible in modernism, the Prince of Wales's lecture to the Royal Institute of British Architects in 1984 earnestly conveyed something of Wolfe's caustic polemic that architecture had lost touch with its history and the people who live and work in modern buildings. An article by Ada Louise Huxtable, a leading American architectural critic, was published the same year as Wolfe's book and lent its title to a ten-part British television series, *Architecture at the Crossroads* (1986). The series opened with scenes of 'architectural murder' – the demolition of old buildings – and panoramas of wind-swept high-rise offices and flats that were accompanied by agonized questions: 'What happened?' 'Why have modern cities and buildings failed us?'

Starting from zero: the International Style, 1930s to 1970s

In 1932 MOMA held an exhibition on 'Modern Architecture', organized by the art historian, Henry-Russell Hitchcock, and the critic and head of the museum's recently formed architecture department, Philip Johnson. The exhibition introduced Walter Gropius, Ludwig Mies van der Rohe, Richard Neutra, and other European architects to an American audience, but coverage of American architecture was limited mainly to Frank Lloyd Wright. The parallel is with the Armory Show of 1913. In entitling the exhibition catalogue *The International Style: Architecture Since 1922*, after Gropius's *International Architecture* of 1925, Hitchcock and Johnson christened what would become the dominant movement in twentieth-century American architecture.

From the 1920s onwards, Austrian-born Richard Neutra brought to the United States a view of architecture which integrated the technology of steel frames, clarity of line in aesthetics, and a progressive social philosophy. He illustrated his outlook in a number of relatively inexpensive houses, and in the Corona Avenue School, Los Angeles (1935) and the design for the Ring Plan School (1928). The arrival of Gropius, Marcel Breuer and Mies van der Rohe in 1937, fleeing from Nazi Germany, had more impact, however, because the 1920s and early 1930s had been such a vital period in European architecture, and America in the Depression was more receptive to a socially conscious architecture. Gropius became chair of the Harvard Department of Architecture, and Breuer also taught there, while Mies was appointed dean of the School of Architecture at the Illinois Institute of Technology. Before emigrating, all had distinguished careers in Germany, especially Gropius. In 1919 he named the Bauhaus ('House of Building') and became its director. Six years later he designed the School's new building at Dessau, before leaving in 1928. Since the Bauhaus was in the forefront of modernism in general, the architects were accompanied in their flight to America by, among others, the painter, Josef Albers, who went on to Black Mountain College in North Carolina, and Laszlo Moholy-Nagy, who accepted an invitation from Chicago's Association of Arts and Industries to set up a new Bauhaus.

Occupying important academic positions and starting their own practices as American architects, these emigré intellectuals decisively influenced American architecture, which had lost the self-consciousness and sense of purpose it had possessed forty years earlier in the Chicago School. The interruptions in Frank Lloyd Wright's career had restricted his influence from spreading in the intervening period. The New Deal ethos of public service was a welcoming context but, ironically, the full impact of European modernism was only felt from the affluent late 1940s onwards. Federal development schemes stimulated a building boom in housing and highway construction, while downtown, and especially downtown New York, multinational corporate capitalism came fully into its own, its power accentuated by Europe's post-war economic troubles. The unofficial Bauhaus motto, 'starting from zero', which, in a European context, referred to the break with existing styles and a bourgeois society, and to the start of a period of utopian vision in architecture, took on a concrete reality in this prosperous vacuum after the Second World War. The outcome, though, was very different from what had been envisaged in the Weimar Republic of the 1920s.

Tom Wolfe's interpretation of the migration of European architects to America is more partisan than the above account:

> [It] was like a certain stock scene from the jungle movies of that period. Bruce Cabot and Myrna Loy make a crash landing in the jungle and crawl out of the wreckage in their Abercrombie & Fitch white safari blouses and tan gabardine jodhpurs and stagger into a clearing. They are surrounded by savages with bones through their noses – who immediately bow down and prostrate themselves and commence a strange moaning chant.
>> *The White Gods!*
>> *Come from the skies at last!*

Of Mies's appointment as dean of architecture at Illinois Institute of Technology, Wolfe adds:

> And not just dean; master builder also. He was given a campus to create . . . Twenty-one large buildings, in the middle of the Depression . . . for an architect who had completed only seventeen buildings in his career –
>> O white gods.[1]

From 1939 through into the 1950s the Illinois Institute of Technology project revealed Mies's extraordinary concern for detail, from the planning of spaces between the buildings to the efficiency of the window-sashes. The glass and black steel frame design of the Metallurgy and Chemical Engineering Buildings is commonplace now; in 1946 the design expressed the structure as rarely before. However, Mies is better known for the Lake Shore Drive apartment towers in Chicago (1949–51), and the Seagram building in New York City (1954–58). On the latter, Mies had the assistance of Philip Johnson, since the early 1940s a qualified architect who had studied, as Tom Wolfe puts it, 'at [Gropius'] feet' and 'didn't get up until decades later'

(p. 11). The thirty-nine-storey Seagram building epitomizes the 'glass box', the International Style's most distinctive achievement, in which structure and fenestration are integrated and the surface is free from gargoyles and corner supports. In Mies's dictum, 'Less is more' (Plate 14). A comparison would be the drive towards object-hood and the removal of elements extraneous to the medium in the post-painterly abstract art of Kenneth Noland, Jules Olitsky and Frank Stella. More pertinent to the paradoxes of the modern movement in architecture is the double echo: of Frederick Winslow Taylor's time-and-motion studies of late nineteenth-century American capitalism; and the socialist Bauhaus philosophy which Walter Gropius expounded in 1923:

> We want a clear, organic architecture, whose inner logic will be radiant and naked, unencumbered by lying facades and trickeries; we want an architecture adapted to our world of machines, radios and fast motor cars, an architecture whose function is clearly recognizable in the relation to its form.[2]

Though I have picked out Mies and Johnson's Seagram Building from the proliferation of glass boxes, it was by no means the first construction to emphasize space rather than mass in a tall building. After the first, rather modest glass box – Pietro Belluschi's Equitable Savings and Loan Association building in Portland, Oregon (1944–48) – Skidmore, Owings and Merrill (SOM) got going, drawing, in part, upon Mies's early 1920s designs for the glass curtain wall. SOM's sleek glass boxes quickly became the badge of corporate status for Union Carbide, Chase Manhattan Bank, Lever Brothers, among many others. Their first important Miesian box was the Lever House (1951–52). It is a landmark in New York City because, courtesy of a change in the zoning law, an unbroken slab could be erected for the first time, as long as space was left between the building front and the street. Hence the small plaza in front of the Lever Building. Previously, the dominant style had been the stepped-back skycraper illustrated dramatically in Hugh Ferriss' *The Metropolis of Tomorrow* (1929). The success of SOM in the International Style, gave them a similar corporate status to their clients.

Over the next two decades, Mies and his followers produced, in Tom Wolfe's witty description, the 'Rue de Regret: The Avenue of the Americas in New York. Row after Mies van der row of glass boxes. Worker housing pitched up fifty stories high' (p. 4). Domestic architecture polarized into high-rise blocks and the low-slung suburban tract houses of the 'crabgrass frontier', the latter left to developers rather than architects. Meanwhile, up in the air, the residents of Mies's Lake Shore Drive towers were not allowed to break up the curtain wall with air conditioning units, even though the apartments' central system

could not cope with Chicago summers. Britain has its own horror
stories, but in the United States the fabled (and televised) end of
modernism came in July 1972, when the 1950s Pruitt–Igoe public
housing project in St Louis was demolished because people could not
live in it.

From Bauhaus to Our House touched a nerve inside and outside the
architectural profession and takes us to the heart of a debate about
modern architecture. None the less, some caveats may be entered, if
only because Tom Wolfe's populism is less wide-eyed than it seems.
First, whatever the losses, the modern movement has a record of
remarkable achievements – which we take for granted – and a view of
architecture that can still be defended, even by revisionary critics like
Charles Jencks:

> Modern architecture is a *'universal' international style stemming from
> the facts of the new constructional means, adequate to a new industrial
> society, and having as its goal the transformation of society, both its
> taste, or perception, and social make-up.* (*Modern Movements in
> Architecture*, p. 373)

By dropping back to the earlier American modernism of the Chicago
School and then of Frank Lloyd Wright, we may be able to put the
relationship between form, function and society into a historical
context. This will help us to explain how socially conscious European
architecture became the badge of corporate capitalism. The longer view
will also put into perspective the question of post-modern architecture
and so provide a comparison with the contemporary situation in other
art forms. When the modern movement is rejected, we ought to ask
from what aesthetic and political standpoint. Charles Jencks was so
anxious for the end of modernism that his report of the demolition of
Pruitt–Igoe advanced the date by two months.

Into the 'ibid.' thickets: the Chicago School, 1880s to 1920s

> Within three years [of the arrival of Gropius and Mies], every so-
> called major American contribution to contemporary architecture
> – whether by Wright, H.H. Richardson . . . or Louis Sullivan,
> leader of the 'Chicago School' of skyscraper architects – had
> dropped down into the footnotes, into the 'ibid.' thickets. (*From
> Bauhaus to Our House*, p. 50)

The situation of these earlier American architects is more complicated than Wolfe makes out, as well as more revealing of the relationship between architecture and society. For one thing, European modernists cited Sullivan and Wright, and the American technology which fostered the skyscraper, as valued influences upon their functional machine aesthetic. And on their part, Sullivan and Wright were not fighting European modernism but the Ecole des Beaux-Arts in Paris, and the Classical, Renaissance, Georgian, Jacobean, and Gothic revivals which punctuated American architecture between 1870 and 1930.

With Henry Hobson Richardson's Marshall Field Wholesale Store (1885–87) and then Dankmar Adler and Louis Sullivan's Auditorium building (1887–89), the Chicago School became the first modern style in American architecture. Daniel Burnham and John Root's Monadnock of 1889–91 is closer to the clean lines of post-1920s modernism, though, because while it was the last of the important tall masonry buildings in Chicago, it has none of the Romanesque solidity of the Auditorium and Marshall Field buildings (Plate 15). Indeed, it was planned as a steel-framed structure. The Monadnock also exemplifies a distinction between pattern, which is spread over the whole of the building, and ornament, which is usually concentrated at corners, entrances and roof. In the case of the Monadnock its slab-like shape has a slight inward curve at first floor level and an outward curve which becomes the parapet.

The Monadnock pushed at the limits of masonry construction. The thickness and overall mass of wall needed for support reduced the size of the windows, though Root partially met this drawback with an undulating shape consisting of projecting bay windows from the second to the penultimate storey, with further windows in the piers. Its slender shape also gives all of the offices outside windows. In responding to the basic requirement for maximum light, Burnham and (mostly) Root achieved a variety that is yet part of the regularity which was insisted upon by the client. The Monadnock anticipated Sullivan's essay, 'The Tall Building Artistically Considered' (1896), which begins with an account of the 'practical conditions' but concludes in ringing tones:

> What is the chief characteristic of the tall office building? And at once we answer, it is lofty. This loftiness is to the artist-nature its thrilling aspect . . . It must be every inch a proud and soaring thing, rising in sheer exultation that from bottom to top it is a unit without a single dissenting line.[3]

However, it was the technology of the load-bearing steel frame which gave substance to Sullivan's Whitmanesque aspirations for the tall building. In his *Autobiography of an Idea* (1924), Sullivan remarks that 'the architects of Chicago welcomed the steel frame and did something with it. The architects of the East were appalled by it and could make no contribution to it.'[4] Among Sullivan's most important steel frame skyscrapers of the Chicago School were the Wainwright building in St Louis (1890–91), the Guaranty building, in Buffalo (1894–5), and the Carson Pirie Scott Store (1899), which Burnham extended in 1903–4 and 1906. Of the Reliance building (1894–5), on which Burnham employed Charles Atwood as designing architect, Carl Condit remarks: 'One short step further in the design of the Reliance and [Atwood] would have produced the transparent tower that Mies van der Rohe imagined in his Berlin project of 1919'.[5]

These buildings could literally, rather than metaphorically, rise, with repercussions for both the space within and around tall buildings. The piers had been up to fifteen feet thick to support the sixteen storeys of the Monadnock, but the steel frame converted the outside wall into the curtain or envelope that became so basic to the International Style. In other words, in Chicago in the 1880s and 1890s we see the style emerging from the technology and from the motor of economic imperatives. With the outside wall no longer bearing the load of the building, so that each section of the outside wall was supported at each floor, windows could be larger. The Carson Pirie Scott and Reliance Buildings both have clear horizontal and quite decorative divisions between floors, so are not glass curtains, but their 'Chicago windows', so-called, are large and separated not by piers but thin mullions (Plate 16).

Sullivan's well-known antipathy towards Eastern architects dates from around 1893 when, under the direction of Daniel Burnham, they brought a neo-classical aesthetics into the design of the major buildings of the Chicago World's Fair. Burnham correctly predicted that the effect of this year-long event would be to reinstate traditional European styles. Looking back from the obscurity of his later life over the successes of Burnham, Sullivan saw it differently, and recalled 'a violent outbreak of the Classic and the Renaissance in the East, which slowly spread westward, contaminating all that it touched . . . The damage wrought by the World's Fair will last for half a century from its date, if not longer . . . Architecture, be it known, is dead (Autobiography of an Idea, p. 324).

The incipient modernist relationship between form and function was riven by the contradictions of the World's Fair, for example between its official, decorative centre and the Midway Plaisance, the forerunner of Coney Island. Richard Hunt's Administration Building dominated the former but the Great Wheel of George W.G. Ferris lifted people higher still, from where they could see not only the nearby re-creation of a temporary, hybrid European city but, in the distance, the 'black' city of Chicago, location of the Auditorium and Monadnock. The other main architectural contrast was between the facade and the structure of the individual buildings within the Fair. Some of the most up-to-date technology was used for the steel frames, but this was then covered by white plaster, called staff, which kept falling off only to be replaced by maintenance gangs overnight. There are few more revealing photographs of a much-photographed Fair than one of the Administration Building under construction. The neo-classical super-structure rises above the foundation girders, while the tracks of a works railroad to the side of the building site signify other technological features of the American industrial landscape in the 1890s.

Burnham carried this paradoxical combination of form and function over into his other career as a city planner in the City Beautiful Movement, which lasted until 1909 and his and Edward H. Bennett's *Plan of Chicago*. That book contains Jules Guerin's pastel illustration of Upper Michigan Avenue as a stately boulevard stretching into the hinterland, and another of the sun setting over the monumental civic centre. This was quite deliberate. 'Beauty has always paid better than any other commodity and always will,' was one of Burnham's axioms. Neatly, Thomas Hines terms this, and not the 'commercial style' of the Chicago School, the 'architecture of capitalism.'[6]

In *The Theory of the Leisure Class*, a book written out of Chicago, Thorstein Veblen pinpoints capitalism's interest in architecture and specifically in:

> the construction of an edifice faced with some aesthetically objectionable but expensive stone, covered with grotesque and incongruous details, and designed, in its battlemented walls and turrets and its massive portals and strategic approaches, to suggest certain barbaric methods of warfare. The interior of the structure shows the same pervasive guidance of the canons of conspicuous waste and predatory exploit.[7]

Through institutions like a world's fair, power relations between financial and cultural elites could be forged. As a mixture of entrepreneur and Progressive reformer, Burnham was instrumental in making such connections. His ideology was that of a new, less obviously rapacious, but ultimately more powerful, phase of capital-ism. To this extent, the vision of the city promoted by the Fair compares with the ambiguities of Edward Bellamy's *Looking Backward* (1888), a utopian novel which seeks to resolve the severe crisis of late nineteenth-century American capitalism but, as Arthur Lipow notes, does not contain the word 'democracy'. Quite appropriately, the best description of the architecture of the World's Fair is given by Bellamy's time-traveller five years before the Fair opened:

Miles of broad streets, shaded by trees and lined with fine
buildings, for the most part not in continuous blocks but set in
larger or smaller enclosures, stretched in every direction. Every
quarter contained large open squares filled with trees, along
which statues glistened and fountains flashed in the late-afternoon
sun. Public buildings of a colossal size and architectural grandeur
unparalleled in my day raised their stately piles on every side.
Surely I had never seen this city nor one comparable to it before.
8

Since much of the architectural eclecticism of the pre- and immediate
post-First World War years was was in the domestic and governmental
spheres, the competition in 1922 to design a skyscraper for the *Chicago
Tribune* attracted a fairly restrained entry. Yet it still seemed as though
many of the architects had visited the back lots of the recently founded
Hollywood studios just before submitting their final designs. There
were motifs culled from Greek, Roman and Egyptian architecture and
the Italian and English Renaissances had been dipped into. Given that
the competition was to design a skyscraper, however, the Gothic
revival was the style most in evidence, in both the winning entry by
Howells and Hood and even in the third-place design submitted by the
Chicago School firm, Holabird and Roche. As in the architecture
inspired by the World's Fair, then, there was a tension, if not a
contradiction, between the technology and the style.

One of the unsuccessful entries was by Bauhaus director, Walter
Gropius, and his partner and part-time tutor at the Bauhaus, Adolf
Meyer. Two points may made about their design. First, that bar the
asymmetry of the horizontal caesuras, its austere shape anticipates the
International Style skyscrapers (Plate 17). For this reason it was
included in the 1932 MOMA exhibition. And second, this is Carl
Condit's point – the design suggests that Bauhaus modernism was the
successor and not the usurper of the Chicago School tradition:

> The starting point appears to have been the newsprint warehouse
> on the northside of the river behind the present Tribune Tower.
> The warehouse is a heavy-handed and strictly utilitarian example
> of the commercial architecture of the Chicago School. (*The
> Chicago School*, p. 217)

Montgomery Schuyler, a very perceptive architectural critic of the
late nineteenth century, made a claim on behalf of the Monadnock
which could be extended to much of the Chicago School, including
both the Burnham responsible for some of the best Chicago buildings
and the Sullivan who attacked him:

It may seem easy enough to leave off all ornament from a tall building . . . and so indeed it is. That is a common scheme in factories which are not works of architecture at all. The point is to produce, by means or in spite of this extreme austerity, an architectural work which shall be as impressive as it clearly is expressive. This is the rare success which seems to me to have been attained in the Monadnock Building. Whoever assumes that it must be very easy to do and that it requires no more than merely the omission of architecture makes a great mistake.[9]

Veblen's 'instinct of workmanship' would have led him to agree with Schuyler that it is the economy of modern architecture – truth to materials and function – which permits an engagement with the non-architectural, the non-artistic, the functional, that is to say, with mass production. From this engagement – the *aesthetic* engagement that Schuyler calls 'architecture' – can come the modernist aspiration for social and political change. This is not a rejection of the world of factories, but a critique along the lines of 'is that all there is to a factory?' (Or a skyscraper?) Of course, there is a fine line between architecture that is capable of engaging with the processes and materials of modernization and an architecture that simply reflects modernization, becomes its monument, its corporate image. While Sullivan's 'form follows function' is a seminal tenet, only the historical context can tell us how that fine line was to be drawn.

We have seen that Tom Wolfe lays the blame for the demise of American architecture on the 'White Gods' of the Bauhaus, but he ignores a much more significant reason: the interest which was shown in architectural aesthetics by American capitalism in its transitional phase between laissez-faire and corporate forms. Wolfe's other objection to the Bauhaus influence is that it led to the worst excesses of the Miesian glass box, and it is on this basis that he, and others too, have dismissed the modern movement. This is a more difficult objection to meet but the route from Weimar to the Avenue of the Americas is convoluted. Wolfe focuses upon the effect of Gropius and Mies upon American architecture; it could be more enlightening to focus on the effect of America upon Bauhaus ideals.

Space, time and architecture: the skyscraper in the 1930s

One of the consequences of the emphasis upon formal beauty in the guidelines for the *Chicago Tribune* Competition was that the spatial characteristics of the entries received even less attention than the functional ones. Spatial, in this instance, refers to the relationship of the building to the spaces around it. However, Gropius' design, though tempted by the Faustian desire for autonomy that undoubtedly inhabits modernism, also evinces a concern for relations – not simply with the immediate street, though that was part of the intellectual context of the Bauhaus and also Le Corbusier's modernism, but with neighbouring issues as well, notably housing and the environment. Le Corbusier's cities in the sky were motivated by an obsession with the environment rather than with height. When he talks of his tower blocks it is in the context of the green fields that will surround the block once the space is cleared. I make this point not to defend Le Corbusier necessarily but to underline how different was the concept of the skyscraper which was developing in Europe in the late 1910s and the 1920s, from that in the United States. The question of the space around the skyscraper – and especially the American skyscraper locked into the grid of Manhattan or the Chicago Loop – precipitates all the other, often troubled, questions asked of this architectural phenonemon. This is because the skyscraper has very little possibility of creating space around it in the literal meaning of 'around'. All its freedom is in the third dimension, but the more it rises, the more it adversely affects the street upon which it stands, by blocking out light or the opportunity for a park or square. And not just the street; the city, too, as more people are brought in to work in the skyscraper.

The question, as we go into the 1930s, with all of the leading Chicago School architects dead, is how did the European and American traditions mix. This is both a broad question about the relationship between traditions in which the degree of state control differed noticeably; and a specific question to do with the influence of Gropius and Mies van der Rohe. The two traditions appeared to mix well, and in 1938–9 Siegfried Giedion gave the Charles Eliot Norton Lectures at Harvard. They were published in 1941 as *Space, Time and Architecture*, and authoritatively reinterpret an amalgam of planning, design and architecture since the Middle Ages in the light of the modern movement. The lectures coincided with the New York World Fair which, unlike the Chicago Fair of 1893, but following on from the 1933 Chicago World's Fair, was an unashamed celebration of modernity. The Court of Honour in Burnham's Fair was replaced by the Trylon and the Perisphere; and the Cultural Congresses by General Motors' Futurama and, inside the Perisphere, by Democracity. Also in 1939, MOMA followed its 'Modern Architecture' exhibition of 1932 with a retrospective of the Bauhaus. Modernism, known in American architectural terminology as the International Style, had arrived and would, from then on, literally, look down on American cities from New York south-west to Houston, north-west to Los Angeles and east to Chicago. In an effort to understand what happened or, as it is usually phrased, what went wrong, we need to look more closely at the 1930s, as in other art forms, the crucial decade.

The most notable first reactions against the eclecticism of the 1920s were George Howe and William Lescaze's Philadelphia Savings Fund Society building (PSFS), Philadelphia (1932) and Raymond Hood's Daily News building (1930) and his McGraw-Hill building (1932), both in New York City. Though the curved glass and polished metal base of the PSFS suggests the influence of 'moderne' design, rather than the cubism of the International Style, Howe and Lescaze largely do without decoration – and certainly avoid the medievalism that had dominated Howe's earlier work. This was an important step since it was decoration, though of a different kind, that denoted the continuing gothicism of the American, and especially the New York, skyscraper tradition. By 1930, William Van Alen's Chrysler building, and Shreve, Lamb and Harmon's eighty-five storey Empire State building (1929–31) were the chief neo-gothic rivals to the famous Woolworth building of 1911–13 (Plate 18). The height of the two later skyscrapers meant that they were technically advanced, but they resisted the leap towards abstraction attempted by the PSFS and Raymond Hood's buildings, the Chrysler building through its aluminium 'hub-caps' tapering towards the spire, and the Empire State building through its more American-style Art Deco spire. David Handlin confirms the connection that we have been tracing, when he remarks of Art Deco that it 'was a style that architects trained at the Ecole des Beaux-Arts could use for commercial buildings instead of the traditional languages of ornament'.[10]

Raymond Hood, like Howe, was important because of his conversion to the International Style, especially since he had won the *Chicago Tribune* Competition for his neo-gothic skyscraper and had built the Art Deco American Radiator building, in New York in 1924, and the Rex Cole Showroom, New York, 1931. Hood's International Style skyscrapers are very different and the McGraw-Hill building, with its cubist, 'stepped' shape and expanse of glass resembles another of the German entries in the *Tribune* competition, by Max Taut. Hood's use of metal-covered piers and sheet steel and steel tubes in the entrance hall contributes to the modernity of the building: 'like a fire raging inside an iceberg; the fire of Manhattanism inside the iceberg of Modernism', according to Rem Koolhaas.[11]

But what of space? Raymond Hood also took up this modernist theme in the project for the Rockefeller Center, which began formally in 1931, ran for the whole decade, and is another of those meeting places between commerce and culture which make twentieth-century America so richly contradictory. Mass communications were represented in Radio City Music Hall and the NCB studios; art and design came together in the pervasive Art Deco of the Center and in a mural by Diego Rivera (destroyed because it contained the face of Lenin), and another by Stuart Davis (a tribute to the communications industry); architecture developed a new form, the skyscraper plaza; and everywhere there was the tension between modernism and, in Berman's words, 'modern capitalism . . . that has set and kept the pot boiling'.

In the Rockefeller Center the single skyscraper is extended into the first of the American skyscraper plazas, a twelve-acre complex of eight blocks and fourteen buildings (the RCA building rose to seventy stories). The whole project was unified in its conception and its design of modest set-backs and uniformly spaced limestone verticals. As Giedion acknowledges when bringing his massive survey up to date with a discussion of 'Space-Time in City Planning' in the 1930s, the Rockefeller Center attempts to re-create the public spaces of classical and medieval cities in the congestion of free-enterprise Manhattan. The theatres, restaurants, shops, studios, roof-top gardens, and offices are linked by pedestrian walks. At one stage in the long process of planning and construction, the Center might have been linked, through another plaza, with the MOMA building and Sixth Avenue which was where Frank Lloyd Wright's Guggenheim Museum was built between 1943 and 1959. The sheer difficulty experienced in intervening in both the literal grid of Manhattan and the metaphorical grid of the market economy thwarted these and other civic plans. The Rockefeller Center, though an extraordinary achievement, and especially in the 1930s, became more inward-looking, though never as 'closed' as some of the shopping and hotel schemes of the 1970s and 1980s. However, it did not fulfil Giedion's hope that the creation of space would transform the city 'not in the interest of single individuals but for the sake of the community as a whole'.[12]

Standards of living in a new mode of living: Frank Lloyd Wright

As an index of modernity and also a way of reaching some aesthetic and political conclusions about buildings, we have started to focus on the theme of space in architecture. In a long and interrupted career

Plate 1. George Wesley Bellows, *Stag at Sharkey's* (1907)

Plate 2. George Wesley Bellows, *Dempsey and Firpo* (1924)

Plate 3. Charles Sheeler, *Offices* (1922)

Plate 4. Georgia O'Keeffe, *Black Iris* (1926)

Plate 5. John Marin, *Lower Manhattan (Composing Derived from Top of Woolworth)* (1922)

Plate 6. Joseph Stella, *Battle of Lights, Coney Island* (1913)

Plate 7. Grant Wood, *Stone City, Iowa* (1930)

Plate 8. Edward Hopper, *Nighthawks* (1942)

Plate 9. Willem de Kooning, *Woman I* (1950–52)

Plate 10. Jackson Pollock, *Mural* (1943)

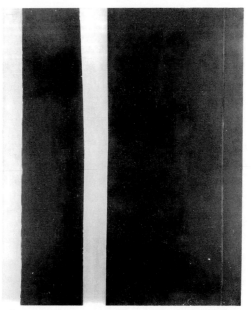

Plate 11. Barnett Newman, *Adam* (1951–52)

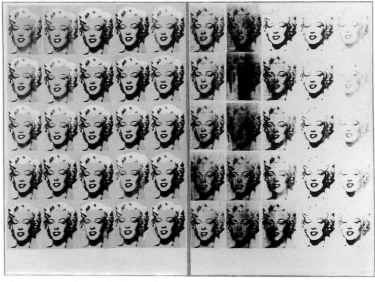

Plate 12. Andy Warhol, *Marilyn* (1962)

Plate 13. Barbara Kruger, *Untitled* Your Gaze Hits the Side of My Face (1981)

Plate 14. Mies Van der Rohe and Philip Johnson, Seagram building, New York City (photographer V. Bennett)

Plate 16. Louis Sullivan, Carson Pirie Scott store, Chicago (photographer R. McCabe)

Plate 15. Daniel Burnham and John Root, Monadnock building, Chicago (photographer H. T. Cadbury–Brown)

Project for Chicago Tribune Tower Competition (1922)   Walter Gropius (b.1883) with
Adolf Meyer (1881-1929)

Plate 17. Adolf Meyer and Walter Gropius, Design for the
Chicago Tribune competition, 1922

Plate 18.   Cass Gilbert, Woolworth Tower, New York City (photographer
A. Higgott)

Plate 19. Frank Lloyd Wright, Larkin building, Buffalo, New York

Plate 20. Frank Lloyd Wright, Frederick C. Robie house, Chicago (photographer A. Minchim)

Plate 21. Michael Graves, Public Services building, Portland, Oregon (photographer Tom Clark)

Plate 22. Susan Griggs, *American Sign* (photographer George Hall)

Plate 23. SITE, Indeterminate Facade Showroom, Houston, Texas

from 1887 to 1959, Frank Lloyd Wright, more than any other architect, recognized that architecture could create space. The 1910 publication of his drawings in Berlin provoked some of the theoretical and practical work on this theme by Gropius, Mies, and Neutra, at a time when he was neglected in the United States in consequence of his well-publicized domestic upheavals and tragedies. Le Corbusier and the Bauhaus architects went on to articulate explicitly the politics of architecture, whereas Wright, like Sullivan, remained trapped in vague transcendental assertions about architecture and the spirit of American democracy. Yet Wright's conception of a building as space rather than mass defined by its walls implicitly turned architecture into a political, as well as an aesthetic, practice. The new technology of early modern architecture, first in Chicago and then more widely through Wright's work, compares in its potential with the new technology of mechanical reproduction that so interested Walter Benjamin. In suggesting such a comparison, Benjamin anticipates post-1960s research into defensible space as a mediation between the private and public domains, and into gender as a factor in the design of interior and exterior space. As Benjamin remarks, 'Buildings are appropriated in a twofold manner: by use and by perception . . . Such appropriation cannot be understood in terms of the attentive concentration of a tourist before a famous building.'[13]

In spite of being dismissed from the firm of Adler and Sullivan in 1893, Wright was undoubtedly influenced by Sullivan's 'form follows function'. For example, in the Larkin building in Buffalo (1904), the towers accommodate the ventilation shafts and the stairs are in the corner piers. Though he objected later to the uniformity of the glass box, Wright was more in tune with the logic which suspected surface ornamentation than was Sullivan. Like Sullivan, though, Wright voiced his criticism of the post-Chicago Fair eclecticism most effectively through his architecture. The Larkin building followed shortly after Wright's 1901 lecture, 'The Art and Craft of the Machine' in which he stated that 'in this age of steel and steam the tools with which civilization's true record will be written are scientific thoughts made operative in iron and bronze and steel and in plastic processes which characterize this age, all of which we call Machines'.[14] The Larkin building is less purely mechanical and instead aspires to be a model of economy that would articulate the relationship between a building and the 'community' which used it. The central interior court has balconied offices all around, not to facilitate surveillance but to transform the workplace into a complete environment. Wright designed much of the furniture as well (Plate 19).

Wright had been building suburban houses since the beginning of his career but with the Ward W. Willets house, Highland Park, Illinois (1900–2) he moved away from the formality and closed design of the

Winslow house, River Forest, Illinois (1893–94), and explored what he called 'the quiet level' which became a keynote of the Prairie Style that attracted such architects as Marion Mahoney Griffin, Walter Burley Griffin, and George Grant Elmslie. Wright's Robie house, Chicago (1909) is one of the best examples of the Prairie Style, the dominant impression being of horizontal lines which parallel the lines of the land (Plate 20). In the Robie House we are drawn to the low street wall, the inner garden wall, the balcony wall, and the two levels of low-pitched roof. Though mostly confined to private, middle-class suburban houses, Wright's horizontal emphasis appears in the 'sculptured' and also Cubist-like succession of terraces, arcades and a winter garden in the Midway Gardens, Chicago (1914).

Inside the Robie House, Wright replaced the room, as a bounded space, with open space, using screens or panels as divisions that do not impede light. Outside, he explored the relationship between the building and the street and aimed for a mixture of the private and the public through lawns that run into the sidewalk, and terraces that are part house, part garden, part interior and part exterior space. Much later, in the Johnson Wax Administration building (1936–9) the transition between the outside and the inside is managed in a commercial building through a carefully designed route. During this spell of renewed activity in the 1930s, Wright pursued his interest in the *site*, and in the Kaufmann house, known as 'Falling Water', in Connesville, Pennsylvania (1935), he built into the side of a hill over which flowed a waterfall. The verticals of rough stone are the vernacular element in the building and pick up the bedrock outcrop; while the smooth cantilevered concrete slabs are pure modernism, comparable with Le Corbusier's in the Villa Savoye, Poissy (1929–31).

A common criticism is that Wright's democratic ideals were compromised not just by his largely middle- and upper-middle class clientele, but by a domestic ideology which was manifested in the importance attached to the hearth as the physical centre of family life, and the suburb as the ideal meeting place of nature and the city. Possibly, though, the isolation that the integrated family can engender, especially in the suburbs, may have struck Wright by the 1930s when he expanded his perspective and began a four to five year meditation on what he called Broadacre City (plans, 1935). It is a micro- as well as a macro-vision, and is built up from the individual 'Usonian' house, a small but carefully designed house on a one-acre site. Though very few were built – one example is the Herbert Jacobs house, Madison (1936) – and then not in communities, the Usonian house reveals a minute attention to the possibilities for prefabrication, and to progressive use of interior spaces. For example, the kitchen is designed as part of the larger space made up of the dining room and the patio, the aim being to minimize the isolation of the housewife; unlike Charlotte Perkins

Gilman in *Women and Economics* (1898), Wright could not bring himself to conceive of the kitchenless house as a solution to the isolation of women in kitchens.

The Usonian house has financial, as well as spatial economy to the fore, and compares interestingly with the public housing schemes of the 1930s and early 1940s, which had attracted the interest of Gropius and Neutra, their ideas, in turn, influencing less well-known European architects, like Alfred Kastner and Oskar Stonorov. In Kastner and Stonorov's Carl Mackley Houses in Philadelphia (1934) the social utopianism of European modernism is apparent in the shared recreational facilities, club-rooms, garage, and library, and in the bridges and passageways which encouraged residents to meet and benefit from the external colours and designs. In this connection, Stonorov referred to 'standards of living in a new mode of living quite different from what individual speculative activity has created'.[15]

In Germany, Gropius' high standards for accommodation and services were dependent upon the interventionist state in the Weimar Republic. He ran into the inflation of the late 1920s and 1930s, and then into the Third Reich. In the United States there was much less drama, but with no significant history of state-supported housing, real estate values gradually returned, even under the wing of the New Deal. As in skyscraper design, there was no programme sufficiently well financed or thought through that would escape the existing pattern of the cities. It was, therefore, quite appropriate and very revealing, that at the 1932 MOMA Exhibition, the housing and architecture sections were mostly self-contained. 'Housing' was organized by Clarence Stein, Catherine Bauer and Henry Wright, and had a separate catalogue written by Lewis Mumford. Hitchcock and Johnson concentrated upon formal issues and upon the skyscraper, and their section was entitled 'Architecture'. This separation was alien to the philosophy and the practice of European and Chicago modernism in all their variants, since the belief in social change through architecture had to involve where people lived as well as where they worked or spent their leisure time.

The need for a new monumentality: a coda to the International Style, 1940s to 1970s

The division between 'Housing' and 'Architecture' at the 1932 MOMA exhibition was a step towards formalizing the International Style, even before it was underway, and well before the New Deal gave way to the multinational corporate capitalism of the Eisenhower years. It is of some significance that Philip Johnson, who became the leading home-grown American modernist, should eventually gravitate towards Mies rather than Walter Gropius. For while the two emigré German architects led the way in the Bauhaus emphasis upon machine age aesthetics, cubic blocks, glass curtain walls, and clean corners free of support, and while they were both involved with public housing projects in Germany, there is a difference between their respective politics of form. Or, at least, there was a difference before Gropius, like Mies, turned towards formalism and away from the Bauhaus ideal of architecture as a service to society. An indication of the incorporation of the modern movement by its American offshoot, the International Style, is the interest in what Sigfried Giedion called in 1943 a 'new monumentality'. Monumentalism became particularly evident in the urban financial centres of the United States from the 1960s onwards.

Monumentalism was prominent in the tradition of ceremonial architecture of palaces, government buildings, and banks that became the staple of the Ecole des Beaux-Arts by the late nineteenth century. It had influenced American architecture of the early Republic but made a comeback after the Chicago World's Fair of 1893. American modernism, led by the Chicago School in mainstream architecture, but also by the more lowly architecture of grain elevators, barns and factories celebrated in Sheeler and Demuth's Precisionist paintings of the 1910s and 1920s, interpreted Beaux-Arts monumentalism as undemocratic. However, it was left to European modernists, rather than Sullivan and his contemporaries, to formulate this interpretation as an *aesthetics* of what Corbusier called the 'House-Tool', meaning, broadly, the building which would be mass produced: the more than just-a-factory of Gropius' Fagus Shoe Factory of 1911. 'I would prefer to design a good building than an original one', Mies declared, following Adolf Loos's more polemical insistence that '*the evolution of culture is synonymous with the removal of ornament from utilitarian objects*'.[16]

The twist in the story is that monumentalism then re-appeared in a modernism sponsored by American capitalism. Far from dismissing modernism as subversive of capitalism, the big corporations, or wealthy citizens for domestic commissions, became its clientele, perhaps reasoning that the Nazi suppression of the Bauhaus meant that modern architecture shared the same values of freedom and progress that were so vigorously promoted in the United States in the immediate post-war and McCarthy eras. There would seem to be a general similarity, at least, to the situation in the post-1945 art world described in the previous chapter.

Context apart, the glass box had always had the potential for turning in on itself. Manfredo Tafuri puts this well, when defining the skyscraper as 'a structure that does not wholly identify with the reasons for its own existence, an entity that remains aloof from the city'.[17] Mies went in this direction because he had less of Gropius' interest in planning the space around the glass box. But Tafuri's fears were, in any case, more likely to materialize in American cities where the grid-plan concentrated attention upon the third dimension. The progressive revelation of the steel structure of the skyscraper, which reached a new level in the Lever and Seagram Buildings, was interpreted, for example by Philip Johnson, as a symbolic statement about society as a monument. In this connection, Kenneth Frampton talks of 'the monumentalization of technique as form' in Mies.[18] He means that the attention to details, however minor, is so intense in the Seagram Building or the Lafayette Towers and Court Houses in Detroit (1955–63), that the building makes a statement about the values of its society by seeking to *be* itself, rather than, according to Beaux-Arts monumentalism, by commemorating values through the manipulation of symbols. Though this is an intricate notion, it possibly explains why abstract architecture at the pitch of Mies's resists interpretation, or, same difference, polarizes it: 'an adequate symbol or . . . just a very exquisite farce', Charles Jencks wonders (*Modern Movements*, p. 105).

Lewis Mumford, who first picked up the connections between modernist formalism and the International Style, turns Mies's 'Less means more' back to the architect by describing his 'steel and glass' boxes as 'elegant monuments of nothingness.'[19] This vacuum of signification – a very different meaning for the modernist dictum of 'returning to zero' – is taken to the extreme of monumentalism in the late International Style super-skyscraper. Examples of this new form include: the twin towers of the World Trade Center (1972) by Minoru Yamasaki, and the 110 storeys of black aluminium of the Sears building (1970–74) and the 100 storeys of the John Hancock Center (1965–70), both in Chicago and both by Skidmore, Owings and Merrill. On the new architectural frontier of Dallas and Houston, colonized in the absence of strict zoning laws by Johnson, I.M. Pei, and SOM, we find such astounding late 1970s constructions as Johnson and Burgee's thirty-six-storey Pennzoil Building and their Post Oaks Central, two towers of streamlined black-grey glass with rounded edges. The isolation of the super-skyscraper is very apparent even in Pei's fairly modest 740 feet, sixty-storey John Hancock Tower in Boston. Its mirrored surface protects the integrity of the building, even to the extent that it incorporates into itself the image of the space around it, part of which is occupied by the previous headquarters of the company.

Less is a bore: post-modernism, 1960s to 1980s

Whether because Mies and his progeny had reached a pitch that could not be sustained, or whether because of the sheer number of very similar high-rise blocks in downtown areas, the effects of the modern movement upon the urban fabric began to dawn on architects and critics from the mid-1960s onwards. Post-modernism is still just about serving as a descriptive label for the work of those, like Venturi, Brown and Rauch, Cesar Pelli, Michael Graves, Architectonica, Charles Moore, Robert Gehry, Robert Stern, Helmut Jahn, and, after a change of direction, Philip Johnson, all of whom have sought to find ways out of the contemporary crisis of architecture. It may be, though, that the dominant and very recognizable form of post-modernism is itself the sign of the crisis rather than its resolution.

As with modernism, so, with post-modernism, the Museum of Modern Art quickly picked up the signs in the streets in its Complexity and Contradiction in Architecture exhibition, based around Robert Venturi *et al.*'s 1966 book of the same name. Venturi's is 'a gentle manifesto' compared with Giedion's *Space, Time and Architecture*, and accepts the futility and the danger of utopian modernism. Instead Venturi takes 'the limited view', though the rejection of 'the visionary view' of the modern movement does not necessarily mean an abandonment of social concern or a modest architecture.[20] Firms like Architectonica from Miami respect the importance of the surrounding neighbourhood, while attempting to add to it. Their four colourful town houses in Houston do just this, while their Miami building, Atlantis, promotes the humorous side of architecture. Sections of the building are cut out and appear elsewhere in the building or around it, for example as a squash court. Post-modernism is a licence not to be so serious as the modernists. Where Mies van der Rohe took the view that 'Less is more', Venturi responded with 'less is a bore'. And Philip Johnson sounds like T.S. Eliot's Prufrock – but minus his hang-ups – when saying goodbye to *his* modernist mentor: 'Mies is such a genius! But I grow old! And bored!' (quoted in Jencks, *Modern Movements*, p. 198). As for Venturi, he anticipated the playful tone of post-structuralist colleagues in the Yale English department when he described the end-result of modernist building as a 'duck', that is to say a shop selling decoy ducks which is constructed as a giant duck. Venturi prefers the post-modernist 'decorated shed', based on the billboard principle of attaching ornament to a simple structure.

The term post-modernism initially described the shocking and anarchic fiction of William Burroughs, among others, but was turned around by Charles Jencks 'to mean the opposite of all this: the end of avant-garde extremism, the partial return to tradition and the central role of communicating with the public – and architecture is *the* public art'.[21] Literature then moved towards architectural definitions of post-modernism. In 'The Literature of Replenishment' John Barth looks for a more democratic, less original fiction. He has no qualms about re-using the techniques and symbols of the past to achieve communication. This is what Jencks is getting at when he defines post-modernism as *'double-coding': 'the combination of Modern techniques with something else (usually traditional building) in order for architecture to communicate with the public and a concerned minority, usually other architects'* (*What is Postmodernism?*, p. 14).

To see what post-modernism means in practice, we can look at Michael Graves's Public Services building in Portland, Oregon (1979–82), which survived protests that it was a Las Vegas building and not one for Oregon and became the flagship for post-modernism (Plate 21). Reacting against his modernist leanings when part of the New York Five in the 1960s, Graves followed the lead of his own highly colourful painting. The Portland Building also answers Venturi's call for contradictions and complexity. It is eclectic, picking up high art motifs (for example, the dark red/brown vertical strips resemble flat columns), as well as modernist and pop art motifs. Pietro Belluschi, who started off the glass box tradition in Portland thirty years before, described the Portland Building as 'an enlarged juke box or the oversized beribboned Christmas package'.

The building did gain a measure of acceptance in Portland, but this probably owed little to Graves's explanation of its pedantic symbolism (the green base as a reference to nature) and more to simply being there. It 'grew on people', even Belluschi: 'I'm getting used to it. I've seen it from a distance and it has its own character. Frankly, I'm sorry I made any adverse comment at all.'[22] Peter Eisenman, like Graves a former member of the New York Five, was less conciliatory and made the most trenchant criticism of Graves's work: 'A house, for example, is no longer conceived as a house (a social or ideological entity) or as an object (in itself) but rather as a painting of an object' (quoted in K. Frampton, *Modern Architecture*, p. 308). Giving priority to the surface of the building – painting it in effect – can have unfortunate consequences. For instance, the windows of the cream middle section of the Portland Building are very small and have the effect of shutting in the occupants as well as shutting out the light. The large windows elsewhere on the building turn out to be partly pure facade: a tinted glass 'skin' but covering the walls rather than constituting the walls as in the glass box.

In addition to reacting against the modernist movement by use of colour, by an arbitrary relationship to function, and by a return to mass – all are evident in the Portland Building – post-modernism also dresses up the glass box. Philip Johnson, who was professional consultant to the committee which awarded Michael Graves the Portland Building commission, follows all of these routes, often with disarming directness, given the gargantuan scale of this stylistic experimentation:

> The Republic Bank [in Houston] is not a building that fits well in that neighborhood. But since there isn't any neighborhood for it to fit into I felt perfectly free, in this marvelous frontier community, to do what I pleased. Pennzoil was the last of the modern buildings that we built, and so they look at each other with rather great enmity, it seems to me. I mean, I would not like to stand in the doorway of Republic Bank and look across at that old-fashioned building across the street. And vice-versa. If I'm in that building I'd say 'What's that fussy building across the street with all those little pyramids on top, and all those little scoops and enormous gables. What do they all mean?'[23]

Johnson and Burgee's AT & T Building, New York, completed 1984 but designed in 1978, was Johnson's first clear venture into post-modernism. Three features of the building provoke comment: first, and most famous, the pediment on the top, taken from the design of Chippendale furniture but on a vast scale and flung up 660 feet; second, the substitution of masonry for the glass curtain to the extent that pale pink Connecticut granite accounts for two-thirds of the surface and glass for the remainder; and third, the return to the tripartite structure of base, middle and top of the 1920s skyscrapers. The building counts as post-modernist because of its historical references and its witty quality, though by the time it was finished, the wittiness even perturbed supporters of post-modernism, who were unsure whether Johnson was a serious post-modernist or not.

Along with Graves's Portland Building and Charles Moore's Piazza d'Italia (1975–9) (the two most cited examples), the AT & T announces that there is a whole architectural thesaurus to hand and it can be quoted from at will. As Philip Johnson remarks, in an interview with Susan Sontag, 'I'm a plagiarist man – you see, you must take everything from everybody' (quoted in Jencks, *Modern Movements*, p. 210). Charles Moore, especially, derives some of his architectural language from local architects and the Italian community in New Orleans, but he still seems to end up with ethnic stereotypes that go well with the Hollywood-set appearance of the Piazza. These stereotypes point to one of the contradictions of post-modernism, that it claims local references yet most of its projects are financed by global rather than national movements of capital.

Another way to understand post-modernist architecture is to see it in the context of an urban/suburban division or even as an attempt to bring middle America into architectural, rather than merely commercial, prominence. High modernism of the 1950s looked down on suburban growth and left the shopping mall and that hyperbole of mass culture, the 'strip', to the attention of developers. But according to Venturi *et al.* in their next book, *Learning from Las Vegas* (1972), post-modernism adopts a 'positive, non-chip-on-the-shoulder view' of 'the commercial vernacular'.[24] It shares the anti-intellectual pluralism expressed by Pop Artists, Claes Oldenburg and Andy Warhol. In place of the seriousness of Mies and Gropius, we have the bizarre side of architecture. For Venturi *et al.* this means the casinos, wedding chapels, gas stations, motels, and billboards of the Las Vegas 'strip', but also of strip-development across America (Plate 22). In contrast to the utopian imposition of a building upon the landscape, such roadside vernacular architecture as a hot-dog stall in the shape of a hot-dog, or a coffee shop in the shape of a coffee pot, cannot be avoided, so it should be enjoyed. It is also part of an architect's education, keeping the architect attuned to 'the cacaphonic context of our real landscape' and therefore aware of 'the individual need for intimacy and detail'. This, Venturi *et. al.* polemically add, is 'unmet by Modern design but [is] satisfied by the five-eights scale reproductions in Disneyland, by the caricatures of human scale in the patios of garden apartments, and by the seven-eights scale furnishings of the fancy interiors of Levittown model homes' (pp. 139 and 148).

To argue against architectural populism risks the charge of elitism, of purporting to know what people want better than they do themselves. Yet Venturi *et al.* are a little casual in their idea of what is 'real' about the contemporary landscape, and they are positively cavalier about the economics of post-modernism compared with the perspective of pre-Second World War modernists, and certainly compared with Thorstein Veblen, an earlier afficionado of cultural ephemera. Veblen's remark, quoted in the Introduction, that 'the signature of one's pecuniary strength should be written in characters which he who runs may read' explains the initial impetus behind the architecture of the Macdonald's, Burger King and Wendy fast food chains. Venturi *et al.* do acknowledge, however, that:

> Service stations, motels, and other simpler types of buildings
> conform in general to this system of inflection toward the
> highway through the position and form of their elements.
> Regardless of the front, the back of the building is styleless,
> because the whole is turned toward the front and no one sees the
> back. (p. 35)

Learning from Las Vegas is itself a text of post-modernism in that it refuses to judge: 'The analysis of a drive-in church . . . would match that of a drive-in restaurant, because this is a study of method, not content' (p. 6). There is, though, a danger of being cocooned, not so much in sign-systems, since that may well be our lot, but in particular sign-systems, such as Disneyland. Describing Orange County, Los Angeles, in *At the Edge of History* (1971), William Irwin Thompson asks an important question of both post-modern architecture and its analysts:

> As one moves through this shattered landscape in which the mountains are invisible from the exhausts of four and a half million cars and the orange trees have been eliminated for real estate speculation, how is he to gain any sense of history except through the artificial monuments he sees nearby in Disneyland . . . [itself] a shattered landscape in which the individual moves through a world of discontinuities: Mississippi riverboats, medieval castles, and rocket ships equally fill the reality of a single moment.[25]

If the experience is similar inside and outside an architecturally themed environment, then what concept of history is being invoked?

Mall time

The most significant feature of Johnson and Burgee's AT & T Building, could be the least obvious. In return for greater height the AT & T, like Mies's Seagram, provided space at ground level, but undercover. There is a grand lobby with an eight-storey arch, and most of the remainder of the ground floor is given over to a galleria. The architect who is best known for the creation and enclosure of downtown public space is John Portman, and it is in his Peachtree Center in Atlanta, Georgia, the Hyatt Regency hotel in San Francisco, the Los Angeles Bonaventure Hotel, and Detroit's Renaissance Center, that the relationship between post-modernism and its society, a post-industrial society according to many commentators, can best be analysed. Portman's lavishly decorated atriums are known for their space-age elevators; balconies with luxuriant trailing plants which create the impression of a mountain wall; tastefully designed nooks and crannies for eating and drinking; and glass roofs which magnify the limited sunlight that still manages to filter down between the canyons of skyscrapers. These structures, then, are the heirs of the Rockefeller Center of the 1930s, and Portman, especially, demonstrates a desire to humanize the environment which was fired by his trip in 1960 to the modernist nightmare of Brazilia.

However, post-1960s downtown plazas have as part of their lineage, the suburban shopping malls. Dating from the Southdale Mall, Edina, Minnesota, in 1956, malls have become (in Walter Benjamin terminology) the sites of the pre-history of post-modernity. Developers have few of the ideals of Victor Gruen, who, like the Bauhaus architects, arrived in America in the late 1930s and envisaged the suburban mall as a communal response to the anonymity of America's car culture. In the 1970s and 1980s, downtown plazas like Water Tower Place in Chicago and Portman's Renaissance Center have copied the malls, creating multi-purpose sites which aspire to be self-contained, often for the very good reason that the outside temperatures make the streets uncomfortable. The RenCen, as it is called, contains a hotel, shops, offices, entertainments, and restaurants in its shining, futuristic cylindrical towers.

The RenCen did revitalize a downtown area that was declining and was scarred by the riots of 1967. And, in the absence of public spaces, the atria of the IBM Office Tower in Manhattan and Portman's complexes all over America have become the new meeting places. But, with some exceptions – for instance the IDS Center in Minneapolis which retains its contact with the streets – the plaza architecture sets itself against the city around it. Paul Goldberger describes the RenCen, protected by the concrete berms that contain its utilities, as more like a 'suburban development . . . tall instead of short . . . dropped within the city limits instead of outside them. . . To many tenants, the chance to hop from car to elevator and never set foot on a city sidewalk is ideal'.[26] It recreates suburban behaviour where the private is valued and the public spaces are either bisected by freeways or are simply dangerous.

Such is the power of international financial speculation that the idea of a national or regional architecture becomes almost nonsensical: these places could be anywhere, and, once in place and in use, they seek to create their own environment through mirrored interiors, Muzak, and the provision of services. With more space available, suburban malls have expanded their offerings in ways that seem quite extraordinary unless, or until, the logic of consumption is acceded to:

> We've mixed amusement with retail and comprised them together to make it one component. And what we've done is basically to take every major tourist attraction in the world put it under one roof in one place making a weather-protected environment. We have the Water Park . . . the largest indoor water park in the world . . . We also have Fantasy Land, in Fantasy Land we have twenty-five rides and attractions . . .[27]

Mega-malls emulate Disneyland, Marriots Great America, and, in Britain, Alton Towers or the Great American Adventure, and are 'themed'. Just as Walter Benjamin's flaneur wandered the Parisian arcades and Alfred Kazin detailed his travels in New York in *A Walker in the City*, so now we have mall-walkers: 'I used to walk with the Sierra Club . . . around Los Angeles . . . but they walked . . . in the *rain!*' (*Mall Time*, 1987); and mall-watchers, such as Joan Didion in an essay in *The White Album* (1979) and David Byrne in the film, *True Stories* (1986).

The interaction between the Rockefeller Center and the city streets was never as successful as originally intended, but the plaza is still an open public space, used as a shopping area in summer and a skating rink in winter. Rockefeller Center came out of the idealism of the 1930s. The new wave of downtown centres came in the wake of urban riots of the 1960s and early 1970s, and also had to meet the counter-attraction of suburbia. The result has been an often very attractive privatizing of potential public realms downtown, following the pattern of the suburban shopping malls, which are guarded and under electronic surveillance. The six-storey atrium of Trump Tower on 5th Avenue in New York City, makes few concessions to the populist intentions of some downtown malls and atria. It is exclusive and the decorative surface is on the inside – which makes something of a nonsense of post-modernism's desire to communicate more widely. It has defined its population so carefully through market research that it can afford to turn its forbidding side to the city. As Fredric Jameson says of Portman's 'mini-city' in Los Angeles:

> [The] Bonaventura [sic] ought not to have entrances at all, since the entryway is always the seam that links the building to the rest of the city that surrounds it: for it does not wish to be a part of the city, but rather its equivalent and its replacement or substitute. That is, however, obviously not possible or practical, whence the deliberate downplaying and reduction of the entrance function to its bare minimum.[28]

'What a dump', says the professor of architecture in Jim McBride's *Breathless*, on entering the Bonaventure. 'You know Frank Lloyd Wright? This is Frank Lloyd Wrong.'

Looking at this architecture of our present, we can readily appreciate the attraction of safety, especially when expressed by elderly couples who frequent the suburban malls. Redevelopment and gentrification of downtown areas have also brought considerable benefits, not least in conserving old buildings or their shells anyway. But we should not ignore the disorientating experience of being in these places where maps of the various levels absolutely fail to function. We should also not overlook the sifting and segregating of the population that the interior architecture of post-modernism physically manifests, together with the effects on the surrounding landscape of freeways and open spaces that are shut off from, rather than linked to, the interior landscape of the city. The message of *Mall Time* is not entirely hyperbole:

> Someone in a mall will grab onto somebody else and ask them: 'What year is it? You know, I've been here for ages and I just want to know, what is it like "out there". And the response will be: 'There is no "out there" '.

The critical present

Tom Wolfe has revitalized the architectural debate, but has missed the point. It is not the excess of theory but the lack of it that is the most worrying facet of contemporary architecture. There is plenty of aesthetic analysis, but it has been corralled by Venturi's promotion of 'the limited view', which interprets modernist intervention as an imposition upon 'the people' of 'rationalist' utopian visions. There is something in this but the result has been to convert architecture into something akin to the surfaces of much post-modern architecture: a cover for the redevelopment of cities in ways that modernists barely dreamed about. Kenneth Frampton:

> The ambivalent manner in which Venturi and Scott-Brown exploit this [populist] ideology as a way of bringing us to condone the ruthless kitsch of Las Vegas, as an exemplary mask for the concealment of the brutality of our own environment, testifies to the aestheticizing intent of their thesis . . . The irony with which architects . . . have sought to transcend through wit the contradictory circumstances under which they are asked to build here seems to degenerate into total acquiescence; and the cult of 'the ugly and the ordinary' becomes indistinguishable from the environmental consequences of the market economy.
> (*Modern Architecture*, p. 291)

A more telling irony is that the difficulties facing a contemporary avant-garde derive not from restrictions placed upon architects – whether political or arising from early twentieth-century mass production – but from the sheer variety of styles which a post-industrial technology permits. There is seemingly no critical leverage available in a pluralistic environment, a theoretical conclusion which is entirely compatible with the lack of positional sense which we can experience in a large shopping mall or downtown plaza. The somewhat elitist, moralistic tone adopted by the BBC television series, *Architecture at the Crossroads*, towards, for example, the architecture of Graves and Johnson, is not, in the end, an adequate critical response, and falls prey to the persuasive populism of post-modernism without ever confronting its ambiguous politics. Aside from critics of post-modernism, there have been some responses, however, within post-modernism itself, and while these are often so recent that they do not rank with some of the architecture we have surveyed, they are worth mentioning to indicate that architecture is not completely stalled at the crossroads.

The Best Product stores designed by SITE are an attempt to do more than simply accept the cash nexus which throws up and then replaces the architecture of the strip – on a weekly basis, or so it can seem. The first of these was the Peeling Wall, Richmond, Virginia (1972), but the most astonishing is the Indeterminate Facade showroom in Houston (1974–5). It led to emergency calls to the police to report a collapsing building and comments from shoppers like 'That's just what I've always wanted to do. Kick the s––– out of one of those buildings' (Plate 23). The Best Store in Sacramento, California (1977) has a fourteen foot 'notch' cut out of one corner. Every day the wedge of bricks moves out into the parking lot and the notch becomes the entrance to an entirely conventional store. James Wines of SITE confirms that one of the sources of this 'de-architecture' is the ubiquitous Marcel Duchamp, and SITE's work is undoubtedly a careful re-thinking of the relationship between architecture and capitalism. Whether the avant-garde can function in the same way in architecture as in painting, however, is a real issue, one pinpointed by someone passing by the Indeterminate Facade and remarking that 'If they ever fixed it, it wouldn't look normal.'[29]

Tom Wolfe is wholly scornful of another development, the work of the New York Five of Peter Eisenman, Michael Graves (before his Portland Building), John Hejduk, Richard Meier, and Charles Gwathmey. They took their name from a joint publication of 1972, *Five Architects*, and sought links with modernism through a purified architectural language, evident in, for example, Eisenman's House series. House VI, Cornwall, Connecticut (1972–6) takes its lead from Le Corbusier, both in its simple white exterior of intersecting verticals and horizontals, and its light and airy interior. As in Frank Lloyd Wright's Prairie and Usonian houses, interior space is not constrained by designated room-space. The difference, as Kathleen Enz Finken remarks, is that 'because of the lack of conventionally planned rooms, inconvenient or unsettling spaces sometimes result and, indeed, the building might seem to be a house only after the fact'.[30]

The mixture of rigour and the inconsequential in Eisenman found expression in the 1988 International Symposium on Deconstruction and Architecture at the Tate Gallery in London. Eisenman figured as prominently as Jacques Derrida, the French philosopher who coined the neologism, deconstruction, and resorted to an architectural metaphor when defining its activity as turning 'against the edifice the instruments or stones available in the house'.[31] At one level, the idea of an architect who reads Derrida and designs a bedroom floor with a hole in it (House VI again), asks for the kind of response that only Tom Wolfe can provide:

> Eisenman was beautiful. He could lead any man alive into the
> Gulp in a single sentence. Eisenman was such a purist that in the
> few instances when houses he designed were built, he did not
> refer to them by the names of the owners . . . He referred to
> them by numbers . . . His confrere Hejduk referred to his houses
> by numbers for a different reason. None of them had ever been
> built'. (p. 122)

At another level, and in the context of the decline of the avant-garde, it is reasonable to argue that the projects (mostly not built) are less important than the fact that in journals, exhibitions, internecine disputes, and cross-disciplinary studies, an avant-garde is once again operational. Moreover, as in literary criticism, deconstruction is a critique of any culturally dominant position from within; in this case a consumer society that has accelerated to overtake, and therefore absorb, even the avant-garde's production of 'the new'. The calm atmosphere of consumerism in the malls is precisely the site in which deconstruction as critique, if not as alternative design, can operate.

Less esoterically, another of The Five, Richard Meier, has sought in his High Museum in Atlanta, Georgia (1980–83) to combine the purity of line of Le Corbusier and the Frank Lloyd Wright of the Guggenheim Museum, with some of the humanism that post-modernism purports to offer. Meier is also a determinedly public architect known for his museums rather than for corporate headquarters. In this connection, I should also want to defend 'high-tech' late modernism, though the main proponents are European, with the best example being Richard Rogers and Renzo Piano's inside-out Pompidou Centre, Paris (1972–7).

In domestic architecture Frank Gehry has drawn on the anti-art of Duchamp in his Gehry house, Santa Monica, California (1977–8), a reconstructed two-storey house which plays interestingly upon the old and the new house and upon the process of construction, which is revealed by the odd angles and peeled back surfaces. Gehry also revealed the house in person by giving conducted tours to irate neighbours and city officials. The Gehry house became a national and, eventually, an international talking point.

These suggest only some of the possible directions which American architecture is taking. Yet, like Tom Wolfe but for different reasons, this survey keeps coming back to the worrying figure of Philip Johnson. His free-floating, urbane, ironic viewpoint dominated the television series, *Architecture at the Crossroads*, in which he appeared as a Miesian modernist, a late-modernist, and a post-modernist, who could yet declare himself still a Miesian at heart. He also helped to organize MOMA's Deconstructive Architecture exhibition, a follow-up to the Tate exhibition. The worries are precipitated not so much by the variety of his work, since this can be applauded; indeed, projects such as the water gardens in Fort Worth or Trinity Square in Houston should be applauded. The worries stem from his easy acceptance that 'our masters are businessmen', not because this isn't true but because this is what allows him to be an artist. After insisting that we must 'differentiate between the building of cities and the design of architecture as an art', he sharply reminded the interviewer that 'I am not . . . joking. I'm very serious about my architecture'. It is quite a chilling statement.

Notes

1. Tom Wolfe, *From Bauhaus to Our House* (1982), pp. 46 and 46–7.

2. Quoted in Charles Jencks, *Modern Movements in Architecture* (Harmondsworth, 1985), p. 109.

3. Louis H. Sullivan, 'The Tall Office Building Artistically Considered', in his *Kindergarten Chats (revised 1918) and Other Writings* (New York, 1947), p. 206.

4. Louis H. Sullivan, *The Autobiography of an Idea* (New York, 1956), p. 313.

5. Carl Condit, *The Chicago School of Architecture: A History of Commercial and Public Building in the Chicago area, 1875–1925* (Chicago, 1964), p. 66.

6. Quoted in William H. Wilson, 'The Ideology, Aesthetics and Politics of the City Beautiful Movement', in *The Rise of Modern Urban Planning, 1800–1914* (1980), p. 172; Thomas Hines, *Burnham of Chicago: Architect and Planner* (Chicago, 1979), ch. 13.

7. Thorstein Veblen, *The Theory of the Leisure Class: An Economic Study of Institutions* (1970), pp. 226–7.

8. Edward Bellamy, *Looking Backward, 2000–1887* (New York, 1960), p. 43. See Arthur Lipow, *Authoritarian Socialism in America: Edward Bellamy and the Nationalist Movement* (Berkeley, 1982).

9. Montgomery Schuyler, *American Architecture and Other Writings*, edited by William H. Jordy and Ralph Coe (Cambridge, Mass., 1961), Vol. II, pp. 410–11.

10. David P. Handlin, *American Architecture* (1895), p. 188.

11. Rem Koolhaas, *Delirious New York: A Retroactive Manifesto for Manhattan* (1978), p. 142.

12. Siegfried Giedion, *Space, Time and Architecture: The Growth of a New Tradition* (Cambridge, Mass., 1967), p. 757.

13. Walter Benjamin, *Illuminations*, edited by Hannah Arendt, translated by Harry Zohn (1973), p. 242.

14. Frank Lloyd Wright, *Modern Architecture: Being the Kahn Lectures for 1930* (Princeton, NJ, 1931), p. 8.

15. Quoted in Richard Pommer, 'The Architecture of Urban Housing in the United States During the Early 1930s', *Journal of the Society of Architectural Historians*, 37 (1978), pp. 242–3.

16. Quoted in Robert Hughes, *The Shock of the New: Art and the Century of Change* (1980), p. 168.

17. Manfredo Tafuri, 'The Disenchanted Mountain: The Skyscraper and the City', in Giorgio Ciucci *et al.*, *The American City: From the Civil War to the New Deal*, translated by Barbara Luigia La Penta (1980), p. 389.

18. Kenneth Frampton, *Modern Architecture: A Critical History* (1985), p. 232.

19. Lewis Mumford, *The Highway and the City* (1963), p. 156.

20. Robert Venturi, *Complexity and Contradiction in Architecture* (New York, 1966).

21. Charles A. Jencks, *The Language of Post-Modern Architecture* (1984), p. 6.

22. Quoted in David L. Gilbert, 'The Portland Building', in *The Critical Edge: Controversy in Recent American Architecture*, edited by Tod A. Marder (Cambridge, Mass., 1985), pp. 166 and 168.

23. Quoted from *Architecture at the Crossroads: Instant Cities*. BBC Production, in conjunction with G. and J. Film and Polython, Germany, 1986.

24. Robert Venturi, Denise Scott-Brown, Steve Izenour, *Learning from Las Vegas: The Forgotten Symbolism of Architectural Form* (Cambridge, Mass., 1977), pp. 3 and 6.

25. William Irwin Thompson, *At the Edge of History: Speculations on the Transformation of Culture* (New York, 1972), pp. 11 and 12.

26. Paul Goldberger, 'A Modern Center in Detroit Sets Itself Apart from City', *New York Times*, 15 March 1977, p. 16.

27. Quoted from *Mall Time*, Hai Productions for Channel Four, 1987.

28. Fredric Jameson, 'Postmodernism, or the Cultural Logic of Late Capitalism', *New Left Review*, 146 (July–August 1984), p. 81.

29. Quoted in Michael J. Bzdak, ' "Indeterminate Facade", Best Products Showroom', in Tod Marder (see Note 22), p. 140.

30. Kathleen Enz Finken, 'House VI, Cornwall, Connecticut', in Tod Marder (see Note 22), p. 126.

31. Jacques Derrida, *Margins of Philosophy*, translated by Alan Bass (Brighton, 1982), p. 135.

Part Two
The Culture of Politics

Chapter 4
From Victorianism to Modernism

Progressivsm, Pragmatism and the Search for Order c. 1890 to 1917

Progressivism was a largely city-based political reform movement, which began in the 1890s and, effectively, ended with the First World War. Progressivism was also a broad reorientation of thought away from the chaos and the inequities of nineteenth-century laissez-faire liberalism towards modern, progressive liberalism. The new *zeitgeist* could be seen in the rationalizing of the economy, and, less visibly, in the disciplining of knowledge within new spheres of professional life: city planning, dominated by Daniel Burnham; the law, where legal realism was promoted by Justice Oliver Wendell Holmes Jr; social work, in which Jane Addams and the Settlement House Movement were pioneers; and, in university departments: sociology (Lester Ward and, in the second decade and 1920s, the Chicago School headed by Robert Park); the new history (James Harvey Robinson, Frederick Jackson Turner, and then Charles Beard); anthropology (Franz Boas); education (John Dewey); and philosophy (William James, Josiah Royce, George Santayana at Harvard and John Dewey at Chicago and then at Columbia).

The motivations of these reformers and (increasingly profes-sionalized) thinkers varied, but Robert Wiebe's characterization of Progressivism as a 'search for order' encapsulates the dislike of, and attack on, urban-industrial capitalism, with its widening divisions between agricultural and commercial interests, and between capitalists and workers.[1] The desire for order was also motivated by the reformers' anxiety about their own role in the middle of American society. Critical of big business, their concern for the working classes was mixed with concern about them should they be provoked to violence and even revolution. Committed to modernization, they sought 'to humanize the emergent industrial-capitalist order by infusing it with a measure of social responsibility, strict personal morality, and respect for cultural standards.'[2] Since this description comes from Daniel Howe's account of American Victorianism, it is clear that the modern does not simply replace the traditional in American thought and culture.

In this chapter we shall be tracing, in different spheres, this transition from Victorianism to modernism. We can begin to explain their complex inter-relationship by examining the underpinnings of Progressive, liberal reform in the quintessentially American philosophy of Pragmatism. It was Pragmatism which provided a philosophical answer to the leading Social Darwinist, sociologist William Graham Sumner, who stated that it was as pointless to intervene in the market and in society, as it was to alter the course of evolution in the natural world. Although Pragmatism originated with Charles Sanders Peirce, and John Dewey had most to do with the Progressive movement, it was William James who defined the limitations of nineteenth-century thought. In concentrating on James's *Pragmatism* (1907), however, I want to show that its 'modern' quality is double-edged. At the same time that James gives a philosophical rationale for Progressive reform and for getting ideas into a better relation with an urban-industrial society than someone like Sumner offered, James's philosophy also had an impact upon the aesthetic and cultural movement of modernism, a dimension of modernity that is far from compatible with Progressivism and its Victorian allegiances.

The 'present dilemma in philosophy' which James outlines in chapter one of *Pragmatism*, was a philosophical stand-off between Idealism and Empiricism which stymied the relating of thought to action. James accuses 'tender-minded' adherents to Idealism of failing to recognize the reality of evil because of the assumption that there is an ultimately unified universe. While, in many ways, himself continuing Emerson's brand of radical Idealism or Transcendentalism earlier in the nineteenth century, James objects that such a philosophy is practically useless in the face of contemporary urban deprivation, misery, deaths and suicides, all of which he illustrates by quoting from newspaper reports. In contrast, to this 'genteel tradition in American philosophy' (and culture), as George Santayana famously described it, was 'tough-minded' Empiricism, which received a boost with Darwin's and Herbert Spencer's theories. The 'American will', to borrow Santayana's terminology again, was so in touch with the material changes in American life that, in the hands of an advocate of extreme laissez-faire like Sumner, it became a mirror-image of the society, and so had no critical potential. It postulated a 'block universe', no less predetermined than that of Idealism, which envisions the world as the image of a single mind. At which point, James offers 'the oddly-named thing pragmatism as a philosophy that can . . . remain religious like the rationalisms, but at the same time, like the empiricisms, it can preserve the richest intimacy with facts.'[3]

It is easy to see why James so annoyed philosophers and provoked charges that Pragmatism was an anti-philosophy, peculiarly American in its anti-intellectualism. He presents Pragmatism as a *method*, rather than as a philosophy. An idea was to be measured by consequences and not by its inherent true-ness, and since this involved taking contexts into account, James encouraged a pluralist, relativist understanding of truth. God is true so long as God has useful consequences. Truth becomes a sub-species of what is good, because what matters to James is the practical difference it makes in conducting oneself in the world:

> There can *be* no difference anywhere that doesn't *make* a
> difference elsewhere – no difference in abstract truth that doesn't
> express itself in a difference in concrete fact and in conduct
> consequent upon that fact, imposed on somebody, somehow,
> somewhere, and somewhen. (*Pragmatism*, p. 45)

Making a difference means communicating, and getting oneself going when the prevailing atmosphere is one of quiescence, whether endorsed by Darwinian determinism or outmoded Transcendental Idealism. We see the Pragmatic influence in, for example, Jane Addams's decision to leave Rockford Seminary and, later, to establish the Hull-House settlement in Chicago. Abstract religion had no meaning for her until it came into relationship with the complexity of social existence in Chicago in the 1880s. Applied to the city, a Pragmatic, experimental philosophy saw possibilities for change which did not involve looking backward to the agrarian past unless, that is, those older truths were of use in dealing with the anomie of urban life.

In *Pragmatism*, James summarizes his *provisional* understanding of truth:

> If you follow the pragmatic method, you cannot look on any . . .
> word ['God,' 'Matter,' 'Reason,' 'the Absolute,' 'Energy'] as
> closing your quest. You must bring out of each word its practical
> cash-value, set it at work within the stream of your experience. It
> appears less as a solution, then, than as a program for more
> work, and more particularly as an indication of the ways in
> which existing realities may be *changed*.
> *Theories thus become instruments, not answers to enigmas, in which
> we can rest.* (p. 46)

Admittedly, in less honest hands, Pragmatism could lean too far towards context, so that talk of 'the cash-value' of an idea assumed a literal meaning in a materialistic society. Nevertheless, what James (and Dewey) undoubtedly achieved, was a philosophy of action, a redefinition of nineteenth-century Emersonian Idealism. Without action, freedom could become solipsistic and practically useless – at a time when material changes threatened to dwarf individuals.

Before following William James and Pragmatism out of Progress-ivism and into the modernism of the immediate pre-First World War years, we should take the opportunity James gives us to pick up a broadly religious line of thinking, which needs to be related to the growing secularization of American society. As Alexis de Tocqueville recognized in the 1830s, America is at once the most secular and religious of countries. At first, James's *The Varieties of Religious Experience* (1902) appears an eccentric book, certainly in the context of Pragmatism, with its explicit orientation to the material world and its links with Progressive reform. However, we ought not to overlook the important connections between James and mid-nineteenth-century Transcendentalism, coming by way of his father, Henry James Sr, a friend of Emerson and Thoreau and a convinced Swedenborgian philosopher. These connections kept philosophy personal; it was John Dewey, James's philosophical successor, who developed the institu-tional side of Pragmatism and incurred the sharp criticism of neo-orthodox theologian Reinhold Niebuhr (see pp. 229–31 below).

The specific dilemma in philosophy which James addresses at the beginning of *Pragmatism* was part of a broader 'dilemma of deter-minism', as James referred to the post-Darwinian controversy between science and religion. In *The Will to Believe* (1897), James argues that no deterministic model – whether spiritual or materialist – can remove elements of indeterminacy or chance. 'There is no possible point of view from which the world can appear an absolutely single fact', he announces in the Preface, adding, in a later chapter, that:

> Indeterminism [or chance, as he also calls it] . . . says that the parts [of the universe] have a certain amount of loose play on one another, so that the laying down of one of them does not necessarily determine what the others shall be. It admits that possibilities may be in excess of actualities, and that things not yet revealed to our knowledge may really in themselves be ambiguous.[4]

In *The Will to Believe* James ranges through other examples, the most emphatic being in the chapter, 'Great Men and their Environment', to conclude that the universe is open and that what matters is the action of the *will*. The non-technical sources of this argument date from James's nervous breakdown in 1869–70 when, in his late twenties, he seriously thought of suicide. It was, so he reports, a conscious decision to change his life which took him out of that crisis. 'My first act of free will shall be to believe in free will', he wrote in a letter of April, 1870.[5] The 'will to believe' became a powerful motor for action, especially when allied to the concept of experience and to the Pragmatist tenet of effects. Religious experience had to be taken as seriously as any other experience.

The Varieties of Religious Experience is possibly the most famous of all American books on religion, not least because James once stated that 'I can't possibly pray – I feel foolish and artificial', and, when asked whether he had ever felt God's presence, answered 'Never' (*Letters*, vol. 2, pp. 214–15). Consistent with his pluralistic outlook, however, James attends carefully to the confessions of St Augustine, to instances of despair and conversion among literary figures, and to a series of (much more interesting) psychological cases, many concerning women. James's Pragmatism intersects with his interest in religion in his insistence upon attending to the consequences of religious belief, rather than its physical, psychological, social, and ontological aspects. If there were consequences (rather than merely results), then the religious belief had existence. Moreover, it could then be argued that believing and acting shaped reality.

Here it may be objected that James simply dodges the question of whether God exists but, at the time he was writing – a materialist age in both the popular and philosophical senses of the word – it may be sufficient that he succeeded in making religious questions worth pursuing once again. A further objection – but one which at least has a subsequent history to it – is that James stands, somewhat unfairly, near the beginning of a therapeutic tradition in American thought and culture.[6] In concentrating upon the effects of religion, including, of course, effects upon the believer, James paves the way for the mind-cure philosophy of Mary Baker Eddy, Bruce Barton, Dale Carnegie, Norman Vincent Peale and others. It is no coincidence that enormously popular books such as Carnegie's *How to Win Friends and Influence People* (1936) and Peale's *The Power of Positive Thinking* (1952), with their emphasis not on Calvinist salvation and damnation, or even on the reality of God, but on healthy-mindedness and positive thinking, took over from the more secular success manuals of the nineteenth century. Both kinds of success are motivated by a 'what works' philosophy which, ironically, must be counted a consequence of Pragmatism, even though it is a travesty of James's intentions. Though George Santayana was a colleague at Harvard and an admirer of James, he had reservations and even slipped into parodying James's religious modernism:

All faiths were what they were experienced as being, in their capacity as faiths; these faiths, not their objects, were the hard facts we must respect. We cannot pass, except under the illusion of the moment, to anything firmer or on a deeper level. There was accordingly no sense of security, no joy, in James's apology for personal religion. He did not really believe; he merely believed in the right of believing that you might be right if you believed.'[7]

In common with many American thinkers, from Benjamin Franklin onwards, who have sought to engage with contemporary life, James taught worse than he knew. Looked at closely, the key chapters in *Varieties* on 'the religion of healthy-mindedness' and 'the sick soul' are much more complex and circumspect than they appear. Briefly, James concludes that the sick souls know more of reality because they have confronted evil. Thus, he faults Walt Whitman, whom he otherwise admired, because Whitman refused to acknowledge 'the sad mortality of this sunlit world'.[8] The superficialities of healthy-mindedness, which James found much in evidence in American culture, may well be the real sickness. In his excellent book, *The Positive Thinkers*, Donald Meyer puts James in more appropriate company, and also anticipates the next phase in American thought:

> James's orientation was remarkably similar to Nietzsche's conception of health as the capacity to withstand disease . . . Most of all [though] he resembled Freud . . . Neither James nor Freud sought to guarantee that the world and society and people would provide immediate gratification, but both rejected the alternative of rejecting them. The sure sign of sickness was denial – of disease, evil, conflict, disharmony, of trying out new life. (p. 300)

The first years of our time: the pre-war intellectual rebellion, 1908 to 1917

A Progressive/Pragmatist alliance remained influential in American thought up to 1917 and then resurfaced in the 1930s, transmuted into New Deal welfare liberalism. Yet even as James's *Pragmatism* was published, a challenge to its account of modernity was germinating. Interestingly, this intellectual rebellion counted William James himself as a mentor, even as it looked back to Tom Paine, Emerson, Whitman, and Thoreau, before finding, in the critic Randolph Bourne, a contemporary voice.

The pre-war intellectual rebellion, which Randolph Bourne symbolizes in so many ways, was contemporary with Progressivism so we cannot easily talk of breaks or even transitions. However, we can identify changes of emphasis and tone in some representative younger intellectuals. For example, in *The Promise of American Life* (1909) and in some essays published a little earlier in *Architectural Record*, Herbert Croly insists on a double focus: 'What the United States needs is a nationalization of their intellectual life comparable to the nationalizing, now under way, of their industry and politics.' Similarly, Walter Lippmann, who was a co-editor with Croly on *The New Republic*, draws on Progressive-Pragmatist ideas but goes beyond Croly in stressing the importance of creativity: 'The goal of action is in its final analysis aesthetic and not moral – a quality of feeling instead of conformity to rule.'[9]

To Croly, Lippmann and Bourne's slightly younger generation, the Progressives were overly tied to their society through their professional affiliations and to existing political machinery, to the point that their ideals could be compromised. Though a Progressive reformer like Jane Addams addressed the problems of modernization, and more practically than any of the new generation of critics, she was not particularly interested in a *cultural* revolution that would affect male-female, class, race, and generational relations. However modern Progressives were in some respects, they did not embrace this kind of diversity. Their aim was to bring marginal or exploited groups into the middle-class WASP world through such literal half-way houses as the Hull House settlement in Chicago. Culturally, then, Progressivism was still pervaded by Victorianism, defined by Henry May in terms of 'three central doctrines . . . first, the certainty and universality of moral values; second, the inevitability, particularly in America, of progress; and third, the importance of traditional literary culture.'[10]

In *A Preface to Politics* (1913), Lippmann is drawn to William James's emphasis upon experience and openness rather than to the well-known Pragmatic method. He mixes James in with Freud's discovery that beneath rationality were more fundamental drives; with Nietzsche on the importance of the will; and with Henri Bergson's *élan vital*. These thinkers testify to the inroads being made by modernist thought and, in Randolph Bourne's phrase, they signal 'the twilight of idols', meaning the intellectual amalgam of Progressivism and Pragmatism. There is, it should be stated, no clear-cut division between Lippmann's Progressivism and his modernism, and indeed in *Drift and Mastery*, published only a year after *A Preface to Politics*, Lippmann seems less enamoured with European modernism. The preferred route to modernity is through Dewey and his more 'instrumental' variety of Pragmatism.

How, then, could Jamesian Pragmatism undermine the 'modern', socially-conscious Progressive/Pragmatist amalgam which it helped to forge, and do so in the name of modernism? Undoubtedly, James makes a lot of the practical side of Pragmatism and its directing of intelligence towards useful action. In doing so, however, he particularly stresses experience, movement and experiment. Ideas are never absolute in Pragmatism, but are constantly in flux. In a famous chapter in his *Principles of Psychology* (1890), entitled 'The Stream of Thought', James anticipates the attempts by modernist novelists to represent consciousness. James maintains that 'within each personal consciousness thought is sensibly continuous' in spite of periods of sleep and violent external interruptions. In linguistic terms, James points out that nouns and adjectives are not the only names for the contents of experience. Prepositions and conjunctions are also required: 'The relations that connect experiences must themselves be experienced relations, and any kind of relation experienced must be accounted as "real" as anything else in the system.' We ought to recognize 'a feeling of "and", and a feeling of "if", a feeling of "but" and a feeling of "by" quite as readily as . . . a feeling of "blue" or a feeling of "cold".' In his enthusiasm to dissolve entitative differences into relational ones, James occasionally overstates his case. When he claimed that 'the "I think" which Kant said must be able to accompany all my objects' is less important than the '"I breathe" which actually does accompany them"', Charles Peirce retorted that he, at least, always held his breath when thinking.[11] But James was in tune with the times and, in filtering the ideas of Bergson into American thought, he spread the idea that reality is always changing and can only be apprehended by immersing oneself in it. The primacy accorded experiential subjectivity and what Bergson called vitalism, worked against the Progressives' confidence in reason, organization, planning, and efficiency.

Croly, Lippmann, Bourne and their generation came from middle-class backgrounds and had been intellectually brought up on Progressive politics and Pragmatist ideas. Yet they took American thought in different directions. Generically, the reaction against Progressivism, or, rather, the reaction from within it, produced what I shall be calling 'criticism', a style of intellectual activity which distinguished radical intellectuals from what was going on in the more sober tradition of social thought and in the professions. The new radicals were in a continual ferment of ideas, positions and programmes which consistently found expression in literary and broadly cultural concerns. It is a reasonable generalization to say that a lot of twentieth-century American intellectual history follows the pattern of this pre-war rebellion. Little magazines, particularly in New York, were at the heart of what was going on, and their format and frequency permitted a sharp response to the events which punctuated the seemingly inexorable process of modernization up to the mid-1930s: the First World War, the Bolshevik Revolution of 1917, the Stock Market Crash of 1929 and the massive Depression which followed, and the revelations about Stalinism during the 1930s. If, with the exception of James and Dewey, there are few major thinkers discussed in this chapter and the next, the compensation is in the level of engagement with events and contemporary preoccupations, and in the excitement generated by intellectuals thinking on their feet.

These 'pre-war rebels' or 'critics of culture' were self-conscious intellectuals, people (in Christopher Lasch's definition) 'for whom thinking fulfills at once the function of work and play [and] . . . whose relationship to society is defined . . . principally by [their] presumed capacity to comment upon it with greater detachment than those more directly caught up in the practical business of production and power'.[12] Aside from the degree of self-consciousness, the new radicals typically worked in bohemia (ideally, Greenwich Village) and not in university or government departments or settlement houses. And they wrote for 'little magazines', rather than professional journals.

The pre-war years were an in-between time: after Victorian culture's heyday and yet, in America at least, before modernism had set in. In such periods ('the first years of our time', as Henry May calls them), when old idols are being eclipsed but no one can predict the new canon, intellectual activity is likely to be quick-fire, even frenetic, rather than measured. And it is true that these years were extra-ordinarily varied in their output, with new excursions in political journalism, criticism of literature, painting, architecture, music and the new arts of photography and cinema. The shifting population of Mabel Dodge's salon on Fifth Avenue indicates the range of activity:

> Socialists, Trade-Unionists, Anarchists, Suffragists, Poets, Relations, Lawyers, Murderers, 'Old Friends', Psychoanalysts, I.W.W.'s, Single Taxers, Birth Controllists, Newspapermen, Artists, Modern-Artists, Club-women, Women's-Place-is-in-the-Home-Women, Clergymen, and just plain men all met there and, stammering in an unaccustomed freedom a kind of speech called Free, exchanged a variousness of vocabulary called, in euphemistic optimism, Opinions![13]

We can make some sense of the bewildering mixture of visitors to Mabel Dodge's salon by talking about two main groups. The first group consisted of Randolph Bourne, Van Wyck Brooks, Waldo Frank, James Oppenheimer, and Paul Rosenfeld, critics whose main interests were with the arts and with what Brooks called, in the title of a 1915 book, *America's Coming of Age*. They were also all on the editorial board of the short-lived magazine *The Seven Arts*. A second magazine, *The Masses*, attracted Crystal Eastman, Max Eastman, Emma Goldman, Floyd Dell, John Reed, Joan Sloan, and Art Young, all of whom had declared socialist or anarchist politics. Lippmann, Croly and Walter Weyl's *New Republic* will concern us only indirectly. When Croly refers in *The Promise of American Life* to ideas as 'weapons', he anticipates the return of the applied intelligence of Pragmatism during debates over entry into the First World War. With Lippmann's socialism being very much an early phase of his thinking, *The New Republic* became the liberal wing of Progressivism rather part of the cultural reaction against it. After the initial attention given by the magazine to the hoped-for renaissance in American culture, this theme declined in importance in its pages.[14]

The range of visitors at Mabel Dodge's was greater than at Alfred Stieglitz's 291, but both were meeting-places, part of the institutional structure of bohemia, places where intellectual collisions could occur in the midst of a city. Meeting-places of this kind had barely existed ten years earlier. In *The Spirit of the Ghetto* (1902), Hutchins Hapgood, who bridged the gap between the generations at Mabel Dodge's, had only encountered this cultural infrastructure when he had visited the cafes of the Jewish Lower East Side in New York City. As immigrants from mostly urban areas in Eastern Europe, transplanted intellectual Jews set a pattern of cosmopolitan life that the young intellectuals later emulated, and which Randolph Bourne expressed:

> Who can walk the lighted streets of a city at night and watch the flowing crowds, the shining youthful faces, the eager exhilaration of the sauntering life, or who can see the surge of humanity on a holiday or a Sunday, without feeling the strange power of this mass-life? This mysterious power of the city which sucks out the life of the countryside, which welds individuals into a co-operative life, is not this the basal force of the age, and does it not suggest the stirrings of a new civilization, socialized and purified? In this garish, vulgar, primitive flow of Broadway, are not new gods being born?[15]

As well as drawing upon city life (*not* the business districts), the pre-war intellectuals looked to European modernism for allies in the fight against repressive puritanism, the philistinism of middle-class life, and the commercial ethics that had to do with both, but had been fostered by a frontier history. Yet, like Alfred Stieglitz at 291, and unlike the expatriates of the 1920s, the new radicals were in search of a home-grown, rather than imported, American culture. A national cultural 'coming of age' would, they hoped, heal the split, described by

William James as between the tender- and tough-minded, by George Santayana as between the American intellect and the American will, and, by Van Wyck Brooks in equally well-known terms:

> What side of American life is not touched by this antithesis [between the 'highbrow' and the 'lowbrow']? What explanation of American life is more central or more illuminating? In everything one finds this frank acceptance of twin values which are not expected to have anything in common: on the one hand, a quite unclouded, quite unhypocritical assumption of transcendent theory ('high ideals'), on the other a simultaneous acceptance of catchpenny realities.[16]

In *America's Coming of Age*, Brooks sought to recreate a 'usable past', an American cultural tradition that would anchor the present and, hopefully, resolve the division between 'high' and 'low'. Ironically, though, his important redisovery of Poe, Hawthorne, Melville, and the Transcendentalists revealed that they were, themselves, starved of a sustaining social context. This was hardly a usable past. A more serious flaw in Brooks's enquiry into an American culture poised on the verge of full-blown modernity, is suggested by the contrast between his optimistic title, which was echoed by James Oppenheimer's editorial to the first issue of *The Seven Arts* in 1916, and his account of an apparently culturally impoverished present. Contemporary developments in poetry (Imagism, the beginnings of William Carlos Williams' work, the Others Group in New York City); in fiction (Theodore Dreiser, Kate Chopin, Abraham Cahan, Willa Cather); and in painting, photography, architecture, music, and film, which, arguably, did herald America's 'coming of age', all go largely unmentioned.

In particular, among these new developments, Brooks misses the opportunity to reinterpret positively the fragmentation of nineteenth-century American culture then underway in the work of regional, ethnic, and feminist writers, artists and thinkers. Instead, in the manner of Matthew Arnold, Brooks looks for a unified culture based upon a national myth. Henry James, for all his cultural snobbishness and self-imposed exile in Europe, at least caught a glimmer of what was going on when he visited New York City in 1904. In *The American Scene* (1907), James tells of going to a Jewish theatre on the Lower East Side, and though his precious reaction to the noises and smells exposes his own prejudices, he was acutely aware that all the cultural life was in the audience. On the stage all that was worst in genteel culture was paraded. This was the same Lower East Side Jewish ghetto where the journalist and novelist Abraham Cahan was working for the *Jewish Daily Forward*, one of the most important of the local cultural institutions that had grown up in the ghetto to support Yiddish religion, theatre, music and politics. Cahan's *Yekl* (1896) and *The Rise of David Levinsky* (1917) are the forerunners of the Jewish-American tradition of Henry Roth, Saul Bellow, Bernard Malamud, Philip Roth and many more.[17]

Similarly, Brooks has nothing to say about black culture. By the mid-1920s, Brooks's trawl of modern American culture had still only brought in Henry James and Mark Twain, and, as he wrote on into the 1950s he continued to ignore black poetry and fiction, from the Harlem Renaissance writers – Countee Cullen, Claude McKay, Langston Hughes, Jean Toomer, and Zora Neale Hurston – through to Richard Wright in the 1940s. Carl Van Vechten, Emilie Hapgood and others who frequented Mabel Dodge's salon were more interested in black culture but tended to idealize what they took to be its 'primitive' quality as an antidote to modernization. There was never any question of a parallel relationship between the American modernism based in Paris or Greenwich Village and in Harlem.

Twilight of idols: Randolph Bourne

Randolph Bourne has taken a long time to recover from his own legend. It took off from his deformed appearance and his death of pneumonia at the age of thirty-two in 1918, and found an early expression in one of the vignettes in John Dos Passos' novel, *Nineteen Nineteen* (1932), published as part of *U.S.A.* in 1938:

> If any man has a ghost
> Bourne has a ghost,
> a tiny twisted unscared ghost in a black cloak
> hopping along the grimy old brick and brownstone streets still
> left in downtown New York,
> crying out in a shrill soundless giggle:
> *War is the health of the state.*[18]

Important though this image of alienated youth has become in American radicalism, Bourne deserves to be known for his perceptive grasp of the relationship between culture and politics. At a time when modernization had fragmented Victorian culture and was replacing it with mass culture, Bourne, more than any other American critic, went after general, even theoretical interpretations of modernity. He did so, however, while reflecting the diversity of American life in essays on town planning, education, literature, photography, politics, and current events, notably the First World War.

Writing about immigrants in 'Trans-National America' (1916), Bourne sounds like Van Wyck Brooks and other critics of mass culture:

> Letting slip from them whatever native culture they had, they have substituted for it only the most rudimentary American – the American culture of the cheap newspaper, the 'movies,' the popular song, the ubiquitous automobile. The unthinking who survey this class call them assimilated, Americanized. (*The Radical Will*, p. 254)

Bourne, however, acknowledges the importance of the immigrants' own culture, and warns against the washing out at the periphery of 'self-conscious cultural nuclei', which possess their own schools, vernacular literature, and presses.

Bourne's objection is not cultural in the narrow sense. The perhaps surprising context for his anti-melting pot and pro-cultural pluralism thesis is the controversy over American entry into the First World War. The outbreak of war in Europe in 1914, Bourne notes, gives the lie to assimilation by bringing to the surface existing but subdued national and cultural sentiments. Far from signalling the failure of American democracy, this divisiveness ought to have stimulated an enquiry into 'what Americanism may rightly mean'. That it did not had to do with the cultural power exerted by a dominant political and economic elite, 'a ruling class, descendant of those British stocks which were the first permanent immigrants' (pp. 248 and 249). He had first come across this group during his visit to Britain in 1913, but it took the war to make him aware of its authority.

In the period between 1914 and 1917, American neutrality was being tried by a sequence of diplomatic and naval manoeuvres by Britain and Germany and by dramatic events, for example the sinking of the Lusitania in 1914 with 128 Americans among the 1200 drowned. In 1917 Bourne directly entered the debate over the United States's position in two articles published in *The Seven Arts* in 1917: 'Twilight of Idols' and 'The War and the Intellectuals'. In comparison with the great events occurring on an international stage, a debate about culture and politics in a short-lived Greenwich Village magazine may appear unimportant. It is often the case, though, that in a major crisis the ideas that finally matter get aired only on the margins. Bourne's work, I want to argue, establishes the central concerns of American intellectuals right through to the 1980s.

Bourne was replying to a number of articles by John Dewey which signal a move away from Dewey's own touchstone of the intelligent and peaceful resolution of any dilemma. In accepting the necessity for American intervention in the war, Dewey argues that intelligence and force could be reconciled under certain conditions. Where violence was wasteful, force, understood as energy, could be directed towards certain ends, at which point the Pragmatic test of truth according to its outcome could be applied. Many of Bourne's contemporaries agreed with Dewey. *The New Republic*, with Croly, Lippmann and Walter Weyl at its head, moved from supporting neutrality at the beginning of 1916 to an interventionist position later that year, and this confirmed Bourne in his apparently exaggerated conclusion that this was 'a war made deliberately by the intellectuals!'. He continues:

> An intellectual class, gently guiding a nation through sheer force of ideas into what the other nations entered only through predatory craft or popular hysteria or militarist madness! A war [here Bourne paraphrases President Wilson – *the* intellectual among American presidents] free from any taint of self-seeking, a war that will secure the triumph of democracy and internationalize the world! (p. 307)

Bourne charges intellectuals with playing a strategic role in changing public opinion, which had been typically isolationist. However, the succession of exclamation marks in Bourne's accusation reflects his anger and amazement at the nature of the argument for intervention advanced by Dewey and *The New Republic*, and what it revealed about the role of the intellectuals and their aspiration to move nearer the centre of power and influence. Bourne seizes on the irony that these intellectuals who, as Progressive reformers or as the students of Dewey, opposed big business and 'the richer and older classes of the Atlantic seaboard' and 'those upper-class elements in each section [of the country] who identified themselves with this Eastern ruling group', should be siding with them in promoting the war. (p. 308)

Bourne's insight into how intellectuals, and with them much American thought and culture, had been 'conscripted' by the banker class, is the broader context for his objection to the assimilation of immigrant cultures in the domestic arena. He recognizes, in 'Trans-National America', that the issue is a subtle exertion of power:

> If freedom means a democratic cooperation in determining the ideals and purposes and industrial and social institutions of a country, then the immigrant has not been free, and the Anglo-Saxon element is guilty of just what every dominant race is guilty of in every European country: the imposition of its own culture upon the minority peoples. The fact that this imposition has been so mild, and, indeed, semi-conscious does not alter its quality. (p. 252)

During a war, Bourne argues, the usual emergency measures solidify the different classes, ethnic groups, and sections. Hence his biting aphorism '*War is the health of the State*' (p. 360).

Bourne's criticism of the intellectuals goes beyond their ethno-centrism. His attack on the philosophical rationale of the 'war intellectuals' decisively marks his era off from the Pragmatist-Progressive one. The argument for intervention was that if they remained on the sidelines, intellectuals had no hope of influencing either the course of the war as sources of expert advice, or the kind of society that would emerge from the war – hopefully one in which some of the controlling power of the State over a market economy would be retained. However, Bourne retorts, their Pragmatism serves them badly. There was something about the all-enveloping quality of war – 'the sewage of the war spirit' – that skewed the Pragmatic equation of the value of an idea with its results. Pragmatism may work in peacetime, when reform of the city or the trusts was on the agenda, but, Bourne points out, war was different because it co-opted thought, turned it into propaganda. Bourne was proved correct. The justifica-tion for some of the *New Republic* intellectuals' support for Woodrow Wilson's claim that the war would 'make the world safe for democracy' grew skaky after the Treaty of Versailles. There was also no evidence that the Progressive ideal of a planned economy would have any staying power after the war.

Pragmatism's commitment to action rather than abstract thought turned into an emotional release for intellectuals who, Bourne argues, could not stand the 'suspense' of 'the knots of thought'. Once again Bourne unpicks the logic of the intellectuals: if the war was too powerful to resist – too real – then how can it be controlled from within? Pragmatism's emphasis upon means rather than ultimate ends could easily be turned towards technical efficiency by the will to power unleashed by the war. Bourne does not underestimate the pressures to conform but he insists that if intellectuals do not ask the difficult questions at such a time, then, who will in the reversion to primitive instincts in the face of a war? 'Criticism flagged and emotional *propaganda* began' (p. 314), he observes.

For Bourne, then, the war had a cultural significance with ramifications in communities far beyond Washington and New York. It was also a philosophical crisis for Pragmatism, to which American thought was wedded. And, finally, it threw down a challenge to the new-found role of the American intellectual as a critic, the answers to which shaped much of subsequent American intellectual history. Specifically, the war took the radicalism out of Pragmatism and sent intellectuals after other forms of adversarial radicalism, akin to that exemplified by Tom Paine and Henry David Thoreau. As Bourne remarks in 'Twilight of Idols': 'One has a sense of having come to a sudden, short stop at the end of an intellectual era' (p. 242).

Bourne's criticism of the war intellectuals is that they had stopped actively thinking. In response, he advocates a strategy rather than a position:

> The deadliest way to annihilate the unoriginal and the insincere is to let it speak for itself. Irony is this letting things speak for themselves and hang themselves by their own rope. Only, it repeats the words after the speaker, and adjusts the rope. (p. 138)

Irony is not a superior, safe and personal point of view. 'If the ironist is destructive, it is his own world that he is destroying; if he is critical, it is his own world that he is criticizing. And his irony is his critique of life.' This defence of 'the life of irony' is against the charge that it is 'a purely aesthetic attitude towards life'. 'The ironist', Bourne insists, 'is ironical not because he does not care, but because he cares too much' (p. 143).

Against a background of the decline of American working-class movements in the wake of the First World War, Bourne's interest in intellectuals as critics ('malcontents') and as ironists, together with his insights into culture as power exerted by an economic elite, can be seen as anticipating a search on the Left for a different perspective on capitalism. Bourne concludes that intellectuals could take a lead, provided they remained involved with American life but acutely aware of the question of power and how the search for it could disarm criticism. On the other hand, this involvement should not simply be with America's arts, as Van Wyck Brooks, Robert Frost and other members of *The Seven Arts* board decided it should be when Bourne's war essays were published and caused a withdrawal of financial backing. For Frost:

> The Arts are but Six!
> You add Politics
> And the Seven will die a-Bourneing[19]

Bourne's is an inside/outside position that could not accept the latent tendencies of *The New Republic* (pragmatic liberalism), *The Seven Arts* (a nationalist aesthetics rather than the cultural studies approach that Bourne pioneered), and, as we shall see, of the *Masses* (faith in the revolutionary potential of the proletariat). From his uncomfortable position, he speculates upon what his contemporaries ought to have been doing between 1914 and 1917: in an international sphere, using the power of neutrality and the unrecognized 'privilege of [their] cosmopolitan outlook such as no other nation of today in Europe can possibly secure'. American intellectuals should raise issues of dual citizenship, and examine America as a model not of 'a nationality but a trans-nationality'. Where Van Wyck Brooks's optimism for an American renaissance was based upon a unified culture, Bourne's hopes lay in a dynamic version of cultural pluralism.

A revolutionary and not a reform magazine: the *Masses*, 1912 to 1918

In 1911 the *Masses* was founded by Piet Vlag, a socialist interested in the co-operative movement. In 1912, though, it was revitalized and a 1913 editorial announced it was to be 'A REVOLUTIONARY AND NOT A REFORM MAGAZINE'. Max Eastman became editor and Floyd Dell associate editor. In a list of very talented contributors, John Reed, Mike Gold, Amy Lowell, Sherwood Anderson, William Carlos Williams, Stuart Davis, George Bellows, John Sloan, Art Young, and Mary Heaton Vorse stand out; so does the range of subjects covered: suffragism, socialism, syndicalism, anarchism, free love, and birth control.

1912 was also renowned for Eugene Debs polling almost a million votes as the Socialist candidate for the presidency, while over a thousand socialists held public office from Berkeley to Schenectady. More dramatically, 1912 was the year when the International Workers of the World (the IWW or the 'Wobblies') led the Lawrence, Massachusetts strike of textile workers.

The *Masses* was drawn to the romantic activism and violence of the syndicalist socialism of the Wobblies rather than to the American Socialist Party and electoral politics. There was no place in the Socialist Party's philosophy of economic determinism for the broad cultural perspective offered by the new radicals, or indeed, as the Party's leader, Daniel DeLeon made very plain, for intellectuals. When 'Big Bill' Haywood, the Wobblies' leader, forcefully reminded intellectuals that their privileges depended upon the steelworker in Pittsburgh, he did so in Mabel Dodge's salon and through the *Masses*. Eastman claimed of the *Masses*, that it 'provided for the first time in America, a meeting ground for revolutionary labor and the radical intelligentsia'.[20] The IWW and the young intellectuals – beyond just those who wrote for the *Masses* – came into contact during the Lawrence Strike, and then in 1913, at Paterson, New Jersey. In support of the latter strike, and under a giant red IWW rooftop sign, John Reed produced a pageant in Madison Square Garden which re-enacted the silkworkers' strike, using the workers and Haywood and Elizabeth Gurley Flynn of the IWW as actors. The coincidence in 1913 in New York City of the pageant and the Armory Show also gives some idea of the new mood of excitement and innovation.

The IWW recreated the older tradition of the restless individual: Emerson's 'endless seeker with no past at my back', but armed with a political commitment. The hobo, as in the songs of Joe Hill for example, and the socialist artist and journalist were the culture heroes of the *Masses*. The contemporary hero was John Reed, who had reported on the Mexican Revolution, been arrested at the Paterson Strike, and, in 1917 went to witness the Bolshevik Revolution. Reed was the most involved of the *Masses* radicals but 'direct action' politics, in Haywood's phrase, chimed broadly with the commitment of other pre-war intellectuals to the openness of experience. It was the experimentalism of the Marxian dialectic rather than its iron-clad truth which attracted Eastman, Dell and Reed. Only Eastman did any serious writing about Marx, however.

One of the *Masses*'s recurring themes was feminism, as is apparent in the art work, which contrasted sharply with the images of the flapper, the Gibson Girl, and the modern housewife which dominated the glossy magazines of the time. For example, the *Masses* in May 1915 contained a drawing by John Sloan of the dancer, Isadora Duncan, who symbolized a rejection of bourgeois repressiveness in the name of artistic and political freedom. In November of that year, the *Masses* brought out a special 'Woman's Citizenship Number' with a cover drawing by Stuart Davis depicting a woman standing up in a subway train, presumably on her way to work. Art Young's cartoons often took the theme of prostitution, juxtaposing prostitutes with disapproving and cruel 'respectable' women, or connecting prostitution with capitalism. 'Defeated', a cartoon in the May 1913 issue, depicts a prostitute driven to suicide by her particular experience of the marketplace.

The 1910s and early 1920s, at least, were an important phase in the women's movement, but the feminism that thrived in Greenwich Village was noteworthy precisely because it did not focus primarily on the vote, though New York City was the location for much of the campaigning that eventually brought women the vote in 1920. The anarchist writer, Emma Goldman, was so antagonistic to American democracy that she opposed woman's suffrage on the grounds that it was a distraction and, if achieved, would be yet another way of binding women into democratic capitalism. Birth control was a more compelling issue than the vote because it gave women more control over their bodies. The *Masses* supported Margaret Sanger, the leading figure in the campaign to educate the public about birth control and a visitor to Mabel Dodge's salon.

For all their consistent commitment to feminist causes, Floyd Dell, Max Eastman, and other male contributors to the *Masses* tended to use issues like prostitution and birth control to symbolize their attack on capitalism and the genteel tradition which, they realized, was its cultural accompaniment. The iconoclastic journalist H.L. Mencken illustrates a double-standard shared by the leading male feminists of the Village. In *In Defense of Women* (1918) Mencken rejected puritanical stereotypes – a theme common to most of his writing – but was patently nervous about feminists, and especially about their claims for economic equality and for independence once married. A generous estimate of the male feminists of the 1910s and 1920s is that they failed to see the specificity of feminist arguments and, implicitly, incorporated feminism into socialism and a bohemian reaction against Victorian society.

The significance of the *Masses*, along with that of *The Seven Arts* and the IWW, was confirmed when it was suppressed as a dissenting voice in the national crisis of war. Outlets through newstands and stores, and through the post, were blocked under the 1917 Espionage and Sedition Act. Eastman, Reed, Dell, Young and three other staff members were tried for conspiracy, though eventually acquitted. However, their denunciation of the war as a capitalist war was rejected by William English Walling and the artists, Sloan and Bellows. The *Masses'* argument became further confused, in a way that Bourne's did not, when Germany threatened the recent Revolution in Russia to which the magazine was so committed.

The *Masses* revolved around too imprecise an alliance of philosophies to prevent splits and defections, often over the role of art, but between 1912 and 1918 it did create the conditions in which cultural and political activities could be interwoven in the cause of consciousness-raising.

Exile's return: the post-war intellectual rebellion

Entry into the First World War curtailed the cultural and political renaissance, and the settlement at Versailles confirmed the intellectuals' disillusion. Among those who had supported intervention, Walter Lippmann spoke out against the Treaty. At home, the 'Red Scare' and the Palmer Raids of 1919–22 were the extreme manifestation of public hostility towards radicals when the mood was for 'normalcy', meaning business. At the peak of the raids in January 1920, more than 6000 people were arrested. Robert La Follette's defeat at the 1924 election indicated the odds stacked against even Progressive, let alone socialist, reform politics. Socialist and Communist Party membership fell away throughout the 1920s. Feminism as a radical critique of the basis of society virtually disappeared after 1920 and the 19th Amendment to the Constitution, which gave the vote, but not much else, to women. America also proved how inhospitable it was to ideas during the revival of religious fundamentalism, which had its high points in the meetings of Aimee Semple McPherson, and in the Scopes Trial in Dayton, Tennessee in 1925 when a local schoolteacher was put on trial for teaching Darwinism. H.L. Mencken had a point when he generalized: 'Heave an egg out of a Pullman and you will hit a fundamentalist almost anywhere in the United States.'

One group of slightly older intellectuals, including George Santayana (an expatriate European), Van Wyck Brooks, H.L. Mencken, and Lewis Mumford responded to the crassness of American society in Harold Stearns's 1922 collection of essays with the ironic title, *Civilization in the United States*. A younger group, including Stearns himself, expatriated themselves on the Left bank in Paris. In *Exile's Return: A Literary Odyssey of the 1920s* (1934; revised 1951), Malcolm Cowley tells the story of this 'lost generation': Ernest Hemingway, John Dos Passos, Hart Crane, e.e. cummings, and, from the earlier group of expatriates, T.S. Eliot and Ezra Pound. They were in sharp reaction to the cultural and political wasteland of America, and opted, instead, for devotion to art. Nothing could be done about society, but good sentences could at least be written.

Exile's Return is an unusual book. Written by a critic and writer who was part of the expatriate/modernist movement in American literature, it is a first-hand literary history which students of American literature understandably raid for its many revealing anecdotes of the important expatriate generation. However, as a book published during the Depression when Cowley, like many intellectuals was moving to the left, *Exile's Return* is an important analysis of the modernist claim that literature has an autonomous status. Literature is not – so these claims go – to be defined by its self-referentiality (as in Imagist poetry for example), or its spatializing of time (Joyce and Hemingway's epiphanic short stories are the usual examples). An illuminating comparision can be made with Georg Lukács, the leading Marxist critic of modernism and Cowley's contemporary. In 'Narrate or Describe' (1936), Lukács examines literary form as an index of economic and social relations. Cowley prefers a leisurely, untheoretical sociology of one group of American modernists, in which he follows them from their middle-class, mid-western backgrounds through the war to Paris and then home when the Great Crash revealed the underlying instability of the economy. The war was an important episode in the story of American modernists. As volunteer ambulancemen, Hemingway, Dos Passos, e.e. cummings, Dashiell Hammett and others, were neither involved, in the manner of the 'war intellectuals', nor involved in Bourne's ironic manner. Cowley writes of a *'spectatorial* attitude', which finds expression in, for example, the discontinuous modernist prose of Hemingway. Cowley's definition and exemplification of modernism is firmly integrated into a historical account of the process of 'deracination' from home town, country and national culture. This process is itself part of 'the great drama' of 'the productive forces of society'.[21] Cowley also parallels Lukács' better known Marxist critique when discussing modernism in terms of commodity production, in which (to borrow Lukacs' vocabulary) the work of art becomes reified, cut off from its economic relation. Commenting upon the transition from a production to a consumption economy, Cowley writes:

> It happened that many of the Greenwich Village ideas proved
> useful in the altered situation. Thus, *self-expression* and *paganism*
> encouraged a demand for all sorts of products – modern
> furniture, beach pajamas, cosmetics, colored bathrooms with
> toilet paper to match. *Living for the moment* meant buying an
> automobile, radio or house, using it now and paying for it
> tomorrow . . . Everything fitted into the business picture.
> (pp. 62 and 63)

Cowley plays down the importance of socio-economic relations in the Prologue, which was written for the revised edition, published in the very different political climate of the 1950s.

Reasonably enough, we can object that this sociology of modernism fails to do justice to the work itself. Yet the status of 'the work itself' is exactly what Cowley is addressing, and *Exile's Return* is a key text in the reorientation of criticism in the direction of explicitly political criticism. Back with his narrative after the section on modernism and the war, Cowley tells the now-familiar story of the rehabilitation of the expatriates, with the execution in 1927 of the anarchists, Sacco and Vanzetti, as the event which radicalized them. From his perspective in the early years of the Depression, Cowley remarks of Sacco and Vanzetti that:

> For a time it seemed that [they] would be forgotten, in the midst
> of the stock-market boom and the exhilaration of easy money.
> Yet the effects of the case continued to operate, in a subterranean
> way, and after a few years they would once more appear on the
> surface. (p. 221)

Before following the logic of radicalism into the 'red decade', we must stop and discuss the Southern intellectual tradition of the 1920s and 1930s and define its very different relation to modernity.

Tell about the South: modernity and anti-modernity in the Southern tradition, 1920s to 1940s

Changes in material conditions had a lot to do with what came to be known as the Southern Renaissance, but one individual played an important part. In a number of essays, but especially in 'The Sahara of the Bozart', published in *The Smart Set* in 1917, H.L. Mencken mercilessly satirized the South:

> It is, indeed, amazing to contemplate so vast a vacuity . . .
> Nearly the whole of Europe could be lost in that stupendous
> region of fat farms, shoddy cities and paralyzed cerebrums . . .
> And yet, for all its size and all its wealth and all the 'progress' it
> boasts of, it is almost as sterile, artistically, intellectually,
> culturally, as the Sahara Desert.[22]

From a cosmopolitan, enlightened and scientific point of view (a Northern point of view, according to Southerners), the South did appear to correspond with Mencken's twisted account. After the Scopes trial in 1925, the South was further exposed as an intellectual backwater, and criticism sharpened accordingly. There were, of course, specific rebuttals: for instance, in *The Advancing South* (1926), Edwin Mims, the chair of the English Department at Vanderbilt University, insisted that the South was progressing, and that the religious temperament of the South amounted to more than fundamentalism of the Monkey Trial variety. In retrospect, though, we can see the Southern *literary* Renaissance as the most comprehensive, if indirect, answer to the charges levelled by Mencken and others. The first wave of writers included Ellen Glasgow, William Faulkner, Erskine Caldwell, Caroline Gordon, Lillian Smith, James Agee, Katherine Anne Porter, Thomas Wolfe, Allen Tate, and Robert Penn Warren. Their achievement was consolidated in the post-war years by Tennessee Williams, Walker Percy, William Styron, Carson McCullers, Truman Capote, and Flannery O'Connor. The more strictly intellectual history of the modern South does not reach the heights of its remarkable literary history but, in the context of debates over modernity is undoubtedly very important.

In Faulkner's novel, *Absalom, Absalom!* (1936), Quentin Compson responds to the need to '*Tell about the South. What's it like there. What do they do there. Why do they live there. Why do they live at all.*'[23] Faulkner adds another historical layer to his novel by making the present of the narrative 1909–10, because from then onwards, but especially after the First World War, it was plain that the South was going the way of the North – but sadly in its wake. Manufacturing was expanding in Southern cities while agriculture was suffering competition from Western states, which were uninhibited by the South's uneconomic sharecropping system. The full recognition of the impact of modernizing processes brought the Southern intellectual tradition together. More straightforwardly than Faulkner in his most complex fiction, the twelve Southerners who wrote the essays on history, culture, education, religion, philosophy, politics, and religion which make up *I'll Take My Stand* (1930), set themselves against the drift in the South towards industrial culture. They rejected the idea of a 'new South' and all that the opportunistic Snopes family represent in Faulkner's trilogy, *The Hamlet* (1940), *The Town* (1957) and *The Mansion* (1959). *I'll Take My Stand* received plenty of critical notice when it appeared (even if the Depression curtailed sales), and, in effect, became the manifesto of the Southern Agrarian movement of the 1930s. That movement sought to reinstate social and aesthetic values that were disappearing or disintegrating, much as Faulkner's older Compson family do in *The Sound and the Fury* (1929) as well as in *Absalom, Absalom!*.

In the sudden and enthusiastic discussions between Donald Davidson, John Crowe Ransom and Allen Tate in 1927 we can see the formation of that branch of the Southern intellectual tradition which, as it metamorphosed into New Criticism, would rival the New York Intellectuals who coalesced around *Partisan Review* after 1937 (see pages 184–205). Tate never looked or acted like a New Yorker but was as involved with modernism as Clement Greenberg, Lionel Trilling, Dwight Macdonald, and the two chief editors of *Partisan Review*, Philip Rahv and William Phillips. After 1924, when Tate moved from the South to New York City, he came into contact with Hart Crane, Malcolm Cowley and many of the Greenwich Village intellectuals, some back from Paris. Then, in 1928–9, when he was in London and Paris, he knew T.S. Eliot, Ford Madox Ford, Gertrude Stein, and Ernest Hemingway. But Tate would have little or nothing of the irreligious European modernism which the New Yorkers took up in the late 1930s, and which we have noticed developing alongside the Pragmatist route into 'the new'. Tate chose Eliot for his modernist hero, less because of Eliot's Southern background and more for his metaphysics of history. Tate's ideal, undissociated culture was not

Eliot's seventeenth-century England, but the Old South. Together with the other Agrarians, with the possible exception of Robert Penn Warren, Tate held on to some founding myth of unity located in the Confederacy.

Between 1922 and 1925 the four poets who contributed to *I'll Take My Stand* – Davidson, Ransom, Warren, and Tate – published in a little magazine, *The Fugitive*. Though it came out of Nashville, *The Fugitive* was not a Southern literary magazine. Rather, the youth of the contributors led them to react against the cultural establishment in the South. However, as the state of their region came together with their work as poets, so poetry (and a way of reading poetry) was thought to encapsulate the qualities of the Old South: a culture opposed to the dehumanizing machine; to capitalist rationalization and notions of progress defined according to the tenets of Protestantism; to the acquisition of possessions; and to mass culture; and standing for non-material ideals and tradition, for 'the aesthetic life', in Ransom's phrase.

Together with the Chicago Renaissance of the 1910s, the Harlem Renaissance of the mid-1920s, and the beginnings of Jewish-American literature with Cahan's *Yekl* in 1896, the Southern Renaissance was part of the fragmentation of an Anglo-American cultural tradition located in New England and the North-east. But to a much greater extent than these cultural developments, the Southern Renaissance emphasized tradition, even as it helped to forward a modernist literary and critical movement which broke with the past. Compared with the vague cultural nationalism of Van Wyck Brooks in *America's Coming of Age*, the Agrarians had a culture and a history from which to draw inspiration. However, if they knew where to look for their 'usable past', they still had to come to terms with Southern history. That is, they had to work out a relationship between space/place/region on the one hand and time/events/history on the other.

We can come to some understanding of the tensions in their work by focussing upon the way the Civil War is interpreted. The title phrase of *I'll Take My Stand*, is from the song, 'Dixie', and points to the historical paradigm that informs the book. This is most evident in an essay by the Vanderbilt historian, Frank Owsley, author of *States Rights in the Confederacy* (1925) and *King Cotton Diplomacy* (1927). In 'The Irrepressible Conflict' Owsley interprets the Civil War as an economic conflict between an industrializing North and a rural South. The date of publication of *I'll Take My Stand*, near the beginning of the Great Depression, gave a certain power to this anti-Marxist but, none the less, economic interpretation of the flaws of industrial capitalism. However, it is significant that the macro-argument used to explain the Civil War in *I'll Take My Stand* is never allowed to become a micro-argument applied to the slave economy. In the work of later historians, such as Eugene Genovese in *The Political Economy of Slavery* (1967) and

The World the Slaveholders Made (1969), the slave South emerges as pre-capitalist yet caught up in the modernizing processes that eroded self-sufficiency. In the work of the Agrarians, the Old South is, quite simply, different, yet unified within its borders. This latter point hardly stands up when critics and historians cannot agree upon what, geographically, constitutes the South, and when continuing work on the South reveals its religious diversity and the hitherto unacknowledged history of the slaves from their point of view. On the last of these themes, Genovese's *Roll Jordan, Roll: The World the Slaves Made* (1974) is exemplary.

In the Agrarians' re-telling of Southern history, the Civil War functions as the Fall. Owsley's economic interpretation is prefaced by the bitter 'memory of defeat':

> But after the military surrender at Appomatox there ensued a
> peace unique in history. There was no generosity. For ten years
> the South, already ruined by the loss of nearly $2,000,000,000
> invested in slaves, with its lands worthless, its cattle and stock
> gone, its houses burned, was turned over to the three millions of
> former slaves, some of whom could still remember the taste of
> human flesh and the bulk of them hardly three generations
> removed from cannibalism. These half-savage blacks were
> armed. Their passions were roused against their former masters
> by savage political leaders like Thaddeus Stevens, who advocated
> the confiscation of all Southern lands for the benefit of the
> negroes, and the extermination, if need be, of the Southern white
> population.[24]

Owsley's earlier reference to 'churches, universities, and state capitols with their archives' being used as 'stables for horses and mean men' (p. 62) suggests a connection between the post-war economic and cultural assaults on the South.

Ransom, in 'Reconstructed but Unregenerate', Lyle Lanier, in 'A Critique of the Philosophy of Progress', Tate, in 'Remarks on Southern Religion', and Andrew Lytle, in 'The Hind Tit', manage the equation between the War and the Fall more subtly than Owsley. So much so that Richard Gray maintains that the *language* of *I'll Take My Stand* can be read in a literary or non-discursive manner to reveal not the real historical conditions but 'a version of pastoral'.[25] Lytle, a farmer as well as a writer, introduces the familiar division early in his essay: 'Since 1865 an agrarian Union has been changed into an industrial empire bent on conquest of the earth's goods and ports to sell them in.' And, later: 'it is committing a mortal sin to persuade farmers that they can grow wealthy by adopting [industrial] methods. A farm is not a place to grow wealthy; it is a place to grow corn' (pp. 202 and

204–5). Here, America is equated with agrarianism to suggest that the South remains the true carrier of the ideal, that ideal itself being linked with Eden. Machinery, fertilisers, market ways, and envy of the planter class – all of these are juxtaposed with a different way of life:

Andrew Lytle

> On this rock [industrialism's] effort to urbanize the farm will probably split – to convince the farmer that it is time, not space, which has value. It will be difficult because the farmer knows that he cannot control time, whereas he can wrestle with space, or at least with that particular part which is his orbit. He can stop, set, chaw, and talk, for, unable to subdue nature, it is no great matter whether he gets a little more or a little less that year from her limitless store. He has the choice of pleasant conversation, the excitement of hunting, fishing, hearing the hounds run, or of the possibility of accumulating greater spoils. (pp. 211–12).

This is reminiscent of the idyllic description of the farm in a Southern text near or at the beginning of the the American agrarian tradition, Thomas Jefferson's famous Query, 'Manufactures', in *Notes on the State of Virginia* (1784–5). Jefferson conducts half of the discussion in the logical language of agrarian political economy since, at the time he was writing, an abundance of land – soon to be dramatically increased with the Louisiana Purchase of 1803 – made agrarianism a reality. But Jefferson's historical consciousness reveals the impossibility of maintaining an agrarian economy in the face of increasing urban and industrial growth, at which point his language becomes highly metaphorical, drawing imagery primarily from the Bible:

> Those who labour in the earth are the chosen people of God, if ever he had a chosen people, whose breasts he has made his peculiar deposit for substantial and genuine virtue. It is the focus in which he keeps alive that sacred fire, which otherwise might escape from the face of the earth. Corruption of morals in the mass of cultivators is a phaenomenon of which no age nor nation has furnished an example.[26]

As for Jefferson, so for the Agrarians, we may interpret the recourse to pastoral in the midst of agrarian political and social economy as an attempt to convey another way of knowing (besides the logical and scientific) which keeps alive an ideal against all the odds which modernity stacks against it. A more critical though some would say blunt view is that too many contradictions and injustices have to be overlooked for the ideal to hold. The myth of the Old South operates ideologically to allow, for instance, many Old Souths to co-exist, but in particular those symbolized by the sturdy yeoman farmer at the centre of Lytle's essay and the leisured, cultured, honourable plantation owner of Donald Davidson and Allen Tate. Historically as well as economically, the populist and aristocratic positions were, if not actually at odds, then potentially so. The 'irrepressible conflict' made it difficult to maintain the two ways of life within the image of the organic community of the South, static in its social hierarchies and consistent in its loyalties. At one point in his deliberations after the publication of I'll Take My Stand, John Crowe Ransom exposes the extent of divisions within the South when he concludes that it was 'the darkey' who kept the South together.

In spite of Owsley's orthodoxy that 'slavery as a moral issue is too simple an explanation' (p. 68) for the Civil War (a view that many historians would accept without reaching Owsley's interpretation of the conflict), it is the 'Negro question' which the myth of the Old South has to manage. In I'll Take My Stand race is only confronted seriously by one of the contributors, Robert Penn Warren in 'The Briar Patch', though Tate, Davidson, Herman Clarence Nixon, and Warren, himself, took up race in later writings, the first two in closed-minded fashion, the second two in the growing recognition that reform had to come. Warren's Segregation (1956) and Who Speaks for the Negro? (1965) are paramount in the second camp. In the collection itself, there are simply the routine references to slaves as property, so it is hardly surprising that Warren's essay provoked disagreements. Davidson and Owsley thought that it contravened established Southern thinking about race by its 'progressive' approach, though it is mostly of its time, being basically a segregationist argument. On the other hand, Warren at least faces the question of what would result from educating black people. He finds an answer in the philosophy of education advanced by the black leader, Booker T. Washington, in his Atlanta Address of 1895 (see pp. 254–55, below). Warren, though, applies Washington's programme of industrial (as opposed to academic and non-vocational) education to agriculture and, in the process, succumbs to the a-historical mythology:

Warren

> the Southern negro has always been a creature of the small town and farm. That is where he still chiefly belongs, by temperament and capacity; there he has less the character of a 'problem' and more the status of a human being who is likely to find in agricultural and domestic pursuits the happiness that his good nature and easy ways incline him to as an ordinary function of his being. (pp. 260–1)

There is, Warren further claims, a 'community of interest between the owner and the "cropper"' (p. 262) which does not exist in the more rationalized capital-labour relations of a Northern city. However, where Booker T. Washington stressed gradualism in the move towards full citizenship – a strategy which at least presupposed equality – Warren just recommends 'unselfishness' and 'patience' to blacks and looks, finally, to some restorative quality in the Southern way of life to resolve the problem. Here, too, in the most forward-looking of the essays the myth of an ideal community reappears. In this context, John Dollard's case study, *Caste and Class in a Southern Town* (1937), is the counterpart to Robert and Helen Lynd's *Middletown* in demythologizing the Southern community.

While the contributors to *I'll Take My Stand* wrote less polemically in their individually authored books, it is reasonable to generalize that constructing a social and political theory, indeed a history, on the basis of an image was still a project fraught with difficulties. William Faulkner is, once more, an instructive example, and one that suggests a connection with the cosmopolitan and international dimension of modernism recorded by Malcolm Cowley in *Exile's Return*. Cowley was a friend of Allen Tate and Caroline Gordon and had completed *Exile's Return* while staying at their farm in Tennessee. Tate and Gordon encouraged Cowley's project for a *Portable Faulkner* (published 1954), which would try to rescue Faulkner from virtual oblivion by reconstructing the geography of his modernist uncertainties (the time shifts in *The Sound and the Fury*, for example). It was then only a short step from Faulkner's map of the imaginary country of Yoknapatawpha ('William Faulkner, Sole Owner and Proprietor') to the universalizing of geography in critical orthodoxy, as in this statement by Hugh Holman in *The Roots of Southern Writing*:

> [The] place of highest honor . . . is reserved [by Faulkner] for the imagination of the artist, which can transmute the data of history into the enlarged reality of art, which can translate sociological data into the eternal problems of human culpability and compassionate feeling. Faulkner's 'postage stamp of earth' has stretched out to the four corners of the world, and the middle class planters and farmers and storekeepers of Yoknapatawpha Country can body forth man's enduring tragedy.[27]

There can be no argument about either the great service Cowley did Faulkner's reputation or the high standard of critical writing on Faulkner which followed, for example in Cleanth Brooks's *William Faulkner: The Yoknapatawpha Country* (1963). Yet the spatializing or mapping of time does some disservice to Faulkner's texts, where the relationship to the Southern past is painful and contradictory. When history proved too intractable for myth and the ideal of the organic community – Robert Penn Warren's later books on race acknowledge this – then a theory of literature took over this conserving and conservative role, while the task of engaging with history passed to the Civil Rights generation. Lawrence Schwartz has reconstructed the politics of the rediscovery of Faulkner and concludes that the combination of aesthetics, the regional and the universal role of literature in the Cowley–Faulkner–Southern Agrarians relationship was 'an aspect of the general retreat from the overt political concerns and engaged social realism of the [1930s]'.[28] At first sight the seminal New Critical statements, like Ransom's *The New Criticism* (1941), Cleanth Brooks's *The Well Wrought Urn* (1947), and Brooks and Warren's *Understanding Poetry* (1938) and *Understanding Fiction* (1943) seem to have little in common with Southern polemics. New Criticism is tight, professional and even scientific, with W.K. Wimsatt and Cleanth Brooks legislating against the vagaries of intentionality, affectivity and paraphrase.[29] Equally, New Criticism seems a long way from the organicism of Agrarianism and, in fact, in I.A. Richards and William Empson has British not American connections, while in the United States Yale University in Connecticut became a New Critical stronghold. Yet on closer inspection there are affinities.

There have been a number of studies of the New Criticism and its Agrarian dimension, but we can short-cut their conclusions by noting Allen Tate's use of Baudelaire's theory of correspondences in his 1950 lecture, 'The Symbolic Imagination':

> The symbolic imagination conducts an action through analogy, of the human to the divine, of the natural to the supernatural, of the low to the high, of time to eternity . . . The symbolic imagination takes rise from a definite limitation of human rationality which was recognized in the West until the 17th Century; in this view the intellect cannot have direct knowledge of essences.

He adds:

> My literary generation was deeply impressed by Baudelaire's sonnet *Correspondances* . . . We were impressed because we had lost the historical perspective leading back to the original source.[30]

Just as the Old South is categorically not to be explained either by other socio-economic systems (especially the North's) or by historical causes, so, by analogy, the poem (if it is genuine literature and not propaganda) is explicable only in its own terms. The science or, more accurately, the professionalism of criticism lies in 'understanding poetry' as poetry. Such understanding can recreate in the reading the present of the poem, just as the ideal traditional society can live again. As Frank Kermode has pointed out in *Romantic Image*, it is at least cause for scepticism that there seem to be so many golden ages, T.S. Eliot's Middle Ages and Ransom and Tate's Old South being just two of the most famous candidates. We should also note that the principle of unity varied: for some critics it was the image, for others ambiguity or paradox; for Eliot it was the 'objective correlative'. When Tate and Caroline Gordon in *The House of Fiction* (1950) and Brooks and Warren in *Understanding Fiction* applied New Critical principles to the short story rather than the poem, then structural tension – often expressed through irony – or the epiphanic moment which collapsed narrative time into space took over from more poetic criteria. That we can find the same criteria in non-Southern critics, such as Cowley in his post-war writing and Leslie Fiedler in *An End to Innocence* (1955) and in someone like Ransom who abandoned agrarianism in 1945, suggests that it is the a-political and a-historical orientation of New Criticism that is definitive. However, an awareness of where the highly political Southern New Critics came from is also the basis for a reintroduction of context into a textual criticism which began in the political glare of the 1930s and flourished in the 1950s, when politics of the ideological kind was thought to be deader than the Confederacy.

The red decade: the 1930s

The Depression was a crisis of massive proportions. Following the stock market crash in 1929, the national income dropped from 81 billion dollars to 41 billion dollars in 1932. 85,000 businesses went bankrupt between 1929 and 1932, 5761 banks failed, and 9 million savings accounts disappeared. In the depths of the Depression in 1932–3, somewhere between 13 and 16 million were unemployed, roughly a quarter of the labour force, and despite the measures of Roosevelt's New Deal and the more substantial economic recovery stimulated by the Second World War, there were still 10 per cent unemployed in 1940. As with the First World War, we shall not deal with political and institutional responses, but with intellectual responses, two in particular. The first is the continuation of the radicalism based upon degrees of commitment to Marxism, whose story we have traced back to the pre-war years. The second is a revamped liberalism that tried to steer a course between Marxism and New Deal liberalism.

The Depression precipitated a reaction by radical intellectuals against the liberal tradition and its belief in individual freedom and in reform through the electoral process and through the kind of planning which did not necessitate collective ownership of the means of production. Mike Gold emerged as one of the most outspoken critics of liberalism. Gold, in common with other literary intellectuals like Joseph Freeman and V.F. Calverton, maintained that only a radical restructuring of society could address the root causes of the Depression in a capitalist system daily revealing its contradictions and the inability of the Hoover administration to cope with rising unemployment.

After all the betrayals and disappointments of Soviet history, it is difficult to acknowledge just how important the USSR was to the American Left. The lack of an industrial proletariat in the USSR also interested American intellectuals since it demonstrated that intellectuals were capable of playing a decisive role. Lenin and Trotsky became important as models of the engaged intellectual. American intellectuals once again visited the USSR, as they had in the post-1917 period, among them Waldo Frank, Joshua Kunitz and Louis Fischer. Mostly, they confirmed the statistics which stated that Stalin's first Five-Year Plan had been successfully completed. A contemporary poster by Fred Ellis contrasts 'two civilizations'. In one, a gaunt, threadbare American stretches out to grab a bone from a rubbish bin before a dog can get it while, in the background, protesters rush towards what looks like the White House. In the other, against a background of smoking factory chimneys, modern, functional architecture and orderly well-dressed workers, a giant Soviet worker stretches out to turn on the power.[31]

The radicals of the 1930s are often lumped together as the 'Old Left', to distinguish them from the 'New Left' of the 1960s. Yet it was a coalition of those like Cowley, Edmund Wilson, John Dos Passos, and Sherwood Anderson, who had links with 1920s modernism; those who had remained political during the 1920s – Mike Gold, Joseph Freeman, and Max Eastman; and the new intellectuals of the 1930s, for instance those, like Philip Rahv, William Phillips and Dwight Macdonald who gathered around the magazine, *Partisan Review.* Within these groupings there were differences, but in the early years of the Depression the crisis brought them together and fifty-two intellectuals signed a statement supporting the 1932 Communist presidential candidates, Foster and Ford.

Among intellectuals who had either retained a belief that aesthetics could not be separated from politics, or had come around to this view as a result of the experiences of the late 1920s and events like the Sacco and Vanzetti trial, the debates typically took place in magazines like the *New Masses* and V.F. Calverton's *Modern Quarterly*, and in the chapters of the John Reed Club for young writers and artists which originated in the offices of the *New Masses* in 1929. The analysis of Marxism – as the only plausible explanation of the catastrophe that had overtaken the world's foremost capitalist nation – had a spin-off in the dual questions of how art in the broadest sense ought to relate to ideas and social change, and what was the social function of the artist. Mike Gold, who went to the Kharkov in the USSR for the second Congress of Revolutionary Writers, brought back answers: respectively, a more determinedly proletarian art that viewed the world from the worker's perspective, and an artist who subordinated aesthetic objectives to political ones. The results included the Social Realist paintings of John Reed Club members William Gropper and Moses and Raphael Soyer and the proletarian fiction of Edward Dahlberg and Jack Conroy. The question of the proletarian novel dominated the first American Writers Congress in 1935, though the broader question that brought novelists, painters, photographers, and critics together was that of power, since the Depression had persuaded intellectuals that ideas and art could be a weapon.

Individualism, old and new: John Dewey in the 1930s

A discussion of what R. Alan Lawson calls 'Independent Liberalism', poised between Marxism and New Deal liberalism, makes an appropriate point to conclude this chapter since it was very much a second act of the Progressive Movement of the 1890–1917 period.[32] The connection between the first and second act is made through the *New Republic* group, George Soule, Bruce Bliven and, especially, John Dewey. Others who come under this umbrella include Stuart Chase, Alfred Bingham, and Lewis Mumford. By concentrating upon John Dewey we can convey something of the philosophical basis of the new liberalism, while attempting to do a little justice to the most important American philosopher this century.

Dewey is known for so much more than his contribution to 1930s liberalism, but the Depression was extremely important in redefining the liberal tradition. The limitations of Dewey's concept of 'creative intelligence' had been shown up by Randolph Bourne in 1917, and then by the waste of the First World War, and the failure of the Treaty of Versailles to come anywhere near matching the outcome anticipated by Dewey and *The New Republic*. Yet, to turn Bourne's criticism round, an economic depression, unlike a world war, did offer scope once again for Pragmatism. But Pragmatism itself had to be re-examined. In the first half of the 1920s, when laissez-faire attitudes underwent a revival, and Progressivism as a political movement died, Dewey moved out of the centre ground which his philosophy had occupied during the Progressive era proper. But he nonetheless published a number of books which continued to analyse 'creative intelligence' in different spheres: for example, philosophy itself in *Reconstruction in Philosophy* (1920), and art in *Human Nature and Conduct* (1922). *The Public and its Problems* (1927) marks the return of a more explicit social focus and deals with the relationship between local communities and larger organizations. From 1929, just before the stock market crash, through the worst years of the Depression to 1933 and Roosevelt's inauguration, Dewey showed a renewed readiness to be involved, to test out ideas in institutional programmes, though he had hardly been reclusive in his support during the 1920s for such organizations as the League for Industrial Democracy and the Committee for the Outlawry of War.

Through the League for Independent Political Action, which he joined in 1929, Dewey attempted, as William James did with nineteenth-century philosophical traditions, to find a way around the two-party system and give an organizational structure to liberalism. This was an apparent contradiction, but one which the extent of the collapse of capitalism made worth confronting, and it is partly the theme of *Individualism, Old and New* (1929). The welfare liberalism which emerged out of debates in and around the League and in the pages of the *New Republic* in 1931 differed from nineteenth-century free-market liberalism by recognizing a collective dimension to life. This dimension arose from what people have in common as citizens that will make them act in public together:

> Are the people of the United States to control the government and to use it on behalf of the peace and welfare of society; or is control to pass into the hands of small, powerful economic groups which use the machinery of administration and legislation for their own purposes?[33]

Collectivity was not based upon any idea of a mass movement. Dewey had warned against the threat represented by religious absolutism in *The Quest for Certainty* (1929), but the totalitarian implications of mass politics only became fully apparent later in the 1930s, so that, up until mid-decade, at least, public political action retained its connection with democracy and could appeal to the 'people' without suggesting the blind masses.

The Depression required, in Dewey's view, a determined attempt to move away from individualism as the basis for action. As in William

James, so in Dewey, Pragmatist experimentalism allowed for activity while yet recognizing the external constraints upon freedom. With production and distribution of goods organized on a vast scale in a capitalist economy, only a flexible experimental outlook firmly allied to efficient planning based on a scientific model could deal with the collapse of that system. Experimentalism was vital in order to understand an unprecedented economic crisis, and then respond to events and to the different groups in need of different kinds of assistance. Unwilling to follow a class analysis, Dewey argued that Americans could be educated into a new social philosophy which accepted co-operation as the only context in which to realize liberal ideals.

There is undoubtedly a managerial point of view in Dewey's liberalism and he shared, with Thorstein Veblen, an admiration for the professional expert. George Soule and Stuart Chase were more outspoken in their admiration for specialist planning groups, and Dewey found it necessary, in *Liberalism and Social Action* (1935), to balance their elitism with support for the kind of co-operation in public action that he had set out in *The Public and its Problems*. Dewey also countered the utilitarian side of Pragmatism by insisting that to question the truth value of ideals, whether religious or political ones, did not rule out their usefulness as a spur to action. To dismiss the possibility of utopia was as un-Pragmatic as to endorse it irrespective of context. In this he was still following William James's Pragmatism. It has to be said, though, that his philosophy lacks James's willingness to entertain individual idiosyncrasy – to the point of James being open to some quite unusual 'varieties of religious experience'. Deweyan creative intelligence was not sufficiently visionary to answer the basic need for ideals, even a faith, that was accentuated by the uncertainties of the Depression. But, then, the coming experience of totalitarianism in the USSR and Germany suggests that Dewey's strength lay precisely in his prosaic qualities.

In the next chapter we can trace the decline of Marxist radicalism from the mid-1930s onwards, beginning with such events as the Moscow Trials, the Spanish Civil War, the Nazi-Soviet Pact, and the movement known as the Popular Front, one cause of which was the overwhelming support for Roosevelt's New Deal in the 1936 election. This election also marked a downturn in the attempt by Dewey, Soule, Chase and others to provide their version of a radical alternative to the New Deal. The League for Independent Political Action folded in 1937 leaving the two-party system intact. With the Democrats firmly in control, a watered-down collectivism prevailed, leaving the new liberals with only a choice between Roosevelt and a Marxism that would be far more vulnerable to the course of events than either independent or New Deal liberalism.

Notes

1. Robert H. Wiebe, *The Search for Order, 1877–1920* (New York, 1967), chs 5–7.

2. Daniel Howe, 'Victorian Culture in America', in *Victorian America*, edited by Daniel Howe (Philadelphia, 1976), p. 12.

3. William James, *Pragmatism* (New York, 1974), p. 33.

4. William James, *The Will to Believe and Other Essays in Popular Philosophy* (New York, 1956), pp. ix and 150.

5. *The Letters of William James*, edited by Henry James, 12 vols. (Boston, 1920), Vol. 1, p. 147.

6. On the therapeutic culture, see T.J. Jackson Lears, *No Place of Grace: Antimodernism and the Transformation of American Culture, 1880–1920* (New York, 1981); Donald Meyer, *The Positive Thinkers: Religion as Pop Psychology from Mary Baker Eddy to Oral Roberts* (New York, 1980); Philip Rieff, *The Triumph of the Therapeutic: Uses of Faith after Freud* (Chicago, 1987); and Christopher Lasch, *The Culture of Narcissism: American Life in an Age of Diminishing Expectations* (1980).

7. George Santayana, *Character and Opinion in the United States, with Reminiscences of William James and Josiah Royce and Academic Life in America* (1920), pp. 76–7.

8. William James, *The Varieties of Religious Experience: A Study in Human Nature* (1960), p. 99.

9. Herbert Croly, 'The New World and the New Art', *Architectural Record* 12 (1902), p. 153; Walter Lippmann, *Preface to Politics* (New York, 1913), p. 200. See Paul F. Bourke, 'The Social Critics and the End of American Innocence, 1907–1921', *Journal of American Studies*, 3 (July 1969), pp. 57–72.

10. Henry F. May, *The End of American Innocence: A Study of the First Years of Our Own Time, 1912–1917* (Chicago, 1964), p. 6.

11. William James, *Principles of Psychology* (1890), vol. 1, pp. 225, 245–6; William James, *Essays in Radical Empiricism* (1912), pp. 42 and 37.

12. Christopher Lasch, *The New Radicalism in America (1889–1963): The Intellectual as a Social Type* (New York, 1965).

13. Mabel Dodge, *Movers and Shakers* (New York, 1936), p. 83.

14. On *The New Republic*, see Charles Forcey, *The Crossroads of Liberalism* (New York, 1961); Paul F. Bourke, 'The Status of Politics, 1909–1919: *The New Republic*, Randolph Bourne and Van Wyck Brooks', *Journal of American Studies*, 8 (August 1974), pp. 171–202; and Richard Crockatt, 'American Liberalism and the Atlantic World, 1916–17', *Journal of American Studies*, 11 (April 1977), pp. 123–43.

15. Randolph Bourne, *The Radical Will: Selected Writings, 1911–1918*, edited by Olaf Hansen (New York, 1977), p. 522.

16. Van Wyck Brooks, *Three Essays on America* (New York, 1970), p. 17. See, also, George Santayana, 'The Genteel Tradition in American Philosophy', in *Santayana on America: Essays, Notes, and Letters on American Life, Literature, and Philosophy* (New York, 1968), pp. 36–56.

17. On the beginnings of the Jewish cultural renaissance, see Hutchins Hapgood, *The Spirit of the Ghetto: Studies of the Jewish Quarter of New York* (New York,

1976); and Moses Rischin, *The Promised City: New York's Jews, 1870–1914* (Cambridge, Mass., 1978), chs 5, 7 and 8.

18. John Dos Passos, *USA* (Harmondsworth, 1966), p. 426.

19. Quoted in Arthur Frank Wertheim, *The New York Little Renaissance: Iconoclasm, Modernism, and Nationalism in American Culture, 1908–1917* (New York, 1976), p. 219.

20. Max Eastman, *Enjoyment of Living* (New York, 1948), p. 409.

21. Malcolm Cowley, *Exile's Return, A Literary Odyssey of the 1920s* (Harmondsworth, 1986), p. 35.

22. H. L. Mencken, *Prejudices: A Selection*, edited by James T. Farrell (New York, n.d.), p. 70.

23. William Faulkner, *Absalom, Absalom!* (Harmondsworth, 1971), p. 143.

24. Twelve Southerners, *I'll Take My Stand: The South and the Agrarian Tradition* (New York, 1962), p. 62.

25. Richard Gray, *The Literature of Memory: Modern Writers of the American South* (Baltimore, 1977), pp. 46–7.

26. *The Portable Thomas Jefferson*, edited by Merrill D. Peterson (Harmondsworth, 1977), p. 217.

27. Hugh Holman, *The Roots of Southern Writing: Essays on the Literature of the American South* (Athens, Georgia, 1972), p. 176.

28. Lawrence Schwartz, 'Malcolm Cowley: Paths to William Faulkner', *Journal of American Studies*, 16 (1982), p. 242.

29. See W.K. Wimsatt, Jr, *The Verbal Icon: Studies in the Meaning of Poetry* (1970), pp. 3–39; and Cleanth Brooks, *The Well Wrought Urn: Studies in the Structure of Poetry* (New York, 1947), chapter 11.

30. Allen Tate, *Collected Essays* (Denver, 1959), pp. 412 and 413. On New Criticism, see John Fekete, *The Critical Twilight: Explorations in the Ideology of Anglo-American Literary Theory from Eliot to McLuhan* (1977), and Paul de Man, *Blindness and Insight: Essays in the Rhetoric of Contemporary Criticism*, revised edn (1983), ch. 2.

31. See John Diggins, *The American Left in the Twentieth Century* (New York, 1973), pp. 112–13.

32. See R. Alan Lawson, *The Failure of Independent Liberalism, 1930–1941* (New York, 1971).

33. John Dewey, 'Policies for a New Party', *The New Republic*, 66 (April 18, 1931), p. 202.

Chapter 5
From the Old Left to the New Left

Communism is twentieth-century Americanism: the Popular Front, 1935 to 1939

In 1935, two years after Hitler had become Chancellor of Germany, the Seventh Congress of the Comintern announced the formation of a Popular Front against fascism. Confronted by the spread of fascism, the USSR could not remain isolated, and had already joined the League of Nations the year before the Congress.

Earl Browder, the American Communist Party (CPUSA) general secretary, gave such a liberal translation of the new policy towards Western democracies that, during the 1936 presidential election, he often made use of the slogan 'Communism is Twentieth-Century Americanism'. When the Communist and Socialist candidates polled only one million votes between them, while Roosevelt was returned with 60.8 per cent of the popular vote, there was a good domestic, as well as international, reason for a conciliatory position towards the New Deal. A Popular Front against fascism might also, it was reasoned, be the platform for a more successful challenge from the Left in 1940.

The Popular Front was already courting intellectuals as well as Left and liberal party organizations. The first move was to disband the John Reed Clubs and then, at the first American Writers' Congress in New York City in 1935, to replace them with the eclectic League of American Writers. Anti-fascism and defence of the Soviet Union took precedence over the creation of a radical culture, though culture remained an important area of political activity, requiring ingenuity if not genius. The *New Masses*, for instance, enlisted the reputations of Thomas Jefferson and Abraham Lincoln and even the popular appeal of Paul Revere's ride against the British in its campaign against fascism. 'The Star-Spangled Banner' was heard at some CPUSA events, and intellectuals went out of their way to show an interest in Hollywood, popular radio series and sport.

In a convoluted analysis of 'revolutionary symbolism' at the first American Writers' Congress, the literary critic, Kenneth Burke, unwittingly anticipated the expediency of the Popular Front: 'The symbol I should plead for, as more basic, more of an ideal incentive, than that of the worker, is that of "the people." ' He added: 'I think that the term "the people" is closer to our folkways than is the corresponding term, "the masses." '[1] Writers, like Sherwood Anderson, John Dos Passos, James Rorty, and Edmund Wilson, photographers, like Dorothea Lange, and the painters on the Works Progress Administration (WPA) projects – most with at least Leftist sympathies – updated their American knowledge by literally travelling the land making contact with 'the people'. The result of this activity was a remarkable record of America in the Great Depression, but, as we noted in Chapter 2, a decided lack of analysis or awareness of the ideology of realism which dominated the Popular Front. An aesthetics which assumed that all art had to do was get back to basic expression corresponded with a widespread feeling that solutions to the crisis also lay in basic patterns of behaviour. Sometimes, the call for simplicity also carried with it a certain kind of content, a pre-industrial, pre-cosmopolitan notion of the good person and the good life, as Richard Pells explains in *Radical Visions and American Dreams*:

> Ironically, in the midst of an urban–industrial depression, when intellectuals were eagerly awaiting the emergence of working-class consciousness and a strong labor movement, the documentaries often concentrated on and romanticized the *agrarian* victims of capitalism. It was as though the crisis had inspired in many writers a renewed reverence for America's past, for its frontier heritage, for its nineteenth-century small towns and farms rather than for its socialist future.[2]

The fate of the left: *Partisan Review* in the 1930s

Partisan Review (*PR*) started in 1934 as a companion journal to the *New Masses*, with a brief to protect the cultural wing of the Communist Party. Within three years, and after a short break in publication, *PR*'s editors, William Phillips and Philip Rahv, were marking their distance from the Party, and more particularly from the Popular Front as a cultural movement. The interconnections between 'the fate of the left' and cultural activities (right down to book-reviewing), were later summarized by Phillips in this way:

> For political thinkers and for publications like *Partisan Review* [questions about 'the fate of the left'] are not purely abstract. They involve making constant decisions not only about basic policies but also concrete ones about trends and individual works in criticism and politics and even about fiction and poetry.[3]

PR appeared during, and was formed by, the startling events of the second half of the 1930s: the Spanish Civil War, the Moscow Trials, the Nazi-Soviet Pact, and the onset of the Second World War. The Spanish Civil War of 1936–9 was the great cause of the Left, with the Communists supporting the Loyalists against Franco, who, in turn, was supported by Hitler. So much was invested in the war, with intellectuals joining the International Brigades on the Loyalist side, that defeat was a crushing disappointment. John Dos Passos' already wavering commitment to the Left ceased with the news that anarchists amd Trotskyites in Spain had been suppressed by their supposed Communist comrades.

In 1936–7 news also leaked out about the Moscow Trials. Intellectuals were faced with defending Stalin, as the embodiment of the USSR and the enemy of fascism, and reviling him for his persecution of Bolshevik heroes, among them Bukharin, Zinoviev and Radek. Dating back to 1934, the trials, were a public purge of anti-Stalinist elements in the USSR, and outside it too, since the exiled Leon Trotsky had long since been accused of treason and hounded around the world. Besides those who featured in the show trials and confessed to crimes they could not possibly have committed, millions of lesser officials, workers, peasants, and intellectuals were also executed or imprisoned.

The American Left was thrown into turmoil, and intellectuals divided between those, like Malcolm Cowley, Granville Hicks, Louis Fischer, Jack Conroy, Lillian Hellman, Langston Hughes, Henry Roth, Dorothy Parker, and Dashiell Hammett, who either defended or at least did not outrightly condemn the trials, and those, like Dwight Macdonald (in an interchange with Cowley), Max Eastman, and Rahv and Phillips, who opposed them. The first group turned themselves inside out to avoid facing the appalling reality of the Soviet Union under Stalin, of which the Moscow Trials were only the most public manifestation. Granville Hicks took a common line in deciding that the ends outweighed the dreadful means, given the danger of Fascism in

Europe and the importance of the USSR in the fight against Hitler. The Moscow Trials and defences of Stalin did immeasurable harm to American intellectual life.

The sequence of events continued apace. In August, 1939, in a complete reversal of Popular Front policy, Stalin signed the Nazi-Soviet Pact with Hitler, and followed it in 1939–40 with the bloody invasion of Poland and Finland. The death count for the invasion is still being completed, so it was the Pact which did most immediate damage to any idea of a Popular Front against fascism – or, at least, it did until June 1941 when the Germans broke the Pact and invaded the Soviet Union. At that juncture, *Life*, among other mass circulation magazines, went beyond mere praise for the bravery of Russians and brought Stalin back into the family as 'Uncle Joe'.

Meanwhile, *PR* was moving away from the Party line, and an anti-Stalinist stance was being formulated by the main editors, Rahv and Phillips, but also by novelist, Mary McCarthy, and, from Yale, Dwight Macdonald, Fred Dupee, and George Morris. Their position was not simply anti-Stalinist, however, though fifteen years later it became just that for many of those who would become better known as the New York Intellectuals. In the late 1930s *PR* made a temporary alliance with such official and unofficial American Trotskyites as the philosophers Sidney Hook, George Novack and James Burnham, the historian Louis Hacker, literary critic Lionel Trilling, art critic, Meyer Schapiro, novelist James T. Farrell, and Max Eastman, the veteran of the old *Masses*. Together they articulated a very precise and important position. To be opposed to the totalitarianism of Stalinist bureaucracy, as evidenced by the Trials, and to be a supporter of Trotsky – an intellectual and an activist who had been ousted by Comintern apparachiks – was to be a *radical* and not a reactionary. This effort to re-think radicalism contrasts with the bluntness of later analyses. One of the worst of the latter was Eastman's for the *Reader's Digest* in the early 1940s, in which the concept of 'conflict' was lifted free of historical circumstances and located in 'human nature' as proof of the impossibility of socialism.

In *Radical Visions and American Dreams*, Richard Pells argues that the anti-Stalinist radicals were obsessed with their radical credentials, and, in an otherwise invaluable book, he rather hurries through the crucial years between 1937, when *PR* was re-founded, and 1943, when its editorial board split. To appreciate the importance of Rahv, Phillips, and Macdonald in particular, and also to see how *PR* radicalism became the much broader grouping known as the New York Intellectuals, we have to slow down.

For *PR*, Stalinism was the corruption of the Bolshevik Revolution, culturally as well as politically. Art under Stalinism compared badly with post-Revolutionary Soviet poetry, theatre and cinema. It is very revealing that Dwight Macdonald's rejection of Stalinism should have been tied up with his interpretation of what had happened to Eisenstein and avant-garde Soviet film in the 1930s. In essays published in *PR* in 1938 and 1939, he attacked the ruination of the Soviet film industry when it was enlisted in the service of the Five Year Plan and put under the official surveillance of a high-up official of the secret police. Macdonald's opinion of Hollywood *kitsch* was that it was virtually a cultural manifestation of Stalinism.

From 1937 onwards, the connection of the Popular Front as a cultural phenomenon with Stalinism was the stimulus for a sudden and quite surprising revaluation of modernism. For instance, against Mike Gold's categorizing of modernism as 'part of the signs of doom that are written largely everywhere on the walls of bourgeois society', the *PR* editors and writers argued that the sheer difficulty of even a politically conservative poet like T.S. Eliot or novelist like Henry James at least made their works less susceptible to use as propaganda.[4] Moreover, modernist literature did more than respond to the issues of the moment, and this itself could be interpreted as a political response when 'issues' were thought by many intellectuals to be largely the creation of the media, and therefore of capitalism. As a result, in the pages of *PR* between 1937 and the late 1940s, Mann, Kafka, Dostoyevsky, Proust, Yeats, Silone, as well as the expatriate Americans, James and Eliot, were read for their radical potential. The parallel in art would be the Abstract Expressionists.

It was entirely appropriate that Stalin's opponent, Leon Trotsky, could be called upon for theoretical support in such an interpretive strategy:

> Artistic creation has its own laws – even when it consciously
> serves a social movement. Truly intellectual creation is
> incompatible with lies, hypocrisies and the spirit of conformity.
> Art can become a strong ally of revolution only insofar as it
> remains faithful to itself.[5]

When Phillips and Rahv recognized in Trotsky a political revolutionary who was willing to accord a significant degree of independence to art, there was a flurry of correspondence between the magazine and Trotsky. In 1938, *PR* did succeed in publishing an important article, 'Manifesto: Towards a Free Revolutionary Art', written by Trotsky and the surrealist André Breton; it appeared, however, under the names of Breton and the Mexican muralist, Diego Rivera, perhaps because of Trotsky's doubts about the revolutionary credentials of *PR*. Shortly afterwards Trotsky did publish in the magazine under his own name: a letter to Breton on the degradation of revolutionary art under the influence of Stalinism.

As the stock of European modernists rose, so estimates of a number of American authors were revised downwards. When Philip Rahv criticized the sentimentalism and lack of political bite of Steinbeck's *Of Mice and Men* (1937), it was more than a piece of literary criticism. Rahv was writing in *New Masses* and attacking the novelist who, if not in 1937 then certainly in 1939 with *The Grapes of Wrath*, best represented the Popular Front's anti-capitalist but anti-revolutionary and decidedly anti-modernist stance. John Ford completed the move from the myth of the worker to that of the people when he chose to end his 1940 film of Steinbeck's novel with Ma Joad's speech:

> Rich fellas come up, an' they die, an' their kids ain't no good and they die out. But we keep a comin'. We're the people that live. They can't wipe us out. They can't lick us. We'll go on forever, Pa, because we're the people.

Behind *PR*'s opting for European modernism, or at least the editors' view that American literature had to learn from it, is not simply the political significance of 'difficulty' (T.S. Eliot's allusiveness or Henry James's 'late style'), but a theory of the artist as alienated from society. This made for a potentially radical perspective, analogous to that exemplified politically but also intellectually by Trotsky. It differed from the endorsement of modernism by the conservative Southern Agrarians and, later, the New Critics, who rewrote alienation into the principle of the autonomous work of art, free from political commitment. Commentators on the *PR* critics and the New York Intellectuals have pointed out that their immigrant Jewish backgrounds made them sympathetic to outsider and European perspectives. And also to the plight of European intellectuals in the 1930s. *PR*'s Fund for European Writers and Artists offered concrete aid to modernism by assisting those who were trying to escape from fascism to the USA. A particularly significant link between politics and modernism was made when *PR* identified itself with the Bolshevik intellectuals accused during the Moscow Trials. 'But it is not only the old Bolsheviks who are on trial', Philip Rahv reasoned. 'We too, all of us, are in the prisoners' dock. These are trials of the human mind and of the human spirit. Their meanings encompass the age.'[6] Radicalism, Rahv and Phillips were among the first of their generation to argue, could not originate with 'the people', because 'the people' were subject to cultural massification. After witnessing the effects of the Popular Front, they were prepared to argue that the very idea of 'the people' was itself a product of the mass media. To offset this lack of an articulated point of view, there had to be an avant-garde made up of intellectuals, who would not be hamstrung by any theory of proletarian literature or social organization.

In some respects the destination *PR* reached by the late 1930s recalls that of Randolph Bourne and his generation. Clement Greenberg's definition of the function of the avant-garde as finding 'a path along which it would be possible to keep culture *moving* in the midst of ideological confusion and violence', sounds like Bourne pinning his hopes on cosmopolitan 'malcontents' who lived 'the life of irony'. And yet, the paragraph which closes Greenberg's 1939 essay, 'Avant-Garde and Kitsch', which we made use of in Chapter 2, conveys a passive, defensive quality as against Bourne's highly active model for the avant-garde. Here it should be remembered that the pre-First World War rebellion was closely accompanied by large political and social movements which had *not* all run their course by 1918 when Bourne died. It was exactly the case that movements were ending when the *PR* writers took the modernist cause.

Since 1939 was a watershed between radicalism and the move towards a consensus and even neo-conservative politics of culture, Greenberg's words are worth examining:

> Capitalism in decline finds that whatever of quality it is still capable of producing becomes almost invariably a threat to its own existence. Advances in culture, no less than advances in science and industry, corrode the very society under whose aegis they are made possible. Here, as in every other question today, it becomes necessary to quote Marx word for word. Today we no longer look towards socialism for a new culture – as inevitably as one will appear, once we do have socialism. Today we look to socialism *simply* for the preservation of whatever living culture we have right now.[7]

Greenberg begins straightforwardly enough and the amalgam of Marxism and modernism that was the achievement of late 1930s radicalism is apparent in the view of art as revolutionary. The difficulties arise when Greenberg moves from the general or theoretical to the particular and historical in the last two sentences. Here, he adopts a backward and static viewpoint. Outside of their historical context these two sentences defy interpretation. But in the context of the threat to art represented by Nazism and Stalinism, and especially the Nazi threat to Paris as the capital of art, we can see why Greenberg should arrive at the paradoxical conclusion that the socialist avant-garde should operate conservatively. In the present dire circumstances, Greenberg is saying, this is all that socialism can achieve. Greenberg is not denigrating socialism in 1939; '*simply*' means something like 'it is patently obvious that only socialism can achieve the task'. However, Greenberg has, in effect, substituted for a revolutionary view of socialism as an avant-garde a view of it as a preserving agent of modernism. What was an option in modernism of the 1890–1930 period, that is, the inward, self-referential turn, is on the point of becoming not just the dominant feature of modernism but of the avant-garde. Whereas, the usual view of the avant-garde (held by supporters and detractors) is that it is the anti-art element within modernism, capable of incorporating aspects of mass culture for critical purposes.

It is an indication of the complexity of Greenberg's thought at this time – and of other *PR* writers – that, in a 1941 essay on Berthold Brecht's poetry, Greenberg allows that there is 'a kind of modernist poetry that gets its special character from an infusion of folk or popular attitudes', and which, consequently, is not so embattled and defensive. (*Art and Culture*, p. 252). Brecht needs mentioning in this context because he is the prime example of a Marxist who wrote in a modernist, experimental way. However, it was the embattled outlook – just discernible at the end of 'Avant-Garde and Kitsch' – which came to dominate *PR* and, later, the New York Intellectuals' understanding of modernist culture. The political activity that is so much a part of the avant-garde's role interested American intellectuals less and less during and after the Second World War, certainly compared with their stance in 1938 when Rahv and Phillips published Trotsky. The most likely reason for the separation of culture and politics was an equation of organized politics with Stalinism and, while fully understandable, this did make for a self-preoccupied avant-garde.

The failure of nerve: the culture of the Cold War

The Second World War was another turning point in the de-radicalization of the intellectuals. In 1936, Sidney Hook had opposed any diversion from socialism in support of an imperialist war. The main reason for Hook's change of position was that the Second World War was a popular one, or at least it became so after the Japanese attack on Pearl Harbor in 1941, and when the horrifying persecution of the Jews began to be reported at the end of 1942. But, as Alan Wald points out 'to change one's characterization of the essence of the war from that of a fundamentally inter-imperialist conflict to a fundamentally antifascist struggle had a logic of its own', which has to do with the process of de-radicalization we have been tracing.[8] Responding to Sidney Hook's 'The New Failure of Nerve' (1943), which accused intellectuals of going soft on communism, art critic Meyer Schapiro was quick to identify Hook's shift to the right and the context in which it had occurred:

> He taxes with failure of nerve individuals who have courageously maintained, at the risk of persecution, the same unpopular views about the war that they held before it began. At the same time he is silent about those who have abandoned the camp of socialism for a shallow and palpably false doctrine of a new managerial society. (quoted in Wald, *The New York Intellectuals*, p. 216)

Along with Greenberg, Mary McCarthy, Edmund Wilson, and James T. Farrell, Schapiro was one of the few prominent intellectuals to maintain an anti-war position, though it was Macdonald who explicitly took on the role of Randolph Bourne in an essay published in *PR* in 1939: 'War and the Intellectuals: Act II'. When Rahv and Phillips turned to support for the war in 1943, as the only way to combat fascism, Macdonald left the magazine. The following year, with Nancy Macdonald, he founded *Politics* and, during the 1950s, maintained a much more independent position than other *PR* intellectuals.

The threat of communist world domination receded during the Second World War and in the immediate aftermath of the creation of the United Nations. It was, however, revived in the post-war years, with the Red Army's domination in the Balkans, Poland and elsewhere in Eastern Europe; the coup against the Czechoslovak government in February 1948; and the Berlin Blockade, beginning in the June of the same year. In March, 1946, speaking in the United States, Winston Churchill referred to the 'iron curtain' across Europe, yet the instability of devastated Western Europe suggested that the 'curtain' was really very flimsy. The Popular Front finally ended in 1946. At the same time, Americans also looked anxiously across the Pacific at the Chinese Revolution, leading to Mao Tse Tung's victory in 1949, and, with more urgency, at the Korean War, which began when North Korean troops, armed by the USSR, invaded the South in June 1950.

The Truman doctrine of March 1947 began as a request to Congress for $400 million of aid for Greece and Turkey to assist them in resisting Communist pressures from within and abroad. The Truman Doctrine was then broadened into a foreign policy of combatting Soviet expansion and communist influence worldwide. The Marshall Plan for $12.5 billion of American economic aid to Europe was passed by Congress as the European Recovery Program in 1948, but the USSR rejected the American offer of Marshall aid and compelled her Eastern European satellites to do the same. The formal establishment of NATO in April 1949 completed the redrawing of the world map only four years after the end of the War. When the USSR made up lost time and, in September 1949, exploded its own atomic bomb, to be followed by American and Soviet hydrogen bomb explosions in 1952 and 1953, respectively, superpower rivalry entered a new phase. The level of tension and anxiety escalated accordingly.

A wartime ally, the Soviet Union rapidly came to represent all that was not as it should be for a victorious America. As early as 1947, a polarized image of the world, in which every troublespot in the third world was evidence of Soviet intentions, turned into a domestic atmosphere of suspicion. One spy trail was followed from Klaus Fuchs, an atomic scientist, and David Greenglass, a machinist, at the atomic energy centre at Los Alamos, to a New York couple, Ethel and Julius Rosenberg. They were accused of organizing the conspiracy to pass atomic secrets to the Russians. Another trail linked Whittaker Chambers, underground courier for the Communist Party in the 1930s, and Alger Hiss, the President of the Carnegie Endowment for International Peace. However, it was the accompanying and far less justifiable hounding of suspected communists and fellow-travellers, which took its name from Senator Joseph McCarthy from Wisconsin, which stands as the low point of the Cold War. McCarthyism might be regarded as the twisted image of hopes that were disappointed when the rest of the world, including European allies, proved recalcitrant in the face of American offers to redesign the world along the lines of freedom and democracy. To underline the sense of frustration and even incomprehensibility felt by many Americans, it is worth making the simple point that in the late 1940s there had been no Vietnam, nor even Korea, no oil crisis, Bay of Pigs, Watergate or Irangate, or massive budget deficit; no shocking political assassinations, no AIDS, and no hard-drug and urban crime waves.

The House Un-American Activities Committee (HUAC) had been in operation since 1938, but reached the public's attention in 1947 when it seized upon communist infiltration of the film industry. The link between culture, the media and the Cold War was thus firmly made from the outset. The first victims were the 'Hollywood Ten' (mostly scriptwriters) who were sentenced to up to a year in prison for contempt of Congress. On release, only the director, Edward Dmytryk, named names and so avoided the blacklist which wasted careers and lives. In 1948 HUAC's investigations led to an indictment of twelve members of the Communist Party under the Smith Act, and to the investigations into William Remington and Harry Dexter White, both important federal officials. Beginning in March 1947, during President Truman's first term of office, government workers were investigated by 'loyalty boards', and four years later over 2000 employees had resigned and over two hundred had been dismissed. During Truman's second term and then into Eisenhower's first in

1952, the FBI amassed information and compiled lists of subversive organizations. Congressional hearings and judicial trials were held; absolutions were given to those who co-operated; and formal and informal sentences were meted out to those who would not.

McCarthy, himself, came to public and national attention in February, 1950 when he wàved his 'list of 205' alleged members of the Communist Party employed in the State Department in front of the Republican Women's Club, Wheeling, West Virginia. Though McCarthy was less important than McCarthyism, he asked exactly the kind of question to which Americans in the 1950s were most vulnerable: 'How can we account for our present situation *unless* we believe that men high in this government are concerting to deliver us to disaster? This *must* be the product of a great conspiracy.' Or as Reverend Parris puts it in *The Crucible* (1953), Arthur Miller's allegory of McCarthyism, 'we must look to cause proportionate'.[9]

Those who resisted McCarthyism were a mixture of maverick intellectuals, Communist Party members who did not try to hide their allegiances, or those who were simply provoked to action. In no particular order: Dashiell Hammett, Lillian Hellman, I.F. Stone, Arthur Miller, Henry Steele Commager, Dwight Macdonald, Mary McCarthy, Michael Harrington, Meyer Schapiro, Harold Rosenberg, Albert Einstein, Hannah Arendt, and Irving Howe. By refusing to co-operate they – or at least those not tainted with whitewashing the Moscow Trials – maintained the tradition of intellectual independence inaugurated by Thoreau, continued by Randolph Bourne, and then adopted by the New York Intellectuals themselves at the time of the Moscow Trials.

The middle of the journey: the New York Intellectuals in the 1940s and 1950s

'In the middle thirties people watched each other very closely for signs of weakness.'[10] This observation, from Lionel Trilling's novel of radicals and liberals, *The Middle of the Journey*, fitted the post-war period, too. By 1947, when the novel was published, the old habits of vigilance were being tuned not to the clash of ideologies, but to the muted hint of conviction and the occasional zealous overstatement. The new vigilance, even at its worst in the behaviour of the McCarthyite right, barely compares with the political atmosphere that surrounded the Moscow Trials. The fact that we can document and illustrate the culture of the Cold War at such length also warns against glib comparisons. Rather, it is the contradiction between the claims for freedom in post-war America and something like McCarthyism which is still shocking.

Like others caught up in the ramifications of the Cold War, and especially McCarthyism, intellectuals were subject to considerable private as well as public pressures to conform, which meant, in effect, to forfeit their adversarial stance. The record suggests that they were no weaker or stronger than other groups. Nevertheless, because it was a Cold War, fought with ideas; because of the role some intellectuals played in giving at least partial intellectual credence to the witchhunts; and because the Cold War played such an important part in their collective career, there are good reasons for treating the Cold War and McCarthyism as a major crisis in American intellectual history.

During the latter part of the 1930s, *PR* stuck to its marginal point of view. It was ironic, therefore, to find the magazine staking out the *middle* ground among intellectuals in the post-war years. Communists were a security risk and could not be trusted, even to admit they were communists in some cases. Against this, *PR* disapproved of so-called 'anti-anti-Communism', and criticized the excesses of McCarthyism. *PR* writers also feared that legitimate dissent would be outlawed along with what they agreed were treasonable actions. This fear was well grounded, leading to the conclusion, voiced by Christopher Lasch, that heresy was indeed too often seen as conspiracy and that some of the sharpest minds around at the time 'lent themselves to purposes having nothing to do with the values they professed – purposes, indeed, that were diametrically opposed to them'.[11]

These ex-Communist Party members (in a few cases), ex-Trotskyites, and fellow travellers, together with *PR*, continued their intellectual migration and moved towards the centre of American life on the authority of their 1930s experiences. They were in a privileged position to provide an *intellectual* framework for a response to the Soviet threat. At the very least, they could claim to be realists, who had seen through the innocence of utopian illusions and who now had the kind of insider knowledge which encouraged William Phillips to urge that 'the Left must not permit the struggle against Stalinism to be appropriated by the Right'.[12]

In *The End of Ideology: On the Exhaustion of Political Ideas in the Fifties* (1960), the sociologist, Daniel Bell, links the new realism with the retreat from socialism. He writes of 'an end to chiliastic hopes, to millenarianism, to apocalyptic thinking – and to ideology'. 'Ideology', he continues, 'which once was a road to action, has come to a dead end.'[13] It had been left high and dry, along with Marx's prediction that a revolution would come out of the contradictions in the most developed nations of the world. Plans and blueprints would not work and could have dire consequences, as the twin examples of Stalin's Russia and Hitler's Germany proved.

However, an early indication of the way that Cold War conditions interfered with the objectivity of intellectuals supposedly at the end of ideology, was the editorial to the 1946 issue of *PR*. Entitled 'The "Liberal" Fifth Column', it attacked *The New Republic* and *The Nation*, among other liberal outlets, for giving excessive support to the Soviet Union's activities in Eastern Europe and for jeopardising democratic freedoms. Irving Howe, himself a late-comer to the *PR*/New York group of intellectuals, cited the *Partisan* editorial as an example of '*Stalinophobia*, a disease common among intellectuals who were once radicals.'[14] The low level of argument, certainly for an editorial in *PR*, and the proto-McCarthyite rhetoric were signs of a very particular outlook upon the world which reappeared in James Burnham's attack on Henry Wallace's campaign for the democratic nomination against Truman: 'A vote for Wallace is a vote for Stalin.'[15]

The distance some intellectuals had travelled is illustrated by Sidney Hook, who in 1933 had accused the Communist Party of being anti-revolutionary, but in 1953 was the most prominent of the Cold Warriors who had learned from their radical pasts, and was zealous in attacking communism in general rather than simply the Party. He was especially severe on fellow-travelling liberals and Western European intellectuals, who equated American capitalism with Soviet communism. In his attacks on communists, Hook supported the use of the Smith Act of 1940 which made it illegal to advocate violent overthrow of the government. From mere membership of the Communist Party, Hook and others concluded that a person was conspiring forcefully against the American government. The Constitutional protection of free speech and political assembly did not apply to communists, not because there had been a treasonable act, but because they held a set of ideas. For Hook, a communist academic was a contradiction in terms, and this was the view of the American Committee on Academic Freedom, on which Hook served. Some 80 per cent of the academics who were accused eventually lost their jobs.

Hook's retreat from his high standards of analysis in the 1930s was very obvious in his proposal in a 1949 *PR* article, that American writers should engage in self-censorship because of the possible consequences of their work. Disturbed by the image of America to be found in William Faulkner or Sinclair Lewis, Hook recommended that writers should stress the positive and not the negative side of American life so as to combat Soviet propaganda.

James Burnham – along with Sidney Hook the toughest of those up from communism – shattered any golden age theory of communism that his contemporaries may have harboured when he declared, in a 1945 article in *PR*, that 'Stalinism is Communism'. Burnham's most important book of the period, *The Managerial Revolution* (1941), substituted for class an analysis of power in large organizations within a world of superpowers. From the 1950s onwards, in the writings of Daniel Bell, C. Wright Mills and other sociologists influenced by Max Weber, Burnham's insights into bureaucratic corporatism were refined, often brilliantly, into the main theme in mid-century American thought: political pluralism. Burnham's own preoccupation with anti-communism left him an unexpected casualty of the Cold War curtailment of intellectual enquiry. Though starting out in *The Managerial Revolution* from a position of no great affection for the United States, Burnham's central concept was applied increasingly just to the USSR and melded with the larger concept of totalitarianism to become yet another expression of Cold War orthodoxy.

Burnham was one of a number of prominent intellectuals from the United States and Europe to attend the 1950 Congress for Cultural Freedom held in West Berlin, and then a year later he was on the rollcall for the American Committee for Cultural Freedom (ACCF). Up until 1954 the ACCF was virtually a Who's Who of American intellectuals: from the older 1930s generation, Sidney Hook, the former Socialist Party presidential candidate, Norman Thomas, William Phillips, Whittaker Chambers, and novelists James T. Farrell and John Dos Passos; and from those who came to prominence after the war, social theorists, Daniel Bell, Irving Kristol, David Riesman, J.K. Galbraith, Nathan Glazer, and Norman Podhoretz, the atomic scientist, J. Robert Oppenheimer, historian, Arthur Schlesinger Jr, and film director, Elia Kazan. It says something of the strength of the consensus (or of the perceived threat from the USSR) that the ACCF could accommodate this diversity.

Through the Congress and then the ACCF, intellectuals formally committed their skills to combatting the propaganda from Moscow which culminated in the Cultural and Scientific Conference for World Peace, held in New York in 1949. An equally important landmark in the rehabilitation of intellectuals was the *PR* symposium, 'Our Country and Our Culture' of 1952, at which it was asked whether there was any longer a good reason for taking intellectual cues from Europe, when it was American culture that had avoided the terrors of fascism and Stalinism. Though participants made their dislike of American mass culture very plain, in the final analysis they distinguished it from the manipulation of culture for political ends in the totalitarian states of the Soviet Union and Nazi Germany of the 1930s. That mass culture did not rule out high culture in the United States was just one of the recognized advantages of a democratic capitalism which was still under the influence of New Deal reformism. The substantive results of this very significant reorientation of American intellectuals' attitude towards their 'country and . . . culture' will be considered in the next chapter. For the moment, though, we can observe that the Berlin Congress signalled a return to commitment – in the name of free speech – and an abandonment of the detached critical role of the intellectual so valued when the Moscow Trials discredited commitment to the Soviet Union in the late 1930s. The irony of the new commitment on the party of intellectuals was compounded since the literal audience at the various congresses was often European intellectuals. Their unwillingness to accept the polar oppositions of East and West as givens, in any attempt to understand the post-war world, closely resembled the American anti-Stalinist radicalism of the late 1930s.

We also know now that the commitment formalized in the Congress for Cultural Freedom and in *Encounter* and other foreign-based journals linked to the Congress, was compromised through secret CIA funding. Michael Josselson 'represented' the CIA in the Congress for Cultural Freedom, and did so from the front: he was the Congress's executive director from its founding. Melvin J. Lasky, a former employee in the American Information Services, was on *Encounter*'s editorial board before taking over from Irving Kristol as editor in 1958. *Encounter* was clearly regarded by the CIA as helping to establish an outpost of American intellectual anti-communism in Britain, where there were disturbing signs of anti-Americanism. In the magazine's first editorial in October 1953, Irving Kristol and the British critic and poet, Stephen Spender, caught only too well the underside of worry and suspicion in the mood of the prosperous 1950s: 'The dark side of the moon may no longer be mistaken for the rising sun, but it is still there and still dark. And shadows move among us; almost too many to count and sometimes even hard to name.'[16]

CIA support (which few knew about, including, by their own statememts, Kristol and Spender) only cemented an intellectual connection that many had already made with American foreign policy and which continued through to Vietnam. When intellectuals changed tack and supported Truman in 1947, seeing in his domestic policy a second act in the New Deal's reform of capitalism, those who formed Americans for Democratic Action (ADA) were in no doubt that Truman's anti-Communist foreign policy was equally correct.

Not all intellectuals made a pact with American foreign policy; nor did all cultural institutions, even those within the orbit of the newly-founded subject of American Studies, where cultural imperialism ought to have had a natural home. In 1947 the first of the Salzburg seminars in American Studies had espoused a much more open-minded attitude towards Eastern Europe, and a more detached view of American culture, than the Congress for Cultural Freedom. However, signs of top level interest in cultural gatherings can be gleaned from the experience of F.O. Matthiessen, one of the academics who travelled to

Austria for the first Salzburg seminar. Known as the author of a seminal study of mid-nineteenth-century American literature, *The American Renaissance* (1941), Matthiessen was thought to be a communist and was prevented from attending subsequent seminars.

In contrast, Burnham, Hook, Kristol and other Cold War intellectuals, along with *Commentary*, *Encounter* and – certainly compared with its pre-Second World War position – *Partisan Review* were no longer on the margins. Their activities confirm the meaning of the Cold War, defined by Thomas Braden, a former CIA official, as a war 'fought with ideas instead of bombs' (quoted in Bernstein (ed.), *Towards a New Past*, p. 356).

An end to innocence: Leslie Fiedler, Harold Rosenberg and the trial of Alger Hiss

In 'The Mood of Three Generations', Daniel Bell formally introduces his own, younger generation of New York Intellectuals. Usually included in this group are the historian, Richard Hofstadter, the novelist, Saul Bellow, the literary and cultural critics Irving Howe, Leslie Fiedler, Alfred Kazin, and Robert Warshow, and the political scientists, Seymour Martin Lipset and Irving Kristol. Not all were from New York City or lived there, but they shared the general ethos that we have been describing; all, in Irving Kristol's term, were 'Newyorkintellectuals'. 'Ours, a "twice-born" generation', Bell writes in *The End of Ideology*, 'finds its wisdom in pessimism, evil, tragedy, and despair. So we are both old and young "before our time." '[17]

We meet the same experienced tone in the Preface to Leslie Fiedler's 1955 collection of essays, *An End to Innocence*:

> I have lived (deeply, though somewhat grudgingly, involved) through a crisis in liberalism which seems to me a major event in the development of the human spirit. This crisis I feel peculiarly qualified to describe, precisely *because* I am a literary man, immune to certain journalistic platitudes and accustomed to regard men and words with a sensibility trained by the newer critical methods. It is a 'close reading' of recent events that I should like to think I have achieved, a reading that does not scant ambiguity or paradox, but tries to give the testimony of a witness before a Senate committee or the letters of the Rosenbergs the same careful scrutiny we have learned to practice on the shorter poems of John Donne.[18]

It is a very interesting passage. Fiedler presents the idea of vigilance, which was endemic to the Cold War, as professional competence, in his case as a literary critic. Moreover, professionalism pertains to the relationship between innocence and experience that was part of the intellectuals' genealogy of disaffection with communism. Professionalism allowed them to distinguish 1950s commitment not just from the propaganda of the Soviet Union, but also from their own 1930s commitment, full of naivety and utopian ideals. In order to catch the nuances of an apparently crass era, as well as the criss-crossings of texts (including literary texts) and contexts, we can consider the essay on Hiss and Chambers; the other explicitly political essays are on Ethel and Julius Rosenberg and McCarthy and the intellectuals.

At the HUAC hearings beginning in August 1948, Whittaker Chambers described communist activity within the New Deal. In telling of his membership of the Communist Party (he had also written for the *New Masses*), he named others, including, not just as a member of the Party but also as a spy, Alger Hiss. After various posts within the New Deal, Hiss had been at Roosevelt's side at the Yalta Conference in 1945, and his success continued after the war when his friends and associates included Adlai Stevenson, the Democratic Presidential candidate in 1952, and Dean Acheson and John Foster Dulles, Secretaries of State under Truman and Eisenhower respectively. Hiss's status made him a test-case for HUAC activities and, more broadly, for the Cold War climate of suspicion. Chambers, too, assumed a symbolic importance in relating his radical past through the media, the HUAC hearings, a libel action brought by Hiss, and two perjury trials. At the second trial Hiss was convicted and sentenced to five years in prison. Chambers' confession dramatized in an exaggerated way the stories of many intellectuals who had lost their innocence.

Fiedler tracks this theme indirectly in the literary essays in *An End to Innocence*: now that European thought and culture had so disastrously failed the world, Americans had to grow up and assume responsibility. American liberalism had been too innocent, too tied to myths of freedom and the absence of limiting conditions. Hence, Fiedler's injunction to that most attractive of American literary innocents, Mark Twain's Huckleberry Finn, to 'come back to the raft ag'in', that is, come back to society and face responsibilities. Fiedler's essay on Hiss and Chambers is more direct. It soon becomes a *mea culpa* for any intellectual who held childish ideals of collective brotherhood in communism. Absolution – and the religious terminology is quite apt – will yet bring maturity: 'The qualifying act of moral adulthood is precisely this admission of responsibility for the past and its consequences, however undesired or unforeseen' (p. 4). This is why

Fiedler, in effect, has to sentence Hiss and, in the companion essay, the Rosenbergs, over again:

> It is not necessary that we liberals be self-flagellants. We have desired good, and we have done some; but we have also done great evil. The confession in itself is nothing, but without the confession there can be no understanding, and without the understanding of what the Hiss case tries desperately to declare, we will not be able to move forward from a liberalism of innocence to a liberalism of responsibility. (p. 24)

When one of those liberals, the art critic, Harold Rosenberg, replied to Fiedler, he categorically refused Fiedler's beguiling invitation, on the grounds that Chambers was never a liberal. Such is the seductiveness of confession, that Fiedler manufactures a 'liberal' who, by definition, must share in Stalin's guilt. To confess will effectively rewrite the past, a skill previously thought to be the monopoly of totalitarian regimes. As Rosenberg remarks, 'A single full-scale blast and the years 1932–1952 could have been turned into the desert of "twenty years of treason"', rather than a key chapter in the culture of politics.[19]

Hiss is condemned by Fiedler for lying; he allows that Hiss could have admitted passing classified information to Chambers and yet justified his actions on behalf of the Soviet Union in the context of 'those years of betrayal leading to Munich'. However, another of Chambers' informants, Henry Julian Wadleigh, is denied moral adulthood precisely because 'he admitted passing documents to Chambers but insisted that his course had been justified by history'. Wadleigh is disqualified from absolution by Fiedler because he fails to look the part: 'the cartoonist's pink-tea radical, with his thick glasses, disordered hair, and acquired Oxford accent' (pp. 5 and 7). Hiss is therefore put in the position of both having to tell the truth and be guilty of treason.

Where Wadleigh fails to learn because his experiences are, Fiedler decides, not really experiences, and Hiss fails to grow up, Whittaker Chambers assumes an almost tragic status. Fiedler's is such a particular and, in its way, compelling, interpretation that it sends us not to Chambers' own testimony, given to support his charges against Hiss, but to the conclusion of Lionel Trilling's *The Middle of the Journey* (1947). In the Preface to that novel, Trilling confirms that he created Gifford Maxim out of Whittaker Chambers (whom he knew) and then – at least a year ahead of the Hiss trial – brought him through the novel's story to the point where, in the name of the doctrine of personal responsibility, he could challenge the powerful environmental explanation for human action favoured by the Left. Referring to a man who has accidentally killed his daughter, Gifford Maxim concludes that:

> I believe that Duck Caldwell – like you or me or any of us – is
> wholly responsible for his acts . . . That is what gives him value
> in my eyes – his eternal, everlasting responsibility . . . And when
> [he] breaks the moral law of the whole universe, I consider that
> his punishment might be infinite, everlasting. And yet in my
> system there is one thing that yours [the communist one] lacks.
> In my system, although there is never-ending responsibility,
> there is such a thing as mercy. (p. 299)

Trilling is a much cooler and experienced figure than Fiedler, and
through his main character, John Laskell, he keeps some distance from
Maxim's new religion, while still accepting that communism has
failed. Laskell is just *so* prophetic of the McCarthy era in his summary
of Maxim:

> [Laskell] was thinking that Maxim . . . would not religiously
> retire from the world but would go where worldly power lies
> waiting for men to pick it up. He had been seeing the great
> executive force that lay behind Maxim's expression of his view of
> the nature of guilt and responsibility. It seemed to him that the
> day was not very far off when Maxim's passions would suit the
> passions of others. (p. 300)

Fiedler is drawn into the Christian rhetoric of confession. But his
certainty – leading him to wonder why on earth Hiss lied – is based
upon unexamined assumptions. Specific to the case, Hiss is assumed to
be guilty and to have no hidden motives, for example protecting
others, like his wife, who may have been involved; more generally,
Fiedler assumes an a-historical model of interpretation. Here he merely
echoes the official investigators' view of the 1930s. Gossip could be
turned into evidence without any account being taken of the way of
being political in that decade: the meetings, the disputes, the necessity
for constant contacts to respond to events. There is also the assumption
that the past only has meaning in relation to the immediate present, to
the extent that, when an individual's past was reconstructed in an
investigation, the past took on a purely psychological meaning. The
content of the past is completely ignored: what it meant to choose and
then support a radical social programme in the 1930s. To give such
content little or no attention is historicism gone wild, with the idea of
guilt subsuming both the differences between forms of radicalism in
the 1930s and the serious interpretation of the relationship between
actions and results. Had these matters received attention, had 'guilt'
not subsumed 'responsibility', then the present might have been
examined more carefully, including the scale of the communist threat

to the fabric of American life. In 1944 the membership of the Communist Party had been 80,000; in 1950 it had been halved and it dropped to 10,000 by 1957. But for many intellectuals the reality of communism could not be questioned because it had become part of them, part of their radical past. They saw the world in terms of stark oppositions that bore hardly any resemblance to the domestic situation. In the essay mentioned earlier, Harold Rosenberg carefully compares and contrasts the McCarthy investigations with the Moscow Trials:

> Since America lacked an agency for the effective extraction of confessions – the threats of McCarthy fell far short of inducing the profound self-doubt that was the speciality of Russian interrogation – the potential confessor had to heckle himself into it. In the United States psychoanalysis assumed the function of the secret police. Americans, too, spoke in order to escape from a dungeon, but it was from the dungeons of their own selves. (pp. 225–6)

Rosenberg suggests that Fiedler's insistence on a collective confession of guilt is just as much a desire for community as that which informed the Popular Front which Fiedler so dislikes. Confession enables the intellectual to rejoin a society re-imagined under the threat of the USSR in terms of a community whose address 'is not the library, the study or the cafe but Main Street'(p. 230). Membership depends upon confessing not simply to a radical past but to being an intellectual. It was in this broad context that Rosenberg coined the phrase a 'herd of independent minds' to describe the New York Intellectuals.

They are, or until some time ago were, radicals: the New York Intellectuals in retrospect

There were some steadfast performances before the House Un-American Activities Committee (HUAC) and elsewhere, and Dwight Macdonald (not least in his magazine, *Politics*) and Harold Rosenberg were exemplary in their criticism of attempts to rewrite the recent past. This tradition of radical independence also produced *Dissent*, which Irving Howe and Lewis Coser founded in 1954. While the editors accepted that 'in America today there is no significant socialist movement and that, in all likelihood, no such movement will appear in the immediate future', *Dissent* at least kept inspecting socialism to see whether there was some life in it.[20] Others were poking it to ensure it was dead. To borrow the title of Howe's autobiography, *Dissent* retained a 'margin of hope'. Contributors to *Dissent* included many of those who would prove influential in the 'break out' of the 1960s – Michael Harrington, Herbert Marcuse, and Norman Mailer (though Mailer's 'The White Negro' was hardly a typical *Dissent* article) – as well as Dwight Macdonald, the most radical (or stubborn?) of the New Yorkers.

It is a measure of the achievements and importance of the New York Intellectuals since the mid-1930s that it would simply not have been possible to follow so many ideas and themes in American intellectual history without reference to them. It is only fair, therefore, to conclude discussion of them, not with McCarthyism but with Irving Howe's assessment in an essay published in *Commentary* in 1967. If Harold Rosenberg's 'herd of independent minds' remains the most perceptive brief characterization, then Howe encapsulates both their history and their style:

> They are, or until recently have been, anti-Communist; they are, or until some time ago were, radicals; they have a fondness for ideological speculation; they write literary criticism with a strong social emphasis; they revel in polemic; they strive self-consciously to be 'brilliant'; and by birth or osmosis they are Jews.

Howe has little that is positive to say of the 1930s – 'a "low dishonest" time' – but he confirms the decade's crucial significance for the New Yorkers:

> By comparison with competing schools of thought, the radicalism of the anti-Stalinist left, as it was then being advanced in *Partisan Review* seemed cogent, fertile, alive: it could stir good minds to argument, it could gain the attention of writers abroad, it seemed to offer a combination of system and independence.[21]

In his comprehensive study, *The New York Intellectuals*, Alan Wald agrees, arguing that 1930s anti-Stalinism should not be confused with post-1945 anti-communism. One was a radical critique of what communism had become under Stalin; the other a blanket attack on radicalism that made it synonymous with the crimes of Stalin.

It is sometimes said that for all their brilliance, the *PR* critics failed to achieve a level of theoretical sophistication comparable with their contemporaries in the Frankfurt School, or with Brecht and Lukács debating the relationship between Marxism and modernism. The New Yorkers were too busy, constantly reacting to events, thinking on their feet as it were. Yet the story of their development suggests that they were at their most sophisticated – at their most potentially theoretical – when they *were* constantly responding to events. Then they achieved a considerable degree of insight into the relationship between culture and politics, and a range of sophisticated discriminations between radical and reactionary tendencies. It was when they relied upon what they took to be a mature reflection upon the world – in effect their anti-communism – that they stopped thinking so fruitfully. Sidney Hook and James Burnham make good test-cases for this hypothesis. Their failure, post-war, to keep examining their anti-communism emptied communism of the content that it had for them in the 1930s. It is one of the telling features of Lionel Trilling's *The Middle of the Journey* – still the major political novel of the period – that it translates ideas into psychologies, and by means of its isolated setting in New England, separates the drama of the intellectuals from the economic and political drama of the 1930s.

Looking back on Irving Howe looking back, the other point to make is that the New Yorkers have been there or thereabouts from the 1930s until the early 1970s. In Howe's phrase, they have maintained an 'alertness towards the public event'. On the other hand, there is a narrowness, if European and 'New York' American high culture is construed as narrow. Their defence of European modernism led them to stringent criticism of the 'Redskin' tradition in American literature (roughly, the Twain–Hemingway–Steinbeck line), but modernist preoccupations have left little room for regional and ethnic literature (bar Jewish literature). Also, the women's movement and its literature seem to be missing even from a 'late' New Yorker like Irving Howe. In his 1967 retrospective, he is more upset about a failure to engage with the intellectual challenge of Norman Mailer than with the emerging protest movements.

Howe's fear in 1967 that the New Yorkers would not rouse themselves to occupy once again the critical margins of American thought has proved correct. *The New York Review of Books* has shown itself more attuned to the time than *Partisan Review*, while the success of neo-conservatism since the 1970s, arising as it did from within the New Yorkers' ranks in the persons of Bell, Kristol, Lipset, and Midge Dexter and Norman Podhoretz, confirms Howe's prediction. Nevertheless, the longer view that we have taken makes it possible to agree with Howe's conclusion, in which he reinstates those he has time for in an important American tradition of radical dissent:

For the values of liberalism, for the politics of a democratic radicalism, for the norms of rationality and intelligence, for the standards of literary seriousness, for the life of the mind as a humane dedication – for all this it should again be worth finding themselves in a minority, even a beleaguered minority, and not with fantasies of martyrdom, but with a quiet recognition that for the intellectual this is likely to be his usual condition. (*The New York Intellectuals*, p. 265)

Two postscripts before we get to the New Left. In the '50th Anniversary' *Partisan Review* (1984), Daniel Bell distanced himself from Irving Kristol, thereby refusing the depressing inevitability of a radicalism (innocence?) to neo-conservatism (experience?) trajectory. And, second, in 1988, Bell, Howe, Galbraith, and Schlesinger signed 'A Reaffirmation of Principle', along with fifty-eight other liberals, in protest against the vilification of liberalism led by President Reagan during the Bush/Dukakis campaign.

There IS an alternative to the present: the New Left

In concluding this story of intellectuals with the New Left, I shall be concentrating, rather narrowly, upon relations (or lack of them) between Students for a Democratic Society (SDS) and the Old Left. In the latter category I shall include those who experienced the crisis of the Old Left and came 'up from communism' – an ex-Old Left.

In spite of coming at the tail end of the Old Left and, indeed, being part of the break with the 1930s, Irving Howe had difficulty responding to the New Left of the 1960s and 1970s. Overall, relations between the New Left and those who could not forget the disasters of the 1930s, were hostile. It was not simply the unexpectedness of a new Left arising out of the affluent late 1950s and 1960s. It was (and this applies to the movements of blacks, women and colonial peoples as well as to youth or students) that the analytical vocabulary of an Old and an ex-Old Left was not adequate. What happened within families – and could barely be described by parents and their children – happened in the wider society, too. Of course, for its part, the New Left did not understand its forerunners, dismissing both Marxism and liberalism too quickly. The New Left thought the Old Left bereft of idealism (experienced in the wrong sense), in many cases too professorial, and just too old.

The main text of SDS, early on at least, was *The Port Huron Statement* (1962). Written by Tom Hayden, especially, and Al Haber, both leading activists, it sums up the idealism of the movement. At an abstract level, the *Port Huron Statement* is a critique of the false reality of American society. For the Old Left in the Depression, reality pressed upon them; it was palpably there in the unemployed and the closed factories, and it could be acted upon. The ex-Old Left also had no problem with reality. They had come to accept it as a marked improvement and had settled into it. The New Left thought reality was a sham, beset with contradictions, and capable of being transcended – through drugs, cultural events, like rock concerts and communes, but more importantly through ideals which, ironically, came to be articulated when economic reality did not press so heavily upon middle-class youth:

> There *is* an alternative to the present . . . In suggesting social
> goals and values . . . we are aware of entering a sphere of some
> disrepute . . . [But] a first task of any social movement is to
> convince people that the search for orienting theories and the
> creation of human values is complex but worthwhile.[22]

The experienced, ironic outlook on life (referred to by Daniel Bell in 'The Mood of Three Generations') had even managed to explain Hiroshima and Nagasaki as part of a story, which began in the 1930s and reached perfect clarity of exposition in 1944 and 1945. (It was the Danish atomic scientist, Niels Bohr, who sounded crazy when, after a visit to Los Alamos, he urged that the bomb's secrets be shared with the USSR.) Paul Buhle outlines the outlook of his, the New Left, generation:

> Compared [to the nuclear threat], even the failures of Socialism
> in the East and the West which obsessed our predecessors seemed
> rather less alarming. They had been so entrapped in the pre-
> Hiroshima frameworks, the expansion of Socialism or the battle
> against reverse-Marxist expansion of Stalin's barbarism, that
> Armageddon became a mere extension of the old logics.[23]

The New Left was not a total break from the liberal democratic story, and in most of the elections at all levels during the 1960s and 1970s, groups within the New Left sought change through reform and the vote. However, the assassination of President Kennedy in 1963 was a symbolic break with electoral reform, while experiences in the Civil Rights organization, SNCC, provided further evidence of the 'system' geared up against democratic change. As Tom Hayden remarked in *Rebellion and Repression* (1969), 'federal government and Democratic Party could not and would not offend Southern officials'.[24] The disillusion with traditional politics combined with social alienation and the experiences in the Civil Rights Movement to create in SDS a new logic of radicalism. For one thing, as Paul Buhle suggests, the opposition between the USA and the USSR which so preoccupied the intellectuals we have been looking at, was deconstructed by the logic of nuclear arms. The meaning of 'us' changed when the idea of a winnable nuclear war was discredited by the very build-up of arms that, in previous wars, could be a factor in eventual victory. 'Us' got mixed up with 'them', and the 'tough' nationalistic language of liberal anti-communism gave way to a more ethical, international vocabulary which, when it looked back, looked back to the International Workers of the World.

There was also a change in the sociological constituency. The Old Left had been fixed on the working class, Marx's proletariat, while those who came up from communism had come either to define 'us' as a radical avant-garde forged in opposition to mass politics, or as a non-radical amorphous network of interest groups. In New Left politics, there was a freewheeling Counter-Cultural individualism that the liberal anti-communists disapproved of: Bell wrote critically of 'the sensibility of the sixties' and Howe of 'the collective naif' and 'the *psychology of unobstructed need*'.[25] Individualism was combined with an ideal of 'participatory democracy' which assumed that popular politics and the syndicalism of the Wobblies were good things. Democracy was a grass roots thing, to be found in health clinics, sanitation schemes, job projects and so forth, though the base of the movement was the university campus. All of which confirms that the New Left was difficult to define in relation to a particular constituency.

The common denominator of the New Left constituency was alienation. For middle-class youth 'growing up absurd' (Paul Goodman's phrase), alienation began at home, but then found its first object in the plight of blacks. When the New Left or the Movement, as it came to be called, coalesced in the *Port Huron Statement*, the Civil Rights movement was recognized as crucial, but there was a more general identification with minorities, the third world, and the poor – each a 'surrogate proletariat', according to Peter Clecak.[26] The working class tended not to be identified as a block, and here the influence of Herbert Marcuse, C. Wright Mills and Paul Goodman were important – in a positive way, in that they opened up the radical possibilities of the new groupings.

There was also a change in the 'how' of radical action. In the scarcity-economy (of the 1930s), the motor force looked to be with the determining objective economic conditions. The New Left, however, was a political response to a world in which abundance was more visible, if not fairly distributed, and in which mass culture and mass communications were an everyday reality. In these changed circumstances, consciousness-raising became the means to political change, aimed at better distribution of wealth but, more importantly, aimed at materialism itself. So, where the Old Left had been born out of not-enough, and the ex-Old Left saw social progress arising from plenty, the New Left was a protest against too-much.

A different relationship between politics and culture was also presupposed. The more austere conditions in which the Old Left was formed partly explain its functional view of culture: art as a representation of reality and/or art as propaganda. Nineteen-sixties performance art and 'happenings', as discussed in Chapter 2, operated differently, and sought to shock the audience into awareness, while rock concerts were thought to create 'togetherness'. Both also symbolized the notion of an 'anywhere' art, neither 'in' the Party nor the museum but composed of 'experiences'. Street art is the clearest example, but alternative or 'underground' magazines would come into the category of 'anywhere' culture as well.

Protests took on an 'anywhere' and 'anywhen' form. This does not mean the issues were not taken seriously or that the stakes were not high. In 1964 the Berkeley Free Speech Movement set a pattern of sorts: there was a diffused objective, rather than a wage-claim at stake, and it was a media event in which both the mass of people and the speakers performed. There was also what George Katsiaficas calls 'the *eros* effect', in which apparently leaderless demonstrations occurred, again in contrast with the organizational politics of the Old Left. Within a few days of President Nixon's televised announcement on 30 April, 1970, of the invasion of Cambodia, over a hundred campuses had demonstrations, the first less than an hour after Nixon came on television. In all, over 400 campuses were disrupted. Taking into account other demonstrations, notably those that followed the killing of four Kent State University students on the 4th May, 1970, over 80 per cent of American universities and colleges experienced protests or strikes in May, involving around 50 per cent of students.[27]

New Left politics had a different narrative: more dispersed and multi-centred, so more difficult to evaluate. The betrayal of communism in the Soviet Union which we have discussed in some detail, and the complexities which affluence brought to class relations in the 1950s, in different ways challenged the straightforward Old Left view of progression towards a revolution. Faced with this loss of faith, but critical also of those of the Old Left who had travelled so far that they ended up acquiescing in corporate, bureaucratized America, with its Cold war mentality, there was (as Gramsci said in a very different context) 'a revolt against *Capital*'.

A lack of faith (or interest) in classic Marxian historical materialism did not mean that the New Left lacked ideals. Quite the reverse. If there is one distinguishing feature between the 1950s 'end of ideology' generation and the New Left, it is the re-emergence of utopianism. In some ways, the New Left drew more on what John Diggins calls 'the lyrical left' of Randolph Bourne and the intellectuals (like John Reed and Floyd Dell) who gathered round the *Masses*, than they did the Old Left of the 1930s; or, for that matter, the reforming Left best represented by Michael Harrington's exposé of poverty, *The Other America*, published in 1963.[28]

The difficulties in institutionalizing so much diversity was one reason for the decline of the New Left. The eclecticism of the Movement was a strength but there was no common agent of change. Second, the escalation of the Vietnam War after 1965 (with the draft, inflation of the war budget at the expense of domestic reforms, and eventually the invasion of Cambodia) produced a dramatic increase in protest: April 1965 in Washington, and the biggest protest in American history; 400,000 in San Francisco and New York in April 1967; then, in October, the famous march on the Pentagon, and many more campus protests in support of organized draft resistance. SDS membership rose from around 1000 in 1964 to around 4300 in 1965, and that was part of the problem. While it was a crowning achievement for New Left organizations to help stop the war, and bring the withdrawal of troops in 1973, the ideological direction of SDS had been changed by the influx of new members and by the sheer numbers demonstrating. The Kent State killings, the My Lai massacre, and the invasion of Cambodia so shocked students in general and the liberal sections of society that Vietnam became part of mainstream political action. Meanwhile, the third reason for the break-up of SDS in 1969 was developing: factionalism, mostly involving the Progressive Labor Party which had joined SDS in 1965.

Rather than detail the institutional in-fighting which marked the end of the New Left, and seriously compromised if it did not destroy the *Port Huron* idealism, an appropriate coda in a book of this kind is a brief consideration of the most important intellectual legacy of New Left thought – the work of Noam Chomsky. Although he is a major figure in the field of linguistics, Chomsky's analysis of American power in *American Power and the New Mandarins* (1969), *At War With Asia* (1970), *Reasons of State* (1970), and *The Culture of Terrorism* (1988) is more pertinent here. Often involved in grassroots protest against American involvement in Asia, the Middle East and Central America, Chomsky differs from the New Left leaders in his *long* view of the global aspirations of the United States, pursued, without notable differences but with escalating violence or the potential for such, across a number of administrations. Where the New Left eased off on economic analysis, Chomsky traces American foreign policy back to American business needs and to the need for free movement of capital into another country for investment and out of it back to the US as profit. Finally, where the New Left broke from Cold War preoccupations, Chomsky analyses the shared aims of the US and the USSR in balance-of-power politics, and maintains an independent left-position which at least bears comparison with that of the early *Partisan Review*. For Chomsky, elite power-mongering is common to the USSR and the US: both have needed the other for global economic stability since 1945. It will be interesting to see how the triumph of American capitalism in the wake of the current collapse of the Soviet empire is managed at an ideological level when so much of its ideology depends upon anti-communism, the detection of the hidden hand of Moscow in the Third World, and propaganda gifts like the building of the Berlin Wall.

In two books of 1988, *The Political Economy of the Mass Media* and *The Culture of Terrorism*, Chomsky examines the representation of American ambitions at home. For example, not only did the US government ignore the World Court's pronouncement that American involvement in Nicaragua was against international law, but so, largely, did the American media. Chomsky has reserved some of his most biting criticisms for intellectuals who, wittingly and unwittingly, delivered up both technical and humanistic justifications for American actions, most unforgettably the US's mass bombing of Vietnam. When the State Department's policy is 'found out', Chomsky argues, the 'secular priesthood' of intellectuals perms a number of explanations, especially versions of the pure-intentions and wise-change-of-policy lines. His 'The Responsibility of Intellectuals' chapter from *American Power* begins with an acknowledgement of Dwight Macdonald but he might justifiably have added to the pedigree of his essay by mentioning Randolph Bourne's 'War and the Intellectuals' of 1917. In the specific context of the Vietnam War, which destroyed the Cold War consensus, Chomsky's statements bring to a head many of the concerns of the past two chapters:

> Intellectuals are in a position to expose the lies of governments,
> to analyze actions according to their causes and motives and often
> hidden intentions. In the Western world at least, they have the
> power that comes from political liberty, from access to
> information and freedom of expression.[29]

Too many American intellectuals, Chomsky insists, have been too busy expressing appreciation of those freedoms and not busy enough living up to the responsibilities they entail.

Notes

1. Kenneth Burke, 'Revolutionary Symbolism in America', in *American Writers' Congress* (New York, 1935), pp. 89–90.

2. Richard H. Pells, *Radical Visions and American Dreams: Culture and Social Thought in the Depression Years* (New York, 1974), p. 199.

3. Quoted in Brian Morton, 'Far from Iowa', *Times Higher Educational Supplement*, 12 June, 1987.

4. Michael Gold, *Change the World!* (New York, 1936), p. 26.

5. *Leon Trotsky on Literature and Art*, edited by Paul Siegel (New York, 1970), p. 114.

6. Philip Rahv, 'Trials of the Mind', *Partisan Review*, 4 (1938), p. 10.

7. Clement Greenberg, *Art and Culture: Critical Essays* (Boston, 1961), pp. 5 and 21.

8. Alan M. Wald, *The New York Intellectuals: The Rise and Decline of the Anti-Stalinist Left from the 1930s to the 1980s* (Chapel Hill, North Carolina, 1987), p. 147.

9. Quoted in Richard Hofstadter, *The Paranoid Style in American Politics and Other Essays* (1965), p. 7; Arthur Miller, *Collected Plays* (New York, 1957), p. 282.

10. Lionel Trilling, *The Middle of the Journey* (New York, 1976), p. 31.

11. Christopher Lasch, 'The Cultural Cold War: A Short History of the Congress for Cultural Freedom', in *Towards a New Past: Dissenting Essays in American History*, edited by Barton J. Bernstein (New York, 1969), p. 323.

12. Letter to Arthur Koestler, quoted in James B. Gilbert, *Writers and Partisans: A History of Literary Radicalism in America* (New York, 1968), p. 261.

13. Daniel Bell, *The End of Ideology: On the Exhaustion of Political Ideas in the Fifties* (New York, 1960), p. 393.

14. Irving Howe, 'How *Partisan Review* Goes to War', *Partisan Review*, 13 (1947), p. 109.

15. James Burnham, 'The Wallace Crusade', *Partisan Review*, 15 (1948), p. 704.

16. Quoted in Peter Steinfels, *The Neoconservatives: The Men Who Are Changing America's Politics* (New York, 1977), pp. 83–4.

17. Irving Kristol, 'Newyorkintellectuals', *The Washington Times Magazine*, 7 April, 1986, p. 4M; Bell (see Note 13), p. 300.

18. Leslie Fiedler, *An End to Innocence: Essays on Culture and Politics* (Boston, 1962), p. ix.

19. Harold Rosenberg, *The Tradition of the New* (Chicago, 1965), p. 222.

20. *Dissent*, 1 (Winter 1954), p. 3.

21. Irving Howe, *Decline of the New* (New York, 1970), pp. 211–12 and 220.

22. SDS, *The Port Huron Statement* in *The New Radicals: A Report With Documents*, edited by Paul Jacobs and Saul Landau (Harmondsworth, 1967), pp. 157 and 158.

23. Paul Buhle, *Marxism in the USA: Remapping the History of the American Left* (1987), p. 221.

24. Tom Hayden, *Rebellion and Repression* (New York, 1969), p. 24.

25. Daniel Bell, *The Cultural Contradictions of Capitalism* (1979), Chapter 3; Irving Howe (see Note 21), pp. 255 and 253.

26. Peter Clecak, *Radical Paradoxes: Dilemmas of the American Left, 1945–1970* (New York, 1973), p. 248.

27. George Katsiaficas, *The Imagination of the New Left: A Global Analysis of 1968* (Boston, 1987), pp. 119–20.

28. John P. Diggins, *The American Left in the Twentieth Century* (New York, 1973), ch. 4.

29. *The Chomsky Reader*, edited by James Peck (1988), p. 60.

Chapter 6
America at mid-century

The best years of our lives

A bout of nostalgia for the years between 1945 and the early 1960s has
created an image of simplicity and calmness, of a society in which a
basic consensus reassuringly underlay healthy adolescent rebelliousness.
Post-war American society has been depicted as free from the need to
think deeply and at length about big questions. This composite image
of 'the best years of our lives' (to borrow the title of the 1946 film) has
doubtless been firmed up by an increasingly widespread view of 'the
sixties' as little more than a diversion from a consensus about society's
aims and values.

This stereotype of America at mid-century has damaged our view of
the major texts of the period. There was plenty going on, as we have
seen in the previous chapter, but there was more to post-war American
thought and culture than the point and counterpoint of Cold War
debate. Many of the central ideas in twentieth-century American
thought were explicitly analysed: totalitarianism, individualism, conformity, political pluralism, and utopianism. It is hardly surprising that
the academic subject of American Studies should have had its
beginnings in the 1950s. One way to remedy the denigratory estimate
of what I take to be the most important intellectual period this century
is to slow the narrative down. We can take a cue from some of the
writers, who, after the Depression and the Second World War, seemed
themselves to be taking a close look at modernity as a political concept
– though not in the narrow institutional meaning of politics.

The calm that settles after all hopes have
died: Hannah Arendt

The totalitarianism of Nazi Germany, Fascist Italy and Stalinist Russia
was translated into American terms so that it became the most

pervasive theme in post-war thought. Invariably the translators were exiled European intellectuals, with Germans prominent. In *Refugee Scholars in America*, Lewis Coser restricts himself to the careers of German-speaking intellectuals, says little about artists, and still ends up with around fifty names. Later, we shall come to Herbert Marcuse, and we have already made some use of two other members of the Frankfurt School, Theodor Adorno and Max Horkheimer. However, their work, and indeed twentieth-century thought as a whole, is thrown into relief by another German exile, Hannah Arendt, and her 1951 book, *The Origins of Totalitarianism*.

Arendt is sometimes thought of as a late recruit to New York Jewish intellectual circles. She was published in *Partisan Review*, *Commentary*, and *Politics* and, like many of her American intellectual contemporaries, her politicization dated from the 1930s. So, too, did her comparison of Nazi and Soviet atrocities, which made frightening sense to the New York Intellectuals whose political education had been dominated by Stalinism but whose family histories, as Jews, were overshadowed by the Holocaust. Nevertheless, *The Origins of Totalitarianism* came out of a different context and tradition of thought, and it also points in a different direction from the route taken by most of the New Yorkers.

As a Jewish refugee, who had been arrested by the Nazis in 1933 before escaping to France and then the United States in 1941, Hannah Arendt drew upon experiences that had given her a closer view of totalitarianism than Americans up from communism. *Origins* cast a shadow over the post-war euphoria in which American intellectuals were ready to share. The tone is set in the 'Preface to the First Edition', where Arendt writes of 'the burden which our century has placed on us':

> Two world wars in one generation, separated by an
> uninterrupted chain of local wars and revolutions, followed by
> no peace treaty for the vanquished and no respite for the victor,
> have ended in the anticipation of a third World War between the
> remaining world powers. This moment of anticipation is like the
> calm that settles after all hopes have died.[1]

Totalitarianism is described by Arendt as 'a way . . . to set the desert itself in motion, to let loose a sand storm that could cover all parts of the inhabited earth' (p. 478). Totalitarianism eradicates existing cultural differences and social formations, typically converting 'classes into masses' (p. 460). She is sure that it is something 'entirely new and unprecedented', a dimension of modern experience which 'none of our traditional legal, moral, or common sense utilitarian categories could any longer help us to come to terms with' (pp. 461 and 460). Her first concern, then, as a political philosopher, becomes that of distinguishing totalitarianism from despotism, tyranny and dictatorship, on the grounds that it is not arbitrary and not lawless; not just another pogrom. It draws its authority from fundamental laws which underlie mere legislation or 'positive laws':

> Totalitarian lawfulness, defying legality and pretending to establish the direct reign of justice on earth, executes the law of History or of Nature without translating it into standards of right and wrong for individual behavior . . . Totalitarian policy claims to transform the human species into an active unfailing carrier of a law to which human beings otherwise would only passively and reluctantly be subjected. (p. 462)

At the centre of Arendt's explanation of totalitarianism, is the idea that 'all laws have become laws of movement'. It is a deeply disturbing idea, and goes far beyond the ambivalences of the most thoughtful home-grown analyses of the post-war period, chiefly because Arendt is highlighting the negative potential of our modern acceptance of, and even commitment to, change. The law of movement becomes the essence of totalitarianism and not the measure of its legality or illegality, its degree of progression or regression. For the Nazis talking of the 'final solution' and the triumph of the Aryan race, it was the law of Nature; it was the law of History for followers of Marx and Lenin.

The Origins of Totalitarianism is a canonical text of modern times, though its genre is easily overlooked because we are so used to talking about literary and artistic modernism. Arendt's definition of totalitarianism gives another meaning to the concept of 'the new', and her understanding is at one with Freud's, Kafka's, and especially Max Weber's, in depicting modernity as burdened by the weight of the past and fixed on the phenomenon of homelessness. The modernist, existential tradition in which Arendt was trained as a philosopher is reinterpreted. Where the aloneness of the existential hero (in Camus and Sartre, and then less sombrely in Saul Bellow's *Dangling Man* of 1944) is a stimulant to thought, for the modern masses loneliness has become a daily experience. The fact that it is the Jews who have come to represent the international culture of modernism, and yet who have come to exemplify the homeless, self-less, condition of modern people, makes Arendt's analysis of modernity cut even deeper.

The opening of chapter nine, 'The Decline of the Nation-State and the End of the Rights of Man', is reminiscent of the announcements of modernism by Willa Cather, T.S. Eliot, D.H. Lawrencee, and Virginia Woolf thirty or forty years before:

It is almost impossible even now to describe what actually
happened in Europe on August 4, 1914. The days before and the
days after the first World War are separated not like the end of an
old and the beginning of a new period, but like the day before
and the day after an explosion. (p. 267)

This is no mere rupture in aesthetic sensibility. Arendt is interested in
the breakdown of the public political realm of the nation-state and its
replacement by ideas of nationhood that drew upon ethnicity and race.

An intermediary stage, or perhaps a cause, was the steady vacating
of the public arena as a place of common interests by the nineteenth-
century European middle classes. The place of the political was taken
by social concerns, notably property, which was transformed from a
private and social principle to a public and political one:

Private interests which by their very nature are temporary,
limited by man's natural span of life, can now escape into the
sphere of public affairs and borrow from them that infinite length
of time which is needed for continuous accumulation. This seems
to create a society very similar to that of the ants and the bees
where 'the Common good differeth not from the Private' . . .

Since, however, men are neither ants nor bees, the whole thing
is a delusion. Public life takes on the deceptive aspect of a total of
private interests as though these interests could create a new
quality through sheer addition. (p. 145)

This passage resonates today even more than when Arendt wrote it.
Hers is a damning critique of an individualism that survived the 1930s
because it was assumed to be the opposite 'state' to totalitarianism. It
could then re-surface in the 1950s. Signs are, however, that
individualism has saved its greatest appeal for the United States (and
Britain) in the 1980s, when the idea of public service and action has
rarely been so discredited – because that idea is interpreted as an
interference in the private concerns of individuals and their families.

In Arendt's account, by the early twentieth century, the idea of a
public realm defined by the common good was seriously diminished.
The exclusion of those who had been denationalized by the massing of
people in ethnic or folk groups, as opposed to political groups, then
became possible. Arendt describes the movements of people who
'remained homeless . . . became stateless' and, 'once they had been
deprived of their human rights . . . were rightless, the scum of the
earth' (p. 267). Looking ahead again, we should note that Arendt's call
for a Jewish homeland in Palestine was hedged with warnings that
ethnicity should not dominate political structures lest a new homeless
group – the Palestinians – be created.

Totalitarianism did not necessarily follow from the neglect of public space, of course, but it became a possibility, though one that had to be instituted through its twin techniques of ideology and terror. Terror, Arendt argues, created the seamless web of an ideology, turning it into reality, but a peculiarly and recognizably modern reality of movement. It was the reign of 'total terror' which revealed the limitations of positive laws and, instead, instituted the reality of the underlying laws of Nature or History: 'If lawfulness is the essence of non-tyrannical government and lawlessness is the essence of tyranny, then terror is the essence of totalitarian domination' (p. 464). Terror acts upon the spaces between people which, in the normal way of things, precipitate communication. Terror presses them together so that they became agents of a process which identified not the guilty or the innocent, but, rather, those who are in the way of the process: Jews or a decadent class.

Before pursuing this explanation of the origins of totalitarianism, it must at least be remarked that Arendt's equation of the laws of Nature and History rests upon a very partial reading of Marx (mostly via the links between Marx and Darwin which Engels insisted upon). It is a reading that ignores Marx's explanation of how consciousness (or, as Arendt might have it, political action) emerges from labour. In *The Human Condition* (1958) Arendt is dismissive of labour; it is only drudgery, whereas for Marx it is both the manifestation of an alienated state and the source of awareness of that state. Whatever else it is, then, Marx's theory of ideology must be about levels of consciousness. Arendt's very particular understanding of ideology as 'the logic of an idea' (p. 469) and her tendency to treat the form rather than the content of totalitarianism when comparing the USSR and Nazi Germany, confirms a common view – then as now – that totalitarianism was embraced by right and left with no distinction. *Origins* therefore underwrote an American reaction against messianic politics, which, as we have noted, was voiced most succinctly by Daniel Bell in *The End of Ideology* (1960).

However, just as Bell, by the 1980s, had proved to be more than a negative thinker, known only for one catch-phrase, so the decline of politics is not the only conclusion to be drawn from *The Origins of Totalitarianism*. Arendt, herself, anticipated, and warned against, this obvious reading in the late 1940s when commenting upon the loose and reactionary use of 'anti-Stalinism'. A more substantial discussion point is the one already mooted, that, in tracing the origins of totalitarianism and the triumph of ideology, Arendt took account of the decline of political activity of the European nineteenth-century middle classes and their withdrawal into self-interest, as well as the excessive politicization of life in the 1930s. Two of her later works may be mentioned in this connection.

First, and most notoriously for some, there is *Eichmann in Jerusalem*. Its sub-title, *The Banality of Evil*, is an unexpected response to an idea she broaches in the Preface to *Origins*:

> And if it is true that in the final stages of totalitarianism an absolute evil appears (absolute because it can no longer be deduced from humanly comprehensible motives), it is also true that without it we might never have known the truly radical nature of Evil. (pp. viii–ix)

Inasmuch as *Eichmann in Jerusalem* is an indirect sequel to *Origins*, its argument takes us in quite a different direction from that taken by the New York Intellectuals, in which they redefined their liberalism or abandoned it in the neo-conservatism of the 1970s and 1980s. The Eichmann book caused a furious outcry among Jews, and especially New York Jews when it was published in 1963. In Eichmann, Arendt saw not a monster or an evil genius, the embodiment of perverted thinking, but a banal, cliché-spouting bureaucratic murderer, whose crime was his inability to think. Arendt appears to take at face value Eichmann's own defence at his trial that he was not responsible, but was just diligently obeying orders. The alternative interpretation of her argument is that she was resisting the easy explanation – that this was evil incarnate – and, instead, was contemplating the possibility that what happened is much closer to us, to ordinary life and in particular to the bourgeois life that Eichmann led in a mass society. This is Arendt making us think the unthinkable, namely that totalitarianism is not to be explained (away) according to the character of Hitler or Stalin or a theory of their lawless seizure of power. The implication, then, is that totalitarianism could not be expected to disappear when they died. This is a more compelling and more defensible argument than the one Arendt also controversially explored, that Jewish leaders in the ghetto were complicit in the extermination of their people.

The other text to consider is *On Revolution* (1963). Far from disabusing intellectuals out of any lingering Depression-bred illusions about political action, Arendt seems to be in at the beginning of a '1960s' view of politics as public participation. This is a position which we associate more readily with others who contributed to Dwight Macdonald's *Politics*, notably C. Wright Mills and Paul Goodman. In an article that looks for these connections between Arendt's early and later work, Richard King argues that what Arendt suggests resembles the republican ideal of a life in which people must appear, debate and act in public with other people.[2] Public participation is an aim in itself rather than the means to some end. Arendt ought to have been entirely disenchanted with this public realm, since another definition of totalitarianism is that it replaces any kind of private life with the public glare. Her understanding of the public dimension none the less stresses the importance of the spaces between people, the places where communication can go on.

The hope, Arendt suggests in the 'Epilogue' to *Origins*, and then confirms in *The Human Condition*, *On Revolution* and some of the essays in *Between Past and Future* (1961) lies in the resuscitation of political action as the expression of whatever freedom still exists, in opposition to the massification that totalitarianism induces. There are only hints of this freedom in the 'Epilogue', but, as a text written after the rest of *Origins*, it does point to a 'way out' of this most terrifying of twentieth-century iron cages. The most important hint of freedom from what Arendt calls 'the iron band of terror', is in her reference to human birth as 'a new beginning':

> The suprahuman force of Nature or History has its own
> beginning and its own end, so that it can be hindered only by the
> new beginning and the individual end which the life of each man
> actually is . . . With each new birth, a new beginning is born into
> the world, a new world has potentially come into being. (pp. 466
> and 465)

This may seem insufficient, but in the conditions of the camps, the results of a new beginning were less important than the sheer fact of its possibility, of something new, something different, of freedom as 'an inner capacity of man' (p. 473). In the article referred to above, Richard King maintains that this was also the beginning of Arendt's concept of political action as 'precisely freedom in its highest form' (King, p. 245).

Individualism reconsidered: David Riesman

In 'The Culture Industry' (1944), Theodor Adorno and Max Horkheimer predicted that the mass communications industry would extend its hegemonic control over American society, the more so since they barely included television in their analysis. The United States would be a continuation of the cultural and political totalitarianism which they had seen in Germany in the 1930s. It is clear that in *Origins* Hannah Arendt saw totalitarianism as the general and seemingly inescapable 'burden' of modernity. Later, we shall find that, in different ways and with varying definitions of 'totalitarianism', both Herbert Marcuse and C. Wright Mills agreed that the political and cultural dimensions of modernity have, at the very least, totalitarian overtones. Marcuse's view of the 'one dimensionality' of American society was confirmed and popularized in the form of 'the technocracy', Theodore Roszak's term from his 1969 book, *The Making of a Counter-Culture*. In other words, the theme grew stronger and continued to lose its implicit or explicit reference to Europe in the 1930s.

In contrast, a number of prominent writers who came to the fore in the post-war years, but 'grew up' in the 1930s, took the warning seriously, but concluded that developments in the United States were a break – though not always a clean break – with the horrific tendency towards totalitarianism. The writers who come to mind are Daniel Bell, Arthur Schlesinger Jr, Lionel Trilling, Seymour Martin Lipset, Richard Hofstadter, Louis Hartz, J.K. Galbraith, and David Riesman. Proclamations of 'The Failure of Socialism' (one of Bell's essay titles), may have been made more shrill by Cold War ideology, but, equally, the sense of being at the end of the era of great narrative explanations (progressive and regressive, Left and Right), became a stimulus for many of the considerable intellectual achievements of the 1950s, spread across five or six disciplines. A book like David Riesman's *The Lonely Crowd* (1950), written with the assistance of Nathan Glazer and Reuel Denney, in tandem with Riesman's 1954 collection, *Individualism Reconsidered*, demonstrates that new issues were being explored from within the overall position that the United States after 1945 was more than simply post-war; it was, arguably, post-industrial, perhaps even post-modern, though this term did not circulate widely until the 1970s. As *The Lonely Crowd* reveals, the metropolitan society then emerging was not necessarily one that drew approval, but its ambiguous qualities of amorphousness and indeterminacy were what distinguished it from the totalitarianism of other mass societies.

There are common strands in all of the books under consideration but their authors tap their way into the post-war world by different routes. Riesman's route is through 'social character', a concept he takes over from his former teacher, the neo-Freudian psychologist, Erich Fromm:

> In order that any society may function well, its members must acquire the kind of character which makes them *want* to act in the way they *have* to act as members of the society or of a special class within it. They have to *desire* what objectively is *necessary* for them to do. *Outer force* is replaced by *inner compulsion*, and by the particular kind of human energy which is channelled into character traits.[3]

On the level which is, finally, the most absorbing one, Riesman mulls over the contradictions between activity and passivity, and individualism and social control in Fromm's definition. But before engaging with this problem, Riesman and his co-researchers extensively illustrate and give a history to Erich Fromm's definition of social character. They investigate child-rearing and educational practices; peer group activities; the mass media; the world of work (corporations rather than factories); politics; consumption (including eating); and sexual relations. It is the sheer interest in private as well as public behavioural patterns which puts *The Lonely Crowd* into a rich tradition of sociological investigation into American life that begins with Alexis de Tocqueville, comes through Thorstein Veblen to the Lynds' *Middletown* (1929), and continues in Erik Erikson's very influential *Childhood and Society* (1950) and the work of social anthropologists, Ruth Benedict, Margaret Mead, and Geoffrey Gorer. In the 1970s and 1980s, this tradition has been given added weight by Christopher Lasch's books, and, most recently, by Robert Bellah *et al.*'s *Habits of the Heart: Individualism and Commitment in American Life* (1985).

Besides Erich Fromm, Riesman is influenced by Max Weber's theory of ideal types. In the now-familiar terminology of *The Lonely Crowd*, there are three dominant types of social character, which correspond to phases of Western, but especially American, societal development, and are correlated with demographic changes: persons who are tradition-directed, inner-directed and other-directed. In seventeenth-century townships in New England, for instance, there was barely a hint of the American Dream of success; rather, children were brought up simply to succeed their parents. Conformity, not individual expressiveness, was the rule and was ensured through the operation of a shame culture. The inner-directed character type is a much more recognizably American figure, the carrier of the Protestant Ethic and the mythology of the self-made man from late eighteenth-century mercantile capitalism through to industrial capitalism in the early twentieth century. A sometimes skewed version of this figure appears in American fiction, from the lonely heroes of Hawthorne and Melville, through the more socially constructed characters of Howells, Dreiser and Henry James, to those of Fitzgerald and Hemingway, uneasily poised between a production and consumption ethic. Finally, with the greater stress on consumption under corporate capitalism, the other-directed figure appears and populates the novels and stories of John Cheever and John Updike.

For all of the sociological neutrality and functionalist terminology, mid-century America and Americans are on the line in *The Lonely Crowd*. Here, Riesman's distinctive contribution is his delineation of a contemporary 'other-directed character', who also appears in the white-collar environment of the corporation described in Sloan Wilson's *The Man in the Gray Flannel Suit* (1955), William Whyte's *The Organization Man* (1956), and a series of books on advertising and occupational mobility by Vance Packard. In this environment, Riesman explains, '*other people* are the problem, not the material environment' and there is 'an increased consumption of words and images from the new mass media . . . Increasingly, relations with the outer world and with oneself are mediated by the flow of mass communication'. Out of this information-rich society come people who must constantly communicate themselves, and so must be sensitive to the signals given out by other people. For the inner-directed person the 'control equipment' is 'like a gyroscope'; for the other-directed person it is 'like a radar' (pp. 18, 20–1 and 25).

In a society of multiple effects, it is hard to be self-reliant in the nineteenth-century Emersonian manner. When anxiety sets in because there is no definable cause which produces the effects, the other-directed person must look to a peer group for reassurance. The peer group becomes the mediator, part-way between the private nuclear family and the anonymous institutions of the society where the person must work. Riesman's descriptions conjure up a world of suburban housing, high schools, and downtown corporations and government agencies, the world of work being reached by means of the freeways which were being built at a phenomenal rate in the wake of the Highways Act of 1956. There is a more direct evocation of the 1950s in Whyte's *The Organization Man*, part of which is a case study of the new housing development of Park Forest on the outskirts of Chicago. Just as other-directed people are always alert to the existence of another peer group to which they must look for approval, so Park Forest is inhabited by 'transients', junior executives on the move, and by their wives, who attend 'kaffee-klatches'. This is the breeding ground for what Betty Friedan would later call 'the problem with no name', but, as with most 1950s books, there is a blindness to women in *The Lonely Crowd* and *The Organization Man*.

On the question of individualism, which is never far from the centre of American thought, Riesman's fears of excessive conformity and superficiality suggest that he regrets the passing of the inner-directed person. Yet, in discussing childrearing, he comments unerringly on the inability of the inner-directed parents to allow their children to relax, adding that the inner-directed are 'frequently quite incapable of casual relationships' (p. 43). A profit and loss account of both personal relations and the spending of time leaves inner-directed people defenceless against the time-and-motion ethos of a rationalized world. Aside from these observations, it is clear that inner-directedness is itself a 'mode of conformity'. There is a definite mechanical quality in the image of the psychological gyroscope.

When it comes to other-directedness, Riesman welcomes a society that has such a large educated middle-class in a period of population decline. More directly, he acknowledges the widespread desire that a job be more than a passport to material success. Riesman is critical, though, of the shallowness of other-directedness and the manipulative outlook which it fosters, especially since even the most practiced manipulator is not immune to the atmosphere of anxiety. The 'radar' may be fine-tuned to pick up subtle signals, but there is no fixed principle of truth or even of what is good, against which to measure the signals. The loneliness (in the middle of a crowd) that can result is harder to bear because, in contrast to inner-directed society, there is nothing positive about loneliness. Not to be liked spells failure.

The Lonely Crowd cannot be mistaken for a eulogy to post-war America, and it leaves us with troubling images, most memorably that of the 'lonely crowd', developed by Philip Slater in *The Pursuit of Loneliness: American Culture at the Breaking point* (1970). What can be said, though, is that Riesman does not see the modes of conformity in America as comparable with those in the totalitarian states which Hannah Arendt describes, in which it is precisely the lack of possibilities arising from a relational view of the world that ensures conformity. We cannot even imagine that the loneliness so vividly depicted by Arendt could be remedied by mind-cure courses or a deodorant.

The final section of *The Lonely Crowd*, 'Autonomy', is the least satisfactory in the book. It is as though Riesman has so immersed himself in American society that he has difficulty formulating a positive alternative. The best he can manage is to hold back some quality in the self that will resist the three types of conformity. The sources of this resistance and its manifestations are quite different from those associated with the more famous literary rebellions of the 1950s: by Jack Kerouac, Allen Ginsberg and the Beats, and by Norman Mailer's hipster rebel in 'The White Negro'. Riesman struggles to preserve some notion of autonomy. So disillusioned is he with the public dimension, populated by conscience-mongerers at times of crisis and by compromising conformists at times of abundance, that he is obliged to look to 'private lives' and to pin hopes of a revival of utopian thinking upon people becoming 'more attentive to their own feelings and aspirations'. Creative consumption might, Riesman is even driven to speculate, be a preparation for 'the larger package of a neighbourhood, a society, and a way of life' (p. 307).

The problem seems to be that whereas in dealing with earlier phases of social development, Riesman makes some connections between material factors (mostly demographic ones) and psychology, in concluding, he has only the psychology and a vague confidence that abundance will give the necessary space to re-form the self. The feelings of alienation which *The Lonely Crowd* expresses, far from being related to economic conditions, are mistaken by Riesman for individual freedom. This freedom to choose in the contemporary period is only possible because economics is not even treated as a significant issue. When Riesman claims that there is no principle that would distinguish 'those to be aided from those to be opposed', one reason lies in his methodology, borrowed from Erich Fromm, which, in effect rules out conflict. The link between social character and population provides, in Riesman's words, 'a kind of shorthand for referring to the myriad institutional elements that are also – *though usually more heatedly* – symbolized by such words as "industrialism," "folk society," "monopoly capitalism," "urbanization," "rationalization," and so on"' (p. 9, my emphasis). His model of explanation therefore offers no way out of the self-regulating system, which Fromm presents as a balance between activity and passivity in social character: '[People] have to *desire* what objectively is *necessary* for them to do.' No credence can be given to the view that the self can be re-made in action, in transforming the material environment because, basically, the material environment is at the very least satisfactory.

For an explanation of what is going on in *The Lonely Crowd*, beneath the surface descriptions of social types, we need to broaden the focus to include other 1950s thinkers, most of whom concerned themselves with a redefinition of politics, and especially American politics. The chapter in *The Lonely Crowd* entitled 'Images of Power' can serve as a bridge to some of the other key texts of the period.

The American political tradition: David Riesman, Daniel Bell, Reinhold Niebuhr, Lionel Trilling, Arthur Schlesinger Jr, Daniel Boorstin, and Richard Hofstadter

When David Riesman looks at American politics through the lens of his theory of social character, the inner-directed person confronts us once again but in the guise of the 'moralizer'. Other-directedness appears in 'the style of an "inside-dopester"' (p. 163), a joiner of groups but not a committed advocate of any one group. Personalized into style, with means more interesting than ends, politics is *consumed* by the middle and upper-middle classes.

Though his modified vocabulary still conveys a note of criticism, the section on politics in *The Lonely Crowd* proves to be the most positive in the book. Riesman shares much the same view of politics as Bell, Lipset, Galbraith, and a number of historians, principally Arthur

Schlesinger Jr, who looked sympathetically upon the American political system from the late 1940s onwards. These writers transcended their academic specialisms and came together in a very influential formulation of the concept of political (rather than primarily ethnic or cultural) *pluralism*. Because 'pluralism' and 'America' function as rough synonyms, especially when Schlesinger, Daniel Boorstin, David Potter and other historians give the subject a historical dimension, there continued to be something at stake beyond political theory, a sub-text with its own historiography and its own politics or ideology.

The chief tenet of the texts of post-war political pluralism is that power has been dispersed, from a ruling class or party into a plurality of veto groups. These represent religion, neighbourhood, occupations, and other 'issues which divide men and create the interest conflicts that involve people in a sense of ongoing reality: labor issues, race problems, tax policy, and the like'. This is Daniel Bell, who goes on to ask 'Is this not the meaning of power to people as it touches their lives?'[4] In place of old-style class politics, Bell recommends the institutionalization of political pluralism based on communities of interest. Since this view of politics is so central to our understanding of the United States in mid-century, and, as such, has both a great deal of appeal and has attracted criticism, it will be worth reconstructing the reasoning behind it.

One route to political pluralism is via Bell's rejoinder to the widespread assumption – by no means limited to conservative thinkers like Ortega Y Gasset – that America epitomizes a mass society and so is ripe for totalitarian politics. Bell begins his essay on 'America as a Mass Society: *A Critique*' (1956) by paraphrasing the standard explanation for the coming of mass society. This explanation links the integration of formerly autonomous communities which comes with modernization, and especially with mass communications, with the diminution of the individual. In a search for an alternative source of identity and stability, the individual, in a 'world of lonely crowds', becomes vulnerable to manipulation, and, as in Nazi Germany but also in America in the Depression, is liable to embrace the 'charismatic leader, the secular messiah' (*End of Ideology*, p. 22). Bell, however, is intent upon exempting the United States from the overall theory of the mass society and certainly from any imputation that it is even a proto-totalitarian one.

In common with many other post-war thinkers, Bell objects to the paucity of any theory compared with the complexity of reality, as evidenced by the plurality of interests and the relative absence of polarized classes. In 'America as a Mass Society' and, more extensively still, in 'Is There a Ruling Class in America?' (a review of C. Wright Mills's *The Power Elite* of 1956), Bell denies that there has been in

America a consolidation of power at the top and, at the bottom, the kind of fragmentation of social structure and individual personality that could conceivably lead to totalitarianism. In political shorthand, Bell opts for Alexis de Tocqueville rather than Marx. While he was aware of potential massification, Tocqueville looked to the 'free associations' which, as he observed during his visit to the United States in the 1830s, formed around particular issues:

> It is difficult to draw a man out of his own circle to interest him in the destiny of the state, because he does not clearly understand what influence the destiny of the state can have upon his own lot. But if it is proposed to make a road across the end of his estate, he will see at a glance that there is a connection between this small public affair and his greatest private affairs; and he will discover, without its being shown to him, the close tie that unites private to general interest.[5]

For Daniel Bell, the associations which, Tocqueville claimed, Americans formed and joined more than any other people, mitigated against the dangers of anomic individualism. Associations also mitigated against the consolidation of power in the state which can result from the isolation of individuals, and therefore answered the gloomy prognostications of Ortega Y Gasset that a cultural order (in his case based upon ruling elites) would be smashed by a revolt of the manipulated masses. The associations for which Tocqueville held out such high hopes were not territorially based, or at least they did not have to be. Consequently, they were not as vulnerable to modernization as were the small towns or neighbourhoods around which so much of the mythology of community revolves in the United States. Tocqueville's associations anticipated the communities of interest described, with varying degrees of enthusiasm by Riesman, Bell, Lipset and their contemporaries. 'In the here and now', Bell writes, 'people do not live at the extreme . . . but they live "in parts," parceling out their lives amidst work, home, neighborhood, fraternal club, etc.' (p. 298). By his estimate, in 1955 there were over 200,000 associations, with a membership of approaching 80 million. This evidence of increasing participation outside of class politics is, Bell states with cultural activities foremost in mind, 'almost an inevitable concomitant of the doubling – *literally* – of the American standard of living over the last fifty years' (p. 33). That is to say, communities of interest were a product of the very modernization which destroyed communities of place. And – Bell hammers home the point qualitatively as well as quantitatively – these associations, along with their redefinition of democracy, are to be found in their most developed form in the most developed nation of the world, the United States. This is the gist of his objection to the theory of mass society being applied to America.

The only conclusion to be reached, Bell and others decide, is that politics in a democracy should be a round of lobbying, manoeuvring, and competition between groups. These groups should be organized around interests, rather than the ideologies which gathered up and integrated localized interests. Politics should *not* be organized around Marxism or any of the emotive attachments that Max Weber sees as giving way to the rationalized procedures of a modern society. In the new circumstances of a modern society, no group can become dominant. Rather, groups have to make alliances that are particular rather than general and extreme. 'Compromise is the "soul if not the whole of politics . . . and progress is along diagonals' (p. 298), Bell explains. In similar vein, David Riesman talks of veto politics, while, in *The Vital Center* (1949), Arthur Schlesinger Jr evaluates trade unions in terms of the specific benefits they have brought their members, and not as agents of class-politics.

In approving the interpretation that 'power in America' is 'situational and mercurial', David Riesman adds a reassuring note:

> But people are afraid of this indeterminacy and amorphousness in the cosmology of power. Even those intellectuals, for instance, who feel themselves very much out of power and who are frightened of those who they think have the power, prefer to be scared by the power structures they conjure up than to face the possibility that the power structure they believe exists has largely evaporated. Most people prefer to suffer with interpretations that give their world meaning than to relax in the cave without an Ariadne's thread. (p. 223)

The labyrinth without Ariadne's thread to lead to the exit is an image to pause over, one that has taken on different meanings since the late 1960s with the advent of post-structuralism and post-modernism.[6] Riesman's main philosophical source is American Pragmatism, and in particular, William James's recognition that it is impossible to provide a transcript of the reality of which one is a part. For Bell, Riesman and Schlesinger, class cannot be the Ariadne's thread because, 'the prism of "class" is too crude to follow the swift play of diverse political groups' (*End of Ideology*, p. 66). The task, then, is to inhabit the system, looking for incremental gain rather than an all-or-nothing transformation.

Instead of the passion of what Bell calls 'ethics', in a modern society we have the tolerance, civility and (Bell does not apologise) simple routine of 'politics', all of which frame provisional conclusions to the big questions. In *The Vital Center*, his major contribution to the redefinition of liberalism, Schlesinger endorses the advice of the nineteenth-century American historian, George Bancroft, on the perennial feud between haves and have-nots: 'he who will act with moderation, prefer fact to theory, and remember that everything in the world is relative and not absolute, will see that the violence of the contest may be stilled' (p. xvi).

Although the quotations have been taken from just a few sources, they are representative of a majority view among mid-century intellectuals, who accepted that, for all its faults, the welfare capitalism of the United States provided the parameters for achievable rather than utopian progress. Corporate America, with Truman still in the White House after the 1948 election, was not exciting, though more exciting than America would be in the Eisenhower years; but it seemed permanent and was producing the kind of economic growth that allowed the administration to return to the theme of a general welfare and so, in Schlesinger's words, 'confound Marx's prediction of increasing proletarian misery' (*The Vital Center*, p. 153).

In an essay on the New York Intellectuals, Irving Howe jokingly remarks on Arthur Schlesinger Jr's 'moony glances at Kierkegaard.'[7] The combination of European modernist angst and a tough and optimistic re-definition of liberalism in *The Vital Center* is sufficiently unexpected and yet widespread enough among Schlesinger's contemporaries to warrant discussion. It also confirms that what we are talking about here is a *culture* of politics and not political history or even political theory.

Schlesinger's first modernist note is his epigraph, taken from W.B. Yeats's 'The Second Coming', which contains the famous line, 'Things fall apart; the centre cannot hold'. In describing the experiences and sensibility of radicals up from communism, Daniel Bell similarly resorts to the language of modernism, even as he argues that America has not succumbed to totalitarianism and, through veto politics, has found a way of being political that avoids extremism. For Bell, 'the key terms which dominate discourse today [are] irony, paradox, ambiguity, and complexity' (p. 300). He further checks any rash celebration of the liberal rationality of interest-group politics with the aid of Weber: 'Max Weber, more than forty years ago, in a poignant essay entitled "Politics as a Vocation", posed the problem as one of accepting the "ethics of responsibility" or "the ethics of ultimate ends"' (p. 302). Bell was fond enough of Weber to quote him as one of the epigraphs to his position-taking essay of 1952, 'The Failure of American Socialism': ' "He who seeks the salvation of souls, his own as well as others, should not seek it along the avenue of politics"' (p. 275). We can go some way towards unravelling the unusual (because contradictory) mixture of modernism, religion, and the political pragmatism that both Bell and Schlesinger were after, by introducing another key figure of mid-century American thought, the existentialist theologian, Reinhold Niebuhr.

As the pastor of a Detroit congregation between 1915 and 1928, Niebuhr had tried out the reformist theology of Washington Gladden and Walter Rauschenbusch. Their Social Gospel had its sources in a critique of late-nineteenth-century laissez-faire economics and was thus a source of twentieth-century, Progressive-Pragmatist liberalism (see pages 147–50). The liberalism of the Social Gospel and its active, 'sociology-minded pastors', as Donald Meyer describes them, was further distinguished by its distance from the rampant fundamentalism of the 1920s, of which the Scopes trial was simply the highlight.[8] Niebuhr was far from a fundamentalist; indeed, in his study of 'the religion of civility' in America, John Murray Cuddihy accuses Niebuhr of favouring 'tact' more than 'truth'.[9] Yet Niebuhr did react against liberal theology and signalled his move towards a powerful neo-orthodox position when he left Detroit in 1928 to join Union Theological Seminary, where he remained until his retirement in 1960. We cannot pursue the detail of Niebuhr's theology but we can examine him as an anti-modernist modernist and then return to the question of his considerable influence in defining the culture of mid-century American politics.

Where Social Gospellers looked out from their churches and saw scope for action, Niebuhr, while remaining one of the most involved of theologians, saw in the crises of the First World War and the Depression, and then in the polarizations in Europe during the 1930s, the challenge to any naive liberalism, religious or secular. His attack was directed not only at liberal religion but at John Dewey, whom he described in *The Children of Light and the Children of Darkness* (1944) as 'the most typical and greatest philosopher of American secularism'.[10] Niebuhr's *Reflections on the End of an Era* (1934) anticipated similar post-war books by Schlesinger, Bell and others which announced a change of mood. From the late 1920s, well in advance of the new generation of chastened liberals, many of them up from communism, Niebuhr tempered his own socialism with a Protestant neo-orthodoxy that took the Social Gospel to task for overlooking the doctrine of original sin. This line of thinking was hardly going to be popular among radicals, at least, during the Depression. It became very influential after the war, however, not because intellectuals suddenly became more religious, but because the 'reality of sin' was consistently related by Niebuhr to the failures of urban-industrial society and to the evidence of evil thrown up by the 1930s.

Niebuhr insisted that any belief in purposeful rationality, such as liberalism and some versions of socialism share, must be tempered by an acknowledgement of original sin. In *The Irony of American History*

(1952), he presents original sin as the explanation for the 'historical' quality of ideas and actions:

> [The self] has an organic unity of rational, emotional and volitional elements which make all its actions and attitudes historically more relative than is realized in any moment of thought and action. The inevitability of this confusion between the relative and the universal is exactly what is meant by original sin.[11]

There appeared to be no other explanation for the errors in social and political thought, especially when these ideas came from reformers whom Niebuhr supported. In the 1930s, an awareness of these errors led him to interpret Marx's analysis of power relations as that which, in local terms, defies rational goodwill. This was quite different from the understanding of Marx which inspired radicals who saw, in Depression conditions, the working out of the rational analysis which they found in Marx's dialectical explanation for historical change. But Niebuhr saw conflict all around and, for him, it was precisely the point of Marxism that its ultimate vision had little to do with local events and signs of order and rationality. The catastrophe of Stalinism therefore affected Niebuhr differently from someone like Sidney Hook, because Niebuhr had nothing much invested in rationality and, as a religious thinker, the vision always related to what was beyond, rather than at the end of history.

An indication of the importance of Niebuhr for post-war intellectuals is apparent in the quotation below from *The Vital Center*, especially if its rhetoric and tone, as well as content, are compared with the explicitly secular analysis of American liberalism which is more typical of the book:

> We have found no angels, whether in the form of kings, gauleiters or commissars; and we know too well what happens when mere humans claim angelic infallibility. Despotism is never so much to be dreaded as when it pretends to do good: who would act the angel acts the brute.
>
> The people as a whole are not perfect; but no special group of the people is more perfect: that is the moral and rationale of democracy. Consistent pessimism about man, far from promoting authoritarianism, alone can innoculate the democratic faith against it. 'Man's capacity for justice makes democracy possible,' Niebuhr has written in his remarkable book on democratic theory [*The Children of Light and the Children of Darkness*]; 'but man's inclination to injustice makes democracy necessary.[12]

Liberalism had been too hopeful, too ambitious in the face of things as they are, too precipitous in its attempts to resolve contradictions. There had been an optimism about advances in human understanding in the nineteenth century, but the greater leaps forward in knowledge in the twentieth century could not be evaluated without reference to the Somme, Dresden, Auschwitz, and Hiroshima and Nagasaki. The correct response to these contradictions appeared to be Niebuhr's reminder of a tragic universe – to which religion was the only guide – but a universe to which there must be a human response. That response, however, was always likely to produce evil in its efforts to do good.

Niebuhr's ironical message influenced Lionel Trilling, who developed it in the sphere of literary criticism. In the Preface to *The Liberal Imagination* (1950), Trilling calls for a less complacent, more self-critical liberalism than that of the 1920s and 1930s. He takes the long view of literary history to argue that our current failings and successes are illuminated by those encapsulated in earlier literary texts. In spite of historical and cultural differences, there is a tradition – the humanist tradition – that transcends time and space, so that Jane Austen or Matthew Arnold can still speak to us; Austen is the subject of one of the key essays in Trilling's 1965 collection, *Beyond Culture*, and Arnold the subject of a 1939 monograph. 'The word liberal', Trilling writes in *The Liberal Imagination*, 'is a word primarily of political import, but its political meaning defines itself by the quality of life it envisages, by the sentiments it desires to affirm. This will begin to explain why a writer of literary criticism involves himself with political considerations.'[13] Trilling is saying that to approach politics via literature is necessarily to accept certain kinds of limits.

The universal truth of 'the liberal imagination' is that we are bound to be at least partly in error. Broadly speaking, this was what Trilling meant by 'tragic realism', and his criticism can be read as an attempt to find an answer to two more lines from W.B. Yeats which also appear as part of the epigraph to Schlesinger's *The Vital Center*:

The best lack all conviction, while the worst
Are full of passionate intensity.

Trilling derives the notion of tragic realism from Freud, or at least an interpretation of Freud which has him telling us that the human condition is beset with limitations. These could not simply be overcome – Trilling rejected a view of psychoanalysis as cure, just as he rejected overly optimistic Marxian blueprints for the social and political resolution of contradictions. Where Niebuhr looked, in the final analysis, beyond society and history for transcendence, Trilling, as a literary critic, looked to the trope of irony and to modernist authors, among them Henry James, for at least an awareness of transcendence but one that, in the nature of literature, could not be actually realized in full. It may help to recall, by way of contrast, the late 1930s defence of modernism by Rahv, Phillips and *Partisan Review*, which accorded James a more radical edge, in revealing the deep-seated conservatism of Popular Front aesthetics, than Trilling's 'realism' would permit.

The consistent intersection of progressive and sceptical impulses amounts to more than busy American intellectuals going 'moony' on European high culture in their spare time. In an earlier chapter, I quoted from Howard Brick's study of Daniel Bell which identifies in Bell 'a special acuity for grasping static contradictions or antinomies – unconquerable polar tensions of being'. It is an insight which applies more widely to the post-war mood of 'irony, paradox, ambiguity, and complexity' (Bell's words).[14] Thirty years after its high point in literature, painting and music – when, incidentally, few American intellectuals favoured it – modernism made a comeback in American *political and social* thought. Brick proposes that a modernist sensibility was belatedly embraced because, while modernism does not necessarily turn its back upon conflict, it seeks to contain conflict in a tense relationship. This relationship is often described as an ironic relationship between the kinds of oppositions that, outside of art, would be manifested in crude and dangerous ideological divisions.

Schlesinger and Bell, but also Richard Hofstadter – none of them literary critics like Trilling – were drawn to modernism because it appeared to describe how any articulated political philosophy contained within it the seeds of its own destruction. In the subtle hands of these intellectuals, liberalism itself was subjected to a modernist critical interrogation in order that, as Trilling puts it, liberalism should be 'aware of the weak or wrong expressions of itself' (*Liberal Imagination*, p. 10). It was recognized that liberalism's claims for progress rested on ideas of rationality that had also released regressive movements in the 1930s, and then again in the 1940s with the beginnings of the arms race. Niebuhr comments upon this dilemma in *The Irony of American History*: 'Our [American] dreams of a pure virtue are dissolved in a situation in which it is possible to exercise the virtue of responsibility toward a community of nations only by courting the prospective guilt of the atom bomb' (p. 2).

In case the connections with, for instance, literary modernism still appear remote, we can compare the ironic outlook of the post-war liberals with a definition of how irony functions in a literary text. The definition comes from Cleanth Brooks and Robert Penn Warren's primer for New Critical analysis, *Understanding Fiction*, published in

1943. Writing as 'the editors' they state that 'they would not endorse an irony which precluded resolution but they would endorse an irony which forced the resolution to take stock of as full a context as possible'.[15] Unlike in Randolph Bourne, irony has lost much of its sharpness, become implicitly quietistic, so conscious of the complexity of existence that the idea of significant social change seems pathetically inadequate. Glossing the story of *Partisan Review* from the late 1930s, and of Daniel Bell in the 1940s, Brick writes: 'Modernism . . . answered estrangement with reconciliation, providing a framework for the discontents of radical intellectuals while denying the possibility of resolving them' (p. 208).

That Bell's is only one understanding of modernism, however, should be apparent from discussions in preceding chapters of this book. The particularity of the post-war liberals' definition of modernism also became clear when the New Left of the 1960s pursued a modernist immediacy of experience. This revival of an adversarial role for modernism drew a sharp *aesthetic* rebuke from Bell in a later book, *The Cultural Contradictions of Capitalism* (1976):

> Erasing the boundary between art and life was a further aspect of
> the breakup of genre, the conversion of a painting into a
> happening, the taking of art out of the museum into the
> environment, the turning of all experience into art, whether it
> had form or not. By celebrating life, this process tended to
> destroy art.[16]

In the Conclusion to this book we can return to the debate over the end of modern culture, in which Bell and also Trilling have played a prominent part. In the context of the 1940s and 1950s, the point is that for modernism to play a reconciliatory role, whether in literary or political disputes, a canonic view of modernism must be presupposed, one which allows modernism to contain all points of view. This is consistent with Brooks and Warren's definition of irony, the idea being that irony allows even a strong moral claim to be stated (the words of the claimant can actually be quoted) and yet contextualized so that its force is dissipated by the superior ironist.

Many of these post-war writers read each other carefully, despite working in different disciplines. It was not surprsing, then, that with the rethinking of the nature of politics in post-war America – in summary, a redefinition of pluralism into liberal consensus politics – went a revaluation of the American past. Schlesinger led the way in this cross-fertilization with his hybrid book, *The Vital Center*, part history, part political theory, and part 'criticism'. One of the few younger intellectuals without a radical past in the 1930s, he encouraged the search for *American* sources for the new liberalism in the American political tradition, giving that tradition a monumental quality in *The Age of Jackson* (1945) and his series, *The Age of Roosevelt*. More schematically, in *The Vital Center* he openly describes the Jacksonians in the 1820s and 1830s and the New Dealers in the 1930s as 'our left' (p. 159), before going on to differentiate between 'the politicians, the administrators, the doers' and the 'Doughface progressives . . . the sentimentalists, the utopians, the wailers', the latter group so often becoming 'the willing accomplice of Communism' (pp. 159 and 160). Though the accent is tougher in Schlesinger we can recognize the oppositions which structure Daniel Bell's opposition between those who opt for politics and those who insist on ethics, meaning ideology. There is less of Riesman's inner and other distinction but it, too, is there in Schlesinger.

Other texts in the new consensus history, as it came to be known, included Louis Hacker's *The Triumph of American Capitalism* (1946); Richard Hofstadter's *The American Political Tradition* (1948) and *The Age of Reform* (1955); Daniel Boorstin's *The Genius of American Politics* (1953); David Potter's *People of Plenty* (1954); and Louis Hartz's *The Liberal Tradition in America* (1955). As with some twentieth-century literary criticism, it is instructive to read these studies as texts in their own right, coming out of a distinct period. A few brief, interlinked examples will have to suffice, however.

The Genius of American Politics works an old theme in a novel way. The old theme was stated in 1914 by the historian Frederick Jackson Turner: 'American democracy was born of no theorist's dream; it was not carried in the *Sarah Constant* to Virginia, nor in the *Mayflower* to Plymouth. It came out of the American forest.'[17] Boorstin refines Turner and claims that Europe has been prominent in political theory because it needed to be, whereas the United States had the inestimable advantages of abundance and difference: 'A pretty good rule-of-thumb for us in the United States is that our national well-being is in inverse proportion to the sharpness and extent of the theoretical differences between our political parties' (*Genius of American Politics*, p. 3).

David Potter's *People of Plenty* also reinterprets Turner's frontier thesis as a lesson for the present. In his seminal essay, 'The Significance of the Frontier in American History' (1893), Turner describes free land as a unifying factor at a time when agitation for reform, first by Populists and then by Progressives, was becoming intense. Yet the reliance upon land at the very time when the frontier was officially closing made Turner's essay implicitly pessimistic and suggested the potential for further conflict over scarce resources. Potter's rewriting of 'land' as 'abundance', which could be created by industrial and technological means, revives optimism that social divisiveness can be avoided. Similarly, Schlesinger asserts that the mixed and affluent society of post-war America 'can overcome the internal contradictions which in Marx's view doomed it to destruction' (p. xi), just as, in politics, liberalism is also the future because it, too, is constantly reconstructing itself, never fixed on any one principle.

Richard Hofstadter also forged a consensus view of American history in reaction against a Marxist but also an American Progressive theory of history as a series of conflicts. In *The American Political Tradition* (1948) Hofstadter objects that the common ground had been ignored in these versions of the American past:

> It is generally recognized that American politics has involved, among other things, a series of conflicts between special interests – between landed capital and financial or industrial capital, between old and new enterprises, large and small property – and that it has not shown, at least until recently, many signs of a struggle between the propertied and unpropertied classes. What has not been sufficiently recognized is the consequence for political thought. The fierceness of the political struggles has often been misleading; for the range of vision embraced by the primary contestants in the major parties has always been bounded by the horizons of property and enterprise. However much at odds on specific issues, the major political traditions have shared a belief in the rights of property, the philosophy of economic individualism, the value of competition; they have accepted the economic virtues of capitalist culture as necessary qualities of man.[18]

For all its drama, dirty tricks and literal and rhetorical violence, the American political tradition is surprisingly uniform. Even Andrew Jackson, the hero of 'the common man' in the 1820s and 1830s, and the centre of Jacksonian Democracy, turns out, in Hofstadter's revisionist interpretation, to be a 'peculiar blend of pioneer and aristocrat' (p. 57), in effect, a self-made man with a capitalist outlook, albeit a Western capitalist haranguing Eastern capitalists in the frontier language of egalitarianism.

In many respects, Hofstadter's account squares with that of his contemporary historians. But whereas Boorstin celebrates what is absent from American political history, Hofstadter's is a sceptical re-vision, which acknowledges the lack of conflict but suggests that it denotes literally a lack of thought. He also speculates on the quality of a political history (and theory) which is coterminous with capitalism, and so does 'not foster ideas that are hostile to [its] fundamental working arrangements' (p. xxxviii). With no real conflicts in the

American past, there was surely no problem which post-war American abundance and the mixed society could not handle, a conclusion questioned by hindsight, and by Michael Harrington's indictment of poverty in *The Other America* (1962). In *The Liberal Tradition in America*, the only other historical account to express such doubts, Louis Hartz similarly argues that the missing feudal stage in American history renders Americans blind to the most fundamental sources of conflict, those that Europeans have encountered through the opposition between socialism and capitalism.

The next generation of 1960s' historians would seek to discover those sources of conflict by rewriting American history 'from the bottom up', in Jesse Lemisch's phrase.[19] Hofstadter himself, while perceiving a crucial shortcoming in the American political tradition in his 1948 book, none the less went on to help close off possible alternatives in his major study of 1955, *The Age of Reform: From Bryan to F.D.R.* Despite the sub-title, political movements rather than the individuals who made the tradition are more in view, and Hofstadter's position has shifted. Intent, as were Trilling, Bell and Schlesinger, upon stiffening the liberal tradition which had proved susceptible to the cultural politics of the Popular Front, Hofstadter turned his critical eye on the Populists, the agrarian radicals of the 1890s. Arguably, the Populists have been the most important grass-roots political movement in American history, possessed of a coherent critical position on industrial capitalism, but Hofstadter emphasizes their 'provincialism . . . nativism and nationalism' and 'anti-Semitism'. 'Populist thought', Hofstadter writes (though he believes that their conspiratorial view of the world is thought-less), 'often carries one into a world in which the simple virtues and unmitigated villanies of a rural melodrama have been projected on a national and even an international scale'.[20]

Intellectuals influenced by *The Age of Reform* saw in Populism a harbinger of McCarthyism. They saw agrarian populism gone sour when faced with modernity, and moralism tinged with paranoia. Hofstadter's 1965 study, *The Paranoid Style in American Politics*, along with *Anti-intellectualism in American Life*, published in 1963, reinforced the lesson that liberal intellectuals ought to be wary of the reactionary qualities of mass movements. In this way, a significant reinterpretation of American political history and political culture became part of the cast of mind of the 1950s, without ever (certainly in Hofstadter's case) degenerating into the kind of apology for Americanism that we came across in the previous chapter.

In *The Intellectuals and McCarthy*, published only just over a decade later than *The Age of Reform*, but written out of a period more open to political populism, Michael Rogin observes of Hofstadter and such contemporaries as Riesman, Lipset, Glazer, Bell, the historian of immigration, Oscar Handlin, and the theologian, Will Heberg – that:

Before they wrote, McCarthyism meant something like character assassination, and Populism was the name of a particular historical movement for social reform at the end of the nineteenth century. Through their influence Populism has become an example of and a general term for anomic movements of mass protest against existing institutions – the type of movement typified by McCarthyism.[21]

Rogin's counter-thesis is that, in spite of all the mythology, McCarthyism was promoted by 'some wealthy and influential political elites' in the Republican Party, mostly on the right wing but including moderates, who saw McCarthy as a way of connecting their local power bases with a national constituency. The intellectuals, Rogin argues, not only missed this explanation for McCarthyism, but also damaged the cause of popular politics. Their interpretation of McCarthyism fed on those aspects of their 1930s experiences which called up a moralistic response to industrial collapse - Hofstadter approved of the organizational, practical response of the New Deal but not its emotional populism. Their interpretation of McCarthyism also cemented the link between the extreme Right and Left that certain readings of the 1930s (for example, Hannah Arendt's) made; and, finally, it smoothed the way for an acceptance of elite leadership in politics. Within elite politics, where leaders, rather than the populace, dealt with conflicts, the intellectual virtues of rationality and analysis could be preserved in the theory of political balance – which we have already discussed from a more sympathetic perspective when considering Bell and Riesman. The consequence in 1950s political theory and practice was a narrowing of the range of public participation in politics, quite the reverse of a traditional understanding of liberal pluralism.

When allied with a fear of the masses, pluralism sets limits that can exclude the 'bottom up' contributions to American democracy made by agrarian and industrial workers, women, and blacks. Those who are not part of the consensus, but are part of 'the other America', and therefore methodologically excluded from Riesman's study of the middle and upper-middle classes, not only have no place in veto politics but do not have moral rights that can be made public. Morality in politics, we recall, is discredited by Riesman, Hofstadter and Bell. Yet without the moral imperatives of, for instance, the Civil Rights Movement under Martin Luther King, important political values would not have become part of the democratic tradition. Veto politics, almost by definition, cannot easily generate visions, or utopias. Once limits are set, veto groups, rather than being the means for opening up politics to new ideas, become part of the two-party system.

The interventionist history of the 1960s has done more than reinstate moral concerns; it has contested a view of American history as homogeneous and lacking real conflict. The so-called 'new social history', which was stimulated by the Civil Rights and Women's Rights movements, and by protest against American foreign policy, has reconstructed communities hitherto hidden from history: communities of blacks (John Blassingame's *Slave Community*, 1972, and Eugene Genovese's *Roll, Jordan, Roll*, 1974); of women (Carol Smith Rosenberg's 'The Female World of Love and Ritual', 1975); and of industrial workers (Alan Dawley's *Class and Community*, 1976). Employing anthropological and/or quantitative approaches which give those who did not leave traditional 'literary' records a voice, these historians have written a small library of community studies. They have written the kind of history where, after two or three hundred pages, we have not left the environs of Lowell, Massachusetts, or the Lower East Side of New York City, but have, by way of reward, appreciated Thoreau's point when he remarks, in *Walden*, that he has 'travelled a good deal in Concord.' Moreover, these close-range studies provide different, and often competing (rather than merely plural), viewpoints on the American past. In Alan Dawley's words, writing about the Jacksonian era which, for many years Arthur Schlesinger Jr made his 'age':

> Because it was so pervasive, the 'Age of Egalitarianism' has
> become a favorite label among historians; however, the label
> blots out the vital differences in the definitions of equality and
> obscures the social conflicts behind the differences. To a frontier
> planter or farmer, equality meant free access to land. To the
> rising entrepreneur, it meant open competition in the race for
> wealth. But to the worker, whose central interests were bound
> up with wage payments – not property, ownership, or capital
> accumulation – equality did not mean an opportunity to win a
> fortune but a chance to live in comfort and dignity.[22]

It is valid to anticipate the 1960s reaction to liberal pluralist politics because, in that quintessential 'fifties' text, *The End of Ideology*, Daniel Bell addresses his thesis to the future as well as to the 1930s. The sudden shift of point of view near the end of that book anticipates a more widespread 'break out' than that which occurred in the writing of American history:

> And yet, the extraordinary fact is that while the old nineteenth-
> century ideologies and intellectual debates have become
> exhausted, the rising states of Asia and Africa are fashioning new
> ideologies with a different appeal for their own people. (p. 403)

Bell admits to a fear that even America will not be immune.

Our theoretical work is indeed utopian: C. Wright Mills

It is remarkable that pluralism, this persuasive combination of theology, aesthetics, recent history as well as American political history back to the Constitution, and sheer practicality, should have coalesced with such authority, only to fall apart in the 1960s. One explanation can be found in the work of of C. Wright Mills. For all his cult-image as a latter-day Thoreau, building his own house, and as a rogue-academic on a motorcycle, in a period of increasing professionalization, Mills had the ability simply to ask different questions. One consequence of Mills's critique, carried on through *White Collar* (1951), *The Sociological Imagination* (1959), 'Letter to the New Left' (1960) and, most controversially, *The Power Elite* (1956) was the very different understanding of pluralism which surfaced in the 1960s.

Leaving aside his 'Letter to the New Left,' with its inspirational rhetoric, and the more polemical late 1950s-early 1960s texts (he died in 1962), then Mills is very much a 1950s writer. A Texan, he came to teach at Maryland (with Richard Hofstadter) and then Columbia University in New York. He wrote for Dwight Macdonald's *Politics* (and suggested the magazine's name), as well as for Daniel Bell's *The New Leader*, and, for a time, lived in the same building as Bell. In *The New Men of Power* (1948), which shares the theme of labor with Bell's early sociology, he is fairly optimistic about the possibilities of unions, white collar workers and intellectuals coming together. By the time of *The Power Elite*, he had come to believe that unions were too mixed up with corporate management to offer any hope of change. This may explain why, in the end, he may not have been able to move beyond critique. With little to latch onto as a source of resistance to the consolidation of power in the upper circles of the military-industrial complex, the difference between Mills and Bell or Riesman may, in the end, come down to a streak of Progressive/Populist era muckraking journalism in Mills, together with what might be described as his will to discover the sources of power.

Nevertheless, in *The Power Elite* Mills directly takes on post-war pluralism or, as he calls it, 'the theory of balance', which, in David Riesman's telling, locates power in the interplay of interest groups, and equates politics with the middle-ground, and the middle-class. Mills steps back to totalize this arena:

> There has developed on the middle levels of power, a semi-
> organized stalemate, and . . . on the bottom level there has come
> into being a mass-like society which has little resemblance to the
> image of a society in which voluntary associations and classic
> publics hold the key to power. The top of the American system
> of power is much more unified and much more powerful, the
> bottom is much more fragmented, and in truth, impotent, than is
> generally supposed by those who are distracted by the middling
> units of power which neither express such will as exists at the
> bottom nor determine the decisions at the top.[23]

There are two interlinked themes here. The first is Mills's response
to the expanded middle of veto politics, leading to his analysis of 'the
power elite'. The second is the hope that Mills holds out for a more
substantial and widespread public participation than he sees in veto
politics; here the relationship between 'classic publics' and the masses is
the issue. Though there is not enough space to pursue the question, it
is not clear why the word 'class' is missing in the passage above or
why, elsewhere in the book Mills is so intent upon eschewing a class
analysis. After all, it is part of his argument that the members of the
power elite are from the same kind of families, go to certain schools,
later attend the same business and social functions, and even share
leisure activities.

But to return to what Mills considered important. He begins *The
Power Elite* by insisting that more is going on than meets the
sociological eye, or at least the eye of the functionalist sociologist:

> The powers of ordinary men are circumscribed by the everyday
> worlds in which they live, yet even in these rounds of job,
> family, and neighborhood they often seem driven by forces they
> can neither understand nor govern . . .
> But not all men are in this sense ordinary. As the means of
> information and of power are centralized, some men come to
> occupy positions in American society from which they can look
> down upon, so to speak, and by their decisions mightily affect,
> the everyday worlds of ordinary men and women. (p. 3)

Mills accepts that most political action goes on in the middle levels.
Instead of idealizing interest group politics in a 'Whitmanesque
enthusiasm for variety' (p. 244), Mills asks for discriminations to be
made between groups: do occupation-based groups exert influence in
the same way and to the same degree as those based on a single issue?
Are there gradations of power within the democratic struggle, so that
the limits and the agenda are set rather than, somehow, setting
themselves, on an analogy with the mechanism of the market in

classical laissez-faire economics? However, the questions Mills pushes most vigorously are Which groups are connected? and How do they then relate to 'the big decisions'? 'Exactly *what*', he asks polemically, 'directly or indirectly, did "small retailers" or "brick masons" have to do with the sequence of decision and event that led to World War II?' (p. 244). Even Congress was by-passed when the decision was taken for the US to enter the Second World War. When it was decided to drop the atom bomb at the end of the war, deliberations were not part of the round of negotiation in the middle realm of politics. Mills's frequent use of the example of the atomic bomb tells us that it is not simply the degree of top-level concentration of power that was new in the post-1930s period, but the nature of power and its means: 'The men of either circle [the USSR's or America's power elite] can cause great cities to be wiped out in a single night, and in a few weeks turn continents into thermonuclear wastelands' (p. 23).

In response to the big decisions that have punctuated this century's history, Mills (in contrast to Riesman, Bell and other liberal pluralists) wants to ask the big questions again. Finding 'Ariadne's thread' or, in his own expression, the 'sociological key', will revive not only American radical criticism but also theories of the Marx and Weber kind which made connections, but which had been thrown into disrepute by the attack on ideology. He is after (in the title of one of his later books) 'the sociological imagination', rather than the empirical study, and this involves taking a historical view. Thus, he traces the beginnings of this incorporation of power to the post-Civil War years when entrepreneurial capitalism began to be superceded by monopoly capitalism, and when the culture heroes were Andrew Carnegie and John D. Rockefeller. However, it was not until the New Deal and the run-up to the Second World War that the recognized and often admired economic elite was joined by a political and military elite. Against this 'triumvirate', interest groups were relatively powerless because they had no 'longer' view.

This conclusion may appear obvious, or paranoid in the manner of Thomas Pynchon's novels of conspiracy. However, a more judicious estimate of Mills's importance in the 1950s debate over pluralism and its apparent alternative, totalitarianism, can be obtained by remembering that Daniel Bell, David Riesman, indeed, the majority of leading liberals were confident that if America still had anything like a ruling class then that class was in decline. Mills further questions received wisdom when claiming that the power elite is not a meritocracy, linked with even the lowest rungs of the social ladder by the stories of diligence rewarded that grew up around the captains of industry of the 1880s and 1890s. The power elite is largely cut off from the middle ranks and, according to Mills in the most striking passages of the book, has developed its own institutions and mechanisms for operating. In its

post-war manifestation 'traffic' between the leading industrial corporations, the state, and the military increases, and decisions in one sphere
are made with other spheres' interests in mind. Ironically, then, the
power elite functions as a genuine community of interest but at the
expense of democracy. Members of one elite appear on the boards of
another and so the interlocking is achieved institutionally rather than as
a conspiracy:

> The higher members of the military, economic, and political
> orders are able readily to take over one another's point of view,
> always in a sympathetic way, and often in a knowledgeable way
> as well. They define one another as among those who count, and
> who, accordingly, must be taken into account. (p. 283)

In his 'Letter to the New Left' Mills conferred on a new and
explicitly young generation of intellectuals the heavy duty of making
connections between different spheres of life as a way of raising
consciousness. The problem was, Whose consciousness? because Mills
subscribes to a fairly standard understanding of the coming of mass
society which leaves those at the bottom in a culturally 'lumpen' state.
Mills's account of the role of the media in *The Power Elite* and 'The
Cultural Apparatus' is influenced by Adorno and Horkheimer's
analysis of Hollywood and radio in 'The Culture Industry', in that it
raises the spectre of totalitarianism. He resists their pessimism, though:
'At the end of that road there is totalitarianism, as in Nazi Germany or
in Communist Russia. We are not yet at that end. In the United States
today, media markets are not entirely ascendant over primary publics'
(p. 304).

In so far as Mills's alternative to the domination of the power elite is
articulated, it seems to involve an informed public – informed by
intellectuals – participating in politics, though not in the circumscribed
context envisioned by Bell and Riesman who both bracket off the top
and the bottom levels. Participation must be on the basis of as full a
knowledge as possible of the existence of the power elite, and an
acknowledgement of how political decisions are vertically linked with
the lowest levels of society. Surprisingly, perhaps, of the figures we
have considered in this chapter it is Hannah Arendt, the source of the
most disturbing picture of the immediate past, who comes out most
strongly in favour of participatory politics. In Mills's case, the
occasional positive statements of an alternative politics – involving
informed publics regaining the power from elites – are kept to himself:
not in the sense of saying little because Mills became more outspoken
between *The Power Elite* and his death, but in the sense, of sticking to
his role of investigative intellectual until such a time that the ideas
could function as part of a counter force. His 1950s books give no

indication of what this will be, but his 'Letter to the New Left' designates youth as the new public. This public is located by Mills not in the restricted foreground of studies of social character, but in the international context of rebellions and protests in Turkey, South Korea, Cuba, Taiwan, Okinawa, Japan, 'and even in our own pleasant Southland'.[24]

What we also notice in this highly influential letter is the re-emergence of utopia from under the term ideology:

> Ultimately, the-end-of-ideology is based upon a disillusionment
> with any real commitment to socialism in any recognizable form.
> *That* is the only 'ideology' that has really ended for these writers.
> But with its ending, *all* ideology, they think, has ended. *That*
> ideology they talk about; their own ideological assumptions, they
> do not. (p. 109)

It took the beginnings of the New Left (whatever its later course) to provoke the following statement from Mills, in which sentences from *The Power Elite* are echoed so that the significance of the whole book changes because of the new context:

> *Utopian* nowadays, I think, refers to any criticism or proposal
> that transcends the up-close milieux of a scatter of individuals,
> the milieux which men and women can understand directly and
> which they can reasonably hope directly to change. In this exact
> sense, our theoretical work is indeed utopian – in my own case,
> at least, deliberately so. What needs to be understood, and what
> needs to be changed, is not merely first this and then that detail
> of some institution or policy. If there is to be a politics of a new
> left, what needs to be analyzed is the *structure* of institutions, the
> *foundation* of policies. In this sense, both in its criticisms and in its
> proposals, our work is necessarily structural, and so – *for us*, just
> now – utopian. (p. 115)

A philosophical inquiry into Freud: Herbert Marcuse

Herbert Marcuse became a cult figure for the New Left and the Counter-Culture, an amazing achievement for a retired, professional philosopher. His theme of liberation from a repressive civilization became their theme. However, before his ideas were taken up by supporters and disciples, and inevitably and rightly changed, he attempted to find a 'way out' of what he later called a 'one-dimensional' society. In this respect, *Eros and Civilization* (1955) may be compared with the different route taken by C. Wright Mills, and, in literature, by Norman Mailer, J.D. Salinger, and the Beat writers, Jack Kerouac and Allen Ginsberg.

Marcuse shared much of the pessimism of colleagues in the Frankfurt School following the defeats of socialism – after both World Wars and at the hands of Stalin. The spread of technological rationality is also a gloomy theme in his work, culminating in *One-Dimensional Man* (1964). Yet, somehow, he sustained his revolutionary optimism.

The name of Marx never appears in *Eros and Civilization*, even though Marx had been central to Marcuse's education, his institutional connections with the Frankfurt School, and his own writings, going back to articles published since the late 1920s and culminating in *Reason and Revolution: Hegel and the Rise of Social Theory* (1941). It is difficult to say whether Marx's omission was tactical, but certainly it was not just tactics. Marcuse's faithful account of Marx on alienation in early essays and in *Reason and Revolution* had to be updated to meet an age of apparent affluence, in which revolution was seemingly not even a possibility. Incidentally, it should be stated here that in this assumption of affluence, Marcuse can be compared, rather than contrasted, with David Riesman and other writers who were at the very least sanguine about post-war America. In consequence, alienation is presented in *Eros and Civilization* as a problem for the affluent as well as for Marx's traditional constituents, the industrial working classes.

From his early writings, Marcuse had focused upon the relationship between the activist and determinist poles in Marxism, between Marx as the inspiration for liberation and Marx as social theorist who gave an account of objective social change. Another way to put this is to say that Marcuse was always alert to the possibilities of the future, even when mired in the most anti-utopian conditions. By the late 1930s, Marcuse had largely lost faith in the working-classes as the active revolutionary force. However, he remained convinced that conscious activity was part of Marx's dialectic of liberation (revolution would not just come of its own accord). He therefore had to look away from Marx's anti-psychology and find other sources of motivation and another image of utopia besides the classic Marxist one.

It should be noted, in this connection, that, following on from Engels' *Socialism: Scientific and Utopian*, Marxism had mostly thought of utopian speculation as a harmful distraction, siphoning off discontent into idealistic plans and projects. However, utopianism comes and goes in Marxist thinking, as Georg Lukács made clear in 1967:

We must essentially compare our situation today with that
in which [utopians] like Fourier and Sismondi found themselves
at the beginning of the nineteenth century. We can only achieve
effective action when we become aware that we find ourselves in
that situation and when it becomes clear to us that there is a sense
in which the development from Fourier to Marx remains, both
theoretically and practically, a task for the future.[25]

Marcuse was in such a situation: located in California in the midst of a
post-war material boom, and in an atmosphere of confidence, shared
by many intellectuals as well as politicians, that the United States could
actually realize the utopias imagined in the nineteenth century. Faced
with abundance, Marcuse sought to redefine 'the negative', that which
would not simply give the lie to claims for progress but, at the same
time, would be a description of a better way of being.

Marcuse had been reading Freud seriously since the late 1930s when
the Frankfurt School had been looking for explanations for the
susceptibility of the working classes to fascist and capitalist propaganda. He returned to Freud in 1950, but the book that resulted – *Eros
and Civilization* – introduces both a more orthodox and a more radical
Freud. Broadly speaking, Marcuse uses Freud, rather than Marx
writing about the nineteenth-century factory system, to define
alienation and loss. Since it is out of Freud that Marcuse also eventually
re-imagines utopia in the form of 'a non-repressive civilization', it is
necessary to give an explanation of this choice of a guide known more
for his message that individuals cannot escape the burden of their
psychic pasts.[26]

Eros and Civilization begins with a paraphrase of Freud's central
cultural proposition: 'Civilization is based on the permanent subjuga-
tion of the human instincts' and 'free gratification of man's instinctual
needs is incompatible with civilized society: renunciation and delay in
satisfaction are the prerequisites of progress' (p. 3). This is the Freud of
Civilization and Its Discontents (1930), a late text in which he moved
openly towards social commentary. Freud does not put the word
civilization in quotation marks; the gains in outward achievement and
in the consolidation of the ego are thought worth the loss of instinctual
freedom. Besides which, the process is inevitable: the reality principle
checks the pleasure principle, according to this scheme:

from:	*to:*
immediate satisfaction	delayed satisfaction
pleasure	restraint of pleasure
joy (play)	toil (work)
receptiveness	productiveness
absence of repression	security (p. 12)

At the point Freud seems most persuasive in diagnosing the limitations of the human condition, Marcuse seeks to historicize him. This means that Marcuse investigates the historical and cultural form which the reality principle has taken in advanced industrial societies. Working from Freud's metapsychology, Marcuse arrives at a specific form of repression: the '*Performance Principle*: the prevailing historical form of the *reality principle*' (p. 35). Within a single important paragraph Marcuse then brings together Freud and Marx, but also the other social theorist who is almost an honorary American thinker, Max Weber:

> The performance principle, which is that of an acquisitive and antagonistic society in the process of constant expansion, presupposes a long development during which domination has been increasingly rationalized: control over social labor now reproduces society on an enlarged scale and under improving conditions. For a long way, the interests of domination and the interests of the whole coincide: the profitable utilization of the productive apparatus fulfills the needs and faculties of the individuals. For the vast majority of the population, the scope and mode of satisfaction are determined by their own labor; but their labor is work for an apparatus which they do not control, which operates as an independent power to which individuals must submit if they want to live. And it becomes the more alien the more specialized the division of labor becomes. Men do not live their lives but perform pre-established functions. While they work, they do not fulfill their own needs and faculties but work in *alienation*. (p. 45)

The echoes of Marx are very clear, but the description of the performance principle and the 'from . . . to' scheme above is exactly what we find in Weber's *The Protestant Ethic and the Spirit of Capitalism*, though Marcuse did not write specifically on Weber until 1964. Marcuse's argument is that the reality principle took the form of asceticism, delayed gratification, and so on in the context of economic scarcity, but has remained unchanged even though the economic conditions have changed. Therefore, Marcuse reasons, there is 'surplus repression' (another echo of Marx on 'surplus value'), and if there is more repression than there needs to be then there is a politics to it.

If, for a moment, we leave *Eros and Civilization* and move to *One Dimensional Man*, we can appreciate that Marcuse includes in his indictment of the performance principle the stress on 'better management, safer planning, greater efficiency, closer calculation', which Bell and others were happy to see replace ideological struggle.[27] Where

American intellectuals sharply distinguished between the United States, on the one hand, and the USSR and Nazi Germany on the other, Marcuse's focus upon technological rationality led him to see similarities that James Burnham had described in *The Managerial Revolution* (1941), before he, too, exempted the United States. Marcuse's broad questions, however, are: Why expand 'the managerial revolution' in a time of acknowledged abundance? If this does not constitute 'surplus repression', what does? And, if, when we have the possibility before us of a victory over scarcity and therefore over the repression that it made necessary, why aren't we considering it seriously?

The evidence of repression amidst abundance was all around. In concluding his chapter on Marcuse in *Marxism and Form*, Fredric Jameson – also dedicated to rescuing utopianism for Marxism – evokes a memorable image of 'the stubborn rebirth of the idea of freedom' by:

> the philosopher, in the exile of that immense housing
> development which is the state of California, remembering,
> reawakening, reinventing – from the rows of products in the
> supermarkets, from the roar of the freeways and the ominous
> shape of the helmets of traffic policemen, from the incessant
> overhead traffic of the fleets of military transport planes, and as it
> were from beyond them, in the future – the almost extinct form
> of the Utopian idea.[28]

The contrasts described by Jameson – abundance and cultural impoverishment, freedom and domination, utopia and dystopia – are basic to Marcuse's analysis. In delineating what is lost, Marcuse allows us to speculate upon what may be achieved. He is not advocating a return to an earlier historical state, on analogy with a return to a time when the pleasure principle reigned. Instead, in the manner of Marx identifying possibilities locked up in capitalism's distortion of, for example, technological potential for the release from drudgery, Marcuse is drawing attention to an alternative narrative of social development which does not overload the reality principle with an excess of the Protestant ethic or performance principle.

Freedom is not entirely lost. It is, however, accessible only through means and activities that are deemed marginal by the existing reality principle: memory and art. While art as aesthetics can be incorporated as a specialized activity into bourgeois society, it none the less brings to conscious life glimpses of another way of being or thinking, besides that dictated by prevailing rationality. To accept 'civilization and its discontents' is not only to deny our psychic pasts, but also what is conscious, the imagination. And 'imagination envisions the reconciliation of the individual with the whole, of desire with realization, of happiness with reason' (p. 143). Art therefore allows for the 'return of the repressed'. When Marcuse links art with life, he does not equate the result with utopia, but sees it as a prefiguration of utopia. It was the understandably enthusiastic and positive conclusion of proponents of the Counter-Culture that utopia was where they were; there was no future tense in much counter-cultural language. Marcuse felt he should endorse the Counter-Culture, though he warned that its activities would be marketed by the 'repressive tolerance' of capitalism.

And then there is memory, a faculty common to us all across classes and other divisions. 'The memory of gratification is at the origin of all thinking, and the impulse to recapture past gratification is the hidden driving power behind the process of thought' (p. 31). To offer such a statement simply as the essence of Marcuse's escape-route from the 1950s is to miss a breadth of concern that derives from Freud but, stylistically, also recalls Marx on religion as 'the sentiment of a heartless world, and the soul of soulless conditions.'

> The mere anticipation of the inevitable end, present in every instant, introduces a repressive element into all libidinal relations and renders pleasure itself painful . . . Man learns that 'it cannot last anyway,' that every pleasure is short, that for all finite things the hour of their birth is the hour of their death – that it couldn't be otherwise. He is resigned before society forces him to practice resignation methodically. The flux of time is society's most natural ally in maintaining law and order, conformity, and the institutions that relegate freedom to a perpetual utopia; the flux of time helps men forget what was and what can be: it makes them oblivious to the better past and the better future.
>
> This ability to forget . . . is an indispensable requirement of mental and physical hygiene without which civilized life would be unbearable; but it is also the mental faculty which sustains submissiveness and renunciation. To forget is also to forgive what should not be forgiven if justice and freedom are to prevail. (pp. 231–2)

Only memory can resist the power of forgetfulness. If there is any justification for refusing the otherwise persuasive reading of Freud as a tragic realist by Lionel Trilling, then this is it. Moreover, it is consistent with the much more assertive statement which Marcuse makes in the 'Preface to the First Edition': 'This essay employs psychological categories because they have become political categories' (p. xxvii). Internal crises and disorders reflect external ones, more than ever now there are routes between the public and private worlds. Through the mechanism of memory, Marcuse insists that there can be movement both ways.

Marcuse began by inquiring whether Freud's proposition about civilization necessarily resulting from repression held true; or at least whether the results were worth the cost of 'intensified unfreedom' (p. 4). In the concluding chapters on sexuality under the reinstated pleasure principle, he considers what non-repression might mean in the sphere where, if we follow Freud, the effects of liberation would be most immediate. 'The notion of a non-repressive instinctual order must first be tested on the most "disorderly" of all the instincts – namely, sexuality' (p. 199).

Marcuse brings sexuality in line with his overall thesis, arguing that the power of the performance principle is manifested in excessive emphasis upon genital sexuality. In common with Norman O. Brown in *Life Against Death* (1959), Marcuse calls for an erotic liberation, a 'polymorphous sexuality' (p. 201) that would not be organized along family and property lines. Against objections that this would lead to 'a society of sex maniacs – that is, to no society' (p. 201), Marcuse refuses the progress/regress opposition which bedevils social theory and talks of 'a *transformation* of the libido: from sexuality constrained under genital supremacy to eroticization of the entire personality' (p. 201).

Marcuse's language makes it hard to appreciate his influence upon the 1960s, and indeed it was less this book than *One Dimensional Man* and *An Essay on Liberation* (1969), and, at a personal level, less Marcuse than Paul Goodman, who made the connection with the new vision of society. Goodman brought the value of sexual liberation down to earth and linked it with youth. If Goodman has not received his dues by now, however, it is unlikely that he will in the foreseeable future. His brief but absolutely explicit exclusion of women as largely irrelevant to the liberationist philosophy necessary to prevent boys from 'growing up absurd' makes it difficult to see *Growing Up Absurd* (1960) being taken as seriously as in other ways it deserves. *Communitas* (1947), co-authored with his brother, Percival Goodman, is likely to wear better.

Marcuse sought to think other than in the terms of his own society. Doing just this as regards sexuality, he hardly makes an extraordinary claim when suggesting that 'free libidinal relations' are not 'essentially antagonistic to work relations' (p. 154); and, a little later, in connection with his main argument, that 'the elimination of surplus-repression would *per se* tend to eliminate, not labor, but the organization of the human existence into an instrument of labor . . . the liberation of Eros could create new and durable work relations' (p. 155). Though it undermines his radical appeal, it would not be difficult to think of historical-cultural contexts in which thinking other than in terms of genital, reproductive sex would actually make good social or economic sense, and in which government advertising and even policy would make that graphically clear.

Incidentally, it is this willingness to reconsider the whole of social as well as private life as capable of transformation which separates Marcuse from Wilhelm Reich, a breakaway in the early 1930s from the Freudian path. Reich anticipated Marcuse in perceiving the revolutionary potential of Freud's instinct theory but concentrated obsessively upon sexual repression, and upon the theory of the orgasm as the form of release. He was so fixed on genital sexuality, and such a militant hetero-sexist, that he barely entertained the diffusion of eroticism that Marcuse drew out of Freud's theory of sexuality.

There is no doubt that Marcuse is serious about a rethinking of sexuality; it is also entirely consistent with his philosophical interpretation of Freud. However, the impact of *Eros and Civilization* could well be greatest upon those who – perhaps well in the wake of the 1960s – regard the chapters on sexuality as weak, a poor pay-off, or an unimaginable utopia deficient in concrete details. By locating Marcuse in a tradition of utopian thinking which, increasingly, has had to take account of the power of ideology, we can read him as a salutary reminder that when we reject utopianism as unrealistic, impractical and even a-political, we may well be accepting our society's definition of what is real, practical and political. We may be accepting society's definition of what is the future: 'The relegation of real possibilities to the no-man's land of utopia is itself an essential element of the ideology of the performance principle' (p. 150). Nor can we take complete refuge in Marcuse's seeming concentration upon America as his test-case. The issue is about what is possible, as he makes very plain:

> The reconciliation between the pleasure and reality principle does not depend on the existence of abundance for all. The only pertinent question is whether a state of civilization can be reasonably envisaged in which human needs are fulfilled in such a manner and to such an extent that surplus-repression can be eliminated. (p. 151)

Notes

1. Hannah Arendt, *The Origins of Totalitarianism* (1986), pp. viii and vii.

2. Richard H. King, 'Endings and Beginnings: Politics in Arendt's Early Thought', *Political Theory*, 12 (1984), pp. 235–51.

3. Quoted in David Riesman, with Nathan Glazer and Ruel Denney, *The Lonely Crowd: A Study of the Changing American Character* (New Haven, 1961), p. 5.

4. Daniel Bell, *The End of Ideology: On the Exhaustion of Political Ideas in the Fifties* (New York, 1962), p. 64.

5. Alexis de Tocqueville, *Democracy in America*, translated by Henry Reeve (New York, 1945), II, p. 111.

6. See, for example, J. Hillis Miller, 'Ariadne's Thread: Repetition and the Narrative Line', *Critical Inquiry*, 3 (1976), pp. 57–78.

7. Irving Howe, *The Decline of the New* (New York, 1970), p. 236.

8. Donald Meyer, *The Positive Thinkers: Religion as Pop Psychology from Mary Baker Eddy to Oral Roberts* (New York, 1980), p. 154.

9. John Murray Cuddihy, *No Offense: Civil Religion and Protestant Taste* (New York, 1978), pp. xiii and 32.

10. Reinhold Niebuhr, *The Children of Light and the Children of Darkness* (New York, 1944), p. 129.

11. Reinhold Niebuhr, *The Irony of American History* (New York, 1952). p. 83.

12. Arthur Schlesinger Jr, *The Vital Center: The Politics of Freedom* (Boston, 1949), p. 170.

13. Lionel Trilling, *The Liberal Imagination: Essays on Literature and Society* (Harmondsworth, 1970), p. 11.

14. Howard Brick, *Daniel Bell and the Decline of Intellectual Radicalism: Social Theory and Political Reconciliation in the 1940s* (Madison, 1986), p. 20.

15. Cleanth Brooks and Robert Penn Warren (eds), *Understanding Fiction* (New York, 1959), p. xix. See pp. 174–76 above for the connections with Southern Agrarianism.

16. Daniel Bell, *The Cultural Contradictions of Capitalism* (1979), p. 121.

17. Quoted in Daniel J. Boorstin, *The Genius of American Politics* (Chicago, 1953), p. 164.

18. Richard Hofstadter, *The American Political Tradition and the Men Who Made It* (New York, 1974), pp. xxxvi–xxxvii.

19. Jesse Lemisch, 'The American Revolution Seen From the Bottom Up', in *Towards a New Past: Dissenting Essays in American History*, edited by Barton J. Bernstein (New York, 1969), pp. 3–45.

20. Richard Hofstadter, *The Age of Reform: From Bryan to F.D.R.* (New York, 1955), pp. 61 and 73. For a different interpretation, see Lawrence Goodwyn, *The Populist Moment* (New York, 1976).

21. Michael Paul Rogin, *The Intellectuals and McCarthy: The Radical Spectre* (Cambridge, Mass., 1967), p. 6.

22. Alan Dawley, *Class and Community: The Industrial Revolution in Lynn* (Cambridge, Mass., 1976), pp. 1–2.

23. C. Wright Mills, *The Power Elite* (New York, 1981), pp. 28–9.

24. C. Wright Mills, 'Letter to the New Left', in *The New Radicals: A Report with Documents*, edited by Paul Jacobs and Saul Landau (Harmondsworth, 1967), p. 118.

25. Quoted in Fredric Jameson, *The Ideologies of Theory: Essays, 1971–1986. Volume 2: The Syntax of History* (1988), p. 76.

26. Herbert Marcuse, *Eros and Civilization: A Philosophical Inquiry into Freud* (Boston, 1966), p. 5.

27. Herbert Marcuse, *One Dimesional Man* (1972), p. 139.

28. Fredric Jameson, *Marxism and Form: Twentieth-Century Dialectical Theories of Literature* (Princeton NJ, 1971), p. 116.

Chapter 7
Black Culture and Politics

The problem of the twentieth century is the problem of the color line

When black youth participated in the sit-ins, bus boycotts, and Freedom Rides which began in the second half of the 1950s, there appeared to be little continuity with the post-Reconstruction black rights movement. It is particularly noticeable that the new generation did not look to W.E.B. DuBois, the major figure in the earlier black rights movement, even though he lived on until 1963 and hardly had a peaceful old age. In his eighties DuBois ran for the United States Senate on the Labor Party ticket, applied to join the Communist Party, renounced his American citizenship, and went to live in Nkrumah's Ghana. Enough, one would have thought, to have aroused more than occasional notice.

In *The Souls of Black Folk* (1903), DuBois announced that 'the problem of the Twentieth Century is the problem of the color line'.[1] Whatever the drawbacks to dealing with blacks in a separate chapter, to do so brings some appreciation, at least, of DuBois's point. More particularly, it helps to make the case for black culture and politics and establishes the necessity for a different narrative within the dominant, white history of events. For instance, we can examine the gap between the Civil Rights movement and the early twentieth century, when DuBois contested the leadership of Booker T. Washington and set a different political and cultural agenda from those we have been following so far. By taking a long view we can also explore the hypothesis that when the later black liberation movements faced dilemmas they needed the example of DuBois and the experience of his founding debates with Washington and Marcus Garvey. Possibly, even, the new generation needed more knowledge of an overlooked event, DuBois's trial in Washington DC in 1951, during the McCarthy era, when he was indicted for being a Soviet agent. His trial reveals the links between capitalism and racism which, as we shall see later, the subsequent movement had to understand all over again.[2]

Property, economy, education and Christian character: Booker T. Washington

Post-Civil War Reconstruction ended when federal troops were withdrawn from the South in 1877. The failings of Reconstruction soon became apparent in the Ku Klux Klan's regime of terror; in the spread of Jim Crow laws; in the disenfranchising of blacks in rewritten state constitutions; and in a share-cropping system that kept black tenants almost as securely tied to the land-owner as under slavery. Blacks had somehow to respond to the realities of the best situation they could hope for, which was the 'separate but equal' ruling handed down by the Supreme Court in the *Plessy vs Ferguson* case of 1896. 1896 was also the date of McKinley's election, effectively the end of the Populist Movement within which, for a time at least, black and white farmers had formed a common front against Northern capitalists.

The message of Washington's *Future of the American Negro* (1899) was that self-help and accommodation to the circumstances and the dominant culture of the work ethic were the only realistic responses:

> There is but one way out . . . one hope of solution; and that is
> for the Negro in every part of America to resolve from
> henceforth that he will throw aside every non-essential and cling
> only to the essential, – that his pillar of fire by night and pillar of
> cloud by day shall be property, economy, education and
> Christian character.[3]

In his autobiography, *Up from Slavery* (1901), Washington grafted his message onto the familiar American story of the self-made man. Like Benjamin Franklin near the beginning of the genre, Washington describes the long journey which he had to make, literally from Malden, West Virginia, to the Hampton Normal and Agricultural Institute 500 miles away, and metaphorically to get him started on the road to economic success.

After founding the Tuskegee Institute in 1881, Washington promoted industrial and agricultural education as the way forward in the New South. The appeal to blacks was that they were pictured free of patently degrading racial stereotypes (slothful, childlike, dependent and so on) and equipped with the useful skills necessary to change their circumstances through their own efforts. The appeal to whites was that blacks were pictured in acceptably subservient roles, but better fitted to serve the needs of the New South. Washington's was a gradualist philosophy of citizenship which made simultaneous reference to traditional values and modern conditions, and carefully controlled the degree to which his audience or readership focused upon means or upon ends. He did not alienate any whites prepared to accept that change had to follow emancipation, especially if they were prepared also to fund educational institutions for blacks. His writings, not surprisingly, have a double-voiced quality: he even builds into his autobiography ideal black and white readers who endorse his message in advance of whatever response is to be elicited from real black and white readers.

Realistic tactics still depend upon an explicit philosophy, and Washington pronounced it in his *Address . . . at the Opening of the Cotton States and International Exposition* in Atlanta in 1895: 'In all things that are purely social we can be as separate as the fingers, yet one as the hand in all things essential to mutual progress.'[4] The segregation against which the later Civil Rights Movement fought is stated as clearly here as in the *Plessy* case the year after.

The Southern press approved of Washington's speech and he became a leader overnight and remained powerful until his death in 1915. In 1895 his conciliatory views were apparently approved of by most blacks. Perhaps they fastened on to the liberationist ends and ignored the racist images. Perhaps, again, more used to 'puttin' on' than whites, blacks would have picked up the strategic quality of Washington's speech. While DuBois was a student at Fisk and Harvard and then a teacher at Wilberforce University, he, too, leant towards self-help philosophy and accommodation, rather than confrontation with whites.

One ever feels his twoness: W.E.B. DuBois

DuBois' career divides chronologically into three periods. From the late 1880s through to 1915, he moved from a Washingtonian position to being the main opponent of an accommodationist philosophy; the publication in 1903 of *The Souls of Black Folk* marked the transition. Then, between 1915 and the mid-1930s, he was the pre-eminent black intellectual, with a base in the National Association for the Advancement of Colored People (NAACP) but, more importantly, in *Crisis* magazine. The third period dates from the later years of the Depression when, along with other radical movements for change, black protest suffered. This decline was accentuated in the post-war period when, as we have seen in the previous chapter, the themes of totalitarianism and the problems of affluence took centre stage. Literary figures, like Richard Wright, Ralph Ellison, and James Baldwin, and academic sociologists, like E. Franklin Frazier and Charles S. Johnson, took over the main responsibility for articulating ideas. In this period, DuBois remained busy but was less influential. At the end of the War he was in his seventies, of course, but his lower profile is better accounted for by the atmosphere of anti-communism and anti-radicalism, especially since DuBois had become a socialist and a pacifist.

The Souls of Black Folk is a founding text of modern black thought. It signals a more critical attitude towards Booker T. Washington than hitherto, with DuBois objecting strongly to Washington's denigration of political and civil rights. Both were essential for the protection of the economic rights which Washington had privileged in his Atlanta *Address*. DuBois was quickly on to the links between racism and capitalism, where Washington's faith in laissez-faire made him blind to factors that interfered with the freedom of the market, the most blatant being 'the color line'. More immediately, in the context of the South at the turn of the century, political rights were being lost and on this Washington's philosophy had nothing positive to offer and may also have done damage. Aside from which, Washington's rejection of a political route to full citizenship in his dealings with whites did not extend to black politics. In his second autobiography, *Dusk of Dawn* (1940), DuBois refers with some feeling to the 'Tuskegee Machine' which swung into action whenever Washington's leadership was threatened.

The Souls of Black Folk sent DuBois in the direction of an organizational split with Washington, first in the Niagara Movement of 1905, and then in the NAACP. Washington saw no gain in apportioning blame for racial strife; if anything, he was inclined to focus upon what blacks had to do, rather than what recompense white society should make. The Niagara Movement, mostly made up of radical black intellectuals, protested openly and called for change on key matters like suffrage and education. They lacked support, however, and Washington blocked avenues of contact with whites and the mass of blacks who followed him. The Niagara Movement folded in 1909, but a year later the NAACP, a bi-racial organization was formed. The NAACP proved to be the institutional link with the post-Second World War era because its greatest legal success was the 1954 Supreme Court ruling in *Brown* vs *Topeka Board of Education* that public schools must be desegregated. By then, the NAACP was in the mainstream, but it has to be emphasized that during the first few years of its existence Washington and his organizations were in the ascendancy; hence the significance of Washington declining to join the NAACP because it was a *political* organization, and because DuBois was prominent, not least as editor of *Crisis*. In addition to their litigation work, both the NAACP and *Crisis* gave sustained publicity to the appalling catalogue of lynchings – 3224 men and women between 1889 and the end of the First World War.

When describing the reaction to his 1950–1 indictment and trial, DuBois admitted great disappointment at the level of support from the 'Talented Tenth'. This reference dates back to *The Souls of Black Folk* and his disagreement with Washington's view that blacks needed a vocational and not an academic education. The Talented Tenth was thought necessary to provide leadership in the professions as well as in politics, and to ensure that more possibilities were kept before blacks than suited white society. They would be the people who argued for political and civil rights where economics preoccupied the mass of blacks. In any case, DuBois argues in *Souls*, blacks had a right to higher education.

Different though they were, DuBois and Washington shared an acute awareness of the doubleness of the black experience. In Washington's autobiography this appears, much as it does in Benjamin Franklin's, in the way that he takes on a role. A critical view would be that Franklin and Washington were so successful in their roles that they lost any other sense of themselves. But, presumably, there is a self in *Up from Slavery*, separate from the one who is the hero of the narrative. That self has chosen not to write an autobiography like *Narrative of the Life of Frederick Douglass* (1845), in which the pain and anger of slavery are directly described.

DuBois's awareness of doubleness makes for one of the most important and influential passages in American writing:

> The Negro is a sort of seventh son, born with a veil, and gifted with second-sight in this American world, – a world which yields him no true self-consciousness, but only lets him see himself through the revelation of the other world. It is a peculiar sensation, this double-consciousness, this sense of always looking at one's self through the eyes of others, of measuring one's soul by the tape of a world that looks on in amused contempt and pity. One ever feels his twoness, – an American, a Negro; two souls, two thoughts, two unreconciled strivings; two warring ideals in one dark body, whose dogged strength alone keeps it from being torn asunder.
>
> The history of the American Negro is the history of this strife, – this longing to attain self-conscious manhood, to merge his double self into a better and truer self. In this merging he wishes neither of the older selves to be lost. He would not Africanize America, for America has too much to teach the world and Africa. He would not bleach his Negro soul in a flood of white Americanism, for he knows that Negro blood has a message for the world. He simply wishes to make it possible for a man to be both a Negro and an American, without being cursed and spit upon by his fellows, without having the doors of Opportunity closed roughly in his face. (pp. 45–6)

Two points convey the complexity of DuBois's thought. The image of the veil, lifted out of the lamentable passage on race in Thomas Jefferson's *Notes on the State of Virginia* (1784–5), and used throughout *The Souls of Black Folk*, suggests at once a deficient and an advantageous point of view. Mostly, it is the former, but again there is doubleness: looking out through the veil – a kind of prison – the world is distorted; for the white person, looking at someone wearing a veil, there is an outline, but no features, no character. This is how Richard Wright depicts Bigger Thomas in *Native Son* (1940), but it is Ralph Ellison in *Invisible Man* (1952) who develops DuBois's image most imaginatively. Ellison's hero is just not there for some of the characters in the novel. The privilege, if it can be called that, of wearing a veil is in seeing the world without being fully seen (again Ellison is DuBois's successor), being inside and outside 'this American world'. The cost of insight is a heavy one, though: a divided self or a self that derives only negative images from the world around it.

The other point to take up is the relationship between the black and white world. Thinking, again, of the differences between DuBois and Washington, it is not entirely clear where each stands. Segregation is seemingly accepted by Washington and the white world is the 'tape' measure, to adapt DuBois's metaphor. On the other hand, integration was the ultimate goal – otherwise Washington would not have received such support from blacks. A further complication is that, in practice, Washington encouraged racial solidarity and self-determination, even though he apparently harboured no sense of racial specialness. Case studies of Northern cities introduce black businessmen and community leaders, like S. Laing Williams and George Cleveland Hall in Chicago, who followed Washington's precepts and helped to mould a sense of identity in the ghetto.[5] The issue then devolves upon the status of the colour line between the ghetto and the surrounding city; if it is drawn, and periodically re-drawn, by the larger society then these are, indeed, ghettoes and not communities. Yet even this apparently reliable interpretive measure does not explain the race-pride that developed within the ghettoes of the 1960s or, for that matter, in the 1910s, 1920s and 1930s in the activities of Marcus Garvey and the Afro-Americanism and Pan-Africanism of DuBois himself.

Up until the 1930s DuBois stood more for integration, because it would be accepting an inferior status not to have demanded this right. Related to the stance he took on integration in the 1910s, was his interest in the common cause of labour. This was shaken, however, by the racism of white unionists in riots in East St Louis in 1917, and by the race riots of the 'Red Summer' of 1919 when 70 blacks were lynched. He joined the Socialist Party in 1911, and there is a Marxist slant in a number of his texts from his novel *The Quest of the Silver*

Fleece (1911) onwards. On other occasions, notably during the Depression when he wrote *Black Reconstruction in America* (1935) and *Dusk of Dawn* (1940), DuBois returned to the relations between class and race. In the 1950s, when he was disillusioned even more with middle-class professional blacks than with black or white workers, he began to think in terms of social and political change coming primarily through a black working class, with leadership being provided, in Leninist fashion, by a black intelligentsia. At this late stage in his thinking, he appeared to distinguish the intelligentsia from the Talented Tenth, which he described as functioning merely as a black economic elite.

DuBois's position on integration changed a number of times. In the late 1920s but, especially, during the Depression, he favoured economic and cultural separation, led by the Talented Tenth, who would organize co-operatives and promote black culture. This was not segregation, he explained, because segregation was separation on the whites's terms. It was also a logical extension of certain passages in *Souls of Black Folk*. The cultural dimension of separatism was shared by the actor and singer, Paul Robeson, when defending his preference for negro spirituals over opera. In doing so, Robeson made a somewhat suspect appeal to blacks as the emotional rather than intellectual side of humanity. The new element in DuBois's thinking, however, was his interest in the black economy. It provoked a final censure by the already exasperated board of the NAACP, and DuBois resigned from the NAACP in 1934, though later rejoined, but only temporarily.

Here we can introduce the militant black nationalism of the West Indian and ex-slave, Marcus Garvey, who came to the United States in 1916, the year after Washington died. His organization, the Universal Negro Improvement Association (UNIA), founded in 1914, made direct appeals to blacks living in urban ghettoes. By Garvey's estimate over 2000 joined UNIA in Harlem alone. In the 1920s, when DuBois's ideas for a black nation within the United States (Afro-Americanism) and his cultural rather than economic (or practical) interest in Pan-Africanism were largely ignored, Garvey had a mass appeal. His appeal was quite different from Booker T. Washington's, even though he followed Washington's example and organized support for black businesses in the city. Garvey's 'Back to Africa' movement linked in with his plans for a black economy when, through UNIA, he established the Black Star Steamship Line. Garvey's 'bottom up' appeal, together with the extremity of his separatism, which actually led him to find common ground with the Ku Klux Klan in 1922, worried the intellectual DuBois. In an article in his magazine, *The Crisis*, DuBois described Garvey as 'without doubt, the most dangerous enemy of the Negro race in America and the world'.[6] As we shall see, the appeal to nationhood, often over the heads of official black leaders (the Talented Tenth were a 'caste aristocracy' according to Garvey), was revived in the late 1960s with black power. The absurdity of Garvey's platform, however, was that his nation was to be in Africa. DuBois was interested in African ancestry and in broadening an international power base, not in resettlement. As he pointed out, also in *The Crisis*, 'Africa belongs to the Africans . . . Liberia is not going to allow American Negroes to assume control and direct her government.'[7] Actually, had DuBois been aware of the larger economic and political context, of which Garveyism was just an element, he would have reached his insights into American capitalism thirty years before his trial in the McCarthy era. The US government, through Secretary of Commerce, Herbert Hoover, was determined that Garvey and his half-a-million followers would never settle in Liberia. This would have blocked the Firestone Company's plans to create a vast rubber plantation to feed its factories if and when the British Government, in an effort to assert its waning economic muscle, cut off supplies from Malaya and elsewhere in the Empire.

In 1927 Garvey was indicted for fraudulent use of the mail service and deported, but he had demonstrated a political and cultural alternative to DuBois and Washington which was revived in the black nationalism of the 1960s.

Before jumping (but not ignoring) the gap between the early black movement and the Civil Rights years, we should discuss the more explicitly cultural mediation of some of the ideas which circulated round DuBois and Garvey. Since Countee Cullen, Langston Hughes, Zora Neale Hurston, James Weldon Johnson, Claude McKay, and Jean Toomer are the major names of the Harlem Renaissance this is, more properly, the subject of literary history. However, it is also an important aspect of the broader cultural renaissance which Van Wyck Brooks called 'America's Coming of Age'. As we have seen, though, Brooks's own work failed even to accommodate black culture, and much of the interest in it by white Greenwich Village intellectuals was a reversed ethnocentrism. In the Harlem Renaissance, however, there was a black counterpart to *America's Coming of Age*. This was *The New Negro* (1925), an anthology edited by Howard University philosophy professor, Alain Locke. The contributors to *The New Negro*, from Albert C. Barnes on art, through J.A. Rogers on jazz, to Kelly Miller on the importance of Howard University, make a determined effort to deal with the culture of submissiveness. Outside of the anthology, in the writings of Cullen, Hughes, and Toomer, the sculpture of Richmond Barthe and the painting of Aaron Douglas, the stereotypes of Uncle Tom and Sambo were further challenged. Techniques and strategies from Afro-American folk art gave the Renaissance a dimension missing in contemporary American modernism, whether based in Greenwich Village or Paris.[8]

However, the difficulties in breaking away from stereotypes while seeking to create an identity – this being the unifying theme of *The New Negro* – produced a kind of naivety, which took the form of an emulation of white aesthetic standards. That is to say, the participants in the Renaissance were often themselves caught up in Brooks's potentially sterile highbrow/lowbrow antithesis. It is revealing that, apart from Langston Hughes, few of the Harlem intellectuals looked to the jazz of Louis Armstrong and Jelly Roll Morton. Literature was the main model for cultural achievement and, as James Weldon Johnson in *Black Manhattan* (1930) and Alain Locke believed, with high culture came the transcendence of race. Though it is a varied anthology, with more than just literary contributions, *The New Negro*, presents breaking away from stereotypes as a necessary prelude to integration in the larger culture. To this extent, it does not anticipate the black consciousness movement of the 1960s, and suggests that black intellectuals were too buoyed up by the possibilities of urban life in the Jazz Age to inspect the economics of black culture closely enough. After all, the precondition for what came to be known as the Harlem Renaissance of the mid-1920s was the great migration of Southern blacks to the north and west between 1890 and the First World War. But the early twentieth-century hopes for Harlem as a prosperous black 'city' were dashed by the sheer numbers of people coming in and the operation of ghetto economics. As Langston Hughes put it, 'Life for me ain't been no golden stair'.[9] Yet in Alain Locke's themes of newness and identity we catch the echoes of Crèvecoeur's famous question in *Letters from an American Farmer* (1783): 'What is the American, this new man?' Clearly, it was difficult for this generation of black intellectuals to think other than through the dominant ideology. There is even, in E. Franklin Frazier's 'Durham: Capital of the Black Middle Class', a version of the self-made man myth. This is a position that Frazier, as a leading black sociologist, later revised, becoming more aware that a history of oppression cannot be shrugged off.[10] When, in their contributions to *The New Negro*, Arthur Huff Fauset and Locke, himself, rediscover a folk heritage we can see both the valuable effort to establish identity and the lack of sustained interest in the oppression which informed folk expression. Jean Toomer's novel, *Cane* (1923), is probably the exception in that, for all its lyricism, it eschews romantic primitivism and faces the history of slavery. Against Alain Locke's optimism that the sudden interest in Harlem pointed to a re-evaluation of blacks, W.E.B. DuBois was more sceptical in concluding *The New Negro*: 'And thus again in 1924 as in 1899 I seem to see the problem of the 20th century as the Problem of the Color Line.'[11] Looking back, in *The Big Sea* (1940), Hughes also remarks on the underlying issue:

I was there. I had a swell time while it lasted. But I thought it wouldn't last long . . . For how could a large and enthusiastic number of people be crazy about Negroes forever? They thought the race problem had been solved through Art plus Gladys Bentley.[12]

I have a dream: Martin Luther King and the Civil Rights Movement

When Martin Luther King Jr emerged from the Dexter Avenue Baptist Church as a leader of the Montgomery, Alabama, bus boycott in 1955, the truth of DuBois's statement on 'the colour line' was about to be more widely recognized. That it had not been, in spite of all that had gone before, is a key factor in understanding and interpreting King's ideas.

The Civil Rights Act of 1957, and the establishment of a Commission which would identify and report on discrimination, seemed to pick up a legislative trail left hanging at the end of the First Reconstruction. The influence of the South over race relations in America remained powerful, however. During the Second World War, for instance, blacks had fought in segregated units and only in 1948 was executive action taken by President Truman to end this practice. The contradiction between fighting the Nazis and continuing to practise racism at home was glaring.

The beginning of the so-called Second Reconstruction was signalled when Chief Justice Earl Warren ruled in *Brown* vs *Board of Education*, 17th May, 1954, that 'in the field of public education the doctrine of "separate but equal" has no place.'[13] In spite of the reversal of the *Plessy* vs *Ferguson* decision of 1896, around 2.4 million black Southern children were still being educated under Jim Crow laws in the mid-to late-1950s. 'All the people of the South are in favor of segregation', declared Senator James Eastland of Mississippi, 'and Supreme Court or no Supreme Court, we are going to maintain segregated schools down in Dixie'.[14] The Southern white backlash reached a pitch in the desegregation process in 1956 when the state's national guard, acting on the orders of Governor Orval E. Faubus, refused nine black students entry to Little Rock Central High School, Arkansas.

This was the context in which Martin Luther King formulated his philosophy of non-violent protest, supported by Bayard Rustin and the

Reverend Ralph David Abernathy. King's ideas were articulated initially as part of the down-to-earth advice given to blacks on how to behave after NAACP lawyers had won a court decision in November 1956 ordering the desegregation of buses in Montgomery:

> Pray for guidance and commit yourself to complete non-violence as you enter the bus.
> Be quiet but friendly; proud but not arrogant; joyous, but not boisterous.
> If cursed, do not curse back. If pushed, do not push back. If struck, do not strike back, but evidence love and goodwill at all times.[15]

After the 382-day bus boycott, King sought to institutionalize this philosophy in the Southern Christian Leadership Conference (SCLC), founded in 1957 with the aim of co-ordinating protest in the South. The important statement which follows is from the pamphlet, *This is SCLC*:

> Christian nonviolence actively resists evil in any form. It never seeks to humiliate the opponent, only to win him. Suffering is accepted without retaliation. Internal violence of the spirit is as much to be rejected as external physical violence. At the center of nonviolence is redemptive love. Creatively used, the philosophy of nonviolence can restore the broken community in America
> . . . SCLC believes that the American dilemma in race relations can best and most quickly be resolved through the actions of thousands of people, committed to the philosophy of nonviolence, who will physically identify themselves in a just and moral struggle . . . The ultimate aim of SCLC is to foster and create the 'beloved community' in America where brotherhood is a reality. It rejects any doctrine of black supremacy for this merely substitutes one kind of tyranny for another . . . Our ultimate goal is genuine intergroup and interpersonal living – *integration*.[16]

King did not advocate separatism, as had, at various times, Washington, Garvey and DuBois, and as would the black power leaders. Looking ahead to other writings, most explicitly *Chaos or Community* (1967), it is clear that while 'community' can mean the local, black community, 'the beloved community' is a universal concept. The redemptive power of love was aimed, therefore, at a racist society as a whole. This did not mean that King lacked specificity in his focus upon blacks. It is important to stress that though he was middle class, he emerged in relation to a local issue; later, as the movement expanded and King became a national leader, he did, inevitably, lose touch with the grassroots and was accused of being a media symbol.

In *This is SCLC*, King identified the vote as the practical aim of the organization: 'SCLC believes that the most important step the Negro can take is that short walk to the voting booth' (quoted in Meier *et al.*, (eds), *Black Protest Thought*, p. 304). Significantly, one of the later protests – against gerrymandering of black voters – was in Tuskegee, the fulcrum of Booker T. Washington's efforts to raise blacks' status through economic and not political action. Over seventy years after Washington took over at Tuskegee, blacks were still without the vote in most of the South, in spite of forty years of NAACP legal pressure. In this connection, it must also be emphasized that while King is in the same tradition as Washington, in that he was seeking to promote a positive self-image for blacks, he accepted none of Washington's humbleness. In his account of the Montgomery bus boycott, King writes about the importance of self-respect, illustrating it with the example of Rosa Parks, whose refusal to move from a 'Whites Only' section of a bus, and subsequent arrest, precipitated the protest.

Non-violence was not passive as King described it. Following Gandhi, but also Thoreau in 'Essay on Civil Disobedience', King regarded non-violence as interventionist: protesters went to where unjust laws were being practised and did so often after meticulous planning. Once in the front line, they openly disobeyed the law and accepted the penalty as part of the protest. This is an appropriate point to resume the narrative of events, but the aim is less to tell the story than to describe King's developing position (and then the positions of those who reacted against his philosophy of non-violence), but also to say more on the general theme of the culture of politics in a mass society.

SCLC was only one of a number of organizations which came together under the umbrella of Civil Rights. The Congress of Racial Equality (CORE) had been formed in 1942 and had used non-violent methods of protest, in accord with its Quaker origins and interest in Gandhi's methods. It had a white, liberal, orientation to it throughout the 1940s and 1950s but, revived after the sit-ins and boycotts of the late 1950s and early 1960s, it attracted more black members. CORE is best known for the Freedom Rides which it organized in the cause of voter registration in the South and in the face of violent retaliation, including from the Ku Klux Klan when one of the buses arrived in Birmingham, Alabama.

CORE had been galvanized into new action by the sit-in movement. This began in Greensboro, North Carolina on 1 February, 1960, when four black students sat in a 'Whites Only' section of a lunchcounter and provoked this kind of response from a white youth:

> Well, it's just not the thing we're used to down here. They come in, and they sit down, and we're not used to them sitting down besides us. Because I wasn't raised with them; I never have lived with them; and I'm not going to start now. (*Eyes on the Prize: 3. Ain't Scared of Your Jails, 1960–1961*)

Soon after Greensboro, in April 1960, and in the midst of thousands of arrests, the Student Nonviolent Coordinating Committee (SNCC) was formed, with Martin Luther King on its adult advisory commitee. SNCC combined with SCLC and NAACP as part of the Albany campaign to register voters and train young blacks, including those from urban ghettos in the South, in non-violent tactics. The accelerated pace of protest and its spread into Northern cities, and into the related issue of poverty, produced diversity within the Civil Rights Movement. Inside a year of formation, SNCC moved away from King, considering him insufficiently radical. NAACP, the leading black organization, was also identified with an older generation, the black middle class, and gradualism and legalism.

1960 was more famous for the presidential election in which John Kennedy defeated Richard Nixon. Black votes had been extremely important in the result and these had, in large part, been secured by Kennedy's strategic action in helping to get Martin Luther King released from a four-month hard-labour sentence in a Georgia prison, after an alleged driving offence. For all Kennedy's rhetoric of a New Frontier and its inspirational effect upon liberals ready for an assault on poverty and discrimination, Kennedy's own pre-election record on Civil Rights had not been impressive. Once elected, his support remained variable, but grew stronger near the end of his short term of office as a result of the activities and the ideas of King and the Civil Rights Movement.

King constantly had his eyes on Washington, keeping Kennedy informed about the violence in Alabama in the immediate wake of the May, 1961, Freedom Rides. Without federal armed support there would have been, at best, local successes, since, too often, victories in the courts meant little in practice. At worst, there would have been even more violence. This pattern of local non-violent action and federal armed support or federal-induced support at state level, confirms the orientation of Civil Rights under King's leadership. It had to be political, national and integrationist in its philosophy and strategies.

The inextricable relation between text and context is apparent if we look at two statements by King from 1963, his 'Letter from

Birmingham Jail' and 'I have a dream' speech delivered in Washington DC. Birmingham was chosen as the target of large-scale desegregationist direct action because it was the most strictly segregated Southern city, policed by Sheriff Eugene 'Bull' Connor and under the state governorship of George Wallace. During the sit-ins, rallies, and marches there was continued use of dogs, hoses, cattle prods, and clubs. Two and a half thousand people were arrested, King among them. From Birmingham Jail, he replied to eight white 'Fellow Clergymen' who had deplored the protest.

In his 'Letter', dated 16 April, King lays out the procedures for a non-violent campaign. Investigations completed, and negotiations stalled, 'we decided to undertake a process of self-purification. We began a series of workshops on nonviolence, and we repeatedly asked ourselves: "Are you able to accept blows without retaliating?" "Are you able to endure the ordeal of jail?"'. 'Direct action', King then explains to the white clergymen, has as its purpose forcing a community to face issues and negotiate. It is therapeutic: 'injustice must be exposed, with all the tension its exposure creates, to the light of human conscience and the air of national opinion before it can be cured.'[17]

In 1956, at the beginning of his public career, King had rebuked a white moderate, the novelist, William Faulkner, for urging even the NAACP to 'stop now for a moment'. To the ministers' question, 'Why didn't you give the new city administration time to act?', King replies as follows:

> We know through painful experience that freedom is never voluntarily given by the oppressor; it must be demanded by the oppressed. Frankly, I have yet to engage in a direct-action campaign that was 'well timed' in the view of those who have not suffered unduly from the disease of segregation. For years now I have heard the word 'Wait!' It rings in the ear of every Negro with piercing familiarity. This 'Wait' has almost always meant 'Never' . . .
>
> We have waited for more than 340 years for our constitutional and God-given rights. The nations of Asia and Africa are moving with jetlike speed toward gaining political independence, but we still creep at horse-and-buggy pace toward gaining a cup of coffee at a lunch counter. (*Why We Can't Wait*, pp. 80–1)

He reprimands the white moderate for caring more for order than justice and for setting 'the timetable for another man's freedom' (p. 84). King was writing from prison, and perhaps was reminded even more directly of the black nationalists, many of whom gained their political experience in Soledad, Folsom and other American prisons, and whose claims were, in 1963, being heard. Consequently, King made his appeal very much to the white moderate clergy with reference to the 'hatred and despair of the black nationalist' and the 'frightening racial nightmare' (p. 87) which threatened unless non-violence prevailed.

King adds a historical viewpoint and a sense of urgency to DuBois's theme of black identity in 'a world which yields [the Negro] no true self-consciousness' (*The Souls of Black Folk*, p. 45). For King, blacks are afflicted with 'nobodiness' and this will not be remedied without intervention. His therapeutic metaphors continue: there is nothing 'in the very flow of time that will inevitably cure all ills. Actually, time itself is neutral; it can be used either destructively or constructively' (p. 86).

Civil Rights was a mass movement by 1963. Manning Marable estimates that 'between autumn 1961 and the spring of 1963, 20,000 men, women and children had been arrested. In 1963 alone another 15,000 were imprisoned; 1000 desegregation protests occurred across the region, in more than 100 cities' (*Race, Reform and Rebellion*, pp. 75–6). We ought to pause to register these figures in the light of the political theory of those who felt America to be at the end of ideology and, hopefully, at the end of mass political movements. It had been Daniel Bell's claim that moralism in politics had been a cause of evil, and that religious fervour ought not to be pursued down the avenue of politics. Very few years afterwards, King openly reinstated moral and religious claims in politics, and did so with a moderate audience in mind.

On 28 August, 1963, a quarter of a million people, roughly one fifth of whom were white, heard King and others speak in front of the Lincoln Memorial. The event had been organized by Bayard Rustin, and by A. Philip Randolph, who had led the March on Washington Movement of 1941. However, whereas the proposal for the earlier march had been trade-union instigated, would have involved only blacks, and was focused on defence industries in the face of growing support for war, the later march took account of new circumstances. It was designed with the media in mind, had received Kennedy's backing once the radical, civil disobedience aims had been ruled out by SCLC and NAACP, and echoed the rhetoric of the American Dream. The SNCC leader, John Lewis, had intended to maintain the grass-roots momentum of his organization and while he included strong criticism of American institutions, his speech had been toned down at the insistence of moderate blacks on the platform.

King's 'I have a dream' speech at the end of the public side of the occasion was an extraordinary performance which accepted the context and therefore the rhetorical, dramatizing function of the occasion. As in his other speeches and open letters, words and phrases are repeated, with very familiar Biblical references and cadences, and there are a series of conceits in which the old-time religion is linked to new circumstances or secular concerns. For instance, the first conceit develops the metaphor of an economic bargain upon which America has reneged. But, King asserts with a skilful slipping between economy and society, the United States does not have a static economy with finite limits:

> America has given the Negro people a bad check; a check which
> has come back marked 'insufficient funds.' But we refuse to
> believe that the bank of justice is bankrupt. We refuse to believe
> that there are insufficient funds in the great vaults of opportunity
> of this nation. So we have come to cash this check – a check that
> will give us upon demand the riches of freedom and the security
> of justice.

With the Civil Rights legislation pending, King insists that 'Now' is the time when the check must be honoured, rather than have the nation return to 'business as usual' (Meier, *et al.*, (eds), *Black Protest Thought*, p. 348).

A comparison, such as Manning Marable suggests, with Booker T. Washington's Atlanta Address is in order because both speakers had two audiences in mind. Having established the obligations of white America, King turns to blacks to reiterate his message of redemptive suffering, self-respect, and non-violence:

> The marvelous new militancy which has engulfed the Negro
> community must not lead us to a distrust of all white people, for
> many of our white brothers, as evidenced by their presence here
> today, have come to realize that their destiny is tied up with our
> destiny and their freedom is inextricably bound to our freedom.
> We cannot walk alone. (*Black Protest Thought*, pp. 348–9)

The last third of the speech links American political culture, the geography of the slave past and the Civil Rights present, and the Christian tradition of endurance and hope. The overall pattern of bringing the particular and the general together is introduced in the famous lines which open this section of the speech:

> I say to you today, my friends, that in spite of the difficulties and
> frustrations of the moment I still have a dream. It is a dream
> deeply rooted in the American dream (p. 349).

By way of three (of many) less hopeful footnotes to the Washington speech, we can note, first, Marable's observation on Kennedy's Civil Rights Bill that 'not a single vote changed in Congress after the march' (*Race, Reform and Rebellion*, p. 82). Senate filibustering also delayed even the legislation to desegregate public accommodation which Kennedy had promised in his election campaign three years earlier. Second, the violence against blacks continued with the deaths of four black girls in Birmingham, when the 16th Street Baptist Church was fire-bombed in September, 1963 (the FBI were allegedly involved); and, the following summer in Mississippi, the fire-bombing by white vigilantes of over twenty black churches and the murder of three Civil Rights workers by a mob that included police. That year the race riots began in Northern cities in the states of New York and New Jersey, and continued through 1968, with thirty-four deaths in Watts in Los Angeles in 1965, ten in Washington DC and thirty-eight in Detroit in 1967 and 1968. Total deaths during the riots were more than two hundred.

The third footnote was more like an afternote, and takes us back to the ideology of black protest. The Washington march took place the day after W.E.B. DuBois died in Ghana, having given up his American citizenship, and also, seemingly, upon his ideal of not opting completely for integration or separatism, but, rather, keeping both options open to avoid the poles of accommodation and the self-destructiveness of some versions of black power. DuBois, we recall, was in at the start of NAACP integrationism while advocating, at different times, Pan-Africanism and cultural nationalism. These possibilities became polarized in the 1960s. Arguably, for blacks, these three footnotes were more significant than the loss of their new champion when Kennedy was assassinated on 22 November 1963.

By any means necessary: Malcolm X and black nationalism

In 1966, four years after he had at last registered as a student at the all-white University of Mississippi, James Meredith was wounded by a white marksman while on his lone 'March Against Fear' through Mississippi. Martin Luther King, representing SLCC but intent upon keeping together a Civil Rights Movement that was becoming more fragmented, joined Stokely Carmichael of SNCC and Floyd McKissick of CORE and completed the march. During the march, Carmichael, who had taken up the expression, 'Black Power', a year earlier, and McKissick began to advocate a more militant approach. In spite of King's continuing authority and his attacks on black nationalism for, as he saw it, its 'hatred and despair', one of the central themes of earlier black protest, dating back to Garvey but also, in different ways, to Washington and DuBois, had re-emerged to challenge the Civil Rights Movement.

In the early 1960s, even before the breakaways from the Civil Rights Movement and the espousal of forms of separatism by CORE and SNCC, Malcolm X was preaching a very different message from King. 'If someone puts a hand on you, send him to the cemetery.' And: 'It won't be blood that's going to flow only on one side.'[18] On the question of violence, there was a wide gap between the Civil Rights movement and those who agreed with Malcolm X's 'by any means necessary' position. 'You cannot integrate a school or get a job with a machine gun', Bayard Rustin objected, and spoke for such as Roy Wilkins of NAACP and Whitney Young of the Urban League.[19] When Robert Williams of the NAACP stated, from within the broadly Civil Rights side of black protest, that blacks should at the very least defend themselves, he was expelled. Huey Newton recalls that he and Bobby Seale were influenced by Williams's *Negroes with Guns* when forming the Black Panthers, itself an organization that looked to the example of Malcolm X. In *Revolutionary Suicide* (1973), Newton states their rationale for forming armed community patrols to keep watch on the police in Oakland:

> As we saw it, Blacks were getting ripped off everywhere. The police had given us no choice but to defend ourselves against their brutality . . . Our program was designed to lead the brothers into self-defense before we were completely wiped out physically and mentally.[20]

Newton reports that Martin Luther King was rejected by the people in Watts, while his murder in 1968 was followed by a wave of violence. 'Nonviolence is a dead philosophy and it was not black people that killed it', Floyd McKissick announced (quoted in John White, *Black Leadership*, p. 143). Carmichael joined the Black Panthers, for a while at least.

It is difficult to evaluate Malcolm X, the figure who has come to represent the various black nationalist movements that took such a different route from Martin Luther King and Civil Rights. As is apparent from *The Autobiography of Malcolm X* (1965), his positions changed and were still doing so when he was murdered in 1965. It is difficult to know quite how to read his autobiography, because it is so American in many ways. However, it tells of his move from a life as a street hustler who had no pride in being black, to a time of growing self-respect and an awareness of black culture and history. There is also a commitment to self-determination through black institutions within America. Taken out of prison and into the black ghettoes of Northern cities, this was the first significant reappearance of black separatism with wide appeal since Marcus Garvey was deported in 1927. One link between Malcolm X and Garvey had been the Reverend Earl Little, Malcolm X's father and a Garveyite minister.

While in prison Malcolm X broke away from his dissolute life and joined the Black Muslim faith. After the Second World War, once under the leadership of Elijah Muhammad, the Nation of Islam had recruited heavily among young lower-class, urban blacks. Many were unemployed; others among the estimated 100,000 members, were petty criminals and drug-addicts. They were transformed into disciplined converts to black capitalism, but in the service of a black nation within the United States to which they contributed a proportion of their incomes. The Black Muslims systematically reversed blacks' traditional points of view. The world of *blacks* (not Negroes) should be celebrated and white mythologies should be attacked.

Later, Malcolm X defended the Black Muslims against Civil Rights leaders who interpreted their doctrine as one of hate, probably financed by Arab groups abroad, and a threat to the progress towards integration which was slowly being made by non-violent direct action. According to Malcolm, though: 'We who are Muslims, followers of the honorable Elijah Muhammad, don't think that an integrated cup of coffee is sufficient payment for 310 years of slave labor' (quoted in Marable, *Race, Reform and Rebellion*, p. 62). Something of this dissatisfaction was, in any case, being expressed wthin the Civil Rights Movement after the apparent high point of the Washington march. This was particularly so within CORE and SNCC as the focus expanded to include economic deprivation, rather than strictly segregationist and therefore predominantly Southern issues.

In spite of the periods spent in prison after demonstrations, Carmichael, McKissick, King and other Civil Rights leaders, were not part of the same world described in *The Autobiography of Malcolm X*, Eldridge Cleaver's *Soul on Ice*, George Jackson's *Soledad Brother*, Newton's *Revolutionary Suicide*, and Seale's *Seize the Time*. They made up an extraordinary 'college' of urban blacks, later black radicals of one kind or another, who kept meeting up 'on the streets' (Newton's repeated phrase) and in prison. In Cleaver's *Soul on Ice*, the section 'Letters from Prison' marks the difference between the Civil Rights and black nationalist leaders:

Nineteen fifty-four, when I was eighteen years old, is held to be
a crucial turning point in the history of the Afro-American – for
the U.S.A. as a whole – the year segregation was outlawed by
the U.S. Supreme Court. It was also a crucial year for me
because on June 18, 1954, I began serving a sentence in state
prison for possession of marijuana.[21]

The significance of Cleaver's very different route to political awareness
is confirmed by Huey Newton, who remarks in *Revolutionary Suicide*
that 'Jail is an odd place to find freedom, but that was the place I first
found mine: in the Alameda County Jail in Oakland in 1964' (p. 99).

Malcolm X's *Autobiography* gave a pattern, and even a rudimentary
philosophy, to the ostensibly individual experiences of Cleaver,
Newton and the others who played prominent parts in the black
nationalist movements of the mid-1960s onwards. Their philosophy
was rudimentary in the sense that it lacked a tradition. Ideas have a
different status when they are articulated out of the context of the
institutional repression experienced by Malcolm X and his contemporaries. When following the careers of the New York Intellectuals in
earlier chapters, there was a sense of them learning on the run, as it
were, certainly compared with the European intellectuals who came to
the United States. But the New Yorkers' careers were stability itself
when compared with the repeated accounts in the prison writings of
what was read by way of a political education. These accounts have the
awkwardness of the autodidact (Malcolm X read the dictionary), and
the reading itself was a startling amalgam of political philosophy: some
Plato, Rousseau, Paine, Marx, Bakunin, Fanon, existentialist writings,
Mao, Che. Despite the seriousness of the engagement with texts –
Marx 'kept me with a headache' (Cleaver, *Soul on Ice*, p. 12), it is not
at all surprising that Huey Newton, to give just one example, should
have repeatedly set the Panthers against 'intellectualizing'.

Having converted to the Black Muslim faith and left prison,
Malcolm X became an organizer and then a minister for the Nation of
Islam. As the minister of the Temple Number Seven in Harlem, he
became more well known than Elijah Muhammad within the sect. He
lectured nationwide and appeared on television and as a preacher came
to rival Martin Luther King. His increasing emphasis upon politics –
that is upon race *relations* – and fears of competition on the part of
Elijah Muhammad, led to him leaving the Nation of Islam in 1964 to
form Muslim Mosque Inc., and then the Organization of Afro-
American Unity (OAAU). By the time of his murder in 1965, by
Black Muslims who believed he had betrayed them, he had come into
his own as a radical spokesperson of urban blacks who recognized his
language in a way that the sources of King's language could be
recognized.

Albeit over a short period, Malcolm X gave a lead to an analysis, continued by other black nationalists, into the connections between racism and capitalism that the achievements of the Civil Rights Movement had only served to reveal. In *Black Power* (1967) a text which marks the coming together of black nationalism of the Malcolm X kind and elements of the more radical wing of Civil Rights, Stokely Carmichael and Charles Hamilton distinguish between two forms of racism. 'Overt' or 'individual' acts of racism maim, kill and destroy property and can be observed and sometimes recorded on television. 'Covert' or 'institutional' racism is 'less identifiable in terms of *specific* individuals committing the acts. But it is no less destructive of human life. [It] . . . originates in the operation of established and respected forces in the society, and thus receives far less public condemnation than the first type.' They add that:

> 'Respectable' individuals can absolve themselves from individual blame: *they* would never plant a bomb in a church; *they* would never stone a black family. But they continue to support political officials and institutions that would and do perpetuate institutionally racist policies.[22]

The interpretation which began to form, even as King's Washington speech was being acclaimed, was that federal reform did not escape institutional racism. It was prompted by a combination of fear of international disapproval and a recognition that it was not in the interest of capitalism to have this much disturbance. The economic argument had, of course, been a powerful one at the time of the Civil War whatever the moral rhetoric of the North. However, desegregation did not address the issue of racism as defined by Carmichael and Hamilton and as manifested in income and unemployment figures. Black unemployment was twice that for whites in the mid-1960s, while the black median income was half that for whites. Arguing against Black Power in 1966, Bayard Rustin makes no effort to disguise the situation:

> *Negroes today are in worse economic shape, live in worse slums, and attend more highly segregated schools than in 1954.* Thus – to recite the appalling, and appallingly familiar, statistical litany once again – more Negroes are unemployed today than in 1954; the gap between the wages of the Negro worker and the white worker is wider; while the unemployment rate among white youths is decreasing, the rate among Negro youths has increased to *32 per cent* (and among Negro girls the rise is even more startling).[23]

The broadening of the black critique of white America was given impetus by the Vietnam War which, at the time of Malcolm X's death in 1965, was an open war with 25,000 American tropps committed. In a forum in January, 1965, Malcolm predicted defeat, adding that 'we're not supposed to say that. If we say that, we're anti-American, or we're seditious, or we're subversive, or we're advocating something that's not intelligent' (*Malcolm X Speaks*, p. 219). Vietnam highlighted the dilemma of the Civil Rights Movement. The NAACP and National Urban League did not want Civil Rights to be linked with a growing protest against Vietnam because to do so would damage their all-important relationship with Lyndon Johnson's administration. In response, SNCC pointed out that the United States had destroyed its claims to be the home of freedom by repeating its opposition to black liberation overseas in Vietnam.

The most important voice against the war was Martin Luther King's in 1966, though he had to withstand criticism within SCLC before he persuaded it, too, to oppose the war. Vietnam and Civil Rights were connected, King concluded. The administration took decisions over intervention in Vietnam where it had been reluctant to act over Civil Rights. Non-violence, even non-violent direct action, eventually won the approval of white society, especially when blacks had Malcolm X as an alternative model. But when King argued for non-violence in American policy towards Vietnam and, in 1967 in New York City, led a protest against the Vietnam war, he was not only openly criticized by Rustin, the NAACP and the Urban League, but incurred the less public attentions of J. Edgar Hoover and the FBI. The surveillance and dirty tricks increased as King made preparations for another march on Washington, in some ways more akin to A. Philip Randolph's proposed march of 1941 than King's own march in 1963. King said of his Poor People's March:

> We'll focus on domestic problems, but it's inevitable that we've got to bring out the question of the tragic mix-up in priorities. We are spending all of this money for death and destruction, and not nearly enough money for life and constructive development. We've seen no changes in Watts . . . (Meier, *et al.*, eds., *Black Protest Thought*)

And in another context, he maintained that 'the black revolution is much more than a struggle for the rights of Negroes. It is forcing America to face all its interrelated flaws – racism, poverty, militarism, and materialism. It is exposing evils that are deeply rooted in the whole structure of our society' (quoted in White, *Black Leadership*, p. 142). For all their differences, the analyses that King and Malcolm X

articulated near the ends of their lives had in common an awareness of
the inter-relatedness of things, including, in Malcolm X's case, the
anti-colonial struggles occurring elsewhere in the world.

Exactly one paragraph long: black culture

When Malcom X encountered American history at Mason Junior High
School, the 'section on Negro history . . . was exactly one paragraph
long' (*Autobiography*, p. 110). Black culture in general was a difficult
and contentious issue. It had been suppressed by Booker T.
Washington, who had seen it as a handicap when he saw it at all. The
migration to northern cities had been an escape from black culture and
the slave past, and an embracing of modernity. In his social history of
Harlem between 1890 and 1930, Gilbert Osofsky includes illustrations
(some of them from *The Crisis* magazine) advertising hair-straighten-
ing (the 'Walker System', for example) and skin-bleaching (Walker's
'Tan-Off').[24] In black culture there were no models of success: where
the Protestant ethic emphasized work and discipline, blacks were
depicted as lazy at worst and happy and contented at best. Success
might come as an entertainer, but at some cost to self-image.
Washington's rival, W.E.B. DuBois was more open to black culture
but vacillated, while the foregrounding of culture during the Harlem
Renaissance was over-optimistic, given the economics of both ghetto
life and support for black writers and artists in the 1920s. Then, in the
1960s, the Civil Rights Movement concluded that progress was
achievable only through the dominant culture, that is, through the
awakening of white consciences or by obliging the federal government
to intervene to ensure citizens' Constitutional rights.

Questions of black culture and identity were only seriously discussed
when black nationalism re-emerged, some thirty years after Garvey
and DuBois. In line with Malcolm X (after his break with the Black
Muslims and the formation of OAAU), the cultural nationalist, Ron
Karenga, argued for the priority of cultural revolution over any other
kind of revolution. To this end, his organization, US, was involved in
the Black Arts Movement, in the promotion of Swahili, in Black
Studies which established links with the Afro- as well as the American
past, and in the more visible badges of cultural nationalism: Afro-
hairstyles, African clothes, black English, and the more ambiguous
because commercially influenced ethos of Soul. 'What is needed',
Karenga insists in less ambiguous vocabulary in his 1968 essay, 'Black

Cultural Nationalism', 'is an aesthetic, a black aesthetic'.[25] It would be based on criteria appropriate to blacks – this a reference to the Harlem Renaissance, perhaps, when white intellectuals set the standards for some black writers. Karenga pursues his theme:

> [The] social criteria for judging art . . . is the most important criteria. For all art must reflect and support the Black Revolution, and any art that does not discuss and contribute to the revolution is invalid, no matter how many lines and spaces are produced in proportion and symmetry and no matter how many sounds are boxed in or blown out and called music. (Gayle (ed.), *The Black Aesthetic*, p. 31)

We can find the black aesthetic in the Black Arts Movement, which took in theatre, dance, music and literature in its search for 'a separate symbolism, mythology, critique, and iconology' (Larry Neal, 'The Black Arts Movement' in *The Black Aesthetic*, p. 257). Imamu Amiri Baraka (LeRoi Jones) helped to found the Black Arts Repertory Theater School in Harlem in 1964. Among the School's productions before funding and internal disagreements led to its closure, was Baraka's *Dutchman* (1964); other productions and poetry readings were taken onto the streets, and the example was followed in many other American cities, especially after the urban riots later in the decade. Baraka also politicized black music, seeing in the blues 'the deepest expression of . . . racial memory'. Music was less amenable to white ideology and so survived slavery to come down to contemporary music: 'What is a white person who walks into a James Brown or Sam and Dave song? How would he function? What would be the social metaphor for his existence in that song? What would he be doing?' (*Black Aesthetic*, pp. 115 and 118). It was not surprising that the aggressive emphasis on power and on art as a weapon would be rejected by more established black writers, like James Baldwin and Ralph Ellison. The extent of the disagreement by 1970 reflected the broader divisions in the black protest movement.

In the remainder of this chapter, we can look at two specific aspects of black culture and consciousness: the writing of black history and the engagement with what, for want of a better word, can be called 'theory'. Although these activities are hardly divorced from politics, their more distanced relationship with protest will fill out the idea of black culture.

Black history figured prominently in the new social history which was an offshoot of the protests of the late 1960s and 1970s. John Blassingame's *The Slave Community* (1972) examines slavery from the slave's point of view, while in *Roll Jordan Roll: The World the Slaves*

Made (1974), Eugene Genovese helps to give black resistance a history, arguing that alongside slave rebellions there was sustained covert resistance. He is especially enlightening on the importance of religion, as an activity which slaveholders encouraged among their slaves (an opiate of the masses), but which the slaves were able to use for their own purposes precisely because it was thought to be harmless by their overseers. Lawrence Levine's *Black Culture and Black Consciousness: Afro-American Folk Thought from Slavery to Freedom* (1977) argues along similar lines for the spirituals and folk songs: these, too, were a cultural expression of politics.

The cumulative effect of these and similar studies was not simply to demonstrate African and then Afro-American roots and continuity with those beginnings, but to reconstruct a culture and a history which blacks did not want to forget. This was particularly important in the aftermath of books like Robert Fogel and Stanley Engerman's *Time on the Cross* (1974), which used quantitative methods to argue that slavery was not a coercive system, and, even more controversially, Stanley Elkins' *Slavery: A Problem in American Institutional and Intellectual Life* (1959). Elkins drew parallels between the slave's life and that of the Jewish prisoner in a concentration camp. Whatever Elkins' aims, his book portrayed blacks (and Jews) as broken and incapable of resistance because of the horrific pressures put upon them. In restoring some autonomy to black culture, Blassingame and others intervened politically as academics. In the context of an expansion in higher education such studies, and the teaching that accompanied the publications, had tangible consequences.

Aware that philosophy is probably the subject which is most susceptible to the loss of engagement that comes with professional and institutional status, Cornel West opens his 1982 book, *Prophesy Deliverance!* by describing the *Afro-American Revolutionary Christianity* of his subtitle as 'a demystifying hermeneutic of the Afro-American experience which enhances the cause of human freedom'.[26] As with any very contemporary material, it is difficult to know quite how to read a book like *Prophesy Deliverance!*: as a primary or secondary text? It could be that West's book is a preface to a more substantial work, so may be more fairly judged as symptomatic of a very interesting confluence of Afro-American studies and critical theory, other examples being Bell Hooks's *Ain't I A Woman: Black Women and Feminism* (1981); Robert Stepto's *From Behind the Veil: A Study of Afro-American Narrative* (1979); Houston Baker's *Modernism and the Harlem Renaissance* (1987), part of a forthcoming trilogy; Gloria T. Hull's reinterpretation of the Harlem Renaissance, *Color, Sex, and Poetry* (1987); *Race, Politics, and Culture: Critical Essays on the Radicalism of the 1960s* (1986), edited by Adolph Reed, Jr; and *Black Literature and Literary Theory* (1984) and *'Race,' Writing, and Difference*, a special issue of *Critical Inquiry* (1985), both edited by Henry Louis Gates. What is initially striking about these books is, first, their base in academic disciplines from which they seek political engagement – Cornel West is exemplary here. And, second, the eclectic mix of influences upon their theorizing, in West's case prophetic Christianity, with its *'principle of the self-realization of individuality within community . . .* both this-worldly liberation and otherworldly salvation' (p. 16); the orientation towards culture, society and history of American Pragmatism, notably John Dewey's version; progressive Marxism; and – an interest he shares with some of the other studies just mentioned – contemporary critical theory: Foucault, Derrida, Fredric Jameson, Raymond Williams, the Frankfurt School, and, from earlier in the twentieth century, Antonio Gramsci. The resulting philosophy, West prophesies, will express 'the particular American variation of European modernity that Afro-Americans helped shape in this country and must contend with in the future' (p. 24).

West, himself, moves speculatively in this direction. He takes seriously what Richard Rorty calls 'a post-philosophical culture', in which philosophers accept the anti-foundational lessons of that line of thinkers from Marx, through Nietzsche, Freud, and Saussure, which culminates in Derrida, Foucault and other post-structuralists. As a philosopher in an adversarial relation to philosophy, West finds Rorty's rather vague advice to forget about Truth and do something more interesting, energizing. Under the influence of Foucault's studies of power and knowledge, he recasts black thought from Washington and DuBois onwards in the light of the discursive formations of modernity, notably the categorizing, classifying and rationalizing paradigm described by Max Weber. His aim is to trace 'the way in which the very structure of modern discourse *at its inception* produced forms of rationality, scientificity, and objectivity as well as aesthetic and cultural ideals which require the constitution of the idea of white supremacy' (p. 47).

The response to the discourse of racism, West states, is through cultural rather than political perceptions. This is a defensible argument, but in underscoring the hegemonic power of capitalist rationality, he is so dismissive of nearly all of the figures surveyed in this chapter that it is difficult to know how a counter-cultural discourse can be constructed. 'The post-modern period', he claims, 'has rendered the framework of the DuBois-Washington debate obsolete, but presently there is little theory and praxis to fill the void' (p. 44). DuBois, it seems to me, has to remain central to any attempt to articulate the relationship between integrationist and separatist philosophies and strategies, particularly if we take his career as the exemplary text rather than the texts of any one of the phases of that career. For the full significance of that career to emerge, we must include his period of

marginality between the mid-1930s and his death in 1963. Mid-way
through that period, a developing connection between black protest
and socialism was symbolically severed by DuBois' indictment for
treason during the McCarthy era.

The trial was preceded the year before by DuBois's campaign in
New York for the US Senate. Since he had no chance of winning, the
more interesting information has to do with the absence of press
coverage, and then the sudden hostile coverage and 'a distinct air of
fear and repression', when he stated his anti-Third World War
message, with its thesis that global war has an economic underpinning.
It was DuBois's involvement with the Peace Information Center in
New York City which brought the attention of the Department of
Justice and the request that the organization be registered as an 'agent
of a foreign principal'. The most significant aspect of this episode was
that the anti-communist atmosphere which, three years earlier at a
hearing of the House Un-American Activities Committee (HUAC),
had led to Paul Robeson being described as 'the black Stalin among
Negroes,' reduced black support for DuBois to a minimum. The
NAACP did very little. DuBois also reached this bleak conclusion
about 'the Talented Tenth':

> Negroes of intelligence and prosperity had become American in
> their acceptance of exploitation as defensible, and in their
> imitation of American 'conspicuous expenditure . . . They hated
> 'communism' and 'socialism' as much as any white American.[27]

DuBois was acquitted but, in the aftermath of the trial, many of his
works were banned from libraries. As Manning Marable argues in
Race, Reform and Rebellion, DuBois' trial symbolized the relationship
between the Cold War and black protest of the post-war years, and
allowed reforms of race relations to be thought of as subversive of
American values. In particular, the trial reveals the links between
capitalism and racism which, as we have seen, the subsequent
movement had to understand all over again. The discontinuity in black
protest in effect obliged the Civil Rights movement and black
nationalism, in their different ways, to create their own origins. The
result, initially at least, was a strong tendency in the universalizing
discourse of Martin Luther King towards the elision of difference. In
black nationalism, it was all difference. The experience of protest and,
it would seem, the effects of the Vietnam war in revealing capitalism as
a common element in racial discrimination and imperial power, did,
however, bring Martin Luther King and Malcolm X nearer to each
other and to a theoretical analysis which included race and class, if not
gender.

Notes

1. W.E.B. DuBois, *The Souls of Black Folk* (New York, 1969), p. xi.

2. See Manning Marable, *Race, Reform and Revolution: The Second Reconstruction in Black America, 1945–1982* (1984), chs 1 and 2.

3. Booker T. Washington, *Future of the American Negro* (Boston, 1899), p. 132.

4. Booker T. Washington, *Up from Slavery* (Harmondsworth, 1986), pp. 221–2.

5. See Allan H. Spear, *Black Chicago: The Making of a Negro Ghetto, 1890–1920* (Chicago, 1967).

6. Quoted in Theodore Draper, *The Rediscovery of Black Nationalism* (1971), p. 51.

7. Quoted in John White, *Black Leadership in America, 1895–1968* (1985), p. 61.

8. See Houston A. Baker, Jr, *Modernism and the Harlem Renaissance* (Chicago, 1987).

9. Langston Hughes, *Mother to Son*, quoted in Gilbert Osofsky, *Harlem: The Making of a Ghetto, Negro New York, 1890–1930* (New York, 1971), p. 3.

10. See G. Franklin Edwards, 'E. Franklin Frazier', in *Black Sociologists: Historical and Contemporary Perspectives* (Chicago, 1974), pp. 85–117.

11. Alain Locke (ed.), *The New Negro* (New York, 1975), p. 414.

12. Langston Hughes, *The Big Sea* (New York, 1945), p. 228.

13. Quoted in C. Vann Woodward, *The Strange Career of Jim Crow* (Oxford, 1966), p. 147.

14. Quoted from *Eyes on the Prize: 2. Fighting Back, 1957–1962*.

15. Martin Luther King Jr, *Stride Toward Freedom: The Montgomery Story* (New York, 1958), p. 158.

16. *Black Protest Thought in the Twentieth Century*, edited by August Meier, Elliott Rudwick and Francis L. Broderick (New York, 1971), pp. 303 and 306.

17. Martin Luther King Jr, *Why We Can't Wait* (New York, 1964), pp. 79 and 85.

18. Quoted in Mary Beth Norton, *et al.*, *A People and a Nation: A History of the United States, Volume II: Since 1865* (Boston, 1982), p. 939; *Malcolm X Speaks: Selected Speeches and Statements*, edited by George Breitman (New York, 1965), p. 48.

19. Quoted in Marable (see note 2), p. 83.

20. Huey P. Newton, *Revolutionary Suicide* (New York, 1973), p. 109.

21. Eldridge Cleaver, *Soul on Ice* (1969), p. 3.

22. Stokely Carmichael and Charles V. Hamilton, *Black Power: The Politics of Liberation in America* (1968), p. 4.

23. Bayard Rustin, ' "Black Power" and Coalition Politics', *Commentary*, 42 (1966), p. 37.

24. See illustrations after p. 148 in Osofsky, *Harlem* (see note 9).

25. *The Black Aesthetic*, edited by Addison Gayle Jr (New York, 1971), p. 31.

26. Cornel West, *Prophesy Deliverance!: An Afro-American Revolutionary Christianity* (Philadelphia, 1982), p. 47.

27. W.E.B. DuBois, *The Autobiography of W.E.B. DuBois: A Soliloquy on Viewing My Life from the Last Decade of its First Century* (New York, 1979), pp. 362, 365 and 370–71. The remark about Paul Robeson is quoted in Marable (see note 2), p. 28.

Chapter 8
Feminism

What happened to feminism?

Betty Friedan's *The Feminine Mystique* was published in 1963 and inaugurated the second wave of the women's movement. Three years later two texts were published which highlight the importance of Friedan's book.

In 1966 Barbara Welter's influential essay, 'The Cult of True Womanhood, 1820–1860', appeared in *American Quarterly*. It informed readers that 'In a society where values changed frequently, where fortunes rose and fell with frightening rapidity, where social and economic mobility provided instability as well as hope, one thing at least remained the same – a true woman was a true woman, wherever she was found.'[1] With only minor differences, the cult of true womanhood and the feminine mystique sound the same, in spite of the century between them. In spite, also, of a women's movement that dates back to the Seneca Falls Convention of 1848, and achieved the vote for women in 1920 with the passing of the Nineteenth Amendment to the Constitution.

In the same year as Welter's essay was published, the major theoretical text of the first feminist movement was reprinted after years of neglect. Charlotte Perkins Gilman's *Women and Economics* (1898) is not mentioned by Betty Friedan and this sixty-year gap – between Gilman's and Friedan's eras – is even more deserving of comment than the discontinuity already discussed in black intellectual history.

The sexuo-economic relation: from Charlotte Perkins Gilman to Rosie the Riveter

Charlotte Perkins Gilman's short story, 'The Yellow Wallpaper', was published in 1892, and she carried on writing through to her death in 1935. The fate of her ideas, as set out primarily in *Women and Economics*, will help to explain the hiatus in twentieth-century American feminism.

Women and Economics stands out from its period because Gilman is *not*, interested in the vote but in women's economic dependence upon men: 'the economic relation is combined with the sex-relation'. And later: 'In spite of her supposed segregation to maternal duties, the human female, the world over, works at extra-maternal duties for hours enough to provide her with an independent living, and then is denied independence on the ground that motherhood prevents her working!'[2]

Gilman makes use of the then standard Darwinian explanation for social development, and does so in three main ways. First, she argues that the male has become the female's economic environment, 'her food supply' (p. 22). Second, she defines people in terms of a changing relationship with the socio-economic environment. Influenced by Bellamy's utopian novel, *Looking Backward* (1888), and the Progressive movement's enthusiasm for planning, she predicted changes in habits and roles and supported schemes for the kitchenless house and the professionalization of housework and childcare. Gilman's third use of Darwinism is to underpin her rejection of sex-specialization, on the grounds that 'sex-distinction in humanity is so marked as to retard and confuse race-distinction, to check individual distinction, seriously to injure the race' (p. 32).

The effects of the sexuo-economic relation are felt everywhere: in the marriage market, which becomes synonymous with a woman's whole world, whereas for men it is one aspect of the social environment; in consumption, where the woman's role as 'the limitless demander of things to use up' harms the economy's ability to answer more important needs (p. 120); and in the kitchen:

> Our general notion is that we have lifted and ennobled our eating and drinking by combining them with love. On the contrary, we have lowered and degraded our love by combining it with eating and drinking . . . Some progress has been made, socially; but this unhappy mingling of sex-interest and self-interest with normal appetites, this Cupid-in-the-kitchen arrangement, has gravely impeded that progress . . . As to science, chemistry, hygiene, – they are but names to [the wife and mother]. 'John likes it so.' 'Willie won't eat it so.' 'Your father never could bear cabbage.' She must consider what he likes, not only because she loves to please him or because she profits by pleasing him, but because he pays for the dinner, and she is a private servant.
>
> Is it not time that the way to a man's heart through his

stomach should be relinquished for some higher avenue? The stomach should be left to its natural uses, not made a thoroughfare for stranger passions and purposes. (pp. 235 and 236–7)

Children were even more in danger at the hands of a maternal instinct untainted by economic and professional considerations: ' "I guess I know how to bring up children!" cried the resentful old lady who was being advised: "I've buried seven!" . . . The experience gained by practising on the child is frequently buried with it' (p. 198).

One criticism invariably levelled against this seminal theoretical text of twentieth-century feminism, is that it is almost unexceptionally middle class. The criticism is an important one, though we might wonder why it is applied more to feminism than to any other protest movement. A more enlightening objection is that Gilman operates with an undifferentiated concept of *work*, and with a rather naive view of capitalist economics as a neutral arena in which sexual difference will play no part. Her solution to wasted women's lives – paid work outside the home – was confounded not by the persistence of Victorian investment in separate spheres but by its apparent demise, as a rapidly expanding capitalist system drew more women than ever before into the labour force. In 1900, two years after *Women and Economics* was published, women made up 17 per cent of the total labour force and just before the Great Crash in 1929 they were almost 22 per cent.

In the 1920s, liberated social and sexual behaviour by short-skirted women with bobbed hair, who were in paid jobs and were potential voters, had the surprising effect of turning Gilman very cranky and reactionary. She referred to 'an unchecked indulgence in appetite and impulse; a coarseness and looseness in speech, dress, manner, and habit of life'. Women were not there for 'enjoyable preliminaries' but to 'cleanse the human race of its worst inheritance by discriminating refusal of unfit fathers'.[3] A combination of Puritan family background and outmoded Darwinist theory is one explanation for her outburst. Yet there is another explanation of her declining importance to the women's movement which also points to perhaps the major problem facing inter-war feminism. The contrast between Gilman's cool analysis in *Women and Economics* and her intemperate polemic against the flapper's social behaviour hints at her realization that a determining factor in women's liberation is not paid work per se, and the emancipated atmosphere of the offices, shops and factories where women found employment, but the *meaning* of work.

Women entered the labour force as individuals in a market economy geared to a certain view of a working life and, in the case of the middle classes, of a career as continuous. Put bluntly, the concept of individual self-determination through paid work had been defined with men in mind. Middle-class women who were optimistic about the new opportunities formed the National Federation of Business and Professional Women's Clubs and the American Association of University Women. Dorothy Bromley, a journalist who thought of herself as a 'feminist – new-style', was typical of professional women in insisting that a woman could have a career *and* a marriage and family. In the professional women's associations and clubs, there was much less interest in supporting the institutional changes Gilman had advocated. Childcare centres were not seen as a priority, so it was presumably up to the individual woman to find individual solutions to the difficulties of combining a career and a home.

Additionally, in all but the top jobs – and very few women were in those in the 1920s – sex segregation was the rule: from the caring professions through office jobs to domestic service and on to industrial occupations. Where the same jobs were performed by men and women, wages were, of course, very different.

The meaning of work for women has also to be understood in the longer view, but even within Gilman's working life women were moved into the workforce while men were at war, moved out of certain occupations when they returned, and urged to move out of (before they were legislated out of) all but the most menial of jobs when unemployment hit in the trough of the Depression. The Federal Economy Act of 1933 stated that if job losses were necessary then only one member of a family could be employed by the Federal government. Women were even on some lists of scapegoats for the Depression and there was a marked reimposition of type with domestic images circulating once more as men demanded the few jobs still available. Marxists and liberals may have been buffetted in the 1930s, but at least something was happening. Feminism was virtually dead. The best that could be hoped for was the isolated figure – a Zora Neale Hurston, Mary Inman, Georgia O'Keeffe, or Lillian Smith; or accidental feminism, as in Mirra Komarovsky's case study, *The Unemployed Man and his Family* (1940), which is very revealing on the woman, employed or unemployed, who had to contend with the psychological and economic consequences when the man lost his job.[4]

Social feminism, which had its roots in Progressive reform, proved to be the most durable kind of feminism in the context of the New Deal. Frances Perkins illustrates the connection between Progressive and New Deal reform, though she herself was not active in social feminism. Once a settlement worker at Hull House (a home away from home, where a woman could do public work while retaining domestic virtues), in the 1920s she became head of the New York State Department of Labor under Governor Roosevelt. When he became President, Roosevelt appointed her as Secretary of Labor, the first woman to hold a cabinet position. Eleanor Roosevelt, together with

Mary Anderson of the Women's Bureau, and organizations like the League of Women Voters were the leaders of social feminists in their campaigns for social welfare and justice in the 1930s. Social feminists accepted that it was necessary to work within, rather than to restructure, existing institutions. Gains included the 1935 Social Security Act which set up maternal and pediatric care with federal funding.

The details of legislative gains, losses and compromises are not directly relevant to this discussion, but they tell us about the dilemmas of feminism. Social feminists were the most effective reformers, yet they consistently opposed the Equal Rights Amendment (ERA), which was kept alive in the 1930s by Alice Paul's Woman's Party. Under ERA, it was argued, the removal of wage discrimination could leave women more vulnerable to competition from men, especially in manual occupations. There was also, among social feminists like Eleanor Roosevelt, a reluctance to have women compete on an equal footing to men, not just for defensive reasons, or for tactical ones of the society-isn't-ready-for-this-yet type, but because they felt that society would be improved if they brought the 'feminine' qualities of service and pacifism to an otherwise rapacious public life. Though the argument was not broached in a theoretical manner by Eleanor Roosevelt or any leading women of the 1930s, at stake is the relationship between the concepts of 'feminism', 'femininity' and 'femaleness' which became so central to the second wave of the women's movement.[5]

At the end of the 1930s when women were needed to replace men who were once more at war, the imagery changed again. Instead of the shopper, who would head the consumer boom that would get America out of the Depression, or, slightly less optimistically, instead of John Steinbeck's strong Ma Joad figure, who would protect the family amidst the insecurity and rootlessness of the Depression, Americans met Rosie the Riveter. Rosie was not merely a woman at work but an industrial worker:

> While other girls attend their favorite cocktail bar,
> Sipping dry martinis, munching caviar,
> There's a girl who's really putting them to shame,
> Rosie is her name.
>
> All the day long, whether rain or shine,
> She's a part of the assembly line,
> She's making history, working for victory,
> Rosie the Riveter.

Under the War Manpower Commission, which began operations in

1942, and with federally funded childcare, six million women came
into the labour force, making up 36 per cent of the working population
at the end of the war, compared with 25 per cent in 1940. Whatever
ambiguities were attached to the meaning of work, the fact that
women continued to enter the work force was a latent cause of the
revival of the women's movement in the 1960s. So, too, were the
contradictions. Women were discarded when men returned and when
the economy demanded consumers rather than producers. The drop
was from 36 per cent in 1945 to 28 per cent in 1947. The official
ideology adjusted to ease the transition, as in this interview, reported in
the documentary, *The Life and Times of Rosie the Riveter*:

> [Commentator:] Edith Stoner's husband is in Alaska. She took
> this job for the duration.
> 'How do you like your job, Mrs Stoner?'
> 'I love it.'
> 'How about after the war? Are you going to keep on working?'
> 'I should say not. When my husband comes back, I'm going to
> be busy at home.'
> 'Good for you.'

It might help to convey the subtlety or complexity of the power
struggle behind the statistics if we think of the newsreels of 1945 and
the many photographs recording the joyful reunions of men and
women after the war. And then we think of the statements made by
women who had experienced independence and job satisfaction in
occupations hitherto closed to them. According to one woman
interviewed in *Rosie the Riveter*, one of the estimated 80 per cent of
women who tried to keep their jobs: 'It was the same old thing. It was
just, you know, being a woman. It was over for us.'

Perhaps the distinguishing characteristic of the post-1945 reimposition of type, compared with that in the 1930s, was the influence of the
media: newspapers, magazines, radio, the movies and, by 1960, around
fifty million television sets. Just as the advertisements and recipes
carried the cult of true womanhood more subtly than the formulaic
stories in the women's magazines of the first half of the nineteenth
century, so the total package for an evening's (or a day's) television –
advertisements, quiz shows, formats for documentaries, as well as soap
operas – disseminated the feminine mystique. The ideology was
alternatively cajoling and coercive. On the one hand, it displayed the
pleasures of suburban life and well-equipped kitchens, together with
the elevation of childcare to a science with Dr Spock's *Baby and Child
Care* (1946). On the other hand, in, for example, the now legendary

and then best-selling *Generation of Vipers* (1942) by Philip Wylie, blame was heaped upon working wives and mothers for the juvenile crimes and adult anxieties of American society. Sociologists and historians added their authority. Marynia Farnham and Ferdinand Lundberg in *Modern Woman: The Lost Sex* (1947) blamed the women's movement, embattled though it was, for women being cut loose from their biological and psychological anchor.

Sometimes feminism was explicitly associated with communism. However, as with the black movement in the post-war years, the near invisibility of feminism was more a result of the preoccupation with conformity that was a spin-off of the general obsession with the USSR. The 'age of conformity' did not just suppress political ideology. It suppressed difference, and generated an image of woman as between twenty and thirty-five, white, middle class and married. The needs and aspirations of lesbians, black, working class, single-parent women, and old or older women were, at best, not considered. At worst, these women were treated as deviants.

The cost of post-war living increased as the range of consumer goods expanded and new houses came on the market in new car-orientated suburbs. Consequently, as middle-class women were being urged to stay home, so they were being pushed out to work to meet the new expenditure demands. Between 1940 and 1960 the percentage of married women in the labour force doubled to 30 per cent, and was up to 50 per cent by 1968 but the motivation for taking a job meant that the 'sexuo-economic relation' had not been broken. These contradictions proved to be a factor in the reappearance of feminism in the 1960s.

Though only a sketch, we can clearly see how women have functioned as a reserve labour force, moved in and out of the economy according to principles that had nothing to do with women's right to work. The purpose of this sketch is to emphasize the limitations of early twentieth-century feminism, stemming from Gilman, and yet the indispensability of feminism if the meaning of work (rather than simply its existence, or non-existence) is to be grasped. The counter-argument which has to be contested is not some up-dated version of the true womanhood ideal, though this did not disappear, but the kind of thesis persuasively put forward by Carl Degler and echoed by historians that the women's movement is a 'revolution without ideology'.[6] Degler argues that the decisive factor in women's improving conditions has not been feminism but increased female participation in the work force: 37.7 per cent of all women 16 years or above were in paid employment at the beginning of the 1960s. One of the tasks of feminist criticism, even moderate feminist criticism, has been to point out that the situation is more complex.

The problem that has no name: Betty Friedan and NOW, 1960s to 1980s

The Feminine Mystique could be classified alongside books like David Riesman's *The Lonely Crowd* (1950) and William H. Whyte's *The Organization Man* (1956), which sought to describe and explain post-war troubles – not in downtown ghettos but in affluent suburbs. Friedan, however, deals with the missing majority, and identifies a discontent that is more fundamental and more consequential than anything experienced by other-directed males:

> The problem lay buried, unspoken for many years in the minds of American women. It was a strange stirring, a sense of dissatisfaction, a yearning that women suffered in the middle of the twentieth century in the United States. Each suburban wife struggled with it alone. As she made the beds, shopped for groceries, matched slipcover material, ate peanut butter sandwiches with her children, chauffeured Cub Scouts and Brownies, lay beside her husband at night, she was afraid to ask even of herself the silent question, 'Is this all?'[7]

From its opening paragraph, *The Feminine Mystique* seems light-weight compared with Simone de Beauvoir's *The Second Sex* or some of the post-1960s Anglo-American and European feminist theory. But theory does not arise in a vacuum: there has to be a history to both the problem and the various solutions offered, and little of women's history and feminist responses were being talked about in the post-war years. The first stage, for Friedan, was to work from what women had, that is, from their experiences and to move towards theory, culture and actions.

Whatever else it does, *The Feminine Mystique* reports 'talk' between women. It creates, within its covers, a latent sisterhood which could coalesce around an event as routine and apparently sex-typed as the 'kaffee klatches' described by William Whyte in his case study of Forest Park. Friedan sets herself the task of finding a language to talk about 'the problem that has no name', adding that 'when a woman tries to put the problem into words, she often merely describes the daily life she leads' (pp. 13 and 27). Although this process of bringing experiences to light by telling stories would be taken much further in later case studies of rape, wife-battering and female sexuality – to the extent that Friedan herself pulled back from the revelations in her revisionist text of 1981, *The Second Stage* – *The Feminine Mystique* establishes the central feminist principle of talking about the personal in some kind of public, but supportive, context.

In spite of possessing everything deemed necessary for her happiness – husband, children, an education, an affluent lifestyle – the middle-class suburban woman was desperate. 'The problem', one respondent remarked, 'is always being the children's mommy, or the minister's wife and never being myself' (p. 25). Yet from doctors (and especially psychoanalysts) to media pundits, authorities united in their opinion that for a woman to be herself meant being feminine, 'accepting [her] own nature, which can find fulfilment only in sexual passivity, male domination, and nurturing maternal love' (p. 38). Nothing much had changed since Gilman concluded that 'everything tells her that she is *she*' (*Women and Economics*, p. 86). Like Gilman, Friedan reacted to sex-typing by talking about women as humans and not as women, defined by their biology.

In the final chapter, entitled 'A New Life Plan for Women', Friedan makes the first step in the direction of theory. However, while talking together is a way to identify 'the problem that has no name', in coming to a conclusion, Friedan does not emphasize the group or women's culture nearly so much as later feminists. Again like Gilman, Friedan's emphasis is upon the career woman. A woman must have a clear idea of where she is going. This will be arrived at and implemented by a decision of *mind*, made by an individual, with the help of education. Friedan and the strain of the women's movement she inspired, evinced a great confidence in the larger society, and even in capitalism, to provide not just any old job but one commensurate with the woman's abilities.

Using language that calls up Weber's theories of modernity (rationalization and the work ethic in particular), Friedan recommends technology to get rid of the chores quickly and efficiently:

> She can use the vacuum cleaner and the dishwasher and all the automatic appliances, and even the instant mashed potatoes for what they are truly worth – to save time that can be used in more creative ways . . .
>
> A woman must say 'no' to the feminine mystique very clearly indeed to sustain the discipline and effort that any professional commitment requires. (pp. 297–8 and 304)

Just as we paused when describing the ambiguities associated with social feminism of the 1920s and 1930s, so we ought to note that Friedan's argument for some kind of androgynous public state assumed that the power relations could be cut through once outside the home. Though the National Organization for Women (NOW) that Friedan helped to found, addressed institutional reforms and the important question of childcare, there is actually less interest in Friedan in structural change than in Gilman, who linked her emphasis upon individual action with schemes for institutionalized cooking and childcare and so on. However, Friedan's was a crucially important denunciation of the feminine mystique, which held that women's nurturing role was a result of biology. Friedan's book was a cue for more trenchant critiques of patriarchal institutions and, from a different perspective, for arguments that would press the claims of sexual difference, but for radical and not conservative, back-to-the-home purposes.

NOW was set up at the Third National Conference of the State Commissions on Women held in Washington DC in 1966. It was the first organization solely devoted to women since the Woman's Party had been started in 1916, and so marks the official beginning of the new women's movement. It picked up the tradition of liberal reform or social feminism, which, as we have seen, had been the most hardy form of feminism between the wars. And it built upon the 1960 Commission on the Status of Women, chaired by Eleanor Roosevelt, and set up by President Kennedy.

Here is a definitive statement about NOW, by Jacqueline Ceballos, President of the New York Chapter of NOW, at the Town Bloody Hall debate in New York City in 1971:

> I'd like to tell you what we do in the National Organization for Women. This is considered the 'square' organization of women's liberation. But we're not too square that we still don't frighten off many, many women and men because they're afraid of the whole women's liberation movement. I don't think it's necesssary to argue about whether women are biologically suited to stay home and wash dishes and take care of men and children all their lives. I don't think that's important. What is important is that the world is changing and that women are at last awakening to the fact that they have a right and a duty to enter into the world and change it and work towards governing the society that governs them.[8]

NOW drew up a Bill of Rights in 1967 which called for an Equal Rights Constitutional Amendment, anti-sex discrimination legislation, maternity benefits and tax assistance for working parents, childcare provision, equal education and job training rights, and women's right to control their own reproductive lives. All of these measures were aimed at helping women to operate in the public world. NOW, rather like the Civil Rights Movement, believed in equality not difference, and so were less interested in ideas of women's distinctive culture, which were beginning to circulate in the late 1960s.

During her research between 1957 and 1963, Friedan was appealing to women at home; this is one reason why the book ends vaguely if optimistically. After 1966, NOW and similar organizations could also appeal to women who were accumulating political experience in the Civil Rights movement and the New Left. This accounts for both the speed with which the new women's movement took off and the divisions that soon appeared when independent younger women refused simply to follow and formed splinter groups, for example, The Feminists in 1968, the New York Radical Feminists in 1969, and Radicalesbians in 1970. However, compared with the Civil Rights and New Left movements, the liberal tradition of feminism has been more open to radical influences. For instance, in the 1970s NOW moved away from its emphaisis on legal equality to address such issues as legalized abortion and the rights of lesbians and the poor.

Move on little girl: women's liberation movements

The women's movement of the 1960s undoubtedly benefited from the greater receptivity to reform stimulated by the Civil Rights and New Left movements. Having examined black protest on its own terms, we can now more fully register the full impact of discrimination against women within the Civil Rights and black nationalist movements.

At the New Left's National Conference for a New Politics in Chicago in 1967 when blacks traded on liberal guilt and demanded 50 per cent of the seats, a radical caucus of women, led by Shulamith Firestone and Jo Freeman, demanded 51 per cent on the grounds that women made up that proportion of the population. This demand was rejected out of hand. Firestone was told by William Pepper, the Conference chair, to 'Move on little girl; we have more important issues to talk about here than women's liberation.' More notorious, still, had been Stokely Carmichael's response to a question about the position of women in SNCC at a conference in 1964: 'The only position for women in SNCC is prone.'[9] At grass roots level, the discrimination was ever-present, confirming housewife and sex-object stereotypes which hindered women from assuming leadership roles.

Although the political experience of organizing was important to women, the greater cause of the Civil Rights Movement and its strategy of provoking action at federal level was inhibiting. Women found something more congenial in the recognition given to individual rebellion in New Left politics. This could, and did, get dissipated into doing one's own thing, especially in the Counter-Cultural side of the New Left. However, the exhilarating combination of personal motives and a public political context, such as the New Left provided, helped to mould the central idea of 'personal politics', to cite the title of Sara Evans' book. Women's Liberation (a media designation after the Miss America demonstration of 1968) took more radical stances than were advocated by NOW. Women in this part of the movement also concurred with the New Left on the importance of consciousness-raising as a necessary prelude to social change. What was less clear in the early stages of dissatisfaction and anger with the then larger political movements, was the relationship between feminism and socialism, whether of the New or Old Left variety.

Consciousness raising was developed by groups such as the Redstockings, who stated in their *Manifesto* of 1969 that:

> We regard our personal experience, and our feelings about that experience, as the basis for an analysis of our common situation. We cannot rely on existing ideologies as they are all the products of male supremacist culture. We question every generalization and accept none that are not confirmed by our experience.[10]

Here we can briefly refer out from the political debates to a number of novels published in the 1970s and 1980s: for example, Marilyn French's *The Woman's Room* (1977), Marge Piercy's *Vida* (1980) and *Branded Lives* (1984), and, in Canada, Margaret Atwood's *Edible Woman* (1969). Although the class and ethnic background of the authors limited the range of women's experience that could be satisfactorily conveyed, these novels reinforced the concept of experience which served as an important substitute for established political and cultural traditions. The coming together of shared and, typically, everyday experiences in some kind of collective institution is also illustrated by Robin Morgan's story of how the seminal anthology, *Sisterhood is Powerful* (1970) got written:

> Five personal relationships were severed, two couples were divorced and one separated, one woman was forced to withdraw her article, by the man she lived with; another's husband kept rewriting the piece until it was unrecognizable as her own; many of the articles were late, and the deadline kept being pushed further ahead, because the authors had so many other pressures on them – from housework to child care to jobs. More than one woman had trouble finishing her piece because it was so personally painful to commit her gut feelings to paper. We were also delayed by occurrences that would not have been of even peripheral importance to an anthology written by men: three pregnancies, one miscarriage, and one birth – plus one abortion and one hysterectomy. (pp. xv-xvi)

The women's movement succeeded in embracing activists and academics. For example, during the 1970s feminist research into the buried history of ordinary American women revealed what practice was telling groups like the Redstockings about the importance of sisterhood, the 'female world of love and ritual', as historian Carol Smith Rosenberg described groups of nineteenth-century Northern middle-class women. Out of their letters and the diaries which record the importance of female networks, Smith Rosenberg reconstructed 'a world in which men made but a shadowy appearance'. Some nineteenth-century female networks, for instance one centred upon the Third Presbyterian Church in New York City, became overt, rather than covert, political movements, protesting against prostitution or taking the temperance cause, since it was invariably women who suffered physically, emotionally and economically from men drinking.[11] Even when these nineteenth-century networks had no direct political outlet, a case can be made for their importance simply for consciousness-raising, based upon the sharing of personal experiences.

Consciousness-raising activities were often formalized within academic programmes. Women's Studies became institutionally as well as intellectually part of the women's movement. Courses grew in popularity, from 100 to over 15,000 between 1969 and 1976, according to Rochelle Gatlin.[12] They generated their own teaching materials and feminist publishers grew up to meet the demand. The (by definition) inter-disciplinary nature of Women's Studies courses undoubtedly stimulated more important theoretical considerations than in any of the other political movements of the 1960s. Women's Studies also had their own institutional context against which to react. Pedagogical practice in colleges and universities was subjected to criticism, notably the use of lectures in which a clear hierarchy was assumed between, typically, a male lecturer imparting information to a passive class – in the Arts, Humanities and Social Sciences the classes would have a large proportion of women. The appointment of female faculty became an important issue, as did sexual harrassment.

The personal is political: radical feminism

Kate Millett

Concluding a survey of the first phase of the second wave of the women's movement (roughly from 1960 and Kennedy's Commission on Women to the splits in the New Left and black protest movements), Sara Evans lays out the next phase:

> In its insistence that 'the personal is political,' contemporary feminism has moved beyond a focus on public or legal inequities to the broader questions of sex roles, socialization, and the economic function of women's work in the home. The issue is not simply discrimination. It penetrates to the underlying cultural definitions of *femaleness* and *maleness*. The sources of this renewed examination of basic meanings lie both in social changes that render patriarchal tradition less tenable and in particular experiences that precipitate a new consciousness.[13]

NOW attended to some of these questions, for example in its Bill of Rights which stated that women should have control over their own reproductive lives; in its partial conversion to consciousness-raising groups as a strategy; and in its eventual support for sexual preference as a feminist issue. Even so, distinctions between the liberal or reformist tradition and radical feminism and socialist feminism were emerging, focused on the relationship between the personal and the political. We have seen that *The Feminine Mystique* was such a breakthrough because it began with personal experiences that a great many women recognized. Others did not, of course, and we can examine the theoretical repercussions of a feminism that starts with the differing experiences of white and, especially, black working-class women, and of lesbians. Moreover, although Friedan does begin with the personal, she has to leave it behind because it is apparently a dead-end. Identity will come when women are free from the home and join 'the mainstream'. NOW, as introduced by Jacqueline Ceballos, sets out to change the mainstream, that is the public world, so that it will accommodate women, but in accepting the necessity of working within the system it does not fundamentally challenge it.

For Kate Millett in *Sexual Politics* (1969), power relations are not so amenable to reason. Sex roles in the public world duplicate roles within the personalized world of the home, family and bedroom. Where Friedan and the equal rights feminists turned away from home, family, and personal, including sexual, relations, because the logic of simple emancipation dictated this move, radical feminists, like Millett, Mary Ellman (in *Thinking About Women*, 1968), Shulamith Firestone, and, in Britain, Germaine Greer, had to deal with the traditional concerns because they saw them as the root of the problem. Women's problems, in other words, did have a name and a cause: the all-pervasiveness of patriarchy, meaning the structural oppression of women by men through institutions, formal and informal: 'Radical feminism is political because it recognizes that a group of individuals (men) have organized for power over women, and that they have set up institutions throughout society to maintain this power.'[14] This statement does not come from *Sexual Politics*, but from 'Politics for the Ego: A Manifesto for N.Y. Radical Feminists' (1969). Like other post-1967 organizations, the New York Radical Feminists concentrated on particular dimensions of patriarchy: rape, incest, pornography and health care to cite the most pressing concerns. Their collective efforts revealed the extent of *sexism* in American society. Millett comes to the same conclusion but, along with Mary Ellman, she initiated debate about the power of literary and other media stereotypes of women.

Millett's literary instances (notably from Henry Miller, D.H. Lawrence and Norman Mailer) present sexual actions as 'a charged microcosm of the variety of attitudes and values to which culture subscribes'.[15] Women are described by these male authors as totally dominated by men. Moreover, women's self-images arise from the man's fundamental 'point of view', and therefore in the pages of these male texts women assume the most passive and degrading sexual positions. Incidently, Millett is sometimes accused of unsophisticated literary criticism, of being unaware of the narrative structures or points of view which forestall a straightforward identification of author and character and/or narrator. But this is to overlook her own ironic point of view which reveals the extent to which both our everyday language and the language critics use to deal with literary texts are permeated by the rhetoric of sexual power. It is this male point of view which functions as the norm throughout society. As the *Redstockings Manifesto* has it:

> Male supremacy is the oldest, most basic form of domination.
> All other forms of exploitation and oppression (racism,
> capitalism, imperialism, etc) are extensions of male
> supremacy. . . *All men* have oppressed women. (Robin Morgan
> (ed.), *Sisterhood is Powerful*, p. 599)

Millett politicizes 'scenes of intimacy', with politics defined not as the 'relatively narrow and exclusive world of meetings, chairmen, and parties', but as 'power-structured relationships, arrangements whereby one group of persons is controlled by another' (p. 23). Millett's examples also free pornography from the confusions that attend liberal and conservative responses and reveal it as an expression of power over women. In one respect, though, her shocking examples – especially from Miller and Mailer – work against the key insight of radical feminism, which is that patriarchy prevails less because these and other individuals enforce it, and more because it is the foundation of institutions and habits of thought. Patriarchy is at the bottom of things because it carries with it the authority of nature, with which culture does 'no more than cooperate' (p. 27). In the more theoretical sections of *Sexual Politics* Millett responds by distinguishing sexual difference from gender difference, the latter being the social organization of the former through socialization and institutions.

When Millett deals with the primary patriarchal institution of the family, she treats the relations between personal and public very differently from Friedan, who seems to believe that the family can be kept separate from the world of work. Millett sees it as the link between the two spheres: 'the family effects control and conformity where political and other authorities are insufficient' (p. 33). Control is exerted directly – over the wife – and is perpetuated into the next generation through socialization.

The problem that Millett comes up against is probably the central one in second wave feminism: having located representative instances of patriarchy (for example in literary descriptions of the sexual act), Millett is intent upon shifting our attention from sex to gender; that is, from the biology of maleness and femaleness to the social constructions of masculinity and femininity and how these constructs are reinforced and perpetuated. This is a major theoretical advance on Friedan. However, the cumulative effect of the instances of patriarchal power which she so devastatingly exposes is to present patriarchy as a 'universal', unchanging even in the historical overview which she provides. Patriarchy is so ever-present and – bar the alternately angry and mocking tone of the book – so irresistible, in both the literal and popular meaning of the word, that – contra Millett's intentions in the book – it might almost be biological. A related objection to the book is that when Millett proposes instances of resistance, she turns to the gay writer Jean Genet. It has been the task of 'gynocritics', in the hands of a literary critic like Elaine Showalter in *A Literature of their Own* (1977), to rediscover and re-assess women writers. Millett mostly restricts herself to a feminist critique of male writers, and is dismissive, in passing, of women writers.

Shulamith Firestone

Shulamith Firestone was a founder of the New York Radical Feminists and Redstockings, and in 1970 published *The Dialectic of Sex: The Case for a Feminist Revolution*. Although this book appeared within a year of *Sexual Politics*, and both can be classified as radical feminism, Firestone looks for a different resolution of the question of patriarchy.

Firestone, too, examines the institutionalization of masculinity and femininity and in ways that resemble Millett's and serve to differentiate both thinkers from Friedan and her emancipatory project:

> To so heighten one's sensitivity to sexism presents problems far worse than the black militant's new awareness of racism: feminists have to question, not just all of *Western* culture, but the organization of culture itself, and further, even the very organization of nature. Many women give up in despair: if *that's* how deep it goes they don't want to know. Others continue.[16]

In common with radical feminists generally, Firestone insists that women are the most oppressed class. She differs from Millett in directly confronting, rather than forgetting, biology (or nature), maintaining that it is the basic link between women and reproduction which is at the root of oppression: social, economic and emotional oppression.

It is therefore not surprising that *The Dialectic of Sex*, from its title and its epigraph (from Engels) onwards, should call up Marxism, but that Firestone should proceed to argue that reproduction and not production is 'the base'. The fundamental class division is between men and women. Hence Firestone's rewriting of Marx's *Communist Manifesto* and, more directly, of Engels's *Socialism: Utopianism or Scientific*:

> Historical materialism is that view of the course of history which seeks the ultimate cause and the great moving power of all historical events in the dialectic of sex: the division of society into two distinct biological classes for procreative reproduction, and the struggles of these classes with one another . . .
>
> The sexual-reproductive organization of society always furnishes the real basis, starting from which we can alone work out the ultimate explanation of the whole superstructure of economic, juridical and political institutions as well as of the religious, philosophical and other ideas of a given historical period. (pp. 20 and 21)

Whether what women have in common outweighs social and economic class differences or can transcend 'the colour line' or can finally justify the exclusion of all men became the crux of other disputes within feminism which we can touch on shortly. What is clear, though, is that radical feminism, by placing women at the centre of concern, rectifies a quite extraordinary blindness in even the most advanced social theory.

Going back to Engels, it is interesting that Firestone should have chosen that particular text to re-write, because *The Dialectic of Sex* itself ends by returning to the utopian vision that Engels discards in favour of historical materialism, or scientific socialism as he calls it. In a way not so different from Herbert Marcuse in *Eros and Civilization*, Firestone looked to the utopian rather than the dystopian, totalitarian potential of technology and speculated on artificial child-bearing: 'It is only recently, in the most technologically advanced countries, that genuine preconditions for feminist revolution have begun to exist.' These conditions point to '*the freeing of women from the tyranny of reproduction by every means possible, and the diffusion of child-rearing to the society as a whole, to men and other children as well as women*' (pp. 206 and 221).

The very mention of 'test-tube' babies is likely to stymie any further discussion, so emotive is the idea. Moreover, as Alison Jaggar suggests when trying to explain the relative lack of interest in Firestone's solution:

> Women in general are not trained in technology, and they know that it is controlled by men. Radical feminists observe that technology, especially reproductive technology, has been used in the past against women and to reinforce male dominance; they do not see how women could take control of advanced technology, at least in the short term, and use it for their own ends.[17]

As a way of appreciating Firestone's contribution to radical feminism, it may be helpful to reiterate something of the defence of Marcuse's utopianism at the end of chapter six. There it was argued that in the analysis of Eros in *Eros and Civilization*, Marcuse was not providing a blueprint but, in the midst of abundance, was defending the possibility of *thinking otherwise*. Firestone, as it happens, does outline 'some "dangerously utopian" concrete proposals', because, she explains, 'there are no precedents in history for feminist revolution . . . Moreover, we haven't even a literary image of [a feminist] future society; there is not even a *utopian* feminist literature yet in existence' (p. 211). This isn't strictly true but in American literature, which is one of the most utopian of national literatures, it is very nearly true. In the golden age of American utopian fiction at the end of the nineteenth century, there were very few utopian novels by women. Gilman's *Herland* came out in *The Forerunner* in 1915 but was not published as a book until 1979. As if in response to Firestone's statement about the lack of feminist utopianism, there was a flurry of important texts during the 1970s, among them Ursula Le Guin's *The Left-Hand of Darkness* (1969) and *The Dispossessed* (1974), Marge Piercy's *Woman on the Edge of Time* (1976) and Sally Miller Gearhart's *The Wanderground* (1979). All follow brief suggestions in Firestone's utopia for redesigned living facilities that attack the family.

More important than the blueprints, however, is the concerted effort to estrange oneself from prevailing modes of thought. Firestone's book begins with the sentence 'Sex class is so deep as to be invisible' (p. 11). The lived utopianism of the 1960s – communes, drugs and so on – lacked the self-conscious reflection which we meet at the end of Firestone's book and, to take one comparable example, in Ursula LeGuin's work. Fredric Jameson, who has written provokingly on Marcuse's reinvention of the idea of the future, has this to say about what LeGuin calls her 'thought experiment':

> [It] is based on a principle of systematic exclusion, a kind of surgical excision of empirical reality, something like a process of ontological attenuation in which the sheer teeming multiplicity of what exists, of what we call reality, is deliberately thinned and weeded out through an operation of radical abstraction and simplification which we will henceforth term *world-reduction*.[18]

In *The Left-Hand of Darkness* world-reduction takes such forms as the ambisexuality of the inhabitants of the planet of Gethen, and the restriction of desire to just a few days in a monthly cycle. Jameson's definition of utopia is a useful reference point when trying to evaluate the controversial solutions proposed in *The Dialectic of Sex*; the success of its critique of a sexist society is not in dispute. According to Jameson: 'Utopia is, in other words, not a place in which humanity is free . . . but rather one in which it is released from the multiple determinisms (economic, political, social) of history itself' (p. 227). Firestone's utopianism is important because, like radical lesbianism, it considered alternatives to existing relations (between men and women, women and children) rather than ways of supporting the traditional family.

Adrienne Rich and Mary Daly

Adrienne Rich, a poet as well as an important feminist thinker, is much less persuaded than Firestone by the idea of functions or roles freed from biological determinations. Millett and Firestone seek to break the link with the body, Firestone more polemically, but in *Of Woman Born* (1976) Rich argues that women must '*think through the body*', the pun suggesting an intellectual project and a grounding of being in nature.[19] Rich also objected to the implication, in the technological decommissioning of anatomy proposed in *The Dialectic of Sex*, that the problem to be remedied was women's biology. Rape statistics and the market for pornography point to the contrary view, that the problem lies with male biology. The conclusion drawn is that women should, to varying degrees, cultivate each other's company, advice that goes back to the female networks of early industrial society in America, and runs through a novel like *Herland*, to the consciousness groups, pro-women groups, and radical lesbians of the late 1960s and 1970s. Adrienne Rich describes this range of experiences as a 'lesbian continuum': from physical sex to day-to-day support. For the Radicalesbians collective in 'The Woman Identified Woman' (1970), lesbianism is a straightforward political issue. The power structures identified by Millett and Firestone have to be met by separation, not simply a recognition of a metaphorical lesbianism.[20]

Mary Daly's work is another illustration of the transition from an integrationist, liberal stance to the varieties of separatism in radical feminism. In *The Church and the Second Sex* (1968), she aroused anger in the ecclesiastical world by arguing that the church should act in public against sexual discrimination. This was still a reformist argument from within the church. In *Beyond God the Father* (1973), however, she adopted the radical feminist line that feminism must concentrate upon women. As a theologian, she argued that God was to be found by pursuing the cause of women because women were closer to the life-spirit that religion sought to respect.

Daly's *Gyn/Ecology* (1978) celebrates womanhood still further by maintaining that female biology, and especially its reproductive capacity, brings a spiritual because natural power, and with it superiority over men. This concept of power is quite different from Millett's understanding of the word, and derives from a radical questioning of values: Why should a male definition of progress, success, rationality, indeed of modernity be accepted? Is it superior because it is forced upon women? This is to simplify Daly's argument and to neglect the religious context of her writing, but it at least introduces the argument (also advanced by Susan Griffin in *Women and Nature*, 1980) that the male/female order of priority can be reversed and from the very biological standpoint that has been the basis for patriarchy. It is not a scientific argument but a poetic, religious one, but this approach is entirely consistent with the questioning of the authority of (male-dominated) science. Daly and Griffin also challenge liberal integrationists, like Friedan, and radical integrationists, like Millett and Firestone, who interpret power in social, political and economic terms, and who react to patriarchy not through a new biologism, but by looking for social and cultural reasons why 'maleness' is privileged over 'femaleness'.

Radical feminism departs from liberalism by its sustained concentration upon women, but it includes Millett and Firestone at one end and Daly, Rich and (in so far as they would want to be included) the Radical lesbians at the other end. Allowing for the tactical and intellectual importance of the celebration of the nature of women at the latter end of the spectrum, to make sexual difference the basis for a politics has limitations and can represent a turning away from the public and political towards the personal world not, as in 'personal politics', to re-engage but to separate.

For all its antipathy to the major existing traditions of liberalism and Marxism, radical feminism was at its strongest when it argued with them, in both senses of the word 'with'. Radical feminist politics allowed movement both ways rather than, as with Friedan and the cultivators of women's culture in just one direction, though opposite directions in these two cases. As younger women came into the radical movement, without the experience of Civil Rights and New Left protests, but with patriarchy firmly installed as the sole enemy, they lost some of the dialectical quality of Millett and Firestone, especially. As radical feminism explored women's culture (spirituality, aesthetics, sexuality) questions of power relations receded in importance, even though the larger social arena remained defined by men. Relations – invariably antagonistic or 'political' ones – gave way to the exploration of essences. In the process some radical feminists were in danger of losing the often difficult 'duality' which defines women's lives (but not only women's lives). The historian, Gerda Lerner, defines that duality as being part of the 'general culture' and 'women's culture' (*The Majority Finds Its Past*, passim). What seems to have happened is that patriarchy, rather than being analysed as a historical and historically variable, phenomenon, has become biologized (quite the reverse of Millett's intention).

Another coup d'état among men?: socialist feminism

The discrimination which women met in the New Left, and the blatant message that, yet again, women's problems would have to be dealt with later, if at all, delayed any serious engagement between feminism and socialism until the mid-1970s at least. However, socialist feminism has never been as significant a strand as in British feminism, partly because of the antipathy to socialism but, more positively, because of the successes of radical and liberal feminism, the latter in exerting real pressure upon the federal government through federal agencies such as the Women's Bureau in the Department of Labor. *Capitalist Patriarchy and the Case for Socialist Feminism* (1979), an uneven collection edited by Zillah Eisenstein, was the first substantial contribution to the post-1960s debate which involved American feminists. The earlier attempts by feminists to examine what the two traditions had in common – Mary Inman's work inside and outside the Communist Party in the 1930s comes to mind – barely informed the revived discussion.[21]

Broadly speaking, socialist feminism locates the oppression of women in the class structure of capitalism. Thus, the struggle for women's liberation is seen as part of the larger class struggle. Feminists are not naive enough to believe that a socialist revolution will meet their demands. As Robin Morgan puts it: 'We know that a male-dominated socialist revolution in economic and even cultural terms, were it to occur tomorrow, would be *no* revolution, but only another coup d'état among men' (*Sisterhood is Powerful*, pp. xxxv–xxxvi). However, many radical feminists, for instance Shulamith Firestone, insist that they are socialists. The British feminist, Juliet Mitchell, who contributed to Eisenstein's collection, argues that historical materialism can be refocused to deal with the relations between the personal and public spheres so as to answer questions posed by feminists.

Khomeini frees women and blacks: black feminism

The most recent challenge to feminism as it enlarges its theoretical scope has come from black feminists, notably Bell Hooks in *Ain't I A Woman?: Black Women and Feminism* (1981) and Gloria Hull and the other editors and contributors to *All the Women are White, All the Blacks Are Men, But Some of Us Are Brave* (1982). Black women, as feminist thinkers, creative writers and activists have probably gained a higher profile as a result of the women's movement than the black movement. This does not mean that they have necessarily defined themselves more by gender than race, so there would be good reasons for including this section in the previous chapter on black protest. The ambiguous headline from the Iran crisis is quoted by Bell Hooks as a way of asking where black women are supposed to be. The only unambiguous answer is that wherever black women have been they have been doubly discriminated against.

The Civil Rights movement began with a black woman, Rosa Parks, refusing to give up her seat to a white man on a Montgomery bus in 1955. SNCC started with the support of SCLC, with Ella Baker, a black woman, rather than Martin Luther King as the chief adult adviser to the students. She later reacted against the strong leadership of King and preferred the group work of SNCC which became the hallmark of the later women's movement. It was also a black woman, Ruby Doris Smith Robinson, followed by two white women, Casey Hayden and Mary King, who protested against the subordinate position accorded women within SNCC and had to put up with Stokely Carmichael's sexist retort. Black women saw in the activities of black men towards white women in the Civil Rights movement a twisted endorsement of the (white) feminine mystique which reinforced the subordinate position of black women and accentuated the difficulties they had in finding positive role models. When Black Power became important from the mid-1960s, the discrimination became blatant in someone like Eldridge Cleaver, with his unremitting talk of black manhood.

The complexities of discrimination appear if we consider the relations between black and white women within the women's movement. Hooks makes a comparison with the origins of the nineteenth-century women's movement:

> 71As if history were repeating itself, [white feminists] also began to make synonymous their social status and the social status of black people. And it was in the context of endless comparisons of the plight of 'women' and 'blacks' that they revealed their racism. In most cases, this racism was an unconscious, unacknowledged aspect of their thought, suppressed by their narcissism – a narcissism which so blinded them that they would not admit two obvious facts: one, that in a capitalist, racist, imperialist state there is no one social status women share as a collective group; and second, that the social status of white women in America has never been like that of black women or men.[22]

Mostly oblivious of black women in its early years, the new women's movement has taken more account of black women since the mid-1970s. But, as Hooks, Gloria Hull and others have shown, misunderstandings have persisted – sometimes because of, rather than in spite of the sympathy. The black woman became the prime example of the victimized but enduring woman. As Hooks remarks, 'We appeared to have been unanimously elected to take up where white women were leaving off. They got *Ms.* magazine; we got *Essence*'

(p. 6). There were other misunderstandings, summarized by Rochelle Gatlin in her excellent survey, *American Women Since 1945*:

> Black women perceived independence and dependence differently. They defined themselves simultaneously in relationship to men and as independent beings. For white women, nurturance and autonomy were polarised; one meant the loss of the other. Independence in the form of political activism or career commitment was incompatible with the privatised wife-mother role. The division between 'public' and 'private' was not as sharp for black women. They were taught to maintain and preserve both their families and their communities. One might say that the survival of the black community was a 'family matter'. Black women could extend the maternal role to supportive work in the movement without experiencing conflict in female identity. (p. 86)

These are by no means the only cultural differences that have to be taken into account, but they suggest the kinds of perspectives that black women have brought to feminism generally. Though outside the purview of this account, the importance of black women novelists must be mentioned: Maya Angelou, Toni Morrison, and Alice Walker have defined an area of black women's experience and history that is distinctive (from black men's experience in particular) but which acts critically on adjacent areas. The work of Hooks and others might be seen as parallel to the work of the novelists. From Hooks's point of view, while gender is not the obvious site for identity, neither is race: 'To both groups [of activists] I voiced my conviction that the struggle to end racism and the struggle to end sexism were naturally intertwined, that to make them separate was to deny a basic truth of our existence' (p. 13).

In her writings and career as an activist, Angela Davis exemplifies the shifting ground of identity, and the necessity, therefore, of examining multiple perspectives. She was a prominent activist in the Black Power movement who was jailed then released with the charges dropped. She was a communist, though, according to Bell Hooks, 'black people did not approve of her communism and refused to take it seriously', in part because they preferred to see her in the stereotypical 'strong black woman' role. Moreover, 'the American public', Hooks adds, 'was not willing to see the "political" Angela Davis; instead they made of her a poster pinup' (p. 183). However, *Women, Race and Class*, published in 1981, is a major text in American feminism. For example, Davis' analyses of housework and in the context of a capitalist society and of race and sex relations indicates how comprehensive a feminist critique can be.

Sexual/textual politics: feminism and post-structuralism

The great insight of feminism is that 'the personal is political', and, in this respect American radical feminism probably led the way. Although the tradition which runs from Charlotte Perkins Gilman through Betty Friedan to NOW, in its purely 'equal rights' phase, begins from the personal, it leaves it behind, believing that the real battles are to be fought in the public domain. Gilman's devastating demythologizing of motherhood and the home, and Friedan's decisive 'no' to the image of the housewife effect that shift of ground. However, the fate of Gilman's important thesis about the 'sexuo-economic relation', and Friedan's return to the nuclear family in *The Second Stage* (1981) equally confirm the shortcomings of liberal feminism, even as it can claim to have had the most impact in practical, reformist terms. The necessity for a radical re-examination of 'the personal' therefore became the central concern of alternatives to the feminist liberal tradition. Alison Jaggar gives this concise summary in *Feminist Politics and Human Nature*:

> On this view, there is no distinction between the 'political' and the 'personal' realms: every area of life is the sphere of 'sexual politics.' All relations between women and men are institutionalized relationships of power and so constitute appropriate subjects for political analysis. Much radical feminist theory consists in just such analyses. It reveals how male power is exercised and reinforced through such 'personal' institutions as childrearing, housework, love, marriage and all kinds of sexual practices, from rape through prostitution to sexual intercourse itself. (p. 101)

What remained contradictory within and across the different radical feminisms, and across socialist feminism as well as liberal feminism, was the 'nature' of 'the personal'. Should it lead to a woman-centred biologism, and to some version of separatism? If socio-economic class was thought to be prior to 'sex class', to recall Shulamith Firestone's term, did this provide adequate feminist answers? If, to follow Kate Millett, attention is directed towards gender, then what of sex and those fixed biological elements? The relationship between nature and culture is not just a feminist preoccupation, of course; it figures in social, political and even aesthetic theory. However, the issue of biological determinism enters discussions about women with depressing regularity.

In an effort to theorize the personal, and so address the nature/culture question, American (and British) feminism of the 1980s has imported ideas from French post-structuralism. Among the figures who are making contributions in this area of 'sexual/textual politics', as Toril Moi neatly describes it, are Gayatri Spivak, Alice Jardine, Shoshana Felman, Barbara Johnson, Jane Gallop, and Teresa de Lauretis.[23] Most are literary, film and cultural theorists. To date, there are no texts to compare with those by Friedan, Millett, Firestone, Daly and Rich, or, from the French tradition, with the writings of Simone de Beauvoir, Julia Kristeva, Luce Irigaray, and Hélène Cixous. For this reason, the brief resume that follows will simply describe the emerging critical practice. No claim is made that it resolves issues raised by earlier versions of feminism.

Two things should be said at the outset to put recent developments into context. First, Robin Morgan, Mary Daly and Adrienne Rich, among others, have resisted the turn towards theory, not least because they see it as another case of male rationality being extended in inappropriate ways to women. This ties in with explorations of a separate women's culture. Initially, at least, the source-texts for much post-structuralist theory tended to be by men (Barthes, Derrida, Foucault, Lacan). In response, it can be pointed out that the anti-theory position – basically an appeal to experience and to action based upon it – is itself a theoretical position. This is very evident when, for example, black feminists point out their differences from white feminists. Theory presses its claims when women's experiences prove *not* to be universal thoughout history and across cultures, or even when day-to-day contradictions provoke thought. Second, the theoretical advances have occurred very much within academic institutions and have been occupied by disciplinary and inter-disciplinary in-fighting. Having theorized experience and action, the temptation is to be more affronted by instances of theoretical impurity, backsliding and revisionism than by the groups, institutions and events which are seemingly immune or oblivious to theory.

The post-structuralist claim that subjectivity is constructed in the web of language, rather than biologically, has, then, induced scepticism about the almost sacred concept of women's experience. For Daly and Rich, among others, this would be counted a loss. However, there is a gain in the undermining of the biological bases of both masculinity and femininity, and in being able to take positive account of the intersections of race and class with gender. For post-structuralists, the meaning of any entity arises relationally, rather than referentially. As the literary critic, Barbara Johnson, argues, 'the differences *between* entities (prose and poetry, man and woman, literature and theory, guilt and innocence) are shown to be based on a repression of differences *within* entities, ways in which an entity differs from itself'.[24] The word or sign 'woman' cannot be defined without reference to another word or sign, for example 'man', and vice-versa. When a sign's meaning appears to be stable, it is an indication of *instituted* power relations at work which have interrupted the endless deferral of meaning through the play of difference. Invariably, this exercise of structural power is attended by the demotion of a historical explanation of the roles men and women play in society in favour of a natural one.

And yet, if sexual identity is constructed in language then attempts to fix identity are capable of being de-constructed. The construction of identity is usually achieved by according priority to one term in the structuralist binary opposition (man over woman, white over black), with an accompanying inscription in metaphor (to 'master' a situation, to 'blacklist' someone). Feminist appropriations of deconstructive strategies of 'reading' texts and institutions, understood as discursive formations, are an important aid in revealing the ideological bases of patriarchy. Since deconstruction works on apparently coherent structures (institutions, philosophical and political statements and so on) by exposing what has to be left out for the structures to retain coherence, and since women are precisely what are left out or assumed, for example in a capitalist economy where they are the 'reserved' element in the labour force, then to 'centre' the marginal figure of woman in any analysis is to introduce a radically disruptive force. Language, or discourse, therefore becomes a crucial rather than secondary issue and, as it appears in post-structuralism, is, in theory, compatible with a Marxist account of subjectivity or consciousness as historically produced. However, within contemporary American feminism, Marxism holds less interest than does contesting the power of such discursive formations as define education (including literary and cultural studies), medicine (particularly psychoanalysis and childbirth), and the family (where all aspects seem central: childcare, housework, sexual relations).

Barbara Kruger (see pp. 110–111) and Cindy Sherman, among other women artists, are pursuing similar ends in visual media. Sherman's photographs of herself in multiple disguises (as a movie star of the 1940s and 1950s, as a *Vogue* model, as a human pig, and so on) have the double effect of questioning the idea of a fixed identity (Who is the real Cindy Sherman?), and criticizing the categories into which women are put or try to put themselves. In selecting a photograph for an exhibition, Sherman choses 'the one that looks like somebody else' or the one that does not quite fit the mould – a *Vogue* model who is awkward or appears victimized.

These varied developments have put feminism more firmly on the theoretical agenda. Of course, there remains a suspicion that high theory is a belated reaction to the disappointments of the 1960s. There is also concern that a decentred self is precisely what women (or members of any exploited group) least need. On the other hand, sexism is, literally, so inscribed in culture that feminist appropriations of deconstruction, Lacanian psychoanalysis and Foucault's analysis of power and knowledge would seem to have more claim to be a politics than some of the 'originals'. Moreover, it is not the case that theory is necessarily isolated from practice, or that more obviously political activity has disappeared. The relationship between nature and culture underlies the Pro-life and Pro-choice controversy surrounding the 1989 Supreme Court decision, *Webster* vs *Reproductive Services*. This decision, which attacked a woman's right to abortion, established in the 1973 case of *Roe* vs *Wade*, provoked a resurgence of feminist activity across the country, notably on 12 November 1989, when hundreds of thousands of women, men and children protested across the country and especially outside the White House home of Pro-life President Bush. That abortion is a key issue in 'personal politics' and a question of power, is also apparent when male prejudice has its say; in this instance, during a phone-in in Fort Wayne, Indiana, location of a current Pro-life 'Operation Rescue': 'They say it's a woman's right because it's her body. As far as I'm concerned, she gives up that right when she's with a man.' Or, in the words of Tom Wyss, an Indiana Legislator: '[Abortion] is a form of birth control.' To which one of the clients at the Women's Health Clinic in Fort Wayne replied: 'Oh, birth control? I don't think so. I think there's a lot less painful birth control than what I just went through.'[25]

Notes

1. Barbara Welter, *Dimity Convictions: The American Woman in the Nineteenth Century* (Athens, Ohio, 1976), p. 21.

2. Charlotte Perkins Gilman, *Women and Economics: A Study of the Economic Relation Between Men and Women as a Factor in Social Evolution*, edited by Carl Degler (New York, 1966), pp. 5 and 21.

3. Charlotte Perkins Gilman, 'Vanguard, Rear-guard, and Mud-guard', *Century Magazine*, 104 (1922), pp. 350, 351 and 353.

4. See Douglas Tallack, 'Women in the Thirties', in *The Thirties: Politics and Culture in a Time of Broken Dreams*, edited by Heinz Ickstadt et al. (Amsterdam, 1987), pp. 85–119.

5. For definitions of these terms, see Toril Moi, 'Feminist Literary Criticism', in *Modern Literary Theory: A Comparative Introduction* (1987), edited by Ann Jefferson and David Robey, rev. edn, chapter 8.

6. Carl N. Degler, 'Revolution Without Ideology: The Changing Place of Women in America', in *The Woman in America*, edited by Robert J. Lifton (Boston, 1965), p. 193.

7. Betty Friedan, *The Feminine Mystique* (Harmondsworth, 1983), p. 9.

8. Quoted from *Town Bloody Hall* (Pennebaker, 1979).

9. Quoted in Sara Evans, *Personal Politics: The Roots of Women's Liberation in the Civil Rights Movement and the New Left* (New York, 1979), pp. 199 and 87.

10. 'Redstockings Manifesto', in *Sisterhood is Powerful: An Anthology of Writings from the Women's Liberation Movement*, edited by Robin Morgan (New York, 1970), p. 600.

11. Carol Smith-Rosenberg, 'The Female World of Love and Ritual: Relations Between Women in Nineteenth-Century America', in *A Heritage of Her Own: Toward a New Social History of American Women*, edited by Nancy Cott and Elizabeth Pleck (New York, 1979), p. 312. See, from the same collection, Carol Smith-Rosenberg, 'Beauty, the Beast and the Militant Woman: A Case Study in Sex Roles and Social Stress in Jacksonian America', pp. 197–221. See, also, Gerda Lerner, *The Majority Finds Its Past: Placing Women in History* (Oxford, 1979).

12. Rochelle Gatlin, *American Women Since 1945* (1987), p. 153.

13. Sara Evans, 'Tomorrow's Yesterday: Feminist Consciousness and the Future of Women', in *Women of America: A History*, edited by Carol Ruth Berkin and Mary Beth Norton (Boston, 1979), p. 400.

14. 'Politics of the Ego: A Manifesto for N.Y. Radical Feminists', in *Radical Feminism*, edited by Anne Koetd et al. (New York, 1973), p. 379.

15. Kate Millett, *Sexual Politics* (New York, 1971), p. 23.

16. Shulamith Firestone, *The Dialectics of Sex: The Case for Feminist Revolution* (1979), p. 12.

17. Alison M. Jaggar, *Feminist Politics and Human Nature* (Sussex, 1983), p. 93.

18. Fredric Jameson, 'World Reduction in LeGuin: The Emergence of Utopian Narrative', *Science Fiction Studies*, 7 (1975), p. 223.

19. Adrienne Rich, *Of Woman Born: Motherhood as Experience and Institution* (New York, 1976), p. 284.

20. See Adrienne Rich, 'Compulsory Heterosexuality and Lesbian Existence', *Signs: Journal of Woman in Society*, 5 (1980), pp. 631–60; and Radicalesbians, 'The Woman Identified Woman', in Koedt (see Note 14).

21. See Mary Inman, *In Woman's Defense* (Los Angeles, 1940) and *Two Forms of Production Under Capitalism* (Los Angeles, 1964).

22. Bell Hooks, *Ain't I A Woman: Black Women and Feminism* (Boston, 1981), p. 136.

23. See Toril Moi, *Sexual/Textual Politics: Feminist Literary Theory* (1985) and Chris Weedon, *Feminist Practice and Poststructuralist Theory* (Oxford, 1987).

24. Barbara Johnson, *The Critical Difference: Essays in the Contemporary Rhetoric of Reading* (Baltimore, 1980), pp. x–xi.

25. Quoted in *Everyman: The Politics of Life* (BBC 1, 1989).

Conclusion: Post-modernity

Modernity and its discontents

In *Modernity and its Discontents*, a British television series first screened in 1985, Michael Ignatieff led into one of the discussions this way:

> Perhaps the most painful price we've had to pay is the loss of community and neighbourhood. In a world of strangers we seem to withdraw more and more to the family and home, our haven from a heartless world.[1]

Ignatieff's discussants, French psychoanalyst and social theorist, Cornelius Castoriades, and American historian and cultural theorist, Christopher Lasch, went on to raise other questions (which I liberally paraphrase): In the event that there is a qualitatively different future ahead of us, where do we look for the agents of change? How have we got increased unfreedom and irrationality out of the Enlightenment project of rationality, which had, after all, broken the fetters of feudal tradition? What has happened to the self, narcissistically preoccupied with itself in American tellings, or decentred and deconstructed in other, mostly European, ones? Aesthetics, the problematics of representation, and the relationship between modern*ism* and post-modern*ism* were discussed in other programmes in the series, and have been very important whenever the question of whether we are at the end of modernity or in a post-modern age is broached.

I have begun with more explicitly theoretical material than in previous chapters, not because I have any concluding ambitions in that direction, but because I want to convey a very marked trend in American thought and culture: the full emergence of 'theory', as outlined by the renegade philosopher, Richard Rorty:

> Beginning in the days of Goethe and Macauley [sic] and Carlyle and Emerson, a kind of writing has developed which is neither the evaluation of the relative merits of literary productions, nor

intellectual history, nor moral philosophy, nor epistemology, nor social prophecy, but all of these mingled together in a new genre.[2]

The questions being asked by Americans like Christopher Lasch are also the ones that haunt the end of Max Weber's *The Protestant Ethic and the Spirit of Capitalism* (1904–5), and especially the passage which I made so much of in my Introduction:

> This order is now bound to the technical and economic conditions of machine production which to-day determine the lives of all the individuals who are born into this mechanism, not only those directly concerned with economic acquisition, with irresistible force. Perhaps it will so determine them until the last ton of fossilized coal is burnt . . . No one knows who will live in this cage in the future, or whether at the end of this tremendous development entirely new prophets will arise, or there will be a great rebirth of old ideas and ideals, or, if neither, mechanized petrification, embellished with a sort of convulsive self-importance. (pp. 181 and 182)

Weber wrote this before most of the events or developments which have given a dramatic chronology to twentieth-century thought and culture: two world wars, the second ending with the dropping of two atomic bombs which, in turn, inaugurated the Cold War and the nuclear age; the Nazi and Stalinist terrors, and, in our own time, escalating violations of human rights all around the world; imperialist military ventures in Eastern Europe, Asia and Latin America; 'the 1960s' and subsequent retrenchment, particularly in the United States and Britain; the precious but precarious social and socialist democracies emerging in the wake of perestroika, vulnerable to embattled but still entrenched communist parties and, as we have seen in West Berlin, to the ambiguous but desired freedoms of capitalism; the quite incredible growth of state bureaucracies and multinational capitalism (IBM now operates in some 130 countries); AIDS and the punitive mentality that co-exists with the hope that medical advances bring; and, finally, Chernobyl and 'the greenhouse effect' as the cost of liberating technologies. If we reflect on even a little of our own history, then the perplexities of Lasch, Castoriades and others interviewed by Michael Ignatieff is less likely to be dismissed as a peculiarity of intellectuals. In particular, 'the cultural contradictions of capitalism' are going to be even more to the forefront as the free market spreads into Eastern Europe.

Weber is invariably present in current deliberations about the fate of modernity because he, more than anyone, confirms that we have constructed our own iron cage, and, in the process, made it difficult to return to the classical objective/subjective dualism upon which our thinking is traditionally based. Weber explains that rationalization had its source in subjectivity: the inner turmoil of the late sixteenth- and seventeenth-century Puritan saint in New England. The effects of rationalization (see pp. 10–17, above) were then externalized in bourgeois individualism: the Protestant work ethic from Benjamin Franklin through to the later nineteenth-century popular fiction of Horatio Alger Jr. Finally, in Weber's own time, rationalization was institutionalized under monopoly capitalism into an objective, impersonal system. The decline of positive community which, as Ignatieff confirms, is a pervasive contemporary theme, is shadowed by a realization that individualism, the alternative for which community is invariably given up, is also in deep trouble.

In *The Cultural Contradictions of Capitalism* (1976), Daniel Bell concentrates upon the other figure produced by modernity. Alongside entrepreneurs, whose conservative cultural tastes seemed suited to their adventurous economics, the late eighteenth- and nineteenth-century market released artists from patronage and instigated an interaction between modernism and modernization. In his study of modernity, *All That Is Solid Melts Into Air* (1982), Marshall Berman, for one, pins great hopes on a dynamic relationship between visions and forces. In contrast, Bell sees modernism as part of the problem rather than the solution. High modernists, such as Joyce, Mallarmé, Pound, Stein, and Woolf disrupted the unity of traditional religious, bourgeois culture by 'insisting on the autonomy of the aesthetic from moral norms; by valuing more highly the new and experimental; and by taking the self (in its quest for originality and uniqueness) as the touchstone of cultural judgment'.[3] For explanation, we can, like Bell himself, turn to the critic, Lionel Trilling.

In 1961 Trilling's essay, 'On the Teaching of Modern Literature', appeared in *Partisan Review*, and in 1965 was reprinted in his *Beyond Culture*. Trilling had been exercised by the seemingly minor task of having to teach the modern literature course at Columbia University. Students had demanded that they be allowed to study the literature of their century: Yeats, Eliot, Joyce, Proust, Kafka, Lawrence, Mann, and Gide are mentioned by Trilling, who adds that his 'uneasiness . . . arises . . . from my personal relation with the works that form the substance of the course'. He wonders how a literature which asks 'if we are content with ourselves, if we are saved or damned', can be taught and examined, when it undermines the very order that the university, in Trilling's view, rightly embodies. Trilling's illustration is Joseph Conrad's *Heart of Darkness*, in which Marlow interprets the horror of Kurtz's 'unnameable acts' in the Congo as marking the difference between the ordinary person and the artist. The artist prefers to mine 'that hell which is the historical beginning of the human soul', rather than acquiesce to the bland lies of the civilization that has overlaid it.'[4]

In the Preface to *Beyond Culture* Trilling explains what has been worrying him. The dramatic expansion of higher education has meant many more people going around believing in and, worse, acting upon, modern literature's 'actually subversive intention . . . of detaching the reader from the habits of thought and feeling that the larger culture imposes' (p. 12). Removed from its personal, private encounter with the older, educated reader whom Trilling has in mind, and to whom modernism brings knowledge of the human condition (and therefore social responsibility), the 'adversary culture' encourages the transgression of limits and the cultivation of experience.

These troubled thoughts helped to crystallize a neo-conservative reaction against modernism which has accompanied the rightward move of a number of the New York Intellectuals. A decade after Trilling, Bell incorporated the idea of 'mass modernism' into an attack on 'the sensibility of the sixties' (at the time Trilling was writing, Bell was still defending modernism as the last bastion of cultural freedom against the threat of totalitarianism):

> In the cry for the autonomy of the aesthetic, there arose the idea
> that experience in and of itself was the supreme value, that
> everything was to be explored, anything was to be permitted – at
> least to the imagination, if not acted out in life. In the
> legitimation of action, the pendulum had swung to the side of
> release, away from restraint.
>
> Modernism has thus been the seducer. (*Cultural Contradictions of Capitalism*, p. 19)

Bell received support for this strand of the end of culture debate from many sources, including the artist and art critic, Suzi Gablik, in her 1984 polemic, *Has Modernism Failed?* Among Gablik's illustrations of the extremity of late modernism are Chris Burden's *Transfixed* (1974) and the performances in New York City of Tehching Hsieh. Gablik quotes Burden's description of *Transfixed*:

> Inside a small garage on Speedway Avenue . . . I stood on the
> rear bumper of a Volkswagen. I lay on my back over the rear
> section of the car, stretching my arms onto the roof. Nails were
> driven through my palms into the roof of the car. The garage
> door was opened and the car was pushed half-way out into
> Speedway. The engine was run at full speed for two minutes.
> Then it was turned off, and the car was pushed back into the
> garage. The door was closed.[5]

The nails were later sold on the New York art market. Gablik does not comment upon what, if any, financial rewards Tehching Hsieh received when he stayed outdoors for the whole of 1981.

Gablik's thesis is that the innovative logic of modernism has come to resemble the drive to product differentiation in capitalism. Modern art also shares a 'bureaucratic megastructure' with capitalism that would have astounded even Max Weber. In 1945, when the Abstract Expressionists were getting going, Marcel Duchamp's estimate of the audience for modern art was 'maybe ten in New York and one or two in New Jersey'. At time of writing, Gablik reports 'a two-billion-dollar-a-year art market in New York City alone, and . . . 14,000 artists with gallery affiliations' (pp. 13 and 12).

The question, What is art?, which Chris Burden posed when he had himself nailed to a VW, can only be answered if we have 'values that resist change' (p. 116). Scanning the current debate over modernity, it is apparent that commentators working in other spheres have reached a similar conclusion to Gablik: what we need is *community*, meaning a consensus of opinion capable of resisting the 'retreat into privatism and self-expression' (p. 118), with its contradictory relationship to a capitalism which can find unusual value in a few nails. Such a community would say 'No' to Burden, and to sculptor, Walter de Maria's one-kilometre deep hole in the ground, which was covered over so that it cannot be seen. (To indicate that I am paraphrasing an argument, rather than necessarily agreeing with it, I should say I have heard one of my students give an entirely convincing explanation of why de Maria's hole in the ground is his favourite work of art.)

Revisionism – the feeling in Gablik's art criticism that things have gone too far – is pervasive in discussions of the end of modern culture. Quite correctly, Martin Marty identifies the new mood with a resurgence of religion in America. We shall be concerned with what Marty calls the 'diffusion' of religion, rather than the evangelical revolution that has taken people from the pews to the polls.[6] The evidence for a new paradigm is considerable. Over twenty years and three books (*The Making of a Counter-Culture*, 1969, *Where the Wasteland Ends*, 1973, and *The Cult of Information*, 1988), Theodore Roszak has looked away from the technocracy to the transcendent realm of 1960s youth culture. As we have seen, twenty years after declaring the end of all ideology, including messianic religion, Daniel Bell looked towards the old certainties and 'The Meaning of the Sacred' in *The Cultural Contradictions of Capitalism* and *The Winding Passage* (1981). Another leading sociologist, Peter Berger, has continued working in the Weber tradition but in search of re-enchantment; witness his *A Rumour of Angels: Modern Society and the Rediscovery of the Supernatural* (1969). However, one of the most interesting instances of the revival of religion in intellectual quarters thought to be thoroughly secularized, is the work of political and cultural commentator, Peter Clecak. In *America's Quest for the Ideal Self: Dissent and Fulfillment in the 60s and 70s* (1983), Clecak contests the orthodoxy that 'in the seventies . . . America allegedly deliquesced into a squalid time of personal "selfishness" (Tom Wolfe's "Me Decade"); "narcissism" (Christopher Lasch); "decadence" (Jim Hougan); political incoherence and political "reaction" (Henry Fairlie . . .).[7] On the (at least partial) rebound from his own socialism, Clecak identifies a 'a central cultural theme' which connected the supposed radicalism of the 1960s with the supposed reaction of the 1970s: 'a quest for personal fulfillment, a pursuit of a free, gratified, unalienated self within one or more communities of valued others' (p. 6). His renewed affection for liberal Christianity gives a direction to this 'quest' and a principle by which to interpret as 'salvation' the contemporary search for meaningful experience which Lasch denigrates as narcissism and the merely therapeutic. This quest incorporates alternative lifestyles, consumerism, political protest; it involves 'elements of the population as diverse as born-again Christians and atheistic feminists, gay-rights activists and red-neck males, mainline Protestants and hard-line conservatives' (p. 9).

It is an attractive argument in many ways and certainly makes a change from Lasch's doom-and-gloom and his overdetermined model of cultural conformity. Lasch seems to credit ordinary people with no desires that are not induced by the media. On the other hand, Clecak is far too reluctant to discriminate between desires; if nothing else gives pause for suspicion of his 'central cultural theme' then the diverse manifestations of the quest for personal fulfilment ought to: jogging, political activism by Marxist lesbians and religious revivalism? The freedoms of this broad church – America's 'civil religion', in Robert Bellah's phrase – are too generalized and fail to acknowledge the context of inequality and the fact that one group or individual's liberation is at the expense of, or at least compromises, others'. In a review of Clecak's book/quest, Richard Crockatt gets to the point of this and other accounts of what Clecak calls 'the wonderfully rich, albeit cacaphonic possibilities for personal expression and democratic action that marked American culture by the late seventies' (p. 31):

> Clecak has taken pluralism to its logical conclusion and ended up with an unrecognizable picture of the potential and actual conflicts within American society. In Clecak's America the barriers to self-fulfillment are provided more by carping critics than by the stubborn realities of power and economic circumstances. But it takes little reflection to see that the American political economy continues to dispense differential rewards to its citizens and that capitalism still marks the boundary within which social and political goals are pursued.

This surely is one of the continuities between the 60s and 70s which demands full consideration.[8]

Community is a key concept in all of this. Community is the location of genuine fulfilment, not just for Clecak but also, as we have noted, for other critics reacting against modernity. Yet community functions as universal – we all know what it means – at the same time as the diversity of community experience defines contemporary American life and signals its sites of conflict or its propensity to fragment into self-satisfied enclaves or outposts of resistance to the dominant culture. Any concept which, as Raymond Williams notes, 'seems never to be used unfavourably, and never to be given any positive opposing or distinguishing term' is capable of disguising deep social and economic divisions.[9] Community (but also 'the self') is also a concept which (as Clecak's book reveals) permits a response to America in the 1970s that simultaneously succeeds in criticizing modern culture from the point of view of traditional, communal and religious values while it describes the diffusion and difference which are the hallmarks of post-modern society.[10] Undoubtedly, religion and its relationship to community are once again high on the intellectual agenda and a vital, because contentious, part of the end of modern culture debate.

The triumph of the therapeutic: Philip Rieff

In rehearsing the current debates it is impossible to avoid the conclusion that the figure who was there first and who set the parameters of discussion is the neo-conservative sociologist, Philip Rieff. Readers of Rieff's first book, *Freud: The Mind of the Moralist* (1959), realize after a while that this is not just a very fine exposition of Freud. It is also a book about the end of modern culture, with a special American resonance. Rieff tells of visiting the church in Rome where Freud went to look at Michelangelo's Moses, the inspiration for *Moses and Monotheism*, in which Freud finally acknowledged his psychological membership of the Jewish community. Rieff, however, 'having had the American experience of detachment from all communities' saw Michelangelo's Moses and not Freud's Jewish (communal) Moses.[11] Rieff only gives himself over to the American connection in the final chapter, 'The Emergence of Psychological Man', though he analyses it at length in *The Triumph of the Therapeutic* (1966) and *Fellow Travellers* (1973).

The pace of modernization in the United States from the 1870s overwhelmed pre-modern communities but then, through the operation of the market, left individuals stranded. Marx talks about this alienated state through economics and a theory of ideology, and offers active commitment to a positive community in the making as a remedy. Freud steps in, where Marx is silent on private fears and turmoil, and diagnoses these individuals as 'unwell'. In ministering to their needs, however, Freud only succeeded in compounding the problems of individualism because he had no viable concept of community to tender to patients. Instead, he recommended analysis, which sought to buttress the ego and eventually detach the patient from the analyst. Concluding the above account, Rieff notes that the fee is part of the ethos of therapy because dependence, which, when mutual, is the woof and warp of any community, is made impersonal by the money that changes hands.

Under the influence of Freud, people are led away from the religious community as well as the secular community of socialists. A certain ironic attitude is fostered towards anything that is not the self, even if, in daily life, most people readily identify themselves as part of this (occupational) community or that (neighbourhood) community. However, therapy gives rein to the cultivation of what Freud tells us are the *real* relations: not Marx's socio-economic ones but those with the self. To accept Rieff's interpretation is not necessarily to reject Freud's aim of reconciling individuals with society. It is a matter of degree but, for Rieff, Freud has bequeathed such a fine, and finely tuned, methodology for learning more, that he has bred 'pedants of the inner life' (p. 329).

Since Rieff's account gets us quickly to the important relationship between individualism and community in modern and post-modern theory, we must, in fairness, acknowledge the other nine chapters and the three Prefaces in *Freud: The Mind of the Moralist*. Before he puts Freud into an American context, Rieff at least suggests that Freud's insights have not been entirely lost; in spite of the exertions of 'psychological man', who 'has talked Freud's sacred reticences into the prevailing profanation of candor' (p. xxiv). On the other hand, Rieff's Freud should not be confused with the Freud of the sexual radicals, Herbert Marcuse, Norman O. Brown and Wilhelm Reich, the Freud tapped for the wellsprings of a rebellion against the repressiveness of modern society. Rieff's Freud is the author of 'what is perhaps the most important body of thought committed to paper in the twentieth century', but he brings 'none of the consolations of philosophy or the hopes of religion' (p. x). All Rieff will gnomically add is that 'Freud's one small hope, reason . . . cannot save us, nothing can; but reason can mitigate the cruelty of living, or give sufficient reasons for not living' (p. xii). Freud has brought this sobering news and a means for coping with it. He has not, Rieff is adamant, supplied a way of transforming private knowledge into a politics. Rieff defines himself as a conservative thinker, who leaves Freud to deal with Marx. 'Freud recognized that in fact the silent vote of the psychic world had never been silent,' Rieff pointedly remarks (p. 345).

The final chapter of *Freud* and Rieff's next book consider the consequences for a whole society of this preoccupation with the self. 'In the emergent democracy of the sick', he witheringly observes, 'everyone can to some extent play doctor to others, and none is allowed the temerity to claim that he can definitively cure or be cured. The hospital is succeeding the church and the parliament as the archetypal institution of Western culture' (p. 355). Rieff was writing in advance of the 'Me' decade, as Tom Wolfe called the 1970s, and well before Christopher Lasch introduced 'the final product of bourgeois individualism', the 'new narcissist . . . haunted not by guilt but by anxiety'.[12] Rieff, as should be apparent, develops David Riesman's character types in *The Lonely Crowd*, and confirms that, whatever its European roots, the hegemony of therapeutic culture is at its most powerful in the metropolitan centres of the United States.

Most of the individual 'true stories' that Robert Bellah and his team collect in *Habits of the Heart* are similarly deficient in communal, public awareness. 'Brian Palmer', a successful Californian businessman, survives a divorce and reassesses his devotion to the work ethic: 'My [new] family life is more important to me . . . and the work will wait.' Bellah suspects that this is not enough:

> Despite the personal triumph Brian's life represents, despite the fulfillment he seems to experience, there is still something uncertain, something poignantly unresolved about his story . . . His new goal – devotion to marriage and children – seems as arbitrary and unexpected as his earlier pursuit of material success. Both are justified as idiosyncratic preference rather than as representing a larger sense of the purpose of life . . . When Brian describes how he has chosen to live . . . he keeps referring to 'values' and 'priorities' not justified by any wider framework of purpose or belief.[13]

Later, 'Brian' puts 'communication' at the top of his list of principles: 'Given open communication and the ability to think problems out, most problems can be solved' (p. 7). The authors of *Habits of the Heart* are sceptical, because there seems to be nothing over and above individual communication which will permit collectivities to coalesce. We can add in Rieff's remark that 'the analytic attitude is a doctrine developed for the private wants of men, and shifts with the individual.'[14] This makes commitment and communality difficult to achieve, though this is the stated hope of someone like Suzi Gablik: 'It is only as individuals that we can find the way back to communal purposes and social obligation – and reconstitute the moral will' (p. 127).

The problem, though, is that even if communication gets started, frequently it peters out. Castoriades says as much, in discussion with Lasch, when he makes the cryptic observation that 'society, essentially, has no address. You can't meet it.' There is no common language, least of all, Castoriades and Lasch agree, a common language of protest: blacks, women and any victimized group insisted one by one, that no one could represent them. Formerly, public projects with a common language and a totalizing narrative, had animated lots of people beyond the politics of the next election. Current voter apathy in the USA (just over 51 per cent voted in the Bush/Dukakis election of 1988) suggests that even a Presidential election fails to mobilize and direct interest.

Questions of communication or lack of it have raised questions about narrative. Philip Rieff reports 'a major question about the motor by which new purposive energies might be generated' (*Triumph of the Therapeutic*, p. 237). Traditional, pre-modern cultures tended not to ask Where next?, while modern cultures have usually had confidence in different kinds of narratives of progress and in their respective motor forces. But in many late- or post-modern narratives, including the narrative of an election campaign or an administration, our attention is on spectacle and isolated, constructed, scenes rather than on progression. More colloquially, there is talk of not going anywhere, of a 'windless' quality, akin to being permanently in a vast shopping mall. Or a library, since the compulsive rewriting and beginning over (and over) again in the post-modernist fiction of John Barth, Donald Barthelme, Robert Coover, and Thomas Pynchon is a corrollary of the lack of narrative. There is movement, of course, but no change, only a constant circulation of signifiers and recycling of narratives, a process facilitated by computer technology.

While not using the word post-modernity, or its variants, Philip Rieff, too, describes, but does not pursue, the circularity of surface motion and blatant self-referentiality that we find explicitly foregrounded in the work of post-modernist writers:

> The therapy of all therapies is not to attach oneself exclusively to any particular therapy, so that no illusion may survive of some end beyond an intensely provate sense of well-being to be generated in the living of life itself. (p. 261)

Somehow or other, we have derived this interest in surfaces from Freud's knowledge of the depths. Rieff, a determined modernist, has arrived at a post-modernist insight.

Post-modernity: back to the future?

Habits of the Heart is set to become the *Middletown* of the late twentieth century, and while I would probably opt for one of Rieff's books rather than Lasch's, there is no doubt that *The Culture of Narcissism* also hit a nerve when it came out in 1979 and was reinforced by *The Minimal Self* in 1984. Clearly, then, Bellah, Lasch and Rieff, in particular, have written weighty analyses of where American culture has come out in the 1980s. And yet these commentators on the end of modernity present us with a profligacy of the emotions, which leaves us with a point of view from which vaguely to disapprove but not much else. They tend to look back – to community and unmediated communication, to nineteenth-century individualism, and to moral restraint. These metaphysical 'simples' are real, but lost or stranded on the other side of a great divide created by world events, technological inventions, and revolutions in modes of thinking. Of the intellectual divides, the most marked has been what Jacques Derrida has called, the structuralist 'event' when, in his words, 'language invaded the universal problematic'.[15]

We might get discussion moving again by examining some of the overlaps between the end of modernity and the post-modernity debate. It is not at all a coincidence that the self-obsessed 1970s and 1980s should have seen the release of a succession of 'retro' films which look back to the lost communities of 1950s small towns: *Back to the Future*, *Peggy Sue Got Married*, *Diner*, *American Graffiti*. Then there is the great success of Garrison Keillor's book and radio show, *Lake Wobegone Days* (1985), with its funny but oddly disturbing aside that 'Left to our own devices, we Wobegonians go straight for the small potatoes . . . We feel uneasy at momentous events.'[16] Community, it would seem, is now being constructed by, and in, the discourse of the very individualism which has superseded it. This lack of self-reflection extends to the search for community on the part of Lasch, Gablik and Bell. None of them accept post-modernity as a category to be analysed but, instead, treat it as modernity which has gone over the top. Suzi Gablik, for instance, reports a second act in the saga of Marcel Duchamp's *Fountain* (1917) when 'a urinal quite similar to Duchamp's was found, by chance, in Alaska, where it had been mysteriously abandoned in a woods [sic] sixty miles from the nearest highway' (p. 38). She objects to too much confusion of the boundaries between the standard dualisms of art and non art; self and society; nature and culture; and the past and the present.

If the title of the leading American journal of post-modernism – *Boundary 2* – is at all significant then we can expect a rephrasing of the end-of-modernity issue, along the lines of this portmanteau question:

What can possibly delimit an entity (the self, a historical period, a community, a politics), in a world of indeterminacy and in the absence of clearly defined boundaries; or, at least, in the absence of boundaries that might still repel invaders but not 'space invaders' or the free-flow of information? Something does seem to have changed and ought to be accounted for, rather than assuming we can only look back to a pre-modern world.

Todd Gitlin's post-modernist 'canon' contains some dubious candidates and unfortunate omissions, but has the kind of familiarity which suggests that in 1989 anyone interested in contemporary culture could easily give a rival 'run-down':

> 'Postmodernism' usually refers to a certain constellation of styles and tones in cultural works: pastiche; blankness; a sense of exhaustion; a mixture of levels, forms, styles; a relish for copies and repetition; a knowingness that dissolves commitment into irony; acute self-consciousness about the formal, constructed nature of the work; pleasure in the play of surfaces; a rejection of history. It is Michael Graves's Portland Building and Philip Johnson's AT & T, Rauschenberg's silkscreens and Warhol's Brillo Boxes; it is shopping malls, mirror glass facades, William Burroughs, Donald Barthelme, Monty Python, Don DeLillo, *Star Wars*, Spaulding Grey, David Byrne, Twyla Tharp, the Flying Karamazov Brothers, George Coates, Frederick Barthelme, Laurie Anderson, the Hyatt Regency, the Centre Pompidou, *The White Hotel*, *Less Than Zero*, Foucault, and Derrida; it is bricolage fashion, and remote-control-equipped viewers 'zapping' around the television dial.[17]

Gitlin refers to 'a rejection of history'. In post-modern architecture this means the rampant 'quoting' of history, which has the effect of displacing a building from its place, both its literal place in a city with a past and its place in architectural history. Where is it? would also be an apposite question to ask of David Lynch's film *Blue Velvet* (1986), which we discussed in Chapter 1. A re-make of a 'retro' film in its evocation of an innocent community of the 1950s, *Blue Velvet* effectively destroys any of our lingering innocence because we have been to the past in so many of the films that Lynch has raided for striking images. *Blue Velvet* is a cinematic version of the heterotopia which intrigues Michel Foucault in *The Order of Things* (1966), and which I referred to in the Preface to this book. David Byrne's *True Stories* (1986) also explores post-modern concepts of space in the traditional setting of a small community. Here, the economy of a small town depends on the giant computer corporation which has its offices just outside the town. The implication is that in the 1980s the limits or boundaries of such a contemporary community (very 1950s-ish in many ways) are the limits of a seemingly limitless system. Certainly, compared with the invisible communications of a global network, the mere roads that the David Byrne character keeps driving in the film are meaningless, neither going anywhere nor integrating the community.

We may see in the stories of *True Stories* and in the instances of inconclusive communication a connection with 'the post-modern condition', defined by the influential contemporary French theorist, Jean François Lyotard, as a loss of belief in the meta-narratives of Christianity, Marxism, science, and Western metaphysics in general. Effects are not explained so straightforwardly by causes. As Thomas Kuhn controversially argues in *The Structure of Scientific Revolutions* (1962), in the test-case of science as a cumulative narrative, there is no continuity between classical and quantum physics but, rather, a rupture in ways of thinking which we signal by the name 'Einstein'.

Lasch and others notwithstanding, it would seem, then, that there are still interesting things to talk about. However, the politics of the post-modern refusal of grand narratives or its interest in heterotopias are ambiguous. For example, in Chapter 5 we discussed the decline of radicalism as post-war American intellectuals lost faith in the grand narrative that Marx tells. Yet, far from restoring faith (or reason for that matter), the radical rewriting of history 'from the bottom up' which went on in the 1960s and 1970s only highlighted the deficiencies of totalizing narrative explanations, Marxist or otherwise. The very genre in which many younger historians chose to write – the local community study – implicitly contests any conclusive and comprehensive historical scheme. As historians dug deeper in local records in search of true origins to set off against the degeneration of the communal ideal, they found difference: one little place differed from another: a native American village from a slave community or an ethnic ghetto, and each came down to the present by a different historical route, marked out by a 'fall' into modernity.

Here, though, we can perhaps see some way of examining the claims of end-of-modernity and post-modernity theorists. On the reasonable assumption that community history is paradigmatic of other less specific quests for standards, the fact that each community fell into modernity at different times suggests that 'difference' is not that which separates a technological from a non-technological society, an inhuman from a human society, but comes whenever we, individually or as groups, enter the circuit of representations.[18] To this extent, the image of the fall, which pervades any number of small town stories, from those told by historians about Colonial New England, through the Lynds' *Middletown* to *Back to the Future*, is misleading, and in ways that, in our own time, bedevil critiques of modern times. A 'classic', and very pertinent, example is the most important blueprint for a community in America: John Winthrop's lay-sermon, 'A Modell of Christian Charity', delivered in 1630 and known as the 'City upon a Hill' speech. Examined closely, though, Winthrop's organic language of community is entangled with metaphors derived from the legal system, the marketplace and even the city, those modern institutions normally regarded as the antithesis of community life. This is not really surprising, because Puritanism was itself a surrogate community for people whose religious 'habits of the heart' were inescapably bound up with land sales, the expansion of domestic and international markets, and migrations from provincial villages to towns and cities, London especially. The 'where' of a seventeenth-century New England township was at once a potential source of stability (the community's sense of place) and of change: no place is nowhere, however utopian the project, but is connected with other places. Community is not a timeless ideal, just as modernization is not an undifferentiated and monolithic force. Community is an effect of a continuing, yet changing, relationship between the local and the general, with neither side of this unstable opposition 'given' in advance.[19]

It is because of this difficulty in decisively situating ourselves that the terms of debate have shifted away from the dichotomies of 'the modern' and 'the traditional' which dog the jeremiads of Lasch and Gablik. However, if traditional verities and established analytical concepts ('community', 'class', 'progress', 'truth' itself) are problematic, what would count as a post-modern politics? Can there be public projects or community, the latter understood by Robert Bellah *et al.* as 'commitment' and by Richard Rorty as 'solidarity'? The answers being given from within the post-modern condition are much more varied than we should expect from our already rather clichéd definitions of post-modernity (as 'lumberton', 'mall time', 'the funhouse', 'the literature of exhaustion', and so on). Also, the answers confirm that the debates cannot now be understood other than on a European/American axis.

Scratching where it does not itch: Richard Rorty

Instead of an absolute commitment to ends (the modern form of community), Jean-François Lyotard, as the leading international proponent of post-modernism, recommends that we look to means, to little or provisional narratives and to a self-reflexivity *vis-à-vis* communication. Asked to give truths in answer to a question, we are liable to tell stories about how we arrived at this truth. Frequently, the stories told in local language games are more interesting than the general truth, and Lyotard merely summarizes what many post-modernists affirm, that these scaled-down ambitions are worth defending: 'Most people have lost the nostalgia for the lost [grand] narrative. It in no way follows that they are reduced to barbarity.'[20]

In American culture, grand narratives seem to have faltered more noticeably than elsewhere, not least as a result of the apocalyptic events of the 1930s. These were theorized (in the main by Daniel Bell) as the end of theory and 'the exhaustion of utopia', a theme echoed by John Barth's post-modernist literary manifesto, 'The Literature of Exhaustion' (1968). Among the figures covered in this book, C. Wright Mills is probably the last to have told big stories – to the point that *The Power Elite* (1956) provoked accusations that he was paranoiac.

An American who is at quite the other extreme from Mills is Richard Rorty, ex-philosophy professor from Princeton, and currently professor of Humanities at Virginia. Students of literature might be aware of the ways in which American literary critics, like J. Hillis Miller, Geoffrey Hartman, and Paul de Man have extended and modified the deconstructive criticism of Jacques Derrida. In the broader context of post-modernity, the Yale School, as these critics are collectively known, is of less relevance than Richard Rorty's *Philosophy and the Mirror of Nature* (1979), *Consequences of Pragmatism* (1982) and *Contingency, Irony, and Solidarity* (1989). In the two latest books, especially, Rorty translates Derrida, Foucault and post-structuralist scepticism and historicism into an American idiom. When Rorty argues that what we have is not Truth but descriptions and re-descriptions of truth, we catch the affinity with Derrida's reinscription, and with literary post-modernism's re-telling of old stories.

In common with Lyotard, Rorty is happy enough to live with a plurality of narratives, none of which make grandiose claims to Truth. Legitimacy for these provisional narratives must be sought in more contingent structures. These structures are interpretative or discursive communities, where agreement can be reached on 'common purposes (for example, prediction and control of the behavior of atoms or people, equalizing life-chances, decreasing cruelty)'.[21] Instead of a universal standard against which to measure important proposals, Rorty is content with free and open discussion. Philosophers, of all people, ought to know that no one is going to agree on a universal standard, least of all if it has anything to do with 'the principle of subjectivity'. Echoing more famous post-structuralist pronouncements on the 'end of man' and the 'death of the subject', he goes on to designate subjectivity as 'just a side-show, something which an isolated order of priests devoted themselves to for a few hundred years, something which did not make much difference to the successes and failures of the European countries in realizing the hopes formulated by the Enlightenment'.[22]

Yet the French and American traditions are not entirely compatible, and it is Rorty who, at the end of the 1980s, is carrying the American banner. First, there is a difference of style, tone and tactics. This is Jacques Derrida giving a working definition of deconstruction in *Of Grammatology* (1967):

> Within the closure, by an oblique and always perilous movement, constantly risking falling back within what is being deconstructed, it is necessary to surround the critical concepts with a careful and thorough discourse – to mark the conditions, the medium and the limits of their effectiveness and to designate rigorously their intimate relationship to the machine whose deconstruction they permit.[23]

In comparison, Rorty completely lacks what verges on a modernist angst in Derrida, even as he confirms textuality and Lyotard's strictures on over-narratives:

> We need to make a distinction between the claim that the world is out there and the claim that truth is out there. To say that the world is out there, that it is not our creation, is to say, with common sense, that most things in space and time are the effects of causes which do not include human mental states. To say that truth is not out there is simply to say that where there are no sentences there is no truth, that sentences are elements of human languages, and that human languages are human creations.
> (*Contingency, Irony, and Solidarity*, pp. 4–5)

Rorty's relaxed manner antagonizes the French (and Francophiles), but also other highly theoretical European thinkers. Typically, he advises the Frankfurt School theorist, Jurgen Habermas, against 'scratching where it does not itch' (Bernstein (ed.), *Habermas and Modernity*, p. 164), and volunteers the heretical opinion that when we have negotiated the tortures of Foucault we find John Dewey waiting. Rorty is quite persuaded by Derrida's deconstruction of metaphysics, but he prefers the Pragmatist de-capitalizing of Truth. Following James and Dewey, therefore, he sees no profit in labouring the deconstructive point and simply advises intellectuals to forget the philosophical search for Truth and do more interesting things, like 'the humanities'.

In *Contingency, Irony, and Solidarity* there is more than a difference of style and tone between American and French post-modernist theory. The difference surfaces in connection with the idea of 'common purposes', the theme of community in a post-modern world which we have been intermittently following: 'I want to see these common purposes against the background of an increasing sense of the radical diversity of private purposes, of the radically poetic character of individual lives' (p. 67). It is in this private realm that Rorty welcomes the contribution of Derrida, and others, like Nietzsche and Heidegger, whom he calls ironists:

> As *public* philosophers they are at best useless and at worst dangerous, but I want to insist on the role they and others like them can play in accommodating the ironist's *private* sense of identity to her liberal hopes. All that is in question, however, is accommodation – not synthesis. My 'poeticized' culture is one which has given up the attempt to unite one's private ways of dealing with one's finitude and one's sense of obligation to other human beings. (p. 68)

Different varieties of post-modernism have their character types. The French or French-inspired one gives us the bricoleur, quoting from cultures present and past to create new configurations out of both the canonical texts and cultural detritus. Rorty's candidate is the liberal ironist, who:

> faces up to the contingency of his or her own most central beliefs and desires – someone sufficiently historicist and nominalist to have abandoned the idea that those central beliefs and desires refer back to something beyond the reach of time and chance', and someone who counts as an 'ungroundable' desire the 'hope that suffering will be diminished, that the humiliation of human beings by other human beings may cease.' (p. xv)

Rorty's liberal ironist accepts that the private and the public worlds do *not* have to be brought together. There is no metaphysical place where all of our subjectivities could meet and agree on an absolute answer to fundamental questions, such as 'Is it right to deliver n innocents over to be tortured to save the lives of m x n other innocents? If so, what are the values of n and m?' (p. xv). And yet, Rorty continues, to adopt an ironical attitude is not to forego the possibility of solidarity or community. He sketches a 'liberal utopia' or 'post-metaphysical culture' in which ironism is everywhere (p. xv):

> A liberal society is one which is content to call 'true' (or 'right' or 'just') whatever the outcome of undistorted communication happens to be, whatever view wins in a free and open encounter. This substitution amounts to dropping the image of a

preestablished harmony between the human subject and the object of knowledge, and thus to dropping the traditional epistemological-metaphysical problematic. (p. 67)

By way of clarification, I should say that the 'traditional epistemo-logical-metaphysical problematic' is the subject/object scheme to which someone like Lasch or Gablik adheres, but which post-modernism questions.

The connection between liberalism and anti-foundationalism is one that would be frowned upon by Derrida and Foucault. Yet this is Rorty's answer to many of the questions we have been posing, in particular, how to be committed while being persuaded that there is no absolute basis against which to measure commitment. William James and John Dewey gave 'consequences' as their answer and Rorty draws on them, while refining the idea of a *discussion* among interested and serious parties in which the participating self is only partly there: the doubts are kept private, while the self acts in public.

When concluding our account of the end of modernity debate, the sense was of a dead-end, allowing for variations between Lasch, Rieff, Gablik and Bellah. Rorty's is an alternative state-of-the-culture diagnosis, in which the loss of an essential (meta-physical) self has the reverse effect: it opens up possibilities. Rorty's is an attractive proposition, not least because it drops back, but not in a nostalgic manner, to two of the earlier figures we have considered, William James and John Dewey, and updates American liberalism on the way. There are, however, problems with Rorty's position and, in exploring them, we can formulate a third stopping point for this survey.

An initial difficulty lies in the behaviour of the ironic self. As described by Rorty this figure is far from private; indeed, s/he behaves rather like David Riesman's other-directed person, evincing a fear of being trapped in 'the vocabulary of any single book' (p. 81). Rorty's textual metaphor reminds us of his full acceptance of 'the linguistic turn' (his phrase) in philosophy, so it is hard to imagine how the distinction between private and public can be sustained when entities are acknowledged as linguistic through and through. 'Nothing is ever fully private', Castoriades remarks in his discussion with Lasch. 'Even when you dream, you have words, and these words you have borrowed from the English language . . . What we call individual is in a certain sense a social construct.' Rorty's anti-foundationalism ought to confirm, rather than reject this position.

Perhaps it is the association of the private with the 'poetic' which leads Rorty to think that the self can pick and choose among activities. His remarks on literature in *Contingency, Irony, and Solidarity* are flat-footed compared with the skill he demonstrates in negotiating philosophical arguments. Rorty seems to regard literature as the source of moral values overlooked by philosophy in its quest for truth. Derrida, too, brings literature to the attention of philosophy but for a different purpose (one that Rorty appears to accept in *Consequences of Pragmatism*), namely, that philosophy, like literature never gets beyond being a form of language.

A second problem is raised by what I take to be the most significant insight to come out of feminism, that the personal is political. For all Rorty's sensitivity (the ironist is self-consciously a 'she' in Rorty's text), the fenced-off private sphere has not, on the whole, been a source of much rest or self-development for women, as well as being the site of a good deal of pain. Irony might help, but not much. This example of women and the politics of private life complements Richard King's criticism that Rorty's 'separation of private morality from social and political morality depletes rather than enriches our vocabulary of "self-realization" *and* of "justice". No description of the self that neglects the *public* opportunities for self-realization can be considered adequate.'[24] In other words, the private must find its way out into the public world.

While Rorty's insights into the constructedness of community get us out of the cul-de-sac of pessimism created by Christopher Lasch's anti-modernism (and even more vehement anti-post-modernism), there is a curious lack of conflict in his contingent liberal community. Curious, that is, because conflict is implicit in his model of a society made up of communities each with their own small but important narratives. Rorty by-passes this danger by attaching his ideal of reasonable discussion to the one community whose ethnocentrism is, by definition, not going to be a problem:

> *We* have to start from where *we* are . . . What takes the curse off this ethnocentrism is not that the largest such group is 'humanity' or 'all rational beings' – no one, I have been claiming, *can* make *that* identification – but, rather, that it is the ethnocentrism of a 'we' ('we liberals') which is dedicated to enlarging itself, to creating an even larger and more variegated *ethnos*. It is the 'we' of the people who have been brought up to distrust ethnocentrism. (p. 198)

The good sense of Rorty's claim for toleration should be evident, but it ought to be measured against his admission in *Consequences of Pragmatism* that 'we should be more willing than we are to celebrate bourgeois capitalist society as the best polity actualized so far, while regretting that it is irrelevant to most of the problems of most of the population of the planet' (p. 210).

When Lyotard (more enthusiastically than Rorty) discards meta- or general narratives his objection is to the idea that a transcendent Truth lies at the end (or the origin) of the story. Yet the meta-narrative is not necessarily the Truth – it is the dominant discourse. Consequently, it is not at all a metaphysical question to ask how we relate the local to the general, the private to the public. It is a question of power.

A post-modernism of resistance/A post-modernism of reaction

The terrain of post-modernist politics and culture is treacherous. There are, for example, demonstrable similarities between Daniel Bell's and David Riesman's end-of-ideology, liberal, pluralist concept of politics, with its particular roots in the Cold War years, and the small narratives and cultural bricolage associated with post-modernism thirty years later. Riesman, as we noted in passing in an earlier chapter, anticipates the indeterminacy of post-modernism, and even employs the typically post-modern image of the labyrinthine web of social relations that must be traced and retraced in the absence of the Ariadne's thread of political commitment.

Undoubtedly, there is critical potential in Rorty's work, though his use of 'solidarity' is a sleight of hand, given his very particular understanding of community and the relationship between public and private. For others who want to remain critical of their society, who cannot fully relax and enjoy the release from seriousness that architect Philip Johnson prescribes, but who accept that there is no going back, not even to Marshall Berman's modernism, what would oppositional thinking consist of? What would a post-modern or textual politics be when there is no firm foundation upon which to base projects?

In answering these questions, a lot depends upon how we understand 'textuality', Jacques Derrida's 'il n'y a pas de hors-texte' (there is nothing outside of the text). The argument which Derrida formulates, in contra-distinction both to Rorty and the end-of-modernity critics, is that textuality is shorthand for our (human) situation in language. Representation is not what we have to get out of (back to real face-to-face presentation or an art that presented 'the real thing') but 'where' we are historically. I take this to be a key point in Edward Said's essay, 'Opponents, Audiences, Constituencies and Community', in Hal Foster's *Postmodern Culture*:

> No single explanation sending one back immediately to a single origin is adequate . . . There is no center, no inertly given and accepted authority, no fixed barriers ordering human history,

even though authority, order and distinction exist. The secular intellectual works to show the absence of divine originality and, on the other side, the complex presence of historical actuality.[25]

Far from textual politics being opposed to representation (as in 'the death of the author' notion), it recognizes the inescapability of language, and therefore the way that power relations are necessarily inscribed in representations, not least representations of minority groups and women. (This has, in any case, been the consistent message of the modernist avant-garde, dada in particular.) When Jean Baudrillard claims that 'the monopolistic stage [of capitalism] signifies less the monopoly of the means of production (which is never total) than the monopoly of the code', he allows for post-modernism to be considered as a critique of representation, rather than as a crisis of representation.[26] The crisis is in the monopoly of about 90 per cent of the collecting, processing and dissemination of the world's information by Western multinational conglomerates – IBM and AT & T in the lead – in a political climate of militant deregulation of state control.

It is in this context that Hal Foster refers in *Postmodern Culture* to the need for 'a post-modernism of resistance', which will contest the appropriation of the language of freedom. We have considered some examples in earlier chapters, but Foster's discrimination within post-modernism deserves to be quoted in its own right:

> In cultural politics today, a basic opposition exists between a
> post-modernism which seeks to deconstruct modernism and
> resist the status quo and a post-modernism which repudiates the
> former to celebrate the latter: a post-modernism of resistance and
> a post-modernism of reaction . . . A post-modernism of
> resistance . . . arises as a counter-practice not only to the official
> culture of modernism but also to the 'false normativity' of a
> reactionary post-modernism . . . A resistant post-modernism is
> concerned with a critical deconstruction of tradition, not an
> instrumental pastiche of pop- or pseudo-historical forms, with a
> critique of origins, not a return to them. (pp. xi–xii)

The 1960s are the sub-text of so many of the current debates. However, far from seeing them as a time of innocence (which we have now grown out of), we should see them as instigating a move towards the analysis of racism and sexism, rather than solely of civil rights, out of which has come what is now being recognized as a distinctive theoretical critique. For example, the analysis of racism in, say, the work of Cornel West and those critics whom he recommends, is precisely concerned with sites of discourse in Foucault's sense. The point is to reveal *conflicting* cultural discourses, not a plurality of interests. In contrast, the pluralism of Riesman's and Bell's veto group politics assumed an underlying consensus – if only a consensus that we were at the end of ideology, and that we could (and should) separate economics, politics and culture. 'I am a socialist in economics, a liberal in politics, and a conservative in culture', Bell announces in the 1978 Foreword to *The Cultural Contradictions of Capitalism* (p. xi). Any post-modernism which takes seriously a textual politics cannot respect a demarcation which would sanction the autonomy of these spheres, and which allows Bell to condemn post-modernism as the worst excesses of modernism, while providing the socio-economic analysis which supports the view that post-modernism is a different phase of culture.

The growth of an information or knowledge society with new linguistic sites at once 'embodies' post-modernity and makes the need for a critique of representation more urgent. As Herbert Schiller asks (in the title of a 1981 book), *Who Knows: Information in the Age of the Fortune 500* (1981). One answer is that, after 'disintermediation', 'the Big Bang' and *zaiteku* (the American, British and Japanese versions of this latest 'event'), it is multinational corporations who 'know'. Their possession of the requisite technology allows money to 'flow' across national boundaries, often with dramatic consequences for local economies and cultures. Access to the most recent technologies of communication is a political question. According to a 1985 Carnegie Report on international training programmes in I.T. run by American corporations, the target is the McLuhanite 'interdependent global community'. Quoting this phrase from the report, Herbert Schiller asks: 'Is it not remarkable how the language of cooperation and community is utilized to describe a process that might more truthfully be viewed as a blatant means of cultural indoctrination of service primarily to the national companies?'[27] In similar vein, a number of American critics joined Jacques Derrida in a special issue of *Diacritics* (1984) to argue that even the nuclear arms race – the most fundamental of issues – is arguably, the most textual.[28] Where common sense tells us that language describes pre-existing realities, a post-modernist theory of representation treats language as constituting those realities under ideological pressures.

Edward Said takes up the questions of expertise and centralization of knowledge – the latter occurring amidst apparent post-modern devolution and dispersal – which Lyotard, in the end, puts to one side. Said argues that 'the cult of expertise and professionalism, for example, has so restricted our scope of vision that a positive (as opposed to an implicit or passive) doctrine of non-interference among fields has set in' (Foster, *Postmodern Culture*, p. 136). Interestingly, for Said (and anyone interested in contextual analysis of literature and the arts), the genuine 'humanities' are not – as is sometimes thought – the repository of traditional values and canonical works, but are a form of activity which does not respect disciplinary expertise, and may therefore, in his word, 'interfere'.

Notes

1. Quoted from *Voices: Modernity and Its Discontents: The Culture of Narcissism* (Channel 4, 1985).

2. Richard Rorty, *Consequences of Pragmatism (Essays: 1972–1980)* (Minneapolis, 1982), p. 66.

3. Daniel Bell, 'Foreword: 1978', in his *The Cultural Contradictions of Capitalism* (1979), p. xxi.

4. Lionel Trilling, *Beyond Culture: Essays on Literature and Learning* (Harmondsworth, 1967), pp. 23 and 33.

5. Suzi Gablik, *Has Modernism Failed?* (1984), p. 49.

6. See Martin E. Marty, 'Religion in America Since Mid-Century', *Daedalus*, 111 (Winter 1982), pp. 149–63; and Robert N. Bellah, 'Civil Religion in America', reprinted in his *Beyond Belief: Essays on Religion in a Post-Traditional World* (New York, 1970), pp. 168–89.

7. Peter Clecak, *America's Quest for the Ideal Self: Dissent and Fulfillment in the 60s and 70s* (New York, 1983), pp. 4–5.

8. Richard Crockatt, 'Salvation and Criticism in Contemporary America', *Over Here: An American Studies Journal*, 4 (Spring 1984), pp. 18–19. For a remarkable attempt to theorize the broader economic continuity between modernity and post-modernity, see David Harvey, *The Condition of Postmodernity: An Enquiry into the Origins of Cultural Change* (Oxford, 1989).

9. Raymond Williams, *Keywords: A Vocabulary of Culture and Society* (Glasgow, 1976), p. 66.

10. On community, see Frances Fitzgerald, *Cities on a Hill: A Journey Through Contemporary American Cultures* (1986); and Charles H. Reynolds and Ralph V. Norman (eds), *Community in America: The Challenge of 'Habits of the Heart'* (Berkeley, 1988). For the way that anti-modernism helped to manage an earlier paradigm shift, see T.J. Jackson Lears, *No Place of Grace: Antimodernism and the Transformation of American Culture, 1880–1920* (New York, 1981).

11. Philip Rieff, *Freud: The Mind of the Moralist* (Chicago, 1979), p. xx.

12. Christopher Lasch, *The Culture of Narcissism: American Life in an Age of Diminishing Expectations* (1980), p. xvi.

13. Robert N. Bellah, Richard Madsen, William M. Sullivan, Ann Swidler, and Steven M. Tipton, *Habits of the Heart: Individualism and Commitment in American Life* (Berkeley, 1985), pp. 3, 5 and 6.

14. Philip Rieff, *The Triumph of the Therapeutic: Uses of Faith after Freud* (Chicago, 1987), p. 50.

15. Jacques Derrida, *Writing and Difference*, translated by Alan Bass (1978), pp. 278 and 280.

16. Garrison Keillor, *Lake Wobegone Days* (1985), p. 7.

17. Todd Gitlin, 'Postmodernism: Roots and Politics', in *Cultural Politics in Contemporary America*, edited by Ian Angus and Sut Jhally (1989), pp. 347–8.

18. For a comparable argument in literary theory, see Frank Kermode, *Romantic Image* (1971), ch. 8.

19. In his influential study of Colonial America, *A New England Town: The First Hundred Years, Dedham, Massachusetts, 1636–1736* (New York, 1970), Kenneth A. Lockridge sets a pattern in community studies by missing the point about the 'fall' into modernity.

20. Jean-François Lyotard, *The Postmodern Condition: A Report On Knowledge*, translated by Geoff Bennington and Brian Massumi (Manchester, 1984).

21. Richard Rorty, *Contingency, Irony, and Solidarity* (Cambridge, 1989), p. 67.

22. Richard Rorty, 'Habermas and Lyotard on Postmodernity', in *Habermas and Modernity*, edited by Richard J. Bernstein (Oxford, 1987), p. 171.

23. Jacques Derrida, *Of Grammatology*, translated by Gayatri Chakravorty Spivak (Baltimore, 1976), p. 14.

24. Richard H. King, 'Self-Realization and Solidarity: Rorty and the Judging Self', in *Pragmatism's Freud*, edited by J. Smith and W. Kerrigan (Baltimore, 1986), p. 40.

25. Edward W. Said, 'Opponents, Audiences, Constituencies and Community', in *Postmodern Culture*, edited by Hal Foster (1985), pp. 145–6.

26. Jean Baudrillard, *The Mirror of Production*, translated by Mark Poster (St Louis, 1975), p. 127.

27. Herbert I. Schiller, 'The Privatization and Transnationalization of Culture', in *Cultural Politics in Contemporary America*, edited by Ian Angus and Sut Jhally (1989), p. 320.

28. See *Diacritics*, 14, 2 (1984) and Ben Taylor, 'Nukespeak: Better Read than Dead', *Over Here: Reviews in American Studies*, 9, 1 (1989), pp. 47–55.

Chronology

Key: d = drama, f = fiction, p = poetry

DATE	POETRY, DRAMA, FICTION	OTHER 'WORKS'	HISTORICAL/CULTURAL EVENTS
1890	Howells *A Hazard of New Fortunes* (f)	W. James *Principles of Psychology* Riis *How the Other Half Lives* Mahan *The Influence of Sea Power upon History* Sullivan Wainwright building, St Louis – 1891	Disenfranchisement of blacks – 1898 Ellis Island opens Frontier officially closes
1891	Whitman *Leaves of Grass* ('deathbed' edition) (p) Garland *Main-Travelled Roads* (f)	Burnham and Root Monadnock building, Chicago (completed 1891)	Development of the Kinetoscope Private Viewer – 1894
1892	Gilman *Yellow Wallpaper* (f)	Page *The Old South*	Homestead Steel strike Grover Cleveland elected president Populist Party formed
1893	Crane *Maggie* (f)	Turner *The Significance of the*	Chicago World's Fair

DATE	POETRY, DRAMA, FICTION	OTHER 'WORKS'	HISTORICAL/CULTURAL EVENTS
		Frontier in American History Wright Winslow house, Illinois – 1894	
1894	Howells *Traveller from Altruria* (f) Twain *Pudd'nhead Wilson* (f)	Lloyd *Wealth Against Commonwealth* Adler and Sullivan Guaranty building, Buffalo – 1895 Burnham (Atwood) Reliance building, Chicago – 1895	Sears Roebuck mail-order begins Pullman strike ended by federal troops
1895	Crane *Red Badge of Courage* (f)	Washington Atlanta *Address*	Lumières' first public showing of Cinématographe, Paris *Variety* founded
1896	Jewett *Country of the Pointed Firs* (f) Cahan *Yekl* (f)	Sullivan *The Tall Office Building Artistically Considered*	Edison's large screen exhibition, Koster and Bial's Music Hall, NYC *Plessy vs Ferguson* ('separate but equal' decision) McKinley elected president
1897	H. James *What Maisie Knew* (f)	W. James *The Will to Believe*	Klondike Gold Rush Boston subway completed
1898	H. James *The Turn of the Screw* (f)	Gilman *Women and Economics*	Spanish–American War
1899	Chopin *The Awakening* (f) Norris *McTeague* (f)	Veblen *Theory of the Leisure Class* Shinn	Treaty of Paris (Philippines, Guam and Puerto Rico to US)

DATE	POETRY, DRAMA, FICTION	OTHER 'WORKS'	HISTORICAL/CULTURAL EVENTS
		Sixth Avenue Elevated after Midnight	
		Sullivan Carson, Pirie, Scott store, Chicago – 1904	
		Dewey *The School and Society*	
1900	Dreiser *Sister Carrie* (f)	Wright Willets house, Highland Park, Illinois – 1902 Roosevelt *The Strenuous Life*	McKinley re-elected president 8 million immigrants arrive – 1910 8000 automobiles registered
1901	Norris *The Octopus* (f)	Washington *Up from Slavery* Wright *The Art and Craft of the Machine* (lecture) Royce *The World and the Individual*	McKinley assassinated T. Roosevelt becomes president Debs's Socialist Party formed First transatlantic radio signal
1902	H. James *Wings of the Dove* (f) Wister *The Virginian* (f)	Hapgood *Spirit of the Ghetto* W. James *Varieties of Religious Experiences*	Pacific cable completed First radio message
1903	H. James *Ambassadors* (f) Norris *The Pit* (f)	DuBois *Souls of Black Folk* Porter *The Great Train Robbery*	Ford Motor Company formed First World Series Wright brothers' flight
1904	H. James *Golden Bowl* (f)	Wright Larkin building, Buffalo Steffens *Shame of the Cities*	Roosevelt elected president New York subway opened

DATE	POETRY, DRAMA, FICTION	OTHER 'WORKS'	HISTORICAL/CULTURAL EVENTS
		Weber *Protestant Ethic and Spirit of Capitalism* Veblen *Theory of Business Enterprise*	
1905	Wharton *House of Mirth* (f)		Niagara movement IWW formed
1906	Sinclair *The Jungle* (f)		San Francisco earthquake
1907	London *The Iron Heel* (f)	Adams *Education of Henry Adams* W. James *Pragmatism* Rauschenbusch *Christianity and Social Crisis* H. James *The American Scene* Bellows *Stag at Sharkey's* Sloan *The Wake of the Ferry*	Immigration at its highest: 1,285,000
1908			The Eight's exhibition, New York City Gallery 291 exhibition Taft elected president First nickelodeon
1909	Stein *Three Lives* (f)	Wright Robie house, Chicago Croly *Promise of American Life* W. James *Pluralistic Universe*	NAACP founded Freud's visit to US

DATE	POETRY, DRAMA, FICTION	OTHER 'WORKS'	HISTORICAL/CULTURAL EVENTS
		Burnham and Bennett *Plan of Chicago*	
1910		Addams *Twenty Years at Hull-House*	First Model T Ford marketed
		Marin *Brooklyn Bridge*	
1911	Wharton *Ethan Frome* (f)	Taylor *Scientific Management*	*Masses* founded
		Gilbert Woolworth building, New York City – 1913	
		Sennett First Keystone Cops comedy	
1912	Dreiser *The Financier* (f)	Robinson *The New History*	Roosevelt runs for president on Progressive ticket
	Antin *The Promised Land* (f)	Sloan *Six-O'Clock Winter*	Wilson elected president Debs polls nearly a million votes
		Bellow *The Cliff Dwellers*	Warner Bros and Fox studios founded US troops enter Cuba
		Duchamp *Nude Descending a Staircase, No. 2*	US troops occupy Nicaragua Lawrence, Mass. strike
		Johnson *Autobiography of an Ex-Colored Man*	*Poetry* founded *Masses* (Eastman as editor)
1913	Cather *O Pioneers* (f)	Stella *Battle of Lights, Coney Island*	The Armory Show Patterson, NJ, strike First moving assembly line at Ford
		Lippmann *Preface to Politics*	Federal Income Tax
		Wilson *The New Freedom*	

DATE	POETRY, DRAMA, FICTION	OTHER 'WORKS'	HISTORICAL/CULTURAL EVENTS
		Eastman *Enjoyment of Poetry*	
		Bourne *Youth and Life*	
		Santayana *Winds of Doctrine*	
		Beard *An Economic Interpretation of the Constitution*	
1914	Frost *North of Boston* (p) Stein *Tender Buttons* (f)	Wright Midway Gardens, Chicago *Des Imagistes* Lippmann *Drift and Mastery* Reed *Insurgent Mexico* Veblen *Instinct of Workmanship*	First World War begins *New Republic* founded Garvey's UNIA formed Margaret Sanger indicted and forced to leave US for sending birth control information through the mail US troops invade Mexico Panama Canal opened
1915	Masters *Spoon River Anthology* (p) Gilman *Herland* (f)	Griffith *Birth of a Nation* Chaplin *The Tramp* Weber *New York at Night Rush-Hour, New York* V.W. Brooks *America's Coming of Age* Lindsay *The Art of the Motion Picture*	First transcontinental telephone Provincetown Players Lusitania sunk Great migration of blacks to Northern cities – 1920
1916	Twain *Mysterious Stranger* (f)	Griffith *Intolerance* Bourne *Gary Schools*	*Seven Arts* founded – 1917 Women's Party formed Wilson re-elected president on peace

DATE	POETRY, DRAMA, FICTION	OTHER 'WORKS'	HISTORICAL/CULTURAL EVENTS
		Dewey *Democracy and Education*	programme Pancho Villa attacks US US invades Mexico National Defense Act Peak of 245,000 miles of railroad
1917	Eliot *The Love Song of J. Alfred Prufrock* (p) Cahan *The Rise of David Levinsky* (f) O'Neill *The Long Voyage Home* (d)	Stella *Brooklyn Bridge* Duchamp *Fountain* Rauschenbusch *A Theology for the Social Gospel* Bourne *War and the Intellectuals* Mencken *A Book of Prefaces*	US enters First World War Bolshevik Revolution Race riots, East St Louis, Illinois Espionage Act Eighteenth Amendment (Prohibition) *The Liberator* founded Independents exhibition, New York City
1918	Cather *My Antonia* (f) Tarkington *Magnificent Ambersons* (f)		First World War ends Sedition Act Debs imprisoned for violating Espionage Act *Masses* ceases publication
1919	Anderson *Winesburg, Ohio* (f)	Duchamp *L.H.O.O.Q.* Reed *Ten Days that Shook the World*	Bauhaus founded in Weimar Versailles Peace Conference/League of Nations Race Riots, Chicago CPUSA formed Volstead Act enforces Prohibition First tabloid newspaper
1920	Lewis *Main Street* (f) Anderson *Poor White* (f)	Dewey *Reconstruction in Philosophy* Marin *Lower Manhattan*	Nineteenth Amendment Votes for women Palmer Raids and Red Scare

DATE	POETRY, DRAMA, FICTION	OTHER 'WORKS'	HISTORICAL/CULTURAL EVENTS
	Wharton *Age of Innocence* (f)		Harding elected president
	Fitzgerald *This Side of Paradise* (f)		First commercial broadcasting from Pittsburgh station
	Dell *Mooncalf* (f)		
	O'Neill *The Emperor Jones* (d)		
	Pound *Hugh Selwyn Mauberly* (p)		
1921	Dos Passos *Three Soldiers* (f)	Chaplin *The Kid*	Sacco and Vanzetti trial Immigration quotas set
	O'Neill *The Hairy Ape* (d)	Davis *Lucky Strike*	Federal Highway Act *Broom* founded
1922	cummings *The Enormous Room* (f)	Flaherty *Nanook of the North*	Creation of USSR Mussolini becomes dictator
	Lewis *Babbitt* (f)	Marin *Lower Manhattan (Composing Derived from Top of Woolworth)*	*Chicago Tribune* competition *The Fugitive* founded
	Eliot *The Waste Land* (p)		*Secession* founded
	O'Neill *Hairy Ape* (d)	Stearns *Civilization in the United States*	
		Dewey *Human Nature and Conduct*	
1923	Cather *A Lost Lady* (f)	Cruz *The Covered Wagon*	Harding dies Coolidge becomes president
	Toomer *Cane* (f)		Height of Ku Klux Klan activity
	W.C. Williams *Spring and All* (p)		*Time* founded *Reader's Digest* founded
	Stevens *Harmonium* (p)		
	cummings *Tulips and Chimneys* (p)		

DATE	POETRY, DRAMA, FICTION	OTHER 'WORKS'	HISTORICAL/CULTURAL EVENTS
1924	Melville *Billy Budd* (f) O'Neill *Desire Under the Elms* (d)	Ford *The Iron Horse* Rosenfeld *Port of New York* Sullivan *Autobiography of an Idea* Mumford *Sticks and Stones* Bellows *Dempsey and Firpo*	New immigration quotas Coolidge elected president LaFollette defeated on Progressive ticket Columbia Pictures formed Soviet Constitution adopted Hoover appointed head FBI Lenin dies
1925	Anderson *Dark Laughter* (f) Cather *Professor's House* (f) Dos Passos *Manhattan Transfer* (f) Dreiser *American Tragedy* (f) Fitzgerald *Great Gatsby* (f) Glasgow *Barren Ground* (f) Pound *Cantos* (p) Stein *The Making of Americans* (f) Hemingway *In Our Time* (f)	Locke *The New Negro* W.C. Williams *In the American Grain* Von Stroheim *Greed* Hart *Tumbleweed* Vidor *The Big Parade*	Scopes Trial KKK membership 3 million
1926	Hughes *The Weary Blues* (p) Faulkner *Soldiers' Pay* (f) Hemingway *Sun Also Rises* (f) Van Vechten *Nigger Heaven* (f)	Warner Bros *Don Juan* O'Keeffe *Red Poppy* *Black Iris* Mumford *The Golden Day*	Vitaphone premier NBC founded Rudolph Valentino dies *New Masses* founded

DATE	POETRY, DRAMA, FICTION	OTHER 'WORKS'	HISTORICAL/CULTURAL EVENTS
1927	Cather *Death Comes for the Archbishop* (f)	Keaton *The General*	Sacco and Vanzetti executed
		Al Jolson in *The Jazz Singer*	Lindbergh's flight from New York to Paris
	Hemingway *Men Without Women* (f)	Dewey *The Public and its Problems*	Marcus Garvey deported
	Rolvaag *Giants in the Earth* (f)		Federal Radio Commission
		Parrington *Main Currents in American Thought Vol. 3*	Babe Ruth hits sixty home runs
			transition founded
		Eastman *Marx and Lenin*	*Hound and Horn* founded
		Murnau *Sunrise*	
1928	McKay *Home to Harlem* (f)	Mead *Coming of Age in Samoa*	Hoover elected president
			RKO formed
		Disney First Mickey Mouse cartoon	Trotsky exiled
			Rise of Stalin
		Von Stroheim *Wedding March*	First television broadcast
1929	Faulkner *Sound and Fury* (f)	Lynds *Middletown*	Stock Market Crash
			MOMA formed
	Hemingway *Farewell to Arms* (f)	Ferriss *Metropolis of Tomorrow*	John Reed Clubs started
			Stalin's Five Year Plan
	Wolfe *Look Homeward Angel* (f)	Shreve, Lamb and Harmon Empire State building	
		Dewey *Individualism, Old and New*	
		Hopper *Chop Suey*	
		Krutch *The Modern Temper*	

DATE	POETRY, DRAMA, FICTION	OTHER 'WORKS'	HISTORICAL/CULTURAL EVENTS
1930	Dos Passos *42nd Parallel* (f) Faulkner *As I Lay Dying* (f) Gold *Jews Without Money* (f) Porter *Flowering Judas* (f) Crane *The Bridge* (p) Eliot *Ash Wednesday* (p) Hammett *Maltese Falcon* (f) Pound *Cantos* (cont.) (p)	O'Keefe *Black Hollyhock, BLue Larkspur* Twelve Southerners *I'll Take My Stand* Sheeler *Classic Landscape* Benton *City Scenes* Wood *American Gothic* *Stone City, Iowa* Hopper *Early Sunday Morning* Hood Daily News building, New York City Van Allen Chrysler building, New York City Josephson *Portrait of the Artist as American*	*Four million Americans unemployed*
1931	Buck *The Good Earth* (f) Cather *Shadows on the Rock* (f) Faulkner *Sanctuary* (f) O'Neill *Mourning Becomes Electra* (d)	Hood Rockefeller Center project, New York City Mumford *Brown Decades* Wellman *Public Enemy* Chaplin *City Lights* Steffens *Autobiography* Wilson *Axel's Castle* Peirce *Collected Papers* – 1951	Scottsboro Affair

DATE	POETRY, DRAMA, FICTION	OTHER 'WORKS'	HISTORICAL/CULTURAL EVENTS
1932	Caldwell *Tobacco Road* (f) Dos Passos *1919* (f) Farrell *Young Lonigan* (f) Faulkner *Light in August* (f)	Hawks *Scarface* Davis *Men Without Women* *American Painting – 1951* Howe and Lescaze PSFS building, Philadelphia Hood McGraw-Hill building, New York City Niebuhr *Moral Man, Immoral Society*	Roosevelt elected president March of 'Bonus Army' on Washington DC Lindbergh kidnapping case MOMA 'International Style' exhibition Radio City Music Hall opened Ford Hunger March, Dearborn, Michigan Drought made Great Plains a 'dustbowl' – 1934
1933	West *Miss Lonelyhearts* (f) Stein *Autobiography of Alice B. Toklas* (f)	Hook *Towards an Understanding of Karl Marx* Cooper and Schoedsack *King Kong* Marx Brothers *Duck Soup*	First New Deal – 1935 'Roosevelt's Hundred Days' Agricultural Adjustment Act National Industrial Recovery Act Public Works Administration National Recovery Administration Tennessee Valley Authority Federal Economy Act Federal Arts Projects begin Roosevelt's first 'fireside chat' Hitler chancellor Bauhaus closed by Nazis Chicago World's Fair Thirteen million Americans unemployed Twenty-first Amendment: Repeals Prohibition Black Mountain College opens

DATE	POETRY, DRAMA, FICTION	OTHER 'WORKS'	HISTORICAL/CULTURAL EVENTS
1934	Farrell *Young Manhood of Studs Lonigan* (f) Fitzgerald *Tender is the Night* (f) Miller *Tropic of Cancer* (f) Cain *The Postman Always Rings Twice* (f) H. Roth *Call It Sleep* (f)	Mumford *Technics and Civilization* Kastner and Stonorov Carl Mackley houses, Philadelphia Cowley *Exile's Return* Niebuhr *Reflections on the End of an Era* Capra *It Happened One Night*	DuBois resigns from NAACP Huey Long's Share Our Wealth Society established Catholic Legion of Decency begins film censorship John Dillinger shot Moscow Trials – 1938 *Partisan Review* founded
1935	Steinbeck *Tortilla Flat* (f) Wolfe *Of Time and the River* (f) Rukeyser *Theory of Flight* (p) Odets *Waiting for Lefty* (d) Moore *Selected Poems* (p) *An Objectivist Anthology* (p) Farrell *Studs Lonigan* (f)	Wright Kaufmann house, Conn. Broadacre City (plans) Dewey *Liberalism and Social Action* DuBois *Black Reconstruction in America* Hicks *et al.*, (eds) *Proletarian Literature in the United States* Gilman *Living of Charlotte Perkins Gilman* Marx Brothers *A Night at the Opera*	First American Writers' Congress League of American Writers Seventh World Congress of the Comintern Second New Deal – 1938 Wagner Act Social Security Act Wealth Tax Committee on Industrial Organization (CIO) formed Huey Long assassinated Italy invades Ethiopia Popular Front announced
1936	Dos Passos *The Big Money* (f) Faulkner *Absalom, Absalom!* (f) Mitchell *Gone With the Wind* (f) Santayana *The Last Puritan* (f)	Chaplin *Modern Times* Capra *Mr Deeds Goes to Town* Wright Johnson Wax Building Racine, Wisc. – 1939	MOMA – Cubism and Abstract Art exhibition – 1937 MOMA – Fantastic Art, Dada, and Surrealism exhibition Roosevelt returned for second term as president Spanish Civil War – 1939

DATE	POETRY, DRAMA, FICTION	OTHER 'WORKS'	HISTORICAL/CULTURAL EVENTS
	Steinbeck *In Dubious Battle* (f)	Herbert Jacobs house, Madison	News of Moscow Trials
		Dodge *Movers and Shakers*	Hitler occupies Rhineland
		Freeman *An American Testament*	*Life* founded
		Benjamin *Work of Art in the Age of Mechanical Reproduction*	
		D. Carnegie *How to Win Friends and Influence People*	
1937	Hemingway *To Have and Have Not* (f) Steinbeck *Of Mice and Men* (f) Hurston *Their Eyes Were Watching God* (f)	Lynds *Middletown in Transition*	Mies and Gropius arrive in US Farm Security Administration United Auto Workers' sit-down strikes Japan invades China Second Writers' Congress *Partisan Review* re-launched
1938	Hemingway *The First Forty-nine Stories* (f) Wilder *Our Town* (d) Dos Passos *USA* (f) Tate *The Fathers* (f)	Mumford *The Culture of Cities* Davis *Swing Landscape* Ransom *The World's Body* Brooks and Warren *Understanding Poetry*	AFL expels CIO unions CIO reorganizes as Congress of Industrial Organization Munich conference 10.4 million Americans unemployed Welles's *War of the Worlds* broadcast Hitler's persecution of the Jews
1939	Steinbeck *Grapes of Wrath* (f) Hellman *The Little Foxes* (d) West *The Day of the Locust* (f)	Ford *Stagecoach* *Young Mr Lincoln* C. Brooks *Modern Poetry and the Tradition* Mies begins Illinois	Nazi-Soviet Pact Second World War begins Ernst, Matta, Dali, Masson, Breton begin arriving, New York City New York World's Fair

DATE	POETRY, DRAMA, FICTION	OTHER 'WORKS'	HISTORICAL/CULTURAL EVENTS
	Porter *Pale Horse, Pale Rider* (f) Chandler *The Big Sleep* (f)	Institute of Technology Campus Greenberg *Avant-Garde and Kitsch* Stone MOMA's new building Selznick (prod.) *Gone With the Wind* Fleming *Wizard of Oz*	MOMA retrospective for Bauhaus Soviet invasion of Poland and Finland – 1940
1940	Wright *Native Son* (f) Faulkner *The Hamlet* (f) Hemingway *For Whom the Bell Tolls* (f) McCullers *The Heart is a Lonely Hunter* (f) Wolfe *You Can't Go Home Again* (f) cummings *Fifty Poems* (p) Chandler *Farewell My Lovely* (f) LeSeuer *Salute to Spring* (f)	O'Keeffe *From the White Place* Ford *Grapes of Wrath* DuBois *Dusk of Dawn* Komarovsky *The Unemployed Man and his Family* Inman *In Woman's Defence* Hook *Reason, Social Myths and Democracy* Wilson *To the Finland Station* Rahv *Image and Idea* Chaplin *Great Dictator*	Smith Act Piet Mondrian comes to US Hitchcock comes to Hollywood Roosevelt elected president for the third time Germany conquers Norway, Denmark, Belgium, France, Holland and Luxembourg AXIS alliance formed American Artists' Congress endorses Soviet invasion of Finland; 17 members withdraw from AAC Ad Reinhardt and others leaflet spectators, and picket MOMA with banner: 'How modern is modern art?'
1941	McCullers *Reflections in a Golden Eye* (f)	Welles *Citizen Kane* Giedion *Space, Time and Architecture* Burnham *Managerial Revolution*	Germany invades USSR Pearl Harbor bombed by Japanese USA declares war on Japan Germany and Italy declare war on USA Arendt comes to USA

DATE	POETRY, DRAMA, FICTION	OTHER 'WORKS'	HISTORICAL/CULTURAL EVENTS
		Matthiessen *American Renaissance*	March on Washington Movement
		Marcuse *Reason and Revolution*	Lend-Lease Act Atlantic Charter meeting of Churchill and Roosevelt
		Agee and Evans *Let Us Now Praise Famous Men*	Manhattan Project begins
		Huston *The Maltese Falcon*	Hitler begins extermination of the Jews
		Ransom *The New Criticism*	
1942	Faulkner *Go Down, Moses* (f)	Hopper *Nighthawks*	Artists for Victory Exhibition, Metropolitan Museum, New York City
	Stevens *Notes Toward a Supreme Fiction* (p)	Wylie *Generation of Vipers*	Peggy Guggenheim's Art of this Century Gallery, New York City
		Kazin *On Native Grounds*	CORE formed War Manpower Commission
		Wilson *The Shock of Recognition*	110,000 Japanese–Americans interned on West Coast
			Battle of Midway
			First self-sustaining nuclear reaction
			Rothko's first solo exhibition, Artists' Gallery
			Duchamp establishes permanent residence in NYC
			Fall of Singapore
1943		Pollock *Mural*	Pollock's first solo exhibition at Art of this Century
		Gorky *Waterfall*	Soviets stop Germans at Stalingrad
		Wright Guggenheim Museum – 1959	California, Detroit and Harlem race riots
			'Big Three' at Teheran

DATE	POETRY, DRAMA, FICTION	OTHER 'WORKS'	HISTORICAL/CULTURAL EVENTS
		Brooks and Warren *Understanding Fiction* Curtiz *Casablanca* Hitchcock *Shadow of a Doubt*	
1944	Bellow *Dangling Man* (f) W.C. Williams *Paterson* – 1958 (p) L. Smith *Strange Fruit* (f) Porter *The Leaning Tower* (f)	Lang *The Woman in the Window* Belluschi *Equitable Savings and Loan building,* Portland – 1948 Adorno and Horkheimer *Dialectic of Enlightenment* de Kooning completes first Women series Niebuhr *The Children of Light and the Children of Darkness*	*Politics* founded Normandy invasion Roosevelt re-elected for fourth term as president Dumbarton Oaks conference GI Bill of Rights MOMA makes first purchase of Pollock and de Kooning
1945	T. Williams *Glass Menagerie* (d) Thurber *Thurber Carnival* (f) G. Brooks *A Street in Bronzeville* (p)		Roosevelt dies Truman becomes president Atomic bombs dropped on Hiroshima and Nagasaki Second World War ends Yalta conference Potsdam Conference UN founded Soviets install communist rule in Poland Discovery of horrors of the concentration camps Demobilization of twelve million GIs

DATE	POETRY, DRAMA, FICTION	OTHER 'WORKS'	HISTORICAL/CULTURAL EVENTS
1946	Warren *All the King's Men* (f)	Pollock *Eyes in the Heat* Spock *Baby and Child Care* Hawks *The Big Sleep* Wyler *The Best Years of Our Lives* Pollock begins all-over poured paintings Mills and Gerth *From Max Weber* Hopper *Approaching a City*	Popular Front ends American television begins broadcasting Churchill's 'iron curtain' speech Paris peace conference Betty Parsons opens gallery in New York City Beginning of baby boom
1947	Trilling *The Middle of the Journey* (f) T. Williams *Streetcar Named Desire* (d)	P. and P. Goodman *Communitas* Farnham and Lundberg *Modern Woman* Capra *It's a Wonderful Life* C. Brooks *A Well-Wrought Urn* Chaplin *Monsieur Verdoux*	HUAAC investigations of Hollywood Americans for Democratic Action formed Truman orders FBI to locate security risks CIA created Cold War begins Communist take-over in Hungary Kennan appeals for 'containment doctrine' National Security Act Truman Doctrine Construction of Levittown, New York
1948	Capote *Other Voices, Other Rooms* (f) Hawkes *The Cannibal* (f) Faulkner *Intruder in the Dust* (f) Mailer *The Naked and the Dead* (f)	Hawks *Red River* Gorer *The Americans* Hofstadter *American Political Tradition* Mills *New Men of Power*	Soviet coup in Czechoslovakia Marshall Plan approved Truman elected president State of Israel founded de Kooning first solo exhibition Gorki commits suicide MOMA buys its first de Kooning

DATE	POETRY, DRAMA, FICTION	OTHER 'WORKS'	HISTORICAL/CULTURAL EVENTS
	Pound *Cantos* (cont.) (p)	Fromm *Escape from Freedom*	Berlin airlift
		Newman *Onement I*	
		Hyman *The Armed Vision*	
		Kinsey *Sexual Behavior in the Human Male*	
		Giedion *Mechanization Takes Command*	
		Welles *Lady from Shanghai*	
1949	Miller *Death of a Salesman* (d)	Walsh *White Heat*	Mao's victory: PR China established
		Rothko *Number 22*	NATO established West Germany formed First Soviet atomic
		Mies Lake Shore Drive apartments, Chicago – 1951	bomb MOMA establishes Department of American Painting and
		Schlesinger *The Vital Center*	Sculpture Rauschenberg at Black Mountain College with Albers, Cage and Cunningham
1950	Olson *Projective Verse* (p)	Riesman *The Lonely Crowd*	Korean war begins – 1953
		de Kooning *Woman I* – 1952	McCarthy's speech in West Virginia
		Pollock *Mural on Indian Red Ground*	McCarran (internal security) Act passed in spite of Truman's veto
		Trilling *The Liberal Imagination*	Hiss convicted of perjury Sino–Soviet Treaty Newman's first solo
		Erikson *Childhood and Society*	exhibition MOMA, Whitney and Institute of
		Wilder *Sunset Boulevard*	Contemporary Art

DATE	POETRY, DRAMA, FICTION	OTHER 'WORKS'	HISTORICAL/CULTURAL EVENTS
		Wright Johnson Wax Tower	reject 'the assumption that art which is esthetically an innovation must somehow be socially or politically subversive, and therefore un-American' Congress for Cultural Freedom, West Berlin
1951	Salinger *The Catcher in the Rye* (f) Jones *From Here to Eternity* (f) Styron *Lie Down in Darkness* (f)	Newman *Adam* Arendt *Origins of Totalitarianism* SOM Lever House, New York City – 1952 Mills *White Collar* Kennan *American Diplomacy*	American Committee for Cultural Freedom DuBois tried for treason Rauschenberg's first solo exhibition
1952	Ellison *Invisible Man* (f) Hemingway *The Old Man and the Sea* (f) O'Connor *Wise Blood* (f)	Kazin *A Walker in the City* Niebuhr *The Irony of American History* Galbraith *American Capitalism* Zinneman *High Noon* Rosenberg *American Action Painting* Peale *The Power of Positive Thinking*	First US hydrogen bomb *Partisan Review* symposium: 'Our Country and Our Culture' Eastman colour introduced Eisenhower elected president Warhol's first solo exhibition, New York City
1953	Miller *The Crucible* (d)	Rauschenberg *Erased de Kooning Drawing*	First Soviet hydrogen bomb

DATE	POETRY, DRAMA, FICTION	OTHER 'WORKS'	HISTORICAL/CULTURAL EVENTS
	Wright *The Outsider* (f) Baldwin *Go Tell It On the Mountain* (f) Bellow *Adventures of Augie March* (f)	Boorstin *The Genius of American Politics* Hook *Heresy, Yes – Conspiracy, No!* Hitchcock *Rear Window*	Cinemascope and 3-D introduced Korean War ends Ethel and Julius Rosenberg executed for espionage Oppenheimer's security clearance suspended Stalin dies *Encounter* founded
1954	Faulkner *A Fable* (f) Jarrell *Pictures from an Institution* (p) Chandler *The Long Goodbye* (f)	Riesman *Individualism Reconsidered* Potter *People of Plenty* Feidelson Jr *Symbolism and American Literature* Wimsatt *The Verbal Icon* Mies and Johnson Seagram building, New York City – 1958 *The Wild One* (starring Marlon Brando)	Cage's happening at Black Mountain College *Brown* vs *Board of Education* Army–McCarthy hearings Senate condemns McCarthy Housing Acts – 1959 French defeated at Dien Bien Phu Bikini nuclear explosion Eisenhower signs bill outlawing Communist Party
1955	Nabokov *Lolita* (f) Gaddis *Recognitions* (f) Barth *The Floating Opera* (f) Pound *Cantos* (cont.) (p) Donleavy *The Ginger Man* (f) S. Wilson *The Man in the Grey Flannel Suit* (f)	Mies Lafayette Towers and Court Houses, Detroit – 1963 Hartz *The Liberal Tradition* Fiedler *An End of Innocence* Rauschenberg *Bed* *Rebus* Marcuse *Eros and Civilization*	Montgomery bus boycott Martin Luther King emerges Civil Rights Act SLCC formed James Dean dies Warsaw Pact formed AFL and CIO merged

DATE	POETRY, DRAMA, FICTION	OTHER 'WORKS'	HISTORICAL/CULTURAL EVENTS
		Lippmann *Essays in the Public Philosophy*	
		Lewis *The American Adam*	
		Rebel Without a Cause (starring James Dean)	
		Hofstadter *The Age of Reform*	
		Baldwin *Notes of a Native Son*	
1956	Ginsberg *Howl* (p) O'Neill *A Long Day's Journey into Night* (d)	Ford *The Searchers* Whyte *The Organization Man* Mills *The Power Elite* Mailer *White Negro*	Federal Highway Act USSR invades Hungary Eisenhower re-elected president Interstate Highway Act
1957	Kerouac *On the Road* (f) Malamud *The Assistant* (f)	Chase *American Novel and Its Tradition* Rauschenberg *Factor I* and *Factor II*	Federal troops enforce desegregation at Little Rock, Arkansas, High School USSR launches Sputnik Peak of Baby Boom (4.3 million births)
1958	Barth *The End of the Road* (f) Albee *Zoo Story* (d)	Arendt *The Human Condition* King Jr *Stride Toward Freedom* Hitchcock *Vertigo* Galbraith *The Affluent Society*	
1959	Burroughs *Naked Lunch* (f)	Kaprow *Eighteen Happenings*	Castro overthrows Batista regime in Cuba Guggenheim Museum

DATE	POETRY, DRAMA, FICTION	OTHER 'WORKS'	HISTORICAL/CULTURAL EVENTS
	Lowell *Life Studies* (p)	Rieff *Freud*	opens its Frank Lloyd Wright building
	Purdy *Malcolm* (f)	Brown *Life Against Death*	
	Pound *Cantos* (cont.) (p)	Hitchcock *North by Northwest*	
		Mailer *Advertisements for Myself*	
		Rosenberg *The Tradition of the New*	
		Mills *Sociological Imagination*	
1960	Barth *The Sot-Weed Factor* (f)	Johns *Painted Bronze*	SDS founded Greensboro, NC lunch counter sit-in SNCC formed
	Lee *To Kill a Mockingbird* (f)	Dine *Car Crash* Bell *The End of Ideology*	J.F. Kennedy elected president Commission on the status of Women
	Albee *American Dream* (d)	Mills *Letter to the New Left*	Birth-control pill F. Stella's first solo exhibition
	O'Connor *The Violent Bear it Away* (f)	Goodman *Growing Up Absurd*	Twenty-two artists, including Hopper, and Raphael and Moses
	Updike *Rabbit Run* (f)	Hitchcock *Psycho*	Soyer, protest against the Whitney's emphasis on
	Snyder *Myths and Texts* (p)	Fiedler *Love and Death in the American Novel*	non-representational art
	Olson *Maximus Poems* – 1975 (p)		U-2 incident
1961	Percy *The Moviegoer* (f)	Greenberg *Art and Culture*	Bay of Pigs invasion of Cuba Berlin Wall built
	Heller *Catch 22* (f)	Trilling *On the Teaching of Modern Literature*	Kennedy sends US troops to Vietnam Peggy Guggenheim
		Jacobs *Life and Death of Great American Cities*	sues Lee Krasner, charging that she and Pollock failed to turn

DATE	POETRY, DRAMA, FICTION	OTHER 'WORKS'	HISTORICAL/CULTURAL EVENTS
		Booth *The Rhetoric of Fiction*	over works in accordance with agreement of 1945–6
		McLuhan *Guttenberg Galaxy*	CORE's Freedom Rides Yuri Gagarin orbits the world
		Mumford *The City in History*	
1962	Hawkes *The Lime Twig* (f)	Ford *The Man Who Shot Liberty Valence*	Cuban missile crisis All the major Pop Artists exhibit
	Albee *Who's Afraid of Virginia Woolf* (d)	SDS *Port Huron Statement*	
	Kesey *One Flew Over the Cuckoo's Nest* (f)	Harrington *The Other America*	
	Faulkner *The Reivers* (f)	Kuhn *The Structure of Scientific Revolutions*	
	Nabokov *Pale Fire* (f)	Macdonald *Against the American Grain*	
	Porter *Ship of Fools* (f)	Warshow *The Immediate Experience*	
		Warhol's soup cans, coca-cola bottles, dollar bills, etc.	
1963	Plath *The Bell Jar* (f)	Lichtenstein *Whaam!*	J.F. Kennedy assassinated
	M. McCarthy *The Group* (f)	Warhol *Thirty are Better than None*	Johnson becomes president DuBois (b. 1868) dies
	Pynchon *V* (f)	Arendt *On Revolution*	Civil Rights demonstrations in Birmingham,
	Baldwin *The Fire Next Time* (f)	King Jr *Letter from Birmingham Jail*	Alabama, and Washington DC
	Rich *Snapshots of a Daughter-in-Law* (p)	*I have a dream . . .* speech	Attorney general, Robert Kennedy, enforces integration of state universities in
		Friedan *The Feminine Mystique*	Mississippi and Alabama

DATE	POETRY, DRAMA, FICTION	OTHER 'WORKS'	HISTORICAL/CULTURAL EVENTS
		Kubrick *Dr Strangelove*	
		Mumford *The Highway and the City*	
1964	O'Hara *Lunch Poems* (p)	Lichtenstein *As I opened fire . . .*	Berkeley Free Speech Movement
	Berger *Little Big Man* (f)	Riesman *Abundance for What?*	Congress passes Civil Rights Act
	Baldwin *Blues for Mister Charlie* (d)	Marcuse *One-Dimensional Man*	Race riots start in New York State – 1968
	Purdy *Cabot Wright Begins* (f)	Rauschenberg *Break-Through*	Johnson elected president
	Bellow *Herzog* (f)	Marcuse *One-Dimensional Man*	Gulf of Tonkin Resolution: offensive war in North Vietnam
	Selby Jr *Last Exit to Brooklyn* (f)	Inman *Two Forms of Production Under Capitalism*	China explodes atom bomb
	L. Jones (Imamu Amiri Baraka) *Dutchman* (d)	Eastman *Love and Revolution*	Johnson announces 'War on Poverty'
	Barthelme *Come Back Dr Caligari* (f)	King Jr *Why We Can't Wait*	
		McLuhan *Understanding Media*	
		Ellison *Shadow and Act*	
		Fiedler *Waiting for the End*	
		Ford *Cheyenne Autumn*	
1965	Plath *Ariel* (p)	Oldenburg *Store Days*	Vietnam demonstration, Washington DC
	Berryman *77 Dream Songs* (p)	SOM *John Hancock Center Chicago* – 1970	Race riots continue (Watts)
	Mailer *An American Dream* (f)	Malcolm X *Autobiography*	Malcolm X assassinated
	Capote *In Cold Blood* (f)	Trilling	Johnson orders bombing of North Vietnam

DATE	POETRY, DRAMA, FICTION	OTHER 'WORKS'	HISTORICAL/CULTURAL EVENTS
		Beyond Culture Kazin *Starting Out In The Thirties* Cox *The Secular City* Tom Wolfe *Kandy-Kolored Tangerine-Flake Streamline Baby*	Economic Opportunity Act: Johnson's 'Great Society' legislation Peggy Guggenheim drops law suit against Lee Krasner Civil Rights march Selma to Montgomery, Alabama Teach-ins protesting American intervention in Vietnam
1966	Malamud *The Fixer* (f) Baraka *Black Art* (p) Pynchon *The Crying of Lot 49* (f) Barth *Giles Goat-Boy* (f) Gass *Omensetter's Luck* (f)	Venturi *Complexity and Contradiction in Architecture* Rieff *Triumph of the Therapeutic* Gilman *Women and Economics* (republished) Sontag *Against Interpretation* *Yale French Studies* Special Issue on Structuralism	MOMA Complexity and Contradiction in Architecture exhibition NOW founded James Meredith March Against Fear, Mississippi US bombs Hanoi Race riots in seven major cities Language of Criticism and Sciences of Man symposium, Johns Hopkins
1967	Brautigan *Trout-Fishing in America* (f) Styron *The Confessions of Nat Turner* (f) Barthelme *Snow White* (f)	Nichols *The Graduate* King Jr *Chaos or Community* Carmichael and Hamilton *Black Power* Cruse *The Crisis of the Negro Intellectual* Penn *Bonnie and Clyde* Hirsch Jr *Validity in Interpretation*	Vietnam demonstrations in New York City and San Francisco March on the Pentagon Race riots continue NOW's First National conference, Washington, DC New Left's National conference for a New Politics, Chicago Three US astronauts killed in Apollo launching

DATE	POETRY, DRAMA, FICTION	OTHER 'WORKS'	HISTORICAL/CULTURAL EVENTS
1968	Updike *Couples* (f) Barth *Lost in the Funhouse* (f) Mailer *Armies of the Night* (f)	Brown *Love's Body* Kubrick *2001* Cleaver *Soul on Ice* DuBois *Autobiography* Ellman *Thinking About Women* Daly *The Church and the Second Sex* Barth *The Literature of Exhaustion* Tom Wolfe *Electric Kool-Aid Acid Test* Didion *Slouching Towards Bethlehem*	USSR invades Czechoslovakia The Feminists formed Miss America Pageant Democratic National Convention, Chicago Martin Luther King assassinated Robert Kennedy assassinated Nixon elected president Tet offensive by North Vietnam Valerie Solanis shoots and seriously injures Andy Warhol My Lai Massacre Race Riots in 168 towns and cities
1969	Roth *Portnoy's Complaint* (f) Vonnegut *Slaughterhouse Five* (f) Coover *Pricksongs and Descants* (f) Le Guin *Left-Hand of Darkness* (f) Pound *Cantos* (cont.) (p)	D. Hopper *Easy Rider* Peckinpah *The Wild Bunch* Barry *Telepathic Pieces* Millett *Sexual Politics* Redstockings *Manifesto* Chomsky *American Power and the New Mandarins* Marcuse *An Essay on Liberation* Cleaver *Post-Prison Writings*	New York Radical Feminists formed Woodstock and Altamont rock festivals Americans, Armstrong and Aldrin, land on the moon

DATE	POETRY, DRAMA, FICTION	OTHER 'WORKS'	HISTORICAL/CULTURAL EVENTS
		Sontag *Styles of Radical Will*	
		Hill *Butch Cassidy and the Sundance Kid*	
		Hayden *Rebellion and Repression*	
		Wexler *Medium Cool*	
		Angelou *I Know Why the Caged Bird Sings*	
		Roszak *The Making of a Counter-Culture*	
1970	Bellow *Mr Sammler's Planet* (f) Ashbery *Double Dream of Spring* (p) Didion *Play It As It Lays* (f) Levertov *Relearning the Alphabet* (p) Hemingway *Islands in the Stream* (f)	Penn *Little Big Man* Altman *M★A★S★H* SOM Sears building, Chicago – 1974 Slater *Pursuit of Loneliness* Morgan *Sisterhood is Powerful* Firestone *Dialectics of Sex* Radicalesbians *The Woman-Identified Woman* Sennett *The Uses of Disorder* Rubin *Do It!* Marcuse *Five Lectures* Seale *Seize the Time*	Invasion of Cambodia Killing of four students at Kent State University and two at Jackson State 448 universities and colleges 'on strike' or closed Women's employment 31.2 million (compare 18.4 million in 1950) More people live in suburbs than in central cities 60.6 million families own television sets (compare 8000 familes in 1947) Radicalesbians formed Congress repeals Gulf of Tonkin Resolution Rothko commits suicide Feminist Press formed

DATE	POETRY, DRAMA, FICTION	OTHER 'WORKS'	HISTORICAL/CULTURAL EVENTS
1971	Heller *Something Happened* (f) Doctorow *Book of Daniel* (f)	Altman *McCabe and Mrs Miller* de Man *Blindness and Insight*	Town Bloody Hall debate, New York City Lt Calley Jr found guilty of My Lai massacre 'Bussing' of students Pentagon Papers leaked to press by Daniel Ellsberg George Jackson killed
1972	Reed *Mumbo Jumbo* (f)	Yamasaki World Trade Center, New York City Venturi, *et al.* *Learning from Las Vegas* Coppola *The Godfather*	Yamasaki's Pruitt-Igoe public housing project, St Louis, demolished ERA passes both Houses of Congress Watergate break-in Nixon visits China Nixon re-elected SALT I agreement *Boundary 2* founded
1973	Pynchon *Gravity's Rainbow* (f) Vidal *Burr* (f) DeLillo *End Zone* (f) Morrison *Sula* (f)	Altman *The Long Goodbye* Scorcese *Mean Streets* Newton *Revolutionary Suicide* Daly *Beyond God the Father* P. Berger, B. Berger and H. Kellner *The Homeless Mind* Rieff *Fellow Teachers* Bell *Coming of Postindustrial Society* Portman Renaissance Center, Detroit – 1981 Bloom *Anxiety of Influence*	Vietnam cease-fire agreement Vice-president Agnew resigns Arab oil embargo Watergate crisis – 1974 Abortion legalized in *Roe* vs *Wade*

DATE	POETRY, DRAMA, FICTION	OTHER 'WORKS'	HISTORICAL/CULTURAL EVENTS
1974	Le Guin *The Dispossessed* (f)	Coppola *The Conversation* *Godfather, II* Polanski *Chinatown* SITE Indeterminate Facade Showroom, Houston – 1975 Bernstein and Woodward *All the President's Men*	Nixon resigns Ford becomes president
1975	Waldman *Fast Spending Women* *and Other Chants* (p) Rothenberg *Poems for the Game of* *Silence* (p) Doctorow *Ragtime* (f) Gaddis *JR* (f)	Altman *Nashville* Tom Wolfe *The Painted Word* Moore Piazza d'Italia, New Orleans – 1979	South Vietnam falls to Communists
1976	Piercy *Woman on the Edge of* *Time* (f)	Rich *Of Woman Born* Bell *Cultural Contradictions* *of Capitalism* Krieger *Theory of Criticism*	Carter elected president HITE report on Female Sexuality
1977	Morrison *Song of Solomon* (f) French *Women's Room* (f) Didion *Book of Common* *Prayer* (f)	Gehry Gehry house Santa Monica – 1978 Berger *Facing Up To* *Modernity* Lucas *Star Wars*	*Roots* serialized on television Resurgence of evangelical Christianity

DATE	POETRY, DRAMA, FICTION	OTHER 'WORKS'	HISTORICAL/CULTURAL EVENTS
1978	Rich *The Dream of a Common Language* (p) Irving *The World According to Garp* (f)	Malik *Days of Heaven* Johnson AT & T building – 1984 Daly *Gyn/Ecology* Cimimo *The Deerhunter* Kazin *New York Jew*	Supreme Court upholds affirmative action in Bakke vs University of California California voters approve Proposition 13 Mass suicides by Rev. Jim Jones's followers in Guyana
1979	Gearhart *The Wanderground* (f) Heller *Good as Gold* (f) Mailer *Executioner's Song* (f) Roth *Zuckerman Bound* – 1985 (f) Rich *On Lies, Secrets and Silence* (p)	Coppola *Apocalypse, Now* Graves Public Services building, Portland Evans *Personal Politics* Lasch *The Culture of Narcissism* Rorty *Philosophy and the Mirror of Nature* Chicago *The Dinner Party* Wolfe *The Right Stuff* Didion *The White Album*	Nuclear accident at Three Mile Island, Penn. Rev. Jerry Falwall establishes the 'Moral Majority' Americans held hostage in US Embassy, Teheran Soviet troops invade Afghanistan Shah of Iran exiled Congress refuses to ratify SALT II Camp David meeting
1980	Welty *Collected Stories* (f)	Meier High Museum, Atlanta Rich *Compulsory Heterosexuality and Lesbian Existence*	Mission to save hostages in Iran fails Reagan elected president Race riots in Miami and Chattanooga

DATE	POETRY, DRAMA, FICTION	OTHER 'WORKS'	HISTORICAL/CULTURAL EVENTS
1981	Morrison *Tar Baby* (f) Irving *Hotel New Hampshire* (f) Wharton *Dad* (f)	Tom Wolfe *From Bauhaus to Our House* Hooks *Ain't I A Woman* Davis *Women, Race and Class* Friedan *The Second Stage* Jameson *Political Unconscious*	Fifty-two hostages in Iran released after 444 days US more involved in San Salvador Congress cuts taxes and increases defence budget
1982	Walker *Color Purple* (f) Bellow *The Dean's December* (f)	Rorty *Consequences of Pragmatism* Anderson *United States* Berman *All That Is Solid Melts Into Air* Gilligan *In a Different Voice: Psychological Theory and Women's Development*	AIDS cases reported in US
1983	Kennedy *Iron Weed* (f)		249 marines killed in car-bomb attack in Lebanon US troops invade Grenada STAR WARS
1984	Heller *God Knows* (f) Ashbury *A Wave* (p) Phillips *Machine Dreams* (f) Erdrich *Love Medicine* (f)	Lasch *The Minimal Self*	Reagan re-elected president

DATE	POETRY, DRAMA, FICTION	OTHER 'WORKS'	HISTORICAL/CULTURAL EVENTS
	Didion *Democracy* (f) DeLillo *White Noise* (f)		
1985		Bellah *et al.* *Habits of the Heart* Foster *Postmodern Culture/The Anti-Aesthetic*	Reagan meets Gorbachov in Geneva
1986	Leavitt *Lost Languages of Cranes* (p) Reed *Reckless Eyeballing* (f)	Lynch *Blue Velvet* Byrne *True Stories*	Iran–Contras scandal US planes bomb Libya
1987	Morrison *Beloved*	Stone *Platoon* Kubrick *Full Metal Jacket*	INF Treaty
1988	DeLillo *Libra* (f) Wolfe *Bonfire of the Vanities* (f)	Levinson *Rain Man* Chomsky *Culture of Terrorism*	Bush elected president MOMA exhibition: Deconstruction in Architecture USSR troops begin withdrawal from Afghanistan
1989		Rorty *Contingency, Irony, and Solidarity* Robinson *Field of Dreams*	Abbie Hoffman dies De Kooning's *Interchange* sold for $20.7 millions *Webster* vs *Reproductive Health Services* Pro-Life 'Operation Rescue' e.g. Fort Wayne, Indiana Pro-abortion marches in Washington DC

DATE	POETRY, DRAMA, FICTION	OTHER 'WORKS'	HISTORICAL/CULTURAL EVENTS
			Berlin Wall starts to come down Malta Summit between Bush and Gorbachov US troops invade Panama

General Bibliographies

Note: Each section is arranged alphabetically. Place of publication is London, unless otherwise stated.

(i) Intellectual and Cultural History

A. 1890s–1940s

Aaron, D.   *Writers on the Left* (New York, 1965). (Informative survey of debates, manifestos, magazines, and events from 1912 to the Second World War.)

Allen, F.J.   *Only Yesterday: An Informal History of the Nineteen-Twenties* (New York, 1931). (An easy narrative covering 'normalcy', 'the red scare', changing patterns of social behaviour, the revolt of the intellectuals, prohibition and gangsters, and the Crash.)

Buhle, P.   *Marxism in the United States: Remapping the History of the American Left* (1987). (Coming out of the New Left, himself, Buhle provides a partisan overview.)

Cash, W.J.   *The Mind of the South* (Harmondsworth, 1973). (Published in 1941, it is impressionistic and speculative – e.g. on the guilt of the white South – but an important book in its own right.)

Clebsch, W.A. *American Religious Thought: A History* (Chicago, 1973). (Good overview but relatively thin on the later twentieth century.)

Conn, P. *The Divided Mind: Ideology and Imagination in America, 1898–1917* (Cambridge, 1983). (An interesting selection of figures, e.g. Henry James, Washington, DuBois, Ives, Goldman, Wharton, Stieglitz, and Frank Lloyd Wright, in the context of modernism and anti-modernism.)

Cooney, T.A. *The Rise of the New York Intellectuals: Partisan Review and its Circle, 1934–45* (Madison, 1987). (Tells the story from the 'daily' life of the magazine outwards.)

Covert, C.L. and J.D. Stevens (eds) *Mass Media Between the Wars: Perceptions of Cultural Tension, 1918–1941* (Syracuse, 1984). (Variable collection but some neglected figures and topics covered, e.g. William Lyon Phelps, local radio, newspapers.)

Cowley, M. *Exile's Return: A Literary Odyssey of the 1920s* (Harmondsworth, 1976). (A rich source of contemporary insight into the 'lost generation', and very much a part of his own intellectual biography.)

Czitrom, D.J. *Media and the American Mind: From Morse to McLuhan* (Chapel Hill, 1982). (The early communications revolution; cinema, popular culture, radio, and social thought.)

Diggins, J.P. *The American Left in the Twentieth Century* (New York, 1973). (Definitely not a narrow political history; uses the categories of 'Lyrical', 'Old' and 'New' Left to make sense of the subject.)

Fass, P.S. *The Damned and the Beautiful: American Youth in the 1920s* (New York, 1977). (Overlong, but a good social history of the new phenomenon of 'youth'.)

Fox, R.W. and T.J.J. Lears (eds) *The Culture of Consumption: Critical Essays in American History, 1880–1980* (New York, 1981). (An exciting collection, advertising to Henry James.)

Frisby, D. *Fragments of Modernity: Theories of Modernity in the Work of Simmel, Kracauer and Benjamin* (Cambridge, 1985). (Allowed the luxury of two non-American studies of modernity, this would be one and Stuart Hughes' book the other – see below.)

Gilbert, J.B. *Writers and Partisans: A History of Literary Radicalism in America* (New York, 1968). (A fine study of *Partisan Review's* editors and contributors from the 1930s into the 1950s.)

Giedion, S. *Mechanization Takes Command: A Contribution to Anonymous History* (New York, 1948). (A wholly

fascinating book, linking industrialism, modes of
perception and ways of living.)

Hoffman, F.J.   *The Twenties: American Writing in the Postwar Decade*
(New York, 1949). (Dated, but still the standard
literary/cultural history.)

Hughes, H.S.   *Consciousness and Society: The Reorientation of European
Social Thought, 1890–1930* (1959).

Kaplan, J.   *Lincoln Steffens: A Biography* (1975). (Steffens seemed
to know most people, so a biography of American
radicalism from the 'Muckrakers' to the mid-1930s.)

Kasson, J. F.   *Amusing the Million: Coney Island at the Turn of the
Century* (New York, 1978). (Mass amusement as a
'harbinger' of modernity.)

Kazin, A.   *On Native Grounds: An Interpretation of Modern
American Prose Literature* (New York, 1942). (A
wonderful literary history by a New York
intellectual unfortunately not covered in the present
book.)

Kern, S.   *The Culture of Time and Space, 1880–1918* (1983).
(European/American modernism: Frank Lloyd
Wright, William James, Gertrude Stein discussed, but
the analysis of modernism is primarily conceptual.)

King, R.H.   *A Southern Renaissance: The Cultural Awakening of the
American South, 1930–1955* (New York, 1980). (The
best kind of cultural history in its combination of
history and theory; discusses literary figures but also
social thinkers, historians and those that are difficult
to classify, e.g. W.J. Cash and Lillian Smith.)

Lasch, C.   *The New Radicalism in America (1889–1963): The
Intellectual as a Social Type* (New York, 1965). (At
its worst, explains away important ideas as
attributable to 'the social history of intellectuals'; at
its best, subjects radicals like Addams, Bourne and
Mailer to uncomfortable scrutiny.)

Lawson, R.A.   *The Failure of Independent Liberalism, 1930–1941* (New
York, 1971). (Manages to do justice to a very worthy
but not especially exciting group trying to find a path
between Marxism and the New Deal.)

Lears, T.J.J.   *No Place of Grace: Antimodernism and the
Transformation of American Culture, 1880–1920* (New
York, 1981). (A formidable book with a genuinely
innovative way of thinking about reformers,
occultists, the arts and crafts movement, militarists,
Henry Adams, and how they helped America
accommodate itself to the twentieth century.)

Leighton, I. (ed.)   *The Aspirin Age, 1919–41* (Harmondsworth, 1964).
(An eclectic mixture of contemporary accounts, e.g.
of the Lindberg flight, the Jack Dempsey fights (by
Gene Tunney) Sacco and Vanzetti, Aimee Semple
McPherson, and Huey Long.)

Marchand, R. *Advertising the American Dream: Making Way For Modernity, 1920–1940* (Berkeley, 1985). (Advertising as index to cultural values.)

May, H.F. *The End of American Innocence: A Study of the First Years of Our Own Time, 1912–1917* (Chicago, 1959). (Rediscovered the forgotten pre-war period of the *Seven Arts, Masses* and early *New Republic*.)

Meyer, D.M. *The Positive Thinkers: Religion as Pop Psychology From Mary Baker Eddy to Oral Roberts* (New York, 1980). (Originally published in 1960, has taken on new importance with recent attention to the therapeutic culture.)

Mowry, G. E. (ed.) *The Twenties: Fords, Flappers and Fanatics* (Englewood Cliffs. NJ, 1963). (Compare with Allen and Leighton's books, above.)

Noble, D.W. *The Progressive Mind, 1890–1917* (Chicago, 1970). (Response of social and political thinkers, novelists, architects, artists and musicians to industrialization, rural decline, blacks in the North and South, and the First World War.)

O'Brien, M. *The Idea of the American South, 1920–1941* (Baltimore, 1979). (The chapters on Southern sociology and Agrarianism are worth reading alongside studies of the literary Renaissance.)

O'Brien, M. *Rethinking the South: Essays in Intellectual History* (Baltimore, 1988). (Combative collection with Part II devoted to the New South.)

Parrington, V.L. *Main Currents in American Thought: Volume 3: The Beginnings of Critical Realism in America: 1860–1920* (New York, 1930). (A 'classic' in American intellectual history; good on the reaction to Romanticism, and on liberalism and Progressivism but too close to modernism to grasp the next 'current' of thought.)

Pells, R.H. *Radical Visions and American Dreams: Culture and Social Thought in the Depression Years* (New York, 1974). (Focuses mostly on intellectuals and literary figures on the broad Left; excellent study which analyses texts as well as contextualizing them.)

Rosenfeld, P. *Port of New York* (Urbana, Illinois, 1966). (Published in 1924; impressionistic, personal, and full of insights into early American modernism in painting, photography, music, literature, and criticism.)

Santayana, G. 'The Genteel Tradition in American Philosophy', in *Santayana on America: Essays, Notes, and Letters on American Life, Literature, and Philosophy*, edited by R.C. Lyon (New York, 1968). (Still the best way to understand the transitions from Transcendentalism to genteel Victorianism to modernism.)

Singel, D.J. *The War Within: From Victorian to Modernist Thought*

	in the South, 1919–1945 (Chapel Hill, 1982). (A valuable study which helps to compensate for the urban bias of the present book.)
Stott, W.	*Documentary Expression and Thirties America* (New York, 1973). (Covers a great deal left out of literary and intellectual histories of the 1930s.)
Susman, W.I.	*Culture as History: The Transformation of American Society in the Twentieth Century* (New York, 1984). (Required reading for anyone who wants to respect the range of American culture and yet raise theoretical questions about how it hangs together – or does not, in some cases.)
Wertheim, A.F.	*The New York Little Renaissance: Iconoclasm, Modernism, and Nationalism in American Culture, 1908–1917* (New York, 1976). (Updates Henry May's study and has more to say about the arts.)
White, M.	*Social Thought in America: The Revolt Against Formalism* (New York, 1976). (A valuable counter weight to synthesizing cultural histories; close analysis of Oliver Wendell Holmes, Jr, John Dewey, Thorstein Veblen, James Harvey Robinson, Charles Beard.)
Wiebe, R.H.	*The Search for Order, 1877–1920* (New York, 1967). (Essential for understanding Weber's rationalization theory in action and important background for post-1920s social thinkers.)
Wilson, E.	*The American Earthquake* (1958); *The Shores of Light: A Literary Chronicle of the Twenties and Thirties* (1952); and *Classics and Commercials: A Literary Chronicle of the Forties* (New York, 1962). (A great range of essays and observations on American culture from the 1920s through the 1940s.)
Wilson, H.T.	*The American Ideology: Science, Technology and Organization as Modes of Rationality in Advanced Industrial Society* (1976). (A difficult book but one that keeps being mentioned.)

B. *1950s–1980s*

Angus I. and S. Jhally (eds)	*Cultural Politics in Contemporary America* (New York, 1989). (The politics of advertising, information technology, race, gender, automobiles, 'shredding', and television.)
Berman, M.	*All That Is Solid Melts Into Air: The Experience of Modernity* (New York, 1982). (Theoretically loose,

but Berman is energetic and engaged – with Marx as well as(Robert) Moses.)

Berman, R.   *America in the Sixties: An Intellectual History* (New York, 1968). (History of intellectuals in the New Left, black movements, and religion.)

Bloom A.   *Prodigal Sons: The New York Intellectuals and their World* (New York, 1986). (An unusual study in tracing this group to their immigrant origins.)

Bouchier, D.   *New Ideologies of Liberation in Britain and the United States* (1978). (A comparative and philosophical perspective which takes the 1960s seriously.)

Boyer, P.   *By the Bomb's Early Light – American Thought and Culture at the Dawn of the Atomic Age* (New York, 1985). (Dicusses the influence of this ultimate threat.)

Brookeman, C.   *American Culture and Society Since the 1930s* (London, 1984). (Useful chapters on, among others, Bell, New Criticism, Eliot, Frankfurt School, Riesman, McLuhan, Mailer, and Sontag, linked by theme of mass culture.)

Caplan, A.L. (ed.)   *The Sociobiology Debate: Readings on Ethical and Scientific Issues* (New York, 1978). (Caplan's Introduction and the selections that follow – e.g. by Edward O. Wilson and Marshall Sahlins – indicate the scope of this 1970s re-run of Darwinism.)

Carroll, P.N.   *It Seemed Like Nothing Happened: The Tragedy and Promise of America in the 1970s* (New York, 1982). (A determined attempt to revise our view of the 'Me-Decade'.)

Carter, D.   *The Final Frontier: The Rise and Fall of the American Rocket State* (New York, 1988). (Reads post-Sputnik American culture in a highly eclectic way via Pynchon's *Gravity's Rainbow*.)

Caute, D.   *The Great Fear: The Anti-Communist Purge Under Truman and Eisenhower* (1978). (Authoritative study, both in command of detail and argument.)

Clecak, P.   *America's Quest for the Ideal Self: Dissent and Fulfillment in the 60s and 70s* (New York, 1983). (Updating the Emersonian quest; a rather odd, even evangelical book, certainly when compared with his *Radical Paradoxes*.)

Clecak, P.   *Radical Paradoxes: Dilemmas of the American Left: 1945–1970* (New York, 1973). (Good, detailed readings of Mills, Marcuse, Swezey, Baran, and New Left texts to reveal the relationship between power and intellectuals.)

Coser, L.A.   *Refugee Scholars in America: Their Impact and their Experiences* (New Haven, 1984). (A vital aspect of post-1930s American thought and culture; see also books by Fleming/Bailyn, Jay, and Heilbut.)

Cuddihy, J.M. *No Offense: Civil Religion and Protestant Taste* (New York, 1978). (A lively attack on 'civil religion' and its parallel in political culture.)

Daedalus Special issue on religion in America, 111 (1982).

Dickstein, M. *Gates of Eden: American Culture in the Sixties* (New York, 1977). (Has to do the 1950s down to establish the credentials of the 1960s but, that apart, a lively study of such topics as the New Journalism, Black writing and nationalism, rock music, and fiction.)

Diggins, J.P. *Up from Communism: Conservative Odysseys in American Intellectual History* (New York, 1975). (More evidence, in a well-argued book, of the importance of American conservative thinkers.)

Fleming D. and *The Intellectual Migration: Europe and America,* B. Bailyn *1930–1960* (Cambridge, Mass., 1969). (eds)

Fitzgerald, F. *Cities on a Hill: A Journey Through Contemporary American Culture* (1987). (Four contemporary communities: the gay community in San Francisco, a retirement community in Florida, Jerry Falwell's evangelical church in Virginia, and a utopian community in Oregon.)

Foster, H. (ed.) *Postmodern Culture* (1985). (US title is *The Anti-Aesthetic*; a seminal collection with essays by major American and European intellectuals on architecture, sculpture, art, and theory.)

Foster, H. *Recodings: Art, Spectacle, Cultural Politics* (Washington, 1985). (Good to see post-modern art given as close a reading as post-modern theory.)

Gilbert, J.B. *Another Chance: Postwar America, 1945–1968* (Philadelphia, 1981). (Lacks the involvement of his book on *Partisan Review*, but a good social/cultural history.)

Gitlin, T. *The Sixties: Years of Hope, Days of Rage* (Toronto, 1987). (Very lively reinterpretation of the 1960s.)

Gunn, G. *The Culture of Criticism and the Criticism of Culture* (New York, 1987). (Advances the claims of Trilling, Wilson, Rorty, Burke, and Geertz over Derrida, Foucault and Lacan.)

Harvey, D. *The Condition of Postmodernity: An Enquiry into the Origins of Cultural Change* (Oxford, 1989). (Brilliant study by Marxist geographer of changes in perceptions of space and time in contemporary culture, and how they relate to developments in capitalism.)

Heilbut, A. *Exiled in Paradise: German Refugee Artists and Intellectuals in America, from the 1930s to the Present* (New York, 1983).

Hodgson, G. *America in Our Time: From World War II to Nixon: What Happened and Why* (1977). (Along with Issel, this is a reliable starting point for the historical background.)

Huyssens, A. *After the Great Divide: Modernism, Mass Culture and Postmodernism* (1986). (The best monograph on this amalgam; plenty of American material, e.g. Pop Art and Hollywood.)

Issel, W. *Social Change in the United States, 1945–1983* (1985).

Jameson, F. *The Ideologies of Theory: Essays, 1971–1986* (1988). (Volume 2 has essays relevant to recent and contemporary America, e.g. on re-thinking the 1960s and on post-modernism.)

Jameson, F. 'Postmodernism, or the Cultural Logic of Late Capitalism', *New Left Review*, 146 (1984), pp. 53–92. (Obligatory stopping point; some exciting, if elliptical analyses, e.g. of the Bonaventure Hotel and Herr's *Dispatches*.)

Jay, M. *The Dialectical Imagination: A History of the Frankfurt School and the Institute of Social Research, 1923–1950* (Boston, 1973).

Kaplan, E.A. *Rocking Around the Clock: Music Television, Postmodernism, and Consumer Culture* (1987). (Study of the cultural context of MTV by a critic who has written widely on post-modernism.)

King, R. *The Party of Eros: Radical Social Thought and the Realm of Freedom* (Chapel Hill, 1972). (Studies of uses of Freud by Goodman, Marcuse and Brown.)

Kroker, A. and D. Cook *The Postmodern Scene: Excremental Culture and Hyper-Aesthetics* (1988). (American culture figures prominently in this 'panic' book: 'panic sex, panic art, panic bodies, panic noise, and panic theory.')

Kuhns, W. *The Post-Industrial Prophets: Interpretations of Technology* (New York, 1973). (A sound account of Mumford, Giedion, Ellul, Innes, McLuhan, Wiener, Fuller.)

Lasch, C. *The Culture of Narcissism: American Life in an Age of Diminishing Expectations* (1980). (An excellent way in to the malaise of contemporary America; the problem is in finding a way out again.)

Lasch, C. *The Minimal Self: Psychic Survival in Troubled Times* (1984). (Lasch's second jeremiad.)

Lentricchia, F. *After the New Criticism* (1980). (A sharply argued interpretation of American critical theory: Krieger, Hirsch, de Man, Bloom.)

Nash, G.H. *The Conservative Intellectual Movement in America Since 1945* (New York, 1976). (Clear analysis of magazines, 'think tanks', research foundations, and of William F. Buckley, James Burnham, Milton Friedman, Russell Kirk, and Irving Kristol.)

O'Neill, W.L.   *A Better World. The Great Schism: Stalinism and the American Intellectuals* (New York, 1983). (A hostile account which, even in the 1980s, provoked diametrically opposed reviews in New York intellectual circles.)

Pells, R.H.   *The Liberal Mind in a Conservative Age: American Intellectuals in the 1940s and 1950s* (New York, 1985). (Continues his study of the 1930s; the best book on post-war intellectuals.)

Rogin, M.P.   *The Intellectuals and McCarthy: The Radical Spectre* (Cambridge, Mass., 1967). (A case-study of McCarthyism which is vitally important to understanding the rejection of popular politics by the 'end-of-ideology' intellectuals.)

Ross, A.   *No Respect: Intellectuals and Popular Culture* (1989). (A more eclectic coverage of the topic than in Part II of the present book; John Waters, Bill Cosby, Mick Jagger, Grace Jones, as well as the New York Intellectuals.)

Roszak, T.   *The Making of a Counter-Culture: Reflections on the Technocratic Society and Its Youthful Opposition* (New York, 1969); *The Cult of Information: The Folklore of Computers and the True Art of Thinking* (1988); *Where the Wasteland Ends: Politics and Transcendance in Postindustrial Society* (New York, 1973). (Roszak's trilogy of largely anti-technocratic studies; more important as symptoms of their periods than as analyses.)

Sayres, S. *et al.*, (eds)   *The 60s Without Apology*, (Minneapolis, 1984). (At last a new wave of interpretations of the 1960s; an excellent collection/anthology.)

Skotheim, R.A.   *Totalitarianism and American Social Thought* (New York, 1971). (Helpful overview of reaction to the 1930s, though much less useful on the relevance of the concept of totalitarianism to analysis of American society.)

Steinfels, P.   *The Neoconservatives: The Men Who Are Changing America's Politics* (New York, 1979). (Critical of Bell, Glazer, Kristol, Lipset, and Moynihan for their assumptions about economic power and negative outlook; they still come out miles ahead of anything British neo-conservatism can offer.)

Wald, A.M.   *The New York Intellectuals: The Rise and Decline of the Anti-Stalinist Left from the 1930s to the 1980s* (Chapel Hill, 1987). (A very critical interpretation of most of the New Yorkers, with some unfair mini-biographies; on the other hand, a perceptive analysis of the larger move from the Left to centrist positions.)

Weinstein, A. *Perjury: The Hiss-Chambers Case* (New York, 1979). (Authoritative account of this important cultural event.)

Wills, G. *Nixon Agonistes: The Crisis of the Self-Made Man* (Boston, 1969). (Dissects a political culture.)

(ii) Black Culture and Politics

Baker, H.A. Jr *Modernism and the Harlem Renaissance* (Chicago, 1987). (Important, if elliptical, study: European modernism does not have a cultural monopoly.)

Blackwell, J.E. and M. Janowitz (eds) *Black Sociologists: Historical and Contemporary Perspectives* (Chicago, 1974). (Deals with some neglected black thinkers, e.g. Charles S. Johnson and E. Franklin Frazier.)

Bracey J.H. Jr, A. Meier and E. Rudwick (eds) *Black Nationalism in America* (Indianapolis, 1970). (Important documents and writings from the nineteenth and twentieth centuries.)

British Broadcasting Corporation *Eyes on the Prize: America's Civil Rights Years* (Blackside Inc., 1986). (An excellent six-part television series.)

Carson, C. *In Struggle: SNCC and the Black Awakening of the 1960s* (Cambridge, Mass., 1981). (An authoritative study of SNCC; plays down role of Civil Rights leaders.)

Cruse, H. *The Crisis of the Negro Intellectual* (New York, 1967). (A key text, which combines close involvement with black intellectual movements with a tough-minded analysis of, e.g., Harlem in the 1920s, DuBois, Garvey, Wright, Hansberry, and Robeson, plus a postcript on black power.)

Davis A. *Women, Race and Class* (see Feminism section).

Draper, T. *The Rediscovery of Black Nationalism* (1971). (Links black nationalism of Malcolm X, the Panthers, black power, and black studies, with its origins in colonization, emigration and Garveyism.)

Fullinwider, S.P. *The Mind and Mood of Black America: 20th Century Thought* (Homewood, Illinois, 1969). (Relates black intellectual history to origins in myth and historical circumstances.)

Franklin, V.P. *Black Self-Determination* (Westport, Conn., 1984). (Study of black American political culture; good analysis of the active – and not passive – importance of religion in protest.)

Gates, H.L. Jr   *Black Literature and Literary Theory* (1984). (More than a literary study: essays deal with such cultural issues as the naming of slaves and the choosing of a name, e.g. by Malcolm X; relations between Afro-American writing and the dominant Western culture; and the role of recent theory.)

Gates, H.L. Jr (ed.)   *'Race,' Writing, and Difference* (Chicago, 1986). (Not restricted to Afro-Americans; a strongly theoretical collection, with contributions from, among others, Jacques Derrida, Gayatri Spivak, Edward Said, Houston Baker, and Barbara Johnson).

Gayle A. Jr (ed.)   *The Black Aesthetic* (New York, 1971). (A crucially important anthology, with essays by Alain Locke, Ron Karenga, Langston Hughes, Richard Wright, and Ishmael Reed, on e.g. the theory of cultural nationalism, music, and literature.)

Harding V.   *There is a River* (New York, 1983). (Compare Franklin).

Harris, L. (ed.)   *Philosophy Born of Struggle: Anthology of Afro-American Philosophy from 1917* (Dubuque, 1983). (A collection which seeks to open up the canon of philosophy to Douglass, DuBois, Holmes, Locke, King, and Malcolm X.)

Hooks, B.   *Ain't I A Woman: Black Women and Feminism* (see Feminism section).

Huggins, N.   *Harlem Renaissance* (New York, 1971). (The standard study.)

Hull G.T., P.B. Scott and B. Smith (eds)   *All the Women are White, All the Blacks are Men But Some of Us are Brave* (see Feminism section).

Hull, G.T.   *Color, Sex, and Poetry: Three Women Writers of the Harlem Renaissance* (Bloomington, 1987). (Makes a case for the women whom men, including black men, sought to exclude: Alice Dunbar Nelson, Angelina Weld Grimke, and Georgia Douglas Johnson.)

Marable, M.   *Race, Reform and Revolution: The Second Reconstruction in Black America, 1945–1982* (1984). (An informative and clearly organized survey with a strong, and persuasive, thesis about the relationship between capitalism and race.)

Meier, A.   *Negro Thought in America, 1880–1915: Racial Ideologies in the Age of Booker T. Washington* (Ann Arbor, 1978). (A lucid analysis which relates the ideas of Washington and DuBois to social forces and institutions.)

Meier, A. and E. Rudwick   *CORE: A Study in the Civil Rights Movement, 1942–1968)* (New York, 1973). (Very good and now standard study of this important organization.)

Meier A. and E. Rudwick	*From Plantation to Ghetto: An Interpretive History of American Negroes* (New York, 1969). (Provides both history and analysis of ideas.)
Meier, A., E. Rudwick and F.L. Broderick (eds)	*Black Protest Thought in the Twentieth Century* (New York, 1971). (A comprehensive anthology of documents and writings.)
Reed, A. Jr (ed.)	*Race, Politics, and Culture: Critical Essays on the Radicalism of the 1960s* (Westport, Conn., 1986). (A difficult but rewarding collection of essays on such topics as cultural nationalism, New Left political culture, and the family.)
White, J.	*Black Leadership in America, 1895–1968* (1985). (Straightforward accounts of Washington, DuBois, Garvey, King, and Malcolm X.)

(iii) Feminism

Banner L.W.	*Women in Modern America: A Brief History* (New York, 1974). (A well-organized and clearly-written overview, which tends to favour social feminism over radical feminism.)
Berkin, R.B. and M.B. Norton (eds)	*Women of America: A History* (Boston, 1979). (Goes back to Colonial times, but has good essays and documents on, e.g., Gilman; union organizer, Lillian Roberts; women and the anti-lynching campaign in the South; and feminist consciousness, the last of these by Sara Evans.)
Chafe, W.	*The American Woman: Her Changing Social, Economic, and Political Roles, 1920–1970* (New York, 1972). (Banner's book – above – draws on Chafe's for its broad approach but is more lively and engaged.)
Cott, N.F.	*The Grounding of Modern Feminism* (New Haven, 1987). (A new look at the period in which feminism was thought to be dead, by a well-known historian who has mostly written on nineteenth-century feminism.)
Davis, A.	*Women, Race and Class* (1982). (Written out of both the black protest movement and feminism; a key text in its own right.)
Eisenstein, H.	*Contemporary Feminist Thought* (1984). (A very good overview which concentrates on ideas.)
Eisenstein, H. and A. Jardine (eds)	*The Future of Difference* (Boston, 1980). (Mostly a theoretical study, with comparisons between Anglo-American and French strands of feminism.)

Evans, S.
Personal Politics: The Roots of Women's Liberation in the Civil Rights Movement and the New Left (New York, 1979). (An insider history but detail and anecdote are integrated into a clear narrative.)

Gatlin, R.
American Women Since 1945 (1987). (A very helpful interpretive survey, dealing with work, the home, the women's movement, health, education, race and class.)

Hooks, B.
Ain't I A Woman: Black Women and Feminism (Boston, 1981). (An important analysis of sexism and female slave experience; imperialism and patriarchy; andracism and feminism.)

Hull, G.T., P.B. Scott and B. Smith (eds)
All the Women are White, All the Blacks are Men, But Some of us are Brave: Black Women's Studies (New York, 1982). (Collection of engaged essays, identifying the contradictions of black women in a number of spheres.)

Jaggar, A.M.
Feminist Politics and Human Nature (Sussex, 1983). (The best analysis of feminism as an intellectual movement; not specifically a study of American feminist thinkers but the discussion of liberal, radical and socialist feminism is very relevant.)

Moi, T.
Sexual/Textual Politics: Feminist Literary Theory (1985). (A concise comparison of French and Anglo-American theory.)

Morgan, R. (ed.)
Sisterhood is Powerful: An Anthology of Writings From the Women's Liberation Movement (New York, 1970). (A seminal anthology of documents; a document in itself.)

O'Neill, W.L.
Everyone Was Brave: A History of Feminism in America (New York, 1976). (Goes back to the 1830s and comes through to the 1960s, so, aside from a brief afterword, there is nothing on radical or Marxist-feminism.)

Ryan, M.P.
Womanhood in America: From Colonial Times to the Present (New York, 1983). (Though not focused on feminism, the cultural and ideological slant makes it the best of the surveys.)

Scharf, L.
To Work and to Wed: Female Employment, Feminism, and the Great Depression (Westport, Conn., 1980) (Valuable analysis of this relatively neglected period in the women's movement.)

Scharf, L. and J.M. Jensen (eds)
Decades of Discontent: The Women's Movement, 1920–1940) (Westport, Conn., 1983). (A re-assessment of the period in which feminism was thought to be dead.)

Sochen, J.
Movers and Shakers: American Women Thinkers and Activists, 1900–1970 (Concise survey of leading figures, e.g. Gilman, Flynn, Eastman, Goldman, Mead, and Friedan.)

Trimberger, E.M.   'Women in the Old and New Left: The Evolution of a Politics of Personal Life', *Feminist Studies*, 5 (1979), pp. 432–50. (An overlooked dimension of American radicalism.)

(iv) Cinema

Adair, G.   *Hollywood's Vietnam* (1981). (From pre-American involvement and *The Quiet American* to *Apocalypse Now* and *The Deerhunter*.)

Adorno T. and M. Horkheimer   'The Culture Industry: Enlightenment as Mass Deception' in *Dialectic of Enlightenment*, translated by John Cumming (1979). (This 1944 essay is a relentless critique of Hollywood – which requires an answer.)

Agee, J.   *Agee on Film* (1963). (One of the few critics to suggest ways round the 'high art'/'mass culture' dichotomy.)

Albrecht, D.   *Designing Dreams: Modern Architecture in the Movies* (1986). (How the modernist utopia of Le Corbusier, Gropius and Mies found its way into Hollywood sets of the 1920s and 1930s.)

Altman, R. (ed.)   *Genre: The Musical: A Reader* (1981). (Very good collection of essays from a variety of critical perspectives; annotated bibliography.)

Balio, T. (ed.)   *The American Film Industry* (Madison, 1984). (A good collection edited by an authority on the subject.)

Bergman, A.   *We're in the Money: Depression America and its Films* (Takes off from the fact that people who could not afford to go the movies in the 1930s, carried on doing so.)

Biskind, P.   *Seeing is Believing: How Hollywood Taught us to Stop Worrying and Love the Fifties* (1983). (Compare Bergman on the 1930s; good on paranoia films like *The Invasion of the Body-Snatchers*.)

Bordwell, D., J. Staiger and K. Thompson   *The Classical Hollywood Cinema: Film Style and Mode of Production to 1960* (1985). (Essential reading, especially for 'auteur' critics, who need to take into account the power of the industry as a determinant of Hollywood's formal practices.)

Bordwell, D.   *Narration in the Fiction Film* (Madison, 1985). (Some excellent close readings; not limited to American cinema.)

Cavell, S.   *Pursuits of Happiness: The Hollywood Comedy of*

Remarriage (Cambridge, Mass., 1981). (An American philosopher analyses a Hollywood genre, with considerable success.)

Dyer R.   *Stars* (1979). (Short but incisively-argued: stars as social products.)

Everson, W.K.   *American Silent Film* (New York, 1978). (Based on extensive viewing; lots of exposition and/but not much theory.)

Feuer, J.   *The Hollywood Musical* (1982). (Makes a strong case for this disparaged genre.)

Gomery, D.   *The Hollywood Studio System* (1986). (More manageable than Bordwell *et al.*)

Haskell, M.   *From Reverence to Rape* (New York, 1974). Standard study; impressionistic but wide-ranging.)

Heath, S.   *Questions of Cinema* (Bloomington, 1981). (Exciting and/but elliptical.)

Jacobs, D.   *Hollywood Renaissance* (New York, 1977). (Argues for the new post-1960s era in cinema.)

Kaplan, E.A. (ed.)   *Women in Film-Noir* (1980). (Goes beyond Haskell and Rosen in re-thinking the relationship between cinema and women.)

Kolker, R.P.   *A Cinema of Loneliness: Penn, Kubrick, Scorcese Spielberg, Altman* (New York, 1988). (An ideological analysis which also considers the formal properties of post-1960s Hollywood film.)

Lauretis, T. de   *Alice Doesn't: Feminism, Semiotics, Cinema* (1984). (An important book on narrative, desire and representation.)

Lee, B.C.   *Hollywood* (Brighton, 1986). (Concise study of the relationship between Hollywood and its products.)

Macdonald, D.   *On Movies* (New York, 1981). (Lines up Hollywood and European cinema within mass-culture debate.)

Madsen, A.   *The New Hollywood: American Movies in the '70s* (New York, 1975). (Compare Jacobs.)

Maltby, R.   *Harmless Entertainment: Hollywood and the Ideology of Consensus* (Metuchen, N.J., 1983). (Thoroughly researched study of relationship between Hollywood – as industry and body of films – and American society.)

May, L.   *Screening Out the Past: The Birth of Mass Culture and the Motion Picture Industry* (New York, 1980). (Shows how cinema arises out of, but works back on, the modernizing processes of the late nineteenth and early twentieth century.)

Monaco, J.   *American Film Now: The People, the Power, the Money, the Movies* (New York, 1979). (Contextualizes the

more director-centred approach of Jacobs and
Madsen to post-classical Hollywood.)

Monaco, J. *How to Read a Film: The Art, Technology, Language
History, and Theory of Film and Media* (New York,
1981). (Provides most of what it offers in the title;
useful glossary of terms.)

Neale, S. *Cinema and Technology: Image, Sound, Colour* (1985).
(The rather repetitive argument is, none the less, a
reminder that cinematic representation *is* different.)

Neale, S. *Genre* (1980). (A short study which manages to
incorporate theoretical perspectives.)

Pye, M. and *The Movie Brats* (1979). (First attempt to deal with
L. Myles Coppola, Lucas, de Palma, Scorcese, and Spielberg.)

Ray, R.B. *A Certain Tendency of the Hollywood Cinema,
1930–1980* (Princeton, NJ, 1985). (Selectively uses
theories of ideology to provide a model for close
readings of classic Hollywood.)

Rosen, M. *Popcorn Venus: Women, Movies and the American Dream*
(New York, 1973). (Compare Haskell.)

Ryan, M. and *Camera Politica: The Politics and Ideology of
D. Kellner Contemporary Hollywood Film* (Bloomington, 1988).
(Ideological analysis of the very close relationship
between film and society.)

Sarris, A. *The American Cinema: Directors and Directions,
1929–1968* (New York, 1968). (Instigated the
wholesale re-evaluation of Hollywood by
discovering, amidst the anonymity of genres and
studios, a pantheon of 'auteurs', e.g. Ford, Hawks,
Hitchcock, Sirk.)

Sitney, P.A. *Visionary Film: The American Avant-Garde* (1974).
(For films omitted from Chapter 1 of the present
book.)

Sklar, R. *Movie-Made America* (New York, 1975). (A cultural
history of American film; concentrates upon a later
period than May.)

Thomson, D. *America in the Dark: Hollywood and the Gift of
Unreality* (1978). (Thomson negotiates a way
between Hollywood cinema as business and as art, to
argue that it is the construction of a certain
'America'.)

Wollen P. *Signs and Meanings in the Cinema* (1969). (Confronts
the 'problem' of Hollywood cinema: how should
studio directors be discussed?)

(v) Painting

Allen, J.S.
The Romance of Commerce and Capitalism: Capitalism, Modernism, and the Chicago-Aspen Crusade for Cultural Reform (Chicago, 1983). (Uses a case study of Aspen, Colorado to argue for the inter-relations specified in the title.)

Ashton, Dore
American Art Since 1945 (1982). (A knowledgeable and reliable survey.)

Brown, M.B.
American Painting from the Armory Show to the Depression (Princeton, NJ, 1955). (The book which opened up the 'early' period; some good, detailed analyses, e.g. of Marin and Dove.)

Buchloh B.H.D., S. Guilbaut and D. Solkin (eds)
Modernism and Modernity: The Vancouver Conference Papers (Halifax, Nova Scotia, 1983). (Clement Greenberg and T.J. Clark in debate, with the best paper Crowe's on 'Modernism and Mass Culture in the Visual Arts'; reprinted in Frascina.)

Burgin, V.
The End of Art Theory: Criticism and Postmodernity (1986). (Not American-based, but an important move from art history to cultural theory.)

Clark, T.J.
The Painting of Modern Life: Paris in the Art of Manet and his Followers (1984). (An indulgence, given no reference to American art, but excellent on modernity, and specific to both the paintings and the history.)

Conrad, P.
The Art of the City: Views and Versions of New York (New York, 1984). (From Walt Whitman's city to Claes Oldenburg's; the chapters on The Eight and early modernists, like Marin and Stella, are especially good.)

Davidson, A.A.
Early American Modernist Painting, 1910–1935 (New York, 1981). (Very thoughtful and thorough account of the Stieglitz and Arensberg Circles, the Precisionists, New York Dada, and much more.)

Foster, H.
Postmodern Culture and *Recodings* (see section i/B).

Foster, S.C.
The Critics of Abstract Expressionism (Ann Arbor, 1980). (A survey of critical positions.)

Frascina, F. (ed.)
Pollock and After: The Critical Debate (1985). (The major texts in the debate over Abstract Expressionism, modernism and the politics of the Cold War.)

Frascina F. and C. Harrison (eds)
Modern Art and Modernism: A Critical Anthology (1986). (Concentrates more on European modernism but some seminal essays – by Greenberg, Popper, Baudelaire, Fried, Gombrich, Trotsky, Benjamin, Brecht, and Clark).

Gablik, S. *Has Modernism Failed?* (New York, 1984). (What we've all thought about contemporary art put into a serious polemic; deserves an answer.)

Greenberg, C. *Art and Culture* (Boston, 1961). (He is out of critical favour but it is difficult to imagine how we would talk about American modernism without these essays and his *Collected Essays and Criticism*.)

Gruen, J. *The Party's Over Now: Reminiscences of the Fifties – New York's Artists, Writers, Musicians, and their Friends* (New York, 1972). (Much more than high-level gossip about this important and, in many ways, tragic group of artists.)

Guilbaut, S. *How New York Stole the Idea of Modern Art: Abstract Expressionism, Freedom, and the Cold War*, translated by A. Goldhammer (Chicago, 1983). (A controversial book which puts Pollock, Newman, Rothko *et al.* into the context of the Cold War to explain their dramatic success.)

Hughes, R. *The Shock of the New* (1980). (Informative and critically acute on all aspects of American and European modernism.)

Huyssen, A. *After the Great Divide* (see section i/B).

Krauss, R.E. *The Originality of the Avant-Garde and Other Modernist Myths* (Cambridge, Mass., 1985). (Krauss takes a strong anti-Greenberg line on modernism, and introduces European theoretical perspectives into her argument.)

Kroker, A. and D. Crook *The Postmodern Scene* (see i/B).

Lippard, L. *et al.* *Pop Art* (1985). (Covers New York and California Pop, as well as examples from Canada and Europe.)

Lucie-Smith, E. *Movements in Art Since 1945* (1985). (Comparable to Ashton in reliability and clarity but goes beyond American art.)

Marling, K.A. *Wall-to-Wall America: A Cultural History of Post-Office Murals in the Great Depression* (Minneapolis, 1982). (Close analysis as well as superior cultural history.)

Nairne, S. *State of the Art: Ideas and Images in the 1980s* (1987). (An exciting mixture of survey and verbal collage of where we are in the 1980s.)

Pollock, G. *Vision and Difference: Femininity, Feminism and Histories of Art* (1988). (Unfortunately, little on American art, but Pollock's rethinking of visual representation is too good to miss.)

Roeder, G.H., Jr *Forum of Uncertainty: Confrontations with Modern Painting in Twentieth-Century American Thought* (Ann Arbor, 1980). (Falls between being good art criticism and good intellectual history, but well-researched and provides a detailed context for American art.)

Rose, B.   *American Art Since 1900: A Critical History* (1967). (Perhaps because there are no surprises, this is a trustworthy overview which gives a coherent pattern to the subject.)

Rose, B.   *Readings in American Art Since 1900: A Documentary Survey* (New York, 1968). (An anthology which can be used in conjunction with Rose's survey.)

Rosenberg, H.   *The Anxious Object* (Chicago, 1982) and *The Tradition of the New* (Chicago, 1982). (Along with Greenberg, the most important post-1945 American critic; his essay on 'The American Action Painters' is a classic itself.)

Rosenfeld, P.   *Port of New York* (see section i/A).

Seitz, W.C.   *Abstract Expressionist Painting in America* (New York, 1983). Seitz was close to the painters and their techniques; therefore, quite the reverse of Guilbaut's study.)

Stangos, N. (ed.)   *Concepts of Modern Art* (1981). (Reassuring to have terms and movements explained.)

Wallis, B. (ed.)   *Art After Modernism: Rethinking Representation* (New York, 1984). (A demanding collection of theoretical essays by, among others, Krauss, Hughes, Kelly, Barthes, Foster, Jameson, Baudrillard, Benjamin, Mulvey, and Foucault.)

(vi) Architecture

Architectural Design   *Deconstruction in Architecture* (1988). (Curiosity alone should make this an obligatory read, but it turns out to be an important sign of intellectual activity.)

Ciucci, G. *et al.*   *The American City: From the Civil War to the New Deal*, translated by B.L. LaPenta (1980). (Long, interesting, mostly Marxist, essays on skyscrapers, urban reform, city planning, and Frank Lloyd Wright.)

Condit, C.W.   *The Chicago School of Architecture: A History of Commercial and Public Building in the Chicago Area, 1875–1925* (Chicago, 1964). (The standard study: full of detailed but clear analyses of key buildings by Burnham, Richardson, Root, and Sullivan.)

Frampton, K.   *Modern Architecture: A Critical History* (1985). (Although American architecture is mixed in with other national traditions, this is an example of how to write an informative survey which yet has an argument and a sense of engagement with the issues. Excellent.)

Giedion, S. *Space, Time and Architecture: The Growth of a New Tradition* (Cambridge, Mass., 1967). ('Giedion's Bible': a wonderfully eclectic account, as much a document of the years of the New York World's Fair as a guide to architecture and planning.)

Handlin, D.P. *American Architecture* (1985). (Along with Roth, below, the best overview, though little on post-modernism.)

Heinemann J. and R. Georges *California Crazy: Roadside Vernacular Architecture* (San Francisco, 1980). (A well-illustrated study of the Toed Inn, the Dog Cafe, Kenyon's Desert Plunge, etc.)

Hines, T.S. *Burnham of Chicago: Architect and Planner* (Chicago, 1974). (A very impressive study of the person too often categorized as the villain of American architecture.)

Hines T.S. *Richard Neutra and the Search for Modern Architecture* (New York, 1982). (A good reason for guilt at omitting Neutra but relief that he has such an excellent critic.)

Hughes, R. *The Shock of the New: Art and the Century of Change* (see Painting section).

Jencks, C. *Modern Movements in Architecture* (Harmondsworth, 1985). (Not as wide-ranging as Frampton, but a lively survey from the major proponent of post-modernism.)

Jencks, C. *The Language of Post-Modern Architecture* (1984). (The best and most lavishly illustrated place to start for definitions and examples.)

Koolhaas, R. *Delirious New York: A Retroactive Manifesto for Manhattan* (London, 1978). (An exciting book, embodying the positive modernism promoted by Marshall Berman.)

Kowinski, W. *The Malling of America: An Inside Look at the Great Consumer Paradise* (New York, 1985). (Amusing and intriguing at first, but gets monotonous after the n-th tour of a mall.)

Marder, T. (ed.) *The Critical Edge: Controversy in Recent American Architecture* (Cambridge, Mass., 1985). (Buildings by Johnson, Portman, Graves, and SITE are analysed in ways that raise pressing social and political questions.)

Mumford, L. *The Brown Decades: A Study of the Arts in America, 1865–1895* (New York, 1971). (A pioneer study in bringing architecture – and other arts – into American Studies.)

Pommer, R.   'The Architecture of Urban Housing in the United States During the Early 1930s', *Journal of the Society of Architectural Historians*, 37 (1978), pp. 235–64. (Shows just why housing was such a crucial but, ultimately, overlooked issue in twentieth-century American architecture.)

Roth, L.M.   *A Concise History of American Architecture* (New York, 1980). (Compare Handlin, above.)

Sky, A. and M. Stone   *Unbuilt America: Forgotten Architecture in the United States from Thomas Jefferson to the Space Age* (New York, 1976). (The 'other' history of American architecture.)

Stern, R.A.M.   *New Directions in American Architecture* (New York, 1977). (A long essay on the move away from modernism by such as Johnson, Venturi, and Moore.)

Venturi, R.   *Complexity and Contradiction in Architecture* (New York, 1966). (The manifesto for postmodernism – before the event.)

Venturi, R. *et al.*   *Learning from Las Vegas: The Forgotten Symbolism of Architectural Form* (Cambridge, Mass., 1986). (A controversial book when it was published in 1972; took 'the strip' seriously as architecture.)

Wolfe, T.   *From Bauhaus to Our House* (1981). (Witty, sharp, full of prejudices; most readers seem to agree with him – as the British seem to agree with Prince Charles – about the state of modern architecture.)

(vii) Music

Blesh R. and H. Janis   *They All Played Ragtime* (New York, 1971).

Charter, S.B.   *The Country Blues* (New York, 1959).

Chase, G.   *America's Music* (New York, 1955).

Griffiths, P.   *Modern Music: The Avant-Garde Since 1945* (New York, 1981).

Heilbut, T.   *The Gospel Sound* (New York, 1971).

Hitchcock, H. Wiley   'Sources for the Study of American Music', *American Studies International*, 14 (Winter 1975), pp. 3–9.

Hitchcock, H. Wiley and S. Sadie (eds)   *New Grove Dictionary of American Music*, 4 vols (1977).

Keil, C.	*Urban Blues* (Chicago, 1966).
Kirkpatrick, J. *et al.*	*New Grove Dictionary of Music and Musicians: Twentieth-Century American Masters* (1988).
Mellers, W.	*Music in a New Found Land: Themes and Developments in the History of American Music* (New York, 1974).
Meyer, L.B.	*Music, the Arts, and Ideas* (Chicago, 1967).
Rockwell, J.	*All American Music: Composition in the Late Twentieth Century* (1985).
Salzman, E.	*Twentieth-Century Music: An Introduction* (Englewood Cliffs, NJ, 1974).
Southern, E.	*The Music of Black Americans* (New York, 1971).
Stearns, M.	*The Story of Jazz* (New York, 1965).

Individual Authors

Notes on biography, major works, and suggested further reading

Note: With the usual exceptions to any rule, I have restricted entries to figures whose careers started prior to 1945. Place of publication is London unless otherwise stated.

ARENDT, Hannah (1906–75), grew up in Koenigsberg, Germany; father died in 1913 and, the year after, family moved to Berlin under threat of a Russian invasion. An uncle supported her education at Marburg, Freiburg and Heidelberg universities; student of Husserl, Jaspers, and Heidegger, with whom she had an affair. In late 1920s, concerned at anti-Semitism in Germany, she became a Zionist (she abandoned Zionism when the State of Israel was formed in 1948, fearful of yet more nationalism). After 1933, gave protection to German Communists; arrested by Gestapo in 1933, but released; and went to Paris where she lived until 1941, mixing with Jewish refugee intellectuals (Walter Benjamin, among them). In 1940 interned in southern France, but reunited in Paris with her (second) husband, the German Communist, Heinrich Bluecher. In 1941 they left for United States. Arendt, still a convinced Zionist, wrote on Jewish themes for various journals; did editorial work with Schocken Books; and wrote for *Partisan Review*; generally part of New York Jewish intellectual circle in the 1950s, sharing its anti-Stalinism and fear of totalitarianism – though from a European perspective. At this time, she became a close friend of Mary McCarthy. *The Origins of Totalitarianism* was published in 1951 and, suddenly, after years of obscurity and straitened circumstances, she was well-known and in demand as an author and lecturer. She remained a 'floating' intellectual (ready to respond to public issues, especially in the 1960s and early 1970s), and did not opt for a full-time academic career; she did hold visiting appointments (for example, at Berkeley, Princeton, and Columbia), and received a number of honorary degrees. Other important books include *The Human Condition* (1958); essays collected in *Between Past and Present* (1961) and *On Revolution* (1963); and *On Violence* (1970). Her reporting of the Eichmann trial in *Eichmann in Jerusalem* (1963) was highly controversial and caused her great difficulty with the New York Jewish community.

See: Canovan, M., *The Political Theory of Hannah Arendt* (New York, 1974).

King, R.H., 'Endings and Beginnings: Politics in Arendt's Early
Thought', *Political Theory*, 12 (1984), pp. 235–51.

Pells, R.H., *The Liberal Mind in a Conservative Age* (New York,
1985), pp. 83–96.

Whitfield, S., *Into the Dark: Hannah Arendt and Totalitarianism*
(Philadelphia, 1980).

Young-Bruehl, E., *Hannah Arendt: For Love of the World* (New
Haven, 1982).

BELL, Daniel (1919–   ), born New York City; brought up by mother when father
died. In 1932, aged thirteen, he joined Young People's Socialist League; in
1937, while at City College, organized the Student Strike Against War. In
1940, having left Columbia, he became a staff writer on the *New Leader* (the
journal of the Social Democratic Federation), and then, between 1941 and
1944, managing editor; also held this position on *Common Sense*, 1944–45. His
next magazine job was as labour editor on Henry Luce's *Fortune* in New York
City. Bell's academic career began at the University of Chicago in 1945, and
he remained there until 1948, teaching the social sciences. After *Fortune*,
returned full-time to academic life in 1958 as professor of sociology at
Columbia. During the 1950s, he published in *Commentary*, *Encounter*, and
Partisan Review, as well as in *Fortune*; and delivered a paper at the Congress
for Cultural Freedom in Milan (1955). In 1960, *The End of Ideology* was
published. Bell's other books of this period include *History of Marxian
Socialism in the United States* (1952), and *The New American Right* (1955) and
The Radical Right (1963) – both as editor. Since moving to Harvard in 1969,
has been known for two more position-taking books, *The Coming of Post-
Industrial Society* (1973), and *The Cultural Contradictions of Capitalism* (1976);
his collection of essays from the 1960–80 period, *The Winding Passage*, was
published in 1980. His neoconservative phase was signalled in 1965 by his
founding of *The Public Interest* with Irving Kristol. Bell has also been on the
editorial board of *Daedalus*, and chair of the Commission on the Year 2000 of
the American Academy of Arts and Sciences.

See: Brick, H., *Daniel Bell and the Decline of Intellectual Radicalism: Social
Theory and Political Reconciliation in the 1940s* (Madison, 1986).

Liebowitz, N., *Daniel Bell and the Agony of Modern Liberalism*
(Westport, Conn., 1985).

Steinfels, P., *The Neoconservatives: The Men Who Are Changing
America's Politics* (New York, 1979), ch. 7.

Waxman, C. (ed.), *The End of Ideology Debate* (New York, 1968).

BOURNE, Randolph (1886–1918), born Bloomfield, New Jersey, into middle-class
family. Deformed during birth, at aged four he was left a hunchback after spina
tuberculosis. He attended local public schools until 1903; then an aimless period
looking for work or in frustrating employment; his parents separated, leading ▸
further financial hardship. In 1909 went to Columbia University on a scholarsh▸
and was influenced by John Dewey, both as philosopher and educationalist. As
editor of the *Columbia Monthly*, and a contributor to *The Atlantic Monthly*, Bou▸
became a defender of youth against authority, and developed a radical Deweyar▸
view of education. In *Youth and Life* (1913) and *The Gary Schools* (1916) he deve▸
these ideas. He travelled in Europe on a Gilder fellowship, 1913–14, and return▸
report on Europe on the eve of war. As one of the new intellectuals in Greenw▸
Village, Bourne wrote first for *The New Republic* (1914–16), and then against it▸
Dewey) for the *Masses* and *The Seven Arts*. Bourne died in the influenza epidem▸
1918, alienated from most of his contemporary intellectuals and with an impor▸
work, *The State*, unfinished.

See: Bourne, R., *The Radical Will: Randolph Bourne, Selected Writings, 1911–1918*, edited (with an Introduction) by O. Hansen (New York, 1977).

Lasch C., *The New Radicalism in America (1889–1963): The Intellectual as a Social Type* (New York, 1965).

Moreau, J., *Randolph Bourne: Legend and Reality* (Washington, DC, 1966).

Schlissel, L., *The World of Randolph Bourne* (New York, 1965).

Paul, S., *Randolph Bourne* (Minneapolis, 1967).

Rosenfeld, P., *Port of New York* (Urbana, 1966), pp. 211–36.

CAPRA, Frank (1897–   ), born Sicily, one of seven children; emigrated with family to Los Angeles in 1903. Graduated as chemical engineer, California Institute of Technology, 1918; enlisted 1918–19. Out of permanent work and very short of money, he contrived to direct a 'short' for a San Francisco company, before moving to Hollywood where he worked as propman and film editor. Worked for Hal Roach, Mack Sennett and Harry Langdon as gagwriter and (for Langdon) as director. In 1927 sacked by Langdon. After spell as stage director in New York City, he was signed up by Columbia in 1931. At Columbia became a leading Hollywood director in the 1930s and early 1940s, with such films as: *It Happened One Night* (1934), *Mr Deeds Goes to Town* (1936), *Mr Smith Goes to Washington* (1939), and *Meet John Doe* (1941). He received three Academy awards. Through heroes played by Gary Cooper and James Stewart, Capra's films celebrate the ordinary American against the 'system'. Capra's populism and patriotism were on show in wartime propaganda films. In post-war America, he was less successful, though *It's a Wonderful Life* (1947) has received critical attention.

See: Carney F., *American Vision: The Films of Frank Capra* (Cambridge, 1988).

Glatzer R. and Raeburn, J. (eds.) *The Cinema of Frank Capra: An Approach to Film Comedy* (Ann Arbor, 1975).

Phelps G., 'The "Populist" Films of Frank Capra,' *Journal of American Studies*, 13, 3 (1979), pp. 377–92.

Richards, J., 'Frank Capra and the Cinema of Populism,' *Film Society Review*, 7 (1972), pp. 38–46 and 61–72.

Sklar, R., *Movie-Made America* (New York, 1975).

CHAPLIN, Charlie (1889–1977), son of music hall entertainers. After father died and mother had mental breakdown, he and his half-brother were on the streets of London or in an orphanage. He went on the stage aged eight and, later, worked for Fred Karno Troupe. After US tour in 1913, signed contract with Mack Sennett's Keystone company and appeared in first film in 1914. His success led to a lucrative contract with Essanay in 1915, the year *The Tramp* was released, Chaplin starring and directing. With Mutual between 1916 and 1918, he made *Easy Street* and *The Immigrant*, among other shorts. Famous, and in search of more control over his films, he formed United Artists in 1919 with Douglas Fairbanks, D.W. Griffith, and Mary Pickford. *The Kid* (1921) was his first full-length feature, and was followed by other major silent (or mostly silent) films: *The Gold Rush* (1925), *The Circus* (1928), *City Lights* (1931), and *Modern Times* (1936). A character similar to the Tramp appears in the anti-fascist film, *The Great Dictator* (1940). *Monsieur Verdoux* (1947), a disconcerting pacifist allegory, brought the attention of the House Un-American Activities Committee. Chaplin's marriages to four young women (between 1918 and 1943), also brought criticism during the conformist 1950s. On his way to the London premiere of *Limelight* (1952),

Chaplin heard he would not obtain a re-entry visa without undergoing further moral and political scrutiny. He went to live in Switzerland, only returning in 1972 to receive a special Academy award. He received a knighthood from Britain in 1975.

> See: Chaplin, C., *My Autobiography* (1964).
> Huff, T., *Charlie Chaplin* (New York, 1951).
> Smith, J., *Chaplin* (Boston, 1988).
> Tyler, P., *Chaplin, Last of the Clowns* (New York, 1947).

DAVIS, Stuart (1894–1964), born Philadelphia, son of the art director of the *Philadelphia News*, which employed Luks, Glackens and Sloan before they came to New York City to form part of The Eight. Between 1910 and 1913 Davis was a student of Robert Henri in New York City; had five paintings in the Armory Show and counted it a great influence upon him. A visit to Paris in 1928 confirmed his commitment to modernism. He did illustrations for the *Masses*, 1913–16, leaving when the editors asked for more direct political art. He maintained a strong political orientation, however, working for the *New Masses* in the 1920s and 1930s; and, in the Depression, for the Federal Arts Project from 1933 (he did two important murals), and the Artists Congress (as national secretary and then national chair). He was editor of *Art Front Magazine* from 1935. Since his first solo exhibition in 1917 at the Sheridan Square gallery, he has gradually been recognized: in 1939 and 1945 MOMA held two exhibitions of his work; the latter was a 'retrospective', as was the 1957 exhibition at the Whitney.

> See: Arnason, H., *Stuart Davis* (New York, 1966).
> Kelder, D. (ed.) *Stuart Davis* (New York, 1971).
> *Stuart Davis Memorial Exhibition, 1894–1964* (Washington, DC, 1965).

De KOONING, Willem (1904–), born Rotterdam, studied in Amsterdam while apprenticed to Jan and Jaap Gidding, a commercial art firm; also worked in art department of large store. Stowed away on board ship and came to US in 1927; worked as house painter, Hoboken, New Jersey in 1927; then to New York City and made contact with Arshile Gorky's group, which included Stuart Davis; worked for Federal Arts Project, 1935–39; completed a mural for New York World Fair, 1939. In 1948, he was an instructor at Black Mountain College, NC; that year, exhibited at Charles Egan gallery, New York City; became unofficial leader of Abstract Expressionists, with Pollock: 'black paintings' around 1950, then Women series; continued as an abstract artist through the 1960s (e.g. *Montauk 1*, 1969); in the 1970s became interested in sculpture. Regularly exhibited, with retrospectives at Stedelijk Museum in Amsterdam, and MOMA and Whitney Museum.

> See: Cummings, P., *et al.*, *Willem de Kooning* (New York, 1984).
> *De Kooning Retrospective*, exhibition catalogue, with Foreword by Clement Greenberg (Boston, 1953).
> *De Kooning-Newman*, exhibition catalogue (New York, 1962).
> Rosenberg, H., *De Kooning* (New York, 1974).
> Waldman, D., *Willem de Kooning* (1988).

DEWEY, John (1859–1952), born Burlington, Vermont; when young, family moved to Virginia where his father was stationed during the Civil War; returned to New England after the war. Attended University of Vermont, and, in 1882, Johns Hopkins University, where he studied with George S. Morris and Charles Sanders Peirce, the founder of Pragmatism; went on to

teach philosophy at Michigan, Minnesota, Chicago (in 1894) and Columbia
in New York City (in 1905). While at Chicago, he was greatly affected by the
atmosphere of urban reform; made link between the University and the
settlement movement, centred on Jane Addams's Hull House. His interest in
education was also fostered while at Chicago (and he married an
educationalist, Alice Chipman) and continued at Columbia, where he
pioneered progressive education in the USA and abroad, making influential
lecture tours of Japan and China between 1918 and 1920. Dewey's impact on
public affairs was also achieved through his regular contributions to liberal
journals, in particular *The New Republic*. He became the leading Pragmatist
(or Instrumentalist) philosopher. Dewey retired from academic life in 1929
but continued his writing and involvement in public affairs: he was
prominent in the American Civil Liberties Union and the American
Association of University Professors; in 1929 he helped to form the League
for Independent Political Action; and in 1938, when nearly eighty, he
travelled to Coyoacan in Mexico to chair the Commission of Inquiry into the
accusations levelled at Trotsky after the Moscow Trials. When he was eighty-
six, he married again, and published two articles in 1952, the year he died.
Dewey worked in the areas of metaphysics, ethics, theory of knowledge,
social philosophy, religion, and aesthetics, publishing more than twenty-five
books. His major works are: *Democracy and Education* (1916), *Reconstruction in
Philosophy* (1920), *Human Nature and Conduct* (1922), *Experience and Nature*
(1925), *The Public and its Problems* (1927), *Individualism Old and New* (1929),
Art as Experience (1934), *Liberalism and Social Action* (1935), and *Logic: The
Theory of Inquiry* (1938).

See: Conkin, P., *Puritans and Pragmatists: Eight Eminent American Thinkers*
(Bloomington, Indiana, 1976), ch. 8.

Hook, S., *John Dewey: An Intellectual Portrait* (New York, 1939).

Hook, S. (ed.), *John Dewey: Philosopher of Science and Freedom* (New
York, 1950).

Kennedy G. (ed.), *Pragmatism and American Culture* (Boston, 1950).

Lawson R.A., *The Failure of Independent Liberalism, 1930–1941* (New
York, 1971), Part 2 and passim.

Novack, G., *Pragmatism versus Marxism: An Appraisal of John Dewey's
Philosophy* (New York, 1975).

Sidorsky, D., Introduction, *John Dewey: The Essential Writings*, edited
by D. Sidorsky (New York, 1977), pp. vii–lv.

DUBOIS, W.E.B. (1868–1963), born a free-black, in Great Barrington in western
Massachusetts; won a scholarship to a black college, Fisk University, in
Tennessee. Attended Fisk between 1885 and 1888; then Harvard, obtaining a
BA, MA and PhD, the last of these in 1895; by then had travelled in Europe
and had started teaching Latin and Greek at Wilberforce University
(1894–96). Between 1887 and 1910 he was professor of Sociology at Atlanta
University; during that period, *The Philadelphia Negro* (1899) was published,
and he moved towards political protest rather than academic life: *Souls of
Black Folk* (1903) indicated a split with Booker T. Washington, especially
over the question of education. A founder member of the Niagara movement
(1905) and the NAACP (1909); also edited *Crisis* magazine from 1910. He
resigned from the NAACP in 1934 and only briefly rejoined in 1945. Since
the teens pursued his interest in socialism and Pan-Africanism; in 1919 he
organized the Second Pan-African Congress in Paris and was heavily
involved in subsequent Congresses. Though he continued to write and be
involved in political issues, he was isolated from the black leadership from

1934 to his death in 1963. He supported peace causes and was indicted for treason in 1951 but acquitted; ran for the Senate in 1950 on the Labor Party ticket; in 1961 sought membership of the Communist party but went to live in Ghana and renounced American citizenship. His principal books in addition to two already mentioned, are *Darkwater* (1920), *Black Reconstruction in America* (1935), *Dusk of Dawn* (1940), and *The Autobiography of W.E.B. DuBois* (1968).

> See: Broderick, F., *W.E.B. DuBois: Negro Leader in a Time of Crisis* (Stanford, 1959).
> Marable, M., *W.E.B. DuBois: Black Radical Democrat* (Boston, 1986).
> Meier, A., *Negro Thought in America, 1880–1915* (Ann Arbor, 1978), chs 10 and 11.
> Rampersand, A., *The Art and Imagination of W.E.B. DuBois* (1976).
> Rudwick, E., *W.E.B. DuBois* (New York, 1969).

FORD, John (Sean O'Feeney) (1895–1973), thirteenth and youngest child of Irish immigrants; brought up in Maine; went to University of Maine for three weeks in 1913 or 1914, before joining brother, Francis, in Hollywood. In Hollywood, worked for Universal as assistant propman, occasionally as actor/stuntman (e.g. as a member of the Ku Klux Klan in *Birth of a Nation*), and as a director (from 1917) under the name 'Jack Ford'. His first feature film was *Straight Shooting* (1917); during the 'silent era', *The Iron Horse* (1924) was his major film. Roughly one third of his 140-plus films were Westerns, and, along with *Young Mr Lincoln* (1939), these best convey Ford's conservative, populist sympathies, and his response to the landscape. His most famous Westerns are: *Stagecoach* (1939), *My Darling Clementine* (1946), *Fort Apache* (1948), *She Wore a Yellow Ribbon* (1949), *Wagonmaster* (1950), and three films which questioned the Western myth: *The Searchers* (1956), *The Man Who Shot Liberty Valance* (1962), and *Cheyenne Autumn* (1964). Known for his 'repertory' company of predominantly male actors: Ward Bond, Harry Carey Sr and Jr, Henry Fonda, Victor McLaglen, James Stewart, and, especially, John Wayne. Received awards for *The Informer* (1935), *Stagecoach*, *The Grapes of Wrath* (1940), *How Green Was My Valley* (1941), *Battle of Midway* (1942), and *The Quiet Man* (1952). During the Second World War, directed propaganda documentaries for OSS; wounded Battle of Midway; later given rank of Rear Admiral.

> See: Baxter, J., *The Cinema of John Ford* (New York, 1971).
> Bogdanovich, P., *John Ford* (Berkeley, 1978).
> Bogdanovich, P., *Directed by John Ford* (film), USA, 1971.
> Browne, N., 'The Spectator-in-the-Text: The Rhetoric of *Stagecoach*,' in B. Nicholls (ed.), *Movies and Methods: An Anthology*, vol. II (Berkeley, 1985), pp. 458–75.
> Editors, *Cahiers du cinéma*, 'John Ford's Young Mr Lincoln', *Screen* 13, 3 (1972), pp. 5–43.
> McBride J. and M. Wilmington, *John Ford* (1975).

FRIEDAN, Betty (1921–   ), born Peoria, Illinois; attended local public schools; then Smith College, obtaining her A.B. in 1942; research fellowship in psychology at Berkeley in 1943. Married in 1947 and brought up three children; divorced 1969. Together with empirical research, her own experiences found expression in *The Feminine Mystique* (1963). That book was the catalyst for the new women's movement; the royalties were used to found NOW; she was the organization's president, 1966–70. Other publications include *It Changed My Life* (1975), an autobiographical account of the women's movement, and *The Second Stage* (1982), a revisionist interpretation. Between 1971 and 1974 she edited *McCall's Magazine*. Has held various visiting academic posts since the early 1970s.

See: Dijkstra, S., 'Simone de Beauvoir and Betty Friedan: The Politics of Omission', *Feminist Studies*, 6 (1980), pp. 290–303.

GILMAN, Charlotte Perkins (1860–1935), born Hartford, Conn., part of the Beecher family of New England. Father left family when Gilman was young; mother and two children moved nineteen times in eighteen years in search of work and the assistance of relatives. She attended the Rhode Island School of Design and was a commercial artist in her late teens; in 1884 married but after birth of child became depressed; recovered somewhat when she amicably separated from husband; eventually she decided he should have custody of the child and this occasioned criticism in Boston and California newspapers. In the 1890s, began writing (e.g. 'The Yellow Wallpaper', 1892) and lecturing as part of reform movement of the time; she was in contact with socialists (Beatrice and Sidney Webb and George Bernard Shaw influenced her) and feminists, and lived for a time at Hull-House in Chicago. *Women and Economics* (1898) a great success; later books include *The Home* (1903) and *The Man-Made World* (1911). From 1909, published her own magazine, *The Forerunner* and serialized her most well-known utopian text, *Herland* (1915). Had close relations with three women, but these seemed to be as difficult for her as those with men. She married again in 1900. Her importance declined in the 1920s. Got breast cancer, and committed suicide in 1934 when she was prevented from working. Her autobiography, *The Living of Charlotte Perkins Gilman*, was published in 1935.

See: Berkin, C., 'Private Woman, Public Woman: The Contradictions of Charlotte Perkins Gilman', in *Women of America: A History*, edited by C. Berkin and M. Norton (Boston, 1979), pp. 150–73.
Degler, C., Introduction, *Women and Economics* (New York, 1966).
Hill, M., *Charlotte Perkins Gilman: The Making of a Radical Feminist, 1860–1896* (Philadelphia, 1980), second volume to follow.

GRIFFITH D.W. (1875–1948), born Kentucky, brought up in Louisville, where, from 1895 onwards, he joined local theatre companies and toured with other companies. Frequently out of work and getting nowhere as an actor, he offered stories to New York film companies, themselves just starting up in the new industry. Edwin S. Porter gave him a star role in *Rescued from an Eagle's Nest* (1907); in 1908 joined Biograph as a director and scriptwriter; first film as director was *The Adventures of Dollie* (1908), one of hundreds of short films made with Biograph up until 1913. In 1909 partnership with cameraman, Billy Bitzer, who helped him develop the first 'language' of cinema, especially in *Birth of a Nation* (1915). By then Grifith was wintering in California for better filming conditions; joined Reliance-Majestic. In 1906 in New York, Griffith had played the lead in the stage-play, *The Clansman*, upon which *Birth of a Nation* was based. The critical interest in *Birth of a Nation* was accompanied by box-office success and controversy for its portrayal of blacks. In 1916 *Intolerance* released: highly experimental, more liberal politically, but its relative commercial failure left Griffith in debt. Having formed United Artists in 1919 (with Chaplin, Fairbanks and Pickford), Griffith made *Broken Blossoms* (1919). In 1919 moved to Mamaroneck, New York, and his own studio, where he made such films as *Way Down East* (1920) and *Orphans of the Storm* (1922). He continued to lose money, returned to Hollywood in 1927 and made five more films. He never regained anything like his earlier position.

See: Geduld H. (ed.), *Focus on D.W. Griffith* (Englewood Cliffs, NJ, 1971).
Griffith D.W., *The Man Who Invented Hollywood: The Autobiography of D.W. Griffith*, edited by J. Hart (Kentucky, 1972).
Henderson, R., *Griffith: His Life and Work* (New York, 1972).
Wagenknecht, E. and A. Slide, *The Films of D.W. Griffith* (New York, 1976).
White, M., '*The Birth of a Nation*: History as Pretext', *Enclitic* (1982), pp. 17–24.

GROPIUS, Walter (1883–1969), born and grew up in Berlin; studied in Berlin and Munich. 1904–15 in army; served again, 1914–18. Between 1907 and 1910 worked in Berlin offices of Peter Behrens; 1910 started his own architectural practice and up to 1914 particularly concerned with designs for workers' housing. With Adolf Meyer, designed Fagus Shoe Factory (1911) and submitted design for Model Factory for Werkbund Exhibition, Cologne, 1914. Joined and named Bauhaus in 1919; director until 1928; designed its new building in Dessau (1925–26). With Meyer submitted innovative proposal for the *Chicago Tribune* competition, 1922, but mostly interested in industrial and domestic architecture. Visited US in 1928. With rise of Nazis, left for London in 1934 and came to US in 1937; went to Harvard Department of Architecture where he had considerable influence on a generation of students. Major writings: *The New Architecture and the Bauhaus* (1935) and *The Scope of Total Architecture* (1956). Set up TAC (The Architects' Collaborative); with TAC designed Temple Oheb Shalom, Baltimore (1957), the Pan-Am building, New York City (1958), and many smaller projects. Fellow, American Institute of Architects, 1954; Member, National Institute of Arts and Letters, 1967.

See: Giedion, S., *Walter Gropius: Work and Teamwork* (New York, 1954).
Jencks, P., *Modern Movements in Architecture* (Harmondsworth, 1985), ch. 3.
Jordy, W., 'The Aftermath of the Bauhaus in America: Gropius, Mies and Breuer', in *The Intellectual Migration: Europe and America, 1930–1960*, edited by D. Fleming and B. Bailyn (Cambridge, Mass., 1969), pp. 485–543.

HAWKS, Howard (1896–1977), born Indiana and moved to California when he was ten. Studied engineering at Cornell University (1916–17), but vacation work in the property department of Hollywood's Famous Players-Lasky had more influence upon him. Spent 1917–19 in the Air Corps, then worked in airplane factory; returned to Hollywood in 1922. He directed his first film, *The Road to Glory*, for Fox in 1925. Over the next 45 years Hawks worked in a highly professional way within the established Hollywood genres: detective/tough-guy films (*To Have and Have Not*, 1944 and *The Big Sleep*, 1946); gangster films (*Scarface*, 1932); comedies (*Bringing Up Baby*, 1938); and Westerns (*Red River*, 1947, *Rio Bravo*, 1959, and *Rio Lobo*, 1970). He is the tough-guy counterpoint to the lyrical John Ford; both shared similar conservative politics, though Hawks seemed to have less doubts about them: *Rio Bravo*, starring John Wayne, apparently made in response to the 'weakness' initially shown by the Gary Cooper figure in Fred Zinnemann's *High Noon* (1952).

See: Bogdanovich, P., *The Cinema of Howard Hawks* (New York, 1962).

McBride, J. (ed.), *Focus on Howard Hawks* (Englewood Cliffs, NJ, 1972).

Wood, R., *Howard Hawks* (New York, 1968).

HITCHCOCK, Alfred (1899–1980), born London. After an education pointing to a career in engineering, he switched to the design and advertising department of W.T. Henley Telegraph Co. In 1919 joined the British studio of Hollywood's Famous Players-Lasky; became a scriptwriter and assistant director in 1922; *The Pleasure Garden* (1926) was his first film as director and *The Lodger* (1926) the first in which he made a 'walk on' appearance. After *The Lady Vanishes* (1938), Hitchcock was signed by Selznick International Studios and made *Rebecca* (1940), which won an Academy award. Hitchcock welcomed the technical expertise in Hollywood and made a succession of thrillers: *Suspicion* (1941), *Shadow of a Doubt* (1943) and, post-war, *Strangers on a Train* (1951), *Dial M for Murder* (1954), *Rear Window* (1954), *Vertigo* (1958), *North by Northwest* (1959), *Psycho* (1960), *The Birds* (1963), and *Torn Curtain* (1966). The comedy-thriller strain in some of these films was pronounced in his last film, *Family Plot* (1980). Hitchcock became an American citizen in 1955. In addition to his popularity in the cinema, he was known to television viewers through two series, *Alfred Hitchcock Presents* (1955–62) and *The Alfred Hitchcock Hour* (1962–65). Box-office success was matched by the critical interest of French New Wave directors, François Truffaut, Claude Chabrol and Eric Rohmer.

See: Bogdanovich, P., *The Cinema of Alfred Hitchcock* (New York, 1962).

Durgnat, R., *The Strange Case of Alfred Hitchcock* (1974).

Phillips, G.D., *Alfred Hitchcock* (1986).

Rohmer, E. and C. Chabrol, *Hitchcock: The First 44 Films*, translated by S. Hochman (New York, 1978).

Spoto, D., *The Art of Alfred Hitchcock: Fifty Years of his Motion Pictures* (New York, 1976).

Truffaut, F., and H. Scott, *Hitchcock* (New York, 1966).

Wood, R., *Hitchcock's Films* (1965).

HOOK, Sidney (1902–   ), born New York City of Jewish parents; brought up in Brooklyn; obtained BS, 1923, from City College, MA and PhD from Columbia in 1926 and 1927. John Dewey supervised his thesis, published as *The Metaphysics of Pragmatism* (1928). He taught in local public schools, 1923–28, and has held academic jobs since then (at New York University, the New York School for Social Research, and the Hoover Institute at Stanford). During the 1930s, when events were shaping his views dramatically, his two books on Marxism led the American field: in 1933, *Towards an Understanding of Karl Marx*, and in 1936, *From Hegel to Marx*. He was involved in a debate over Marxism and Pragmatism with Max Eastman in the early 1930s. In the 1940s and 1950s (having taken very radical positions in the 1930s, for example, on the coming war), Hook adopted a tough anti-communist stance. He was a strong supporter of the American Committee for Cultural Freedom and the Congress for Cultural Freedom in the 1950s. His *Heresy, Yes, Conspiracy, No!* (1953) was a product of the post-war years. Along with the two 1930s books on Marxism, Hook's other major works are: *John Dewey: An Intellectual Portrait* (1939); *Reason, Social Myths and Democracy* (1940); and *Revolution, Reform and Social Justice* (1975).

See: Kurtz, P. ed., *Sidney Hook: Philosopher of Democracy and Humanism* (Buffalo, 1982).

HOPPER, Edward (1882–1967), born Nyack, New York. He studied commercial
art and illustration in New York City, 1889–90, but moved towards fine art
under Robert Henri at the Chase School of Art between 1900 and 1906; he
did not, himself, recognize any influence from Henri or The Eight. Nor was
he sent in a new direction by the next four years spent in Europe. He never
went back, but settled in New York City, spending the summers painting in
Maine. Was a commercial illustrator, 1913–23. Though he had exhibited at
the first Independents exhibition, it was not until 1923 that he devoted
himself full-time to painting. His most famous paintings are of city scenes
(e.g. *Early Sunday Morning*, 1930, and *Nighthawks*, 1942), but he also painted
coastal and suburban scenes. He had a retrospective at MOMA in 1933, and
another at Boston Museum of Fine Arts, 1950. In 1945 he became an
Honorary Member of the National Institute of Arts and Letters; in 1955 a
Member of the American Academy of Arts and Letters; received an Honorary
doctorate from the Art Institute, Chicago, in 1950.

> See: Goodrich, L., *Edward Hopper* (New York, 1956).
> Levin, G., *Edward Hopper as Illustrator* (New York, 1979).

HUSTON, John (1906–87), son of actor, Walter Huston; travelled with him on
vaudeville circuit, and with mother on the racetrack circuit. After spells as a
cavalry officer in Mexico, an actor, a reporter, a scriptwriter in Hollywood
(in the early 1930s), street singer and artist in Paris and London, he returned
to Hollywood in 1937. Only four years later he had his first director credit:
The Maltese Falcon, starring Humphrey Bogart. During the war he made
propaganda films which yet had good documentary qualities. In 1948 *The
Treasure of the Sierra Madre* (based on a B. Traven novel) and *Key Largo* were
released, followed by *The Asphalt Jungle* (1950), *The African Queen* (1952),
and very creditable adaptations of works by major American writers: *The Red
Badge of Courage* (1951, Stephen Crane), *Moby Dick* (1956, Herman Melville),
The Misfits (1961, Arthur Miller), and *The Night of the Iguana* (1964,
Tennessee Williams). With William Wyler formed the Committee for the
First Amendment, defending free speech in McCarthy era. Unlike other
'classic' Hollywood directors, Huston made the transition into the post-1960s
period with one remarkable film, *Fat City* (1970), and two very worthwhile
ones, *The Life and Times of Judge Roy Bean* (1972), and *Wise Blood* (1979).

> See: Pratley, G., *The Cinema of John Huston* (Cranbury, NJ, 1976).
> Ross, L., *Picture* (New York, 1952).

JAMES, William (1842–1910), son of Henry James Sr, a Swedenborgian
philosopher, and the oldest of five children, among them Alice James and
Henry James. Born in New York City and brought up in a cosmopolitan
family; travelled widely in Europe from a young age and while he never
expatriated himself (as did Henry James), he was rarely in the US for
continuous periods of more than five years. In 1861 went to Harvard, initially
to study chemistry, moving towards biology under the influence of Louis
Agassiz, but in 1864 opting for medicine; he took an MD in 1869. Taught at
Harvard for 35 years, in physiology, psychology (*Principles of Psychology*,
1890), and then philosophy; became professor of philosophy in 1885.
Engaged in an intellectual struggle with Spencer's Social Darwinism, on the
one hand, and Josiah Royce's Hegelian Idealism, on the other. With Royce
and George Santayana, James was part of a formidable Harvard Philosophy
Department and the centre of 'classic' American philosophy. His philosophy
of Pragmatism was developed through *The Will to Believe* (1897) and
Pragmatism (1907 – the year he retired from Harvard), and refined in *The*

Meaning of Truth, A Sequel to Pragmatism (1909), *A Pluralistic Universe* (1909), and the posthumously published, *Essays in Radical Empiricism* (1912). Along with Veblen's *Theory of the Leisure Class*, James's *Pragmatism* is the most influential text on later American thought. *The Varieties of Religious Experience* (1901–2) is an important sideline to his main development as a thinker, and a response to the severe personal crises he had experienced since the 1860s (see the chapter on 'The Sick Soul').

See: Allen G., *William James* (1967).
     Conkin, P., *Puritans and Pragmatists: Eight Eminent American Thinkers* (Bloomington, Indiana, 1976), ch. 7.
     Feinstein, H., *Becoming William James* (Ithaca, 1983).
     Kennedy, G. (ed.), *Pragmatism and American Culture* (Boston, 1950).
     Kuklick, B., *The Rise of American Philosophy: Cambridge, Massachusetts, 1860–1930* (New Haven, 1977), chs 9, 10, pp. 14–17.
     Perry R.B., *The Thought and Character of William James* (Boston, 1935).
     Santayana, G., *Santayana on America: Essays, Notes, and Letters on American Life, Literature, and Philosophy*, edited by R. Lyon (New York, 1968), pp. 36–56 and 73–88.
     White, M., *Science and Sentiment in America: Philosophical Thought from Jonathan Edwards to John Dewey* (New York, 1972), ch. 8.

JOHNSON, Philip (1906–   ), born to affluent family in Cleveland, Ohio; educated at Harvard, 1923–30. In 1930 joined the Department of Architecture and Design at the Museum of Modern Art (MOMA) in New York City; later became its director, with another spell in the 1940s and 1950s. Organized the seminal 1932 exhibition, *The International Style: Architecture Since 1932* with Henry-Russell Hitchock. Visited Mies van der Rohe in Germany and was instrumental in bringing Mies to the US. Left MOMA in 1934 and ran (unsuccessfully) for Congress on the ticket of Father Coughlin, a right-wing populist. Also worked for the Louisiana Senator, Huey Long, and formed the organization, Youth and Nation. In 1940, three years after Mies' and Walter Gropius' arrival in US, Johnson went to Harvard to study architecture under Gropius; graduated 1943; published *Mies van der Rohe* (1947), and applied Mies's principles selectively to his own Glass House, New Canaan, Connecticut (1945–49); assisted Mies on Seagram building, New York City (1954–58), the epitome of the International Style. Began developing more eclectic style, however: e.g. Amon Carter Museum, Fort Worth, Texas (1961); Kline Science Tower, Yale University, New Haven, Connecticut (1962–66) and New York State Theater, Lincoln Center for the Performing Arts, New York City (1964), both with Richard Foster. In the 1970s built 'super-skyscrapers' in Houston (e.g. Pennzoil Place, 1972–76, and Post Oaks Centre, 1976, Transco Tower and Republic Bank, both 1981 with his new partner, John Burgee), before 'going post-modernist' with the AT & T building, also with Burgee, New York City (1978–84). Through his private practice, writings (see *Writings*, edited by P. Stern, 1979), and institutional work at MOMA, has become America's leading architect and style-setter; Fellow of Institute of Architects and American Academy of Arts and Letters.

See: Ciucci, G., K. Frampton and C. Owens, *Processes: The Glass House, 1949 and the AT & T Corporate Headquarters* (Cambridge, Mass., 1978).
     Goldberger, P., 'The New Age of Philip Johnson', *The New York Times Magazine*, 14 May, 1978, pp. 26–27, 65–73.

Hitchcock, H-R, Introduction, *Philip Johnson: Architecture, 1949–1965* (New York, 1966).

Jacobus, J., *Philip Johnson* (New York, 1962).

Miller, N. *Johnson/Burgee: Architecture* (New York, 1979).

KING, Martin Luther Jr. (1929–68), born Atlanta, Georgia. His father and grandfather were Baptist ministers; his father was also a member of the NAACP. After studying sociology at Morehouse College (1944–8), King went on to Crozier Theological Seminary, Pennsylvania, where he was read, and was influenced by, the writings of Reinhold Niebuhr and Gandhi. While at Boston University, studying for a PhD he met Coretta Scott. They were married in 1953. In 1955, while in first pastorship, at Dexter Avenue Baptist church, Montgomery, Alabama, the bus boycott started. King was imprisoned on an alleged speeding charge and his house was bombed. In 1957 he helped form SCLC and in 1959 left Montgomery to work for SCLC. At the forefront of major direct action campaigns in Albany, Georgia (1961–2) and Birmingham, Alabama (1962–3), and marches in Washington DC (August 1963) and Selma, Alabama (1965). Planning a march in Memphis, Tennessee, April, 1968, he was killed by James Earl Ray. King's most important writings are: *Stride Toward Freedom: The Montgomery Story* (New York, 1958), *Why We Can't Wait* (New York, 1964), and *Chaos or Community* (1967).

See: Branch, T., *Parting the Waters: Martin Luther King and the Civil Rights Movement, 1954–1963* (1988).

Garrow, D., *Bearing the Cross: Martin Luther King, Jr, and the Southern Christian Leadership Conference* (1988).

Garrow, D. *The FBI and Martin Luther King Jr: From 'Solo' to Memphis* (1981).

Lewis, D., *King: A Critical Biography* (1970).

LANG, Fritz (1890–1976), born Vienna; studied engineering but left home and travelled in Africa, Asia, Australasia, and Europe before the First World War, during which he enlisted in the Austrian army. Married Thea von Harbou, 1924, with whom he had worked on screenplays; they separated in 1933 and she went on to make films for the Nazis. Directed first film in 1919 and, in his German Expressionist period, was known for such films as *Destiny* (1921), *Dr Mabuse, the Gambler* (1922), *Metropolis* (1927) – which he conceived after a visit to New York City – *M* (1931), and *The Testament of Dr Mabuse* (1933). Alternately threatened and courted by the Nazis, he left Germany and, via Paris, went to Hollywood; became an American citizen in 1935. His first American film was *Fury* (1936), followed by (among others): *You Only Live Once* (1937), *The Return of Frank James* (1940), *Hangmen Also Die* (1943), *Ministry of Fear* (1944), *The Woman in the Window* (1944), *Rancho Notorious* (1952), *Clash by Night* (1952), *The Big Heat* (1953), *Human Desire* (1954), and *Beyond a Reasonable Doubt* (1956). Lang retained a 'German' style in many of his films (he worked on *Hangmen Also Die* with Brecht), but combined it with American themes, notably in his gangster film, *The Big Heat* and in his three Westerns. His relations with Hollywood were often strained and, late in his career, he directed films in India and Germany. He died in Beverly Hills.

See: Bogdanovich, P., *Fritz Lang in America* (New York, 1969).

Eisner, L., *Fritz Lang*, translated by G. Marder, edited by D. Robinson (1976).

Jenkins, S. (ed.), *Fritz Lang: The Image and the Look* (1980).

Jensen, P., *The Cinema of Fritz Lang* (Cranbury, NJ, 1967).

MACDONALD, Dwight (1906–82), born New York City, educated at Phillips
Exeter, 1920–24, and Yale, until 1928. In the year before the Stock Market
Crash, Macdonald worked at Macy's, and during the Depression worked for
seven years on Henry Luce's *Fortune Magazine* while, at the same time
developing his amalgam of Left-anarchist politics. By late 1930s he was a
Trotskyite, having resigned from *Fortune* in 1936. He attacked the Popular
Front and Moscow Trials and, in 1937, not surprisingly, found a home on the
editorial board of *Partisan Review*, where he stayed until 1943, when he
resigned in protest against the journal's pro-war stance. In 1939 Macdonald
founded the short-lived League of Cultural Freedom and Socialism – a
reasonable summary of his own position; also joined Socialist Workers Party,
though, post-war, his radicalism became cultural rather than political.
Leading critic of mass culture between the watersheds of the 1930s and 1960s;
his film criticism (*On Movies*, 1971) is particularly important. In 1944, he and
his wife, Nancy Macdonald, founded *Politics*; it lasted until 1949 but
established Macdonald's independence as a critic. From 1967 onwards,
though still critical of the New Left, he revived the political dimension of his
career and campaigned strongly against the Vietnam war. With Noam
Chomsky and others, he founded Resist (1965) to help draft resisters, and
followed another independent critic, Thoreau, in refusing to pay part of his
taxes. His main collections of essays are *Memoirs of a Revolutionist* (1957),
Against the American Grain (1962), and *Discriminations* (1974).

> See: Arendt, H., 'He's All Dwight', *New York Review of Books*, 11 (1
>   August 1968).
>   Gilbert J., *Writers and Partisans: A History of Literary Radicalism in
>   America* (New York, 1968), passim.
>   Pells, R., *The Liberal Mind in a Conservative Age: American Intellectuals
>   in the 1940s and 1950s* (New York, 1985), 174–82.
>   Whitfield, S., *A Critical American: The Politics of Dwight Macdonald*
>   (Hamden, Conn., 1984).

MALCOLM X (Malcolm Little) (1925–65), born Omaha, Nebraska. His father,
Reverend Earl Little, was a Garveyite minister who was murdered by white
racists when Malcolm was six. His mother went insane. At the age of
twenty-one sent to prison for burglary; in prison he converted to the Nation
of Islam and, on release in 1952, changed his name to Malcolm X and became
a Black Muslim minister in Detroit. In 1954 he moved to Harlem and by
1964, when he left the Black Muslims, he had a large following and was in
demand nationally for lectures. He broke with the Black Muslims because his
outlook had become more political than theirs; he then founded the Muslim
Mosque, Inc., and, almost immediately, the Organization of Afro-American
Unity. He visited Africa and the Middle East in 1964 and took the name Al
Hajj Malik al-Shabazz; shortly after his return, he was assassinated by
members of the Nation of Islam. *The Autobiography of Malcolm X*, written
with the assistance of Alex Haley (later the author of *Roots*), was published
posthumously in 1965. His late speeches and interviews have been published
as *Malcolm X Speaks*, edited by George Breitman.

> See: Breitman, G., *The Last Year of Malcolm X: The Evolution of a
>   Revolutionary* (New York, 1968).
>   Clarke, J.H., *Malcolm X: The Man and his Times* (Toronto, 1969).
>   Cleaver, E., 'Initial Reactions on the Assassination of Malcolm X',
>   in *Soul on Ice* (1969), pp. 50–61.
>   Kahn T., and B. Rustin, 'The Ambiguous Legacy of Malcolm X',
>   *Dissent*, 12 (1965), pp. 188–92.

Jones L., 'The Legacy of Malcolm X and the Coming of the Black Nation', in *Home: Social Essays* (New York, 1966).

Ohmann, C., 'The Autobiography of Malcolm X: A Revolutionary Use of the Franklin Tradition', *American Quarterly*, 22 (1970), pp. 131–49.

White, J., *Black Leadership in America, 1895–1968* (1985), pp. 98–120 and 163–4.

MARCUSE, Herbert (1898–1979), the first child (of three) of a Jewish, middle-class, Berlin family. After service in the reserves during the First World War, went to Humboldt University in Berlin (where he was friends with Walter Benjamin and occasionally met Georg Lukács), and then, in 1920, Freiburg University (where he was taught by Husserl and Heidegger). He read Marx seriously in the early 1920s, but did not join the Communist Party, and grew very concerned about Stalinism in the USSR. In 1933 he joined the neo-Marxist Institute of Social Research in Frankfurt (the 'Frankfurt School'), but the same year had to leave Germany to escape the Nazis. He went first to Geneva and then to New York City, where he took out nationalization papers. Between 1934 and 1940 he worked in the re-established Institute and published in its journal, the *Zeitschrift für Sozialforschung*. *Reason and Revolution* was published in 1941. With the Institute in financial difficulties and Horkheimer in California (for medical reasons), Marcuse (and another colleague, Franz Neumann) worked for the federal government in Washington, DC. Marcuse moved more to the Left and refined his insights into totalitarian tendencies in modern society, while in the odd position of analysing German propaganda for the American government. In 1950, he left government service after ten years, and taught at Columbia and Brandeis universities before moving to the University of California, San Diego, in 1967. In 1955 *Eros and Civilization* was published and Marcuse had fully entered his American intellectual career, though *One Dimensional Man* (1964) and *An Essay on Liberation* (1969) were the most influential texts for the New Left and Counter-Culture. His popularity amongst students at San Diego led to attacks on him; Ronald Reagan, then Governor of California, declared him unfit to teach, and he received death-threats. He went on a lecture tour of Europe in 1967 and then during the 'Events' of 1968.

See: Brookeman, C., *American Culture and Society Since the 1930s* (1984), ch. 9.

Clecak, P., *Radical Paradoxes: Dilemmas of the American Left, 1945–1970* (New York, 1973), ch. 6.

Jameson, F., *Marxism and Form: Twentieth-Century Dialectical Theories of Literature* (Princeton, NJ, 1971), pp. 106–16.

Katz, B., *Herbert Marcuse and the Art of Liberation* (1982).

King, R., *The Party of Eros: Radical Social Thought and the Realm of Freedom* (New York, 1973), ch. 4.

Robinson, P., *The Sexual Radicals* (1972), pp. 114–82.

MARIN, John (1870–1953), born Rutherford, New Jersey. Initially, planned to be an architect, but started painting while at Pennsylvania Academy of Fine Art, Philadelphia (1899–1901), and then at the Arts Students' League, New York City (1901–3). In Europe 1905 to 1910; was influenced by Whistler's water colours rather than European modernism; a contact with photographer, Edward Steichen, while in Europe in 1909, led to an introduction to Alfred Stieglitz in New York. He became part of the Stieglitz circle, and had his first exhibition at 291 gallery in 1909; returned to Europe in 1910–11, and this time was influenced by Cubism and Futurism. The Armory Show in 1913 (at which he exhibited) confirmed him in his modernism. *Brooklyn Bridge* (1910), *Lower Manhattan* (1920) and *Lower Manhattan (Composing Derived from Top of Woolworth)* (1922) exemplify his strong interest in New York City in the 1910s and 1920s, but he is also known for his water colors of the Maine Coast. He had a retrospective at MOMA in 1936; his *Selected Writings*, edited by D. Norman, were published in 1949.

> See: Benson, E., *John Marin: The Man and his Work* (Washington, DC, 1935).
> Greenberg, C., *Art and Culture: Critical Essays* (Boston, 1961), pp. 181–83.
> Mackinley, H., *John Marin* (Boston, 1948).
> Reich, S., *John Marin: A Stylistic Analysis and a Catalogue Raisonne* (Tucson, Arizona, 1970).

MIES VAN DER ROHE, Ludwig (1889–1969), born Aachen, Germany. Worked in Peter Behrens' office in Berlin, 1908–11, and involved in the Deutscher Werkbund. In 1919–21 experimented with his revolutionary glass towers; these were not built but can be compared with contemporary German Expressionist interests and also with the sets in Fritz Lang's film *Metropolis* (1927). They were prophetic of the post-1945 'glass box'. His most well-known early building was the German Pavilion, Barcelona International Exposition, 1929. Mies was Director of the Bauhaus 1930–33 and left when it was closed by the Nazis in 1933. He eventually arrived in the US in 1937, and in 1938 became Director of Architecture at the Illinois Institute of Technology, Chicago. From 1939 he designed its new campus. Other projects in 'the International Style' included: 860 Lake Shore Drive, Chicago (1948–51); the Seagram building, New York City (1954–8); Lafayette Towers, Detroit (1963). Mies's most famous domestic work is the Farnsworth House, Plano, Illinois (1945–50). In the late 1980s, his design for a glass skyscraper for the Mansion House site in London was turned down in favour of a post-modernist design. Greatly influenced, as well as contributed to, modern American architecture, though left few written statements; see, for example, 'Mies Speaks', in the *Architectural Review* for December, 1968.

> See: Blake, P., *Mies van der Rohe: Architecture and Structure* (New York, 1960).
> Blaser, W., *After Mies: Mies van der Rohe, Teaching and Principles* (New York, 1977).
> Carter, P., *Mies van der Rohe at Work* (1974).
> Frampton, K., *Modern Architecture: A Critical History* (1985), Part II, chs 18 and 26.
> Johnson P., *Mies van der Rohe* (New York, 1947).
> Jordy, W., 'The Aftermath of the Bauhaus in America: Gropius, Mies and Breuer', in *The Intellectual Migration: Europe and America, 1930–1960*, edited by D. Fleming and B. Bailyn (Cambridge, Mass., 1969), pp. 485–543.
> Pawley, M., *Mies van der Rohe* (1970).

MILLETT, Kate (1934–   ), born St Paul, Minnesota. After local schools, went to University of Minnesota, obtaining a BA in 1956; spent 1956–58 in Oxford. She obtained a PhD in English and Comparative literature from Columbia in 1970. Appointed as instructor in English at the University of North Carolina, then, in 1964 she went to Barnard College, New York. In 1965 she married the Japanese sculptor, Fumio Yoshimura. *Sexual Politics*, which brought her widespread attention, was published in 1969, followed by *Flying* (1974), and *Sita* (1977). Member of Congress of Racial Equality (CORE) since 1965; chair of Education Committee for NOW since 1966. She is also a sculptor.

> See: Kaplan, C., 'Radical Feminism and Literature: Rethinking Millett's Sexual Politics', in *The Woman Question: Readings on the Subordination of Women*, edited by M.S. Evans (1982).
> Moi, T. *Sexual/Textual Politics* (1985), pp. 21–31.

MILLS, C. Wright (1916–62), born in Waco, Texas; grew up in Sherman, Fort Worth and Dallas – an unhappy childhood apparently. After a number of changes of high school, he went on to University of Texas and obtained his BA and MA. In 1939 went to do a Phd at University of Wisconsin, where Edward A. Ross was chair of the Sociology Department, and where Hans Gerth (ex-Frankfurt School) taught. Gerth introduced Mills to European social theory and, together, they produced an important anthology, *From Max Weber* (1946). Mills taught sociology at University of Maryland (1941–45) and at Columbia from 1945. In New York City, he was in contact with many of the New York Intellectuals but led a very different lifestyle: with Ruth Harper, his wife, he built a house in Rockland County, New York, on their (subsistence) farm. His colleagues in the Sociology Department included Robert Lynd, Paul Lazarsfeld, and Robert Merton; the Frankfurt School in exile was also at Columbia. Mills was involved in a number of research projects while at Columbia, among them studies of Puerto Ricans in New York City (1947–8), and health needs of United Automobile Workers, CIO (1948). His major works were published in this period: *The New Men of Power* (1948), *White Collar* (1951) and, most notably, *The Power Elite* (1956). More polemical works followed (*The Causes of World War Three*, 1958, and *Listen, Yankee*, 1960). His 1959 book, *The Sociological Imagination* is a warning against the loss of commitment that comes with professionalization. From the mid-1950s he travelled to Latin America, the USSR, and Western Europe. He was an important inspiration to the New Left ('Letter to the New Left', 1960), and some of the dangers of which he wrote were dramatically manifested just after his death in the Cuban missile crisis of 1962.

> See: Bottomore, T., *Critics of Society: Radical Social Thought in North America* (1969), ch. 4.
> Clecak, P., *Radical Paradoxes: Dilemmas of the American Left: 1945–1970* (New York, 1974), ch. 3.
> Domhoff G. and H. Ballard (eds), *C. Wright Mills and 'The Power Elite'* (Boston, 1963).
> Eldridge, J., *C. Wright Mills* (Chichester, 1983).
> Gillam, R., 'White Collar from Start to Finish', *Theory and Society*, 10 (1981).
> Pells, R., *The Liberal Mind in a Conservative Age: American Intellectuals in the 1940s and 1950s* (New York, 1985), pp. 249–61.
> Scimecca, J., *The Sociological Theory of C. Wright Mills* (New York, 1977).

NEWMAN, Barnett (Baruch Newman) (1905–70), born in Manhattan, New York City, of Polish immigrant parents. Studied at the Arts Students' League. 1922–6 under John Sloan, and at City College of New York, 1923–7. Worked in his father's clothing business; it suffered in the Great Crash of 1929, but Newman kept it going until 1937; he ran (unsuccessfully) for mayor in 1934. During the 1930s, he occasionally worked as an art teacher in the public schools. In the early 1940s he destroyed nearly all of his work, feeling sure that Cubism, Surrealism and certainly American social realism were dead. *Onement 1* (1948) marked the emergence of his new art – the painting is a field of cadmium red with a vertical stripe of orange. His painting was highly controversial, not just its early colour-field style but the size (*Cathedra*, 1951, is eight feet by eighteen feet). Newman was heavily involved in the new American art – he collaborated with Rothko and Motherwell on the Subject of the Artist School, and was associated editor on the *Tiger's Eye*. In 1950 he was exhibited at Betty Parsons' gallery, and again the following year, though was ignored in the 1952 'Fifteen Americans' exhibition at MOMA. Although Clement Greenberg wrote about him in *Partisan Review* in 1955, he was not fully recognized until 1966 and his *Stations of the Cross* exhibition at the Guggenheim Museum.

See: Hess T., *Barnet Newman* (New York, 1969).
Newman, B., *American Modern Artists*, exhibition catalogue (New York, 1943).
Rosenberg, H., *Barnett Newman* (New York, 1978).

NIEBUHR, Reinhold (1892–1971), born Wright City, Missouri; attended Elmhurst College, Eden Theological Seminary, and Yale Divinity School, where he was awarded his BD in 1914 and AM in 1915. After graduating in 1915, he went to Detroit, and worked as pastor to the Bethel Evangelical church until 1928. It was during this period that he became critical of the superficial optimism of the 'social gospel' approach of the Protestant church which, in attending to local, practical needs, seemed not to address larger questions. The year after Niebuhr left Detroit for New York City (to teach philosophy of religion at Union Theological Seminary) the stockmarket collapsed, and the ensuing economic crisis, and, especially, the rise of totalitarianism highlighted the question of original sin that he had begun seriously to reconsider. He stayed at Union Theological Seminary until his retirement in 1960, having an increasing influence upon more secular intellectuals through such major texts as *Moral Man and Immoral Society* (1932), *The Children of Light and the Children of Darkness* (1944), and *The Irony of American History* (1952).

See: Fox, R., *Reinhold Niebuhr: A Biography* (New York, 1985).
Scott, N., *Reinhold Niebuhr* (Minneapolis, 1974).

O'KEEFFE, Georgia (1887–1986), born Sun Prairie, Wisconsin; studied at the Art Institute of Chicago (1905–6), the Art Students' League, New York City (1907–8), University of Virginia (1912), and Teacher's College of Columbia University, New York (1914–16), where she worked under the early American modernist, Arthur Dow. O'Keeffe was a commercial artist in Chicago (1908–10), and taught in the public schools of Amarillo, Texas (1913–16), and at University of Virginia (1913–18). She was never committed to teaching as a permanent career, especially after 1916 when she came to New York City, met Alfred Stieglitz and became part of his circle of early American modernists. O'Keeffe and Stieglitz were married in 1924 (he died in 1946). She travelled widely in the USA after 1932, in Mexico in 1951, and, between 1953 and 1969, in Europe, India, Asia, the Middle East, and the Pacific Islands. By the end of her travels, she was in her eighties. Her first solo exhibition was at Stieglitz's 291 in 1917; others followed, for example at the Anderson gallery in New York City (1923 and 1924, again organized by Stieglitz); regularly in the 1930s at An American Place, New York City; and at the big museums: retrospectives were held at the Chicago Art Institute

(1943), MOMA (1946), and Worcester Art Museum, Worcester, Mass. (1960). She became a Member of the National Institute of Arts and Letters in 1947, the American Academy of Arts and Letters in 1963, and the American Academy of Arts and Sciences, 1966. Known for her large flowers, she also painted New York City and the landscapes of the Southwest. She died in New Mexico.

See: Castro, J., *The Art and Life of Georgia O'Keeffe* (1985).
       Goodrich L., and D. Bry, *Georgia O'Keeffe* (New York, 1970).
       Lisler, L., *Portrait of an Artist: A Biography of Georgia O'Keeffe* (1987).
       Rich, B., *Georgia O'Keeffe: 40 Years of Her Art* (Worcester, Mass., 1960).

POLLOCK, Jackson (1912–56), born Cody, Wyoming; moved to Arizona with family; then back and forth between Arizona (1915–18 and 1923–5) and California (1918–23 and 1925–9). Went to New York City in 1929 and became Jackson Pollock rather than Paul Jackson Pollock. Studied at the Art Students' League in 1929 under regionalist painter, Thomas Hart Benton; during 1930s influenced by regionalism, but more so by Mexican muralists; 1938–42 worked for Federal Arts Project; met painter, Lee Krasner, in 1932 and they were married in 1940; that year they were exhibited together, along with Willem de Kooning; first solo, 1943 at Peggy Guggenheim's Art of this Century gallery, New York City; quickly became her star painter. She subsidized him for two years (£300 a month and loan of £2000 to Pollock and Krasner on their Long Island house) in return for all but two paintings produced 1946–7. In 1947 his famous 'drip' painting style emerged; continued working into the 1950s and had his first retrospective in 1956, the year he died in a car accident; thought to have been deeply troubled in last few months of his life.

See: Frank, E., *Jackson Pollock* (New York, 1983).
       Friedman, B., *Jackson Pollock: Energy Made Visible* (1973).
       Namuth H. and P. Falkenberg, *Jackson Pollock*, film (1951).
       O'Hara, F., *Jackson Pollock* (New York, 1959).
       O'Connor, F., *Jackson Pollock* (New York, 1967).
       Rosenberg, H., *The Tradition of the New* (Chicago, 1960).
       Sandler, I., *Abstract Expressionism: The Triumph of American Painting* (New York, 1970).

RAUSCHENBERG, Robert (1925–   ), born Port Arthur, Texas; later studied pharmacy at University of Texas and then did war service. In 1947, after two years at Kansas City Art Institute, benefitted from the G.I. Bill and went to study at Academie Julian, Paris. That and his subsequent two years (1948–50) at the famous Black Mountain College, North Carolina, under Josef Alpers, prepared him to lead the post-Abstract Expressionist avant-garde; he also taught at Black Mountain in 1952 and was part of a happening with John Cage and choreographer, Merce Cunningham. Had his first solo exhibition in 1951 at Betty Parsons' gallery in New York City. In 1955 began designing sets and costumes for Cunningham's Dance company, and in 1961 joined the company as lighting director as well as stage manager. From the mid-1950s, began to make his combination pictures, such as *Rebus* (1955) and *Monogram* (1959). Continued to have regular exhibitions, including two at MOMA (1966 and 1968) and retrospectives at the National College of Fine Arts, Washington, DC (1977), and the San Francisco Museum of Modern Art (1977). In 1978 he became a Member of the American Academy of Arts and Sciences, but remains better known for his stuffed goat with a rubber tyre around it. In 1966 he started EAT 'Experiment in Art and Technology' with the lazer scientist, Billy Kluver. In Emile de Antonio's film, *Painters Painting* (1972), covering post-war American art, Rauschenberg often seems to be the dominant figure.

See: Forge A., *Robert Rauschenberg* (New York, 1969).

RIESMAN, David (1909–   ), born in Philadelphia into an affluent, German-American family; oldest of three children, he went to Harvard University, graduating in 1931, before going on to Harvard Law School. He worked as a law clerk for Justice Brandeis, 1935–6, then taught at Buffalo Law School (1937–41). Between 1943 and 1946 he was a commercial lawyer, before returning to academic life at University of Chicago, but in the social sciences rather than law. His increasing intellectual eclecticism, and contacts with Erich Fromm, led to the texts for which he is known: *The Lonely Crowd* (1950) (and its companion, *Faces in the Crowd*, 1952), based on research with Nathan Glazer and Reuel Denney. Other works include: *Thorstein Veblen* (1953), *Individualism Reconsidered* (1954); and *Abundance for What?* (1964). Riesman moved to Harvard in 1954 as professor of sociology.

See: Brookeman, C., *American Culture and Society Since the 1930s* (1984), ch. 10.
Gans, H. *et al.* (eds.), *On the Making of Americans: Essays in Honor of David Riesman* (Philadelphia, 1979).
Pells, R., *The Liberal Mind in a Conservative Age: American Intellectuals in the 1940s and 1950s* (New York, 1985), pp. 238–48 and passim.
Wilkinson, R., *The Pursuit of American Character* (New York, 1988).

ROTHKO, Mark (1903–70), born Dansk, Russia; emigrated with family to Portland, Oregon, 1913; studied at Yale, 1921–3; began to paint in 1925, having had little formal tuition, bar a short period under Max Weber at the Art Students' League, New York City. Had his first solo shows in 1933 at the Contemporary Art Gallery, New York City and the Art Museum, Portland, Orgeon; then, in 1945, exhibited at Art of this Century gallery, and in 1947 at Betty Parsons; MOMA in 1961; the Guggenheim Museum in 1963; and a Memorial Show at MOMA in 1970. He became a Member of the National Institute of Arts and Letters, 1968; and received an honorary doctorate from Yale in 1969. Before this success, had been in at the beginning of Abstract Expressionism and, as early as 1935 founded The Ten with Adolph Gottlieb; more typically for the period, he worked for Federal Arts Project, 1936–7. After the war, in 1948, he founded, with Barnett Newman and Robert Motherwell, the Subject of the Artist School, New York City. Between 1951 and 1956, he did some art teaching in New York City, Boulder, Colorado, and New Orleans. Rothko committed suicide in his studio in 1970.

See: Waldron, D., *Mark Rothko (1903–1970)* (1978).

STELLA, Joseph (1877–1946), born near Naples, Italy; emigrated to USA with family in 1902. Later studied at the Art Students' League, New York City and the New York School of Art; worked as illustrator. 1909–12 in Europe; the catalyst for his career was 1912 visit to Paris where he met Matisse and Picasso, and was friends with Modigliani; also in 1912, went to the Futurist exhibition at Bernheim-Jeune's. *Battle of Light, Coney Island* (1913–14) was a direct result of the Armory Show; went on (between 1913 and 1923) to paint a Futurist New York City, for example in his *New York Interpreted* series (1920–22), and in his paintings of Brooklyn Bridge.

See: Baur, J., *Joseph Stella* (New York, 1971).
Jaffe, I., *Joseph Stella* (Cambridge, Mass., 1970).

SULLIVAN, Louis (1856–1924), born Boston. Influenced, when young, by his
grandfather's New England Transcendentalism, he later promoted an organic
architecture. Sullivan was intent on becoming an architect but disliked
academic work; he studied architecture for just a term at MIT in 1873, left
and went, via Philadelphia and employment with architect, Frank Furness, to
Chicago; worked for William Le Barron Jenney, the inventor of the
skyscraper; then to Paris, and the Ecole des Beaux-Arts, which he rejected
even more sharply than MIT; in 1879 he returned to Chicago and Dankmar
Adler's practice. He became a partner in 1881 and for the next twenty years
was the leading architect in the Chicago School. His first major building was
the Auditorium of 1886–90 (Romanesque/Commercial on the outside but
very ornamental inside, the latter a Sullivan trait, defended in many of his
writings). The Auditorium was followed by the Wainwright building, St
Louis (1890–91); the Guaranty building, Buffalo (1894–95), and the Carson,
Pirie and Store Store (1899–1904). He was responsible for the only eccentric
official building at the Chicago World's Fair in 1893 – the Transportation
building. In the mythology of American architecture, Sullivan was broken by
the neo-classicism of the Fair, though his period of decline came after Adler's
death in 1900. Between 1907–19 he built a number of Midwestern banks,
however. He was one of the judges in the other Chicago architectural 'event',
the 1922 *Chicago Tribune* competition. His *Autobiography of an Idea*, like his
1896 'The Tall Office Building Artistically Considered' (and other essays in
Kindergarten Chats and Other Writings, edited by I. Athey, 1947), was much
influenced by Walt Whitman's concept of a democratic, organic culture.

See: Bush-Brown, A., *Louis Sullivan* (New York, 1960).
Condit, C., *The Chicago School of Architecture: A History of Commercial
and Public Building in the Chicago Area, 1875–1925* (Chicago, 1964),
passim.
Mumford, L., *The Brown Decades: A Study of the Arts in America,
1865–1895* (New York, 1971), ch. 3.
Twombly, R. *Louis Sullivan: His Life and Work* (Chicago, 1987).
Van Zanten, D. *et al.*, *Louis Sullivan* (New York, 1987).

TRILLING, Lionel (1905–75), born and brought up in New York City, in an
orthodox Jewish home. He studied at Columbia, receiving his AB in 1925,
his AM, 1926 and his PhD, 1938. The delay in completing his PhD,
published in 1939 as *Matthew Arnold*, had something to do with his own
position as a Jew at Columbia; he was the first Jew to be appointed to a
permanent position in the English Department. After he left the *Menorah
Journal* in 1931, he had little to do with the Jewish community, though
returned to the theme occasionally in his writing. From 1932 onwards,
Trilling taught at Columbia, becoming professor of English in 1948. From
this apparently narrow base, Trilling has significantly influenced intellectual
life through such books as *The Liberal Imagination* (1950), *The Opposing Self*
(1955), *Beyond Culture* (1955), and *Sincerity and Authenticity* (1973). His essays
and reviews from the period 1965–75 have been published as *The Last Decade*
(1979), edited by Diana Trilling, his wife and an important literary critic. His
literary and cultural criticism, like his novel, *The Middle of the Journey* (1947),
chart a representative (but in his case, very thoughtful) move away from
1930s socialism to a chastened liberalism and, by the 1960s, a cultural neo-
conservatism.

See: Boyers, R., *Lionel Trilling: Negative Capability and the Wisdom of Avoidance* (1977).

Brookeman, C. *American Culture and Society Since the 1930s* (1984), pp. 112–22.

Chate W., *Lionel Trilling: Criticism and Politics* (Stanford, 1980).

Gunn, G., *The Culture of Criticism and the Criticism of Culture* (New York, 1987), passim.

Krupnick, M., *Lionel Trilling and the Fate of Cultural Criticism* (Evanston, 1986).

VEBLEN, Thorstein (1857–1929), sixth child of parents who had emigrated from Norway ten years before his birth; brought up in Norwegian-American community of Cato, Wisconsin; sent to Carleton College, Minnesota, where, between 1874 and 1880, he was the 'bright but unsound' kind of student (his college address was 'A Plea for Cannibalism'); went on to study philosophy at Johns Hopkins and Yale universities; PhD awarded, 1884, but with no job to be had, returned to Wisconsin and the farm for seven years. Eventually began his teaching career at University of Chicago in 1891, where he was known for his untidiness, indifference to students (typically all received a 'C' grade), and affairs with Faculty wives; in 1899, out of the intellectual excitement of Chicago in the 1890s, he published his major work, *The Theory of the Leisure Class*, an ironic attack on the culture of capitalism. Other texts include: *The Theory of Business Enterprise* (1904), *The Instinct of Workmanship and the State of the Industrial Arts* (1914), *The Higher Learning in America* (1918), and *The Engineers and the Price System* (1921). During the First World War, he worked briefly for the federal government in Washington, DC, and from 1919 at the New School for Social Research; also held academic appointments at Stanford University (1906–09) and the University of Missouri (1911–17), but seemed to go out of his way to fail at his career. His first wife divorced him in 1911. Had a short period of popularity among alienated intellectuals in the 1920s but remained, to the end, more alienated, and certainly more eccentric, than any of his few supporters. His second wife had a mental breakdown in the 1920s. Veblen went to live in a cabin in Palo Alto, California, and died in 1929. A major figure in American social thought (a particular influence upon C. Wright Mills and David Riesman), and anticipated recent cultural critiques of capitalism and the structuralist interest in sign systems.

See: Aaron, D., *Men of Good Hope: A Story of American Progressives* (New York, 1951), ch. 7.

Diggins, J., *The Bard of Savagery: Thorstein Veblen and Modern Social Theory* (Hassocks, Sussex, 1978).

Dorfman, J., *Thorstein Veblen and his America* (New York, 1934).

Riesman, D., *Thorstein Veblen: A Critical Interpretation* (New York, 1953).

White, M., *Social Thought in America: The Revolt Against Formalism* (New York, 1976), ch. 6.

WARHOL, Andy (1928?–87), born near Pittsburg, Pennsylvania, parents Czechoslovakian immigrants. Between 1945 and 1949, he was at the Institute of Technology, Pittsburg, studying pictorial design. He was a commercial artist in New York City, 1950–57, though in 1952 had a solo show at the Hugo Gallery. By the early 1960s, he and his Campbell Soup cans, Brillo Pad boxes, and green Coca-Cola bottles were famous. Warhol was fascinated by the repetitiousness of mass production, and used commercial techniques, notably silk-screening. The name of his studio, The Factory, also questioned the uniqueness of the work of art. In 1965, he stated that he was retiring as an artist to concentrate on film-making. He made over fifty films, the most controversial being *Sleep* (1963), in which a man sleeps for six hours; *Empire* (1964) in which a camera steadily watches the Empire State building for eight hours; and *Chelsea Girls* (1966), which was thought pornographic by some. In addition to making films, Warhol opened a night club, 'The Exploding Plastic Inevitable', and had a house band, which he managed: The Velvet Underground. In 1968 he was shot and badly wounded by one of the actresses in his films. In time, this added to his cult-figure quality. No doubt he would have been pleased to hear *The Andy Warhol Diaries* (1989) described by a reviewer as 'stupefyingly tedious'.

> See: Coplans, J., *Andy Warhol* (Pasadena, 1970).
> Crone, R., *Andy Warhol* (1970).
> Bockris, V., *Warhol* (1988).

WELLES, Orson (1915–85), born Wisconsin of wealthy and artistic parents; decided not to go to college but, at the age of sixteen travelled to Ireland, Britain, Spain and Morocco working desultorily in the theatre. In 1935 appeared on Broadway, directed a short and performed on radio – all for the first time; was the first voice of the radio character, 'The Shadow'. Directed and produced plays for Federal Theater Project (federal agents blocked his production of Marc Blitzstein's Left-wing play, *The Cradle Will Rock*). In 1937 formed Mercury Theatre, working on stage and on radio. On Halloween, 1938 the company's *War of the Worlds* was broadcast. RKO signed Welles in 1939 and after abortive projects the extraordinarily innovative *Citizen Kane* was released in 1941, with Welles as director, star and scriptwriter. After controversy (the Hearst organization tried to stop *Kane* and the Writers Guild argued that Herman J. Mankiewicz was at least the co-scriptwriter); critical acclaim; and lack of box-office success, Welles' artistic freedom was curtailed, e.g. in heavily cut 1942 film, *The Magnificent Ambersons*. Fired by RKO in 1947, he went on to make *The Lady from Shanghai* (1948) with Columbia, which failed commercially and was the final cause of the marriage breakdown between Welles and co-star, Rita Hayworth. After *Macbeth* (1949), with Republic, Welles left Hollywood and starred as Harry Lime in the British film, *The Third Man* (1949). His only other Hollywood film has been the remarkable 'noir' thriller, *Touch of Evil* (1958).

> See: Bazin, A., *Orson Welles: A Critical View*, translated by J. Rosenbaum (1978).
> Gottesman, R. (ed.), *Focus on Orson Welles* (Englewood Cliffs, NJ, 1975).
> Heath S., *Questions of Cinema* (Bloomington, Indiana, 1981), passim.
> Kael, P., *The Citizen Kane Book* (St Albans, 1974).
> McBride, J., *Orson Welles* (1972).

WRIGHT, Frank Lloyd (1867–1959), born and grew up mostly in Wisconsin, father an itinerant preacher but mother greater influence on his artistic interests; studied engineering (briefly) at the University of Wisconsin, but in 1889 he began work in Adler and Sullivan's Chicago architectural firm. Married Catherine Lee Tobin in 1889 and built their home in Oak Park, Chicago (1889). Dismissed by Sullivan for moonlighting, he set up his own practice in 1893. Developed Prairie School of architecture, high point being the Robie house, Chicago (1909). Three important public buildings in his 'first' period: Unity Temple, Oak Park (1904–06); Larkin building, Buffalo (1904); and Midway Gardens, Chicago (1914). Almost as influential, were Wright's lecture, 'The Art and Craft of the Machine', first delivered at Jane Addams' Hull House, 1901, and the publication of his writings in Berlin, 1910–11, where they were read by European modernists. For all his middle-class, family values, Wright left his family in 1909 and went to Europe with Mamah Bortwick Cheney, who was married to a neighbour. The scandal made his return difficult, but he established a practice at Taliesin, Spring Green, Wisconsin. In 1914 his house was set fire to by a crazed cook; Cheney was killed, as were other occupants. Between 1915 and 1920 he was in Tokyo working on the Imperial Hotel. In his 'second' period, Wright's major works were: the Kaufmann house ('Falling Water'), Bear Run, Pennsylvania (1936); the Johnson Wax Administration building (1936–9) and Laboratory Tower (1950), Racine, Wisconsin; a few 'Usonian' houses; the 1930s utopian project, Broadacre City; the Price Tower, Bartlesville, Oklahoma (1953–5); and the Guggenheim Museum, New York City (1943–59). When Wright began his 1930 Kahn Lectures at Princeton University with his 1901 'Art and Craft of the Machine' lecture, it indicated how far ahead of his time he had been (see *An American Architecture: Frank Lloyd Wright*, edited by E. Kaufmann (1955)). Among his most important texts are: *An Autobiography* and *The Disappearing City* (both 1932) and *The Living City* (1958).

See: Brooks, H., *The Prairie School, Frank Lloyd Wright and his Midwest Contemporaries* (New York, 1976).

Ciucci, G., 'The City in Agrarian Ideology and Frank Lloyd Wright: Origins and Development of Broadacres', in G. Ciucci *et al.*, *The American City: From the Civil War to the New Deal*, translated by B. La Penta (1980), pp. 293–387.

Fishman, R., *Urban Utopias in the Twentieth Century: Ebenezer Howard, Frank Lloyd Wright and Le Corbusier* (New York, 1977).

Gill, B., *Many Masks: A Life of Frank Lloyd Wright* (1988).

Jencks, C., *Modern Movements in Architecture* (Harmondsworth, 1985), pp. 124–40.

Twombly, R., *Frank Lloyd Wright: An Interpretive Biography* (New York, 1975).

Hitchcock H-R., *In the Nature of Materials, 1887–1941: The Buildings of Frank Lloyd Wright* (New York, 1942).

Skully, V., *Frank Lloyd Wright* (New York, 1960).

Index